MOVIES IN
AMERICAN HISTORY

MOVIES IN AMERICAN HISTORY

AN ENCYCLOPEDIA
Volume 2

Philip C. DiMare, Editor

 ABC-CLIO

Santa Barbara, California • Denver, Colorado • Oxford, England

Copyright 2011 by ABC-CLIO, LLC

All rights reserved. No part of this publication may be reproduced, stored in a retrieval system, or transmitted, in any form or by any means, electronic, mechanical, photocopying, recording, or otherwise, except for the inclusion of brief quotations in a review, without prior permission in writing from the publisher.

Library of Congress Cataloging-in-Publication Data

Movies in American history : an encyclopedia / Philip C. DiMare, editor.
   p. cm.
Includes bibliographical references and index.
Includes filmography.
ISBN 978–1–59884–296–8 (hardcopy (set) : alk. paper) — ISBN 978–1–59884–297–5 (ebook (set))
1. Motion pictures—United States—Encyclopedias. 2. Motion picture actors and actresses—United States—Biography—Encyclopedias. 3. Motion picture producers and directors—United States—Biography—Encyclopedias. 4. Motion picture industry—United States—Encyclopedias. I. DiMare, Philip C.
PN1993.5.U6M68   2011
791.430973′03—dc22   2011006901

ISBN: 978–1–59884–296–8
EISBN: 978–1–59884–297–5

15 14 13 12 11   1 2 3 4 5

This book is also available on the World Wide Web as an eBook.
Visit www.abc-clio.com for details.

ABC-CLIO, LLC
130 Cremona Drive, P.O. Box 1911
Santa Barbara, California 93116-1911

This book is printed on acid-free paper ∞

Manufactured in the United States of America

CONTENTS

Contents

Contents

Contents

Contents

N

NIXON.   Oliver Stone has been one of the most controversial directors in Hollywood since the mid-1980s. Key to this controversy has been the director's claim to be doing history in films such as *Born on the Fourth of July* (1989), *JFK* (1991), and *The Doors* (1991). This claim has sparked widespread debate, increasing the director's and his work's exposure, and helping to increase his box-office revenues. One of Stone's most controversial films was *Nixon* (1995), his dramatization of the life and volatile career of one of America's most infamous political figures.

Nixon purports to be a psychological biography of the only man in history to resign the presidency of the United States. Beginning by examining his meager beginnings as the son of a failed lemon farmer father and a devout Quaker mother, Stone depicts Nixon's youth as sadly dysfunctional, and likely responsible for the many psychological foibles that eventually led to his political downfall. Stone goes on to reiterate a theory that had been suggested in a number of his other "historical" films: that during the 1960s, particularly after the assassination of President John F. Kennedy, the government of the United States was taken over by unscrupulous, and dangerous, members of what Dwight Eisenhower called the "military-industrial complex." In *Nixon*, Stone goes so far as to imply that Nixon himself actually had knowledge of conspiratorial activities swirling around Kennedy's death, and that he may ultimately have benefited from these shadowy activities as he moved along his path toward the White House.

As with all of Stone's pictures that claim to be historically based, *Nixon* elicited comment from highly regarded historians such as Stephen Ambrose and Arthur M. Schlesinger Jr. Ambrose, whose historical views tend toward the conservative, attacked Stone's work as a gross—even fraudulent—misrepresentation of the former president. Schlesinger, whose work represents the more progressive side of the historical debate, thought that the film, although certainly taking some dramatic license, was basically correct in its portrait of the tortured former president. For his part, Stone staunchly defended the accuracy of his film, pointing out that he had done extensive research, including interviewing many former Nixon staffers and listening to hours of previously unreleased Nixon White House recordings. Indeed, said Stone, beyond engaging in hours of labor intensive research simply because he wanted to make *Nixon* a first-rate film, he also conducted this research because he knew that he would be subject to attacks from historians once the picture was released.

Nixon was such a complicated figure—odd looking, even he had to admit, and frequently off-putting—"When they look at you," he says to a portrait of Kennedy in *Nixon*, "they see what they want to be; when they look at me, they see what they are"—it is difficult to know who could possibly be successful in playing him onscreen. Rip Torn tried it in the 1979 mini-series *Blind Ambition*, based on the John Dean book of the same name; and more recently, Frank Langella portrayed the post-White House Nixon in Ron Howard's *Frost-Nixon* (2008). Interestingly, though, the lead role in *Nixon* did not go to an American-born actor but to the Welshman Anthony Hopkins. Transforming himself into a perverse caricature of Nixon—who at times during his political career almost seemed to be a caricature of himself—Hopkins earned one of his many Academy Award nominations for Best Actor. Hopkins portrays Nixon as a sympathetic character, deeply affected by the deaths of his two brothers when he was young, close to his Quaker mother, and often bound up by the almost oppressive strictures of his faith. Politically astute—he became one of the most sought-after advisors for Republican candidates late in his life—and disgustingly coarse in his personal relationships with his male companions, Nixon seemed almost painfully shy in public, especially given that he was a nationally recognized politician. Some of the most poignant moments in *Nixon* are shared between Nixon and his wife, Pat, played with élan by Best Supporting Actress nominee Joan Allen. Unsure of himself, even in this most intimate of relationships, Nixon seemed always haunted by his crippling insecurities. Indeed, the Stone/Hopkins Nixon is a profoundly private man who so desperately wanted to be loved that, ironically, he entered the most public of professions, politics. Ultimately, suggests Stone, it was Nixon's insecurities that led to his downfall. Fearful of his enemies—both real and imagined—he made choices that today seem bizarrely self-destructive, especially in regard to Watergate.

Perhaps less accurate than his film portrayals of the Doors or Alexander the Great, and less compelling than his political thriller *JFK*, *Nixon* remains an important film, examining as it does the life and career of an important, tragically flawed, and often misunderstood leader in American history.

See also: JFK; Politics and Film; Stone, Oliver

References

Ambrose, Stephen E. "*Nixon*: Is It History?"; Schlesinger, Arthur J. Jr. "On *JFK* and *Nixon*"; and Stone, Oliver. "On *Nixon* and *JFK*." In Toplin, Robert Brent, ed. *Oliver Stone's USA: Film, History, and Controversy.* Lawrence: University Press of Kansas, 2000.

Kunz, Don, ed. *The Films of Oliver Stone.* Lanham, MD: Scarecrow Press, 1997.

Silet, Charles L. P. *Oliver Stone: Interviews* (Conversations with Filmmakers Series). Jackson: University Press of Mississippi, 2001.

—Richard A. Hall

NO COUNTRY FOR OLD MEN.　　In the stories of the ancient Greeks, tragedy was marked by the unfolding of fate, brought down on the protagonist because of one tragic flaw, the mortal weakness within the hero that allowed the gods to have their way with him. Sometimes the gods acted directly. At other times the Furies would be unleashed to wreak their terrible and implacable vengeance. Set against a hardscrabble landscape, and richly cruel in its depiction of fate, the harsh tragedy of the 2007 film, *No Country for Old Men*, is like one of those ancient tales brought to life in the American Southwest. As in ancient tragedy, the hero brings his fate on himself, in this case by performing an act of mercy, and as in Greek tragedy his fate is personified by a frighteningly unstoppable personal Fury.

Directed by Ethan and Joel Coen, and based on a 2005 novel of the same name by Cormac McCarthy, *No Country for Old Men* won four Oscars including Best Picture, an unusual award for a film in which nearly all the characters with whom one would ordinarily identify are killed. But even the best of the characters in this film come across as hard-edged, existing in a West Texas desert landscape, a trailer park of the soul.

Llewelyn Moss, played by Josh Brolin, is out hunting on foot when he comes across deserted vehicles, bodies, bags of drugs, and a case containing a great deal of money. The only survivor is inarticulate with pain and dehydration, and can only beg Moss for a drink of water. Moss has no water, and he pragmatically leaves the wounded man at the scene while taking the bag with the money for his own. In the harsh rules of this dog-eat-dog land, Moss has done well for himself. He has left little trace of himself at the scene and has come away with a life-changing amount of money. Nevertheless, his survivor sensibilities are overcome by pity, and Moss drives into the desert to bring water to the wounded man, only to find him dead. No good deed goes unpunished, and it is this foolhardy act of kindness that sets the hunters on his trail.

The primary and ultimately successful hunter is one of the most frightening villains in film, a smoothly coiffed hitman named Anton Chigurh, played by Javier Bardem. Chigurh is inscrutable, unstoppable, unemotional and reasonable, as only a madman can be. If he were merely venial and greedy as so many movie villains are made out to be, he would be much less chilling. It is his deranged but logical personal ethic that drives him ruthlessly forward. His twisted sense of justice leads him to kill not only Moss, but anyone who interferes with his prey. He even goes out of his way to kill Moss's wife, not as revenge but as a kind of insane justice. If given a chance to speak before they are killed, his victims try to convince the killer that he doesn't "have to do this," that the future is not fixed, that events are not inevitable. But Chigurh must kill. As the inexorable hand of fate, his actions are fixed, a theme underscored by Chigurh's habit of tossing a coin, heads or tails, to offer his victims the hope of a 50-50 chance at mercy.

Meanwhile, circling the edge of this vortex of violence and inescapable fate is the enigmatic character of Sheriff Bell, played by veteran actor Tommy Lee Jones. The sheriff serves as witness and storyteller, narrator and commentator. Like the ancient Greek bard Homer, who set his tales of fate and the cruel and inexplicable will of the gods in a mythic era, the sheriff narrates these events as a tragic and completed past. The film is bracketed by his reminiscences, buttressing the inevitability of the characters' actions and reactions with the immutability of the perfected past tense. Like a solo version of the ancient Greek theatrical device, the chorus, Sheriff Bell's comments provide distance, context, and monumentality. Through the soft Texas drawl of his words, the story is framed as an epic tragedy, beyond the law of man even as represented by the office he holds and the badge he wears. And yet, in the country that is no place for the old, it is the voice of Sheriff Bell, the old man, that survives to tell the tale.

See also: Coen Brothers, The

References

Corrigan, Robert, ed. *Classical Tragedy, Greek and Roman.* New York: Applaus, 1990.
Nussbaum, Martha Craven. *The Fragility of Goodness: Luck and Ethics in Greek Tragedy and Philosophy.* Cambridge, UK: Cambridge University Press, 2001.
Visser, Margaret. *Beyond Fate.* Toronto: House of Anansi Press, 2002.

—Helen M. York

OFFICER AND A GENTLEMAN, AN.   Written by Douglas Day Stewart and nominated for an Academy Award, *An Officer and a Gentleman* grossed nearly $130 million after its 1982 release. Directed by Taylor Hackford and distributed by Paramount Pictures, the film stars Richard Gere, Louis Gossett Jr., and Debra Winger. An engaging, military love story, *An Officer and a Gentleman* is a tale of immutable challenges, acquired valor, self-actualization, and sensitivity.

Basically a traditional coming-of-age story set in the context of a war film, the picture's narrative unfolds on several complex levels. A Naval Aviation Officer candidate, Zack Mayo (Gere), is a talented college graduate, though a socially maladjusted young man. The son of an enlisted Navy man, who must endure his mother's suicide and the failed parenting of his alcoholic and womanizing father, Zack has grown into a displaced loner, searching for a purpose in life. His quest takes him to a 13-week Aviation Officer Candidate School program, during which he will be trained, and parented, by Marine Corps Gunnery Sergeant Emil Foley (Gossett). There is a love interest, a woman, blue-collar factory worker Paula Pokrifki (Winger). Paula is young and ethical, and clearly relegated to the social and economic fringes of American culture, with little hope of self-empowerment. She and her good friend Lynette Pomeroy (Lisa Blount) remain optimistic that they will find husbands from among the candidates training in their hometown, young men who will take them away from the debilitating drudgery of their community.

In his typical fashion, Zack attempts to use his superior intellect, physical skills, and charm to make his way through the program with as little effort as possible. He cons his classmates and uses Paula: "I've loved you since I met you," says Paula. "I don't want you to love me. I don't want anyone to love me," responds Zack. He even tries to fool Sergeant Foley: "In every class," says Foley, "there's always one joker who thinks that he's smarter than me. In this class, that happens to be you. Isn't it, Mayonnaise?" Realizing his tremendous potential, however, Foley rides Zack to the breaking point. In one of the film's most poignant scenes, with Foley trying to force Mayo to quit, Zack begs Foley, through tears of anguish and despair, not to kick him out of the program:

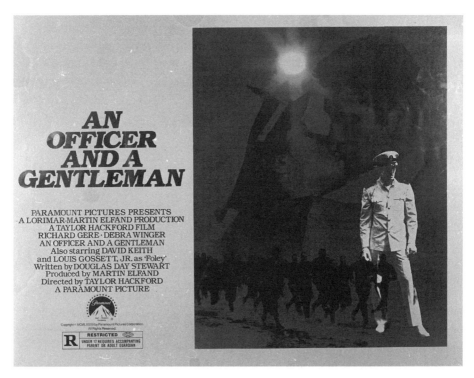

Movie poster for the film *An Officer and a Gentleman* featuring actors Richard Gere and Debra Winger, 1982. (Hulton Archive/Getty Images)

"DON'T YOU DO IT! DON'T! YOU ... I got nowhere else to go, I got nowhere else to g ... I got nothing else."

Allowed to stay in the program, Zack becomes the leader, and the friend that the other candidates, and Paula, desperately need. Maintaining a thematic balance among romance, action, and drama, the film winds toward a rather predictable conclusion: Officer Zack Mayo, resplendent in naval whites, and having come to understand loyalty, heroism, and self, strides into the local factory, sweeps Paula up in his arms, and carries her off to the cheers of those who must remain behind.

The film fits neatly within the cultural, political, and economic context of Reagan-era America. Suffering through the ignominy of a humiliating defeat in Vietnam, the Watergate scandal and failed presidency of Richard Nixon, and the "malaise" of the Carter administration, American's were in the mood for redemptive narratives, especially those that were framed by a thematic of military heroism. Expressing the possibility that the hopes and dreams of those who had been relegated to the margins of American society could indeed be realized, the film was an overwhelming success, cashing in at the box office and garnering a Best Actress nomination for Winger and Oscars for Best Supporting Actor for Gossett and Best Song for "Up Where We Belong."

References

An Officer and a Gentleman. http://en.wikipedia.org/wiki/An_Officer_and_a_Gentleman.
An Officer and a Gentleman. Available at http://www.fast-rewind.com/.

—*Gloria Sawyer*

ON THE WATERFRONT.   Hollywood and organized labor were both among the earliest targets of the Cold War's witch hunts for communist subversion. It is not surprising, then, that the 1954 working-class drama *On the Waterfront* did not depict a strike or other solidarity movement, and instead celebrated apolitical individualism while condemning union corruption. Based in part on a series of prizewinning newspaper articles about New Jersey longshoreman's unions, *On the Waterfront* relocates the action to Brooklyn. The narrative revolves around the question of whether dockworker Terry Malloy (Marlon Brando) will testify against labor bosses after he witnesses the murder of another worker who had provided information about union racketeering to the Waterfront Crime Commission. Directed by former Communist Party member Elia Kazan, who in 1952 angered many when he revealed the names of former communist associates to the House Un-American Activities Committee, *On the Waterfront* raised questions about the filmmaker's motives; some argued that Kazan made the movie to justify his own willingness to name names. In any case, audiences and critics applauded, and *On the Waterfront* became American cinema's most decorated labor film, winning eight Academy Awards in 1955, including Oscars for best picture, director, screenplay, actor (Brando), and supporting actress (Eva Marie Saint).

Although *On the Waterfront* stands as a representative product of Cold War Hollywood, the film has endured largely because of its ability to both draw on and transcend conventions of mid-1950s popular culture. Enlivened by a sophisticated Leonard Bernstein soundtrack, the movie successfully combines elements of film noir, contemporary urban television shows, and live theater. Kazan and screenwriter Budd Schulberg have said that they wanted to make an "eastern"—a film featuring themes common to westerns but set on the East Coast. Indeed, in many ways the picture recalls *High Noon* (1952), also the story of a principled man taking action while others do nothing, and a film that was interpreted by many as an allegory about public submissiveness during the Cold War.

On the Waterfront may indeed function as a New York western; however, the film's protagonist exhibits something more complicated than the rugged individualism of the typical western hero. Brando's much-celebrated rendering of the hard-edged and sensitive sides of ex-boxer Terry Malloy represents a landmark among Hollywood's portrayals of American masculinity. In the film's iconic scene, Malloy rides in a taxi with his brother Charley, a union insider assigned to convince him not to testify or, if unsuccessful in that effort, to kill him. Terry disarms Charley by reminding him that years ago, determined to win a lucrative bet, he asked Terry to deliberately lose a fight and thus ruin his boxing career. "You don't understand," he says, "I coulda had class, I coulda been a contender, I coulda been somebody. . . ." While that is the most oft-quoted moment, Brando's performance flourishes over the course of the several scenes depicting Terry's courtship with Edie (Saint), the sister of the murdered worker. Edie has no reason to trust Terry but nevertheless seems drawn to him. Connecting viscerally in the silences of their awkward conversations, their love is based on pure intuition, the same kind of animal instinct that compels Edie's love for her cat and inspires Terry to care for a flock of pigeons on an apartment rooftop. So there is solidarity in *On the Waterfront* after all, but a kind not based on any ideology nor impelled by struggles for group rights.

On the Waterfront was as much a postwar film as it was a Cold War production, for it reflected anxieties about rapid modernization and urbanization. It appealed to yearnings for a society based on instinctual moral decisions rather than the wheelings and dealings of labor bosses, corporations, and city bureaucracies. Still, the film remains a cultural artifact of American Cold War liberalism: Poor working conditions are blamed not on employers but on corrupt unions, the film celebrates the power of individuals who counter groupthink, and in the climactic scene the workers' triumph is that they no longer have to bribe union officials to be able to answer the shipping company magnate's call, "Let's go to work!"

See also: Brando, Marlon; Hollywood Blacklist, The; HUAC Hearings, The; Kazan, Elia

References

Bodnar, John. *Blue-Collar Hollywood: Liberalism, Democracy, and Working People in American Film.* Baltimore: Johns Hopkins University Press, 2006.

Bromwich, David. "Brando and *On the Waterfront*," *Threepenny Review* 65, Spring 1996: 19–21.

Zaniello, Tom. *Working Stiffs, Union Maids, Reds, and Riffraff: An Expanded Guide to Films about Labor.* Ithaca, NY: ILR Press, 2003.

—Kenneth F. Maffitt

ORDINARY PEOPLE. Opening his 1980 film *Ordinary People* with a series of dazzling dissolves reminiscent of those used by Orson Welles to guide us into the mysterious realm of Xanadu in *Citizen Kane*, first-time director Robert Redford draws us seductively into a pristine upper-class world of manicured lawns and perfectly appointed Colonial homes. Redford lingers over these shots, as if to make us envious of this wonderfully safe and secure space, one that seems so different from those that most of us inhabit simply because it is anything but ordinary. There are secrets to be revealed, though, about the perfect families that populate this world and that initially appear all but immune to the dross and strain of everyday life.

The film centers on the three remaining members of an emotionally tortured family trying to deal with the death of a son and a brother. Conrad (Timothy Hutton), or sometimes Connie or Con, as his father and best friends call him, struggles to reconcile the loss of his older, heroic brother, Buck (Scott Doebler), who died tragically in a boating accident. Anxious, unable to concentrate, distraught—we learn that Connie tried to kill himself and spent months in a psychiatric hospital after his brother's death—Conrad is gently prodded by his well-meaning father, Calvin (the superb Donald Sutherland), to keep their agreement and to visit the psychologist who has been recommended to the family. Connie reluctantly agrees to go, and so begins his relationship with Dr. Berger (Judd Hirsch), who will slowly, sometimes painfully draw out Conrad's story.

Although he loves her dearly and desperately seeks her approval, Conrad's relationship with his mother, Beth (Mary Tyler Moore playing as far against type as one can imagine), is distant, at best. Haunted by memories of her golden boy Buck, Beth seems incapable of feeling anything for anyone else in her life. Seeking merely to exist, she orders every minute detail of her life—her house, her clothes, her appearance, the lives of her husband and son, indeed of her sons, as Buck's room remains just as it was before he died, a shrine to the extraordinarily gifted athlete, student, friend that he was. Conrad tries everything he knows to break through the barriers that his mother has erected, but there is no way in for him. It is as if Beth believed that she and her family, and especially Buck, were somehow not "ordinary people," that the unique qualities they possessed, and that had allowed them to rise above so many others, would forever keep the world at bay. Beth knows different now, though; for, since she lost her son, she understands the fragility of human existence—"Ward," she cries hysterically to her brother, "you tell me the meaning of happy. But first you better make sure your kids are good and safe, that they haven't fallen off a horse, been hit by a car, or drown in that pool you're so proud of."

The problem, of course, is that Beth and her family, despite what they have accomplished, *are*, in fact, ordinary people; and just like the rest of us, they must deal with what life gives us over to—heartache, sickness, death. Beth, finally, cannot cope with what has come her way. As her husband says to her: "You're determined Beth; but you know something? You're not strong. . . . We would have been all right if there hadn't been any mess. But you can't handle mess. You need everything neat and easy. I don't know. Maybe you can't love anyone."

Because his father is right, because his mother cannot love him, and especially because she is not strong but merely determined, Connie turns to two other figures in his life for support: his doctor and a budding love interest, Jeannine Pratt (Elizabeth McGovern). Dr. Berger, an avuncular, terribly gifted analyst, is able to bring Connie to the point where he comes to realize, to his great surprise, that he is still alive and his brother dead because Buck—much like their mother, it seems—was just not strong enough: "It hurts to be mad at him, doesn't it?," asks Dr. Berger. "God I loved him. It's not fair. You just do one thing wrong," says Connie. "And what was the one wrong thing that you did?" "I hung on. I stayed with the boat."

While his relationship with Dr. Berger gives Connie what he needs to survive, his relationship with Jeannine gives him what he desires. Lovely, talented, and self-possessed enough to be self-deprecating, Jeannine seems hopelessly out of Connie's league—and yet, she is drawn to him because of all the things that make him so wonderfully special in his ordinary way. Unlike glorious, tragic Buck, Connie represents the best of us.

See also: Melodrama, The

References

Ebert, Roger. *Four-Star Reviews: 1967–2007*. Kansas City, MO: Andrews McMeel Publishing, 2007.
Grant, Barry Keith, ed. *Film Genre Reader III*. Austin: University of Texas Press, 2003.
Kawin, Bruce F. *How Movies Work*. Berkeley: University of California Press, 1992.

—Philip C. DiMare

P

PAPER CHASE, THE. Based on the 1970 novel by John J. Osborn Jr., *The Paper Chase* tells the story of Harvard Law student James T. Hart (Timothy Bottoms), who struggles to perform while maintaining his integrity in the face of withering attacks by a storied professor. An insider look into the lives of Ivy League law students during the 1970s, *The Paper Chase* received three Academy Award nominations, with the brilliant John Houseman winning the Oscar for his supporting role as Professor Charles W. Kingsfield.

The film opens with first-year students filing into their first session of Kingsfield's course on contract law. Setting the scene for what is to come, Kingsfield calls on Hart, requesting that he recite the facts of a particular case. When Hart reveals that he has not read the assignment, Kingsfield reprimands him for his lack of preparedness. Recognizing the amount of pressure he and his classmates are under, and seeking to ensure that he is never again unprepared, Hart locks himself in his dorm room and studies for hours on end. Based on terrifying stories he has heard about Kingsfield from third- and fourth-year students, Hart comes to idolize, and fear, this intimidating mentor. Realizing that they can never cover every element of the law themselves, the students divide up into study groups, each member agreeing to outline the material for one legal area. Hart's group is comprised of Ford (Graham Beckel), Brooks (James Naughton), Anderson (Edward Herrmann), Bell (Craig Nelson), and O'Connor (Robert Lydiard). Methodical in producing his outlines, Hart nevertheless takes time to relax, swimming in the university pool and sometimes breaking into campus buildings.

As he moves through the term, Hart's reverence for Kingsfield turns into an obsession to impress this mentor. In preparation for spring exams, Hart breaks into a restricted area of the library and steals Kingsfield's legendary notes on contract law, notes that the professor had created when he was a Harvard law student. By the end of the school year, overwhelmed by the pressures of a law program, several members of Hart's study group have either dropped out of the group or out of Harvard altogether; Brooks even attempts suicide. Disgusted at what he has become, Hart begins to wonder if a law degree is worth the grueling effort required of those who pursue it.

Though on one level he has come to despise him, however, Hart is still inspired by his teacher. Initially thrilled when Kingsfield takes him on as a student researcher, Hart drives himself to the breaking point in order to complete his assignment. Having stayed up for five straight days, but not quite finished with the task, Hart approaches Kingsfield and shamefacedly asks the professor for more time. Kingsfield dismisses him, informing him that the assignment has now been given to a third-year student and that Hart's contribution is no longer needed.

Stunned and embarrassed, Hart does what he has promised himself he would never do again: he attends class unprepared. After being called on by Kingsfield, he is publicly humiliated. Given a dime by Kingsfield, Hart is instructed to call his parents and to inform them that he will be dropping out of law school. Exiting the lecture hall, Hart pauses, turns to the professor, and yells out: "You are a son of a bitch, Kingsfield." "Mr. Hart," Kingsfield calmly replies, "that is the most intelligent thing you've said today. You may take your seat." After final exams, which he aces, an exhausted Hart goes to Cape Cod to relax. Having been forwarded his grades in the mail, Hart hesitates before opening the envelop that will reveal his future. Leaving the envelop sealed, he swiftly folds it into an airplane and sends it sailing into the sea.

Although no longer in vogue, Kingsfield's intimidating style was practiced by some professors in 1970s law schools. Thought by some the only way to teach lawyers to stand up under fire, legal historians point out that Kingsfield's tactics were nonetheless rare in real law schools (Koch, 1983). Although popular, some critics felt that *The Paper Chase* could have done more to portray the legal profession more positively. Hart, they point out, unlike some of his classmates, seemed interested in the law only because of his obsession with Kingsfield (Kael, 1973).

See also: Melodrama, The

References

Kael, Pauline. "The Current Cinema: Un-People." *New Yorker*, October 29, 1973: 153–59.
Koch, Kevin, James. *Seeing the Light: Law School and the Law Student.* Master's thesis. University of Iowa, 1983.
Ledwon, Lenora, ed. *Law and Literature: Text and Theory.* New York: Garland, 1996.

—*Jennifer K. Morrison*

PASSION OF THE CHRIST, THE.   Released in 2004, actor/director Mel Gibson's *The Passion of the Christ* became the most successful, and the most controversial, religious film in the history of American cinema. Gibson produced *The Passion* through Icon, his own production company, using $25 million of his own money. Acted entirely in Latin and Aramaic with subtitles, and containing extremely graphic and bloody violence, the film seemed an unlikely hit. Nevertheless, *The Passion of the Christ* has become the highest-grossing R-rated film of all time and challenged Peter Jackson's *The Lord of the Rings: The Return of the King* for the top-grossing film of 2004.

Scene from the controversial 2004 film *The Passion of the Christ*, starring James Caviezel. Directed by Mel Gibson. (Photofest)

The film revolves around the last few hours of the life of Jesus (James Caviezel) in which he is arrested, beaten, scourged, mocked, and finally crucified. Gibson leaves little to the imagination in his portrayal of Jesus's torture and death. There are few references in the film to other aspects of the life of Jesus beyond his crucifixion. Tightly edited flashbacks (most under a minute) give the viewer brief moments of respite from the violence.

The *Passion of the Christ* became for some a deeply religious experience, while others found it theologically, historically, and even morally problematic. The themes, implicit and explicit, of the film ensured that it would be at the center of a cultural and religious firestorm. Numerous religious leaders from the both the Jewish and Christian community claimed that the film drew on the centuries-old anti-Semitic tradition of the Passion Play. Staged as part of European liturgical traditions since the late Middle Ages and into modern times, the Passion Play typically portrayed the crucifixion of Christ as the responsibility of "evil Jews." These public spectacles, often performed on Good Friday, frequently led to outbreaks of violence against Jewish communities. Many critics believed Gibson's film drew too freely on this tradition.

Some Christian critics have also suggested that the film's emphasis on the violence of the crucifixion obscured the life and ethical teachings of Jesus. Noted biblical scholar John Dominic Crossan referred to it as "a hymn to a savage God," a celebration of violence for its own sake. The U.S. Conference of Catholic Bishops reissued a 1988 document in which they had urged that any portrayal of the crucifixion of Jesus must, as a matter of conscience, ensure that no imagery or symbolism used could have anti-Semitic overtones, even if that imagery came from the Gospels themselves.

Gibson, a traditionalist Catholic who rejects all of the changes that have come to the Church since the second Vatican Council in the 1960s, argued that the film simply portrayed the final hours of Jesus's life based on the Gospels and, he finally admitted, on the mystical visions of a nineteenth-century nun named Catherine Emerich. In an unlikely cultural alliance, many Protestant evangelical Christians joined Gibson in defending the film. They also rejected the idea that the film contained anti-Semitic imagery and symbolism and viewed attacks on it as part of a generalized secular assault on Christianity in America. Evangelical leaders have been the film's staunchest supporters, and are often fulsome in their praise of its alleged historical accuracy and fidelity to the Gospel accounts.

Critics have admitted that *The Passion* shows flashes of technical excellence while generally decrying the film on other grounds. Some have connected its appeal to the shock cinema of Quentin Tarantino and Gasper Noé. Historian of the American "Jesus film" W. Barnes Tatum praised Gibson's artistic vision while concluding that it was "theologically problematic, historically unlikely and literally uncritical" (Tatum, 2004).

Controversy over the film briefly reignited in the summer of 2006 when Mel Gibson was stopped for speeding in Malibu Beach, California. A drunken Gibson unleashed a tirade at the arresting officers, hurling anti-Semitic epitaphs and claiming that Jews were responsible "for all the wars in the world." He subsequently made a public apology for his statements.

See also: Gibson, Mel; Religion and Nationalism in Film

References

Beal, Timothy K., and Tod Linafelt. *Mel Gibson's Bible: Religion, Popular Culture, and The Passion of the Christ*. Chicago and London: University of Chicago Press, 2006.

Corley, Kathleen E., and Robert L. Webb. *Jesus and Mel Gibson's The Passion of the Christ*. London: Continuum, 2004.

McDannell, Colleen. "Votive Offering: The Passion of the Christ." In *Catholics in the Movies*. Oxford, UK: Oxford University Press, 2008: 317–45.

Tatum, W. Barnes. "*The Passion* in the History of Jesus Films," *Jesus and Mel Gibson's The Passion of the Christ*. London: Continuum, 2004.

—*W. Scott Poole*

PHILADELPHIA. TriStar Pictures and Clinica Estetico released *Philadelphia* on December 23, 1993. Marketed as the first mainstream Hollywood film to deal with AIDS and homosexuality (Connant, 76), *Philadelphia* is a statement about the necessity for social tolerance. It is clear from the film's opening title sequence, a visual exploration of urban Philadelphia accompanied by Bruce Springsteen's somber "Streets of Philadelphia," that the movie is entering into a cinematic discussion of American social ills. *Philadelphia* made AIDS and homosexuality legitimate areas of exploration in the entertainment industry. When *Philadelphia* was released, the medical world, and to a

Scene from the 1993 film *Philadelphia*, starring Tom Hanks (left) and Denzel Washington. Directed by Jonathan Demme. (Photofest)

degree the larger American public, were aware that HIV and AIDS impacted a much larger demographic than the gay community. However, popular culture still associated AIDS primarily with male homosexuality. Significantly, although providing a sympathetic image of those suffering from the disease and opening up a profoundly important social dialogue, *Philadelphia* also reinforced the notion that AIDS was synonymous with male homosexuality and deviant sexual behavior.

Produced and directed by Jonathan Demme (*Silence of the Lambs*) and starring audience-friendly actors Tom Hanks (*Big*) and Denzel Washington (*Glory*), *Philadelphia* is a courtroom drama that tells the story of Ivy League corporate attorney Andrew Beckett (Hanks). Several minutes into the film Beckett is seen in a fraternal environment, smoking cigars, having cocktails, and exchanging workplace jabs with the senior partners at his prestigious Philadelphia law firm. Here, Beckett is dubbed the "golden boy" and informed that he will be the firm's next partner. Shortly after this promotion, the film audience discovers that Beckett has AIDS and is gay; his co-workers only begin to suspect the truth. After working tirelessly on an important brief, Beckett is framed to look incompetent and then fired. Convinced that this abrupt turn of events was an instance of workplace discrimination, Beckett decides to sue his former employer. Unable to find anyone to take his case, Beckett approaches ambulance-chasing attorney Joe Miller (Washington). Initially reluctant to take the case, Miller finally agrees to represent Beckett, bringing cinematic life to the tagline on the movie's one-sheet "No one would take his case . . . until one man was willing to take on the system." In a dramatic courtroom speech, Miller looks directly into the camera and condemns not only the wrongdoings of Beckett's former law firm but also society's fears of AIDS and homosexuality.

Originally named Gay Related Immune Deficiency Syndrome (GRIDS), AIDS was both medically and socially linked with the male homosexual community, at least in the United States. Americans, however, ultimately came to realize that the disease was not exclusive to the gay community, and thus became somewhat more sympathetic to those who contracted it. The highly publicized story of Ryan White captured the hearts of Americans, for instance. Interestingly, though, White was a young boy who acquired the disease through a blood transfusion, and because of this, his story was seen as a socially acceptable anomaly. Images of male homosexuals as sexually deviant remained ubiquitous in the pop culture media. Indeed, Jonathan Demme himself had been criticized for his portrayal of homosexuality in his film *Silence of the Lambs* (1991), in which Jame Gumb (Ted Levine), a psychotic killer, is, among other things, seen cross-dressing in a women's suit made from the skins of his female victims. Given this, some critics felt that *Philadelphia* was simply Demme's way of apologizing for the way he portrayed deviant sexuality in *Silence of the Lambs*. Although the director maintained that Gumb was not supposed to be viewed as being gay, he did admit that audiences could have perceived the character in that way (Green, 1994, 58). Although the portrayal of homosexuality is quite different in *Silence of the Lambs* and *Philadelphia*, the latter film does reinforce the connection between AIDS and male homosexuality. In *Philadelphia*, it is made clear that Beckett contracted HIV/AIDS during a random sexual encounter in a gay porn theater, clearly linking the disease with male homosexuality, sexually deviant behavior, and promiscuity.

For all its controversy, however, *Philadelphia* did usher in an era when television shows and films dealing with homosexuality became more commonplace. The fact that Beckett was played by a nonhomosexual also reinvigorated a conversation about gay and lesbian actors in Hollywood. Hanks won an Oscar for his performance, making the film a significant turning point for his career, as well. After this film, Hanks became a serious A-list actor and Hollywood heavyweight. *Philadelphia*, although on a certain level dangerously stereotypical, was nonetheless a compassionate film that changed both the trajectory of Hanks's career and the discussion of sexuality in American society.

See also: Washington, Denzel

References

Connant, Jennet. "Tom Hanks Wipes That Grin off His Face." *Esquire*, December 1993: 74–83, 146.

Green, Jesse. "The Philadelphia Experiment." *Premiere*, January 1994: 54–58.

—*Laurie Chin Sayres*

PHILADELPHIA STORY, THE. *The Philadelphia Story* premiered in December 1940. It was the fifth collaboration of director George Cukor and star Katharine Hepburn. The film marked Hepburn's return to Hollywood, and initiated the second wave of her career. In 1938, after the box-office failures of two films now considered classics, *Bringing Up Baby* (1938) and *Holiday* (1938), she was labeled "box-office poison" by exhibitors and driven out of Hollywood to Broadway where playwright Philip Barry (who also wrote *Holiday*) wrote *The Philadelphia Story* specifically for Hepburn. It addressed precisely those derided qualities that had become a part of her star persona: articulateness, arrogance, and an upper-class sensibility. The men in the narrative repeatedly accuse Tracy Lord (Hepburn) of arrogance, a theme especially pronounced in a harsh diatribe from her father, whom Tracy chastises for adultery. He, in turn, berates her for maintaining impossibly high standards for herself and others (even blaming her inability to be a "sympathetic daughter" for his infidelity). Tracy's flaw is, essentially, not having any flaws, at least in her own mind; thus, she must learn to "have some regard for human frailty." As viewers, we see her suffer this series of condemnations until, by the end, she feels enough like an imperfect human to declare—as she gets married—"You know how I feel? Like a human, like a human being!" Presumably, audiences transferred Tracy's lessons onto Hepburn, who won widespread critical praise and public acceptance for her performance, paving the way for a series of excellent leading roles in romantic comedies with Spencer Tracy, beginning with her next film, *Woman of the Year* (1942).

The narrative of *The Philadelphia Story* begins days before Tracy's second wedding to George (John Howard), a middle-class employee of her father's company. She divorced, we soon learn, charming, old-moneyed, C. K. Dexter Haven (Cary Grant) two years before. The Lords are a nationally known family living in Philadelphia's affluent "Main Line" suburb. Unbeknownst to Tracy (who prizes her privacy), Dexter has struck a deal with tabloid *Spy* magazine to sneak in a reporter, Macauley "Mike" Conner (James Stewart), and photographer, Elizabeth Imbrie (Ruth Hussey), to her impending nuptials. Tracy immediately catches on, but is unable to evict the guests after learning that Dexter's motives were pure: in exchange for the story, *Spy* has agreed not to print a dirty piece on Tracy's father's affair with a dancer.

Tracy and Mike become infatuated with each other, each discovering that his or her class prejudices may be unfounded. A love square thus emerges among Tracy, Mike, George, and Dexter—who is masterminding the narrative's events in an effort to win Tracy back. In this way, the film confronts class politics explicitly by mapping class onto the romantic leads. Most visibly, Mike must learn that "even if a fellow is born into the pink, he can be a pretty nice guy." Tracy, who early on espouses a liberal attitude toward class difference, is forced to see that George is more interested in using her to climb the social ladder than he is in loving her. At the end of the film, the class order is reestablished: Tracy and Dexter remarry and Mike and Elizabeth are together. Only George is shut out of a romantically happy ending, shunned by both upper and lower classes. It is up to interpretation whether the film is conservative in this respect or whether it offers a bitter take on an immobile system.

James Stewart won his only Academy Award as Best Actor for his performance. Donald Ogden Stewart also won an Academy Award for Best Screenplay. The film was nominated for Best Picture, Hepburn and Hussey were nominated for their performances, and Cukor was nominated for his direction. *The Philadelphia Story* was recently ranked number 44 on the American Film Institute's 100 Greatest Movies list, and as the fifth Best Romantic Comedy in American Cinema. In Stanley Cavell's influential book *Pursuits of Happiness: The Hollywood Comedy of Remarriage*, *The Philadelphia Story* is awarded a prominent place in American cinematic history as a key member of the "comedy of remarriage," which Cavell argues is an influential, and distinctively American, film genre.

See also: Cukor, George; Grant, Cary; Hepburn, Katharine; Romantic Comedy, The

References

Cavell, Stanley. *Pursuits of Happiness: The Hollywood Comedy of Remarriage.* Cambridge, MA: Harvard University Press, 1981.
Hepburn, Katharine. *Me: Stories of My Life.* New York: Random House, 1996.
Phillips, Gene. *George Cukor.* Boston: Twayne, 1982.

—*Kyle Stevens*

PIANO, THE.   *The Piano* (1993) is an important film for the global recognition of Australasian cinema, women filmmakers, and its American distributor Miramax. The film's story focuses on a mute, mail-order bride, Ada McGrath (Holly Hunter), who travels from Scotland to New Zealand during the 1850s to marry a colonist, Alisdair Stewart (Sam Neill). Ada primarily expresses herself through playing her piano, an instrument that is sold by her new husband to a subordinate, George Baines (Harvey Keitel), who offers it back to Ada, key by key, in exchange for escalating physical intimacies with her. Inspired by the subversive work of the Brontës and Emily Dickinson, director Jane Campion ostensibly wished to create a newly wish-fulfilling, female-focused cinematic fantasy, one in which the heroine escapes Victorian constraints to finally express shameless sexuality with a man who physically liberates her (initially against her will).

The Piano emphasizes Ada's threatened position as a pale-faced foreigner in an unfathomable land, sidelining its broader colonial context *and* postcolonial awareness (most troublingly, Maoris are portrayed as comic caricatures of "natives"). New Zealand is viewed through breathtaking crane shots and pans that showcase the diversity of its landscape as from a tourist's photographic perspective, in parallel to Ada's outsider status. Though the film's resonance in terms of New Zealand culture is widely acknowledged, it ironically delocalizes itself by literally combining scenes filmed in the North and South Island. In parallel to this, American critics have focused on the transnational significance of the film in feminist and psychoanalytic terms. Psychoanalytic readings of the film emphasize its use of Gothic elements, its portrayal of repression and desire, and the Oedipal trajectory of its narrative when Ada's daughter Flora (Anna Paquin) rebels against maternal separation. More pervasive, feminist readings of the film dwell on how to view the "bargaining" between Ada and Baines—as enabling the liberation of female desire or, most troublingly, as romanticized prostitution—and how to understand Ada's automutism—as symbolic of female oppression or as ironic self-empowerment through rejection of patriarchal language.

The film's reception raises troubling questions about what it means when a mute heroine is almost unanimously celebrated for representing female empowerment: reviewers repeatedly emphasized Hunter's new beauty *in silence*, praising the "eloquence" of her almost speechless performance. Ironically, Ada's muteness is belied by Michael Nyman's anachronistic soundtrack which, in its modern romanticism, communicates her capacity for emotionally full expression outside time or place. This emphasis is what made *The Piano* such a success for its independent American distributor Miramax, despite its "foreignness." *The Piano* was also the first film by a woman director to win the Palme d'Or at Cannes, a fact much publicized by Miramax, reflecting that company's promotional approach to foregrounding international awards. Miramax aggressively marketed *The Piano* for Academy Awards: that it was nominated for eight Oscars and won three bolstered Miramax's globalizing approach to the promotion of "art-house" cinema during the 1990s. It also increased recognition of women filmmakers by involving a relatively high number of women in fundamental roles: director and screenwriter (Campion), producer (Jan Chapman), editor (Veronika Jenet), and costume designer (Janet Patterson).

The film is also important in relation to Campion's other films, each of which focuses on psychological tensions within female characters. Its complex sexual politics especially resonate with Campion's subsequent adaptation of Henry James (*The Portrait of a Lady*, 1996) and her most recent feature film, a female-focused neo-noir (*In the Cut*, 2003).

In terms of genre, *The Piano* has itself been classified as a contemporary women's film, a period film, a gothic melodrama, and a revisionist historical text. It also resonates with the western because, like that genre, *The Piano* has been repeatedly analyzed in terms of ideologically-loaded frontier mythology, national formation, and cultural definition. Early shots of Ada's prestigious Broadwood piano, transported with her from the Old World (Scotland) and precariously placed over oncoming, " 'savage" waves in the new frontier context, suggest the fragility of "civilization": a visual message that parallels how the isolated houses of the American frontier are shot in numerous westerns. That parallel aside, where women are typically marginalized in westerns, *The Piano* foregrounds the destructiveness of female subjugation (and/or sexuality) in a different historical context of colonial settlement.

See also: Campion, Jane; Women in Film

References

Coombs, Felicity, and Suzanne Gemmell. eds. *Piano Lessons: Approaches to The Piano*. Sydney: John Libbey, 1999.

Dalton, Mary M., and Kirsten James Fatzinger. "Choosing Silence: Defiance and Resistance without Voice in Jane Campion's *The Piano*." *Women and Language* 26(2), 2003: 34–39.

—*Elsie Walker*

PILLOW TALK. *Pillow Talk*, released in 1959, was the first of three movies that Doris Day and Rock Hudson would make together. The other two were *Lover Come Back* (1961) and *Send Me No Flowers* (1964). These three films ushered in a new type of film genre: labeled "no sex sex comedies" or "naughty but nice bedroom comedies," they were long on sexual innuendo—"Pillow Talk," the trailer announced, is "*what goes on* when the lights go off"—but short on sex. As with other films that bumped up against the forbidden topic of sexuality, *Pillow Talk* was still subject to the guidelines laid down by the Hays Code, a set of regulations that had been used to control the content of films for over three decades. The film represented a significant shift in focus for both lead actors. Doris Day, who seemed to embody the idea of the virtuous mother or wife and had consistently been chosen for such roles, was now cast as Jan Morrow, a single, sophisticated, and successful professional. Although Jan was still searching for Mr. Right, she was no longer depicted as merely an asexual homemaker. The film revived Day's career and made her into Hollywood's biggest female box-office draw over the next six years. It also brought the actress her only Academy Award nomination. Hudson's departure from his normal dramatic roles was even more striking, as he was now cast as the romantic lead, Brad Allen, a flourishing songwriter and incorrigible playboy. As a result of the film's success, Hudson began to be offered more and more roles as the leading man in romantic comedies.

In the film, Jan and Brad share what once was called a "party line," where two or more telephone subscribers have to share the same phone line. Jan becomes angry when Brad is constantly on the phone breezily wooing an assortment of women, which makes it all but impossible for Jan to make or receive business calls. Brad eventually finds out who Jan is, adopts a Texas accent, and uses their party line to charm her until she falls in love with him. She later discovers who he really is and walks out on him. Realizing that he has fallen in love with her, Brad begs Jan's forgiveness, but to no avail. Desperately trying to win her back, he hires Jan to redecorate his apartment, telling her that he wants to be rid of everything that smacks of his old life as a playboy. Still hurt that Brad had tricked her, Jan turns the tables on him, making over his apartment into something resembling a Turkish brothel. Angrily confronting her about what she has done, Brad finally carries Jan back to his apartment, where all is made right when he declares his love for her and promises to remain faithful forever.

The telephone plays a critical role in *Pillow Talk*. Because of the auditory, nonvisual relationship between Jan and Brad, they talk without seeing each other—although the audience sees both simultaneously thanks to split-screen photography. When Brad does finally get a look at Jan, he begins to play two roles—his playboy self, in their innuendo-filled party-line conversations, and the honest, hardworking oil tycoon who is every bit the perfect gentleman. This was not the first time that telephones played an important role in films. *Sorry, Wrong Number* used the telephone to create suspense and terror; and in *It's a Wonderful Life*, a telephone call to Donna Reed transforms James Stewart into a jealous lover. But in *Pillow Talk*, its role is in the service of comedy. It allows characters to have conversations from different locations. And unlike most uses of the telephone within movies, where the audience lacks the same visual contact as the caller, through the advanced technology of the split screen, Day and Hudson share the same scene simultaneously.

In addition to the telephone, Hudson's playboy bachelor pad is rigged with the same sorts of cutting-edge predigital technology—buttons to engage door locks, drop LPs onto record player platters, lower lights, transform couches into beds—that could be found in James Bond's Aston Martin, in the 1964 film *Goldfinger*. Playboy bachelor apartments were an important example of modern technology used as part of the art of seduction.

See also: Romantic Comedy, The

References

Cohan, Steven. *Masked Men: Masculinity and the Movies in the Fifties*. Bloomington: Indiana University Press, 1997.

Schantz, Ned. "Telephonic Film." *Film Quarterly* 56(4), 2003: 23–35.

—Rick Lilla

PLACE IN THE SUN, A.   Based on Theodore Dreiser's novel *An American Tragedy*, *A Place in the Sun* was released in the fall of 1951. Dreiser's book had originally been adapted for the screen in 1931, as the nation spiraled into the depths of the Great Depression. Although the 1931 version of the film did poorly at the box office, director George Stevens was able to convince studio heads at Paramount to remake the film. A steamy romance starring Montgomery Clift and Elizabeth Taylor, the remake was widely popular with audiences, proving to be, it seems, a perfect filmic representative of America's post-WWII angst.

The film opens with George Eastman (Clift), the son of poor, uneducated church workers, accepting a job at his wealthy uncle's factory. It is a job with little status and even less pay, but George works hard and shows himself to be reliable. Despite being warned against fraternizing with the women with whom he works, George begins secretly dating another factory worker, Alice "Al" Tripp (Shelley Winters), whom he eventually impregnates. While carrying on his covert affair with Alice, George meets Angela Vickers (Taylor), a beautiful socialite who is intrigued by the handsome, charismatically simple young man. George falls hard for Angela, losing all interest in Alice. He now tries to convince the forlorn Alice to have an abortion; although she tries to accommodate George's request, she cannot find a doctor willing to do the procedure. Sensing George's feelings for Angela, and terribly hurt by his betrayal, Alice threatens to reveal her condition to Angela. Desperate, George contemplates drowning Alice in order to clear the way to marry Angela. Renting a boat, he rows Alice out onto the lake. As night falls, however, he realizes that he cannot go through with his plan. Alice,

Film stars Elizabeth Taylor and Montgomery Clift in the 1951 Paramount film *A Place in the Sun.* (Picture Post/Hulton Archive/Getty Images)

sensing that something is tragically wrong, stands up in order to approach and comfort him. The boat begins to rock, finally overturning; Alice is drowned, but George makes it back to shore. The body is eventually recovered, Alice's pregnancy and their relationship are revealed, and George is convicted of murder. The film ends with George walking to the gallows.

Clift had appeared in a number of unremarkable films before he made *A Place in the Sun—The Search* (1948) and *The Big Lift*—but he had made a name for himself in Howard Hawks's powerful Western *Red River* (1948). Using his method-acting skills, Clift, it seems, inspired even John Wayne's performance in the latter picture. Perfectly cast in *A Place in the Sun*, Clift was emblematic of a new breed of young actors— Marlon Brando, James Dean, Paul Newman—who played existentially tortured men-boys: provocative, childlike subjects of their passions who seem unable to provide direction for themselves or others. Hauntingly attractive, Clift's George Eastman appears directionless and powerless when he interacts with Alice and Angela. It is Alice, after all, who comes to George's room after he has naively informed her of his landlady's restriction regarding guests; and it is Angela who whispers that he should "tell mamma all." Audiences thrilled at the pairing of Clift and Taylor, two of Hollywood's hottest young stars, seemingly unaware that in rooting for the pair, they were ignoring George's immoral and disturbingly irresponsible treatment of Alice and their unborn child.

Interestingly, Paramount feared that *A Place in the Sun* would fail at the box office, and thus delayed its release. The film proved a commercial hit, though; it also received nine Academy Award nominations, and took home Oscars for Best Picture, Best Director for Stevens, Best Actor for Clift, and Best Actress in a supporting role for Winters.

References

Pichel, Irving. "Revivals, Reissues, Remakes, and 'A Place in the Sun.'" *The Quarterly Journal of Film, Radio and Television* 6(4), 1952: 388–92.
Pomerance, Murray, ed. *American Cinema of the 1950s: Themes and Variations.* New Brunswick, NJ: Rutgers University Press, 2005.

—*Rick Lilla*

PLANET OF THE APES. Arriving as it did in 1968, at the height of one of the most culturally important decades in American history, *Planet of the Apes* became more than a mere science fiction adventure; it became a cultural phenomenon, posing important questions for viewers and critics alike. Ground breaking make-up effects and performances from legends like Charlton Heston helped to usher in an era when science fiction films would be taken seriously as entertainment vehicles that could be extraordinarily profitable. *Planet of the Apes* would spawn four successful movie sequels, two television series, massive amounts of merchandise, and a twenty-first-century remake.

The intriguing screenplay for *Planet of the Apes* was originally drafted by Rod Serling, of television's *Twilight Zone*, and then fleshed out by Michael Wilson. The story opens with four astronauts—three men and a woman—on a mission to the stars. Placing themselves in a state of suspended animation within sealed pods, they sleep while their ship travels thousands of years into the future. When the men awaken— the female astronaut's pod was damaged and she is long dead—they find themselves on an Earth-like planet populated by intelligent apes and humans who have yet to learn to read, write, or even speak. The ape population is rigidly divided by caste, class, and race: Orangutans—light-skinned, light-furred and blond-headed—fill elite positions as societal administrators, politicians, and lawyers; chimpanzees—light-skinned, dark-furred, and dark-headed—constitute the learned class of scientists and teachers; while gorillas—dark-skinned, dark-furred, and dark-headed—function as the police and military. Humans are seen as nothing more than mindless animals to be captured, imprisoned and used for purposes of experimentation and entertainment. In the end, after barely escaping with his life, George Taylor (Heston), the only surviving astronaut, heads into the "forbidden" territories in search of a new life with a mostly mute human mate who is indigenous to the planet. What he discovers, in one of the most iconic endings in film history—he uncovers the remnants of the Statue of Liberty in the rubble left after nuclear war—is that he has been on Earth all along.

Charlton Heston is restrained with a leash and collar by two actors playing apemen in a still from director Franklin Schaffner's film *Planet of the Apes*, 1968. (Hulton Archive/Getty Images)

The film raises provocative questions about American society, both as it was during the 1960s and as it is today. While being taken prisoner, Taylor suffers a neck wound and is initially unable to speak, making him seem just like the other humans on the planet. Thrown into a barred cell, he draws the attention of two scientists, Zira (Kim Hunter) and Cornelius (Roddy McDowell), and the animus of their administrative boss, Dr. Zaius (Maurice Evans), Minister of Science and Chief Defender of the Faith. The scientists begin to believe that Taylor—"Bright Eyes," Zira calls him—is different from other humans—he is intelligent, they suggest. Ultimately recovering his voice, he is taken before a three-ape tribunal. Eerily, the hearing touches on both the 1858 Dred Scott case and the 1925 Scopes Trial. Like Dred Scott—whom the Supreme Court decided had no right to bring a suit against his master because he was a slave, and thus not a citizen but merely property—because Taylor is a "man," he has no rights under ape law. If there is to be a trial, however, it will be, like the Scopes Trial, one that concerns an issue of scientific heresy—arguing evolution over creation.

The prosecuting attorney, Dr. Honorious (James Daly), claims that his case is simple, based as it is on the apes' First Article of Faith: that the Almighty created apes in His image; He gave them souls and minds, and made them lords of the planet. Certain unorthodox scientists, though, have chosen to study humans—to study evolution. Zira and Cornelius are accused of tampering with Taylor and making him into a "speaking monster." For their part, the scientists argue that Taylor, who, if the prosecutor is correct, cannot have come from another planet, must be part of their planet's evolutionary chain—a close relative of apes—a notion the tribunal members cannot countenance. One-by-one they literally cover ears, eyes, and mouth in a disturbing expression of hear no evil, see no evil, speak no evil. Zira and Cornelius are charged by the state with scientific heresy. Threatened with emasculation and deadening experimental brain surgery, Taylor, along with his beautiful mate, escapes with the help of Zira, Cornelius, and Dr. Zaius.

Resonant with themes related to 1960s' debates over religion and science, the struggle for civil rights, and the specter of Cold War politics, *Planet of the Apes* struck a powerful chord with audiences. The films that followed in the series would continue to address questions related to issues of class, race, and religion.

References

Behind the Planet of the Apes, documentary. Twentieth Century-Fox DVD, 1998.

Greene, Eric. *Planet of the Apes as American Myth: Race, Politics, and Popular Culture.* Middletown, CT: Wesleyan University Press, 1996.

—*Richard A. Hall*

PLATOON. *Platoon* (1986) was the first film in writer/director Oliver Stone's Vietnam War trilogy, which also included *Born on the Fourth of July* (1989) and *Heaven and Earth* (1993). Shot on location in the Philippines for just $6 million, the film was a critical and commercial success, garnering eight Academy Award nominations, including wins for Best Director and Best Picture, and earning over $130 million in its initial release. It created a sensation in the United States, prompting a special screening for political leaders in Washington, D.C., frenzied national media coverage, and lines around the block. *Platoon* reinvigorated the Vietnam War-film genre and encouraged release of a spate of Vietnam-related films in the late 1980s.

Platoon follows the tour of duty of Chris Taylor, a naive enlistee new to Vietnam in 1967. Modeled loosely on Stone himself, Taylor is a son of privilege who rebelled against expectations by dropping out of college to join the Army. The film is essentially a coming-of-age drama in which Taylor confronts the harsh realities of the Vietnam combat zone and becomes embroiled in a conflict between two sergeants, Barnes and Elias, who represent competing leadership styles, opposing regional and political perspectives, realism and idealism, authoritarianism and rebellion, and, most broadly, darkness and light themselves. The conflict between Barnes and Elias comes to a head during the village sequence, a disturbing portrait of American soldiers run amok in not-so-subtle imitation of the 1968 My Lai Massacre. Barnes kills a Vietnamese woman in cold blood, Elias threatens to report him to military authorities, and Barnes threatens to kill Elias. He eventually succeeds, cutting Elias down in the midst of a firefight. The martyred Elias survives long enough to raise questions about Barnes's role in his death, and Taylor becomes convinced that Barnes must be killed. The film concludes with a chaotic battle involving relentless attacks by a faceless Vietnamese enemy that is blunted only by air strikes directly on the American base. Afterward, Taylor awakens alone in an Eden-like clearing and surveys the destruction all around him. He finds a wounded Barnes writhing in pain and seizes the opportunity to execute

Scene from the 1986 film *Platoon*, starring (left to right) Willem Dafoe, Charlie Sheen, and Tom Berenger. Directed by Oliver Stone. (Photofest)

him. Wounded himself, Taylor returns home altered and scarred, having avenged Elias by becoming like Barnes.

Critics and veterans alike hailed *Platoon* for its authentic portrayal of Americans' struggles in Vietnam. *Platoon's* realism was a departure from the epic expressionism of *The Deer Hunter* (1978), the surrealism of *Apocalypse Now* (1979), and the cartoonish violence of *Rambo I* and *II* (1982 and 1985, respectively), but its authenticity rested not with the melodramatic plot but rather with the textural details of experience: dappled light filtering through jungle canopy, the whine of mosquitoes at night, the casual intimacy of comrades in arms, the whir and chop of helicopters, the sweat and slang and exhaustion. The concept of authenticity lay at the core of the film's marketing strategy, with the original trailer emphasizing Stone's own status as a Vietnam veteran. *Platoon* also launched military technical advisor Dale Dye's Hollywood consultancy and established actor "boot camp" as an essential feature of war film preparation.

Despite its claim to realism, *Platoon* spends no time on the political dynamics of the war, focusing instead on a host of conflicts between American soldiers. The men of the platoon are divided by class, race, regionalism, their drugs of choice, and their relationship to the military, with draftees and lifers coexisting in states of mutual resentment. These literal, historical conflicts are reflected metaphorically in numerous references to "friendly fire," the act of soldiers shooting their own. In his final monologue, Taylor reflects, "We did not fight the enemy, we fought ourselves, and the enemy was within us." These are arguably the most famous lines of the film. Scholars have taken issue with the solipsism of this construction, which posits the reasons for the war—and by extension, critiques of American foreign policy—as essentially irrelevant. With the motives for U.S. intervention and the causes of American defeat in Vietnam so excised, *Platoon* frames the war as an individual's struggle against the elements and his own moral failings. Ultimately, *Platoon* marked a turning point for Vietnam veterans, who found redemption from the war's brutality and futility in the film's portrayal of struggle, sacrifice, and victimization.

See also: Stone, Oliver; War Film, The

References

Kinney, Katherine. *Friendly Fire: American Images of the Vietnam War.* Oxford, UK and New York: Oxford University Press, 2000.

Toplin, Robert Brent, ed. *Oliver Stone's USA: Film, History, and Controversy.* Lawrence: University Press of Kansas, 2000.

—Meredith H. Lair

POSTMAN ALWAYS RINGS TWICE, THE. Tay Garnett's *The Postman Always Rings Twice* (1946) represents the third attempt to bring James M. Cain's 1934 novel of the same name to the screen—the first two were Pierre Chenal's *Le dernier tornant* (1939) and Luchino Visconti's *Ossessione* (1943)—but for most American film aficionados it remains, in spite of Bob Rafelson's 1981 remake, the definitive version of Cain's lurid melodrama. Viewed from a 1940s perspective, however, Billy Wilder's *Double Indemnity* (1943), another Cain adaptation, cast a long shadow over crime films of this era, and its influence on *The Postman Always Rings Twice* was therefore far greater than either its French or Italian predecessors.

As an example of what later critics would call film noir, *Postman* exhibits many (though not all) of the traits that define this genre. Its protagonists, Frank Chambers (John Garfield) and Cora Smith (Lana Turner), are both adulterous and homicidal, and their scheme to eliminate Cora's hapless husband strikes a familiar chord in movies where murders are committed for lust and profit. Noir husbands are generally a disposable commodity, and like their counterparts in *Double Indemnity*, Nick and Cora's attempt to pass off a murder as an accident soon goes awry. As for the mutual distrust that almost derails their relationship, that too is a familiar motif in noir couplings, and while Nick and Cora do not actually try to kill each other, each one's suspicions of the other make it easy for an unscrupulous district attorney (played by Leon Ames) to turn them against each other when their case comes to trial.

Paradoxically, *Postman's* doomed lovers can almost be seen as innocents in crime, and certainly when compared with *Double Indemnity's* Walter Neff and Phyllis Dietrichson, their fumbling attempts to finish off Cora's husband clearly reveal a degree of sheer incompetence that sets them apart from more practiced killers. John Garfield's Frank Chambers is, in fact, a drifter, a basically weak (albeit sensual) character whose first impulse is simply to run off with Cora and take his chances on the road. As for Lana Turner's Cora, her character is more femme than fatale, and compared with Barbara Stanwyck's Phyllis, Turner's Cora possesses comparatively little of the killer instinct; her mood swings throughout the film suggest that Garnett couldn't quite bring himself to transform a celluloid sex goddess into a psychopathic monster. Noir females tend to be far more single-minded—and therefore deadlier—than their male counterparts, while *Postman's* protagonists are almost equally confused by fear and desire, as well as ambivalent about each other and about the crime they are "fated" to commit.

Visually, *Postman* seldom exhibits the preference for low-key lighting, spatial constriction, or disorienting angles of perception that constitute the cinematic signature of noir directors. In contrast to the haunted expressionistic interiors of noirish films like *Key Largo* (1948) or *Kiss Me Deadly* (1955), Sidney Wagner (*Postman's* cinematographer) employs a more realistic lighting scheme throughout, and as a result, our protagonists are able to move about in a bright, sunlit world, oblivious to the deadly traps that both passion and an unseen vengeance have created for them. And though the murder of Cora's husband is shot in pitch darkness, on a treacherously twisty country road—as it should be—virtually every other scene takes place in a series of well-lighted rooms and open spaces.

However, the fierce determinism that rules over human lives and literary plotlines in film noir at last claims both Nick and Cora as its victims, and it is this absurd twist of fate or chance that links *Postman* most directly to the world of noir melodrama. Thus, having been at last reconciled to one another, and having found themselves free from prosecution for crimes for which they cannot be punished, Nick and Cora are nevertheless forced to pay for their sins. Fate first strikes Cora, who suddenly dies in an accidental drowning, and then Nick, who is immediately accused of plotting her death, even though he is guiltless of any criminal intent. And though justice of a rough sort is clearly served here, it is a twisted kind of justice that the noir universe metes out, a system of absurd retributions that parody the very principle of justice they supposedly embody. As Nick observes, ironically, on his way to the gas chamber, the "postman" has indeed rung twice, and he will now be punished for the crime he did not commit. Such an ending, of course, demands a curious suspension of the very empathy for those criminal passions the entire film has labored to elicit, but that is precisely what noir filmmakers appear to demand of their audiences: an emotional detachment that deprives them of whatever moral satisfaction they might have derived from a more conventional and conventionally ritualized spectacle of crime and punishment.

See also: Double Indemnity ; Film Noir; Wilder, Billy

References

Ballinger, Alexander, and Danny Graydon. *The Rough Guide to Film Noir*. London: Penguin, 2007.

Silver, Alain, Elizabeth Ward, James Ursini, and Robert Porfirio, eds. *The Film Noir Encyclopedia*. London: Duckworth Overlook, 2010.

—*Robert Platzner*

PRETTY WOMAN. One of the biggest box-office successes of 1990, *Pretty Woman* marked Julia Roberts's rise to superstardom and the reinvigoration of the "woman's film" in mass culture. The film, a latter-day cross between Cinderella and Pygmalion, updates the classic convention of the damsel in distress saved by a worthy man. This time around, it's Vivian Ward, Roberts's hooker-with-a-heart-of-gold, who comes to the moral and emotional salvation of Edward Lewis, the uptight corporate raider played by Richard Gere. Marketability concerns shaped *Pretty Woman*'s rosy outcome. J. F. Lawton's original script for *3,000*—the amount Edward pays Vivian for a week of her services—ended the pair's weeklong escape on a darker

Scene from the 1986 film *Pretty Woman*, starring Richard Gere and Julia Roberts. Directed by Garry Marshall. (Photofest)

note. Only editing by veteran sitcom-writer-turned-director Garry Marshall gave the film its happy ending: when Edward arrives in a shining white limo to sweep Vivian off her feet, she informs him that the heroine of her fairy tale rescues the hero "right back."

The romance begins as a business transaction. Edward is in Los Angeles for work. Dumped over the phone by his live-in girlfriend, he drives off in his lawyer's sports car, looking to blow off steam. A quick stop to ask for directions from the leggy Vivian turns into a lesson on driving a stick shift as Vivian pilots the odd couple toward Edward's posh Beverly Hills hotel. In the days that follow, Edward exposes Vivian to high culture, chartering a private plane to San Francisco to attend the opera and taking her to a polo match. In return, Vivian teaches Edward to walk barefoot in the park and to express his emotions, until then repressed on account of an unloving father (his third takeover victim). From their week together, Vivian gains an upgraded wardrobe and a new knowledge of flatware etiquette, but it is Edward who emerges the more profoundly changed: breaking with old habits, he negotiates a friendly merger with the owner of a shipbuilding company.

Wildly popular with audiences, *Pretty Woman* was criticized for idealizing prostitution and for its uncomplicated portrayal of money buying respect, if not morality or happiness, for its characters. In one memorable scene, Vivian reenters a Rodeo Drive boutique where earlier, dressed in her Hollywood Boulevard attire, she had been snubbed by a salesgirl. Richard announces to the sales staff that the couple is "going to be spending an obscene amount of money in here." They do. Critics argued that the film dodged the serious inequalities of Vivian's situation and made few connections to the broader picture of women's sexual and economic exploitation. The movie treated the AIDS crisis that had rocked Reagan-era America lightly in a scene where Vivian fans out a rainbow array of condoms for Edward's choosing.

The film also made a splash in the trade and popular presses for its target audience. In the previous two decades, the industry had treated the female demographic as peripheral to the success of big-budget action and horror blockbusters. *Pretty Woman* was interpreted as part of a broader trend in the American film industry to target movies at women. However, the representation of women in this new wave of women's films was ambiguous. A number of modestly budgeted films from the late 1970s and 1980s had cast a skeptical eye on marriage and traditional romance. These films, which included *Annie Hall* (1977) and *Kramer vs. Kramer* (1979), captured the lingering tensions surrounding the push for women's professional and sexual equality. Some commentators viewed *Pretty Woman* as a retreat from the social and political frankness of these films to the timeworn conventions of fairy-tale romance.

Yet critics who dismissed *Pretty Woman* as escapist stumbled over how to explain its smashing success among female viewers. The performances remain memorable. Roberts's portrayal of the free-spirited, sharp-witted Vivian earned her a Best Actress Oscar nomination. Supporting cast member Laura San Giacomo winningly humanized Vivian's drug-addled hooker roommate, as did Hector Elizondo, the punctilious hotel manager who takes Vivian under his wing. Fans of the film have argued that, rather than patronizing women with the old Prince Charming myth, *Pretty Woman* revises it, winking at audiences attuned to Hollywood fairy tales. The film leaves the final word not to Vivian or Edward, embracing on her fire escape, but to a homeless man wandering the streets of Los Angeles. "This is Hollywood," he announces, "land of dreams." With this framing device, *Pretty Woman* signaled its debt to fantasy, and audiences' hunger for the same.

See also: Romantic Comedy, The

References

Garrett, Roberta. *Postmodern Chick Flicks: The Return of the Woman's Film.* New York: Palgrave Macmillan, 2007.

Greenberg, Harvey Roy. "Rescrewed: *Pretty Woman*'s Co-opted Feminism." *Journal of Popular Film and Television* 19(1), Spring 1991: 9–13.
Merkin, Daphne. "Prince Charming Comes Back." *New York Times*, July 15, 1990.

—Diana Lemberg

PRIDE OF THE YANKEES, THE. *The Pride of the Yankees* (1942) is director Sam Wood's dramatic biopic of New York Yankees baseball star Lou Gehrig, whose 1941 death at age 37 from amyotrophic lateral sclerosis (ALS), a disease that more commonly bears his name, is one of the great tragedies in American sports. The film was a critical success, garnering an Oscar for Best Film Editing and earning 10 other nominations, but its long-term legacy is as one of Hollywood's most revered baseball films, an all-American hero story, classic romance, and triumphant meditation on the immutability of the American Dream.

Damon Runyon's prologue introduces the film as the story of a humble hero who carried himself with modest dignity and faced his own untimely death gracefully. Wood's film, however, is more than mere cinematic biography. Gehrig's life story becomes a quintessentially American fable, a soaring affirmation of the American Dream tinged in tragic, but simultaneously triumphal, overtones that resonated with its World War II era audience. It is the story of what an all-American boy could achieve, fulfilling not only his own dreams but those of his hardworking German immigrant parents, as well. In the end, Gehrig courageously confronted his own mortality, exemplified by his famous "Luckiest Man" speech at Yankee Stadium, suggesting that while hard times loomed, Americans could persevere.

Although Wood took some license in telling the story, *The Pride of the Yankees* is a relatively accurate account of Gehrig's life. In particular, the film is faithful to the early life of Lou Gehrig (Gary Cooper)—his relationship with his immigrant parents, devotion to his mother (Elsa Janssen), and the circumstances that led to the start of his professional baseball career with the New York Yankees. On the other hand, there was some fictionalization in the portrayal of Gehrig's romance and marriage to Chicago socialite Eleanor Twitchell (Teresa Wright), his inspirational home-run-hitting exploits for hospitalized children, and other aspects of his baseball career. Several real baseball stars played themselves in the film, including Gehrig's teammates Bill Dickey and the legendary Babe Ruth. Much of the film's success in capturing the essence of its protagonist can be attributed to Gary Cooper. Cooper, despite being an abysmal baseball player who batted from the wrong side of the plate, looked much like Gehrig and his penchant for taking on humble, stoic characters had well prepared him to adopt the persona of the notoriously sober baseball superstar.

The Pride of the Yankees is often regarded as one of the best of Hollywood's baseball films, and is certainly a classic tale of a first-generation American's journey from rags to riches, but it is also a wonderfully crafted love story. In fact, it is the romance of Lou and Eleanor Gehrig, tracing their lives from the height of his career on the diamond through his struggle with a fatal disease, which serves as the narrative backbone of the film. Director Wood later adopted an almost identical format for his 1949 baseball drama *The Stratton Story*, starring Jimmy Stewart and June Allyson. To some degree the emphasis on personal relationships, and the focus on the human elements of the story, was meant to appeal to a largely female wartime audience. Cooper and Wright possessed such a charming chemistry, and so capably captured the simple magic of everyday romance, that they both earned Oscar nominations for their performances. Irving Berlin's "Always," a favorite tune of the real-life Gehrigs, added a personal touch to the movie's romantic tone.

Despite the film's somewhat saccharine tone, it remains a classic example of both sports and wartime cinema. Baseball, the "National Pastime," was at the height of its cultural prominence when *The Pride of the Yankees* was released. There can be no doubt that Wood's film, with a screenplay co-scripted by noted sportswriter Paul Gallico, would remind wartime audiences of ideal American virtues—modesty, fairness, and courageous resilience—embodied in both Lou Gehrig and the sport he played.

See also: Sports Film, The

References

Briley, Ron, Michael K. Schoenecke, and Deborah A. Carmichael. *All-Stars and Movie Stars: Sports in Film and History.* Lexington: University Press of Kentucky, 2008.

Dixon, Wheeler Winston, ed. *American Cinema of the 1940s: Themes and Variations.* New Brunswick, NJ: Rutgers University Press, 2006.

Gehring, Wes D. *Mr. Deeds Goes to Yankee Stadium: Baseball Films in the Capra Tradition.* Jefferson, NC: McFarland, 2004.

Most, Marshall G., and Robert Rudd. *Stars, Stripes, and Diamonds: American Culture and the Baseball Film.* Jefferson, NC: McFarland, 2006.

—Nathan M. Corzine

PRODUCERS, THE. Winning an Academy Award for Best Writing, Story and Screenplay, *The Producers* (1968) is a brilliant satire that made writer-director Mel Brooks a comedic sensation, although Brooks would later claim that *Blazing Saddles* (1974) was his best work. *The Producers*, which Brooks resurrected as a Tony-winning Broadway musical by the same name in 2001 and in a film adaptation of the musical in 2005, broke new ground in American cinema by aggressively mocking Adolf Hitler and his infamous Nazi storm troopers. The satirical play within the film, which the character of Max Bialystock described as "practically a love letter to Hitler," also poked fun at the allegedly naive cheerfulness of *The Sound of Music* (1965), which similarly juxtaposed carefree singing and dancing against a fascist Axis backdrop. Banned in Germany for its relentless parody of the Third Reich, *The Producers* became a cult classic among Jews on both sides of the Atlantic.

"I picked the wrong play, the wrong director, the wrong cast," moans theatrical producer Max Bialystock (Zero Mostel) near the end of *The Producers*. Throwing up his hands and lamenting his fate as an inmate at the state penitentiary, he wonders,

"Where did I go right?" Bialystock's accountant-turned-partner Leo Bloom (Gene Wilder) hysterically casts about for the pair's doctored ledgers and threatens to turn himself into the police in exchange for leniency. "Springtime for Hitler: A Gay Romp with Adolf and Eva in Berchtesgarten," Bialystock and Bloom's patently offensive play, had become "the biggest hit on Broadway." But for Bialystock and Bloom, right was wrong and success meant failure. All that the crooked duo had to do was to produce a flop and they would walk away with $2 million. How hard could it be?

Rated PG-13 for "sexual humor and references," *The Producers* opens with a scene of Bialystock clutching and being clutched by a little old lady (Estelle Winwood) known by the moniker "hold me, touch me." Bloom, an accountant from the firm Whitehall and Marks hired to balance Bialystock's books, walks in on the middle-aged producer and one of his octogenarian investors engaged in sexual role-playing. Pressured by Bialystock to use "creative accounting," Bloom discovers that with a play guaranteed to fail, "a producer could make more money with a flop than he could with a hit." Bialystock quickly convinces Bloom to quit his job in order to co-produce a flop that would make the pair millionaires in unspent seed money. Putting their greed ahead of their antifascist ideals, the once-popular producer and his new partner in crime don swastika armbands in order to acquire the rights to "Springtime for Hitler" from ex-Nazi Franz Liebkind (Kenneth Mars).

Moving to the second phase of Bialystock and Bloom's seemingly foolproof scheme, Bialystock romances little old ladies until he has raised $2 million in checks made out to "cash," and hires Ulla (Lee Meredith), a gorgeous blonde but English-deficient Swede, to be his new receptionist. With Bloom, Bialystock next hires the cross-dressing Roger De Bris (Christopher Hewitt) to direct the production. Finally, "Springtime for Hitler" opens, and smartly dressed theatergoers watch in shock as Lorenzo St. DuBois (Dick Shawn) plays an ostentatiously bisexual Hitler and Brooks himself appears in an acerbically satirical cameo: "Don't be stupid, be a smartie./Come and join the Nazi party." However, even the show's climactic inclusion of a spinning swastika, comprised of leather-garbed storm troopers of the Rockette variety, fails to sufficiently offend the theatergoing masses. Ironically, the play becomes a hit, sending Bialystock and Bloom to Sing Sing where they plot their next production, "Prisoners of Love."

The Producers ranks among the best films ever produced with the goal of focusing attention on the Holocaust. Two decades after the Nazis systematically murdered millions of Jews, homosexuals, gypsies, and dissidents, Brooks effectively recast—through Jewish humor—Hitler as an object of ridicule at the mercy of Jewish producers and commercialization. Confronted with mixed reviews for the film, Brooks explained, "More than anything, the great Holocaust by the Nazis is probably the great outrage of the Twentieth Century . . . if I get on the soapbox and wax eloquently, it'll be blown away in the wind, but if I do 'springtime for Hitler' it'll never be forgotten." Although the 2001 musical proved instantly successful, Brooks deserves more acclaim for taking on Hitler in America in 1968.

See also: Music in Film; Musical, The

Janet Leigh screams in the famous shower scene from the film *Psycho*, directed by Alfred Hitchcock, 1960. (Paramount Pictures/Courtesy of Getty Images)

References

Brooks, Mel, and Tom Meehan. *The Producers: The Book, Lyrics, and Story behind the Biggest Hit in Broadway History!* New York: Hyperion, 2001.

Desser, David, and Lester D. Friedman. *American Jewish Filmmakers*, 2nd ed. Urbana: University of Illinois Press, 2004.

Simpson, Paul, Helen Rodiss, and Michaela Bushnell, eds. *The Rough Guide to Cult Movies*. London: Haymarket Customer Publishing, 2004.

Sinyard, Neil. *The Films of Mel Brooks*. New York: Exeter Books, 1987.

—Alan Kennedy-Shaffer

PSYCHO. At the time of its release in the summer of 1960, *Psycho* was a box-office sensation, shattering attendance records for the year. Although critics initially gave it mixed reviews, Alfred Hitchcock's low-budget black-and-white thriller is now regarded as a cinematic masterpiece.

Based on the Wisconsin serial killer, Ed Gein, *Psycho* first appeared in 1959 as a novel written by Robert Bloch. After purchasing the rights from Bloch, Hitchcock hired Joseph Stefano to write the screenplay, but soon ran into trouble with his studio. Paramount executives could see no commercial potential in a movie that killed off the heroine in the first half, but this was precisely the twist that appealed to Hitchcock. He agreed to finance the film himself once Paramount agreed to distribute it, then shot it using his television crew on a rapid schedule.

Psycho's plot revolves around a series of crimes. After Marion Crane (Janet Leigh) impulsively steals $40,000 from her employer, she drives all day to meet her boyfriend Sam (John Gavin), but becomes tired and stops at the Bates Motel where Norman (Anthony Perkins) gives her a room. That night, she is murdered in the shower by what appears to be a crazy old woman. Later, Arbogast (Martin Balsam), a private detective investigating the case, is also murdered, and Marion's sister Lila (Vera Miles) and Sam try to find out what happened. When Lila tries to speak with Mrs. Bates in the basement, she too is nearly murdered, but Sam rescues her just in time.

Psycho succeeds as a thriller because of its cinematic technique. From the opening credits it is clear that *Psycho* is a strikingly original film. Veteran Hitchcock collaborator

Bernard Herrmann uses only the string section in his orchestral score, starkly complementing the crisscrossing horizontal and vertical lines of Saul Bass's visuals. Following the credits, Hitchcock's camera pans the Phoenix cityscape and penetrates the hotel window where Marion and Sam enjoy a Friday afternoon tryst—half-dressed. It is the first of many instances in *Psycho* where the viewer is positioned as a voyeur. A more overt example occurs after Norman and Marion's mildly flirtatious dinner conversation. When Marion retires to her room, Norman removes a picture from overtop a peephole in the adjacent room and stares at Marion in her underwear. Thanks to the subjective camera shot, we are staring at Marion just as Norman is.

Throughout *Psycho*, Hitchcock plays upon the voyeuristic tendencies of the audience by provocatively revealing some details while carefully concealing others. In 1960, it was still relatively unusual to show a woman on-screen dressed only in a bra and half-slip. Likewise, it was utterly taboo to flush a toilet as Marion does at the Bates Motel after disposing of some scraps of paper. Distracted by these images, audiences are less aware of what they are not seeing. Mrs. Bates, for example, speaks to Norman throughout the film, but the viewer does not see her face until the end.

The most blatant appeal to voyeurism in *Psycho* occurs during the shower scene. One of the most famous sequences in cinematic history, the shower scene powerfully suggests erotic violence without ever really showing anything. At no point in the 78-shot, 45-second sequence does the viewer see any forbidden body parts, and only once does the knife appear to make contact with the body. Instead the violence is achieved through montage, substituting film cuts for cutting of the skin. The high-pitched violin motif that Herrmann devised to accompany the murder is equally renowned and often parodied in popular culture, as in a 1990 episode of *The Simpsons*, entitled, "Itchy & Scratchy & Marge."

Psycho spawned a whole new subgenre of horror, the "slasher," with films like *Halloween* (1978) and *Friday the 13th* (1980) employing many of *Psycho*'s innovations. Slasher films generally feature a psychologically disturbed killer who has a preference for knives and sexually active female victims. *Psycho* has also inspired numerous sequels, homages, and even a shot-for-shot remake by Gus Van Sant in 1998. Tributes to *Psycho* range from lowbrow comedy, such as Mel Brooks's *High Anxiety* (1977) to art-house tragedy in Brian De Palma's *Dressed to Kill* (1980). Arguably Hitchcock's greatest film, *Psycho* continues to surprise, horrify, and elate viewers with its stunning originality and masterful technique.

See also: Hitchcock, Alfred

References

Rebello, Stephen. *Alfred Hitchcock and the Making of Psycho*. New York: First Harper Perennial, 1991

Truffaut, François. *Hitchcock*. With the collaboration of Helen G. Scott. New York: Simon and Schuster, 1985.

—*Joseph Christopher Schaub*

PULP FICTION.   Quentin Tarantino's *Pulp Fiction* (1994) merges classic American crime genre techniques and characters into a single self-reflexive homage. As an example of postmodern cinema, it also includes a barrage of musical, visual, and dialogic popular culture references. The film is made up of three individual but interconnected stories, each introduced with a title card. It is the references themselves that make *Pulp Fiction* so attuned to American audiences, with strictly American cars, books, television, and music constantly shown and heard in the background.

Setting the tone for this uniquely American filmic experience, the first story, "Vincent Vega and Marsellus Wallace's Wife," is preceded by a running commentary on the differences between McDonald's in Amsterdam and in the United States. Told from the American perspective of hitman Vincent Vega (John Travolta), the dialogue reveals several cultural differences between the two countries. Vincent is accompanied by his partner Jules Winnfield (Samuel L. Jackson), and though both men wear black suits and carry guns, they're more humanized than typical hitmen of the crime genre.

In "Vincent Vega and Marsellus Wallace's Wife" Vincent serves as proxy on a date with the wife of his boss, Marsellus Wallace (Ving Rhames). He takes Marsellus's wife Mia (Uma Thurman) to the 1950s-theme restaurant "Jack Rabbit Slim's." Easily the pinnacle of American pop culture references in the film, Vincent and Mia see posters for 1950s and '60s movies, sit in a booth shaped like an old Chrysler, and order the "Douglas Sirk steak" and the "Durward Kirby burger" while interacting with servers impersonating celebrities such as Ed Sullivan, Buddy Holly, Marilyn Monroe, and Ricky Nelson.

Scene from the 1986 film *Pulp Fiction*, starring John Travolta (left) and Samuel L. Jackson. Directed by Quentin Tarantino. (Photofest)

In the prologue for the second story, "The Gold Watch," a close-up of an old TV showing the 1959 American children's cartoon *Clutch Cargo* is shown. Tarantino opted to use this reference to allude to this scene as a flashback, further emphasizing that *Pulp Fiction* is best understood by American viewers.

"The Gold Watch" follows boxer Butch Coolidge (Bruce Willis) after double-crossing Marsellus on a fight. Butch's escape is complicated by his deceased father's gold watch, which was bestowed on him as a child by Captain Koons (Christopher Walken), who was a POW with his father during the Vietnam War. Tarantino chooses *The Losers* (1968)—a film playing on Butch's motel TV about motorcyclists sent by the CIA to rescue a presidential advisor in Cambodia—to abruptly wake Butch from a deep sleep. This cultural reference reminds viewers of his father's war, and now his own war against Marsellus. With his gold watch still on the nightstand in his apartment, Butch risks returning for it. Here Butch's story intersects Vincent's, as the latter is waiting for Butch at his apartment. Butch shoots Vincent, who dies with a copy of the Peter O'Donnell pulp novel *Modesty Blaise* on his lap.

The third story, "The Bonnie Situation," begins where "Vincent Vega and Marsellus Wallace's Wife" left off. This segment contains more up-to-date pop and pulp culture references, especially to Los Angeles. In this story, Vincent mistakenly shoots and kills an informant while he and Jules are driving home from the job in the first story. Exposed in suburban Los Angeles with a bloody car, they stop at Jimmie Dimmick's (Quentin Tarantino) modish house while Winston "The Wolf" Wolfe (Harvey Keitel) is called in to "solve problems." Jimmie is introduced wearing a bathrobe over his Detroit metro magazine *Orbit* T-shirt while giving a speech about drinking gourmet coffee. Jimmie gives Vincent and Jules clean T-shirts of the old comic-strip character Krazy Kat, and the "Banana Slug" campus mascot of University of California Santa Cruz.

The film ends where it began, in the Hawthorne Grill in Los Angeles. Here, Jules makes a final speech of redemption amidst an unrelated robbery. In his speech he references *Happy Days'* "The Fonz" when he tells one of the robbers to "be cool."

Pulp Fiction's effective use of nonlinear storytelling paired with its incredibly diverse cultural references allow it to accomplish more than any traditional crime drama ever could. The film won 43 awards, including an Oscar for Best Writing and the Golden Palm at the Cannes Film Festival. With its extensive use of pastiche, *Pulp Fiction* transcends the crime genre, pulling together references from popular American culture, pulp and hard-boiled crime fiction, French New Wave, Samurai cinema, and more.

See also: Editing; Gangster Film, The

References

Polan, Dana. *Pulp Fiction*. New York: St. Martin's, 2000.
The Internet Movie Database. "Quentin Tarantino." http://www.imdb.com/name/nm0000233/.

—*Adam Dean*

Q

QUIET MAN, THE. With *The Quiet Man* (1952), director John Ford offered an intensely personal film that was the culmination of an infamously extended struggle with the Hollywood studio system. The result, more than 15 years in the making, was a lush homage to the director's Irish roots, combining nostalgia with something heretofore lacking in the Fordian oeuvre: a sprightly romantic love story. The film, arguably Ford's most beloved, earned the director his fourth and final Best Director Oscar.

Ford had tinkered with *The Quiet Man* for years after discovering Maurice Walsh's short story in a 1933 edition of the *Saturday Evening Post*. Although he made several attempts in the 1930s and 1940s to produce a film version, Hollywood's major studio heads insisted that Ford's pet project had no commercial potential. Nevertheless, he continuously played with the story, adding dramatic depth, and casting the film with regulars from his other projects—Maureen O'Hara, John Wayne, and Victor McLaglen among them—years before he actually found a studio willing to back it.

In the end, Ford was able to convince a second-tier studio, Republic Pictures, to take on his Irish "Taming of the Shrew" tale. Although Ford had spent years tweaking the somewhat thin, mood-based plot of the original short story, commentators still argued that his version of *The Quiet Man* was nothing more than a superficial idyll. Many Irish critics despised the film, offended by its unrealistic, stereotyped portrayal of Irish communities and rituals. Studio head Herbert Yates, convinced the project was a mistake, thought the film's Technicolor green was overwhelming. More pointedly, a generation of feminist critics derided the film, despite the presence of a strong-willed central female character, for perceived misogyny.

Beneath *The Quiet Man*'s simple veneer, however, is a well-crafted romance that still connects with contemporary audiences. The plot involves the return to his Innisfree birthplace of Sean "Trooper" Thornton (John Wayne), an Irish American boxer who has killed a man in the ring and who hopes to escape his brutal, materialistic American past by exiling himself to his dimly remembered childhood home. There he runs afoul of local bully Squire "Red Will" Danaher (Victor McLaglen) when he purchases ancestral land coveted by Danaher. This strained relationship is further complicated by

Thornton's courtship of Danaher's sister—the fiery Mary Kate Danaher (Maureen O'Hara). When Mary Kate refuses to consummate her marriage to Thornton until she receives her dowry, held from her by her brother, the former boxer is forced to overcome his personal demons and confront Danaher. Once Thornton chooses to use his fists again, the two men meet in one of Hollywood's most celebrated fight sequences, a bare-fisted brawl that takes them across the Innisfree countryside surrounded by a swarm of local onlookers.

How Green Was My Valley author Richard Llewellyn drafted the screenplay for *The Quiet Man*, and the script's sentimental feel recalls that from Ford's 1941 Best Picture Oscar winner. The setting for this fable of two people who must tame themselves before they can live happily together is a magical community whose values represent the antithesis of the American obsession with individualism and accumulation. Ford's Innisfree is a place where time has no meaning. His Ireland is the sort of dreamscape that could exist only in the mind of the Irish exile—and Ford was exactly that. Cutting elements that would have addressed internecine political conflicts—in one version Sean Thornton would have joined the IRA—Ford instead envisioned a space where Catholics and Protestants lived in relative peace, where pub patrons broke into spontaneous song, and where traditional courtship rituals were painstakingly overseen by local tippler Michaeleen Oge Flynn (Barry Fitzgerald).

Ultimately, *The Quiet Man* served as a semiautobiographical cinematic homecoming for Ford. Although his Ireland was by turns too green, too comic, and too musical, it was also a place that resonated with American audiences eager to escape to a simple and beautiful place after the years of World War II and early Cold War turmoil. Subsequent audiences, beset by different stresses, have proven just as eager to escape, even if only for a while, to Innisfree.

See also: Ford, John; Melodrama, The

References

Eyman, Scott. *Print the Legend: The Life and Times of John Ford*. Baltimore: Johns Hopkins University Press, 1999.

Ford, Dan. *Pappy: The Life of John Ford*. Englewood Cliffs, NJ: Prentice Hall, 1979.

McBride, Joseph, and Michael Wilmington. *John Ford*. New York: Da Capo, 1988.

Roberts, Randy, and James S. Olson. *John Wayne: American*. New York: Free Press, 1995.

—*Nathan M. Corzine*

R

REBEL WITHOUT A CAUSE. *Rebel Without a Cause* (1955), directed by Nicholas Ray, received Oscar nominations for Supporting Actress (Natalie Wood), Supporting Actor (Sal Mineo), and Writing for a Motion Picture Story (Ray). The renowned movie is best known for its lead actor, James Dean, who played the malcontented teenager, Jim Stark. This role, in addition to Dean's tragic death in a 1955 car accident at the age 24, made him into an iconic representative of teenage angst.

Rebel Without a Cause is about juvenile delinquency. More interesting are its sources. The three main characters, Jim, Judy (Wood), and "Plato" (Mineo), are estranged from their parents. Jim refers to his family not as a place of refuge and support, but as a "zoo." He feels alienated from his father's effeteness and his parents' bickering; Judy's father refuses her the affection she needs; and Plato's parents are separated and absent. Yet—viewing the film as an historical source—the teenagers' discontent is also the by-product of 1950s affluence and the resulting cultural emphasis on materialism. This is manifest in the lecture scene at the planetarium. Dr. Minton (Ian Wolfe), commenting on the end of the world, states that "We will disappear into the blackness of the space from which we came, destroyed as we began, in a burst of gas and fire. . . . And man, existing alone, seems himself an episode of little consequence." Surely the monologue, and especially the teenagers' troubled reactions to it, are symbolic of their alienation from their parents (which they perceive); but it also reflects anxiety over the purposeless and superficial existence of a materially driven life (which they do not readily perceive). Industrial-capitalist America's emphasis on the material self at the expense of the spiritual self, it appears, bred a sense of a lack of fulfillment, especially in its more sensitive teenaged members. Jim is dejected despite the fact that his father, Frank Stark (Jim Backus), buys him "everything" he wants. Before the so-called "Chickie Run," Jim asks his antagonist, Buzz Gunderson (Corey Allen), "Why do we do this," to which Buzz replies, "You got to do something." That is, ostensibly, "you got to do something" to divert one's attention from the unfulfilling, one-dimensionality of materialist American life. A more explicit anxiety derived from affluence is reflected in the feminization—synonymous with the weakening—of Jim's father, which expresses a fear that affluence cultivates effeteness. Frank is subject to a domineering wife and

Actors (left to right) Sal Mineo, James Dean, and Natalie Wood in a still from director Nicholas Ray's film *Rebel Without a Cause*. (Warner Bros./Getty Images)

mother, who together, Jim claims, "make mush out of him." This feminization reaches its apogee when Jim discovers his father in an apron.

As a 1950s film, *Rebel Without a Cause* is generally read as a product of the cultural conformity fostered by the so-called second Red Scare—because a direct confrontation with the Soviet Union was not a policy option, anticommunism intensified domestically, which fostered a consensus around conservative values (Whitfield, 1996). Indeed, it may be argued that despite its negative portrayal of middle-class family life, the film actually reinforced Cold War conformity by evaluating personal relationships, rather than assessing economic, political, or social issues (Shaw, 2007). Yet, if the film explores personal relations, it also expresses an anxiety with American affluence and a cultural emphasis on materialism. And it might be—even if it reinforced Cold War militarism—that the feminization of Jim's father was an acute warning that affluence was not only damaging family dynamics, but also was weakening America society during the Cold War—could any 1950s viewer imagine Jim's apron-wearing father as capable of fighting the Soviets? Furthermore, Jim is symbolically a refutation of cultural conformity; the red jacket does indeed represent his angst, but it also marks him as an individual who exists in a metaphorically black-and-white world. He befriended Plato, after all, Judy points out, "when nobody else liked him—[and] that's being strong." Some cultural commentators believe that Dean's fashionable rebelliousness helped precipitate the upheavals of the 1960s; if this is the case, then the film may be understood not merely as a cinematic reflection of 1950s (anti)orthodoxy, but also as a cautionary tale foreshadowing the cultural conflicts that exploded during the 1960s.

References

Shaw, Tony. "Hollywood's Cold War." In *Culture, Politics, and the Cold War*. Amherst: University of Massachusetts Press, 2007.

Whitfield, Stephen. *The Culture of the Cold War*. 2nd ed. Baltimore: Johns Hopkins University Press, 1996.

—Mark D. Popowski

RIO BRAVO.   Director Howard Hawks made no secret of the fact that his film *Rio Bravo* (1959) was a response to the 1952 Fred Zinnemann picture *High Noon*. Hawks found the Zinnemann film politically objectionable, suggesting that it was a thinly veiled attack on the HUAC hearings and the blacklisting of members of the cinematic community. Hawks thought that the adoption of this political position was cowardly, and even dangerously "unpatriotic," as in his mind it failed to take seriously the communist threat issuing from the Soviet Union. He believed that *High Noon* was a cinematic representation of just such a weak-willed political stance, especially in regard to the film's portrayal of its protagonist Will Kane (Gary Cooper), a less than heroic sheriff, who is neither "good enough" to confront a crazed band of killers himself or wise enough to hire real "professionals" to help him turn back the deadly outlaws.

In the end, Hawks found the storyline of *High Noon* absurd, particularly its conclusion, which depicted Kane having to be saved by his "Quaker wife" (Grace Kelly) and ultimately "riding into the sunset," not as the traditional Westerner but as what might be understood by someone like Hawks as an antiviolence liberal, who, in a final act of political defiance, flings his badge into the dust and turns his back on his community. Casting film star John Wayne as his protagonist in *Rio Bravo*, Hawks set out to make what he believed was a real western. Wayne was the perfect leading man for the picture, as he had already established himself as an iconic American film hero; he also agreed wholeheartedly with Hawks's interpretation of *High Noon*.

In *Rio Bravo*, Hawks positioned his protagonist, Sheriff John T. Chance (Wayne), in a similar situation to Will Kane's in *High Noon*. Chance, marshal of Rio Bravo, must confront an angry rancher, Nathan Burdette (John Russell), and his loyal gunmen after Chance arrests the rancher's younger brother Joe (Claude Akins) for murdering an unarmed man during a saloon brawl. Chance must hold the killer in jail until the deputy marshal shows up in six days' time to take him away. Nathan Burdette is not about to let Chance turn his brother over to the marshal, though. Unlike Sheriff Kane in *High Noon*, Chance turns to professionals to deal with his precarious situation, rejecting an offer made by his devoted friend Pat Wheeler (Ward Bond) to let Chance

Actors John Wayne (right) and Ricky Nelson (left) star in the western *Rio Bravo*, 1959. (Archive Photos/Getty Images)

deputize his ranch hands: "Well-meaning amateurs, most of them worried about their wives and kids," grumbles Chance. Chance's deputy, the alcoholic Dude (Dean Martin), and an old, crippled jailer, Stumpy (Walter Brennan), stand beside the sheriff. When Wheeler recklessly tries to convince the town's citizens to help Chance, Burdette's men ambush him. Wheeler's ex-bodyguard, Colorado (Ricky Nelson), ulti-mately joins Chance after rescuing the sheriff in a shoot-out. The sheriff even falls for a mysterious, and wholly un-Quaker-like, woman (Angie Dickinson), who knows how to talk, shoot, and even love him. Eventually, Burdette's gang abducts Dude and arranges an exchange for Joe. In an explosive finale, the resourceful heroes thwart Burdette's plans to free Joe and kill Dude.

When *Rio Bravo* was released in 1959, it was hailed by critics and audiences alike as a superlative western; and today, it is often chosen as one of the best genre films in the history of the American cinema. Interestingly, however, although the picture is clearly an example of a classic western, complete with its traditional "heroic loner" protago-nist, at least on one level it may be understood as a cinematic declaration of the Cold War politics of Hawks and Wayne. Indeed, it may be argued that *Rio Bravo*, with its emphasis on professional men who are called upon to protect the community from murderous interlopers, is expressive of the antipathy both Hawks and Wayne, and many others in the United States, felt toward the Soviet Union, Communism, and what they perceived as unpatriotic Americans, Zinnemann and Cooper included. Wayne had established his own anticommunist credentials in his 1952 thriller *Big Jim McClain*, in which he portrayed a HUAC investigator searching for "Reds" in Hawaii; and in *Blood Alley* (1955), in which he contended with the Red Chinese. But despite the contemporary settings and the clear-cut anticommunist sentiments of these latter two films, it may be that *Rio Bravo* is really the most obvious statement of the Cold War ideology shared by Hawks, Wayne, and many nervous Americans during the 1950s.

See also: Hawks, Howard; Wayne, John; Western, The

References

McBride, Joseph. *Hawks on Hawks*. Los Angeles: University of California Press, 1982.
McCarthy, Todd. *Howard Hawks: The Grey Fox of Hollywood*. New York: Grove, 1997.
Wood, Robin. *Rio Bravo*. London: British Film Institute, 2003.

—*Van Roberts*

RISKY BUSINESS.   *Risky Business* (1983), writer-director Paul Brickman's directorial debut, is many things: among them a satire of the capitalist 1980's; a suburban coming-of-age story; and the film that launched Tom Cruise toward superstardom. Strongly reviewed as more sophisticated than bawdy movies like *Porky's* (1982) that were finding teen audiences at the time, the picture earned 10 times its modest budget and evoked comparisons to what many considered the emblematic coming-of-age film of its generation, *The Graduate* (1967). *Risky Business* remains a classic cinematic work of the 1980s and one of Cruise's best movies.

The film's plot, full of spirited hijinks and serious themes, revolves around Joel Goodsen (Cruise), literally the "good son" raised with all the comforts of the tony Chicago suburbs. He and his friends worry about college admissions, but they also are seriously concerned, as teens often are, about sex. When Joel's parents take an out-of-town trip, they leave Joel home alone, reassuring him of their trust and reminding him of his long-shot interview with a Princeton admissions officer, which is to take place while they are gone.

However, Joel, counseled by his friend Miles (Curtis Armstrong), begins to "say 'what the fuck' " and take chances; which, Miles argues, will "make your future." After dancing around the living room to Bob Seger's "Old Time Rock 'n' Roll" in the film's iconic (and most parodied) scene, Joel begins to break rules: he drives his father's Porsche against strict orders, and he calls Lana (Rebecca De Mornay), the streetwise prostitute who will make him a man sexually and give him his real education. After Joel accidentally dumps the Porsche into Lake Michigan, he accepts Lana's suggestion to bring her prostitute friends together with his rich ones in order to earn the money to fix the car. The plan works, but more than that, it reconciles the competing sides of Joel, the good son who will go to the Ivy League school and the hormone-ravaged teen who wants sex. Joel's interview with the Princeton representative, which mistakenly takes place during a party and appears doomed, actually makes his future by convincing the interviewer that "Princeton can use a guy like Joel."

The film works on several levels and can be interpreted in different ways. Clearly, it satirizes the money-loving 1980's. Joel wants to major in business, and his friends wish to "just make money" in their careers. Joel's main extracurricular activity is "Future Enterprisers," though when Lana calls him a "Little Enterpriser," it is obvious whom the viewer should see as the real businessperson. Furthermore, Joel, whose record is "not really Ivy League" quality, acts excessively and illegally, as many future financiers will, and is rewarded with admission to Princeton. Indeed, if Joel had truly matriculated at Princeton in 1983, he might well have been working for Gordon Gekko, the character from Oliver Stone's *Wall Street* (1987). In this reading, Joel is no longer the good son; rather, he has been corrupted by his no-rules, money-obsessed culture.

However, such a reading seems too dark when the movie is seen as a suburban coming-of-age tale. After all, Joel starts the film as an anxious boy, worried about ruining his future with his natural desire for sex. Indeed, the film's opening scene, his "dream," which is "always the same," is all about his urges ruining his chances at college. But the film also makes it clear that Joel lives in a lifeless suburban culture. Thus, one may ask whether his transformation is corrupting or liberating. After all, while prostitution is illegal, the prostitutes in the movie love these clean suburban boys; Joel's friends, with their sexual urges but limited experience, "need the service" that Lana and her friends provide; and, while Lana is a hooker, she is also Joel's "girlfriend," and there is never a hint that Joel treats her with any disrespect. It may be, then, that as a coming-of-age story, the film reads more positively, as a good boy finding the confidence to take chances and escape a repressive suburban environment.

Risky Business's "corruption or liberation" thematic ambiguity is one among several parallels to *The Graduate*, a film that ends on a strikingly ambiguous, melancholy note. Other commonalities include the generation gap, the protagonists' rule-breaking sexual awakenings, and the lead characters' shared concerns about their futures.

See also: Coming-of-Age Film, The

Reference

Ebert, Roger. "*Risky Business.*" *Chicago Sun Times*, January 1, 1983. Available at: www.rogerebert.com

—*Derek N. Buckaloo*

ROCKY HORROR PICTURE SHOW, THE. The film version of *The Rocky Horror Picture Show* was released in 1975. Over the last 30 years its growing popularity has made it a phenomenon in the United States; indeed it has become a cult classic (Weinstock, 2008). In 1973, a rock-and-roll show, *The Rocky Horror Show*, opened at the Royal Court's experimental Theatre Upstairs in London. Written by Richard O'Brien, the stage version opened to great success and was moved twice to accommodate the increasing number of fans who flocked to see it. It moved to the United States when American film and music producer Lou Adler and producer Michael White agreed to open it at Adler's rock club, The Roxy, in Los Angeles (Weinstock, 2008). This is where Twentieth Century-Fox executive Gordon Stulberg saw the show and decided to invest $1 million to bring it to the big screen. The stage production opened on Broadway before the release of the film, but it was "an unmitigated critical and popular disaster" (Weinstock, 2008). Even though the picture flopped in most areas of the United States when it was released in September 1975, it developed a small but devoted audience that continued to view it—in ritualistic fashion—over and over again. The watershed moment for *Rocky Horror* came when it opened at the Waverly Theatre in New York City's Greenwich Village on April Fool's Day 1976. By the end of the 1970s, the raucous musical had become a pop-culture "must see," with 200 prints of the film circulated in various locations across America (Weinstock, 2008).

Narrated by a criminologist (Charles Gray), the film follows newly engaged couple Brad Majors (Barry Bostwick) and Janet Weiss (Susan Sarandon) as they set out to meet their old science teacher, Dr. Everett V. Scott (Jonathan Adams). On a remote road, in the midst of a driving rainstorm, they experience a flat tire. They decide to set off on foot in order to find help; eventually—and ominously—they spy a castle light off in the distance. When they knock on the door, Brad and Janet are greeted by Riff Raff (Richard O'Brien), the butler, and Magenta (Patricia Quinn), the maid. Invited in, they discover they are unexpected guests at a party thrown by mad scientist Dr. Frank-N-Furter (Tim Curry), a transvestite from the planet Transsexual in the galaxy Transylvania. With his groupie Columbia (Nell Campbell), Frank-N-Furter, on this particular night, unveils his creature, Rocky (Peter Hinwood). Due to their situation, Brad and Janet are forced to spend the night in the eerie castle, where they experience an unsettling world of gender reversal and debauchery. In the finale, the characters come together in an orgy in a swimming pool, which is the fulfillment of a plan devised by Riff Raff and Magenta to return to the planet of Transsexual. While Brad, Janet, and Dr. Scott escape, Riff Raff and Magenta kill Frank-N-Furter and Columbia with a laser that emits "pure anti-matter" before the castle-spaceship lifts off.

On one very important level, *The Rocky Horror Picture Show* maintains its distinctly perverse allure because it continues to function as a sort of filmic doppelganger of the truly bizarre ritualistic ceremonies in which its ecstatic audience members participate. On another level, it seems that the film's popularity has much to do with its connection to two sub-cultures within American society: glam-rock, which it embraces, and science fiction cinema, which it mocks. *Rocky Horror* incorporates drama, satiric humor, and gender role ambiguity, for example, three major elements of the 1970s glam-rock subculture (Marchetti, 1982). These elements have become associated with gay street culture, especially with drag, for which Frank-N-Furter has become a kind of cultic poster boy—the character, after all, spends the entire film in lingerie, fishnet stockings, and platform heels (Marchetti, 1982). In regard to science fiction, the picture-as-phenomenon, unselfconsciously playing on its own outlandish notions of filmic doubling, defines itself, almost vampishly, within what seems to be an orthodox sci-fi framework in the very moment that it consistently acts as a parodic foil to the traditional sci-fi films of the late 1930s (Matheson, 2008). Despite its enigmatic character, however, a generation after it was first released, *The Rocky Horror Picture Show*, at least for one segment of the cinematic public, shows no sign of losing its oddly powerful appeal.

References

Marchetti, Gina. *Film and Subculture: The Relationship of Film to the Punk and Glitter Youth Subcultures*. PhD dissertation. Northwestern University, 1982.

Matheson, Sue. " 'Drinking Those Moments When': The Use (and Abuse) of Late-Night Double Feature Science Fiction and Hollywood Icons in *The Rocky Horror Picture Show*." In Weinstock, Jeffrey A., ed. *Reading Rocky Horror: The Rocky Horror Picture Show and Popular Culture*. New York: Palgrave Macmillan, 2008.

Weinstock, Jeffrey A. " 'It's a Jump to the Left': The *Rocky Horror Picture Show* and Popular Culture." In *Reading Rocky Horror: The Rocky Horror Picture Show and Popular Culture*. New York: Palgrave Macmillan, 2008.

—Jennifer K. Morrison

ROGER & ME. *Roger & Me* (1989) is one of Michael Moore's early documentaries that won international attention. It describes the effects of General Motors' decision to close plants in Flint, Michigan, where Moore is originally from, and to shift work to less expensive manufacturing sites such as Mexico.

At the outset of the documentary, Michael Moore is hired by *Mother Jones* with headquarters in San Francisco. Although Moore quits his job and leaves his beloved Flint to move from the Midwest to the West Coast, he fails miserably and needs to return. Just the fact that he cannot distinguish between all the different coffee flavors offered in fancy cafés in San Francisco aligns him with the blue-collar workers of Michigan, where he feels he belongs. However, ridiculing the working class is also part of his strategy; he shows regular people as foolish and creates a somewhat superior position of observation for himself.

Moore's cinematic style is different from other documentary filmmakers for two main reasons: first, he is present as a highly personal narrator and as a sort of investigative reporter who also asks the tough questions of his subjects. He pursues a political agenda in making his films that has been described as overtly critical of mainstream Republican politics. Secondly, his storytelling is cynical and self-reflexive. Bill Nichols (1991) has remarked, "The use of stylistic devices to achieve a reflexive effect runs the risk of manipulating social actors" (71). Nichols detects the possibility that Moore's characters "will fall into the narrative slots reserved to donors, helpers, and villains" (71). Moore shows the audience how he structures the film and displays openly the building blocks that constitute this genre. He establishes himself as a specialist on the topic in a comedic way by outlining the legacy of his own family and the automobile industry in Michigan.

Moore has been criticized for his exploitative style of interviewing well-intentioned subjects, such as a middle-aged woman who is economically so depressed that she makes additional money by raising and illegally skinning rabbits in her backyard. The filmmaker also shows his failed attempts to contact Roger B. Smith, the former CEO of General Motors, by going to the GM headquarters and trying to get access to the executive suite. When prompted by the security guards to identify himself, Moore pulls out all kinds of insignificant cards he carries in his wallet but fails to provide proper ID. Next, he stops by the country club that Roger Smith frequently visits and engages the front desk clerk in an awkward description of game and alligator dishes that the wealthy clients at this exclusive resort consume. The description of decadent consumption is contrasted with the documentation of evictions of former GM workers, now laid off, who lose their homes. Moore follows the eviction officer, a sleazy and unlikable man who unsympathetically throws entire families out on the street on Christmas day, along with their plastic Christmas trees.

Roger & Me establishes numerous contrasting scenarios. On the one hand, there is the grim reality of GM workers who are losing their jobs and livelihoods and in some cases end up emotionally damaged, such as one of Michael Moore's childhood friends who experienced a mental breakdown. On the other hand, there are the desperate attempts of an economically deprived town to stay optimistic and generate revenue through wacky attempts to attract tourists. Some performers who grew up in Flint still come to visit but are frequently as shady as some of the people who live in the town they are supposedly trying to revive. Moore gets access with his camera team to several exclusive events such as a garden party where living beings pose as statues for the upper middle class. Ultimately, Moore manages to get inside a GM convention where Roger Smith gives the Christmas Message to his employees while laid-off workers continue to be evicted from their homes in Flint. Moore confronts the chairman and is asked to leave. When he refuses, security guards carry him outside of the convention room.

This physical intervention of the filmmaker is a style that Moore continued to perfect in his subsequent films, such as *Bowling for Columbine* (2002), a documentary about gun control in the United States that was successful abroad; the internationally acclaimed *Fahrenheit 9/11* (2004); and *Sicko* (2007), about the health insurance crisis in the United States.

See also: Moore, Michael; Documentary, The

Reference

Nichols, Bill. *Representing Reality.* Bloomington: Indiana University Press, 1991.

—*Karen A. Ritzenhoff*

ROSEMARY'S BABY. Controversial director Roman Polanski's *Rosemary's Baby* appeared in American theatres in 1968. Based on Ira Levin's popular novel of the same name, the film echoed a number of social, cultural, and religious anxieties that emerged as the 1960s drew to a close. Polanski's film both portrayed and critiqued these anxieties, as *Rosemary's Baby* joined a chorus of voices condemning the traditional family and excoriating religion for what was seen by its enemies as its tendencies toward hypocrisy, superstition, and political corruption.

The film opens with the sounds of a comforting lullaby accompanying a camera panning the New York cityscape and stopping over a gothic apartment building (called "the Bramford" in the film but actually the historic Dakota building). A young couple, Guy (John Cassavetes) and Rosemary (Mia Farrow), move into an apartment next door to two elderly, quirky, and garrulous neighbors, and we learn that Guy and Rosemary want to have a child. Polanski managed to keep his late 1960s audience off-balance with these plot points since they all suggested the beginnings of a Doris Day-type romance. The tone of the film quickly becomes dark, however, and we learn that the kindly old couple is part of a large conspiracy of Satanists who have promised Guy success in his acting career in exchange for the use of his wife's womb. In one harrowing scene, Guy drugs and rapes Rosemary while the Satanists watch. The Devil appears to take over Guy's body and impregnate Rosemary. Throughout the rest of the film, the mother-to-be has a growing awareness that her husband and their neighbors are controlling her every movement. Everyone to whom she turns for help appears to be part of the larger conspiracy. She slowly begins to believe that she is giving birth to the Antichrist. At the end of the film, when her child is born, she appears to agree to raise it, even though he has "his father's eyes," which glow a demonic red.

Horror historian David J. Skal views *Rosemary's Baby* as the beginning of a series of films that reflected American society's anxieties over the sexual revolution, the changing nature of parenthood, and the feminist revolution. Polanski released the film eight years after the oral contraceptive Enovin, known popularly as "the Pill," became available and in the same year that Pope Paul VI released the controversial encyclical *Humanae Vitae*, strongly restating the papal condemnation of contraception. Skal further notes that films such as *Rosemary's Baby* began to be released soon after it was revealed that profound birth defects were linked to Thalidomide, a tranquilizer that had been widely prescribed to expectant mothers. Receiving worldwide media attention, the Thalidomide crisis was one of the factors that rekindled the public debate on abortion, a debate that ultimately culminated in the Supreme Court's 1973 *Roe v. Wade* decision. In this context, Skal sees *Rosemary's Baby* as "a brilliant metaphorical distillation of the widespread ambivalence and anxiety over sex and reproduction." Significantly, during the 1970s and 1980s, horror films focused on demonic gynecology or monstrous births—such as *It's Alive* (1974), *The Brood* (1979), and most spectacularly, *Alien* (1979)—would become extremely popular (Skal, 2001).

Beyond being read as a cautionary tale that addresses anxieties about sexuality and reproduction, *Rosemary's Baby* can also be understood as a critique of gender oppression and patriarchal mores. A number of critics have noted that the Satanists who impregnate, supervise, and control Rosemary are merely acting out a slightly altered version of the conservative moral response to 1960s liberalism. Rosemary's effort to escape the clutches of her husband and his satanic allies is an effort to control her body, her sexuality, and the right to bear a child when and if she wishes. The unforgettable end of the film, when Rosemary agrees to care for the child and sees his monstrous eyes, horrifies in part because Rosemary's resistance to the patriarchal pressures pressing in upon her has been turned aside and she quietly accepts her demon-inspired biology as destiny. The frequent references to Catholicism and the use of Catholic symbols further strengthen this theme. As film historian Tony Williams suggests, Polanski sought to show that "Catholicism and Satanism . . . both wish their subjects to be fruitful and multiply" (Williams, 1996).

See also: Polanski, Roman

Mia Farrow, wearing a plaid maternity dress, holds a book in a still from the film *Rosemary's Baby*, directed by Roman Polanski, 1968. (Paramount Pictures/Courtesy of Getty Images)

References

Skal, David J. *The Monster Show: A Cultural History of Horror.* New York: Faber & Faber, 2001.

Williams, Tony. *Hearths of Darkness: The Family in the American Horror Film.* Cranbury, NJ: Associated University Presses, 1996.

—*W. Scott Poole*

S

SAVING PRIVATE RYAN. *Saving Private Ryan* is a 1998 World War II drama about a small group of American infantrymen on a mission in France during the Allied invasion of Normandy. Directed by Steven Spielberg and written by Robert Rodat, it uses characters and situations familiar from 1940s combat films, but overlays them with a distinctly modern sensibility. Along with Tom Brokaw's best-selling book *The Greatest Generation*, published the same year, it became a focal point of popular adulation for the aging veterans of World War II.

The film is framed by scenes set in the present, showing one such veteran on a pilgrimage to the American military cemetery above Omaha Beach—site of the heaviest fighting on D-Day. The old man kneels before a grave marker, the present dissolves into the past, and for the next 23 minutes the viewer is immersed in the struggle to take and hold Omaha Beach on the morning of June 6, 1944. The combat scenes are unrelentingly chaotic, but a company of the 2nd Ranger Battalion, led by Captain Miller (Tom Hanks), gradually becomes the focal point. The beach taken, Miller is assigned a new mission: to locate Private James Francis Ryan—a paratrooper whose three brothers have recently been killed in combat within days of each other—and bring him to safety. Miller chooses five men from his company, and the battalion commander assigns a sixth: a corporal from headquarters who is fluent in French and German.

The small unit thus formed is—like those in countless films made during World War II itself—a collection of stock characters. It includes Reiben (Edward Burns), a wisecracking machine-gunner from Brooklyn; Jackson (Barry Pepper), a pious Southern sharpshooter; Caparzo (Vin Diesel), a tough-looking but soft-hearted Italian American rifleman; and Upham (Jeremy Northam), the bookish translator, who has never seen combat. Miller, the war-weary captain who only wants to go home to his family, and Horvath (Tom Sizemore), the fiercely loyal sergeant who has been at his side for the duration, are—like the melting-pot unit they lead—familiar figures.

The incidents that form the plot of the film are equally familiar. Caparzo, attempting an act of mercy in the midst of a skirmish, is killed by a sniper. Upham, the "new guy," is gradually accepted into the unit and taught the basic skills of a combat soldier. Miller, at a critical moment, lets his men see a glimpse of the human behind the mask

Tom Sizemore and Tom Hanks during the D-Day landing in Steven Spielberg's 1998 film *Saving Private Ryan*. The movie received seven Academy Award nominations and was a major box-office success. (Paramount/Photofest)

of command he usually wears. The group enjoys a moment of rest in a bombed-out town, listening to recordings of Edith Piaf on a salvaged gramophone. The final battle, in which Miller's small unit joins forces with Ryan's to hold a strategic bridge against a German counterattack, echoes the to-the-last-man climaxes of wartime films such as *Wake Island, Sahara*, and especially *Bataan* (all 1943). The battle ends in the best Hollywood fashion, with American reinforcements arriving and routing the Germans just as all hope seems to be lost.

Despite these structural similarities, however, *Private Ryan*'s depiction of the *experience* of war is far removed from that of its 1940s antecedents. War appears—as it does in Vietnam-influenced films from *M*A*S*H* (1970) to *Apocalypse Now* (1979) and *Full Metal Jacket* (1987)—as inherently chaotic and frequently surreal. Death is seldom painless and never clean. The opening combat scenes on Omaha Beach—an unrelenting stream of images of sudden death, agonizing wounds, and paralyzing fear—have the graphic brutality of *Bonnie and Clyde* (1967) or *The Wild Bunch* (1969), but not their terrible beauty. Freed from the Production Code that governed the films of the World War II and postwar eras, the soldiers in *Private Ryan* swear often and inventively. When the naive Upham asks what "FUBAR" means, the answer is not the traditional all-audiences version, "Fouled Up Beyond All Recognition," but the historically accurate "Fucked Up." Even Wade, the gentle and compassionate medic, becomes profane when the man whose wound he has just stabilized is shot through the head by an unseen German rifleman: "Just give us a fucking chance, you son of a bitch! You son of a fucking cocksucker!"

The soldiers in *Private Ryan* occupy a middle ground between the plaster saints of wartime combat films and the tortured nihilists of *Apocalypse Now* or *Full Metal Jacket*. They have much in common with the men of postwar films like *Battleground* (1949), *Flying Leathernecks* (1951), and *Stalag 17* (1953): recognizably human heroes limited, but not crippled, by their flaws. Miller and his men grow weary, frustrated, and confused as the mission drags on without the prospect of an end. They make questionable decisions and outright mistakes—sometimes fatal ones. They gripe about the war and the army, and debate the wisdom of risking eight men to save one. Private Reiben angrily questions Miller's judgment, crossing over the line of insubordination and edging close to mutiny. Corporal Upham is terrified in combat and fails, during the final battle, to carry out his assigned task of bringing ammunition to the others. Ultimately, however, all the soldiers act with dedication and valor. They do what they do—and most of them give their lives—not to preserve democracy or spare Mrs. Ryan the loss of her sole surviving son, but because they see it as their duty.

Duty is, ultimately, the theme that connects *Saving Private Ryan* to *The Greatest Generation* and, more generally, to the public tributes paid to World War II veterans in the late 1990s. A sense of duty—a willingness to do what society expects, no matter the personal cost—was seen as the World War II generation's defining quality, and Spielberg and Rodat use it to define Miller, Ryan, and the others. Miller, dying at the foot of the bridge, gasps out his last words to young Ryan: "Earn this." The scene dissolves back to the present and the Omaha Beach cemetery where the old man—who we now realize *is* Ryan, kneeling before Miller's grave marker—asks his wife, in a trembling voice: "Tell me I'm a good man . . . tell me I've lived a good life." His implied question—"*Have* I been worthy of these men's sacrifices?"—is clearly one that Spielberg and Rodat wish the film's audiences, and the nation as a whole, to ask themselves.

See also: Spielberg, Steven; War Film, The

References

Auster, Albert. "*Saving Private Ryan* and American Triumphalism." *Journal of Popular Film and Television* 30(2), 2002, 98–104.

Bodnar, John. "*Saving Private Ryan* and Postmodern Memory in America." In Martel, Gordon, ed. *The World War Two Reader*. London: Routledge, 2004, 435–48.

Landon, Phil. "Realism, Genre, and *Saving Private Ryan*," *Film and History* 28(2), 1998, 58–63.

—*A. Bowdoin Van Riper*

SCARFACE: THE SHAME OF A NATION (1932). *Scarface* is mysteriously absent from director Martin Scorsese's biopic of Howard Hughes, *The Aviator* (2004), overshadowed instead by the productions of *Hell's Angels* (1930), *The Outlaw* (1943), and Hughes's disastrous ownership of the film studio RKO. Perhaps its absence in *The Aviator* speaks to an anxiety of influence—Scorsese being the contemporary director most associated with the gangster genre—as *Scarface* is not only Hughes's most acclaimed contribution to Hollywood history but a film that continues to influence today's cultural landscape.

When Hughes began work on *Scarface* in early 1931, and hired Howard Hawks to direct, the gangster cycle was already highly contested and the Hollywood studios under the leadership of Will Hays had begun promising to halt the production of gangster films. The situation had only deteriorated in May when a script was readied with the help of Ben Hecht and W. R. Burnett. William Wellman's *The Public Enemy* (1931) had just hit theaters, and it was being widely reported that *Scarface* was going to deal with the life of real-life gangster boss Al Capone, still at large and nicknamed "Scarface," and to include many infamous events, such as the St. Valentine's massacre. Consequently, Hughes was now strongly encouraged not to make the film by the Hays Office or alternatively to make extensive changes to the script. Although Hughes conceded in the end to numerous suggestions—among other things, inserting rhetorical social messages and having the gangster "turn yellow" at the end—*Scarface* was to become the most explosive gangster film of its time, if not of the studio era altogether. It was extensively censored or banned outright, and marked the point at which the excessively violent gangster pictures of the early 1930s declined precipitously.

In a remarkable performance, Paul Muni plays Tony Camonte, who like so many other film gangsters rises from rags to riches, only to be killed at the end of the film. Throughout, he is amply assisted by his faithful friend Guino Rinaldo (George Raft); that is, until Tony discovers Guino has become involved with his sister Francesca (Ann Dvorak) and promptly shoots him dead. If this gangster plot is mostly typical of the early 1930s cycle and has become a standard of the genre today, it is in the psychology of the characters and their interrelations that the film stands out. The incestual desire between Tony and Francesca is almost explicit, strikingly so for a film made during the early 1930s, while Tony's violent behavior is driven by mania and even some sort of psychosis. However, *Scarface* stands out in more ways than one.

Scarface was an independent production developed and fought for by Howard Hughes and inconceivable as a standard studio production. It has few if any of the social problem elements so typical of the gangster films made by Warner Bros.—the studio that specialized equally in gangsters and social problem films. Even if James Cagney had become legendary for playing "psychotic" gangsters from *The Public Enemy* to *Angels with Dirty Faces* (1938), their psychology is explained sociologically, and it is perhaps not until *White Heat* (1949) that one finds in his work a mania comparable to Muni's in *Scarface*.

The extremity of *Scarface*'s characterization finds its stylistic equivalent in the film's mise-en-scène, its lighting in particular. Much has been made of the 1930s gangster cycle's indebtedness to German Expressionism, but arguably only *Scarface* could convincingly be described as expressionistic. Its opening on a dark street with an eerie light post is suggestive of both German Expressionism and its American heir, the horror film, as is Tony's excessive character and conspicuous scar; the visual "X" leitmotiv; the extensive play with shadows; and, in retrospect, the casting of horror icon Boris Karloff as one of Tony's antagonists. *Scarface* is further distinguished by numerous and sometimes elaborate tracking shots more typical of late silent German cinema than the classical Hollywood continuity editing of which director Howard Hawks was the quintessential example. Sound effects help to accentuate the violence at the heart of the film, while also emphasizing its ethnic specificity, as many characters speak with a stereotypical Italian accent and in broken English.

More than any other film, *Scarface* contributed to the temporary elimination of gangster films from the American screen; but it was also the one film that had the greatest impact on the development of violence in American movies. And when the gangster genre returned with a vengeance in the New Hollywood era, *Scarface* was at its center, culminating with Brian De Palma's remake in 1983, the latter also creating something of an uproar and becoming yet another cornerstone of popular American cinema.

See also: Gangster Film, The; Hays Office and Censorship, The; Hawks, Howard

References

Maltby, Richard. "The Spectacle of Criminality." In Slocum, J. David. *Violence and American Cinema.* New York: Routledge, 2001: 117–52.

Munby, Jonathan. *Public Enemies, Public Heroes: Screening the Gangster from Little Caesar to Touch of Evil.* Chicago: University of Chicago Press, 1999.

Prince, Stephen. *Classical Film Violence: Designing and Regulating Brutality in Hollywood Cinema, 1930–1968.* New Brunswick, NJ: Rutgers University Press, 2003.

—*Björn Nordfjörd*

SCHINDLER'S LIST. *Schindler's List*, adapted from Thomas Keneally's book *Schindler's Ark* (titled *Schindler's List* in the United States), dramatizes the story of Oskar Schindler (Liam Neeson), a womanizing German industrialist who employed Jewish slave labor in his enamelware factory outside Krakow, Poland during the Nazi occupation. As the Nazi noose tightens, the initially self-centered protagonist becomes increasingly committed to the laborers and their families. Together with Jewish bookkeeper Itzhak Stern (Ben Kingsley), Schindler conspires against SS commander Amon Göth (Ralph Fiennes) to save the lives of some 1,100 Jews. By the end of the film, as the Jewish survivors are liberated by Soviet troops in the present-day Czech Republic, a penniless Schindler and his wife flee westward, carrying little more than a letter explaining Schindler's efforts on behalf of the Jews.

Schindler's List appeared in 1993, amidst the flurry of 50th-anniversary Holocaust commemorations and World War II remembrances that shaped both popular and academic culture in the mid-1990s. The film won seven Oscars, including Best Picture, Best Director, and Best Original Score (John Williams), and became a lightning rod for discussions on the appropriate way to remember and reproduce Holocaust history. Supporters emphasized the film's attention to historical detail and contextualization of iconic imagery, noting Spielberg's quest for his own Jewish roots and his own description of *Schindler's List* as a cinematic memorial to the millions murdered by the Nazis.

Director Steven Spielberg and actor Liam Neeson on the set of *Schindler's List* in 1993. (Universal/ The Kobal Collection)

Detractors condemned what they saw as a reprehensible attempt to dramatize and profit from an act of terror that defies artistic representation.

Film critics often compared *Schindler's List* with Claude Lanzmann's 1985 documentary *Shoah*. While both films draw on the memories and stories of Holocaust survivors, *Schindler's List* attempts to contextualize historical events and personal memories, dramatizing a specific chapter of the Holocaust and challenging dichotomies of good and evil, victim and perpetrator. Some reviewers accused Spielberg of humanizing the wrong people (i.e., the German perpetrators), reinforcing cultural stereotypes, objectifying the female body, and sensationalizing mass murder, but most appreciated his effort to balance the enormity of the Holocaust with an acknowledgment of individual agency. The final scene, in which both the actors and actual Holocaust survivors climb a hill toward Schindler's grave, reminds viewers that *Schindler's List*, while directed by a master of fantasy, depicts the experiences and memories of real people.

Technically, *Schindler's List* exemplifies late twentieth-century realism, blurring the boundaries among documentary, drama, and art film. Unlike Spielberg's earlier blockbusters, such as *Jaws* (1975), *E.T.* (1982), and *Jurassic Park* (1993), *Schindler's List* engages real-life crises, and embraces narrative complexity; scenes of graphic violence contrast with images of everyday life under Nazi rule. With the exception of a brief introductory scene and fleeting glimpses of a young girl in a red coat, the film is shot in black and white, a decision that was both lauded as emphasizing the bleakness of the subject and criticized as attempting to claim historical authenticity. Numerous point-of-view shots convey the perspective of individual witnesses to public acts of terror in the Krakow ghetto and at Auschwitz, scenes which are juxtaposed against images of opulent dinner parties and the comparatively normal home lives of Göth and Schindler. Heroes, villains, and victims are all depicted as multifaceted individuals whose actions are informed, but not predetermined, by the Nazi regime.

Although not particularly innovative in theme, story, or cinematic technique, *Schindler's List* marked several turning points for American film. Spielberg's own work shifted from a fantasy genre noted primarily for special effects to more serious topics. A similar shift can be seen throughout the film industry, resulting in the release of numerous Oscar-winning historical dramas in the 1990s, as well as greater collaboration between film professionals and trained historians. More broadly, the heated, well-publicized debates about the appropriateness and truth value of *Schindler's List* helped bridge not only the traditional divide between elite and popular culture, but also between academic and lay audiences.

See also: Spielberg, Steven; War Film, The

References

Bernstein, Michael Andre. "The *Schindler's List* Effect." *American Scholar* 63, Summer 1994: 429–32.

Eley, Geoff, and Atina Grossmann. "Watching *Schindler's List*: Not the Last Word." *New German Critique* 71, Spring/Summer, 1997: 41–62.

Manchel, Frank. "A Reel Witness: Steven Spielberg's Representation of the Holocaust in *Schindler's List*." *Journal of Modern History* 67(1), 1995: 83–100.

"Schindler's List: Myth, Movie and Memory." *Village Voice* 39(13), March 29, 1994: 24–31.

—*Kimberly A. Redding*

SEARCHERS, THE.   John Ford's *The Searchers* (1956) was based on Alan Le May's *The Avenging Texan*, a serial published in 1954 in the *Saturday Evening Post*. Considered by many to be Ford's masterpiece and one of the finest westerns ever produced, it recounts the story of Ethan Edwards (John Wayne), a Confederate veteran who returns home to his brother's ranch on the Texas frontier in 1868. His three-year absence since the end of the Civil War is a matter of some concern to his brother Aaron (Walter Coy) and sister-in-law Martha (Dorothy Jordan). Captain Samuel Johnston Clayton (Ward Bond), the leader of a local group of Texas Rangers, even implies that Ethan may be responsible for a string of crimes. For his part, Ethan is happy to be reunited with his nephew Ben and nieces Lucy and Debbie, although he is bothered to see Martin Pawley (Jeffrey Hunter), a young man with partial Cherokee ancestry. (Ethan saved Martin from a Comanche raid when Martin was a child, and Martin subsequently grew up in Aaron's household.) The possibility of a peaceful homecoming is shattered when news of a cattle raid draws the local men and Rangers out into the wilds. The raid turns out to be a ruse engineered by Comanche warriors led by a chief named Scar (Henry Brandon) who slaughter Aaron, Martha, and Ben. Ethan and Martin then spend five years searching for the kidnapped Lucy and Debbie.

The Searchers explores the meaning of masculinity and the civilizing potential of family through the juxtaposition of the different experiences of younger and older men. Similar concerns appear in other westerns of the 1950s and 1960s, including, *The Tin Star* (1957), *The Magnificent Seven* (1960), *The Man Who Shot Liberty Valance* (1962), *Hud* (1963), and *El Dorado* (1967). In *The Searchers*, these themes are embodied in the contrasting attitudes and experiences of Ethan and Martin. Domesticity can be considered the broader of the two themes: the film begins with the image of a door opening and ends with another one closing. We see Ethan for the first time through the first door, but unlike Martin, he remains outside—ever the wandering loner—after the second has closed.

Although David Thomson has accused Ford of invalidating the western as a form, relying on "clichéd panoramas," and creating films whose collective message is "trite, callous, and evasive," even he has acknowledged that *The Searchers* is a moving film that treats its subject seriously (Thomson, 2002). *The Searchers* has been described as being morally ambiguous (Coyne, 1997), especially in relation to its treatment of race and racism, and Ethan Edwards has been called both Ford's first antihero (Buscombe, 1988) and a racist (Coyne, 1997). Such characters were increasingly common in westerns of the 1950s, as were the treatment of racial prejudice and rape and the presentation of more graphic violence (Loy, 2004). In these ways, *The Searchers* was very much a reflection of contemporary American society and culture (Loy, 2004). Scholars do not agree, however, on how to interpret the film's stance toward Native Americans. R. Philip Loy, for example, sees it as anti-Indian (Loy, 2004). Contrarily, Kathryn Kalinak argues that the sheer amount of music associated with Indians in the film— stereotypical though some of it may be—and the use of folk songs from the American South combine to form a complex musical world that demands a nuanced reading of the film's treatment of race, miscegenation, and violence (Kalinak, 2007). Kalinak has also noted that several disintegrated nations—the Confederacy, the Republic of Texas, the Spanish New World, and the Comanche people—haunt the narrative. This is reflected sonically through the interruption of songs (such as "Shall We Gather at the River?") throughout the film (Kalinak, 2007).

The influence of *The Searchers* on American popular culture has been widespread. Ethan Edwards's catchphrase "That'll be the day" inspired a 1957 Buddy Holly song, while directors such as Martin Scorsese, Steven Spielberg, and George Lucas have borrowed from the film's imagery and themes (Fagen, 2003).

See also: Ford, John; Western, The

References

Buscombe, Edward. *The BFL Companion to the Western.* New York: Atheneum, 1988.

Coyne, Michael. *The Crowded Prairie: American National Identity in the Hollywood Western.* London: I. B. Tauris, 1997.

Fagen, Herb, ed. *The Encyclopedia of Westerns.* New York: Facts on File, 2003.

Kalinak, Kathryn. *How the West Was Sung: Music in the Westerns of John Ford*. Los Angeles: University of California Press, 2007.

Loy, R. Philip. *Westerns in a Changing America, 1955–2000*. Jefferson, NC: McFarland, 2004.

Thomson, David. *The New Biographical Dictionary of Film*. New York: Alfred A. Knopf, 2002.

—Stanley C. Pelkey II

SERPICO. Released at the end of 1973, Sidney Lumet's *Serpico* captured an America struggling with a crisis of identity: weary of ineffective leftist political activism, yet distrustful of government authority after stories of local and federal corruption became increasingly common. Adapted from the Peter Maas biography of the same name, the film traces the experiences of New York City police officer Frank Serpico as he works to expose police racketeering from 1967 to 1972. Considered a misfit by both his colleagues and the members of his own private-life community, Serpico fully embraces the antiauthoritarian sentiments of the 1960s counterculture while maintaining an unwavering allegiance to the law and order sensibilities of Nixonian America. Winning a Golden Globe for Al Pacino's lead performance and receiving Academy-Award nominations for Pacino and screenwriters Waldo Scott and Norman Wexler, *Serpico* remains an engaging example of Lumet's ability to depict the contradictions that defined America in the early 1970s.

Deviating from the linear style typical of Lumet's films, *Serpico* is primarily structured as a flashback, beginning with Serpico's rush to the emergency room after he is the victim of a suspicious shooting during a drug bust. Having established the fact that Serpico has developed a less than stellar reputation within the NYPD, the film goes on to explore his early years as a first-generation Italian American patrol cop. Driven to become the best cop he can be, Serpico enrolls in police forensics programs, audits New York University courses, learns Spanish, and cultivates an interest in ballet. Ironically, his inherent curiosity and work ethic, coupled with his adoption of a counterculture lifestyle, eventually make him a pariah among his NYPD partners. Bored with his work and uneasy over his squad commander's accusations that he is a "weirdo cop" and a homosexual, Serpico approaches Captain Inspector McClain (Biff McGuire) and requests a transfer. He fares no better with the members of his new unit, however, as he refuses the free meals and cash payoffs that his colleagues readily accept. Serpico's actions, considered by other cops as not only unorthodox but somehow unethical, give rise to a great deal of hostility. Increasingly marginalized, and beginning to fear for his life, Serpico turns informant with the help of McClain, his corruption-loathing superior; Inspector Lombardo (Ed Grover); and internal affairs officer Bob Blair (Tony Roberts). Although he survives being shot and testifies before a specially organized session of the Knapp Commission, he finally becomes disillusioned with police work. Rejecting the highly coveted detective's shield that he has dreamed of wearing, Serpico resigns from the force. Lumet ends the film with an alienated Serpico standing on a corner with his sheepdog, as title cards explain that he now leads a transient life "somewhere in Switzerland."

Despite clearly sympathizing with his lead character, Lumet refused to present audiences with a sanitized version of Serpico's life. Though his adoption of the

Al Pacino, as officer Frank Serpico, waits in a hallway before apprehending drug dealers in a scene from Sidney Lumet's police corruption drama *Serpico*, 1973. (Paramount Pictures/Hulton Archive/Getty Images)

counterculture ideals of the 1960s allowed him to define a certain foundational ethic, it also seemed to foster in him a somewhat obsessive desire to expose corruption within the NYPD and an inability to entertain the possibility of marrying and having a family. It may be argued that in presenting Serpico as a character unable to succeed either within the legal system or within the nuclear family, the film addresses the precarious status of urban Italian American males in a 1970s America marked by white flight and deindustrialization. Retaining immigrant stigmas despite wider representation in prominent social positions and in Hollywood film, working-class, Italian American males tended to remain tethered to two cultural roles: the neighborhood beat cop, such as Serpico, or, ironically, the underworld crime figure, such as those played by Pacino in the *Godfather* trilogy, *Dick Tracy*, and *Donnie Brasco*. Sadly, unfulfilled as a beat cop and abhorring the corrupt activities of his predominantly Italian colleagues, Serpico is unable to locate a place for himself within American culture, ultimately rejecting the nation altogether.

See also: Lumet, Sidney; Pacino, Al

References

Bowles, Stephen E. *Sidney Lumet: A Guide to References and Resources.* Boston: G. K. Hall, 1979.

Ray, Robert. *A Certain Tendency in the Hollywood Cinema, 1930–1980.* Princeton, NJ: Princeton University Press, 1985.

Wilson, Christopher P. "Undercover: White Ethnicity and Police Exposé in the 1970s." *American Literature* 77(2), June 2005: 349–77.

—*Jerod Ra'Del Hollyfield*

SEX, LIES, AND VIDEOTAPE.   Steven Soderbergh's *Sex, Lies and Videotape* captured the prestigious Palme d'Or at the Cannes Film Festival in 1989. Along with other independent films, such as Atom Egoyan's *Speaking Parts* (1989) and *Family Viewing* (1987) and David Cronenberg's *Videodrome* (1982), Soderbergh's film focused on viewer fascination with video recording, especially in ways that radically reshaped the meaning of public and private space and relationships of power between men and women. Ostensibly a film that instantiates the idea of the "male gaze," as Soderbergh, the male director, records his male protagonist recording his female subjects, the film tropes this notion by placing the video recorder in the hands of a woman who turns her gaze back on the men who seek to control her.

Sex, Lies, and Videotape tells the story of Graham Dalton, played with eerie charm by James Spader, who interviews attractive women about their private lives while he films them. He is in control of the camera, acting to construct the imagistic reality that he is recording. As Laura Mulvey suggested in her seminal 1975 essay "Visual Pleasure and Narrative Cinema," the male observer is the active, dominant partner during moments of scopophilia, whereas the female subject remains passive. Significantly, in a key scene in the film, the camera, and thereby the balance of power, changes hands, when one of Graham's subjects, Ann Bishop Mullany (Andie MacDowell), turns the camera on the filmmaker himself. Stripped of his videographic means of defense, Graham becomes increasingly insecure and self-conscious. As Mulvey suggested, these scenes expose the male gaze for what it is: an expression of patriarchal power that is subject to destabilization when its boundaries are transgressed. Forced to reveal his own sexual inadequacies, Graham develops a perverse visual connection with Ann, who is unhappily married to his college friend John Mullany (Peter Gallagher), a pathological womanizer and liar.

Learning of the unusual relationship between his wife and his friend, John, who has been competing with Graham for years, enters Graham's apartment and discovers a video recording on which Ann has made clear her feelings about her sexually unsatisfactory marriage. Although John has been continually unfaithful to Ann, going so far as to carry on a sexual relationship with her sister Cynthia (Laura San Giacomo), he cannot abide his wife's act of carnal betrayal and divorces her. As the film draws to a close, we learn that John is ultimately punished for his sins by losing his prized position at a prestigious law firm, while it seems that Graham and Ann, with the aid of their video mediator, will eventually be able to negotiate their way through their psychological minefields and end up together.

Demonstrating the potential of independent films to attract large audiences, *Sex, Lies, and Videotape* appeared to seduce viewers by making them into socially acceptable voyeurs. Blurring the boundaries between public and private, and between domains of male and female power, Soderbergh plays on the appeal of the home video market by creating a film that explores complex notions of narrative authenticity.

See also: Feminist Film Criticism; Male Gaze, The; Women in Film

References

Desbarats, Carole. "Conquering What They Tell Us Is Natural." In *Atom Egoyan*. Ontario: Ministry of Culture, Tourism and Recreation, 1993: 9–32.

Mulvey, Laura. "Visual Pleasure and Narrative Cinema." In Erens, Patricia. *Issues in Feminist Film Criticism*. Bloomington: Indiana University Press, 1990: 28–40.

—*Karen A. Ritzenhoff*

SHADOWS. As John Cassavetes's directorial debut, *Shadows* (1961) is remarkable both for its bold portrayal of the complex social issues of 1950s American society and for its mythologized role at the start of the experimental, independent filmmaking tradition. *Shadows* grew from cinematic theories that emerged in the same New York ethos that inspired Charlie Parker's bebop jazz and the Beat literature of Jack Kerouac; as such, it shares a developing rejection of capitalist establishment values and a vital exploration of the visceral emotions and gritty realities of modern urban life. *Shadows* began in Cassavetes's acting workshop as an experiment with his best students where he assigned roles that they used to improvise scenes. These experiments were so effective that Cassavetes soon planned a film project; by appealing for donations, he freed his creative vision from the studio system and became an originator of independent film. Ironically, unable to make *Shadows* a purely improvisational film, he added scenes that were carefully scripted.

Much of the film *is* improvised, however, and as such it tends toward raw emotion and natural reaction instead of carefully plotted narrative development. The central characters are African American siblings of mixed parentage living in New York. The dark-skinned elder brother, Hugh, heads the family; his younger siblings Bennie and Lelia are mixed race, and so light-skinned that they often "pass" for white. This interrelational dynamic frames the film's exploration of a broad spectrum of social concerns, including race, miscegenation, feminism, family, and love. Though narrative threads connect the siblings, at its most basic level the film seeks to record the quotidian lives of this set of sophisticated, urbane, creative African Americans. Although it does not address them directly, *Shadows* resonates with the issues of the nascent civil rights movement of the 1950s—*Brown v. Board of Education*; the Montgomery bus boycott; the Freedom Riders; and the Civil Rights Bills of 1957 and 1960.

Early in the film, we find Bennie in a club, isolated and imperious, seemingly unable to reconcile the racial issues that plague him, and America. Significantly, a central conflict occurs when Lelia, who is young and intelligent but somewhat naive, meets a white man named Tony at a party and sleeps with him soon afterward. Certainly Lelia's willingness to lose her virginity with a man she hardly knows would have upset mainstream audiences during the 1950s, but so too would the portrayal of an interracial sexual relationship. The crisis comes when Tony meets Hugh; thinking that Lelia is white, Tony is shocked when he meets her dark-skinned older brother and realizes that he has slept with a mixed-race woman. Lelia is disturbed not because she has slept with a white man, but because she cannot conceive that race should even be an issue: she sees herself as a vibrant and artistic individual, not as a racialized object subject to a (white) man's approval.

Tony, like so many white Americans, then and now, prides himself on being a progressive thinker; and later, once he has explored his feelings, seems honestly appalled by his rejection of Lelia because of her mixed heritage. For the first time, it seems, he understands his own latent racism and feels genuinely repentant. He goes to Lelia's apartment to rectify things but must entrust Bennie with an emotional message: "I realize now there's no difference between us.... Just tell her that Tony said, 'I'm sorry.'" Bennie's unsympathetic laughter following Tony's departure reveals how much difference he knows really does exist between his sister and Tony.

At the end of the film, Cassavetes once again locates Bennie in a club. Still angry and still isolated, he eventually walks off into the night seeking a "normal life." His shadows remain, however, insuring that his desire for normality will not be easily consummated.

See also: Independent Film, The

References

Carney, Raymond. *Shadows*. London: British Film Institute, 2001.
Cassavetes, John. *Cassavetes on Cassavetes*. London: Faber & Faber, 2001.
Charity, Tom. *John Cassavetes: Lifeworks*. London: Omnibus, 2001.
Fine, Marshall. *Accidental Genius: How John Cassavetes Invented the American Independent Film*. New York: Hyperion, 2005.
Kouvaros, George. *Where Does It Happen? John Cassavetes and Cinema at the Breaking Point*. Minneapolis: University of Minnesota Press, 2004.

—*Kelly MacPhail*

SHAFT. The NAACP gave up trying to persuade Hollywood to cast more African Americans in films and television shows in 1963, ultimately resorting to legal measures and economic sanctions to effect changes. As a result of these efforts, blacks began to appear in both major and minor screen and television roles in greater numbers. Actor Sidney Poitier, for instance, emerged in the late 1960s as the first truly popular African American actor and qualified as an example of "the model integrationist hero." By the 1970s, African Americans had turned up not only in ghetto-themed movies but also in every other film genre and in diverse settings on television shows.

Eventually, the pendulum swung from one extreme to the other, as racist depictions of African Americans as subservient Sambo characters—prevalent before the 1960s— gave way to the portrayal of blacks as Superspades in films representative of what came to be called blaxploitation pictures. The brief golden age of blaxploitation movies stretched from 1970 through 1975, with these pictures targeted primarily at black audiences. Blaxploitation heroes and heroines displayed a social and political consciousness—a street ethic that allowed them to work within the system but also to do whatever it took to improve the African American community. Not surprisingly,

Scene from the 1970 film *Shaft*, starring Richard Roundtree. Directed by Gordon Parks, 1971. (GAB Archive/Redferns)

blaxploitation heroes often clashed with whites; but filmmakers—both white and black—refused to depict whites in strictly monolithic terms. Good whites and bad whites jockeyed for prominence in these films. Although one NAACP official described blaxploitation as just "another form of cultural genocide," African American audiences flocked to see these pictures.

Based on a novel by Chester Himes, director Ossie Davis's urban crime thriller *Cotton Comes to Harlem* (1970), about two African American NYPD cops, Coffin Ed Johnson (Raymond St. Jacques) and Gravedigger Jones (Godfrey Cambridge), paved the way for the production of other films in the short-lived movement. When the film premiered, critics did not categorize *Cotton* as blaxploitation. Interestingly, the term "black exploitation" first appeared in print in the August 16, 1972, issue of the show business newspaper *Variety*, in which the NAACP Beverly Hills-Hollywood branch president Junius Griffin coined the phrase to describe the derogatory impact these films had on the African American community. Later, the phrase black exploitation was abbreviated as blaxploitation.

Two films that historians point to as instrumental in shaping the movement were Melvin Van Peebles's *Sweet Sweetback's Baadasssss Song* (1971) and Gordon Parks's *Shaft* (1971). In his film, Peebles expanded the narrative content of Davis's *Cotton Comes to Harlem* by adding sequences devoted to sex and violence, and *Sweetback's* success—especially with black audiences—triggered the blaxploitation craze, one of the most profitable in cinematic history. Major Hollywood film studios rushed to produce similar films. Metro-Goldwyn-Mayer, for instance, followed *Sweetback's* success with their adaptation of Ernest Tidyman's literary private eye thriller *Shaft* (1971).

Shaft starred model-turned-actor Richard Roundtree as a sort of latter-day, ultrahip version of Humphrey Bogart's Sam Spade character from *The Maltese Falcon*. As a detective movie, the picture observed all the conventions of the genre. The action opens with the trench-coated protagonist wearing out shoe leather in Manhattan to the tune of Isaac Hayes's evocative, Oscar-winning rendition of "Theme from Shaft." The lyrics of the song provided a thumbnail sketch of the hero's persona: private detective John Shaft is "the cat who won't cop out when there's danger all about." An infamous Harlem crime lord, Bumpy Jonas (Moses Gunn), loosely based on real-life criminal Bumpy Johnson, hires Shaft to locate his missing daughter Marcy. Eventually, Shaft discovers that the Italian mafia has abducted her and he assembles a motley crew of black militants to help him rescue Marcy.

Although it became an instant success, African American leaders and film critics excoriated the film for perpetuating the stereotype of young black males as violent and sexually promiscuous. Ironically, some critics complained not about the film's stereotypical characterization of its protagonist, but about the fact that *Shaft* simply substituted blacks in roles that were traditionally played by whites. Yet, for all the criticism that came its way, the picture was wildly popular, ultimately spawning two sequels—*Shaft's Big Score* (1972) and *Shaft in Africa* (1973)—and later, a short-lived television series. It also paved the way for the release of other significant blaxploitation offerings, including *Super Fly* (1972), *Cleopatra Jones* (1973), and *Foxy Brown* (1974), the latter two starring female action stars Tamara Dobson and Pam Grier.

See also: African Americans in Film

References

Lawrence, Novotny. *Blaxploitation Films of the 1970s: Blackness and Genre.* New York: Routledge, 2008.

Leab, Daniel J. *From Sambo to Superspade: The Black Experience in Motion Pictures.* Boston: Houghton Mifflin, 1975.

—*Van Roberts*

SHANE.   Long regarded as one of the classic westerns, George Stevens's *Shane* embodies nearly all of the central myths of this genre, and does so with a simplicity and dramatic economy that distinguish this film from its numerous predecessors. Based on the 1949 novel by Jack Schaefer, adapted for the screen by A. B. Guthrie Jr., *Shane* tells the story of a handsome drifter and ex-gunfighter, of shadowy origins, who frees a small frontier town in Wyoming from the violent and tyrannical rule of the Ryker family, and of its irascible patriarch, Rufus Ryker.

Scene still from *Shane*, starring Alan Ladd (left) and Van Heflin, 1953. (Paramount/The Kobal Collection)

Schaefer's novel is set in 1889, but the conflict between ranchers and homesteaders that lies at the heart of *Shane* is more nearly reflective of the Wyoming range wars of the 1890s, and Stevens draws extensively on the history of this period to give his movie the look and feel of the late nineteenth-century frontier. Shot on location in Jackson Hole, Wyoming, against the majestic backdrop of the Grand Tetons, Stevens clearly hoped to capture some of the grandeur of the natural setting for his drama of second chances and the domestication of the Wild West.

In place of the first-person narration that Schaefer employs throughout his novel, Stevens adopts a subtler and more cinematic device of foregrounding the impressions of eight-year-old Joey Starrett, as he responds to the mysterious stranger in his midst, a man in buckskins known only by one name, "Shane." In what became his signature role, Alan Ladd portrays Shane as a soft-spoken yet potentially menacing figure, who rides out of the mountains one day in search of a new life and finds it, however briefly, within the Starrett family circle. Joe Starrett (Van Heflin) and his wife Marion (Jean Arthur) are drawn to Shane's quiet manner and obvious helpfulness, though it is Marion whose connection to Shane is deepest, and (in spite of herself) clearly romantic. And though Joe insists that he doesn't want Shane to "fight his battles for him," that is precisely the role Shane ultimately plays, as the Ryker brothers, determined to drive the homesteaders from "their" land, hire a gunslinger from Cheyenne named Jack Wilson (Jack Palance) to frighten the few homesteading families that remain into leaving. Shane's shootout with Wilson is one of the most realistically filmed gunfights in the history of a genre that often glorifies gun culture, but it also serves as a sobering climax to a film that seriously weighs the moral costs of violence. Shane's confession to Joey that there's "no going back from a killing" captures perfectly both the poignancy and the tragic heroism of Shane's doomed attempt to leave his gunfighting days behind him.

The actual shooting of *Shane* was completed in 1951, but for the next year and a half Stevens edited and reedited his film until it was released in 1953, leaving Paramount Studios in doubt that the film would ever be released or turn a profit. The film's subsequent success—it was nominated for six Academy Awards and won for Best Color Cinematography—confirmed Stevens's reputation as a director (and in this case, producer as well) who would settle for nothing less than the best his crew was capable of. Cinematographer Lloyd Griggs shot the movie in a widescreen ratio that was later adapted to a CinemaScope format, and the expansive horizontality of the projected screen image was reinforced throughout by Griggs's use of long shots, emphasizing the expanse of the Wyoming grazing lands where much of the action takes place. In an effort to achieve as much dramatic realism as possible, Stevens dressed his actors in period costumes, even to the extent of showing his audience a close-up of a Sears and Roebuck catalog from the 1890s, and having them comment on changing fashions. But in sharp contrast to other western movies of the '50s (and particularly those on TV), *Shane* never glamorizes violence, nor does it unambiguously identify masculinity with the gun. *Shane* is one of the few films set on the western frontier that depicts farmers doing real labor—splitting logs, clearing stumps, and fixing fence posts—as opposed to cowboys on horseback, forever pursuing outlaws in black hats.

However, *Shane* is not deficient in western iconography, nor does it seriously challenge the heroic narrative of westward expansion. Shane himself exists at just one remove from the knight-errant of the romance tradition, and his willingness to sacrifice his happiness (and perhaps even his life) to secure the well-being of a community that only reluctantly accepts him, resonated powerfully with audiences that had begun to demand more of this genre than the familiar "horse opera." Victor Young's soaring score and A. B. Guthrie's often understated dialogue, along with some of the finest screen performances of this decade, will likely ensure *Shane's* place in the hierarchy of western filmmaking for years to come.

See also: Western, The

Reference

Countryman, Edward, and Evonne Von Heussen-Countryman. *Shane*. London: British Film Institute, 2008.

—Robert Platzner

SHAWSHANK REDEMPTION, THE. Frank Darabont's *The Shawshank Redemption* (1994) tells a simple story—almost too simple for contemporary audiences who frequently seek films with adrenaline-like pacing, flashy violence, and soundtracks set to hipster music—but in its simplicity it cuts to the core of some of life's most complex and enduring themes. Among them are hope and friendship. It's also about humanity, which is unusual for a movie that deals almost uniquely with convicted prisoners in a Maine penitentiary. But Darabont does not allow his characters to be defined as criminals; instead, he sees these ostensibly dangerous, misguided misfits for what they truly are: human beings. The warden might not see them as such, nor might the prison guards, but to the audience they become honest, fragile characters who struggle to maintain hope, to be free, and most of all to be human.

Based on Stephen King's novella "Rita Hayworth and Shawshank Redemption," the film chronicles the prison life of Andy Dufresne (Tim Robbins), a banker who is convicted for killing his wife and her lover in cold blood. The narrative is told from the perspective of Shawshank's resident conman, Ellis "Red" Redding (Morgan Freeman), who quickly befriends Andy, striking a bond thicker than the fortified walls, barbed wire, and rusted fencing that surrounds the facility. Through Red's narration, the film unfolds as a series of episodes that depict Andy chafing under the constrictions imposed on him by his surroundings, and the quiet encouragement his disobedience imparts to his friends. As an educated banker, Andy uses his skills to subvert the realities of his environment: he offers his financial services to the head guard in return for some beers to be shared among his comrades; after procuring a large collection of used books and records for the prison, he expands the library and begins administering high school equivalency tests for inmates. All of these subtle cases of defiance build to the grand act of insubordination: Andy's escape. But that is merely a plot point. The real liberation occurs not for Andy but for Red. Andy suffers in prison, but he suffers more as a result of his refusal to acquiesce; Red, by contrast, suffers *because* he acquiesces, yet by the end of the film, through his relationship with Andy, he learns how to be free.

"Prison is no fairy-tale world," states Red, and he is correct. Darabont reveals prison life to be violent, repressive, and dehumanizing; yet he does so dispassionately, never reveling in its abuses. Nor is he concerned with traditional questions of guilt versus innocence. Andy is innocent, Red is not, but none of that matters because Darabont sees his characters as humans first and prisoners second. This is a motif he repeated in his 1999 prison drama *The Green Mile*, and it works. It is also instructive. Just as historians of the 1960s and 1970s illustrated the necessity of uncovering the agency of working people, bondspersons, and women, *Shawshank* raises important points concerning how scholars might approach convicted persons in their studies—that is, with openness and honesty, not nihilism and prejudice. This seems especially pertinent in the post-9/11 world where the troubling revelations of abuse and torture at Abu Ghraib prison and Guantanamo Bay have generated fierce debates about the treatment of prisoners.

The emotional power *Shawshank* generates, however, is not limited to its narrative of prison life. The film's emphasis on humanity and hope are universal themes designed to touch audiences on a multitude of levels, which is a primary reason for its enduring success. Frequently regarded as one of the best films of its time, it is surprising to think that, despite garnering seven Academy Award nominations *Shawshank* was a commercial failure. Today it stands alongside other treasured classics, including *Citizen Kane* and *It's A Wonderful Life*, as an overlooked film saved by the reverence of a few dedicated followers. Like these works, *Shawshank* not only entertains its audience, it inspires and provokes them, as well.

References

Darabont, Frank, Morgan Freeman, and Tim Robbins. Interviewed by Charlie Rose. *Charlie Rose*. PBS, September 6, 2004.

Davis, Angela. *Angela Davis: An Autobiography*. New York: Random House, 1974.

Foucault, Michel. *Discipline and Punish: The Birth of the Prison*. New York: Vintage, 1977.

—*Ryan J. Kirkby*

SHINING, THE.   Released in 1980 and starring Jack Nicholson, *The Shining* is a horror film directed by Stanley Kubrick. Kubrick and screenwriter Diane Johnson adapted the screenplay from Stephen King's 1978 bestseller of the same name. Nicholson plays tortured writer Jack Torrence, who, looking to earn a little extra money while working on his novel, agrees to act as the off-season caretaker at the Overlook Hotel in Colorado. Enthusiastic about the appointment, Jack packs up his wife, Wendy (Shelley Duvall), and their son, Danny (Danny Lloyd), and the family heads off on their winter adventure.

Arriving at the Overlook on the day it is shutting down for the season, the family is taken on a tour of the facility by the hotel's director. As they move through the cavernous spaces of the hotel, the group encounters the hotel's aging chef, Dick Halloran (Scatman Crothers), who offers to take Danny down to the kitchen for some ice cream. While sharing his treat with Mr. Halloran, Danny reveals to him that he is afraid of the hotel, particularly room 237. Mr. Halloran surprises Danny by communicating with the boy telepathically; he also tries to reassure him by telling Danny that his psychic abilities are really a gift, what Halloran calls "shining." Before they leave each other, Halloran warns Danny to stay out of the hotel's abandoned rooms, especially room 237.

Danny's curiosity gets the better of him and he enters the room, where he meets a ghost woman. Jack also ventures into the forbidden room, encountering the same woman, but lies to Wendy about his experience. Jack's madness accelerates as his writing goes nowhere and his supernatural visions increase at an alarming rate. Wendy witnesses this madness when she discovers his manuscript with the words "All work and no play make Jack a dull boy" repeating throughout the pages. When she confronts him, he threatens her. Wendy knocks him unconscious with a baseball bat and drags him to the kitchen's walk-in freezer, locking it behind her. The ghost of the Overlook's

Jack Nicholson in Stanley Kubrick's film *The Shining*, 1980. (Photofest)

previous winter caretaker, Delbert Grady (Philip Stone), releases Jack and sends him after his family. In the bedroom, Danny writes "Redrum" on the door to try to warn his mother. Seeing the word reflected in a mirror, Wendy realizes her son has really written "Murder!," and she rushes to save Danny. Jack hacks his way to her through a bathroom door with an axe and sticks his face through the wood, yelling, "Heeeeeeeeere's Johnny!" Wendy and Danny escape through the hotel's hedge maze, taking Dick's abandoned vehicle, leaving Jack to freeze to death. The final shot of the film is a photograph of the hotel dated July 4, 1921, with a young and smiling Jack front row and center.

The Shining proved to be a great commercial success, but was met with mixed reviews from critics. Roger Ebert concluded that the film was decidedly ambiguous, and that it was difficult to connect with any of the characters. Stephen King publicly disapproved of the picture, arguing that though it was a solid film, it failed to address the major themes of alcoholism and the disintegration of the family that were prevalent in his novel. King also felt that the possession of Jack in the earlier parts of the film denied "the entire tragedy of his downfall."

Of all the film adaptations of King's work, *The Shining* has received the most critical and scholarly attention. Tony Magistrale argues that *The Shining* receives more praise than any other Kubrick film or King adaptation because it must be "read carefully, in a process that is akin to experiencing a poem or viewing a complex oil painting." The subtle nuances of its scenes make it "too artistic to work as a horror film," but "whatever Kubrick sacrifices in visceral or psychological terror, he more than rewards in visual evocative brilliance." Setting the horror in a place of intimacy (the bedroom) allows the characters to expose greater levels of vulnerability, as those places are usually the most private of all spaces, demonstrating that terror comes not from the shadows but from well-lighted areas associated with intimacy and trust (Magistrale, 2003).

The film remains one of the greatest horror pictures of all time. After reconsideration many years later, Ebert added it to his series of "Great Movie" reviews in 2006, and it is on the American Film Institute's (AFI) Top 100 list. Stephen King, though he had softened his views on the Kubrick adaptation, produced his own TV miniseries of *The Shining* in 1997, which starred Steven Weber as Jack. Most recently, Jack's axe from the film helped to break a Hollywood auction record, adding to a $7.8 million dollar profit made by a four-day Hollywood auction.

See also: Horror Film, The; Kubrick, Stanley

References

Falsetto, Mario. *Stanley Kubrick: A Narrative and Stylistic Analysis*, 2nd ed. Westport, CT: Praeger, 2001.

Magistrale, Tony. *Hollywood's Stephen King*. New York: Macmillan, 2003.

Walker, Alexander, Ulrich Ruchti, and Sybil Taylor. *Stanley Kubrick, Director: A Visual Analysis*. New York: W. W. Norton, 2000.

—*Jennie Woodard*

SHREK SERIES, THE. *Shrek* (2001), directed by Andrew Adamson and Vicky Jenson, is the first in a series of American computer-animated films (*Shrek; Shrek 2; Shrek the Third*) about a grumpy, green ogre (voiced by Mike Myers) with certain heroic qualities. The film was based on the book *Shrek!* (1990), by American cartoonist

The animated cast of the 2001 film *Shrek*. Shown (from left) are Donkey (voice: Eddie Murphy), Shrek (voice: Mike Myers), Princess Fiona (voice: Cameron Diaz), and Lord Farquaad of Duloc (voice: John Lithgow). (Photofest)

William Steig, and established Dreamworks Animation as one of the leaders in the world of animated motion pictures. Before this, Disney's Pixar films had dominated the scene. Recognized for its appeal to a wide spectrum of viewers, *Shrek* is an example of narrative and technical innovation. The postmodern features in the film include the subversion of traditional fairy-tale characters and the parodic treatment of film and television culture. The 3D computer animation creates the illusion of visual depth and a paradoxical "realism" in the presentation of these fairy-tale characters. The *Shrek* phenomenon has also gone well beyond the film itself through merchandising efforts, most of which are designed to appeal to the child consumer; the green ogre has been reproduced in everything from *Shrek* backpacks to cans of *Shrek* pasta, and the visibility of this character shows no sign of fading away.

As a computer-animated movie, *Shrek* is certainly reflective of recent artistic and technical developments in computer technology (Hopkins, 2004); however, many basic elements of the storyline are consistent with the narrative patterns of the past, including the tales adapted by Disney early on to the medium of film (e.g., *Sleeping Beauty*, and *Snow White and the Seven Dwarfs*). Shrek, for example, embarks on what may be understood as a hero's journey—in the manner of Joseph Campbell's *Hero with a Thousand Faces*—in this case with the male protagonist in search of a princess. Along the way, the hero meets other characters who assist him in his quest; the film also features a fire breathing dragon as well as an alter-ego villain, Lord Farquaad. However, *Shrek* distinguishes itself as a postmodern variant of the traditional fairy tale in a number of important ways. To begin with, the hero happens to be a green ogre—ogres are usually not the stuff of heroism in fairy tales. The fairy godmother—also presented against type—is a villainous figure, and her equally devious son, Charming, is quite a departure from the noble prince of the traditional fairy-tale narrative.

The very first scene in *Shrek* alerts the viewer to many of these narrative reversals and establishes the film's subversive approach: the story, it is clear, is representative of a nontraditional fairy tale that challenges earlier examples of this narrative form. In this opening scene, a voiceover narrator reads a fairy tale about a princess in search of her true love; however, the narration is soon disrupted by the image of an ogre's hand ripping out a page of the book that is being read. Viewers then hear the sound of a flushing toilet, which they realize is located in Shrek's outhouse. Significantly, these scenes reflect a filmic shift away from an anonymous, nondiegetic narrator who is not a character in the story, to a diegetic narrator, who most definitely is a character—Shrek himself reading the story in his outhouse. Shrek's incongruous appearance in the film's title sequence, then—he takes a mud shower and consumes a bowl full of eyeballs—acts to undercut audience expectations of a "charming" prince.

One of the ways in which *Shrek* represented a breakthrough for animated films was its success in appealing to diverse demographic groups: children, adults, and even film studies scholars. Unlike audiences of the past, which may have dismissed animated films as suitable only for children, contemporary audiences have come to appreciate the fact that animated films may include adult content as well as technical features that computer-savvy audiences can appreciate. *Shrek* is significant in the history of animated film not only because of the number of famous actors who lent their voices to the production (Mike Myers as Shrek, Eddie Murphy as Donkey, Cameron Diaz as Princess Fiona, and Antonio Banderas as Puss n' Boots), but also because of its clever use of pastiche, intertextuality, and innovative cinematography. *Shrek*, for instance, contains countless references to contemporary popular culture; it also uses the visual techniques of live-action film, including long shots, close-ups, high- and low-angle shots, parallel editing and montage—elements that may help to explain why adult audiences appreciate the film.

While *Shrek* has been marketed primarily to children, adult themes are plainly woven through the visual narrative. For example, the Big Bad Wolf is costumed in a pink dress and nightcap, seemingly reinscribing the image of the wolf in grandma's clothing that is a foundational element in the traditional fairy tale "Little Red Riding Hood"; however, because the wolf in *Shrek* is presented outside the context of this formative fairy tale—and within the context of a non-traditional, and on an extremely important level, very adult fairy tale—his transvestism is readily apparent, as are the peculiar proclivities of a cross-dressing bartender who appears in *Shrek II*. Some adult viewers have been critical of the level of sexual suggestiveness that is apparent in these pictures, demonstrating, it seems, the fine line that filmmakers must walk in order to create movies that appeal to inter-generational audiences.

Like Disney's Pixar films, in relationship to which crossover toys were mass-marketed, the *Shrek* movies became even more popular because of the complementary merchandise and bonus features that were marketed to the films' many fans. In addition to DVD versions of the film, which include games and technical bloopers to appeal to the child spectator, Shrek characters have found their way into toy stores and even onto grocery store shelves. Indeed, fans have even had the opportunity to consume Shrek pasta and Shrek Halloween treats.

Film sequels are often less successful than the original films; however, *Shrek 2* (2004) was even more appealing than *Shrek*. Every bit as clever as the original—and perhaps even more subversive in its intertextual references to popular culture—it became the highest-grossing film of 2004. The familiar characters of the original were all back: Shrek and Fiona return from their honeymoon to find an invitation from Fiona's parents to visit them in the land of Far, Far Away. Here, Shrek is transformed into human form, complementing Fiona's earlier hybrid status as woman/female ogre in the original story. *Shrek 2* also caters to adult tastes, with Puss 'n Boots (again voiced by Antonio Banderas) being arrested for holding catnip. The scene functions as a combination of homage and parody, as it is clearly reminiscent of the drug busts featured on the reality television show *Cops*.

Shrek The Third (2007) takes the ongoing Shrek narrative in yet another direction by focusing on the search for a new successor for the kingdom of Far, Far Away. After Fiona's father, King Harold, passes away, Shrek rejects the idea of taking on the role. Instead, he leaves the kingdom, along with Donkey and Puss n' Boots, to search for King Harold's nephew, Arthur Pendragon (Justin Timberlake). The plot of this third installment is more convoluted and less focused than the other two films, involving a host of villainous fairy-tale characters who side with (Prince) Charming against the Shrek contingent in order to apprehend innocent fairy-tale characters. Princess Fiona is relegated to a peripheral role, as she is pregnant and stays far, far away in Far, Far Away while Shrek ventures forth. The introduction of legendary characters such as Arthur and Merlin may have also created a certain sense of confusion in the minds of some viewers that the earlier Shrek films avoided by focusing on the adventures of characters within a circumscribed fairy-tale world rather than introducing characters from distant legends and other fairy tales.

See also: Animation

References

Franceschetti, Donald R. *Growing Up with Science*. Tarrytown, NY: Marshall Cavendish, 2006.

Hiltzik, Michael A., and Alex Pham. "Synthetic Actors Guild." *Los Angeles Times*, May 8, 2001. http://articles.latimes.com/2001/may/08/news/mn-60707.

Hopkins, John. *Shrek: From the Swamp to the Screen*. New York: Harry N. Abrams, 2004.

Parry, Becky. "Reading and Rereading *Shrek*. *English in Education* 43(2), 2009: 148–61.

—*Karin Beeler*

SILENCE OF THE LAMBS, THE. In *The Silence of the Lambs* (1991), FBI trainee Clarice Starling (Jodie Foster) investigates "Buffalo Bill" (Ted Levine), a serial killer who kidnaps, kills, and skins women. Directed by her superior Jack Crawford (Scott Glenn), Starling questions psychiatrist Hannibal Lecter (Anthony Hopkins), a long-imprisoned serial killer who cannibalized his victims. Starling asks Lecter to profile Buffalo Bill, and he proposes a quid pro quo arrangement. He will share his insights if Starling recounts traumatic childhood memories, such as her father's death and witnessing the slaughter of lambs. Meanwhile, Bill kidnaps another woman, setting a timer on the FBI's manhunt. From Lecter, Starling learns that Bill seeks to transform himself, which is why he leaves moth cocoons with his victims—the pupa symbolizes transformation. Later, Starling deduces that Bill intends to fashion a "woman suit" from his victims' skin. By film's end, Lecter escapes confinement, and Starling locates Bill in time to save the kidnapped woman.

Gender issues are central to *Silence*, not only in Bill's gender-bending transformation and the misogyny of his crimes, but in the obstacles Starling faces as a female agent. Several shots and scenes emphasize Starling's small stature next to larger, stronger men. Starling repeatedly attracts the male gaze, which Lecter underscores by asking, "Don't you feel eyes moving over your body, Clarice?" Crawford manipulates a local policeman's sexist desire to shield Starling from gruesome evidence to get him to cooperate. Starling objects but is not above exploiting her femininity or flirting to advance her investigation. Indeed, Crawford strategically chooses a woman for the assignment, as eros partly motivates Lecter's cooperation. After several interviews, Lecter jokes, "People will say we're in love." Many have identified feminist themes in *Silence*, a reading perhaps inflected by Foster's other roles and public persona.

Silence also posits Crawford and Lecter as father figures to Starling, whose biological father, also a policeman, was killed when she was a child. Starling clearly respects

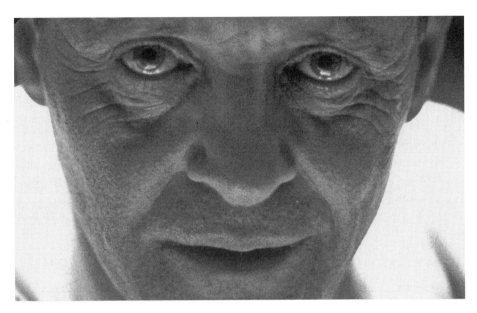

Scene from the 1991 film *Silence of the Lambs*, starring Anthony Hopkins. Directed by Jonathan Demme. (Photofest)

Crawford and reacts proudly to his fatherly praise. The film juxtaposes her first meeting with Lecter with a flashback of her father; the inclusion of similar tracking-shot sequences in both scenes cements the comparison. Both Lecter and Crawford serve as Starling's teachers and advisors. Both also manipulate her for their own ends. Later, when Starling graduates from training, Crawford tells her that her father would be proud, and a close-up of their handshake recalls a poignant shot of Lecter handing Starling a file, their first and only physical contact. In this resonant moment, the film unites all three fathers.

Director Jonathan Demme shot much of *Silence* with craftsmanlike simplicity, but several sequences and techniques are noteworthy. Throughout much of the film, Bill is shot from behind, in long shots, or in close-ups revealing only parts of his body. Like Starling, we must create our own "profile" of Bill from limited information. When we finally see Bill in full shot, the effect is disturbing. He stands naked with his genitals tucked between his legs to resemble a woman; wears makeup and other feminine accessories, including the scalp and hair of his unfinished woman suit; and strikes a pose reminiscent of Lecter's arrangement of a victim's corpse.

Silence utilizes horror film tropes, such as close shots of the female protagonist exploring claustrophobic rooms. These shots create anxiety by preventing us from perceiving offscreen threats. As the FBI closes in on Bill, Demme also tricks us with some horror-film legerdemain. He cuts between interior shots of Bill in his house and exterior shots of Crawford's agents approaching what we assume to be the same house. However, Crawford's men raid a vacant home, and we are surprised to learn that it is Starling, not the FBI team, ringing Bill's doorbell.

The film repeatedly alludes to Alfred Hitchcock's *Psycho* (1960). In fact, both Buffalo Bill and Norman Bates were based, in part, on real-world serial killer Ed Gein. Near the remains of Bill's first victim is a stuffed hawk, an allusion to Bates's stuffed birds. Demme also emulates Hitchcock's technique of cutting between point-of-view tracking shots and reaction tracking shots when Starling walks to her first interview with Lecter and in flashbacks of her father.

Silence received critical acclaim and is one of only three films to win the five most prestigious Academy Awards (Picture, Director, Screenplay, Actor, and Actress). Controversy emerged over the possibly homophobic choice to represent Bill as gay or transsexual, a fact that may have informed Demme's decision to direct *Philadelphia* (1993), which portrays homosexuals positively.

See also: Feminist Film Criticism; Foster, Jodie; Male Gaze, The; Women in Film

References

McQuain, Christopher. "You've Come a Long Way, Baby? Life Outside the Celluloid Closet Poses New Conundrums for Queers Looking for Silver-Screen Mirrors." *The Film Journal* 3, http://www.thefilmjournal.com/issue3/longwaybaby.html 2002.

Mizejewski, Linda. *Hardboiled and High Heeled: The Woman Detective in Popular Culture*. New York: Routledge, 2004.

Niesel, Jeffrey. "The Horror of Everyday Life: Taxidermy, Aesthetics, and Consumption in Horror Films." *Journal of Criminal Justice and Popular Culture* 2(4), 1994: 61–80.

—*Eric L. Sarlin*

SINGIN' IN THE RAIN.   Co-directed by Gene Kelly and Stanley Donen, *Singin' in the Rain* has come to epitomize the MGM musical. Though not a notable critical success when released in 1952, in 2002 *Sight & Sound*'s once-a-decade poll of leading critics ranked it among the top 10 films of all time. A warm and humorous depiction of the genre's origins, the film's reputation grew as critics recognized how it self-consciously refracts that story through a contemporary lens. While on the surface a consummate studio musical, *Singin' in the Rain* also offers a strikingly complex consideration of the nature of musicals at a time when their era was drawing to a close.

Producer Arthur Freed conceived the production as a "catalogue" musical featuring songs he wrote with Nacio Herb Brown for films made in the 1920s and 1930s. As a backdrop, screenwriters Betty Comden and Adolph Green formulated a simple plot driven by the problems facing Don Lockwood (Kelly) and Lina Lamont (Jean Hagen), a silent film duo whose careers are threatened by the transition to sound. In particular, Don is hampered by simplistic dialogue and Lina has an extremely unpleasant voice. These difficulties are winkingly based on anecdotes like the story of John Gilbert's career decline after the arrival of sound—indeed, Gilbert appeared in *The Hollywood Revue of 1929*, in which the song "Singin' in the Rain" debuted.

After a disastrous preview of Lockwood-and-Lamont's first talkie, Don's best friend Cosmo Brown (Donald O'Connor) proposes that they rework the film into a musical, with Don's girlfriend Kathy Selden (Debbie Reynolds) dubbing Lina's voice. Lina is enraged when she learns of this, and also jealous of Kathy's relationship with Don; however, she turns the situation to her advantage by blackmailing studio head R. F. Simpson (Millard Mitchell) into continuing the arrangement without giving Kathy credit. The premiere, with Kathy's voice instead of Lina's on the soundtrack, is a hit, but when the audience insists that Lina reprise "Singin' in the Rain," Don, Cosmo, and R. F. raise the curtain to reveal Kathy singing the part. Don introduces Kathy as the "real star," and the film closes on a billboard advertisement for "Singin' in the Rain with Don Lockwood and Kathy Selden."

Dancer and actor Gene Kelly and Debbie Reynolds in *Singin' in the Rain*, directed by Stanley Donen and Kelly, 1952. (Warner Bros./Getty Images)

As the decision to start with the songs rather than the story reflects, the essence of the film lies in its musical numbers. They serve as an index to major styles from the history of the musical, but all are couched in the form of the "integrated" musical, an approach endorsed by Kelly/Donen. As developed and popularized by Agnes de Mille's Broadway choreography for *Oklahoma!* (1943), this technique integrates performance into the plot rather than bracketing it off. Instead of "pausing" the plot for the sake of singing and dancing, in an integrated musical the plot continues throughout. Thus, Kelly's number "Singin' in the Rain" is *both* symbolic of Don's joy at being in love *and*, quite literally, an impromptu performance taking place in the real world of the film, visible as such to confused passersby. This logic extends throughout: all of the characters who perform are professionals within the narrative, and the characters who are not performers, such as R. F., or are untalented, such as Lina, have no numbers.

The integration of the numbers, despite their unrealistic aspects such as the frequent use of nondiegetic music, underlines the film's self-reflexivity. Interestingly, its openness is itself an illusion: despite the claim that using uncredited vocal talent is reprehensible, for instance, Reynolds's singing voice was dubbed by an uncredited Betty Noyes. Similarly, though the film promotes "spontaneous" performance, in fact Kelly was a perfectionist who rigorously rehearsed the choreography. As Jane Feuer argues, *Singin' in the Rain* employs a putative demystification of the musical only in order to remystify it. While other films in the 1950s pursued greater realism, *Singin' in the Rain* makes use of the trappings of realism as a way of contending that professional "entertainment" is more desirable. Caught between changing tastes and a different economic structure that rendered big-budget musicals less feasible, *Singin' in the Rain* is one of the great achievements of the MGM musical system and, simultaneously, an encapsulation of why that system would not persist.

See also: Music in Film; Musical, The

References

Altman, Rick. *The American Film Musical*. Bloomington: Indiana University Press, 1989.
Feuer, Jane. *The Hollywood Musical*. Bloomington: Indiana University Press, 1993.
Fordin, Hugh. *M-G-M's Greatest Musicals*. New York: Da Capo, 1996.
Wollen, Peter. *Singin' in the Rain*. London: British Film Institute, 2008.

—*Matthew Sewell*

SINGLES. Writer and director Cameron Crowe's 1992 film *Singles* is a snapshot in time, capturing the trials and tribulations of a group of twenty-somethings looking for love in Seattle's fledgling grunge scene. Traffic manager Steve (Campbell Scott) meets environmentalist Linda (Kyra Sedgwick) at a Seattle night club and is smitten; Linda, though, is wary about love, having been hurt too many times in the past. Steve's neighbor and former flame, Janet (Bridget Fonda), is a true romantic and former architecture student who works at a coffeehouse. She's obsessed with Cliff (Matt Dillon), a wannabe rock star who works any number of odd jobs to stay afloat, and who does not appreciate Janet at all. Then there is Debbie (Sheila Kelley), an advertising executive holding onto her 1980s look, who turns to video dating in search of her soul mate, and Bailey (Jim True-Frost), an artsy Bohemian type.

Steve and Linda embark on a romance, enjoying the first days of falling in love and being each other's everything—until they face the ultimate test, an unplanned pregnancy. When Linda loses the baby in an auto accident, she buries herself in her work and the couple breaks up. Steve falls into a deep depression, one that is worsened when the mayor (Tom Skerritt) declines to back his pet project, a "Supertrain" that would change the face of Seattle. Janet, meanwhile, decides to have breast augmentation, thinking it will make Cliff happy. Thanks to her new doctor (Bill Pullman), Janet decides that she is fine just the way she is, thank you, and begins to ignore Cliff. Of course, once Janet stops throwing herself at him, Cliff pulls out all the stops in an attempt to win her over. In the end, the singles are reunited and paired off, with non-committal Bailey the exception. Linda realizes that Steve is the man for her, and Cliff proves his worth to Janet. Even Debbie finds love, despite her disastrous attempt at video dating, a sequence that includes scenes with the forever "thirty-something"—will this guy ever shave?—Peter Horton. The wonderful Eric Stoltz puts in a brief appearance as a Bitter Mime; while Jeremy Piven plays a hyper drugstore cashier—a younger version of Ari Gold from *Entourage*?; and filmmaker Tim Burton, Hitchcocklike, appears briefly on-screen. Even Crowe steps out from behind the camera, showing up on-screen as a journalist interviewing Cliff in a nightclub.

More than just a film about finding love, *Singles* is a chronicle of Generation X—young people raised in the 1960s and 1970s, who came of age in the 1980s. Unlike the baby boomers, many of whom spent their youth in the 1960s indulging in free love and experimenting with drugs, the members of Gen-X faced AIDS, herpes, and crack epidemics, as well as an uncertain economy. The affluence and rampant consumerism of the 1980s gave way to a fiscal crisis in the late 1980s and early 1990s, which in turn resulted in a poor job market, and underemployment for many Gen-Xers. Cynical and perceived to be lacking ambition, members of Generation X reveled in being the stereotypical "slackers"—content to get by with just enough rather than killing themselves in some perverse attempt to keep up with, and outdo, the Joneses. Grunge personified this stereotype, with a physical look that included torn jeans, flannel shirts, knit caps, and unkempt hair. The unofficial king of Gen-X was the tragic Kurt Cobain—who ultimately killed himself—lead singer of the grunge rock group Nirvana, the band that, for many, defined the Seattle music scene during the 1980s and early 1990s.

The rise of grunge marked a return to the popularity of rock-and-roll music after years of chart domination by pop and dance music. A former music journalist who wrote for *Rolling Stone* magazine and was married to musician Nancy Wilson of the rock group Heart, Crowe was no stranger to the music scene. In fact, he claimed that the screenplay for *Singles* was ultimately influenced by another tragic death, the accidental overdose of his friend Andy Wood, the lead singer of Mother Love Bone. As in Crowe's previous films, *Fast Times at Ridgemont High* and *Say Anything*, the soundtrack for *Singles* provided an aural framework for the picture's narrative sequences. Indeed, the film includes performances by grunge bands that were popular in Seattle at the time: Soundgarden, Alice in Chains, and Pearl Jam—whose real-life members portrayed the filmic members of Cliff's band, Citizen Dick. The soundtrack also includes material from the Lovemongers, Mudhoney, Mother Love Bone, and Screaming Trees; and Paul Westerberg offerings bookend the narrative sequences, with his "Waiting for Somebody" opening the picture and his "Dyslexic Heart" playing as the credits roll.

See also: Coming-of-Age Film, The; Music in Film; Romantic Comedy, The

References

Crowe, Cameron. "Making the Scene: A Filmmaker's Diary." *Rolling Stone* 640, October 1, 1992. http://www.cameroncrowe.com/eyes_ears/articles/crowe_jrl_make_scene.html.

Gordinier, Jeff. *X Saves the World: How Generation X Got the Shaft but Can Still Keep Everything from Sucking*. New York: Viking, 2008.

Kallen, Stuart. *The 1990s: A Cultural History of the United States through the Decades*. San Diego: Lucent Books, 1999.

McDonough, Gary, Robert Gregg, and Cindy Wong. *Encyclopedia of Contemporary American Culture*. London and New York: Routledge, 2001.

Rose, Cynthia, ed. *American Decades: Primary Sources*. Detroit: Thomson Gale, 2004.

—Michele Camardella

SIXTEEN CANDLES.   A teenage girl's 16th birthday is supposed to include a big party, the perfect boyfriend, and a shiny new car, all wrapped up with a bright red bow. But what happens when the members of your family forget your big day because they are consumed with planning your older sister's wedding? Ask high school sophomore Samantha Baker (Molly Ringwald), the birthday girl in John Hughes's 1984 romantic teen comedy *Sixteen Candles*. Much to her dismay, Sam awakens on her big day—the day before her sister's wedding—looking exactly as she did yesterday, when she was just 15. Her mother (Carlin Glynn) forgets to make her special carrots for lunch, and no one in her family remembers it is her birthday, much less her Sweet Sixteen birthday! As children's author Judith Viorst might have said, she was having a "Terrible, Horrible, No-Good, Very Bad Day" indeed.

Things go from bad to worse as she struggles with her fear that the object of her infatuation, super-popular senior Jake Ryan (Michael Schoeffling), has learned that she is a virgin and is saving herself for him. To add insult to injury, Sam has been relegated to sleeping on the living room sofa so that her visiting grandparents—they are

Scene from the 1984 film *Sixteen Candles*, starring Molly Ringwald (right). Directed by John Hughes. (Photofest)

there not for her birthday, but for her sister's wedding—can stay in her bedroom, and has been forced to entertain Long Duk Dong (Gedde Watanabe), a nerdy foreign exchange student, at the school dance. Distraught about her birthday and sure that Jake does not know that she exists, Sam hides in the school's auto shop, where the love-sick Geek (Anthony Michael Hall) eventually finds her. His serenades—and fumbling romantic advances—fail to cheer her up; his news that Jake is also interested in her, however, gives Sam hope, so much so that she agrees to loan the Geek her underwear so that he can win a box of floppy computer disks in a bet.

Unable to bring herself to speak to Jake while retrieving her coat in a subtly drawn comic sequence at the end of the dance, Sam returns home, all the more depressed because Long Duk Dong has managed to find an American girlfriend in a mere five hours. A bedtime heart-to-heart with her father (Paul Dooley) also fails to provide solace. Jake, meanwhile, finds that his longtime girlfriend, the perfect Carolyn (Haviland Morris), has invited half the school back to his parents' house for a wild party while Mom and Dad are out of town. Fed up with her antics and disgusted by what his childish friends have done to his parents' house, Jake entrusts Geek with the task of driving an unconscious Carolyn home in his father's Rolls-Royce. The next day, having found the Geek and Carolyn looking a bit too cozy in the back seat of the Rolls, Jake sees an "out" and ends the relationship, showing up at the church where Sam's sister, an overmedicated Ginny (Blanche Baker), has just married Rudy (John Kapelos). Jake whisks bridesmaid Sam away for a romantic birthday party for two, giving her the perfect Sweet Sixteen, after all.

Written and directed by Hughes, *Sixteen Candles* captures the awkwardness and fragility of being a teenager, including the monotony of going to class, the respite provided by hanging out with friends, and the frustration of dealing with seemingly clueless adults who just don't get it. Unlike the serious teen cinema of the mid-1950s, which inevitably dealt with troubled adolescents, the bulk of 1980s teen movies included physical comedy that lightened the overall tone of the films and promised a positive outcome. In her breakout role as Samantha, Ringwald perfectly embodied the angst-ridden teenager—mawkish but not pathetic, sweet, romantic, adorable. Indeed, *Sixteen Candles* launched Ringwald's career—she would also appear in *The Breakfast Club*, *Pretty in Pink*, *The Pickup Artist*, and *For Keeps?* during the 1980s, effectively playing the same role with impeccable charm. For his part, Hughes spoke to teenagers on their own level—he would go on to write and/or direct other iconic teen films: *The Breakfast Club* (1985), *Pretty in Pink* (1986), and *Ferris Bueller's Day Off* (1986). So popular would Ringwald become that she and a number of other hot young actors with whom she co-starred—Emilio Estevez (co-starred in *The Breakfast Club*), Michael Anthony Hall (co-starred in *Sixteen Candles* and *The Breakfast Club*), Andrew McCarthy (co-starred in *Pretty in Pink*), Judd Nelson (co-starred in *The Breakfast Club*), and Ally Sheedy (co-starred in *The Breakfast Club*)—would be dubbed members of the "Brat Pack," a play on Frank Sinatra's 1960s "Rat Pack," which included Dean Martin, Peter Lawford, and Sammy Davis Jr.

See also: Coming-of-Age Film, The; Music in Film; Romantic Comedy, The

References

Grant, Barry, ed. *Schirmer Encyclopedia of Film, Volume 4*. Detroit: Thomson Gale, 2007.

Reed, Joseph. *American Scenario: The Uses of Film Drama*. Middletown, CT: Wesleyan University Press, 1989.

Rollins, Peter, ed. *The Columbia Companion to American History on Film*. New York: Columbia University Press, 2003.

—Michele Camardella

SIXTH SENSE, THE.   The five natural senses are sight, hearing, smell, taste and touch. A sixth sense has always been characterized as beyond natural, conveying an ability to perceive the paranormal. In other words, *The Sixth Sense*, by its title alone, gives rise to an expectation in viewers that they are going to watch a film about the supernatural. While it fulfills this expectation admirably, this film is much more than a simple ghost story.

Written and directed by M. Night Shyamalan, this delicately nuanced film with its unexpected plot twists shook the world of popular culture, earning six Academy Award nominations when it was released in 1999, and winning a number of lesser honors, including the People's Choice Award. Breaking away from the gory, effects-driven horror movies that had dominated the genre for at least a decade, and leaning more toward the nineteenth-century literature of Ambrose Bierce, H. H. Munro, and Henry James,

Scene from the movie *The Sixth Sense*, which received a Best Picture Academy Award nomination in 2000. Shown are Haley Joel Osment (left) and Bruce Willis. (AFP/Getty Images)

the reality-shifting plot had people talking about the film at the watercooler, dragging their friends off to see it, and standing in line to see it again.

The Sixth Sense begins with an expository flashback that introduces award-winning child psychologist Dr. Malcolm Crowe (Bruce Willis) on the night that he is shot by a disturbed former patient. As the action resumes months later, a strangely diminished Dr. Crowe is meeting a new client, Cole Sear (Haley Joel Osment), a painfully shy boy who dreams of being liked and included by his classmates, but who is plagued by the attentions of individuals who have suffered violent deaths—as Cole tells Dr. Crowe, "I see dead people!" Sometimes, Cole reveals, besides scaring him, the dead physically hurt him. The plot at this point is concerned with how Dr. Crowe will come to grips with the presence of the paranormal, and how the boy will ultimately be saved by the adult. But this is not the traditional story of a helpless child-victim being saved by the white-knight professional psychologist. Dr. Crowe is in far more need of help than even he is aware; indeed, it is the boy who will ultimately save the man.

In *The Sixth Sense* Shyamalan suggests that communication, even between those who care for each other—especially between those who care for each other—is difficult, halting, and secretive. Cole keeps the visits from the dead locked away from his confused but supportive mother (Toni Collette); Dr. Crowe seems unable to talk to his former, and formerly supportive and loving wife; and Cole is wary of Dr. Crowe, reluctant to reveal his secret. Eventually, however, Cole feels safe enough to confide in Dr. Crowe, and the barriers to communication begin to crumble. The boy listens to the unwitting ghosts who visit him, helping them resolve unfinished business they have with the world of the living. Cole is empowered, and no longer victimized. He can finally reveal his inner life to his mother, who loves him. In the end, with Cole's help, Dr. Crowe is finally able to talk to his wife, telling her he loves her. Even more importantly, his wife can hear him, even though it turns out that Crowe has been one of the violently dead, a ghost since the attack depicted in the first scene. For the viewer, this epiphany challenges every scene in the movie, as each motivation and action is transformed by this new awareness.

The plot of *The Sixth Sense* is brilliant, but it is the sensitive acting that makes the film believable, heartbreaking, and sweetly triumphant. Bruce Willis is at his best as Dr. Crowe; but it is the performance of young Haley Joel Osment as Cole that holds the film together. Osment is fragile, funny, geeky, brave, and tremblingly human.

This film stays with the viewer long after the closing credits, raising questions that may have no answers: How do we know we are alive? What is real? And perhaps most importantly, what does love have to do with all of this? Maybe the sixth sense is not the ability to see ghosts but the even rarer ability fully to communicate love. It has been said that we are born alone, we live alone, and we die alone—trapped within the cage of our five senses. In this film, Shyamalan gives us a glimpse of another sense, connecting us through bonds of trust, hope, and love throughout and even beyond our mortal lives.

See also: Horror Film, The; Science Fiction Film, The

References

Bierce, Ambrose. "An Occurrence at Owl Creek Bridge." *Tales of Soldiers and Civilians*. Mankato, MA: Creative Education, 1980.

Dyson, Jeremy. *Bright Darkness: The Lost Art of the Supernatural Horror Film*, London and Washington, DC: Cassell, 1997.

James, Henry. "The Turn of the Screw." *The Turn of the Screw and Other Short Novels*. New York: Signet Classics, 1995.

Kovacs, Lee. *The Haunted Screen: Ghosts in Literature and Film*. Jefferson, NC: McFarland, 2005.

Munro, Hector Hugh (Saki). "The Open Window." *The Complete Saki*, New York: Penguin, 1982.

—*Helen M. York*

SLEEPLESS IN SEATTLE.   An unapologetically romantic film, *Sleepless in Seattle* became *the* date movie of 1993, and eventually grossed $125 million. The film opens with Sam Baldwin (Tom Hanks) explaining to his son Jonah (Ross Malinger) how his mother succumbed to cancer. Grief-stricken, Sam moves to Seattle. Eighteen months later and with Sam still mourning, Jonah calls a radio psychiatrist who convinces Sam to talk about his wife. Listening to the broadcast in Baltimore, Annie Reed (Meg Ryan) cries over Sam's story. Annie becomes preoccupied with Sam, despite being engaged to Walter (Bill Pullman). Annie even writes a letter asking Sam to meet her on top of the Empire State Building on Valentine's Day.

Back in Seattle, Sam struggles to rejoin the dating world, sharing a sidesplitting exchange with Jay (Rob Reiner) about the perils of dating in the 1990s. Sam eventually starts dating Victoria (Barbara Garrick), leading Jonah to call the radio psychiatrist and to claim that "my father's been captured by a ho." Listening in Baltimore, a distressed Annie flies to Seattle to find Sam. After unknowingly catching Sam's eye in the airport, Annie mistakes Sam's sister for his girlfriend, believing he is in love with her. Before flying back to Baltimore and attempting to forget about the whole sad situation, Annie again catches Sam's attention by almost being run over.

Unhappy with his father's choice of girlfriend, Jonah pleads with Sam to meet Annie, whose letter he liked. Upset with his father's refusal, Jonah flies to New York by himself, and a panicked Sam follows on the next flight. Jonah and Sam reunite at the Empire State Building in an emotional scene. On the other side of town, Annie breaks off her engagement and rushes to the top of the Empire State Building. There she finds Jonah's forgotten Seattle Mariner's backpack, seemingly knowing to whom it belongs. When Sam and Jonah return for the backpack, Sam recognizes Annie and the two leave hand-in-hand.

Sleepless in Seattle was heavily influenced by another romantic film, *An Affair to Remember* (1957). Throughout *Sleepless*, the characters watch and reference the earlier film, which is where Annie gets the Empire State Building idea. Jay even counsels Sam to "think Cary Grant" while talking to women. That association adds to the film's

Scene from the 1993 film *Sleepless in Seattle*, starring Meg Ryan and Tom Hanks. Directed by Nora Ephron. (Photofest)

sentimentality, which accounts for how it moves the audience. A connection can be made with each character as they are all familiar and likable. Even Walter, who would have been easy for writer/director Nora Ephron to make unlovable, comes across as friendly and affable. The strong friendship between Annie and Becky (Rosie O'Donnell) and the loving relationship between Sam and Jonah add to the film's emotionality and further connect the viewer to the characters. Relatable personalities help overcome the occasionally contrived plot points, creating an atmosphere where the viewer empathizes with the characters. As Roger Ebert wrote, the film is "as ephemeral as a talk show, as contrived as the late show, and yet so warm and gentle I smiled the whole way through."

Significantly, the film turned out to be important for the careers of both Hanks and Ryan. The two had already co-starred in an earlier film—the quirky *Joe Versus the Volcano* (1990). Unfortunately, audiences were baffled by the film, and it ended up being a box-office flop. But Hanks went on to make the extremely successful *A League of Their Own* and Ryan *Prelude to a Kiss*, both of which were released in 1992, and their individual successes helped convince Ephron that reuniting the two popular stars was not as risky as some thought. The pairing worked so well that Hanks and Ryan would join to make *You've Got Mail* (1998).

It may be that what made audiences "smile the whole way through" *Sleepless in Seattle* were its suggestions that within the global village anyone can be your soul mate and that when romance is real, nothing can stand in its way. At least for a brief time in a darkened theatre, viewers could hope that everyone's destiny is to be filled full with love and happiness.

See also: Romantic Comedy, The

References

Ebert, Roger. "*Sleepless in Seattle.*" *Chicago Sun Times*, June 25, 1993. Available at www.rogerebert.suntimes.com.

Pfeiffer, Lee, and Michael Lewis. *The Films of Tom Hanks*. Secaucus, NJ: Carol Publishing, 1996.

—*Sean Graham*

SNOW WHITE AND THE SEVEN DWARFS.   In 1935, Walt Disney thought about turning six cartoon shorts into one feature film. But would audiences patiently watch for 83 minutes? When *Snow White and the Seven Dwarfs*, based on the German fairy tale "Schneewittchen," from the Brothers Grimm's collection, premiered on December 21, 1937, the audience—studded with celebrities—cheered wildly for the first full-length animated feature film in movie history. *Snow White* turned out to be a blockbuster, taking in more money than any movie before. The reviews praised it as a masterpiece of animation. In 1939, Disney received an honorary Academy Award for his pioneer work and significant screen innovation, and in 2008, the American Film Institute called it the greatest animated film of all time.

With *Snow White*, Disney sought to speak to both children and adults, and in the process, completely redefined the nature of movie entertainment. He presented viewers with a simple story and an attractive protagonist with whom they could easily identify. Snow White is forced by her evil stepmother, the queen of the court, to work as a lowly maid. The queen, who continual calls upon her magic mirror to proclaim that she is the "fairest of them all," one day is disturbed to hear the mirror unexpectedly declare that Snow White is more beautiful than she. The queen orders her huntsman to kill the child, but he is unable to do so. In a bravura sequence that recalls German Expressionism, she flees through a dark, terrifying forest in which the trees leer and claw at her. Exhausted, she falls asleep but is discovered the next morning by forest creatures who lead her to the house of the seven dwarfs. Realizing that Snow White is still alive, the queen tricks her into biting a poisoned apple, which causes her to fall into a deep sleep. The dwarfs chase the queen until she falls to her death, and then put Snow White into a glass coffin, watching her body as the seasons change. Finally, a handsome prince spies Snow White, and, captivated by her beauty, kisses her, and she awakens.

Snow White, it seems, functions on multiple levels. For some, it was merely a sweet coming-of-age story; for others it was a Marxist critique of 1920s fiscal conservatism and a Freudian expression of sexual development. Thus, some interpreted the struggle

Snow White is cradled in the Prince's arms as the dwarfs celebrate, in a still from the animated film *Snow White and the Seven Dwarfs*, 1937. (Disney/Courtesy of Getty In Images)

between the queen and Snow White as representative of the battle engaging an older generation's capitalism and fading sexuality and a younger generation's socialism and awakening sexuality: during puberty Snow White lives and matures with the dwarfs, a hardworking, communistic society; ready to become an adult, she is literally suspended until the handsome prince, with his symbolic kiss, makes her into a woman. Taking a very different perspective, the *Christian Century* called Disney an educator of the soul and suggested the picture was really a religious allegory: Snow White and her friends live in a Garden of Eden; the stepmother causes Snow White's "fall"; and the salvific Prince makes possible the triumph of love and the inculcation of family values.

However *Snow White* was understood, the picture's popularity was undeniable. This, it seems, had much to do with Disney's attention to detail and his decision to present the dwarfs as distinct and lovable personalities who balanced the evil of the stepmother-queen. The redemptive quality of the film also appealed to audiences who had been suffering through the Great Depression since 1929. Haunted by unemployment and poverty, the land of opportunity had turned into a nation of despair. Believing that his New Deal programs had successfully turned the economy around, however, Roosevelt slowed government spending after he was reelected in 1936, once again plunging the country into recession. Disney produced a film that responded to the economic desperation of the time, reflecting the value of hard work, the virtue of community among common people, and the triumph of the underdog. It was his most thoroughgoing political statement since his 1933 Depression allegory *The Three Little Pigs*; and by offering his audiences a filmic release from the seemingly inescapable, he provided them with a sort of vicarious power over a world that appeared hopelessly out of control.

See also: Animation; Disney, Walt

References

"American Cultural History, The Twentieth Century: 1930–1939." Lone Star College, Kingwood. http://kclibrary.lonestar.edu/decade30.html.

Gabler, Neal. *Walt Disney: The Biography.* London: Aurum Press, 2008.

Solomon, Charles. *Enchanted Drawings: The History of Animation.* New York: Alfred A. Knopf, 1989.

Watts, Steven. *The Magic Kingdom: Walt Disney and the American Way of Life.* New York: Houghton Mifflin, 1997.

Wells, Paul. *Animation and America.* New Brunswick, NJ: Rutgers University Press, 2002.

—Daniela Ribitsch

SOUND OF MUSIC, THE.   Released in 1965, Twentieth Century-Fox's *The Sound of Music* was nominated for 10 Oscars and won five, including Best Picture and Best Director (Robert Wise). Julie Andrews and Christopher Plummer play the lead roles—a young novitiate named Maria and a widowed Austrian naval officer, Captain von Trapp. Their lives intersect in the late 1930s when Maria is sent to work as a nanny to the captain's seven children. *The Sound of Music* is at once a coming-of-age story, a nod toward the *Heimatfilm* genre (literally the "home-land" film), and a tribute to the masterful musical collaboration of Richard Rodgers and Oscar Hammerstein. Within a year of its release, *The Sound of Music* became the most financially successful film of all time, held that title for five years, and still plays to enthusiastic audiences around the world, epitomizing the international appeal of the American musical.

The Sound of Music is based loosely on the life of Vienna native Maria Augusta Kutschera (1905–1987), who grew up an orphan and studied at Vienna's State Teachers' College before seeking admission as a candidate at the Nonnberg Abbey in Salzburg. Soon after, Kutschera was sent to tutor the daughter of recently widowed Austrian naval officer Baron Georg Ritter von Trapp. According to her memoir, Kutschera fell in love with the family's seven children and married the baron in 1927. During the Depression, the family began singing publicly, and their success at the 1936 Salzburg Music Festival led to international appearances. The staunchly anti-Nazi family immigrated to the United States in 1938, undertaking several national and international tours before settling in Vermont.

By 1958, the von Trapp family's experience in Nazi-occupied Austria had become the basis for two German-language films (*Die Trapp-Familie* and *Die Trapp-Familie in Amerika*), a book by Howard Lindsay and Russel Crouse, and a stage musical by Richard Rodgers and Oscar Hammerstein. Rodgers and Hammerstein sold the movie rights to Twentieth Century-Fox in 1960. Ernest Lehman's screenplay, like the stage musical, takes considerable liberties with the original narrative. For example, the film overlooks Maria's early socialist upbringing in Vienna, turns Captain von Trapp's eldest child into a daughter—Liesl (Charmian Carr)—and overdramatizes the family's flight from Nazi-occupied Austria.

As Maria, Julie Andrews plays a bright, idealistic, if somewhat unfocused young novitiate who arrives at the von Trapp estate with an irrepressible optimism and her guitar. She wins over the Captain's seven children, relaxing the Captain's strict disciplinary code, and introducing them to tunes including "Do, Re Mi," "My Favorite Things," and "The Lonely Goatherd." Frightened by her blossoming romance with the much older Captain Von Trapp, Maria flees back to the abbey; after consulting with the Mother Abbess (Peggy Wood), however, she eventually returns to the family she loves. In a dramatic final scene, shot on location outside Salzburg and accompanied by a choral version of "Climb Ev'ry Mountain," the family hikes over the Alps to escape the Nazi dictatorship.

After warm receptions at previews in Tulsa and Minneapolis, *The Sound of Music* opened in Los Angeles in 1965. Critics described the film as sentimentalized fantasy, but acknowledged the musical prowess of Rodgers and Hammerstein. They also noted that the film avoided the stilted choreography plaguing most Broadway-based films, and lauded Wise's ability to integrate music, plot and a complex array of scenes shot both on location and in Hollywood. In addition to Best Film and Best Director, *The Sound of Music* won Academy Awards for Best Sound (James Corcoran and Fred Hynes), Best Score (Irwin Kostal), and Best Editing (William Reynolds).

The cinematic version of *The Sound of Music* is closely tied to its stage counterpart, largely because Rodgers and Hammerstein contributed to both productions; not surprisingly, given the involvement of the composers, both stage play and film are best known for their infectious melodies. Unlike in many Hollywood musicals, the songs in *The Sound of Music* are an integral part of the picture's narrative flow, contributing to the development of both characters and plot. "Do, Re, Mi," for example, is not simply a gratuitous production number; Maria uses the song to teach her young charges the notes of the scale—in the process freeing both their voices and their hearts.

See also: Music in Film; Musical, The

References

Hirsch, Julia. *The Sound of Music: The Making of America's Favorite Movie.* New York: McGraw-Hill, 1993.

Maslon, Lawrence. *The Sound of Music Companion.* New York: Simon and Schuster, 2007.

Von Trapp, Maria August. *The Story of the Trapp Family Singers.* Philadelphia: Lippincott, 1948.

—*Kimberly A. Redding*

SPLENDOR IN THE GRASS. Looking at the films and plays that challenged conventional moral standards of the 1950s and early 1960s, three names often appear: Tennessee Williams, Elia Kazan, and William Inge. As a journalist in 1944, Inge was assigned by his newspaper to do a feature article on Williams. In the course of this assignment, he realized that being a playwright was his biggest ambition. Before writing the original screenplay for *Splendor in the Grass*, Inge was previously known for his plays *Come Back Little Sheba* (1950), *The Dark at the Top of the Stairs* (1957) and *Picnic* (1953). Elia Kazan, who had previously directed two of Williams's most notable works, *A Streetcar Named Desire* (1951) and *Cat on a Hot Tin Roof* (1958), directed *Splendor.*

Splendor tells the story of Bud Stamper (Warren Beatty) and Deanie Loomis (Natalie Wood), who are high school sweethearts in rural Kansas of 1928, but they and their more closely resemble teenagers of the early 1960s. Bud comes from a wealthy family, whose strong-willed father Ace has made his money from his oil wells, while Deanie comes from a much less affluent home. However, it is not class differences but sex, or rather the lack thereof, that provides the central tension of this story. Deanie's mother repeatedly warns her that to give into sex would taint her reputation and make her someone boys would not want as a wife. The mother presents sex as something unpleasant that has to be endured, not enjoyed. But when Deanie and Bud accompany Bud's sexually promiscuous older sister and her boyfriend on a date, she observes sex as adventurous and fun. From the increasing pressure Deanie feels from Bud, she is torn between becoming the promiscuous self-destructive easy lay or remaining the staid proper virginal good girl. Bud, going through each scene with ever-increasing sexual frustration, asks first his father and then his doctor for advice. The doctor understands Bud's dilemma but declines to advise him. Ace is too busy planning Bud's future to understand his crisis, and suggests finding a "different kind of girl" to satisfy his sexual appetite. Bud initially rejects his advice, saying that he only loves Deanie, but after a pivotal scene in which Bud, his pent-up sexual frustrations at their peak, pushes Deanie to her knees with all the visual cues that he wants her to give him oral sex (but using language that allowed the scene to be approved by the Production Code Administration), Deanie collapses in despair at what he seems to be asking of her. Bud focuses his attentions on a more sexually available girl, and Deanie, sensing his betrayal tries to become this "other type of girl," dressing in red, and trying to seduce a different boy. This act completes her mental unraveling and she attempts suicide. Although rescued, her mental state causes her to be institutionalized. The final segment of the film follows Bud and Deanie's separate paths.

Splendor was released in 1961, on the cusp of the 1960s sexual revolution. Its chief theme of sexual repression and how it affects its two main characters was an important cultural step in removing the taboo of sex, something not talked about to parents or professionals. As the decade continued, several other films continued pushing against the sexual mores of the time, most notably *Lolita* (1962), *Walk on the Wild Side* (1962), *Marnie* (1964), *The Graduate* (1967), and *Bob & Carol & Ted & Alice* (1969).

Hollywood was influenced by the field of psychiatry but altered it to fit its own moral agenda. Nina Leibman compares *Splendor* to another Kazan film, *A Streetcar*

Named Desire, arguing that Hollywood misused Freud's concept of sexual repression to control female sexuality. Unlike Freud's view that the repression of desire *was* the cause of psychological ailments, Hollywood made it appear that the *expression* of such feelings was the core of these maladies. Despite this criticism, however, *Splendor* made a strong statement against ignoring one's sexual urges or attempting to act as if this driving force behind romantic relationships should not be discussed.

Beatty's role as Bud would launch his career. For Wood, it would be one of her highest achievements. Inge too, reached the highest point of his career by winning an Academy Award for his screenplay. *Splendor* epitomizes Inge's major focus—that of lonely lives, unrealized longings, and the hypocrisy of traditional morality.

See also: Beatty, Warren; Kazan, Elia

References

Grant, Barry K., ed. *American Cinema of the 1960s*. Piscataway, NJ: Rutgers University Press, 2008.

Leibman, Nina C. "Sexual Misdemeanor/Psychoanalytic Felony." *Cinema Journal* 26(2), 1987: 27–38.

—*Rick Lilla*

STAGECOACH. In 1937, director John Ford bought the rights to the Ernest Haycox story "Stage to Lordsburg." Two years later, Ford would use the ideas from the story as the foundation for his iconic 1939 western *Stagecoach*. By the time he made *Stagecoach*, Ford had established himself as one of Hollywood's preeminent and most prolific directors. Interestingly, he had made many B-westerns early in his career, but had turned away from the genre for more than a decade before he made *Stagecoach* in 1939. The year proved to be not only an important one for Ford as a director—*Stagecoach* was accompanied by the release of his *Drums Along the Mohawk* and *Young Mr. Lincoln*—but a pivotal year for the screen western, as in addition to *Stagecoach* and *Drums Along the Mohawk*, films such as *Dodge City*, *Destry Rides Again*, *Jesse James*, *Union Pacific*, *The Oklahoma Kid*, *Frontier Marshal*, *Stand Up and Fight*, and *Man of Conquest* also appeared.

Stagecoach was the first of nine films that Ford would shoot in Arizona's ethereal Monument Valley, a vast, southwestern landscape marked by steep-edged mesas and soaring buttes. Shooting there was more than difficult in 1938. As Ford's grandson has pointed out, to get to Monument Valley, which was located 200 miles from Flagstaff, Arizona, the cast and crew were forced to drive over rutted dirt roads that were crossed by numerous streambeds, none of which had bridges. Once there, they were without phones or a telegraph, and at 5,000 feet, the area was brutally cold in the winter and almost unbearably hot in the summer. Still, Ford loved to shoot there; partly because it afforded him protection from studio heads back in Hollywood, but more importantly, because it gave his westerns the otherworldly look and feel that he desired.

Actors (from left) George Bancroft, John Wayne, and Louise Platt on the set of the movie *Stagecoach* in 1939. (Michael Ochs Archives/Getty Images)

Ignoring the use of either a dateline or a scrolling historical explanation, Ford opens the picture with a series of sweeping establishing shots of Monument Valley, in which he crosscuts among cavalry troops, Indian warriors, and a stagecoach crossing the barren landscape. He then cuts to two lone, distant riders galloping straight at us. Using a series of dissolves, Ford takes us into a cavalry camp with its telegraph office, where a group of men wait anxiously for a message. Just before the line goes dead, a single-word missive comes over the wire: "Geronimo." With this brilliantly simple plot device, Ford sets his story in the 1880s, when the Apache chieftain Geronimo fought the last of the battles that constituted the Indian Wars, which had raged since the United States and Mexico signed the Treaty of Guadalupe Hidalgo that ended the Mexican-American War in 1848. He also defines the vast spaces of Monument Valley as uncivilized territory, filled with anonymous savages who must be keep from civilized folk by way of military force.

Cutting from the telegraph office to the bustling main street of a western town, Ford quickly relocates us within the boundaries of civilization. A stagecoach noisily makes its way down the street, stopping across from the Tonto Hotel. It is here, in Tonto, that Ford introduces us to the characters who will populate the stage: Dallas (Claire Trevor), a prostitute, and Doc Boone (Thomas Mitchell), an alcoholic physician, who are being driven from town by the members of the Ladies Law and Order League; Hatfield (John Carradine), a former Confederate soldier and Southern sophisticate, who has been reduced to supporting himself by becoming a drifting gambler; Mrs. Lucy Malloy (Louise Platt), the gentile wife of a Union officer who is desperately trying to locate her husband; Ellsworth H. Gatewood (Berton Churchill), a stuffy, dismissive banker and prominent citizen of Tonto, who, while decrying progressive ideals as the ruination of the market economy, is sneaking out of town with embezzled funds; Samuel Peacock (Donald Meek), a docile, nervous whiskey drummer; Buck Rickabaugh (Andy Devine), the comical stagecoach driver; Marshal Curley Wilcox (George Bancroft), a tough, no-nonsense lawman; and, of course, the Ringo Kid (John Wayne), an escaped convict seeking to avenge the murders of his father and brother.

Given that *Stagecoach* has long been considered a landmark cinematic work because it succeeded in reimagining the formulaic structure of what was then the standard film western, it is surprising to note how conventional the film actually is—Ford even gives us the requisite cavalry-to-the-rescue scene near the end of the picture. Indeed, characters such as those who appear in *Stagecoach* had been seen—in myriad forms—in dozens of B-westerns by the time the picture was released in 1939, and in Ford's film they initially seem to be nothing more than conventional narrative elements functioning within the framework of a traditional western. Early on, however, we begin to realize that Ford will develop these apparently typical western characters against type—or at least as what may be understood as hybrid types. In the beginning, for instance, the civilized, gentlemanly Hatfield and gentile Lucy Malloy prove to be hard-hearted social snobs, while Dallas and Doc Boone, ostensibly savage violators of the social order, turn out to be salvific figures—Doc delivers Lucy's baby and Dallas watches over the new mother during and after the difficult delivery—who teach the rest of the passengers what being civilized really means. Such fictional character types were not new, of course—in fact, they were common stereotypes. Yet Ford provides us with much more: He slowly reveals to us that Hatfield's vocal defense of the elitist South may actually be connected to Hatfield's own disturbing sense of being rejected by his father; Ford also refuses to release Dallas and Doc from their existential struggles with prostitution and alcoholism.

Nowhere is this troping of conventional character types more powerfully articulated than in relation to the figure of the Ringo Kid. Not initially among the passengers who leave Tonto, Ringo halts the stage as it makes its way out of town into the vast reaches of Monument Valley by firing a shot from his carbine into the air. Ford, it seems, positions Ringo here, on the frontier borderline between civilization and savagery, intentionally. Such rogue characters—suitably violent, populist protectors of the people—were also not new; they traced their roots back to the nineteenth-century myths created around real-life figures such as Daniel Boone and Davy Crockett and fictional characters such as Natty Bumppo from the novels of James Fennimore Cooper. In Ford's hands, however, Ringo, although violent enough to help fight off an Indian attack and to avenge the murders of his father and brother, is in many ways an overgrown child, innocent in the ways of the world—he never seems to understand, for instance, that Dallas, with whom he falls in love, is a tainted woman, one, as we said, who will continue to be haunted by her past even as she rides off with Ringo to begin her life anew. Ford even breaks from the code of the western by having Ringo and Dallas ride off into the sunrise—after an unsettling noirish night in Lordsburg—instead of into the sunset. They are headed for Mexico, transgressing, it seems, yet another border. Apparently, there is no place for them in America; as Doc says to Curley as they watch the couple go: "Well, they're saved from the blessings of civilization."

See also: Ford, John; Wayne, John; Western, The

References

Grant, Barry Keith, ed. *John Ford's Stagecoach*. New York: Cambridge University Press, 2003.

Simmon, Scott. *The Invention of the Western Film: A Cultural History of the Genre's First Half-Century.* New York: Cambridge University Press, 2003.

Slotkin, Richard. *Gunfighter Nation: The Myth of the Frontier in Twentieth-Century America.* Norman: University of Oklahoma Press, 1992.

—*Philip C. DiMare*

STAR TREK SERIES, THE.   Created by Gene Roddenberry, *Star Trek* began as a television series that ran on NBC from 1966 to 1969. It became an American phenomenon that continues to influence cultures and inspire fans around the world. *Star Trek* tells a story of adventure, exploration, and utopian communities in space, in a galaxy filled with strange alien beings, some wonderful, others terrifying. It is an adventure that everyone can enjoy; in its imagined future, all can live fulfilling lives, all are included in the community, and none are marginalized or oppressed. Unlike the *Superman* series, which tells of "the never ending battle for truth, justice, and the American way," in *Star Trek*, that battle has been won. Now, a united humanity enjoys peace in the galaxy, justice in society, and truth in the pursuit of happiness. According to *Star Trek's* voiceover, space is the final frontier, and the adventure is to "explore strange new worlds, to seek out new life, new civilizations . . . to boldly go where no one has gone before." This is the backdrop and the dream behind 11 full-length movies, hundreds of television episodes, an animated series, numerous comic book series, and countless novels, video games, fan clubs, and conventions.

Significantly, *Star Trek's* ideal future of truth, justice, and unlimited adventure is defined within the context of the real present using language and imagery that are necessarily products of the past. *Star Trek*, then, is a construction defined by its forward-looking creators; yet this has not diminished its popularity, or its influence. Continuing to fuel imaginations, *Star Trek* has attracted a millions-strong cult following and led to academic studies that explore its different manifestations in regard to myth, religion, sociology, history, law, race, gender, and class.

At the end of *Star Trek: The Motion Picture*, Captain Kirk orders navigator Sulu to set the *Enterprise* in motion: "Ahead Warp 1." Attempting to determine their destination, Sulu asks: "Heading, sir?" Kirk's simple response is instructive: "Out there. That-away." Another adventure has wound down and the *Enterprise* crew is ready for more. The appeal of this imagery is perennial, and it did not begin with *Star Trek*. Space as

Actors George Takei, James Doohan, Grace Lee Whitney, Nichelle Nichols, Stephen Collins, DeForest Kelley, Majel Barrett, William Shatner, Leonard Nimoy, Persis Khambatta, and Walter Koenig pose for a portrait during the filming of the movie *Star Trek: The Motion Picture*, 1979. (Michael Ochs Archives/Getty Images)

the final frontier derives from notions of futurism and American progress. In the nineteenth century, American progress was imagined in terms of westward expansion. It was a dream of unlimited possibilities and endless progress made possible through science, courage, and the spirit of adventure needed to trek across the vast American continent. Though tempered by time and the reality of limited frontier territories, this ideal helped fuel the space race and remains important in shaping America's identity and civic philosophy. Its mythological imagery was first conceived in the literary western, where stories were told about heroic men and women facing and overcoming adversity in order to build civilization from the ground up. It found new life in science fiction, in the hope and expectation of space travel in the future and the reality of unlimited space beyond earth. The image of space as the ultimate frontier was first seen in science fiction novels and comic books, later in 1930s and '40s movie serials like *Flash Gordon* and *Buck Rogers*, and still later in the *Star Trek* television series and in films like *Star Wars* and *Star Trek*.

As a cultural descendant of the western, *Star Trek* emphasizes male camaraderie and values like honor, loyalty, and sacrifice. Although it shares features with heroic narratives like *Superman* and I its vision is grounded in science. It makes forays into fantasy, but it is primarily science fiction; its human characters do not have superpowers, although its alien characters are often endowed with super-strength compared with humans. There tend to be no individual heroes whose sidekicks trail after them; rather, *Star Trek* presents us with groups of characters, each member playing an important role in preserving the stability of the greater community.

In their journeys into outer space, these characters explore the nature of humanity. As Joseph Campbell explained in his work on myth, the journey to outer space is also an inner journey. Curiosity is an important human trait, but it leads to discoveries about the self as much as it does to discoveries of what lies outside the self. This process of introspective exploration takes many turns as the different incarnations of *Star Trek* unfold. It is there from the beginning, however. in the original series through the character trio of Kirk, Spock, and McCoy, whose interactions were a source of humor and tension rarely duplicated elsewhere. They were the boys away from home, bound by loyalty and honor. As career military men, they were friends who brought out the best in each other, a unique, male-oriented family learning and growing together. On a more philosophical level, they represented symbolically three essential elements of human nature: head (Spock), heart (McCoy), and soul (Kirk). More accurately, Spock represents rationality, McCoy emotion, and Kirk a balance between the two. That balance is what makes Kirk a good captain, a role requiring courage, strength, and self-control.

The familial tension in the early series, and then later in the *Star Trek* films, arose mostly out of the clash between Spock and McCoy, out of the struggle between Spock's nearly uncompromising logic and McCoy's explosive emotionality. McCoy is not the only crew member who clashes with Spock, however. Indeed, because his logic makes him so very frustratingly un-human, he becomes a sort of alien touchstone in relation to which humanity is defined. This use of the alien that serves as representational Other to the human self is an important element of science fiction in general and of *Star Trek* in particular. When we look at each of the spin-off crews in *Star Trek*, we find one or two crew members whose "alienness" is defined, at least in part, by a lack of essential human traits, and whose contrast with humanity helps to define us. These characters include Data (*The Next Generation*), Odo (*Deep Space Nine*), the Doctor and Seven of Nine (*Voyager*), and T'Pol (*Enterprise*). Each of these characters lacks or suppresses that most essential of human traits, emotion, and eventually finds or embraces it. As they do so, each journeys closer to his or her own humanity— including Spock.

Delving further into inner space, *Star Trek* explores spirituality. *Star Trek*'s creator excluded religion from the starship and the United Federation of Planets. Only a secular government could support Infinite Diversity in Infinite Combinations (the Vulcan multiracial, multiethnic philosophy at the heart of *Star Trek*). And, any single religion on the starship would inevitably come into conflict with others. Nevertheless, both original and *Next Generation* crews are confronted with alien religions, which they typically debunk. In *Star Trek V: The Final Frontier* (1989), for example, Spock's half brother, Sybok, leads the *Enterprise* across the "great barrier" of space in search of God, who turns out to be an evil alien.

After *The Next Generation*, *Star Trek* is more open to religion. *Voyager*'s Captain Janeway discovers, in "Sacred Ground," that the spirits worshiped on an alien world are real, and in "Concerning Flight," finds science and spirituality compatible. In *Deep Space Nine*, the most religious of the *Star Trek* series, Captain Sisko discovers that the Bajoran gods, "the Prophets," are real, although he calls them wormhole aliens. He serves as an emissary between them and the Bajorans, later discovers he was chosen for that role before his birth and is descended from the Prophets through his mother, and in the end, becomes one of them.

Significantly, *Star Trek* was created in the 1960s, a time of turmoil and social revolution. The civil rights movement, women's liberation, free love, and antiwar protests, all made their way into *Star Trek*. The original series' attempt to depict a future of social justice for all met with mixed success, however. Dramatic requirements conflicted with the series' antiwar ideal, and the need for ratings and advertising dollars pitted the ideal of justice for minorities and women against racism and the attraction of miniskirts. Still, *Star Trek* displayed inclusion in every episode. The cast of characters in the original series was more multicultural than any other group on any other television show or film of the time.

In hindsight, of course, it is easy to see the limitations of the original *Star Trek*—women confined to traditional roles as sex objects, nurturers, and passive listeners; minority males limited to the lower ranks; and leading Caucasian characters shooting barbs at the single alien Commander. Some of the blame for this went to the network and its advertisers. They rejected the first pilot, featuring a female second in command, but accepted the second pilot, which put women "in their place," on the periphery in miniskirts. But blame must also be accepted by the *Star Trek* writers, themselves, as they produced stories such as "Turnabout Intruder," which proclaimed that it was Starfleet policy to exclude women from command.

Series spin-offs made progress. Instead of one woman on the regular crew in the original series (Uhura), there were two in *The Next Generation* (three in its first season). In an imaginary world strongly focused on male friendships, this at least gave women someone in whom they could confide. Women were also more prominent in the films, both as characters and in backdrops, beginning with *Star Trek III: The Search for Spock* (1984). Finally, in the third spin-off, *Star Trek: Voyager*, several women made it to the top. The *Star Trek* series had begun giving women token leadership in *The Next Generation*; Captain Picard's boss, Admiral Nechayev, was a woman who appeared only on rare occasions. In *Voyager*, three main characters were women, two in the top ranks of captain and chief engineer.

Race was dealt with in both storylines and cast. In "Let That Be Your Last Battlefield" (*Star Trek*, season three), for example, racism was the cause of an alien civil war. But the differences between sides were insignificant; one group had white on the right side of the face and black on the left and claimed to be superior to the other group, which had black on the right side of the face and white on the left. Thus, when they destroyed each other, it was for no other reason than blind hatred. Alien crew members were also a resource for exploring racism. McCoy regularly railed against Spock's pointy ears, green blood, and Vulcan logic. And, in "The Galileo Seven" (*Star Trek*, season one), crew members doubted Spock's loyalty as the leader of an away mission. This theme was repeated in later series with Data (android), "The Doctor" (hologram), and Seven of Nine (ex-Borg), all of whom lacked emotion, and, for that reason, were thought by other crew members incapable of loyalty.

The crew of the original *Star Trek* was very diverse. It included two nonethnic white males; alien, Japanese, Russian, and Irish crew members; and a black female. Backdrops, such as Federation Council meetings and alien bars, were scenes of even greater diversity, where humans mingled with strange and exotic species. In a form of tokenism that continued throughout the original series and films, black men were cast as admirals and other higher-ranking officers in occasional scenes depicting conversations between the captain and his superiors. Finally, in *The Next Generation*, a black male was cast as a human crew member, and in *Deep Space Nine*, as the series' leading character.

Star Trek uses aliens and alien societies, symbolically and allegorically, to deal with controversial issues like racism, sexism, homosexuality, and war. This use of the alien is an important part of what makes *Star Trek* what it is, a story combining the futurism of science fiction with a dream of American progress that, unlike its nineteenth-century ancestor, stands against injustice and oppression.

See also: Science Fiction Film, The

References

Campbell, Joseph. *The Inner Reaches of Outer Space: Metaphor as Myth and as Religion*. Novato: New World Library, 2002.

Chaires, Robert H., and Bradley Chilton, eds. *Star Trek Visions of Law and Justice*. Dallas: Adios Press, 2003.

Geraghty, Lincoln, ed. *The Influence of Star Trek on Television, Film and Culture*. Jefferson, NC: McFarland, 2007.

Malmgren, Carl D. "Self and Other in SF: Alien Encounters." *Science Fiction Studies* 20(1), March 1993: 15–33.

Mogen, David. *Wilderness Visions: The Western Theme in Science Fiction Literature*, 2nd ed. San Bernardino, CA: Borgo Press, 1982.

Wagner, John, and Jan Lundeen. *Deep Space and Sacred Time: Star Trek in the American Mythos*. Westport, CT: Praeger, 1998.

—*Susan de Gaia*

STAR WARS SERIES, THE. *Star Wars* is the collective term for a franchise of media texts and products based on a core of six motion pictures. The original trilogy of *Star Wars* (1977), *The Empire Strikes Back* (1980), and *Return of the Jedi* (1983) was followed by a prequel trilogy of *The Phantom Menace* (1999), *Attack of the Clones* (2002), and *Revenge of the Sith* (2005). A seventh all-CGI film, *The Clone Wars* (2008), was inserted into the narrative of the prequels. While many people worked on the production of *Star Wars*, the franchise is typically described as the vision of its creator, George Lucas. *Star Wars* changed the nature of film in America by advancing the idea of the summer special-effects blockbuster and by becoming the gold standard

Scene from the 1980 film *Star Wars Episode V: The Empire Strikes Back*, starring David Prowse (as Darth Vader; voice: James Earl Jones) and Mark Hamill (as Luke Skywalker). Directed by Irvin Kershner. (Photofest)

model in merchandising licensed products. *Star Wars* enjoyed enormous success. According to the Internet Movie Database, three of the films in the franchise (*Star Wars, Phantom Menace*, and *Revenge of the Sith*) placed in the top 10 of all-time top U.S. box-office takes.

The original trilogy revolves around the attempt by the heroic, outnumbered Rebel Alliance to overthrow the repressive Empire. The film centers on the character of Luke Skywalker (Mark Hamill), a young man pursuing his destiny to become a Jedi. Mentoring Luke are Obi-Wan "Ben" Kenobi (Alec Guinness) and the alien Yoda (voiced by Frank Oz). Luke is aided by droids R2-D2 (Kenny Baker) and C-3PO (Anthony Daniels), the independent and resourceful Princess Leia (Carrie Fisher), and the roguish Han Solo (Harrison Ford) and his Wookie first-mate Chewbacca (Peter Mayhew). In the second and third movies, the heroes are also joined by Lando Calrissian (Billy Dee Williams). Opposing these heroes is the intimidating villain Darth Vader (David Prowse, voiced by James Earl Jones), who leads the storm troopers on behalf of the Emperor (Ian McDiarmid).

When *Star Wars* debuted, the film took a different direction than science fiction movies of the past. Unlike the monster and alien invasion films of the 1950s that expressed American Cold War anxieties or the more cerebral fare of movies like *2001: A Space Odyssey* (1968), *Star Wars* struck out in the direction of epic space opera adventure. As with the films that followed in the series, the original movie used space as a backdrop for grand adventure, spiced with visual spectacle. Planets were the exotic backdrops to these quests. Viewers were taken from the twin-sunned desert planet Tatooine to the menacing, moon-sized Death Star, a technological atrocity that destroys other worlds.

Audiences responded enthusiastically to *Star Wars*. The simple morality of the first film no doubt appealed to a nation that had gone through Watergate and was dealing with the cultural malaise during the Carter administration. This melodramatic strain runs through the original trilogy. Good has to work hard, but it generally triumphs against overwhelming odds to defeat evil in the end. Although fairly direct, the narratives of the films did spin out some surprises, most notably the shocking revelation, at the end of *Empire*, that Darth Vader was Luke's father. In *Return of the Jedi*, Luke is able to redeem his father when Vader dramatically sacrifices his own life to save Luke from being killed by the Emperor. Despite their surface differences, Han and Leia find true love. In the *Star Wars* universe, trust in friends is always rewarded.

The films' eye-popping special effects were also a tremendous draw. Audiences were treated to cutting edge special-effects sequences in all the movies. Although modern in effect, Jedi lightsaber duels invoked the swashbuckling swordfights of old Hollywood adventures. Space battles between Rebel X-Wings and Imperial TIE fighters drew on memories of fighter plane battles.

Viewers began to rewatch the spectacle, often bragging of the number of times they'd seen the films. The trilogy demonstrated that well-crafted special-effects blockbusters could earn enormous profits beyond their high production cost. *Star Wars* led directly to the resurrection of the *Star Trek* franchise with *Star Trek: The Motion Picture* (1979) and probably contributed to the success of movies like *Superman* (1978). Such success also bred many imitators. While borrowing heavily from *Star Wars'* space opera feel, films such as *Starcrash* (1978) or *Battle Beyond the Stars* (1980) failed to muster dazzling special effects. Later films such as *The Last Starfighter* (1984) would lift whole plot elements, such as a young man destined to defeat an evil ship with a fatal design flaw.

Many years passed before the next *Star Wars* movie came to the screen. The idea of the prequel stories was hinted at by the opening narrative crawl for *The Empire Strikes Back*, which labeled the film "Episode V." In anticipation of the prequels and in celebration of the 20th anniversary of *Star Wars*, in 1997 the films of the original trilogy were returned to the theaters as special editions. The first film began being known under the new episode title, *A New Hope*. The special editions were not merely rereleased. Lucas changed the films, largely by inserting new special-effects sequences into older scenes. While the narratives went relatively untouched, a controversial change was made to the character of Han Solo in *A New Hope*, when a scene in which Han shot the bounty hunter Greedo was altered to make it appear that Han shot only after being fired upon by Greedo.

The prequel trilogy takes a more tragic direction as the films center on the character of Anakin Skywalker (Jake Lloyd, Hayden Christensen), destined to become the evil Darth Vader. Anakin is mentored in the first film by Jedi Qui-Gon Jinn (Liam Neeson) and then later by young Obi-Wan (Ewan McGregor). Anakin is aided in his adventures, and later has a doomed love affair with Queen Amidala (Natalie Portman).

While the prequels introduce new characters like the Gungan Jar Jar Binks, audiences see earlier versions of favorite characters such as Yoda, R2-D2, C-3PO, Obi-Wan, and Chewbacca.

The narratives of the prequel trilogies establish a more complicated storyline. Senator Palpatine (Ian McDiarmid) is secretly the evil Sith Lord Sidious, the sworn foe of the Jedi. He comes to power by manipulating a war between the Jedi and the clone army of the Republic and battle droid-reliant Trade Guilds (later subsumed into the Separatists) To sow this chaos, Palpatine uses a number of evil agents: Darth Maul (Ray Park) in *Menace*, Count Dooku (Christopher Lee) in *Clones* and *Sith*, and General Grievous (voiced by Matthew Wood). Exploiting the political situation and fears of the power of the Jedi, Palpatine grabs power in the guise of offering order, thus becoming Emperor at the end of the trilogy.

The prequel trilogies have a darker tone as Palpatine also manipulates Anakin with tragic results. Qui-Gon believes that Anakin is the Chosen One, prophesied to bring balance to the Force. Ambitious, Anakin chafes under what he sees as the restrictive training system overseen by Jedi Counselors such as Yoda and Mace Windu (Samuel L. Jackson). Secretly wed to Amidala in *Clones*, Anakin has nightmare visions of his wife's death in *Sith*. Palpatine uses these fears to bring Anakin under his control. Anakin betrays the Jedi, leading a massacre at the Jedi Temple (a controversy among fans as the Temple had youthful trainees). *Sith* concludes on a very down note as Obi-Wan defeats Anakin in battle and a heartbroken Amidala dies giving birth to the twins Luke and Leia. The twins are taken into hiding, establishing the pretext of the original trilogy. The gruesomely injured Anakin is transformed, in a scene reminiscent of *Frankenstein* (1931), into the cyborg Darth Vader.

In 2008, *The Clone Wars* presented an all–CGI adventure set between *Clones* and *Sith*. An accomplished Jedi at this time in the stories, Anakin is given an apprentice of his own to train, the spirited Ahsoka (voiced by Ashley Eckstein).

The Force is an important spiritual concept that runs throughout all of the films. In *Star Wars*, Ben explains that the Force is an energy field that binds all living things. Certain individuals are more connected with the Force than others, allowing them to manipulate the Force. This manipulation grants a number of spectacular powers such as telekinetic and telepathic abilities. Although not antitechnology, the Force is presented as something more useful, and thus more ideal, than technology. The most famous example is Luke switching off his targeting computer and relying on the Force to destroy the Death Star.

The prequels added a more pseudoscientific, and for fans, a more controversial explanation for the Force by introducing the idea of midi-chlorians, microbes that allow the manipulation of the Force. Although not confirmed in the narrative, scenes in *The Phantom Menace* suggest that Anakin may have been a virgin birth, created by the midi-chlorians.

Although Anakin is presented as a messianic figure and the Jedi function in ways similar to the Crusaders in the prequels, the Force is not an orthodox religion along the lines of Western Christianity. In many ways the Force is more like Eastern religions in that it requires contemplative study to master. The Force operates on a simple dichotomy of good and evil. Students must constantly beware the seduction of the Dark Side of the Force, a fate that some, such as the Sith and Darth Vader, were unable to resist. To avoid this temptation, the practitioner must constantly master his or her emotions.

Interestingly, while the Force and the Jedi are important to the *Star Wars* universe, within the narrative most characters react with skepticism to the Force. Since Luke and Leia are born at the end of *Sith*, the time difference between the end of the prequels and the beginning of the original trilogy is only their age. Yet in that short time, many characters, notably Han Solo, are skeptical of the Force. In the prequels, Palpatine is able to use fear of the Jedi's power in order to scapegoat the group in his own bid for dominance.

Star Wars presents other political and moral arguments outside the Force, although the views are sometimes less coherent. In the original trilogy, the Empire is clearly evil and repressive, with the Rebel Alliance taking the role of heroic underdog. Leia's title of Princess also suggests a monarchy akin to those found in fairy tales. In the prequels both the Republic with its clone warriors and the Trade Guild/Separatists with their droid armies are manipulated by Palpatine. While the Republic eventually becomes the Empire, through most of the prequels the clone warriors are on the side of good due to their association with the Jedi. The political universe of the prequels is more demonstrably democratic, although the films are at pains to explain how Amidala is somehow elected queen. The Republic's demise models the shift from the Roman Republic to the Roman Empire. The vulnerability of this democracy to Palpatine's ambitions is a contemporary warning on the fragile balance between freedom and security.

Personal morality is ultimately important in the *Star Wars* universe, where redemption is a powerful theme. Collectively the films may be read as Anakin Skywalker's tragic fall and salvation through self-sacrifice. Other redemptions can be seen in the films, such as Han Solo's renouncement of materialism when he returns to save Luke in *Star Wars* or Lando Calrissian's seeing beyond self-preservation when he joins the Rebels after betraying them in *Empire Strikes Back*.

Technology is another vital element in *Star Wars*, and there is no way this entry could begin to note all the examples. Although the Jedi teach that the Force is something more meaningful and useful in the universe, technology does all the hard work waging the wars in these stars. The Jedi aren't Luddites; they are best identified by their signature weapons, the lightsaber. Sword surrogates, lightsabers feature in many prominent duels throughout all of the films. Travel in the *Star Wars* universe, be it local or intergalactic, is accomplished easily by a dizzying array of vehicles and warships. Technology even provides important characters in the form of droids.

Special effects are a hallmark of the films. Lucas's companies have been on the cutting edge of developing this movie magic for decades. The original films pioneered the use of models and stop-motion animation. In the rereleases Lucas used computer technology to add more effects to complete his vision. The prequels embraced CGI wizardry, creating whole environments and characters electronically. Two notable examples of this transition are the characters of Yoda and Jabba the Hutt. Puppets and animatronics in the original films, the characters appeared in the prequels as CGI animation.

While human characters abound in the *Star Wars* universe, one signature element of the franchise is the inclusion of nonhuman characters. In fact, in some crucial ways the narratives of all the films are structured around the adventures of R2-D2 and C-3PO. The duo has a knack for being in just the right place at the right time. *Star Wars'* Cantina Band scene presented an array of aliens hanging out in a bar on Tattoine, and the trend continued from there. From trusty Wookiee co-pilot Chewbacca to Jedi master Yoda, alien beings abound. Although there is some evidence of droid prejudice in the original trilogy, the *Star Wars* universe is truly diverse. Nonhumans hold important positions and roles. A few problems do exist, most notably in Jar Jar Binks, a character that skews painfully close to minstrel show stereotypes.

Music and sound are two more signature aspects of *Star Wars*. Just as the films promoted visual effects, they have also advanced sound effects. Composer and conductor John Williams created the music for all six of the live-action films. Many of the musical leitmotifs have become well known in American culture, particularly the *Star Wars* theme itself and the Imperial March that often accompanies Darth Vader's appearances. In addition to its official releases, *Star Wars* music has been recorded by a number of orchestras in a bid to raise revenues.

Although this entry has by design focused on the films themselves, *Star Wars* is much more than a cinematic experience. From the beginning, Lucas has licensed this franchise into a wide variety of products such as T-shirts, posters, costumes, and lightsabers. Most notable of these are the *Star Wars* action figures. These figures changed the nature of children's toys by promoting a collectible line of characters, vehicles, and play sets that children could use to reenact scenes from the movies or to create their own adventures. Although the toy company Kenner was unable to produce action figures in time for the 1977 holiday season (instead selling IOUs for the figures), these toys have been sold at every holiday season since, with the line expanding to include new elements from all the films.

Star Wars is also an important force in publishing. Alan Dean Foster's 1978 novel *Splinter of the Mind's Eye* was the first original adventure set in the *Star Wars* universe. Countless other books have followed, fleshing out the events between the movies and recounting the further adventures of characters after the films. Marvel Comics produced *Star Wars* comic book adventures during the original trilogy, but the rights have moved on to other companies. There are also many reference books for the series.

Star Wars was also a source for a number of television programs. *The Star Wars Holiday Special* (1978) centered on Chewbacca's family, but although it featured most of the main characters it is not accepted as canon. Never rereleased, the special is a kitschy prize of collectors everywhere. Saturday morning cartoon *Droids* (1985) chronicled the R2-D2 and C-3PO's adventures before the original trilogy, while *Ewoks* (1985) followed the lives of the fuzzy aliens from *Return of the Jedi*. The Clone Wars carried directly into an all-CGI show on Cartoon Network in 2008. *Star Wars* is referenced in many other media products. Two prominent cinematic parodies were *Hardware Wars* (1977) and *Spaceballs* (1987). Some programs, such as *Robot Chicken* and *Family*

Guy, have produced entire parodies of *Star Wars* with the permission of, and occasional participation by, Lucas.

Not surprisingly, Lucasfilm's video-game divisions have also produced a number of games in the *Star Wars* universe. There is a massive multiplayer online *Star Wars* game. Various platforms have allowed players to reenact battles from the movies (*Star Wars Battlefront*) or pursue narrative adventures within the spaces of the films (*The Force Unleashed*).

Finally, *Star Wars* was referenced politically when President Ronald Reagan unveiled the Strategic Defense Initiative in 1983. SDI planned to use satellite and Earth-based weaponry to destroy incoming ballistic missile attacks. There are no scenes in the *Star Wars* films that display such moments, so the label was merely an attempt to popularize the idea with the American public.

Few movies have won a place in the hearts and imaginations of viewers the way the *Star Wars* films have. While generations of fans can and do bicker over the movies' narrative inconsistencies, the ubiquity of *Star Wars* in American popular culture and the continued success of their associated products are a testament to the loyalty of those fans.

See also: Lucas, George; Science Fiction Film, The

References

Belton, John. *American Cinema/American Culture*. 3rd ed. Boston: McGraw-Hill, 2009.
Lawrence, John Shelton, and Robert Jewett. *The Myth of the American Superhero*. Grand Rapids, MI: William B. Eerdmans Publishing, 2002.
Seabrook, John. "Letter from the Skywalker Ranch: Why Is the Force Still with Us?" *New Yorker*, January 6, 1997: 40–53.

—Michael G. Robinson

STREETCAR NAMED DESIRE, A. Elia Kazan's *A Streetcar Named Desire* (1951) is a film adaptation of the Tennessee Williams play of the same name. The play, also directed by Kazan, won the Pulitzer Prize, the New York Drama Critics' Circle Award, and a Tony Award. Following on the success of the play, the film received 12 Oscar nominations and helped to make Marlon Brando a Hollywood superstar. Except for Vivien Leigh, all of the actors from the original Broadway production played their stage roles on-screen. Working closely on both the theatre and film productions of *Streetcar*, Williams and Kazan pioneered the concept of subjective realism and opened up discussions of the portrayal of male and female sexuality on stage and screen.

The film centers on Blanche DuBois's gradual descent into madness. After losing the family plantation, Belle Reve, as well as her position as a schoolteacher, Blanche moves to New Orleans to share a two-room apartment in the French Quarter with her sister, Stella Kowalski (Kim Hunter), and her brutish, cynical brother-in-law, Stanley Kowalski (Brando). Tennessee Williams described *A Streetcar Named Desire* as a "tragedy of misunderstandings," and the misunderstandings become apparent from

Marlon Brando and Kim Hunter in a dramatic scene from *A Streetcar Named Desire* written by Tennessee Williams and directed by Elia Kazan. (Hulton Archive/Getty Images)

the very beginning of the picture (Murphy, 1992). Blanche makes it seem as though she took a leave of absence from the school, when in fact, she was terminated after becoming sexually involved with a student. She then accuses Stella of only desiring Stanley sexually, instead of truly loving him; an accusation that rings true on one level, as Stella's relationship with Stanley appears at least partially based on her need for his protection to survive the harsh life of the French Quarter.

Significantly, Blanche gives vague answers to questions or avoids them completely, although she claims to tell the truth in regard to really important matters. While on a date with her ultrasensitive and emotionally unaware suitor Mitch (Karl Malden), she reveals that she feels responsible for the death of her husband, Allan Gray, who publically shot himself at a party after revealing his homosexuality to Blanche. When Mitch confronts her about her past indiscretions, Blanche confesses to "many meetings with strangers," but declares that she "never lied in [her] heart." Mitch chooses to believe Stanley's version of the truth, and so he leaves Blanche to endure life alone. What initially seems like conceit eventually reveals itself to be a defensive strategy employed by Blanche in an attempt to survive an unforgiving, post–World War II American society.

For the film adaptation, director Kazan strove to transfer the stage version to the screen, to include its themes, and insisted on using the Broadway cast in order to keep the integrity of the play intact. Warner Bros., though, wanted Kazan to cast someone with more box-office draw than Jessica Tandy in the role of Blanche, thus the choice of Leigh (Freeman, 1995). Although Kazan reluctantly agreed to the requests of the studio, the film still became a victim of the Hollywood Censorship Office. For fear of receiving a "C," or "condemned" rating from the League of Decency, whose morality code inspired the Hollywood production code, Warner Brothers demanded the deletion of lines and scenes, in addition to a changed ending (Freeman 1995). In the stage version, Stella commits Blanche to an insane asylum and remains with Stanley as a means of survival. In the film version, however, we see a more morally and socially acceptable ending where Stella whispers to her new baby that they are never going back to Stanley again (Thomson, 2003). She then takes the newborn baby in her arms and runs upstairs to the neighbor's apartment. Kazan and Williams both felt that the movie's changed ending ruined the story's effectiveness in that Stella's actions seem absurd in the context of the rest of the film (Freeman, 1995, 28–29). As a whole, *A Streetcar Named Desire* remained controversial, regardless of the producer's cuts. In 1993, Fox released the director's cut of the film that includes three minutes of excised footage that underscored the sexual tension between Stanley and Blanche, as well as Stella's passion for her husband. The film remains a landmark in American film for the social issues it raised during a time of moral consciousness in American culture.

See also: Brando, Marlon; Kazan, Elia; Melodrama, The

References

Freeman, Koina. *Derailment of A Streetcar Named Desire: Compromise of a Theatrical Document through Translation to the Screen*. Unpublished master's thesis: California State University, Long Beach, 1995.

Murphy, Brenda. *Tennessee Williams and Elia Kazan*. Cambridge, UK: Cambridge University Press, 1992

Thomson, David. *Marlon Brando*. New York: DK Publishing, 2003.

—Jennifer K. Morrison

SULLIVAN'S TRAVELS.   Writer and director Preston Sturges's *Sullivan's Travels* (1941) explores the complex operations of socially engaged cinema during the Great Depression, offering a satirical vision of Hollywood. The film focuses on the story of young filmmaker John Lloyd Sullivan, who resists his role as a creator of lighthearted comedies. Sullivan wants instead to produce a hard-hitting socially relevant film titled, "O Brother, Where Art Thou?"

Studio executives reject Sullivan's idea, questioning his ability to produce a worthwhile film. Noting that his model in the genre of socially conscious films is director Frank Capra, they ask Sullivan, "What do you know about hard luck?" They argue that

Sullivan has not experienced the life of the common man and therefore cannot produce a meaningful film about his experience.

In response, Sullivan dons the garb of a hobo and embarks on a disastrous adventure in hopes of understanding the plight of the everyday individual. His butler objects to his plan, arguing that the poor value their privacy. He cautions Sullivan, "Poverty is not the lack of anything, but a positive plague, virulent in itself, contagious as cholera, with filth, criminality, vice, and despair as only a few of its symptoms. It is to be stayed away from, even for purposes of study. It is to be shunned."

Nonetheless, Sullivan departs, pairing up with a failed actress (Veronica Lake) who poses as a young man during their journey. The two travel to Kansas City, where they tour a skid-row district, observing a mission, a flophouse, and a soup kitchen. Sullivan decides to end his project. But first, he wants to distribute cash to the poor, out of gratitude for the lessons he has learned. As he distributes five-dollar bills, one homeless man, who had earlier stolen Sullivan's boots, now knocks him out and steals his money. Sturges refuses Capra's frequently romanticized depiction of the nation's poor, instead, portraying some indigent people as both desperate and violent.

The escaping thief is struck and killed by a passing train. Wearing the stolen boots tagged with Sullivan's identification, he is identified as the director. Meanwhile, during an altercation, Sullivan, now an amnesiac, strikes a railroad yard worker with a rock. He is tried and sentenced to six years in prison. As a prisoner, he encounters a life of hard labor on a chain gang, abuse, and misery. He is taken with other prisoners to an African American church to see a Walt Disney cartoon. Through that experience, he comes to understand and appreciate the value of comedy to those who are suffering. Although his life is one filled with pain, he can still find pleasure in the products of Hollywood. He realizes that his destiny is to return to the studio and produce similarly comedic films.

A darker film than those directed in this era by Capra, *Sullivan's Travels* offered a complex vision of the relationship between art, culture, and society during the Great Depression. Sturges seemed to be saying that everyday Americans were not necessarily either heroes or villains, and should not be painted with a broad brush. Cultural products, such as films, Sturges seemed to contend, need not position themselves heavy-handedly as uplifting and educational projects. Instead, they could offer audiences a temporary escape from reality.

Sullivan's Travels demonstrated Sturges's interest in experimenting with narrative structure. Sullivan's four journeys away from Hollywood are each presented in the style of a distinct genre, including physical comedy, melodrama, silent film, and prison film. The film offers audiences a nuanced exploration of the role of cultural production in the lives of everyday Americans. *Sullivan's Travels* received critical acclaim but no Academy Award nominations.

See also: Sturges, Preston

References

Moran, Kathleen, and Michael Rogin. " 'What's the Matter with Capra?' *Sullivan's Travels* and the Popular Front." *Representations* 71, Summer 2000: 106–34.

Peeler, David P. *Hope Among Us Yet: Social Criticism and Social Solace in Depression America.* Athens: University of Georgia Press, 1987.

Pells, Richard H. *Radical Visions and American Dreams: Culture and Social Thought in the Depression Years.* Chicago: University of Illinois Press, 1998.

—Ella Howard

SUNSET BLVD.   Billy Wilder's *Sunset Blvd.* (1950) is one of the great Hollywood movies about movies, rivaled, perhaps, only by *Singin' in the Rain.* While the latter film is pure joy, *Sunset Blvd.* provides us with dark humor and is ultimately a caustic indictment of the business of Hollywood moviemaking.

The story involves a down-on-his-luck screenwriter named Joe Gillis (William Holden), who turns into the driveway of an old mansion on Sunset Blvd. in Los Angeles, while being chased by two men who are trying to repossess his car. The mansion turns out to belong to Norma Desmond (Gloria Swanson), an aging actress who has never been able to acknowledge her star power has long passed. Indeed, when Joe recognizes her, she denies that she has lost any of her movie star brilliance: "You're Norma Desmond," says Joe. "You used to be in silent pictures. You used to be big." "I *am* big," responds Norma crossly. "It's the *pictures* that got small."

When Norma realizes that Joe is a screenwriter, she hires him to help edit a script she is writing that will provide her a vehicle for her comeback (although when Joe calls it a "comeback," she memorably snaps, "I hate that word. It's a *return!*"). The two form an uneasy interdependent relationship—she needs Joe's skills as a writer, he needs her money. Joe moves into the house, and the relationship evolves to the point where Joe begins to provide not just his writing acumen, but what can best be described as companionship.

The movie is essentially about how people in Hollywood use each other and how ruthless they are toward one another once they no longer need each other. Early in the story, Joe asks his agent for help in getting a job, or at least to loan him $200 until he can finish the script that he knows will put him over the top. The agent refuses, telling Joe that the best writing in the world was done on an empty stomach. Although he recognizes that his relationship with Norma is emotionally unhealthy, Joe nevertheless wants Norma's financial support to continue. In order to deal with his peculiar situation, he begins sneaking out at night to work on his own script with another, female, screenwriter. When Norma discovers this, she threatens suicide; when Joe finally decides to leave for good, she ends up killing him.

A darkly incisive character study, the film has an unsettling noirish sensibility. Wilder had already directed one of the great film noirs six years earlier when he made *Double Indemnity.* Like that earlier film, *Sunset Blvd.* is told in flashbacks with voice-over narration—viewers know the outcome of the story from the very beginning, as

Silent screen star Gloria Swanson stars with William Holden in the biting Hollywood satire *Sunset Blvd.*, directed by Billy Wilder, 1950. (Hulton Archive/Getty Images)

the picture opens with a shot of Joe lying face down in a swimming pool: "The poor dope—he always wanted a pool. Well, in the end, he got himself a pool." Marked by the shadowy, uncanny—even creepy—interiors of Norma's mansion, the picture presses in on the viewer, literally and figuratively, as Joe's ill-advised decisions send him spiraling toward his predetermined death.

Interestingly, Gloria Swanson was herself a well-known silent film star who found it difficult to make the switch to sound films; and Erich von Stroheim, who played her butler Max, although one of the truly great directors of the silent era, was never really able to recover from his disastrous production of *Greed*. Wilder even had the legendary silent film star Buster Keaton sit in as one of Norma's guests with whom she plays cards—guests whom Joe calls Norma's "waxworks."

See also: Film Noir; Wilder, Billy

References

Henry, Nora. *Ethics and Social Criticism in the Hollywood Films of Erich von Stroheim, Ernst Lubitsch, and Billy Wilder*. Westport, CT: Praeger, 2003.

Staggs, Sam. *Close-up on Sunset Boulevard: Billy Wilder, Norma Desmond, and the Dark Hollywood Dream*. New York: St. Martin's, 2002.

—Govind Shanadi

SUPERMAN: THE MOVIE.   The 1978 film version of *Superman* was a milestone on many levels: It created a resurgence of a comic book character that had been an icon for 40 years; it established the careers of its stars Christopher Reeve and Margot Kidder; and perhaps most importantly, it ushered in the age of the modern cinematic superhero. The character of Superman had been introduced in *Action Comics #1* in 1938 by creators Jerry Siegel and Joe Shuster. In the four decades that followed, the world's first "superhero" went on to star in a long-running radio show, animated cartoon shorts, live-action movie serials, and a 1951 big-screen adventure starring George Reeves, *Superman and the Mole Men*. This latter film would spawn the popular 1950s television show.

The 1978 incarnation was produced by Alexander and Ilya Salkind, with a script by *Godfather* author Mario Puzo, co-written with David and Leslie Newman and Robert Benton. Directed by Richard Donner, the film featured a score by John Williams, hot off of his award-winning score for *Star Wars*. Wanting relative unknowns to fill the starring roles, the Salkinds chose Christopher Reeve and Margot Kidder as the Man of Steel and his love interest, Lois Lane. Gene Hackman brilliantly portrayed Superman's arch-nemesis Lex Luthor. The role of Superman's father, Jor-El, went to screen legend Marlon Brando, who received top billing even though he made only a cameo appearance in the film.

Born as baby Kal-El on the doomed planet of Krypton, the future Superman is shot into space by his parents in an attempt to save him from their fate. Landing in a field outside of Smallville, Kansas, he is found by an elderly couple, Jonathan and Martha Kent, who take the boy in and raise him as their son. As baby "Clark" grows into adulthood, his "second" father dies, leaving him to make his way in a world that is not his own. He emerges a decade later on the streets of Metropolis, seeking a job as a reporter at the local newspaper, the *Daily Planet*. It is there that he meets Lois Lane, as well as other Superman mainstays: editor Perry White and cub reporter Jimmy Olsen. Once he begins fighting crime as Superman, the hero catches the attention of criminal mastermind Lex Luthor, who has researched Superman's origins and discovered his one weakness: irradiated remnants of his long-dead planet: Kryptonite. Superman soon discovers Luthor's plan to buy up thousands of acres of worthless desert properties in the American west, and, using stolen nuclear weapons, to blow up the San Andreas fault line, sending California into the ocean and making his "desert" properties prime coastal real estate. Though successful in stopping Luthor, and saving the lives of those who had been threatened, Superman discovers he is too late to save Lois Lane, who has died in the earthquakes. Disobeying the one rule set down by his real father, Superman uses his powers to reverse the rotation of the planet and turn back time, which, although it allows him to save Lois, also has the ominous effect of "changing human history."

The success of *Superman* was due in large part to the timing of its release. By the end of the 1970s, American morale had descended to one of its lowest points. Having endured the Watergate scandal; the inglorious loss of the Vietnam War; a stagnant economy, exacerbated by a massive energy crisis; and what was increasingly perceived as the failure of the Carter administration, the United States, for one of the few times

Scene from the 1978 film *Superman*, starring Christopher Reeve. Directed by Richard Donner. (Photofest)

in its history, seemed to be bowing its head in shame. The American people needed a hero . . . and *Superman* provided them with one.

Interestingly, the film was released during the lead-up to the era of flag-waving patriotism that defined the Reagan years. Though Superman would ultimately lose much of his appeal as the 1980s increasingly made way for antiheroes like Batman, Wolverine, and the Watchmen, he would never completely disappear from the landscape of the American psyche. Throughout the 1990s, he would be featured in no fewer than five top-10 pop songs. He would emerge again in the wake of the events of September 11, 2001, when, just one week after that tragic day, the WB television network premiered what would become its most popular series, *Smallville*, a show chronicling the adventures of a young Clark Kent, fulfilling his heroic destiny.

See also: Action Adventure Film, The; Science Fiction Film, The; Superhero, The

References

Burns, Kevin, Dir. *Look, Up in the Sky! The Amazing Story of Superman.* Warner Bros. DVD, 2006.

Daniels, Les. *Superman: The Complete History.* San Francisco: Chronicle Books. 1998.

—Richard A. Hall

T

TAXI DRIVER. *Taxi Driver* (1976) is an Academy Award–winning film directed by Martin Scorsese and starring Robert De Niro as a mentally unstable Vietnam War veteran named Travis Bickle. Bickle drives a cab at night and comes to despise the contemptible people who roam the city streets after dark. The film depicts the tragic consequences of loneliness and alienation as he attempts to "clean up" the streets. *Taxi Driver* is remembered not only for its gritty performances but also as the film that inspired the 1981 attempted assassination of U.S. president Ronald Reagan by John Hinckley, who was obsessed with Jodie Foster, the actress who plays teen prostitute Iris in the film.

Taxi Driver can be defined as a film about failure: personal, cultural, and that of a country engulfed in an unpopular war. While hospitalized, author Paul Schrader was motivated to write the screenplay for *Taxi Driver* while reading newspaper accounts of would-be assassin Arthur Bremer, who shot and paralyzed Alabama governor George Wallace in 1972. After a failed relationship, Bremer began drinking heavily and did not talk to anyone for weeks. Bremer believed that his only means to gain the recognition he coveted was to assassinate someone of distinction, and after failing to penetrate President Richard Nixon's security zone, he targeted Wallace.

In *Taxi Driver*, Bremer is loosely represented by Bickle, an ex-Marine whose insomnia leads him to a job driving a New York City taxicab at night. His diary expresses his harsh view of what he sees as the squalor and sleaze on the streets. Alienated, awkward in his attempts at relationships, and unable to sleep, he visits the Times Square X-rated movie theaters and watches the screen with a dispassionate gaze. The only people he has a minimal relationship with are a group of fellow taxi drivers, whom he occasionally meets for evening coffee. He consults one of them, Wizard (Peter Boyle), and attempts to explain the dark, evil thoughts he is having.

Several defining moments in the narrative act as a catalyst in setting the motivation for Travis. He meets and pursues beautiful blonde Betsy (Cybill Shepherd), who works in the Manhattan office of presidential candidate and U.S. senator Charles Palantine (Leonard Harris). She is a vision of purity, dressed in a flowing white dress. After observing her from the insulation of his taxi, he meets Betsy in the office and convinces

Robert De Niro points a pistol at a firing range in a still from the film *Taxi Driver*, directed by Martin Scorsese. (Columbia Pictures/Fotos International/Getty Images).

her to have coffee with him. Unable to separate Betsy from his routine, alienated lifestyle, he takes her to an X-rated movie on their first date and she rushes out.

His other meeting with a female is by chance, when Iris, a teenage prostitute, suddenly gets into his taxi and tells him to drive away quickly. Before he can react, she is pulled out of the cab by her pimp, Sport (Harvey Keitel), who drops a $20 bill on his seat and tells him to forget about what just happened. In his wanderings, Travis again meets Iris and this time befriends her, attempting to convince her to abandon her lifestyle and return home.

One evening Travis picks up Palantine and his aides on their way to an event. During the ride he tells the senator how he feels about the city being a cesspool and how it must be cleaned up. Palantine humors Travis, realizing that he is deranged. In another self-defining incident, Travis, who has purchased an array of assault weapons, confronts an armed robber in a convenience store and shoots him, leaving the unlicensed gun with the store owner before fleeing. Deciding to organize his life and get his body into shape, Travis begins a regimen of lifting weights and doing push-ups and pull-ups. Visiting a Palantine rally, he approaches a Secret Service agent, who becomes suspicious when Travis asks questions about becoming an agent. Travis blends into the crowd before another agent can photograph him.

Back home, in one of the most famous scenes in film, Travis, wearing a green military fatigue jacket, poses in front of a mirror, posturing as a tough guy and repeating the phrase "You talkin' to me?" while drawing his gun from a forearm spring-loaded holster. Travis begins to set his life in order, writing a final letter to his parents, articulating his fantasy of living with Betsy and working at a sensitive job with the government. He stuffs $500 into an envelope intended for Iris, thinking that he will be dead by the time she receives it. Wearing a Mohawk-style haircut, Travis stalks Palantine at a rally with the intent to assassinate him, but flees after being seen by a Secret Service agent.

In a bloodthirsty scene of retribution and symbolic cleansing, Travis confronts Sport outside Iris's apartment and shoots him. He enters the building, shooting the manager, and is wounded in the neck by Sport, whom he kills. Then he is shot in the arm by Iris's customer, whom he shoots in the face and chest. He wrestles with the manager and, after subduing him in front of Iris, he tries to shoot himself under the chin but is out of bullets. As the police enter he puts his bloody trigger finger to his head and mimics the sound of a shot.

The media pay tribute to him as a hero who rescued the young Iris from her involuntary servitude. He is lauded as a purveyor of vigilante justice, cleaning the city of its filth. In the last scene he is the next taxi in line at the St. Regis Hotel as Betsy enters the cab. They say little, and when they reach her apartment, Travis refuses to accept Betsy's offer to pay the fare and he drives away, taking a last glance of her in the rearview mirror.

Taxi Driver received high critical acclaim and was nominated for four Oscars at the 1977 Academy Awards presentation, including Best Actor (De Niro), Best Supporting Actress (Foster), Best Original Score, and Best Picture.

See also: De Niro, Robert; Scorsese, Martin

References

Schrader, Paul. *Taxi Driver*. London: Faber & Faber, 2000.
Taubin, Amy. *Taxi Driver*. London: British Film Institute, 2008.

—*James Roman*

TERMINATOR SERIES, THE. *The Terminator* (1984), James Cameron's low-budget science fiction film featuring a relentless cyborg killer from the future, captured the zeitgeist of early 1980s America by reflecting the culture's ambivalence toward technology at the dawn of the digital revolution. The surprise success of the film set the stage for numerous sequels, and launched a franchise that continues to generate spin-off products in a wide variety of media formats.

The terminator character has become synonymous with Arnold Schwarzenegger, who played the T-800 cyborg assassin in the first film. Born in the small town of Thal, Austria, Schwarzenegger achieved international fame as a bodybuilder, winning the Mr. Universe title five times and Mr. Olympia title seven times between 1966 and 1980. He began his acting career with *Hercules in New York* (1970) and appeared in numerous other films before becoming a serious box-office draw in *Conan the*

Scene from the 1984 film *The Terminator*, starring Arnold Schwarzenegger. Directed by James Cameron. (Photofest)

Barbarian (1982). For *The Terminator*, Schwarzenegger was initially offered the role of the hero, but chose the role of the flesh-covered robot villain instead, using his muscle-bound physique and thick Austrian accent to define the character of the unstoppable killing machine. Schwarzenegger's portrayal of the terminator made him one of the world's most popular action movie stars of the next two decades.

The film was also a career launcher for James Cameron, who, prior to *The Terminator*, had only directed one feature film, *Piranha II: The Spawning* (1981). After *The Terminator*, Cameron went on to direct many popular Hollywood movies, including the enormously successful *Titanic* (1997), which won 11 Academy Awards and is one of the top-grossing motion pictures of all time. He also directed *The Terminator*'s sequel, *Terminator 2: Judgment Day* (1991). For *The Terminator*, Cameron shares screenwriting credits with Gale Anne Hurd, who also produced the film and married Cameron a year after its release. The story was largely based on two 1964 episodes of the television show *The Outer Limits* written by Harlan Ellison, entitled "Soldier," and "Demon with a Glass Hand." Cameron's influence is most obvious in *The Terminator*'s special effects which, despite a modest budget of only $6.4 million, achieved a convincing vision of a dystopic future that rivaled films with larger budgets, such as Ridley Scott's classic *Blade Runner* (1981).

The Terminator begins in Los Angeles in 2029. A sophisticated computer system called Skynet has started World War III as a way of eliminating all human life. Some humans have survived to wage war against the machines. Skynet has created an army of cyborgs to infiltrate and kill off these human resistors, but it realizes that in order to win against the humans it must eliminate their leader, John Connor, before he is born. Skynet sends the T-800 back in time to kill John's mother, Sarah Connor (Linda Hamilton), before she conceives. To protect his mother from the T-800, John sends

Kyle Reese (Michael Biehn) back in time. Kyle finds Sarah just before the T-800, saying, "Come with me if you want to live." Kyle and Sarah then flee from the T-800 and hide out in a hotel room where Kyle confesses that he has always loved Sarah. They consummate their relationship (conceiving John in the process), and ultimately confront the T-800 in a final showdown in which Kyle is killed, but Sarah manages to crush the T-800 in a compactor.

Like many dystopic science fiction films, *The Terminator* bristles with strong undercurrents of technophobia. Throughout the film there are scenes where machines break down or fail to help human beings. Telephones, a police radio, an answering machine, a walkman, all play a role in either assisting the T-800 in its quest to find Sarah, or preventing victims from recognizing the danger the T-800 presents. In addition, the T-800 consistently uses automobiles and a panoply of weapons against human beings. The most enduring image of the relentless incursion of technology into everyday American life is the T-800 itself, particularly when its flesh is burned off and it continues to pursue Sarah as a robotic skeleton.

Despite its dark, technophobic undertones, *The Terminator* is not without humor, and the credit for this must be given to Schwarzenegger, whose deadpan delivery and heavy Austrian accent turned throwaway lines of dialogue into memorable snippets of popular vernacular. Before crashing a car into the police station where Sarah is being held in protective custody, the T-800 politely asks a clerk if he may see Sarah Connor. When he is told he will have to wait, the T-800 looks around the room, and in a flat mechanical voice says, "I'll be back." The phrase would become not only the signature line of the movie, but also a forecaster of numerous *Terminator* sequels, and an indicator of the cultural longevity of Arnold Schwarzenegger. For legal and technical reasons it took seven years, but eventually the terminator did come back.

Terminator 2: Judgment Day is one of the few sequels that is generally regarded as being superior to the original. Written by Cameron and William Wisher, *T2* was the most expensive movie of its time with a budget exceeding $100 million, but it made more than five times its cost in worldwide box-office sales. Its special effects helped to pioneer a new era of computer-generated imagery that would be seen in later films such as Steven Spielberg's *Jurassic Park* (1993). Along with its popular success, *T2* won Academy Awards for soundtrack, visual special effects, sound effects, and make-up. The key to its success, however, is that it does not merely repeat the themes of the first film. Instead, it takes the technophobic theme and reverses it, showing that technology can also be used to benefit human beings.

T2 takes place 13 years after the original *Terminator*. This time two cyborgs are sent back to present day Los Angeles. One is a T-800 (Schwarzenegger) that the John Connor of the future has captured, reprogrammed, and sent back to protect the 13-year old John Connor (Edward Furlong) from the T-1000, Skynet's newest terminator. The T-1000 (Robert Patrick) is even more dangerous than the T-800. Composed of "liquid metal," the T-1000 can resume its original shape after being shot, burned, or crushed, and can even shape-shift to take the form of other humans of similar size. Robert Patrick's clean-cut looks and policeman's uniform make the T-1000 less menacing than the bulky, foreign accented Schwarzenegger was in the first film.

At the same time, its impressive ability to shape-shift undermines the technophobic subtext of the first *Terminator* with its seductive visual spectacle.

In addition to the T-1000's stunning liquid metal effects, the T-800's role reversal from assassin to protector contributes to an overall positive view of technology in *T2*. Schwarzenegger plays the T-800 like a father figure to the young John Connor, and even sacrifices himself at the end, descending into a cauldron of molten steel so that Cyberdyne, the company that eventually develops Skynet, will not be able to use his technology. This opposite characterization of the T-800 reflected Schwarzenegger's new image as one of the most popular action heroes in the world. He had even proved himself a competent comedian in *Twins* (1988), and *Kindergarten Cop* (1990), and his role in T2 shows this change as well, with many comic lines coming from his imitation of John Connor's teenage slang. In one scene, before shooting the T-1000, he sardonically utters another phrase that would enter the cultural lexicon, "Hasta la vista, Baby."

Another character who changed radically from the original *Terminator* was Sarah Connor, again played by Linda Hamilton. At the beginning of *T2*, Sarah is being held in a maximum-security insane asylum because she is obsessed with trying to prevent World War III. Apart from her mental change, Sarah is also physically transformed. When we first see her, she is doing pull-ups in a sleeveless tank top. She has progressed from a docile, stereotypically feminine woman who needs to be protected by Kyle Reese in the first film, into a lean, muscular killer who, in many ways, takes on the traits of a cyborg terminator. She also has a single-minded ambition to kill Miles Dyson (Joe Morton), the man responsible for the development of Skynet, and sets out to do so with a laser-sighted rifle reminiscent of the laser-sight the T-800 trained on her in the first film. Just before "terminating" Dyson in front of his family, Sarah regains her humanity, and together with John and the T-800, recruits Dyson to help destroy the Cyberdyne offices.

The strong characterization of Sarah Connor in *T2* takes up the latent feminism of the first movie and expands it. Where Sarah requires Kyle's training in the first film before she can kill the T-800, by the second film Sarah has become an action heroine in her own right. Since she is also the narrator of the second film, Sarah has voice-over authority in the depiction of the story events as well. The third *Terminator* movie would go even further in depicting a powerful female character, but it would not be Sarah Connor. Instead, the strong female character is a new cyborg killer.

Terminator 3: Rise of the Machines (2003) was the first *Terminator* film not written and directed by James Cameron. Jonathan Mostow, fresh from helming *U-571* (2000), agreed to direct after Cameron turned it down. The story does not differ substantially from *T2*, but John Connor (Nick Stahl) is older; Sarah Connor has died; and, along with the T-800 (Schwarzenegger), who is sent to protect Connor again, a newer T-X, "terminatrix" (Kristanna Loken), is sent to kill Connor and anyone who might assist him in the future. The T-X has the same shape-shifting abilities that the T-1000 had, but can also remotely control other machines. Connor and his future wife, Kate Brewster (Claire Danes), try to prevent Skynet's nuclear war, but in the end, are only able to hide out in an underground base station and wait it out.

Despite Schwarzenegger's star power, and an enormous budget of $200 million, *T3* was not able to turn a profit during its theatrical run in the United States. For many, the third *Terminator* film had lapsed into parody. A typical example occurs in the beginning. In each film, the naked T-800 confronts the first people it meets in order to acquire clothing. In the original film, the T-800 violently dispatches a trio of street punks. In *T2*, the T-800 enters a biker bar, where the thugs are considerably tougher, but again, defeats them. By the third film, the T-800 repeats this same performance in a club for male strippers, where his nudity is applauded as part of the act, and he is told to "talk to the hand," when he asks for one of the stripper's clothes.

Despite the shortcomings of *T3*, it showed that after two decades, there was still plenty of interest in the franchise. *Terminator 4: Salvation* was released in 2009. It starred Christian Bale as John Connor, with Roland Kickinger, another Austrian bodybuilder, playing the part of the T-800. Beyond the four films, the *Terminator* franchise has produced novels, video games, and a Fox television series entitled *Terminator: The Sarah Connor Chronicles*, which stars Lena Headey as Sarah Connor and Thomas Dekker as a teenage John Connor. With all of these spin-offs, the influence of the time-traveling terminator will likely continue long into the future.

See also: Action Adventure Film, The; Science Fiction Film, The

References

Friedman, Norman L. "*The Terminator*: Changes in Critical Evaluations of Cultural Productions." *Journal of Popular Culture* 28(1), 1994: 73–80.
Mann, Karen. "Narrative Entanglements: 'The Terminator.'" *Film Quarterly* 43(2): 17–27.
Rushing, Janice Hocker, and Thomas S. Frentz. *Projecting the Shadow: The Cyborg Hero in American Film*. Chicago: University of Chicago Press, 1991.

—*Joseph Christopher Schaub*

THELMA AND LOUISE. Directed by Ridley Scott—best known at the time for such slick sci-fi thrillers as *Alien* and *Blade Runner*—*Thelma and Louise* burst on the scene in 1991, garnering immediate, though not universal, critical and popular acclaim. The film tells the story of Thelma (Geena Davis), a housewife whose spirit seems to be largely stifled by her domineering husband Darryl (Christopher McDonald), and Louise (Susan Sarandon), an unmarried waitress whose obvious strength masks a trauma hidden deep within her past; it follows them through a series of serio-comic adventures that begin when they go off on what they think will be a relaxing two-day road trip. Callie Khouri wrote the original screenplay, and wanted to direct the film herself, but was unable to find a studio willing to produce it until Scott agreed to direct it for MGM—an arrangement Khouri approved on the condition that Scott promise not to change her ending. The film features performances by Brad Pitt, in his first role in a major Hollywood production, Harvey Keitel, and Michael Madsen.

Thelma and Louise's little trip takes an unexpected turn when Thelma is nearly raped by a man with whom she's flirted in a bar (Timothy Carhart) and Louise

Scene from the 1991 film *Thelma and Louise*, starring Susan Sarandon (left) and Geena Davis. Directed by Ridley Scott. (Photofest)

intervenes, shooting and killing the attacker. Convinced that their story of self-defense would never be believed by the authorities, Thelma and Louise decide to flee to Mexico. On the way, they meet a charming thief, J. D. (Pitt), who ends up seducing Thelma, teaching her how he commits robberies, and stealing all of the women's money. As their flight gets more desperate, Thelma and Louise embrace the life of care-free outlaws, and for a time manage to evade capture by both the FBI and a sympathetic local detective (Keitel). Ultimately, however, their attempts to escape the authorities prove futile, and they choose the only option that they feel is left to them—they literally fly off a cliff in their car. Although Scott, in a shot reminiscent of George Roy Hill's final shot in another outlaw-buddy-movie, *Butch Cassidy and the Sundance Kid*, freezes the frame with Thelma, Louise, and their car in midflight over a deep ravine, we can only assume that our protagonists have been set free from their tragically oppressive lives by dying.

For the most part, *Thelma and Louise* was received by both critics and the filmgoing public with wild enthusiasm. In particular, it was praised for its appropriation and sub-version of numerous well-established cinematic genres, including the buddy film, the road film, the outlaw-couple-on-the-run film, and the female friendship film. It was hailed as a feminist manifesto, a celebration of Thelma and Louise's refusal to be determined by the demands of a patriarchal society, as embodied in the conventions of both personal relationships and a legal system that all too often fails to protect female victims of male violence. However, it also generated a great deal of controversy, with numerous critics taking it to task for its violence and its derogatory—even, ironically, essentialist—depictions of men.

The question of whether or not *Thelma and Louise* is really a feminist film continues to be debated, particularly in academic circles where scholars have been writing about and discussing the film since it was released two decades ago. Building on the feminist film theory of Laura Mulvey, much of the scholarly criticism related to *Thelma and Louise* focuses on the extent to which the film is or is not successful in contributing to the construction of a female gaze that subverts the male gaze that, for Mulvey and others, structures cinematic viewing pleasure. Khouri herself has argued that Thelma and Louise are not feminists but outlaws, yet she also acknowledges that she wrote the film because she was tired of the predominance of passive roles for women in American cinema—an acknowledgment that suggests the implicit, if not explicit, feminist agenda of the film.

Thelma and Louise received numerous awards, and even more award nominations. Screenwriter Khouri won an Academy Award and a Writers Guild Award for Best Screenplay Written Directly for the Screen, and a Golden Globe Award for Best Screenplay, Motion Picture. Davis and Sarandon were both nominated for the Academy Award for Best Actress in a Leading Role, and for the Golden Globe Award for Best Performance by an Actress in a Motion Picture. The film also received Academy Award nominations for Best Director, Best Cinematographer (Adrian Biddle), and Best Film Editing (Thom Noble), as well as a Golden Globe nomination for Best Motion Picture, Drama.

The 2003 DVD release of *Thelma and Louise* includes a 2001 documentary in three parts, *Thelma and Louise: The Last Journey*, featuring timely interviews with Scott, Khouri, and several key cast members; 30 minutes of footage deleted from the theatrical release; and an alternate ending with commentary from Scott. The DVD continues to generate sales well into the second decade of the film's life, suggesting that *Thelma and Louise* still resonates with the American moviegoing public.

See also: Male Gaze, The; Mulvey, Laura; Scott, Ridley

References

Cook, Bernie, ed. *Thelma and Louise Live! The Cultural Afterlife of an American Film*. Austin: University of Texas Press, 2007.

Fournier, Gina. *Thelma and Louise and Women in Hollywood*. Jefferson, NC: McFarland, 2007.

Hollinger, Karen. *In the Company of Women: Contemporary Female Friendship Films*. Minneapolis: University of Minnesota Press, 1998.

Sturken, Marita. *Thelma and Louise*. London: British Film Institute, 2000.

—*Judith Poxon*

THIRD MAN, THE. Adapted from Graham Greene's novel of the same name, Carol Reed's *The Third Man* (1949) is a noir thriller set in the divided city of Vienna after World War II. Holly Martins (Joseph Cotton), a writer of pulp-fiction westerns, is invited to Vienna by an old school friend, Harry Lime (Orson Welles). Accepting the invitation, Holly arrives in Vienna only to find that Harry has died under mysterious circumstances, apparently related to smuggled penicillin. Unnerved by stories he begins to hear about Harry and the black market trade of penicillin, Holly sets about clearing his friend's name.

Filmed in 1948, shortly after the end of World War II, *The Third Man* was released at the point where the Cold War relationship between the Soviet Union and the United States was becoming increasingly tense. As early as 1946, the prescient Winston Churchill had warned that an "Iron Curtain" was descending across Eastern Europe; and in 1947, George Kennan sent his infamous "Long Telegram" to President Truman, detailing what he called the policy of "containment." By 1949, Mao and the communists had come to power, and Truman was being accused of "losing China."

The film explores what was a real black market in stolen and adulterated drugs in an occupied city. In Vienna, large amounts of these drugs were moved by criminals through the city's massive underground sewer system—the mazelike system was also used by criminals to slip from one sector of the city to another. The Austrian authorities actually put together a special unit of sewer police, which was depicted in the film's climactic chase scenes. Interestingly, because the film's producer, David O. Selznick, felt that the original script was marked by anti-American sensibilities, he insisted that a plotline that had Americans involved in Lime's gang be eliminated and that Lime's nationality not be revealed—leaving Holly Martins as the lone well-intentioned American who would set things right.

Viewers identified with the openness and optimism of Martins, who embodied the notion that American energy and dedication could rescue something worthwhile from tired old Vienna—much as the American military had rescued Europe from its worst wartime nightmare. Martins even characterizes himself as being like the hero of one of his novels, *The Lone Rider of Santa Fe*. Things were not as simple as they seemed, however, as the Vienna of *The Third Man* ended up being considerably darker and wilder than the pulp-fiction westerns penned by the naive Martins.

Interestingly, although the film is marked by an explicit sense of technical and psychological darkness, it is nevertheless redemptive at its core. In the end, *The Third Man* is very much about saving individuals—Anna from life in a communist state, children from the effects of impure drugs, and Martins from being murdered. Indeed, even Martins's misguided attempt to save his friend's reputation, his merciful ending of that friend's suffering, and Anna's steadfast loyalty to her criminal boyfriend and refusal to take up with Martins affirm the value of human relationships.

See also: Hard-Boiled Detective Film, The; Welles, Orson

References

Carpenter, Lynette. " 'I Never Knew the Old Vienna': Cold War Politics and *The Third Man*." In Phillips, William H., ed. *Analyzing Films: A Practical Guide*. New York: Holt, Rinehart, and Winston, 1983: 40–47.

Falk, Quentin. *Travels in Greenland: The Cinema of Graham Greene*. New York: Quartet Books, 1984.

Man, Glenn K. S. "*The Third Man*: Pulp Fiction and Art Film." *Literature/Film Quarterly* 21(3), Summer 1993: 171–77.

—W. M. Hagen

THREE KINGS.   The U.S.-led international military coalition's goal during the Gulf War, Americans were told, was to liberate Kuwait from Iraqi occupation and to prevent further aggression by Iraq's despotic leader, Saddam Hussein. U.S. military action, dominated by Operation Desert Storm, began in mid-January 1991. Six short weeks later, President George H. W. Bush declared victory. Reports of a high civilian death toll, environmental damage caused by oil spills and oil fires, and Hussein's continuing attacks on Kurds and Shiite Muslims dampened the celebration for some on the home front. However, largely because fewer than 300 American troops died, the war did not generate the same level of controversy in the United States as did Vietnam or even Ronald Reagan's interventions in Central America in the 1980s. Desert Storm Commander Norman Schwarzkopf returned home a war hero, and on March 1 President Bush exclaimed, "By God, we've kicked the Vietnam syndrome once and for all." While this triumphalist view permeated American media and popular culture during the decade between the Gulf War and September 11, 2001, David O. Russell's bracing *Three Kings* (1999) represents an important exception.

A unique blend of acerbic black humor and earnest moral inquiry, *Three Kings* is set in the aftermath of Operation Desert Storm. Immediately questioning the idea that the Gulf War represented a clean break from Vietnam, the film's second scene shows soldiers marking their victory by dancing to Rare Earth's 1971 hit "I Just Want to Celebrate." During the party, a journalist tells Special Forces officer Major Archie Gates (George Clooney) a rumor that Iraqis are keeping gold stolen from Kuwait in nearby bunkers; the following day, troops find a map to the bunkers on the body of an Iraqi prisoner. Gates, who earlier tells another officer, "I don't know what we did here," decides that if he is not going to find meaning in the war, he can at least try to find enrichment, and he leads three soldiers on a mission to resteal the gold. What begins like a hijinks-filled heist picture shifts dramatically after the foursome witnesses an Iraqi soldier execute the wife of an anti-Saddam leader. Suddenly, the need to protect refugees begins to compete with the search for gold. "Bush told the people to rise up against Saddam," Gates explains. "They thought they'd have our support—they don't. Now they're getting slaughtered." Will these soldiers do the right thing?

If the most famous Vietnam films retreated from the simple patriotism of World War II movies by portraying troubled soldiers succumbing to the complexity and terror of war, *Three Kings* depicts the immediate aftermath of the Gulf War both as a surreal, media-managed situation and one in which the moral choices are so clear that even four American men looking for action like frat boys on a Saturday night can manage them. Unlike World War II movie heroes or the tortured souls of many Vietnam films, *Three Kings*' protagonists remain average GI Joes throughout, only half-believing they will find the riches that will enable them to quit their low-status jobs back home. Like the Vietnam War, the Gulf War was fought by the working class, yet this film's signifiers of class are humorous and ironic. The soldiers are not Michael Cimino's primal deer hunters or stand-ins for America in the manner of the broken fighting men of *Born on the Fourth of July*. Instead, Vig (Spike Jonze) is shown back home practicing his marksmanship by shooting stuffed animals with a sawed-off shotgun, and Elgin's (Ice Cube) service to his country represents, as a freeze-frame caption reads, "a four-month paid vacation from Detroit."

The comedy in *Three Kings* is complimented by sympathetic portrayals of Iraqi refugees that won accolades from Middle Eastern Americans, and by Russell's anatomical depictions of violence. In one of the film's signature scenes, Gates responds to the troops' desire for action by asking if they know what happens when one suffers a bullet wound. As the camera moves inside the body of one of the soldiers, we see a bullet rip through tissue and generate bright green bile, producing the kind of footage seen regularly over the past decade on television shows such as *CSI* and *House, MD*. Although it can be jolting watching *Three Kings'* unusual blend of realism and surrealism, of satire and sincerity, the film provides strong evidence that post-Cold War warfare demands postmodern filmmaking.

See also: War Film, The

References

Edelstein, David. "One Film, Two Wars, 'Three Kings.'" *New York Times*, April 6, 2003.
McAlister, Melani. *Epic Encounters: Culture, Media, and U.S. Interests in the Middle East since 1945*. Berkeley: University of California Press, 2005.

—*Kenneth F. Maffitt*

TITANIC.   *Titanic* was initially perceived as a disaster waiting to happen—again. During production, rumors circulated about problems on the set, an obsessed director, and production budget overruns. The unprecedented commercial success of the film changed all that. Released in December 1997, *Titanic* was the first movie to gross more than $1 billion worldwide. Reviewers subsequently recast the record-breaking cost of production ($200 million) as a sign of the film's quality. Director James Cameron was heralded as an auteur and a stickler for historical authenticity. The film went on to win 11 Academy Awards, including Best Picture and Best Director.

Critics and scholars offer various explanations for the film's extraordinary popularity with audiences: the mix of genre elements; the lavish visual style; the narrative frame linking past and present; the teen heartthrob status of Leonardo DiCaprio; the savvy marketing of the soundtrack, including the hit song by Celine Dion; and nostalgia for the big-budget epic romances of the past. Although there may be no single explanation for the *Titanic* phenomenon, the film's appeal to both female and male viewers is significant. *Titanic* is representative of a contemporary production trend in Hollywood: female-centered action-adventure films designed to woo female viewers without alienating male viewers, the genre's core audience.

Scene from the 1997 film *Titanic*, starring Leonardo DiCaprio and Kate Winslet. Directed by James Cameron. (Photofest)

In the film, Rose's (Kate Winslet) oppression as an upper-class woman is opposed to Jack's (DiCaprio) freedom as a working-class man. One scene in particular captures the sense of freedom that Jack has and Rose wants. Jack, along with Fabrizio (Danny Nucci), a friend from steerage, climbs up on the bow of the ship in order to experience the exhilaration of speed and movement as the Titanic sets out for America, full steam ahead. As pistons engage, dolphins leap, and heavily synthesized music swells, Fabrizio, the hopeful immigrant, shouts excitedly that he can "see the Statue of Liberty already," while Jack throws his arms open wide and declares himself "the king of the world." This is a sensation scene, designed less for advancing the narrative than to evoke the feelings associated with being alive—with being a male body in the world, specifically. The extent to which that body might be oppressed by virtue of its class status is elided in the film. Instead, oppression is located with Rose and the constraints of her experience as a woman on the "upper deck."

Rose's attempts to fight back against gender oppression are linked with the women's suffrage movement in America. In one scene, Rose and her family members dine with Ismay (Jonathan Hyde), managing director of White Star Lines, and Andrews (Victor Garber), Titanic's designer. Ismay boasts that Titanic is "the largest moving object ever made by the hand of man in all of history," while Andrews, of a more modest demeanor, displaces the credit due to him for having designed the ship by referring to the grandiosity of Ismay's idea: "He envisioned a steamer so grand in scale and so luxurious in its appointments that its supremacy would never be challenged." Rose reacts to the idea of "supremacy that can never be challenged" by doing just that. She lights a cigarette—the sign of a suffragist in 1912 America—as a subtle challenge to the patriarchal supremacy implicit in Ismay's idea. Ruth (Frances Fisher), Rose's mother, immediately chastises her for lighting up, while Cal (Billy Zane), her fiancé, snatches the cigarette out of her mouth and extinguishes it. Ruth and Cal are melodramatic villains, upholding oppressive gender ideologies that the film will work to overcome.

In addition to adopting the attitude of the suffragette, Rose gradually begins to manifest the physical freedom associated with the working-class man. She is transformed into an action heroine—literally becoming like Jack in a type-scene repeat in which she is allowed to become "king of the world" on the soaring bow of the ship. In another scene, Jack is not only trapped within the sinking ship, he is melodramatically trapped within the trap, handcuffed to a pipe on a lower deck that is quickly filling with water. It is up to Rose to save him, which she does, in the nick of time. In another scene, with Rose in the lead, she and Jack attempt to outrun a deluge but are swept underwater and deposited against a locked gate. Miraculously, a steward appears and, with trembling hands, tries to unlock the gate, once again invoking the narrative question central to suspense: will he release them in the nick of time or will he be too late? When the steward drops the keys and flees in a panic, Jack dives underwater and recovers them, escalating the suspense. "What one is it, Rose?" he cries, abiding by the gender politics of the film, which resist letting the male character take over at the expense of the female hero. Rose cleverly identifies the correct key in the nick of time.

In the final scenes of the film, Cameron prepares us for the possibility of Rose's death but also invites us to "let go" via the sensory and emotional experience of film entertainment. "The former world has passed away," announces a priest as passengers kneel and pray while struggling to hold onto him. The next shot depicts the body of a young woman in a diaphanous white gown floating weightlessly in her underwater grave. This image is followed by shots of the ship tipping upright, stern over bow. One after another, passengers let go, screaming, and slide down the deck of the ship, in a manner reminiscent of an amusement park ride. This effect continues as the ship snaps in two. The stern plunges and then is upended once again, giving passengers (and members of the audience) the roller coaster ride of their lives.

The connection between death and film entertainment as conduits for "letting go" is confirmed as Jack climbs over the railings of the ship and positions himself "overboard," as it were, inviting Rose to join him. "Give me your hand. I've got you. I won't let go," he exclaims. The ship bobs momentarily, as if waiting for Jack and Rose to secure themselves in their seats, and then begins its final, spectacular plunge. "This is it!" Jack declares. This is the moment toward which the film has been building: the moment of death, facilitated by the film's most thrilling special effects. The ship plunges vertically into the water and disappears from the horizon for the last time. Pulled along in the ship's wake, Jack and Rose struggle to hold onto each other, but are forced to let go. Making their way to the surface, Jack guides Rose to a piece of floating debris and helps her onto it while remaining nearby, submerged in the icy water. He then enlists her in promising that she'll "survive," that she'll "never give up, no matter what happens, no matter how hopeless," that she'll "never let go." Clutching Jack's trembling hand, Rose agrees to "never let go." The irony, of course, is that in order to keep her promise to survive, she must eventually "let go" of Jack in death. She releases him into the icy depths, and viewers into the experience of pathos and heightened emotion.

Rose is eventually rescued and delivered to the safety of America's harbor. From her position on *Carpathia*'s steerage deck, gazing on the Statue of Liberty, she declares her new name, rejecting the values of her repressive past. As Rose Dawson, she will lead an emancipated life, doing all the things she had once asked Jack to teach her—"to ride like a man, chew tobacco like a man, spit like a man"—all of which depend on the freedom of the non-corseted body. That she does indeed lead a nontraditional life for a woman, a life of adventure, is evidenced by a collection of framed photographs gathered next to her deathbed: Rose deep-sea fishing, Rose piloting an airplane, Rose riding a horse, and so on. The photos are offered as proof that she has experienced the exhilarating sensations associated with being "king of the world."

See also: Melodrama, The; Women in Film

Reference

Sandler, Kevin S., and Gaylyn Studlar, eds. *Titanic: Anatomy of a Blockbuster.* Piscataway, NJ: Rutgers University Press, 1999.

—*Carol Donelan*

TO KILL A MOCKINGBIRD. Based on the Pulitzer Prize–winning novel by Harper Lee, *To Kill a Mockingbird* (1962) explores the role of racism in the South during the Great Depression. Although the novel and the film were set in a fictional town based on Lee's childhood home in 1930s Monroeville, Alabama, the picture debuted at the height of the 1960s civil rights movement and provided audiences a glimpse of southern society struggling with the haunting legacy of perverse tradition, fear, and racial hierarchy. Directed by Robert Mulligan and starring Gregory Peck, *To Kill a Mockingbird* represented an attempt to break free from the destructive stereotypes that had characterized earlier films set in the South. Whereas, for example, pictures such as *Gone with the Wind* had focused on antebellum plantation life, and others, such as *A Streetcar Named Desire*, had portrayed the South as a decadent, repressed region of America, the critically acclaimed *Mockingbird* emphasized the courageous role of Atticus Finch (Gregory Peck), a southern white attorney who acted as a filmic representative of both the civil rights movement and the possibility of the South's eventual integration into national life.

To Kill a Mockingbird revolves around the experiences of Scout, the young daughter of Atticus Finch, who functions as the cinematic bridge figure through whom the film's two parallel narratives are connected. The first of these narratives focuses on the efforts

Actor Gregory Peck, as Atticus Finch, stands in a courtroom in a scene from director Robert Mulligan's film *To Kill a Mockingbird*, 1962. (Universal Studios/Courtesy of Getty Images)

of Scout (Mary Badham), her older brother Jem (Phillip Alford), and a neighborhood friend to uncover the mystery of Arthur "Boo" Radley (Robert Duvall), a young man rarely seen outside his nearby house and assumed to be strange and dangerous. The second narrative focuses on Finch, who, while the children struggle with their fear of the unknown, finds himself defending Tom Robinson (Brock Peters), an innocent black man accused of sexually assaulting a young white woman named Mayella Ewell (Collin Wilcox). Although Finch protects Robinson from a local lynch mob and ably defends him during the dramatic trial, Robinson is convicted for violating the region's racial mores and is eventually killed trying to escape before Finch can appeal the questionable verdict. The children join the town in following the trial and observe the hostility of the larger white community, especially Robert E. Lee "Bob" Ewell, the father of the woman who falsely accused Robinson of rape in order to hide her own romantic and scandalous interest in the defendant. The two narratives intersect to create a pivotal moment in the lives of Scout and Jem when a vengeful Buell attacks the children only to be killed by Boo Radley, the misunderstood recluse.

To Kill a Mockingbird provided 1960s America with a poignant morality tale, one that sought to demonstrate that racial redemption could be achieved through the expression of understanding, tolerance, and compassion. Interestingly, however, even though it raised important questions about race in America, it is clear today that the film still did not go far enough in breaking down the destructive racial stereotypes that had dominated earlier pictures. Tom Robinson, for instance, remains largely a mute and marginalized figure, almost wholly defined by his paternalistic relationship to Atticus Finch; and while the film's description of the explicit injustice of southern society at least hinted at white America's deepest fears of the mythos of black male sexual perversity, the plot almost completely neglects the pervasive structural racism and rigid class hierarchy that often dominated southern life.

Thus, although the film seemed powerful during the early 1960s, as the civil rights movement allowed Americans to embrace the ideal of interracial cooperation, as the movement collapsed and the seemingly intractable challenges of race and class remained unresolved, the film's depiction of the promise of an enlightened white America appear less and less realistic.

See also: African Americans in Film; Ethnic and Immigrant Culture Filmmaking

References

Arnold, Edwin T. "What the Movies Told Us." *Southern Quarterly* 34(3), 1996: 57–65.
Crespino, Joseph. "The Strange Career of Atticus Finch." *Southern Cultures* 6(2), 2000: 9–29.
Lee, Harper. *To Kill a Mockingbird*. New York: Harper & Row, 1960.

—Richard L. Hughes

TOP GUN. The top ticket seller of 1986, *Top Gun*, won an Oscar for Best Original Song for "Take My Breath Away," and received Oscar nominations for Best Sound Effects Editing, Best Film Editing, and Best Sound. Though a box-office success, most critics dismissed it as a blatant representation of Reaganite values—it was anticommunist, individualist, militarist, morally unambiguous, nationalistic, and triumphalist. To be sure, critics also derided it as superficial filmmaking. The movie's success, they believed, was based solely in its pop musical and especially in its visual appeal.

Top Gun reflected President Ronald Reagan's and his right-leaning constituency's desire for a reassertion of American triumphalism. This was a stark contrast from the 1970s political and cultural "crisis of confidence." From a foreign policy perspective, burying the Vietnam War—by attributing the loss to both bureaucrats and an overreliance on technology, not a superior enemy—and reasserting American power were crucial to the reconstruction of American triumphalism. Like Reagan, a devout anticommunist who revived the Cold War, Reaganite cinema reasserted American power by reengaging and even defeating the communists. *Top Gun* epitomized this effort. And like Reagan, who viewed the United States as righteous and the Soviet Union as an "evil empire," *Top Gun* reflected his morally unambiguous view of the Cold War. In the aerial combat scenes, the light-colored (good) American F-14 Tomcats are contrasted against the dark-colored (evil) Soviet MIGs. The MIG pilots' faces are covered by dark visors; they are faceless, whereas we see the faces of the American pilots, and their names are written on the top of their helmets. These factors, in addition to filming

Scene from the 1986 film *Top Gun*, starring Tom Cruise. Directed by Tony Scott. (Photofest)

the MIGs only at a distance, serve to depersonalize and, therefore, dehumanize the enemy—the American pilots are fighting evil, not people (Palmer, 2003).

Yet *Top Gun* is not simply a military contest, but a boast of the supremacy of the American system—that is, the superiority of individualism and democracy over Soviet collectivism and totalitarianism (Palmer, 2003). This is made manifest in the figure of "Maverick" (Tom Cruise). He *is* his call sign's namesake, a trait that is perceived as dangerous by his flight instructors—he is viewed as a "wild card" and "completely unpredictable." Yet his unbridled individualism, from which his creative and courageous flying is derived, makes him an excellent pilot (Sprinker, 1987). He resists becoming the overly mechanical fighter that the Navy demands. Maverick's later decision to temper his individualism with technical acumen—triggered by the tragic death of his best friend and co-pilot, "Goose" (Anthony Edwards)—unites the American Frontier with American technical proficiency. In the climactic aerial combat scene, Maverick saves the excessively mechanical pilot "Iceman" (Val Kilmer), and shoots down three MIGs. Maverick and the United States—that is, individualism and democracy complemented by technical proficiency (who could ignore the technological sophistication of the F-14 Tomcats and that of the pilots who flew them?)—are victorious over Soviet collectivism and totalitarianism, which bred machines rather than humans (Palmer, 2003).

In addition to reflecting and projecting cultural and political triumphalism, *Top Gun* reflected and projected militarism. It was a corollary that if the United States was superior to the Soviet Union, its military, then—protecting the American virtues of individualism, democracy, and capitalism—was virtuous (not evil or fascist, as was suggested by New Left elements; such militarism was also a reaction against New Left pacifism and *anti*-anticommunism). Tony Shaw (2007) notes a link during the Cold War between the Pentagon and the film industry. The former provided technical and material aid in return for a positive portrayal of the military, which promoted militarism. Top Gun flight instructor "Viper" (Tom Skerritt) warns his student-pilots: "although we're not at war, we must always act as though we are at war." *Top Gun* was filmed with the Navy's cooperation, romanticized combat, and was used as a recruitment tool (Sprinker, 1987). If the film is dismissed by the Left as a reflection of grotesque triumphalism and militarism, the Right takes a less critical stance as it indeed views the Cold War as a necessary confrontation with a murderous and totalitarian state with diametrically opposed values.

See also: Action-Adventure Film, The; War Film, The

References

Palmer, William J. *The Films of the Eighties: A Social History.* Carbondale: Southern Illinois University Press, 1993.

Shaw, Tony. *Hollywood's Cold War.* Amherst: University of Massachusetts Press, 2007.

Sprinker, Michael. "Top Gun." In Magill, Frank N. *Magill's Cinema Annual, 1987: A Survey of the Films of 1986.* Pasadena, CA: Salem Press, 1987.

—*Mark D. Popowski*

TOUCH OF EVIL.   Directed by Orson Welles, *Touch of Evil* was released in 1958. Starring Charlton Heston as Mexican law enforcement official Ramon Miguel "Mike" Vargas and Janet Leigh as his wife, Susan "Susie" Vargas, the film is perhaps best remembered for Welles's performance as corrupt American police chief Hank Quinlan. Heavily made up, Welles transformed himself into a bloated, rumpled, sinister screen presence, creating what most agree was his finest characterization since he portrayed Charles Foster Kane in his classic 1941 film *Citizen Kane.*

Touch of Evil begins with one of the most famous opening sequences in film history. In one long—nearly four-minute—take, the camera pans, cranes, and tracks as it simultaneously follows a bomb that is armed and placed in a car alongside of which Mike and Susie casually stroll. Suddenly, the couple's festive idyll is shattered when the car explodes. The sequence has long been celebrated for its technical bravura, but it has deeper implications: with his fluid camera, Welles, it seems, transgresses borders; or perhaps more correctly, he elides borders.

This theme of bordering proves to be the foundational narrative element in *Touch of Evil.* Protagonists Vargas and Quinlan, for instance, constantly cross borders, both geographical and cultural, as they struggle to establish their respective investigative jurisdictions. As it turns out, the case is complicated: a bomb that was placed in a car in Mexico, allegedly by a Mexican national, goes off in Texas, killing two Americans.

Who, then, should head the investigation? The situation is further complicated by the fact that Vargas is married to an American, while Quinlan has been involved with Tanya (Marlene Dietrich), a Mexican prostitute.

Pushing hard against each other, Vargas and Quinlan develop their own theories about the crime. Vargas attempts to solve the case by exploring the clues with which he has been presented, although he is immediately suspicious of the Grandis, a crime family whose members move back and forth between the United States and Mexico with impunity. For his part, Quinlan, based on what he takes to be his finely honed powers of deduction, decides that a young Mexican man, Manelo Sanchez (Victor Millan), is guilty. Excusing his actions by way of his own perverse ethic—Quinlan has adopted an ends-justify-the-means attitude, beating confessions out of his prisoners when they are not appropriately forthcoming—he fabricates a scenario that fits his preconceived notions about the crime and orders that the suspect be broken, by whatever means necessary.

As is the case in many of Welles's films, the ending of *Touch of Evil* is marked by irony. Quinlan's efforts to frame Sanchez (and eventually Vargas), ultimately leading to his own downfall, prove to have been unnecessary, as Sanchez finally confesses; or so it seems, as the question regarding whether the young man was really guilty or just cracked under interrogative pressure is left open—was the confession beaten out of him? We naturally conclude that Vargas's law-and-order sensibilities are more redeeming than Quinlan's obsessive, results-at-all-costs methods, and that this is the point of the film. But there is additional irony—after all, Vargas ends up illegally wiretapping Quinlan in order to expose him. Vargas, then, disturbed by his wife's victimization, resorts to using precisely the same unethical investigative methods that he claims to abhor, and that Quinlan began to use after his own wife was murdered.

The dark, complex exploration of transnational issues that provides the narrative framework for *Touch of Evil* is still resonant today, as Americans and Mexicans continue the bitter debates over immigration, the controversial fence being built between the two countries, and the frightening specter of Mexican drug gangs buying guns in Texas and bringing them back across the border. Filmically, Welles provided us with a playful yet unsettling trope of thematic boundaries: mixing low comedy with violent action, blurring the lines between hero and antagonist, and giving the camera a haunting life of its own. Not surprisingly, conservative studio heads at Universal "simplified" the film—a process that Welles was forced to endure on numerous occasions throughout his career. Even so, the influence of *Touch of Evil* can still be seen in the work of contemporary filmmakers such as Alejandro Gonzalez Inarritu's *Babel* and the Coen brothers' *No Country for Old Men*.

See also: Film Noir; Hard-Boiled Detective Film, The; Welles, Orson

References

Comito, Terry, ed. *Touch of Evil: Orson Welles, Director.* Piscataway, NJ: Rutgers University Press, 1985.

Conrad, Peter. *Orson Welles: The Stories of His Life.* London: Faber & Faber, 2003.

Thomson, David. *Rosebud: The Story of Orson Welles.* New York: Alfred A. Knopf, 1996.

—Dimitri Keramitas

TOY STORY. In July 1991, Disney Studios agreed to a three-feature-film deal with a small computer animation company owned by Steve Jobs, the founder of Apple Computers. Pixar, formally the computer division of George Lucas's Lucasfilms, had, until then, focused on developing computer animated short films and commercials. The deal allowed Pixar to develop its first feature-length film that was completely computer generated. The collaboration with Pixar marked a departure for Disney, long the dominant force in "cell animation," which had been richly praised for its realism. Pixar, realizing its inability to reach that level of animated realism, sought instead to provide a fantasy world that was a caricature of reality.

The company's first film, *Toy Story*, was written by John Lasseter, who also directed; Pete Docter; Andrew Stanton; and Joe Ranft. Inspired by an earlier Pixar short, *Tin Toy*, the film tells the story of a toy cowboy named Woody (voiced by Tom Hanks) who fears being replaced as a little boy's favorite plaything by a

Scene from the 1986 film *Toy Story*. Shown are Sheriff Woody (voice: Tom Hanks) and Buzz Lightyear (voice: Tim Allen). Directed by John Lasseter. (Photofest)

highly coveted toy astronaut named Buzz Lightyear (named after real-life astronaut Buzz Aldrin and voiced by Tim Allen). The film unfolds as a buddy picture, as the two toys learn to look past their differences and to work together to overcome adversity in order to make their owner, Andy, happy.

Production of *Toy Story* occupied a staff of 110 people, including 28 full-time animators, for four years. Using technology developed by Edwin Catmull, three-dimensional wire-frame models were initially scanned into a computer. From there, each model was equipped with articulated variables, "avars" for short, by which animators could show movement. Woody and Buzz contained more than 700 avars each; and to produce Woody's Tom Hanks-like facial expressions, 58 avars were placed on the model's face alone. Animators then added color, texture, transparency, and other specific characteristics to enhance the look of their creations. Interestingly, the decision to wrap the narrative of *Toy Story* around the toys themselves had much to do with the limitations of the technology in 1995; because toys are not expected to possess fluid, lifelike movements, reasoned the film's creators, audiences would be forgiving if animators were not able to achieve such realistic, humanlike effects. In the end, the final cinematic product required the use of 300 Sun microprocessors and 800,000 hours of computing time to complete.

Released on November 22, 1995, *Toy Story* became an instant blockbuster, earning $64.7 million in its first 12 days. Indeed, it became the highest-grossing film of 1995, taking in $192 million domestically and an additional $357 million globally. Although Pixar had never been a particularly successful company before it joined Disney, shortly after the film's release Steve Jobs made the decision to take Pixar public. As he had in the past, Jobs proved to be a business genius, as Pixar became the most profitable IPO of the year; Jobs's share of the company was ultimately valued at over $1.1 billion.

For his work on *Toy Story*, John Lasseter was awarded the Oscar for Special Achievement at the 1996 Academy Awards. The film was also nominated for awards for Best Original Music (Randy Newman), Best Original Song ("You've Got a Friend in Me" by Randy Newman), and Best Screenplay Written Directly for the Film.

The success of *Toy Story* cemented the relationship between Disney and Pixar, and Disney now set out to conquer computer-generated films. Michael Eisner, the visionary CEO of Disney, negotiated a new contract that extended Pixar's commitment to Disney for five more films and that made the two business entities equal partners in future ventures. Jobs, concerned about establishing Pixar's name in the film industry, insisted that all pictures produced by the new company carry both the Pixar and Disney labels. Disney, however, wisely retained control of all sequels and rights to consumer products. The trend that began with *Toy Story* continued over the years, producing one blockbuster after another, including *A Bug's Life* (1998), *Toy Story 2* (1999), *Monsters, Inc.* (2001), *Finding Nemo* (2003), *The Incredibles* (2004), *Cars* (2006), *Ratatouille* (2007), *Wall-E* (2008), and *Up* (2009).

See also: Animation

References

Kanfer, Stefan. *Serious Business: The Art and Commerce of Animation in America from Betty Boop to Toy Story.* New York: Scribners, 1997.

Paik, Karen. *To Infinity and Beyond! The Story of Pixar Animation Studios.* San Francisco: Disney Enterprises/Pixar Animation Studios, 2007

Price, David A. *The Pixar Touch: The Making of a Company.* New York: Alfred A. Knopf, 2008.

Stewart, James B. *DisneyWar.* New York: Simon and Schuster, 2005.

Telotte, J. P. *The Mouse Machine: Disney and Technology.* Chicago: University of Illinois Press, 2008.

—*Robert W. Malick*

TRAFFIC. Based loosely on *Traffik*, a 1990 British television drama about the opium trade between Pakistan and Great Britain, director Steven Soderbergh's multi-stranded film focuses ambitiously on cocaine trafficking at the U.S.-Mexican border and on consumption of the drug in the United States. Released at the end of a decade that saw increased anxiety in the U.S.-Mexican relationship—surrounding both illegal immigration and drugs—*Traffic* (2000) generally avoids the former topic and instead seeks to expose the futility of U.S. policymakers' "war on drugs." In the 1970s and 1980s, cartels in Bolivia, Colombia, and elsewhere expanded to meet escalating demand for illegal narcotics in the United States. President Ronald Reagan responded in 1982 by appointing the first "drug czar," which in 1988 became the cabinet-level Director of the Office of National Drug Control Policy. Following a crackdown on Caribbean trade routes, in the late 1980s South American cartels began to rely increasingly on shipping cocaine through Mexico, enriching Mexican cartels and initiating a wave of corruption in government and law enforcement south of the border.

Unlike those who have perceived little but political grandstanding in the war on drugs, *Traffic* portrays policymakers and agency staffers as sincere combatants in a losing battle. This may explain why several government officials, including Sen. Harry Reid (D-Nev.) and Sen. Dianne Feinstein (D-Calif.), were willing to appear in cameos as themselves in the film. In one of *Traffic*'s three interwoven storylines, the real bureaucrats interact with the character of Ohio judge and newly appointed national drug czar Robert Wakefield (Michael Douglas), an earnest public servant who expresses shock when he learns that the cartels have a bigger budget than he does. In a second storyline, San Diego drug enforcement agents Monte (Don Cheadle) and Ray (Luís Guzmán) find it difficult to take their jobs seriously, especially when, during a stakeout at the plush La Jolla home of the Tijuana cartel's main U.S. connection, the drug dealer's wife (Catherine Zeta-Jones) knocks on the door of their undercover van and brings them lemonade.

In its third narrative thread, *Traffic* attributes much of the futility of drug enforcement to corruption in Mexico. Although the grainy, sepia-toned Mexican sequences have rankled some critics who say they present the country as stereotypically lawless and chaotic, others have praised the film for capturing living conditions in Tijuana without resorting to border-town clichés. For his portrayal of Tijuana police officer Javier Rodríguez, who struggles to advance without selling out to any of the competing drug cartels, Benicio Del Toro won the Academy Award for Best Supporting Actor. Rodríguez offers to share information with U.S. drug agents, but only if they will provide funds to help Tijuana build a new Little League baseball field. Is Soderbergh arguing that Mexico needs traditional American values?

Whatever idyllic era of the American past the baseball field might symbolize is hard to imagine in *Traffic*, which is keen to explore the role of insatiable U.S. demand in fueling the drug trade. The film argues that the principal battleground in the drug war is located not at the border, but in the heart of the American family. *Traffic*'s cocaine addicts are not the crack-consuming, Reagan-era underclass, but Wakefield's 16-year-old daughter, Caroline, and her friends in Cincinnati's posh Indian Hill suburb. These high school students drink, snort cocaine, and trade sarcastic barbs while sprawled on leather couches in family rooms lined with stained glass and shelves full of their highly educated parents' books. The behavior is learned: Wakefield's wife (Amy Irving) withholds information about Caroline's drug problem and accuses her husband of abusing alcohol; Robert tells her he drinks to cope with his "boredom" with the marriage. If the Wakefields serve as the individual problem family in *Traffic*, the basic cleavage in the American Family writ large is one of race and class, signified by the stark difference between tony Indian Hill and the seedy, less convincingly rendered urban neighborhood where the teenagers buy the drugs from an African American dealer. "If there is a war on drugs," Wakefield tells the White House press corps in a concluding scene, "then many of our family members are the enemy. I don't know how you wage war on your own family."

See also: Politics and Film

References

Payan, Tony. *The Three U.S.-Mexico Border Wars: Drugs, Immigration, and Homeland Security.* Westport, CT: Praeger, 2006.

Shaw, Deborah. " 'You Are Alright, But . . .': Individual and Collective Representations of Mexicans, Latinos, Anglo-Americans and African-Americans in Steven Soderbergh's *Traffic*." *Quarterly Review of Film and Video* 22(2005): 211–23.

—*Kenneth F. Maffitt*

12 ANGRY MEN.   Set in a sweltering jury room on the hottest day of the year, Sidney Lumet's film *12 Angry Men* (1957) has a Zenlike simplicity. A young man is on trial for murder, accused of stabbing his father to death in their inner-city tenement. The judge instructs the jury that they must reach a unanimous verdict, and that a finding of guilty will result in the defendant's execution. Eleven of the 12 jurors see the case as open-and-shut, and the evidence as overwhelming. The twelfth is less certain. "Let's talk about it," he says, and for the remainder of the movie the 12 do just that. They muse, reason, speculate, snarl, badger, cajole, disparage, and threaten. Jackets are removed, ties loosened, and sleeves rolled up; unexamined assumptions are exposed, prejudices are laid bare, and deeply buried resentments dragged to the surface. When the talking is over, the vote has swung from 11-1 in favor of conviction to 12-0 in favor of acquittal.

In the film, as in the Reginald Rose television play from which it was adapted, the jurors represent 12 different varieties of American everyman, and the jury as a whole represents a cross-section of American society in the mid-1950s. Underscoring their everyman status is the fact that, in the film as in the play, they have no names, and are identified only by the numbers of the seats they occupy at the jury table. On paper the jurors are broadly drawn "types" defined by a trait or two: Number 2 is meek; Number 4 coldly rational; Number 10 bigoted; and so forth. Impeccable casting—Martin Balsam as Number 1, the consensus-seeking foreman; Jack Warden as boorish Number 7, who cares more about his baseball tickets than the trial; Jack Klugman as Number 5, who grew up on the same mean streets as the defendant—turns them into well-developed characters.

Actor Lee J. Cobb (right), as Juror # 3, wields a switchblade as he threatens Henry Fonda, as Juror # 8, in a scene from the 1957 film *12 Angry Men*, directed by Sidney Lumet. (Getty Images)

The nominal hero of the film is Number 8, who casts the lone dissenting vote and encourages the others to consider whether reasonable doubt exists in the case. Played by Henry Fonda—the lone star in a cast of character actors—he personifies 1950s liberal ideals. He is intelligent without being an intellectual, compassionate without being soft or naive, and persuasive without being slick or insincere. Number 8 is a passionate advocate for social justice, but he is no radical. Polite, soft-spoken, and conservatively dressed, he conforms to social norms rather than challenging them. He believes that the System works *if* everyone involved participates and does so in good faith. He is fierce toward those who neglect that duty (callous Number 3, indifferent Number 7, and bigoted Number 10) and solicitous toward those who feel they have no role to play (meek Number 2, elderly Number 9, and foreign-born Number 11). His deepest, most passionate commitment is not to a particular ideology, but to the integrity of the System. The issue for him is not whether the accused is guilty or innocent, but whether the rules—especially proof of guilt "beyond a reasonable doubt"—have been fairly applied to him.

Number 8's idealistic view of the jury system is also that of Rose the playwright, Lumet the director, and the film itself. The triumph at the end of the film is not the fact that Number 8 wins the jury-room argument or that the accused walks free, but that the jury reaches the 12-0 verdict that the System (personified by the judge) requires. *12 Angry Men*, though structured as a legal thriller and directed as a character-driven drama, is ultimately a political film: a ringing endorsement of the idea that the System can deliver the "justice for all" promised in the Pledge of Allegiance.

The political views expressed in *12 Angry Men* make it a popular supplement for civics classes, but they also make the film something of a period piece. Its faith in the System (expressed, in more complex ways, in Otto Preminger's *Anatomy of a Murder* released two years later) is more in tune with the idealism of *Mister Smith Goes to Washington* (1938) and *The Devil and Daniel Webster* (1941) than it is with the cynicism of subsequent courtroom dramas. Those later films—from *Paths of Glory* (1958) and *Judgment at Nuremberg* (1961) through *And Justice for All* (1979), *The Verdict* (1983), *Scent of a Woman* (1997), and *The Runaway Jury* (2003)—portray the System as noble but irretrievably broken, controlled not by the People (for whom Lumet's jurors stand in) but by a wealthy and powerful few.

See also: Lumet, Sidney; Melodrama, The

References

Ebert, Roger. "12 Angry Men." In *The Great Movies II*. New York: Broadway Books, 2005.
Ellsworth, Phoebe C. "One Inspiring Jury," *Michigan Law Review* 101(6), 2003: 1387–1407.
Munyan, Russ, ed. *Readings on Twelve Angry Men*. Farmington Hills, MI: Greenhaven Press, 2000.

—*A. Bowdoin Van Riper*

2001: A SPACE ODYSSEY.   A landmark science fiction film, *2001: A Space Odyssey* (1968) showcases groundbreaking special effects and explores unusual philosophical and religious themes. Emphasizing scientific accuracy, the film presents a slow and sometimes disturbingly silent image of spaceflight. Based partly on "The Sentinel," a short story by Arthur C. Clarke (co-screenwriter with director Stanley Kubrick), *2001* is a film of startling complexity and scope, especially in the challenging image of the Monolith (mysterious black rectangles of unknown origin). While *2001* resists singular explanations, two themes, evolution and technology, are central to the film's structure.

The Monolith, the most famous image of *2001*, is closely associated with the process of evolution. While Clarke originally imagined the mysterious object as a robotic "intelligence detector" left on the Moon and designed to alert its builders when Earth evolved creatures capable of spaceflight (Clarke, 1999), the film's Monolith is far more potent and abstract. *2001* begins four million years ago at "The Dawn of Man," where a band of hominids encounter a Monolith and experience a sudden evolutionary breakthrough: tool use. The silent Monolith is juxtaposed against the Sun and Moon, both revealing its extraterrestrial origin and also suggesting humanity's future trajectory. Cutting suddenly, *2001* leaps into the space age.

In the second act, the hominids' descendants, technology-wielding humans, excavate a Monolith buried on the Moon. In the finale, astronaut Dave Bowman discovers a giant Monolith orbiting Jupiter. Transported through a colorfully surreal passageway to an unknown destination, and accompanied by yet another Monolith, Bowman rapidly ages (or mutates) and is reborn as the Star Child, a "posthuman" and presumably superhuman entity (Abrams, 2007). Though the Monoliths' origin and the reason for their interest in humankind are not revealed, they *do* appear to be shaping humanity's destiny. An ersatz-God of a secular teleology, the alien Monolith is the superpowerful (but not supernatural) midwife of human evolution. The process of evolution is also a form of birth. "The Dawn of Man," Bowman's journey through the stellar passageway, and the fetus-like Star Child all suggest birth and the creation of new life (Moore, 2001); two characters even mark birthdays. However, *Homo sapiens* is a stage in, not the culmination of, this gestation process.

Actor Gary Lockwood as Dr. Frank Poole in the classic 1968 science fiction movie *2001: A Space Odyssey*, directed by Stanley Kubrick. (Archive Photos/Getty Images)

This vision of evolution reflects the *Übermensch* (Superman or Overman) concept expounded by Friedrich Nietzsche in his philosophical novel *Thus Spoke Zarathustra* (Nietzsche, 1954). Nietzsche imagines humanity as a "rope" stretched between an animal past and a superhuman future (Nietzsche, 1954), a sequence, from "Beast" to "Man," and then from "Man" to "Superman"—precisely the evolutionary process we see unfold in *2001*. The Nietzschean theme is further reinforced by the use of Richard Strauss's Nietzsche-inspired music *Thus Spoke Zarathustra*. Signaling profound transitions, Strauss's slow, rising music appears both at the point where tools are invented and at the point of Bowman's final transformation.

The second key theme in *2001* is the relationship between humans and technology, which the film frames with an ironic tension (Fry, 2003). The film's first act climaxes with toolmaking, specifically, the mental leap necessary to turn a bone into a club for hunting. Ominously, the first tool is also a weapon, which is ultimately deployed against a rival hominid band; the essence of humanity, the "killer-ape," is technology and perhaps violence. The bone-weapon, exuberantly tossed in the air, is transformed via the dramatic cut mentioned above into an orbiting spacecraft, linking primitive and advanced technology (Fry, 2003). Accompanied by Johann Strauss's *Blue Danube,* the scene revels in futuristic, albeit often sterile-looking, hardware. Encased in various technologies, astronauts are apparently scientific supermen who have transcended their biological limitations. The future (from the standpoint of 1968) is complete with commercial passenger spacecraft, a gracefully rotating space station, and a network of lunar bases. Nature itself is domesticated as air, gravity, and food are reworked to serve human needs. Even human metabolism is controllable, as three members of the Jupiter-bound *Discovery* travel in a state of suspended animation.

2001's image of technology remains ambiguous, for while *Discovery* is a life-sustaining cocoon for its crew, it is also the scene of a deadly confrontation between humanity and the product of its genius, the Hal-9000 computer. Hal, who proudly notes the error-free history of 9000-series computers, is eerily emotional in contrast to his stoic human crewmates. He is also capable of humanlike violence, and his rebellion (which is tempting to associate with that of Frankenstein's creature) is a reminder that artifice can threaten the artisan. Technological superman Bowman (the only surviving crew*man*) must confront the super *pseudo*-man of technology, Hal. Trapped outside *Discovery* by Hal, Bowman significantly reenters the ship without his space helmet (i.e., partially denuded of technology). Hal's rebellion and ultimate defeat by Bowman suggests that artificial intelligence is a false path to the Superman. The true destiny of *Homo sapiens*, biological evolution guided by the alien Monolith, finally unfolds in Bowman's metamorphosis into the Star Child. Technology, like the primitive hominids and *Homo sapiens* itself, is ultimately a means to a larger end.

Raising provocative questions and offering some of the most enduring images in cinema, *2001: A Space Odyssey* establishes biological and technological evolution as a teleological journey. In this narrative *Homo sapiens* is one stage in a larger process, the conclusion and meaning of which remains veiled.

See also: Kubrick, Stanley; Science Fiction Film, The

References

Abrams, J. J. "Nietzsche's Overman as Posthuman Star Child in *2001: A Space Odyssey*." In Abrams, Jerald J. ed. *Philosophy of Stanley Kubrick*. Lexington: University Press of Kentucky, 2007.

Clarke, A. C. "Son of Strangelove." In *Greetings, Carbon-Based Bipeds! Collected Essays, 1934–1998*. New York: St Martin's Press, 1999.

Fry, C. L. "From Technology to Transcendence: Humanity's Evolutionary Journey in *2001: A Space Odyssey*." *Extrapolation*. 44.3 (Fall, 2003), 331–343.

Moore, G. "The Process of Life in *2001: A Space Odyssey*." *Images*. Issue 9 (February, 2004). Available at: www.imagesjournal.com.

Nietzsche, Frederick. *Thus Spoke Zarathustra*. In Kaufmann, Walter, ed./trans. *The Portable Nietzsche*. New York: Penguin Press, 1954.

—*Karl Leib*

U

UNFORGIVEN. *Unforgiven* (1992) was the 10th western with which the film's director, Clint Eastwood, had been associated. After starring in the "spaghetti westerns" *A Fistful of Dollars* (1964), *For a Few Dollars More* (1965), and *The Good, the Bad, and the Ugly* (1965), all with Italian director Sergio Leone, and then in other westerns such as *Hang 'Em High* (1968), *Two Mules for Sister Sara* (1970), and *Joe Kidd* (1972) with other directors, Eastwood starred in and stepped behind the camera to direct *High Plains Drifter* (1973), *The Outlaw Josey Wales* (1976), and *Pale Rider* (1985). In a sense, then, Eastwood had been moving toward making *Unforgiven* since early in his career.

According to critic Stephen Hunter, *Unforgiven* "tells the story of how the West was lost . . . lost . . . to pointless, ugly violence, men with guns who couldn't imagine the pain their bullets would cause and had no capacity to conceptualize the vacuum of loss they created when they killed" (Hunter, 1995). William Munny (Eastwood) is a former gunslinger and now a widower with two young children. Since being cured by his wife, as he says, "of drink and wickedness," he has nothing to show for his miserable existence but a squalid pig farm. But when he is approached by the "Schofield Kid" (Jaimz Woolvett) and offered an opportunity to split a $1,000 reward for the capture of two men who have maimed a prostitute, he reluctantly straps on his gun for the first time in more than a decade. Along the way to the town of Big Whiskey, he joins up with his former partner-in-crime, Ned Logan (Morgan Freeman). Preceding them is another bounty hunter, railroad gunman "English Bob" (Richard Harris), who is traveling with his biographer (Saul Rubinek). Opposing them is Sheriff "Little Bill" Daggett (Gene Hackman), himself a brutal "former" badman. What transpires is a series of confrontations among the men that erupt in cold and calculated bloodletting.

Unforgiven is a film—like its director, one might say—of few words. More to the point, it's a collection of *sounds*—the wind rasping across the high plains, a sudden thunderbolt piercing lowering clouds, the reedy screech of a bow scraping across a violin, and the blunt cry of men dying from gunshots at point-blank range. Significantly, among its few words is the cryptic inscription that appears at the beginning of the film: "Dedicated to Sergio and Don." "They were my teachers," Eastwood explains. "In a

CLINT EASTWOOD

GENE HACKMAN

MORGAN FREEMAN

RICHARD HARRIS

UNFORGIVEN

Poster for the 1992 film *Unforgiven*. Shown from top: Richard Harris, Morgan Freeman, Gene Hackman, and Clint Eastwood. Directed by Clint Eastwood. (Photofest)

way the film is a tribute to Sergio Leone and Don Siegel. If you analyze something like Sergio's *The Good, the Bad, and the Ugly*, you see there wasn't a whole lot of *talk* in them, just strong visuals and music and lots of shooting and crazy one-upmanship. They were more or less like operas. And Don was always so prepared and shot fast and brought his films in under schedule. You can learn a lot from that" (Tibbetts, 1993).

It is likely that *Unforgiven* may have been Eastwood's last western. "Whether it's my last western or not, remains to be seen," he said in an interview in 1992. "The western can be a genre that permits you to work in different approaches and moralities and subjects. You can take it in different directions. If you don't, it gets into a rut and there'll be somebody to pronounce 'the western is dead.' That happens every few years. Hollywood is so silly, sometimes, and it'll follow the fad—until somebody comes up with another successful one. I *can* say that if I was going to do just one last western, I think *Unforgiven* might be the one."

Unforgiven won four Oscars, for director, supporting actor (Gene Hackman), and editing (Joel Cox). In its blunt brutality, *Unforgiven* surpasses anything Eastwood had done before. Eastwood has been subject to attacks from the critics for allegedly indulging in gratuitously sensationalized violence. Especially devastating was the criticism leveled at him by the iconic film critic Pauline Kael in regard to his *Dirty Harry* movies. Regarding *Magnum Force*, for example, Kael wrote, "With a Clint Eastwood, the action film can—indeed, must—drop the pretense that human life has any value . . . killing is dissociated from pain; it's even dissociated from life." She dismissed another *Dirty Harry* entry, *The Enforcer*, as "garbage," depicting "a collection of villains so disgustingly cruel and inhuman that Eastwood can spend the rest of the movie killing them with a perfect conscience" (Kael, 1994). Eastwood is careful not to push the idea too far that *Unforgiven* is a "reply" to his critics; yet the film, for all its coruscating and grimly choreographed scenes of slaughter and mayhem, can hardly be characterized as indulging in false heroics or sensationalizing violence. To the contrary.

> People have always tried to see the West as something heroic and glamorous, and one could say that in my pictures I have followed the tradition of glamorizing violence. But in something like *Unforgiven* there's nothing very heroic at all. Now, I'm certainly not doing any penance for any of the mayhem I've presented on the screen over the years. But at the same token, I think it's a time in my life and a time in history where violence should not be such a humorous thing. That there are consequences to both the perpetrator as well as the victim. This is important to address, and if you can do it in a western atmosphere that would be fine. In a nutshell, it's not fun and it's not glamorous. I grew up with *White Heat* and *Public Enemy* and all those Jimmy Cagney films shooting people in the trunks of cars and all kinds of craziness. But it never made us into criminals and we didn't go out and start blowing people away because we saw it on the screen. You always realized it was just a movie. The movie industry has always been an easy target for attack because it always runs scared. (Tibbetts, 1993)

Eastwood's William Munny has tried to put his past as a gunfighter aside to become a farmer. Yet, after protesting constantly that he's "not that kind of killer" anymore, he finds in the moment of confrontation with "Little Bill" Daggett that he has not escaped his demons. "He's back in his mode of mayhem," Eastwood says.

> And he doesn't care. He's his old self again, at least for the moment. Before, he's been very rusty, having trouble getting on his horse, he wasn't shooting very well. He wasn't nailing people with the very first shot (like I would do in my earlier films!). Now, when he goes on this suicidal mission, he's all machine. He's not going to do any of this 'you draw first' stuff. He marches in to the saloon and just says, 'Who owns this place?' And then, Boom! He not only coldly murders Daggett at point-blank range but shoots some bystanders with no more compunction than someone swatting a fly. Munny has been protesting all the time that he's changed, but maybe he's been protesting too much. (Tibbetts, 1993)

Unforgiven is suffused with a fatalistic resignation about life and death. "We all have it comin', kid," Munny warns a frightened young gunslinger. The gunslinging hijinks of Eastwood's spaghetti westerns, for all their carnage, had evaded this implacable truth. In *Unforgiven*, whatever Munny's justifications for killing—he is avenging the cruel torture/murder of his best friend—his deeds are executed with ruthless, cold-blooded precision. It is an image as beautiful in its graceful precision as it is deadly in its horrible finality. "You'll notice," affirms Eastwood, "that Munny is no longer the clumsy has-been you've seen throughout the film—falling from his horse, missing things at target practice, getting beaten up. For the first time, he's back now in full charge of his abilities" (Tibbetts, 1993).

By contrast to this apocalypse, the film's epilogue brings us back to where we began, to a view of a distant horizon line where Munny's farm is starkly outlined against the darkling twilight. On the soundtrack a plaintive tune is heard, picked out on a guitar.

Dwarfed by the sky, Munny's tiny figure is seen for a moment; then it disappears. "I tried to end with the same image that we had at the beginning," observes Eastwood. "The first time he was burying his wife. Now, he's—well; he's leaving. All we know is that he left the place with his two children. Maybe he went to San Francisco. Maybe not." Eastwood shrugs.

> Maybe he's at last put his past behind him, or maybe he's just bought some time against the destruction that will surely catch up with him. When William Munny says, "I'm not the man I used to be," I'm sure there'll be folks out there who think that's me, Clint Eastwood, talking. Whatever they read in that line is fine with me. There may be some validity in that. When Munny says, "I ain't like that no more," it's true enough. Hopefully, all of us mature in some way and learn something from our lives. We hope that characters like Will Munny at last have changed for the good. But sometimes you wonder if all of us aren't really just going in circles, chasing our tails. Maybe, in the end, we haven't really learned anything. (Tibbetts, 1993)

See also: Eastwood, Clint; Western, The

References

Hunter, Stephen. *Violent Screen*. Baltimore: Bancroft Press, 1995.

Kael, Pauline. *For Keeps: 30 Years at the Movies*. New York: Dutton, 1994.

Tibbetts, John. "Clint Eastwood and the Machinery of Violence [An Interview]," *Literature/Film Quarterly* 21(1), 1993.

—John C. Tibbetts

V

VERTIGO.   Received upon its initial release in 1958 with muted admiration, Alfred Hitchcock's *Vertigo* has come to be regarded as one of the cinema's most important and popular works. Its spiraling psychological intensity has left a mark on filmmakers as diverse as the experimental French New Wave director Chris Marker (*La jetée*) and the Dutch director Paul Verhoeven (*Basic Instinct*). But perhaps *Vertigo*'s most significant cultural impact has been on the generations of viewers who return to it repeatedly to connect with its obsessive and claustrophobic power. Seldom has a mainstream American movie created such an uncomfortably addictive emotional connection with its viewers.

Set in a hypnotically beautiful San Francisco, with many of its most famous sequences shot in almost surrealistically evocative locations, *Vertigo*, like other deluxe 1950s Paramount pictures, is a glossy and transfixing wide-screen VistaVision spectacle. But *Vertigo* employs the commercial cinematic apparatus of its day to produce the equivalent of an inner spectacle, a journey into the troubled, endless vortex of unattainable projection and desire. Oddly, for a film that depends so thoroughly on an American locale (San Francisco with its labyrinthine hills and vast expanses of water-spanning steel seems the only place where this drama of the unconscious could unfold), and whose main character fits a classic American movie profile (he's a psychologically wounded former police detective), *Vertigo* transcends any particular American influence and jumps headlong into a world that evokes the power of archetypal dreams.

Each of the film's major acts intensifies its ineluctable spiral into personal tragedy. Act one is prelude: Scottie Ferguson (James Stewart) is a victim of acrophobia; his fear of heights leads to the accidental death of a fellow police officer. Act two is a mystery story: After forced retirement, Scottie is privately employed by an old friend to follow, surreptitiously, his blonde, socialite wife Madeleine (Kim Novak), who has grown morbidly obsessed with a dead woman's past, even taking on the dead woman's personality and suicidal impulses. Before this act is over, Scottie follows Madeleine to museums and flower shops, rescues her from a suicidal plunge into San Francisco Bay, takes her home (and undresses her), and falls in love. In trying to break Madeleine's obsession, Scottie brings her to an old mission that haunts her dreams; but Madeleine,

JAMES STEWART
KIM NOVAK
IN ALFRED HITCHCOCK'S
MASTERPIECE

'VERTIGO'

Poster advertising *Vertigo*, Alfred Hitchock's classic 1961 film starring Jimmy Stewart and Kim Novak. (Library of Congress)

overcome with her need to reenact the dead woman's suicide, bolts from his arms and hurls herself off the mission's tower. Scottie's acrophobia, of course, prevents him from stopping her as she falls to her death.

Act three makes it clear that the film's real theme is about the impossibility of Scottie reclaiming his lost anima figure; now the plot follows a traumatized Scottie, who imagines he sees the dead Madeleine in passing women. Lonely and grieving, walking in a disembodied state, Scottie one day passes Judy Barton, a cheap-looking, brunette, working-class girl whose face nonetheless is a dead ringer for his lost love. Scottie sets out to mold Judy into what he desires: he gets her to dye her hair blonde and to cut it like Madeleine's; he buys her the same color and style of clothing. Indeed, only when the fetishistic transformation has been achieved can he complete an intoxicating, vertiginous consummation of their relationship. In this iconic filmic moment—the camera envelopes the characters in a stunning 360-degree pan—Hitchcock lays bare an obsessive preoccupation with a type, one embodied by actresses such as Madeleine Carroll, Grace Kelly, and later by Eva Marie Saint, Janet Leigh, and Tippi Hedren.

In love with a dead woman whom he has in effect reincarnated through Judy, Scottie discovers the inevitable twist of act four—after it has already been revealed to the audience: Judy *was* Madeleine, or, rather, she played her in order to involve Scottie in the murder of the real Madeleine, whom Scottie never actually met. In the end, Judy falls for Scottie as she works to seduce him into murdering Madeleine; but for whom does Scottie fall? The Madeleine who never was—the archetypal Madeleine? A phantom of projected passion? Enraged when the plot is revealed, Scottie drags Judy back to the scene of the crime, and Hitchcock's tragedy ends in a final desperate apotheosis of the repetition compulsion at the center of lost love: like Scottie, we are left peering into the mystery of eternal unquenchable desire, into a love we always wanted but that never was—and that can never be.

See also: Hitchcock, Alfred

References

Barr, Charles. *Vertigo*. London: British Film Institute, 2008.
O'Brien, Geoffrey. "Magnificent Obsession," *New York Review of Books*, December 19, 1996.
Truffaut, François. *Hitchcock by Truffaut*. New York: Simon and Schuster, 1967.

—*Robert Cowgill*

WAITING FOR GUFFMAN. Christopher Guest has become so identified with the satiric "mockumentary" that a retrospective of his work was held at the Museum of Modern Art in 2005. After appearing in, and co-writing, Rob Reiner's ground-breaking *This Is Spinal Tap* (1986), Guest launched out on his own with *Waiting for Guffman* (1996). Like his subsequent efforts, notably *Best in Show* (2000) and *A Mighty Wind* (2003), *Guffman* utilizes the forms and practices of documentary in order to undermine any claims to truth.

Anyone who has ever participated in a local theater project or a hometown festival will find something gruesomely familiar in *Waiting for Guffman*. Behind its perversely entertaining send-up of homespun theatrics, its gingham-cloth humor, and its cotton-candy satire is a wicked set of jaws with big teeth.

The town of Blaine, Missouri, is celebrating its "sesquicentennial" (that's a century and a half, whispers the town mayor), and it wants to put on a show called "Red, White, and Blaine." The local theater director, Corky St. Clair (Guest), takes on the assignment, rounds up the usual suspects, suffers through the rehearsals, and prepares for opening night. Tension is added by the news that a big-time Broadway scout will attend. His name is "Mort Guffman."

The movie's first 10 minutes sets the stage, as it were, reviewing the history of the town of Blaine: In frontier days a pioneer named Blaine Fabin, bound to a wagon train traveling from Philadelphia to California, stopped at the first scent of salt water. Proclaiming the region to be part of California, he established a town in his own name. No matter the region turned out to be in Missouri, Blaine's noble history had begun. Years later came a visit from President McKinley, whose delight at being presented with a locally manufactured footstool assured the town of becoming "The Stool Capitol of the World." Then in 1946, a UFO landed and abducted one of the local townspeople, leaving him, decades later, remembering the numberless hours he spent enduring the "probing" of aliens.

Corky takes up the challenge of mounting a musical pageant celebrating this glorious heritage. He brings to the task impressive theatrical credentials, like his local production of a stage version of *Backdraft* ("You can *feel* the heat!"), which almost burned down the theater house. Now, with *Red, White, and Blaine* set to go, Corky awaits Mr. Guffman with more than the usual anticipation. Maybe, just maybe, the show can go to Broadway, and Corky will have a chance to return to the Great White Way.

Waiting for Guffman's cast members have their characters securely within their sights—and they take dead aim. Guest's Corky pouts and lisps his way through a gay stereotype that would be outrageous if it were not also occasionally starkly poignant. With his "Judy Tenuta" T-shirts and vest-bolero pants ensembles, he's an exotic fish in a humdrum aquarium. Eugene Levy is Allan Pearl, the dentist, who claims theater legacy from his grandfather's Yiddish theater days; Catherine O'Hara and Fred Willard are Sara and Ron Albertson, theater wannabes and local travel agents who have never ventured beyond Blaine (except for Ron, who once had penis-reduction surgery in Jefferson City); Parker Posey is Libby the Dairy Queen girl, who's willing to quit ice cream confections like Blizzards and Derbys for the footlights; Bob Balaban is Lloyd, the music teacher, terminally timid but a dynamo at the podium; and Lewis Arquette is Clifford, the grizzled town father who is lured out of his trailer and out of retirement.

On opening night the chair reserved for Guffman remains empty until the production is 10 minutes gone. Then a dapper man arrives and sits down. At the postplay backstage festivities, however, after he is introduced to the ecstatic cast, he admits his name is not Guffman but "Roy Loomis," in town on a brief visit. In the manner of Samuel Beckett, it seems, the entire town will have to go on waiting for Guffman.

Red, White, and Blaine both illuminates and alters the lives of Blaine's residents. The dentist and the travel planners leave their jobs and head for the showbiz spotlights, the former to entertain at a Miami nursing home, the latter two to work as extras in Hollywood. The Dairy Queen girl leaves town, as well, but only because her father is now out of prison ("on good behavior," since he didn't kill anybody), and they are on the road together while she dreams of new ways to make fat-free Blizzards. And Corky, well, he returns to New York where he opens up a theater memorabilia shop, featuring such red hot items as "Remains of the Day" lunch boxes and "My Dinner with Andre" action figures.

The film is shot in pseudo cinéma vérité style, with Guest's camera wobbling around the characters, who speak directly into it, shamelessly proclaiming who and what they are. Because the cast and credits are reserved for the end of the film, you almost feel as if you are viewing a real documentary about small-town life. And as for the big musical production itself, never fear—you see it in its entirety, footstools and flying saucers and everything. But hints of pathos, even tragedy, peek through the warp and woof of events. Revelations of Corky's dismal private life (references to a nonexistent "wife" apparently have provided him with the necessary cover to live in Blaine) and theatrical background (he was, he says, "stomped down for years" playing in off-off-off-off Broadway theater productions in New York City) are dispensed intermittently throughout the film. Most moving of all, perhaps, is the town councilman's glittering eyes as he gazes with rapt—and barely concealed sexual—attention at Corky as he performs. In his hungry stare is the real drama, the play-behind-the-play; the hollow dark that lurks behind the brightly painted flats. That is the real meaning of Blaine and the real message behind this film: You can *dream* of California, but you've got to *live* in Blaine.

References

McCreadie, Marsha. *Documentary Superstars*. New York: Allworth, 2008.
Muir, John Kenneth. *Best in Show: The Films of Christopher Guest and Company*. New York: Applause, 2004.

—*John C. Tibbetts*

WAY WE WERE, THE.   In *The Way We Were* (1973), director Sydney Pollack wraps an exquisite love story within an overarching narrative framework oriented around political and cultural issues that emerged during the middle decades of the twentieth century. Set against the backdrop of the lead-up to WWII and the war's aftermath, Pollack's love story focuses on the lives of the tragically mismatched Hubbell Gardner (Robert Redford) and Katie Morosky (Barbra Streisand). One of seven films that Robert Redford and Pollack made together, *The Way We Were* proved to be a critical and box-office success.

We first encounter the indomitable Katie as she scurries across the busy streets of New York City to one of her many jobs, this one as an assistant to radio producer Bill Verso (Herb Edelman). When Bill's date unexpectedly cancels on him, Katie has the good fortune of being taken by her boss to the famous El Morocco nightclub. Filled with servicemen and their dates, the nightclub is a glittering respite from the horrors of war. Mesmerized by the setting, Katie's eyes scan the room until they light upon Hubbell; resplendent in uniform, Hubbell sits with eyes closed, subtly swaying on a bar stool. Smiling, Katie's mind drifts back to when she and Hubbell were students at a prestigious Eastern college.

The two could not have been more different. Hubbell was the all-American golden boy attending school on an athletic scholarship. A star on both the track and rowing teams, seemingly without a care in the world, he is involved with Carol Ann (Lois Chiles), a lovely young woman who comes from money. Katie, on the other hand, must work a host of jobs to support herself. An extraordinarily serious student, she is also a campus radical. Their ill-fated attraction to each other begins to be revealed during an on-campus Peace Rally. The president of the Young Communist League, Katie gives a speech in support of the Soviet Union's resistance to Franco's rise to power in Spain. Decrying Hitler's and Mussolini's use of Spain as a "testing ground for another World War," Katie calls upon her classmates to pledge themselves to "world peace now." In the audience, Hubbell listens with rapt attention.

Significantly, the Young Communist League was a real-life student organization that emerged during the 1930s as a core part of the American Youth Congress. Supported by Eleanor Roosevelt, members of the YCL were some of the most vocal antiwar advocates during the 1930s. In Pollack's film, Katie embodies the YCL movement, and,

Robert Redford and Barbra Streisand embrace in a publicity photo from the film *The Way We Were*, directed by Sydney Pollack, 1973. (Fotos International/Getty Images)

consumed by her political passions, she cannot understand her attraction to the seemingly feckless Hubbell. She begins to change her mind about him, however, when she listens to their professor read aloud one of Hubbell's short stories—"The All American Smile"—in a literature class Katie and Hubbell share: "In a way he was like the country he lived in," the story begins, "everything came too easily to him." Devastated that her story was not chosen to be read, Katie still cannot help but listen—like Hubbell to her speech—with rapt attention. And so their bond is forged.

After bringing us back to El Morocco, Pollack allows us to watch as Katie and Hubbell fall in love. Now a staunch supporter of President Roosevelt and his WWII foreign policies, Katie is surprised that Hubbell, whom she comes to realize is much more than just a pretty face, is not as interested in politics as she: "You'd rather talk politics," says Hubbell, "all the contradictions. . . . It's all a bunch of political double talk, but you hold on. I don't see how you do it." "I don't see how you can't," retorts Katie. As it turns out, not only does Katie stump for Roosevelt, but a number of her jobs—including the one at the radio station—are connected to the Office of War Information, a federal agency that Roosevelt brought into existence when he signed Executive Order 9182 on June 13, 1942. The Office of War Information was established, the order declared, "In recognition of the right of the American people and of all other peoples opposing the Axis aggressors to be truthfully informed about the common war effort." Much like George Creel's World War I–era Committee on Public Information, which had taken advantage of the fledgling film industry by using it to communicate the prowar messages of Woodrow Wilson, the OWI enlisted the aid of radio producers and Hollywood film directors to help give expression to Roosevelt's own prowar messages.

Although her passion intrigues Hubbell, Katie's all-consuming commitment to the world of politics almost drives him away. Having salvaged the relationship, though, the couple marries and relocates to Los Angeles after Hubbell sells his novel to Hollywood. Well-off, with a beachfront house, a boat, and a sports car, the two seem to have reconciled their differences—until Katie gets involved in the cause of the so-called Hollywood Ten. The Hollywood Ten was the name given to a group of real-life writers and directors who were cited for contempt of Congress when they refused to cooperate with the House Un-American Activities Committee (HUAC), which was investigating alleged communist influence in Hollywood. The first official Hollywood blacklist was instituted on November 25, 1947, the day after the 10 men of the group were cited for contempt. In a press release issued a week later by Eric Johnston, then head of the Motion Picture Association of America, 48 of the most powerful studio heads in the industry stated that they "deplore[d] the actions of the 10 Hollywood men who have been cited for contempt by the House of Representatives." Although they claimed that they did not "desire to prejudge their legal rights," they nevertheless declared that they had no choice but to "forthwith discharge or suspend without compensation" each member of the "10 until such time as he is acquitted or has purged himself of contempt and declares under oath that he is not a Communist." All of the members of the group were ultimately fined and jailed for their refusal to bow to the dictates of Congress and industry heads.

Katie is depicted as a fellow traveler of the Hollywood Ten, literally attending their hearings in Washington, D.C. After she and Hubbell are accosted by a group of frenzied anticommunist protestors, the couple exchanges angry words: "You didn't expect to come to Hollywood and get a chance to tell off the world, did you?" says Hubbell. "Is that what you think I'm doing?" responds Katie. "You bet I do," says Hubbell bitterly. Once again, Katie's politics prove too much for Hubbell, and the couple begins to break apart, this time for good. In the film's wonderfully romantic final sequence, Katie and Hubbell encounter each other on a busy New York City thoroughfare. Katie is there to gather signatures and pass out flyers protesting the use of the H-Bomb, the horrible nuclear weapon developed by both the United States and the Soviet Union during the early 1950s; Hubbell, accompanied by his new girl, is there writing a television show. "You never give up," says Hubbell about her continuing protest activities. "Only when I'm absolutely forced to," responds Katie, "but I'm a very good loser." "Better than I am," Hubbell admits. "Well, I've had . . . more practice," replies Katie softly.

See also: Pollack, Sydney; Streisand, Barbra

References

Lewis, Jon. *American Film: A History.* New York: W. W. Norton, 2008.
Meyer, Janet L. *Sydney Pollack: A Critical Filmography.* Jefferson, NC: McFarland, 2008.
Schatz, Thomas. *Hollywood Genres: Formulas, Filmmaking, and the Studio System.* Boston: McGraw-Hill, 1981.

—*Philip C. DiMare*

WEST SIDE STORY.   Like many movie musicals, *West Side Story* (1961) was first a Broadway hit. The play by Arthur Laurents, adapted by Ernest Lehman, is an updating of *Romeo and Juliet*, cleverly set in New York City's Upper West Side with youth gangs in place of the feuding families that complicate young love. Directed by Jerome Robbins and Robert Wise, the United Artists release features choreography by Robbins and music and lyrics by Leonard Bernstein and Stephen Sondheim, respectively. Leading actors, none of whom transferred from Broadway, are Natalie Wood (Maria), Richard Beymer (Tony), George Chakiris (Bernardo), Rita Moreno (Anita), and Russ Tamblyn (Riff); both Wood's and Beymer's songs were dubbed by lesser-known artists.

The story revolves around the doomed love affair of Tony and Maria. Tony is a former member of the Jets, an Anglo gang led by Riff, and anxious to protect their territory from the newly arrived Puerto Rican gang, the Sharks. Maria is engaged to Chino, her brother Bernardo is the Sharks' leader, and Anita is her friend and Bernardo's girlfriend. The film opens with a potential rumble between the gangs being avoided only when the police arrive. Tensions erupt again at a dance attended by the gangs and "their girls," while Tony and Maria fall in love. Meanwhile, a war council is in the works to settle who will dominate the streets. The fight that ends Act I also ends in tragedy: Bernardo has killed Riff and Tony has killed Bernardo. In Act II Tony and Maria still vow to be together despite the quest for revenge on both sides. Anita is assaulted by some Jets and responds by claiming Chino has killed Maria. When Tony hears this he seeks out Chino, telling Chino to kill him, too; at the last minute Tony sees Maria alive but Chino does shoot him as the lovers run toward one another. In a departure from Shakespeare, Maria survives and the film ends on a note of hope as members of the two gangs carry Tony's body away.

Its semi-tragic ending is one of several ways *West Side Story* holds a unique place in movie musical history, continuing many aspects of the postwar genre but in ways geared to then-contemporary themes, music, and politics. The love story, for example, is the staple of the postwar musical, but the film does not deliver the happily-ever-after ending audiences had come to expect. Similarly traditional are memorable tunes that can exist independently of the show, and *West Side Story* delivers many, including "America," "Maria," "Something's Coming," "Somewhere," and "Tonight." The fact that they are Bernstein-Sondheim songs, though, means they depart from the melodic conventions of the earlier musicals while aptly conveying the bittersweet flavor of the show. Finally, dance, a crucial element of plot development since *Oklahoma!*, is used to great effect in scenes both typical (Tony and Maria at the dance) and unusual (dancing gang members).

Undoubtedly the mixture of the familiar and the contemporary contributed to the film's appeal to a wide range of viewers, both in 1961 and after. The specter of the "juvenile delinquent," a perennial American concern, was revived in the fifties, and not just by educators and sociologists, but in films such as *The Wild One* (1953), *Rebel Without a Cause* (1955), and *Blackboard Jungle* (1955). *West Side Story* linked these concerns to issues of immigration and urban ethnic tension, especially in relation to the post-WWII "Great Migration" of Puerto Ricans to New York City. This made *West Side Story* not only timely but also exceptional, in that it allowed the voices of immigrant others to be heard during a time when they were most often silenced. This expressive shift of perspective is seen—and heard—in the film's reimagined version of the production number "America." In the on-screen version, the Sharks' Puerto Rican gang members are included in the number, and answer the overly sentimental pronouncement that "Life is all right in America" with the poignantly cynical refrain, "If you're all white in America."

West Side Story has often been described as the most honored movie musical ever made, and rightly so. It received 11 Academy Award nominations and won ten, including Best Picture, Best Director (for both Robbins and Wise), Best Supporting Actor and Actress, and Best Scoring of a Musical Picture. Only three films have won more Oscars, and only nine other musicals have been named Best Picture. *West Side Story* is on the American Film Institute's Top 100 list, contains three of its Top 100 Songs, and is rated number two on its list of the 25 Greatest Movie Musicals of All Time.

See also: Ethnic and Immigrant Culture Cinema; Musical, The; Music in the Movies

References

Berson, Misha. *Something's Coming, Something Good: West Side Story and the American Imagination*. New York: Applause, 2010.

Knapp, Raymond. *The American Musical and the Formation of National Identity*. Princeton, NJ: Princeton University Press, 2004.

Monush, Barry. *West Side Story: Music on Film Series*. New York: Limelight, 2010.

—*Vicki L. Eaklor*

WHEN HARRY MET SALLY.   Produced and directed by Rob Reiner, and starring Billy Crystal and Meg Ryan, *When Harry Met Sally* is a romantic comedy that exposes the challenges of finding love and staying married. Released in the summer of 1989, the film's edgy and sophisticated screenplay earned writer Nora Ephron an Oscar nomination.

The film opens with Harry Connick's rendition of "It Had to Be You" playing in the background, preparing the viewer for the possibility of romance. Harry (Crystal) and Sally (Ryan) are introduced as they drive all night from Chicago to New York City. During the 18 hours they spend together, they discuss love, sexual relationships, and the differences between men and women. Harry thinks that "Men and women can't be friends because the sex part always gets in the way." When they reach New York City the next morning, they part ways, although we realize that a spark between the two has been lit. They meet again five years later, but both are in committed relationships. After another five years, they meet once more; now, though, their respective relationships ended, they become friends. Harry, surprised at himself, muses, "Great . . . a woman friend."

The extremely intimate yet nonsexual relationship that develops between Harry and Sally is cleverly depicted by Reiner, who shows the pair, through the use of split screen, snuggled in their own beds talking to each other on the phone while they watch the same movie; taking long meandering walks; shopping together; and sharing meals. When their relationship finally does turn sexual, it is Harry who cannot decide how

Scene from the 1989 film *When Harry Met Sally*, starring Meg Ryan and Billy Crystal. Directed by Rob Reiner. (Photofest)

this shift will affect their friendship; in the end, as Harry predicted long before during their fateful car ride to New York City, the friendship cannot survive "the sex part."

Of course, as is the case with all romantic comedy couples, *we* know Harry and Sally are right for each other even if they don't. It takes Harry and Sally another two years to admit to themselves that they are, indeed, perfectly suited, and they quickly marry. As Harry says, "when you realize that you want to spend the rest of your life with somebody, you want the rest of your life to start as soon as possible."

Reiner uses documentary-style interviews with older couples to mark out the filmic points of transitions in the relationship between Harry and Sally. Interestingly, the experiences of love and intimacy discussed by these older couples are all initiated with "love at first sight" moments that lead to lasting marriages. These couples serve to emphasize the idealistic notion that there actually is one "right person" out there for all of us who is just waiting to be found. Even though they don't recognize their own "love at first sight" moment, it was there, and, just like those couples in the interviews, ultimately they do come to love each other deeply. Pictured in their own interview at the end of the film, it appears that their relationship will endure.

According to Reiner, the movie was based on his own tortured experiences. He had discussed the project with Nora Ephron, seeking out a woman who would understand and be able to write about the experiences of other women. Their conversations ranged over topics such as friendship and sex, and they eventually led Reiner to pose the question to Ephron: "Can men and women be friends without having sex?" Based on

Ephron's screenplay, we are never sure about the answer to that question—after all, the "sex part" did get in the way of the friendship between Harry and Sally, at least until they admitted they were in love. Indeed, in one of the most iconic scenes in American film, an older woman (played by Reiner's mother), who is sitting in a restaurant in which Harry and Sally are eating, watches with rapt attention as Sally demonstrates, for all to see and hear, how perfectly a woman can fake an orgasm. When the waiter approaches the women to take her order, she says simply, "I'll have what she's having."

See also: Ephron, Nora; Romantic Comedy, The

References

Emery, Robert J. *The Directors: Take Two*. New York: Allworth, 2007.
Shumway, David R. *Modern Love: Romance, Intimacy, and the Marriage Crisis*. New York: New York University Press, 2003.

—*Vicky Bach*

WHITE CHRISTMAS.   Following the success of *Holiday Inn* in 1942, and the identification of the Academy Award-winning Irving Berlin song "White Christmas" with the Christmas season, Paramount decided to use *Holiday Inn* as the inspiration for a new film and call it *White Christmas* (1954). As with *Holiday Inn*, *White Christmas* featured a soundtrack composed by Irving Berlin; the picture was also intended to be the third screen collaboration of *Holiday Inn* co-stars Bing Crosby and Fred Astaire. After reading the script, however, Astaire decided to pass on the film, and the role was given to Donald O'Connor. Unluckily, O'Connor injured his leg during filming, and the part ultimately went to Danny Kaye.

White Christmas tells the story of a song-and-dance duo, Bob Wallace (Crosby) and Phil Davis (Kaye), who, after meeting in the army, become fast friends and develop a show-business partnership. After returning to the States, the two performers decide to take some much-needed time off. They head to a New England ski resort with two showgirl sisters, Betty (Rosemary Clooney) and Judy Haynes (Vera-Ellen). On arriving at the resort, they discover that the owner, Thomas Waverly (Dean Jagger), is their former army general. Unfortunately, the resort is almost bankrupt, as no snow has fallen that year. In order to help General Waverly, the group decides to stage a benefit gala for him. The benefit is a success, snow starts to fall, the resort is saved, and Bob and Phil find love in the arms of Betty and Judy.

White Christmas is an example of the feel-good, family entertainment common during the 1950s. Its happy, some would say overly sentimental, ending suggests that while the troubles of wartime are hard to overcome, brotherhood, love, and, of course, Christmas, have transformative, even redemptive powers, an idea that was particularly appealing to viewers living in Cold War America. These notions, it seems, are embodied in the film's eponymous title song. Indeed, "White Christmas" is a song imbued with the wartime mood. Sad and wistful, it captures emotions shared by both returning soldiers and civilians at home. The song, like the film, recalls the emotions of wartime; and when it sounds out at the end of the film, it acts as a trigger for nostalgic yearnings for the peace and happiness traditionally associated with Christmas. The song could not be nominated for an Academy Award for its use in *White Christmas*, however, as it had already won that award when it was used in *Holiday Inn*. Instead "Count Your Blessings Instead of Sheep" was nominated for Best Original Song, losing to "Three Coins in the Fountain" from the film of the same name. Nevertheless by the 1980s, "White Christmas" had become the best-selling song of all time.

See also: Musical, The; Music in Film

References

Connelly, Mark, ed. *Christmas at the Movies: Images of Christmas in American, British and European Cinema*. London: I. B. Tauris, 2000.
Hirschhorn, Clive. *The Hollywood Musical*. New York: Crown, 1981.
Woll, Allen L. *The Hollywood Musical Goes to War*. Chicago: Nelson-Hall, 1983.

—*Victoria Williams*

WHO'S AFRAID OF VIRGINIA WOOLF? *Who's Afraid of Virginia Woolf?* was released in 1966 by Warner Bros. The debut film of director Mike Nichols, it was both a critical and commercial hit, grossing more than $14.5 million. The film stars Elizabeth Taylor and Richard Burton, who were, at the time, the most famous couple in the world. Adapted by Ernest Lehman from the play by Edward Albee, *Who's Afraid of Virginia Woolf?* follows a night in the life of married couple George (Burton), a history professor, and Martha (Taylor), the daughter of the president of the university. Filmed in black and white, and composed largely of long takes and facial close-ups, the visual austerity of *Who's Afraid of Virginia Woolf?* is balanced by the density of its dialogue. Nichols's desire to maintain both Albee's rhythm and commentary on language use made *Who's Afraid of Virginia Woolf?* the first picture intentionally shot with overlapping dialogue.

George and Martha have an apparently embittered marriage, but it is on this night that things "snap" and they declare "total war" on each other. Despite the couple's constant bickering, *Who's Afraid of Virginia Woolf?* is a dark romantic comedy. Although their ferocious wordplay suggests nefarious intentions, it is also proof that they are a good match. The story occurs mostly in George and Martha's home in the fictional town of New Carthage, where they host a recently hired biology professor and his wife, Nick (George Segal) and Honey (Sandy Dennis). The young couple becomes instrumental to George and Martha's infighting. The narrative develops through a series of verbal "games" orchestrated by George and Martha to hurt each other and their guests. Martha repeatedly attacks George's lack of ambition, belaboring Nick's status as a biology professor to incite internecine rivalries; she makes sexual advances toward the ambitious Nick, who does not resist since he wants to "plow a few pertinent wives" in order to ascend the university ladder. Over the course of the night, and

Scene from the 1966 film *Who's Afraid of Virginia Woolf?*, starring Richard Burton and Elizabeth Taylor. Directed by Mike Nichols. (Apic/Getty Images)

as the couples become increasingly drunk, secrets appear to be uncovered. However, the film maintains a veil of ambiguity, and never allows the spectator to be certain about the facts of George's and Martha's pasts. We always suspect their stories might be based in some truth but, at the same time, are partially invented to inspire particular reactions in each other (and their guests). The evening culminates in the revelation that the son George and Martha claimed to have is a product of their imaginations.

The film's frank sexual themes reflected the trend toward mature content evidenced by the growing popularity of non-Hollywood films gaining favor in America in the 1960s, but it was its graphic language—including words never before heard on American screens—that made *Who's Afraid of Virginia Woolf?* a milestone cinematic work. It became the first movie to challenge successfully the Motion Picture Production Code established by Will Hays in 1934. Initially, the Code refused to approve the film, but after a series of threats to release the film regardless of the Code's approval, *Who's Afraid of Virginia Woolf?* was finally granted a Code seal as an exemption from its standard strictures based on the belief that it was a "superior picture." Similarly, the influential Catholic Legion of Decency approved the film for adults, as it fit into their "think film" category. Thus, having essentially defeated the Production Code (which would be dismantled only two years later and replaced by the Motion Picture Association of America ratings system), it changed the course of Hollywood cinema, arguably marking the beginning of the period often termed "New Hollywood."

Who's Afraid of Virginia Woolf? was nominated for 13 Academy Awards, and is notable for being one of the few films whose entire cast was nominated for the Oscar. It won five, including Best Actress (Taylor); Best Supporting Actress (Dennis); Best Art Direction, Black and White (Richard Sylbert and George James Hopkins); Best Cinematography, Black-and-White (Haskell Wexler); and Best Costume Design, Black-and-White (Irene Sharaff). Among other accolades, the film won three British Academy of Film and Television Arts Awards, including Best Picture. In 2007, it ranked 67th on the American Film Institute's list of the 100 Greatest Films.

See also: Melodrama, The; Nichols, Mike; Taylor, Elizabeth

References

Belton, John. *American Cinema/American Culture.* New York: McGraw-Hill, 1994.

Gelmis, Joseph. *The Film Director as Superstar.* Garden City, NY: Doubleday, 1970.

O'Steen, Sam. *Cut to the Chase: Forty-Five Years of Editing America's Favorite Movies.* Studio City, CA: Michael Wiese, 2001.

—*Kyle Stevens*

WILD BUNCH, THE. The opening sequence of Sam Peckinpah's *The Wild Bunch* (1969) introduces the film's themes and motifs. A group of men wearing U. S. Army uniforms rides slowly into a small town in South Texas. The members of the group look uneasily at a number of children tormenting scorpions in a pile of red ants, an action foreshadowing the fates of the men. Everything seems normal as they arrive in the town. This tranquility is shattered, however, when the men enter the local bank and pull out their guns as Pike Bishop (William Holden), their leader, shouts, "If they move . . . kill 'em." The robbers soon discover they have walked into a trap. Bounty hunters led by Deke Thornton (Robert Ryan) are waiting on top of a building across the street. Bishop's men wait until the South Texas Temperance Union marches by to open fire, and bodies, most belonging to innocent citizens, begin dropping. Bishop and four of his men escape, leaving the rest behind to crazed scavengers (Strother Martin and L. Q. Jones).

This shockingly violent—for 1969—opening sequence helps to establish the members of Bishop's gang as men who are being left behind in the rapidly changing industrial world of the early twentieth century. Even they realize, it seems, that as the new century dawns, times are changing in America. This theme of displaced men struggling against the reality of a fading frontier began to be played out a decade earlier in John Sturges's *The Magnificent Seven*—one can even see resonances of the idea in John Ford's *The Searchers* (1956)—and Arthur Penn addressed the same subject in *Butch Cassidy and the Sundance Kid*, also released in 1969. In these films, especially in *The Wild Bunch* and *Butch Cassidy and the Sundance Kid*, there would be no romanticization of the American West.

Scene from the 1969 film *The Wild Bunch*, starring (from left) Ben Johnson (as Tector Gorch), Warren Oates (as Lyle Gorch), William Holden (as Pike Bishop), and Ernest Borgnine (as Dutch Engstrom). Directed by Sam Peckinpah. (Photofest)

With no place left for them within American boundaries, the members of Bishop's gang make their way across the border into Mexico. Pursued by Thornton, they find themselves in the midst of the Mexican Revolution, a decade-long revolt spanning the period from 1910 to 1920. They go to the village of Angel (Jaime Sanchez), which has been attacked by the rampaging federal army of General Mapache (Emilio Fernandez). An antisocial opportunist, Mapache uses the peoples' revolt as an excuse to take whatever and kill whomever he wants. Despite experiencing certain ethical misgivings, Bishop eventually agrees to help Mapache by stealing a shipment of weapons from the U.S. Army. This decision is one of several underscoring similarities between Bishop and Thornton, both of whom allow circumstances to release them to violate their codes of conduct.

In Peckinpah's West, the present is always receding too quickly into the past, as history intrudes on the rugged individualists who populate his films. Peckinpah, who co-wrote the screenplay for *The Wild Bunch* with Walon Green, does not overemphasize this point, however, introducing it subtly—the outlaws look on quizzically as an automobile rumbles past, for instance, an ominous sign of encroaching progress.

Casting aging actors such as Holden, Ryan, Borgnine, and Ben Johnson also helped demonstrate how time was catching up with the West. Holden, for instance, who was turning 50 when he made the film, makes Bishop seem increasingly burdened by his awareness of his own mortality.

Another of Peckinpah's westerns, *Ride the High Country* (1962), makes many of the same points made in *The Wild Bunch*; but the former film has an elegiac poignancy lacking in the latter. Just as the Old West was jolted by change, America changed drastically between 1962, when *Ride the High Country* was released, and 1969, when *The Wild Bunch* was released. This was particularly true in regard to the nation's sentiment concerning the Vietnam War. Just as many Americans were unable to reconcile themselves to a seemingly pointless, unwinnable war, Bishop's gang finds itself plunged into a situation that makes little sense. Because Bishop has allowed Angel to take some of the weapons so that his village can better defend itself, Mapache has the young Mexican tortured. The outlaws try to ignore his mistreatment because what, after all, can they do when they are so outnumbered. Then their strange ethical code kicks in—the idea that a man is not a man if he stands by and sees his friend slowly being killed. The outlaws are going to die anyway, so why not go out in a blaze of glory? Oddly violent notions of friendship, loyalty, honor, and being true to oneself—these are foundational elements within Peckinpah's slowly fading West.

See also: Peckinpah, Sam; Western, The

References

Kitses, Jim. *Horizons West: Anthony Mann, Budd Boetticher, Sam Peckinpah: Studies of Authorship within the Western.* Bloomington and London: Indiana University Press, 1970.

Seydor, Paul. *Peckinpah: The Western Films: A Reconsideration.* Urbana and Chicago: University of Illinois Press, 1997.

Weddle, David. *"If They Move . . . Kill 'Em": The Life and Times of Sam Peckinpah.* New York: Grove, 1994.

—*Michael Adams*

WINCHESTER '73.   One of Hollywood's landmark westerns, *Winchester '73* (1950) is marked by a moral and psychological complexity that had rarely been seen in this genre. The picture was also the first of a series of films that emerged from the prolific and productive partnerships that director Anthony Mann established with star James Stewart and screenwriter Borden Chase. Between 1950 and 1955, Mann and Stewart made eight films together, most of them psychological westerns in the mold of *Winchester '73*, with Chase writing three of them.

Winchester '73 follows cowboy Lin McAdam (Stewart), who, alongside his friend "High-Spade" Frankie Wilson (Millard Mitchell), is searching the West for Dutch Henry Brown (Stephen McNally), the man who murdered his father. This quest brings them to Dodge City, the location of a shooting contest that will be presided over by Wyatt Earp (Will Geer). A priceless "One in a Thousand" 1873 Winchester rifle will be awarded as first prize, and McAdam knows that Dutch will be unable to resist competing for it. The depth of the men's animosity is immediately apparent when they first meet, as both men reach for the pistols Earp forced them to surrender upon entering town. Their long-standing and violently intimate relationship is further hinted at during the contest, when they exhibit identical shooting styles. In the final round, McAdam defeats Brown, claiming the Winchester. His victory is short-lived, however, as Brown and his comrades attack McAdam, steal the rifle, and flee town.

At this point, the film breaks into an innovative double narrative. One strand follows McAdam and High-Spade as they pursue Dutch into Texas, helping a cavalry unit fight off an Indian raid and meeting a beautiful showgirl, Lola Manners (Shelley Winters), along the way. The other thread follows the rifle itself as it passes from one owner to the next: from Dutch Henry it goes to a gun trader (John McIntire), an Indian chief on the warpath (Rock Hudson), Lola's cowardly fiancé (Charles Drake), and notorious gunslinger Waco Johnny Dean (Dan Duryea). Waco is a sometime ally of Dutch Henry, and it is here that the strands of the story reunite, for the two outlaws plan to rob a bank together. Seeing Waco in possession of "his" rifle, Dutch demands its return, and the gunslinger agrees. Afterward, he admits to Lola, whom he has kidnapped, that he plans to murder Dutch following the bank heist. McAdam and High-Spade help foil the robbery, gunning down Waco in the process. From Wilson we learn that Dutch is in fact McAdam's brother, and that Dutch killed their father. In the film's climactic showdown, McAdam gets revenge by killing Dutch and reclaiming the Winchester.

As they did in their later westerns, including *The Naked Spur* (1953) and *The Man from Laramie* (1955), Mann and Stewart challenged the traditional conventions of the genre in *Winchester '73*, questioning the use of violence to solve problems, examining the human cost of revenge, and focusing on a psychologically damaged protagonist. McAdam has given up everything to pursue his quarry, and when High-Spade asks what he will do after killing Dutch, McAdam can offer no clear plan for the future; he is consumed by his maniacal quest, rendering him unable to think of anything else. Indeed, while McAdam is clearly drawn to Lola, he is incapable of consummating their romance until he has killed Dutch. His obsession with avenging their father's death, it seems, prevents him from having any semblance of a normal life. Interestingly, though, in a sentimental turn, and one that breaks with the genre convention of the westerner as a loner, once he *has* killed Dutch, McAdam returns to Lola and is able to get on with the life his quest for vengeance had previously denied him.

See also: Western, The

References

Basinger, Jeanine. *Anthony Mann.* Boston: Twayne, 1979.

Kitses, Jim. *Horizons West: Anthony Mann, Budd Boetticher, Sam Peckinpah: Studies in Authorship within the Western.* Bloomington: Indiana University Press, 1969.

—*Bryan Kvet*

WITNESS. *Witness* (1985) was directed by Peter Weir, with screenplay by Earl W. Wallace and William Kelley, and music by Maurice Jarre. At the 1986 Academy Awards, *Witness* was nominated for eight Oscars including Best Actor, Best Director, and Best Music. The movie won two Oscars for Best Film Editing (Thom Noble) and Best Writing, Screenplay Written Directly for the Screen (Earl W. Wallace, William Kelley, Pamela Wallace). The movie was Australian director Weir's first Hollywood film, and Harrison Ford's first Academy Award nomination.

Witness uses the backdrop of a Pennsylvania Amish community to tell the story of an Amish woman, Rachel Lapp, and her son Samuel. Following the death of her husband, Rachel and her son leave their Lancaster County farm and travel to visit her sister in Baltimore. At a stopover en route, Samuel witnesses the brutal murder of a policeman in a Philadelphia train station bathroom. A detective, John Book, investigates the case, and he is wounded by the murderer. Realizing that Samuel is in danger, Book returns with Rachel and Samuel to Lancaster County to recover. Book's entry into the Amish community brings two cultures together—the traditional rural and the violent urban.

Weir uses music and dialogue sparingly, inviting viewers to rely on their senses of sight and sound. He creates scenes that rely only on sounds of the natural world or the voice, bringing the viewer closer to the reality of the Amish world, with its lack of electricity, television, or radio. We hear the sounds of horses' hooves on the pavement and the sound of a typewriter in the police station. On the farm, we hear the sounds of animals and the hammering of nails at a barn-raising. Maurice Jarre provides music on the synthesizer, an inspired instrumental contrast to the simplicity and traditional lifestyle of the Amish community. As the movie opens, we see a windswept field of wheat, and the simple tonal quality of the synthesizer provides a spiritual, transcendent mood to the scene. This mood and music take us through the scenes of the train ride and continue as Samuel wanders through the large train station, underscoring his wonder at these new sights.

Book brings the contemporary urban world into the Amish community. Yet, although he is an outsider, the simplicity of his name, John Book, implies that there is, perhaps, a link between this policeman who lives by violence, and the community for whom violence is anathema. Within this community Book recovers; adopts the plain, black clothing of the Amish; and is faced with the impact of the Amish culture on his life. There are several scenes of growing sexual tension between Book and Rachel, and she is warned of the punishment the community would mete out should she succumb to her desires. Both struggle to come to terms with the choice of leaving their own community. Although they do make love toward the end of the movie, Rachel is aware that in choosing to leave, the harm she would bring on her son and her community would be permanent and beyond repair. When she realizes that Book will return to Philadelphia, she struggles for confirmation when speaking with her father-in-law Eli. "But why?" she asks. "What's he going back to? Nothing . . ." Eli states what she knows to be true: "He's going back to his world, where he belongs. He knows it . . . and you know it too."

The theme of witnessing runs throughout the movie. Initially it is the boy Samuel who witnesses a horrific murder. Book himself is witness to the traditional ways of the Amish community and is drawn into its daily life. The community is witness to the growing relationship between Rachel and Book and is quick to show its displeasure. However, the climax of the film comes when the murderer and his accomplices arrive at the farm to kill Book and Samuel. The entire community is assembled as if "bearing witness" to the destructive force they have actively shunned. Book takes strength from the community around him, and, in the last scenes, instead of using violence, he uses words to end the brutality. As Book finally leaves the farm, Eli says to him: "You be careful out there among the English." This is as close as the two cultures will get— Book has found a different way of reacting to violence, and Eli has expanded his realm of possibilities to include the "English" man Book.

References

Hansen, L. "Perspectives: A New Image of Nonviolence in Popular Film." *Journal of Popular Film and Television* 14(3), 1986: 136–41.

Hentzi, Gary. "Peter Weir and the Cinema of New Age Humanism." *Film Quarterly* 44(2), 1999: 2–12.

McGowan, John P. "Looking at the (Alter)natives: Peter Weir's *Witness*." *Chicago Review* 35(3), 1986: 36–47.

—Vicky Bach

WIZARD OF OZ, THE. *The Wizard of Oz* (1939) is a musical motion picture, directed by Victor Fleming and produced by Metro-Goldwyn-Mayer (MGM). Based on L. Frank Baum's children's novel *The Wonderful Wizard of Oz* (1900), the film tells the story of Dorothy Gale, a troubled young farm girl from Kansas, who is transported on a fantastic journey to the Land of Oz, and ultimately comes to realize that "there's no place like home."

The film juxtaposes drab, sepia-toned images of heartland America against the brilliant Technicolor of Oz, as it delivers an explicit message that the search for happiness only brings the seeker back to his or her roots. The routines and minor heartaches of daily life in Kansas with her Aunt Em (Clara Blandick) and Uncle Henry (Charles Grapewin), seem unbearable to young Dorothy (played by 16-year-old Judy Garland), until she finds herself swept away—house and all—by a raging tornado. Jarred as the house abruptly hits the ground, Dorothy opens the door to discover that she has been delivered into the exquisite Land of Oz. Wandering from the house, she finds that she has killed a wicked witch, come into possession of a pair of magical ruby slippers, and engendered the enmity of the first witch's (even more) wicked sister. Desperate to find her way home, Dorothy—along with her dog, Toto, and her newfound friends, a Scarecrow (Ray Bolger) in need of a brain, a Tin Man (Jack Haley) in need of a heart, and a Cowardly Lion (Bert Lahr) in need of courage—embarks on a quest down the Yellow Brick Road to find the Emerald City, home of the Wizard of Oz.

The MGM adaptation of Baum's book was not the first—it was preceded by two silent films, *His Majesty, the Scarecrow of Oz* (1914) and *The Wizard of Oz* (1925),

The Scarecrow, played by Ray Bolger, and Dorothy, played by Judy Garland, encounter some hazards on the way to Oz in the 1939 film *The Wizard of Oz*. Along with *Gone with the Wind*, *The Wizard of Oz* was one of the most famous movies of the 1930s. (AP/Wide World Photos)

directed by Larry Semon—but it is considered to be the definitive cinematic version of the story. The script, crafted by Noel Langley, Florence Ryerson, and Edgar Allan Woolf, differs from the novel in several ways, with characters and events expanded or deleted to suit the new medium. Most significantly, while the cinematic Oz is cast as a dream, the literary Oz was intended to be an actual place—one to which Dorothy would return in later adventures. Color, throughout the film, precisely delineates the boundaries between fantasy and reality: the scenes in Kansas were shot in black and white but given a uniform sepia tint that suggested both the warm familiarity of old photographs and the sun-bleached grimness of the Dust Bowl. The Oz scenes, on the other hand, have the vibrant, saturated colors made possible by the three-strip Technicolor process. This sharp distinction underscores the film's central message: dusty-brown Kansas is, for Dorothy, preferable to vibrant Oz because it is real and because in the fantasy of Oz, there *is* "no place like home."

Throughout their journey, the seekers experience breathtaking wonders and curiosities: the Munchkins, flying monkeys, talking trees, a horse that changes color (the proverbial "horse of a different color"), and the Wizard himself (Frank Morgan). The Emerald City proves, however, to be a hollow world of spectacle and illusions.

The fearsome disembodied face and booming voice of the Wizard are merely elaborate special effects, and the "wizard" who produces them proves to have neither great powers nor magical gifts to bestow. The Wicked Witch of the West (Margaret Hamilton), who pursues and threatens Dorothy throughout the film, dissolves away into nothingness when accidentally splashed with water, and even Dorothy's main ally, Glinda, the Good Witch of the North (Billie Burke), appears and disappears in a translucent bubble. Oz's lack of real substance reflects the film's central conceit and key departure from Baum's book: the idea that Dorothy's adventures in Oz are elements in some sophisticated dream, with friends and foes that are no more than thinly disguised versions of characters from her real life. The redemptive ending—a symbolic and literal coming-of-age moment that finds Dorothy happily restored to her Kansas home—celebrates her transition from rebellious, dissatisfied child to appreciative young adult, who, possessing a more mature outlook, cheerfully accepts—indeed embraces—her social and familial role.

Far from simply a moral message for children, *The Wizard of Oz* is laden with meaning for adults, as well, reflecting the anxieties and concerns of its era. In fact, at the time of its release, a review in *Variety* magazine observed that "Oz has a message well-timed to current events." Those events—the Great Depression and the enactment of Franklin D. Roosevelt's New Deal—shaped the political-economic landscape from which the film emerged, and for many, were reflected in its allegorical storyline. According to E. Y. "Yip" Harburg, the lyricist honored with an Academy Award for the film's iconic song "Over the Rainbow," the Emerald City was, in fact, the New Deal—the bright, shining hope of Depression-era Americans, desperately in need of the confidence to shape their own destinies. In a way uncharacteristic of most cinematic songwriters, Harburg, who actively supported Roosevelt's policies, crafted lyrics that shaped the film's message, and served as a celebration of the country's benevolent "Wizard" and the New Deal programs that led the American heartland "out of the woods . . . out of the dark . . . into the light."

As Dorothy found, though, that light emanates not from the Emerald City—nor by extension, the promises and programs of Roosevelt's New Deal—but from the values already present in the American heartland. Oz, for Dorothy, is a land of anxiety and confusion, where the norms of everyday life are discarded, and the wonders of prosperity are freely available rather than earned. The Wizard, while "a very good man," is in fact, "a very bad wizard"—a fraud, hidden from view—his power deriving solely from his ability to create beautiful and fearsome illusions. Through her newfound friends, however, Dorothy learns lessons of substance: the values of community, ingenuity, hard work, and faith. Only by making common cause with the Scarecrow, Tin Man, Cowardly Lion, and even Toto is she able to overcome adversity and see through the Wizard's facade. Her belief in his power comes to nothing; her belief in herself and her friends, however, restores order and happiness.

The film made its first appearance on television in 1956, as part of CBS's *Ford Star Jubilee* anthology series, after which the network continued to air it annually, until 1991, establishing the story and its characters as indelible parts of American popular culture. Cited by the Library of Congress as the most watched film in history, it was among the first titles of "cultural, historical, or aesthetic significance" to be named to the National Film Registry (1989). A television event that continues through the present day, *The Wizard of Oz* has been subject to remakes, spin-offs, and commercial tie-ins for decades, ranging from the Broadway hit *Wicked*, to "Dorothy" cookie jars, to bumper stickers that urge "Run, Toto, run!"

References

Nathanson, Paul. *Over the Rainbow: The Wizard of Oz as a Secular Myth of America*. Albany: State University of New York Press, 1991.

Rushdie, Salman. *The Wizard of Oz*. London: British Film Institute, 1992.

Scarfone, Jay, and William Stillman. *The Wizardry of Oz: The Artistry and Magic of the 1939 MGM Classic, Revised and Expanded*. New York: Applause, 2004.

—Cynthia J. Miller and A. Bowdoin Van Riper

WOMAN OF THE YEAR.   *Woman of the Year* features the legendary screen duo Spencer Tracy and Katharine Hepburn in their first film appearance together. Hepburn plays Tess Harding, an international reporter for a New York City newspaper who is wrapped up in the events of World War II. Audiences in the 1940s would have noticed how Hepburn's character mirrored the real life of renowned journalist Dorothy Thompson. Spencer Tracy plays Sam Craig, a sports journalist who takes up the cause of basic American values. *Woman of the Year* was both a box-office and critical success. It earned Hepburn an Academy Award nomination for Best Actress and brought home Oscars for Original Writing and Original Screenplay. (Miller, 2008)

Woman of the Year was produced prior to the United States entry into World War II—its release date was January 1942—yet it revealed the issues presented by wartime exigencies. Tess states in a radio interview that perhaps baseball should be suspended during the war. Sam is incensed with her comments, and the war of the sexes begins in the public and personal lives of the two journalists. Their animosity fades into love and they are married; however, this is not a simple happily-ever-after story. Tess, as the embodiment of 1940s feminism, maintains her independence and public life, much like the characters played by Bette Davis in *Front Page Woman* and Rosalind Russell in *His Girl Friday*. All three of these influential female stars, playing assertive and yet extremely attractive female journalists, reflected significant American cultural trends expressed during this era. Ms. Hepburn's portrayal of an independent career woman, glamorous, opinionated, and sexy in trousers, paralleled the wartime role American women would be asked to assume after Pearl Harbor. Her intelligence, political savvy, and autonomy were as essential to the war effort as the activities of the soldiers, the no-nonsense all-American males portrayed by the stoic Mr. Tracy. In February 1942, *New York Times* film critic Bosley Crowther gave *Woman of the Year* a "triumphant" review. He commented that the film would appeal emotionally to average Americans, both male and female. He described a scene in the film when a radio announcer asked a group of men surrounding Tracy at the local coffeeshop to list the two current topics most frequently discussed by average American citizens. The answer was obvious: war and sports. The romantic comedy played out by Tracy and Hepburn made these topics fair game.

Men of the 1940s respected the hard work and wit of their women, but they still wanted a feminine domestic partner. As historian Nancy Woloch suggests, by the 1940s the image of the intelligent, wage-earning woman gave way to a female heroine who put her traditional gender roles as wife and mother first. Thus, it is not surprising that after Sam leaves Tess because she is too self-centered, she ultimately comes to her senses, offering to give up her career if her husband will have her back. American society expected its women to return to the home and give up their jobs when the war was over. William Mann commented in the *New York Times* (2007) that Katharine Hepburn would always lose in the Hollywood films when she and Tracy engaged in a battle of the sexes. He suggests that the film star understood that American postwar culture might allow some celebration of female independence; but in the end, she would have to give in to male authority.

See also: Hepburn, Katharine; Romantic Comedy, The; Women in Film

References

Mann, William. "Hepburn, Revisited." *New York Times*, May 12, 2007.
Miller, Frank. "Woman of the Year: The Essentials Synopsis." *Turner Classic Movies*. http://www.tcm.com/tcmdb/title.jsp?stid=14145&category=Articles.
Woloch, Nancy. *Women and the American Experience*, 3rd ed. Boston: McGraw-Hill, 2000.

—*Katharina Tumpek-Kjellmark*

WORKING GIRL. *Working Girl*, staring Melanie Griffith as Tess McGill, Sigourney Weaver as Katharine Parker, and Harrison Ford as Jack Trainer, explores the social networks of 1980s corporate America. Tess, a secretary with ambition and "street smarts," finds herself working for Katharine, a no-nonsense captain of industry whose business practices are proven to be questionable. After a skiing accident keeps Katharine out of the office, Tess takes advantage of the situation to forward to Jack a business idea she had originally pitched to Katharine, an idea that Katharine intends to claim as her own. The working relationship between Tess and Katharine is further complicated by the fact that Jack and Katharine have been involved in an ill-fated, and seemingly sterile, personal relationship—one that is ending as Jack and Tess begin their own romantic involvement. Tess's ambition and intelligence ultimately serve her well, and by the end of the film she has become a high-paid executive, while Katharine has been embarrassed in front of colleagues and faces the possibility that she will be forced from her job as a result of her unethical behavior with Tess.

The relatively small percentage of women who made it to the highest positions in corporate America during the 1980s found themselves in the awkward position of being outsiders on the inside. This idea is expressed in the film's opening scene, which focuses on a commuter ferry making its way into Manhattan from the New Jersey

Poster for the 1988 film *Working Girl*, starring Sigourney Weaver, Harrison Ford, and Melanie Griffith, peeking out from behind her two co-stars. Directed by Mike Nichols. (Photofest)

shore—the alternating shots of the crowds of commuters and the Statue of Liberty are meant to remind viewers of the immigrants that built America; just as these foreigners were assimilated into America's burgeoning multicultural society, women during the 1980s were being assimilated into the corporate world and proving themselves to be valuable players in that high-powered community. Yet, even though these women came to be integral parts of the workforce, they still found themselves largely excluded from it.

The character of Tess embodies the struggles facing women and the efforts they made during this period to prove themselves essential components of corporate America. Tess's lack of a degree from a prestigious university, for instance—she received her degree "with honors," but from night school, as she is reminded during the course of the film—is held against her, and although she proves that she is intelligent as well as intuitive, she is still relegated to working as a temp-agency secretary throughout the early part of the picture. In an effort to improve herself professionally, Tess is taking business and diction courses and seeking to land a "serious" job in the upper echelons of the corporate community.

The film sets Tess and Katharine in juxtapositional tension. Katharine has been accepted into the corporate "old boys club" and personifies its practices. Significantly, although she, just like her male counterparts, is every bit the cool professional, in business settings she distinguishes herself by wearing bright-colored clothing and even hinting that sexual favors are in the offing should the right deal present itself. Thus, Katharine is portrayed as having climbed the corporate ladder both by becoming just like her unscrupulous male colleagues and by at least implying that she is willing to compromise her own sense of self by sleeping her way to the top. Tess, on the other hand, although she is portrayed as having a "head for business and bod for sin," struggles to break free from the trap of being valued only for her looks and what she can provide men in the bedroom, instead of being valued for what she has to offer in the boardroom. Interestingly, while finally rejecting everything that Katharine represents, Tess becomes both the executive and the woman she wants to be by embracing, and expressing, the much more ethical, and sensitive, ideals of Jack—the corporate male who is aggressive and yet refuses to compromise his own integrity to "get the deal done." In the end, Tess and Jack, who value each other for all the right reasons, are perfect together.

Working Girl, then, not only depicts the struggle that women faced when they began entering the upper echelons of the business community during the 1980s, it also reminds us, in a wonderfully provocative way, that ability, hard work, and commitment should mean more, even in the corporate world, than do gender and class.

See also: Women in Film

References

Davies-Netzley, Sally Ann. "Women above the Glass Ceiling: Perceptions on Corporate Mobility and Strategies for Success." *Gender and Society* 12(3), June 1998: 339–55.

Tasker, Yvonne. *Working Girls: Gender and Sexuality in Popular Cinema.* New York: Routledge, 1998.

Wajcman, Judy. *Managing Like a Man: Women and Men in Corporate Management.* University Park: Pennsylvania State University Press, 1998.

—Elise Guest

Y

YANKEE DOODLE DANDY. The George M. Cohan biopic *Yankee Doodle Dandy* (1942) illustrates how historical films often reveal as much about the era in which they are made as the one they depict. Ostensibly about the American composer/performer's amazing run of Broadway hits from the 1900s through the 1930s, the success of this biographical film can be explained more by timeliness than the particularity of its take on Cohan. With a release date in early 1942, just after the attack on Pearl Harbor in late 1941, the composer's patriotic World War I–era hits "Over There" and "You're a Grand Old Flag" were newly relevant and ready for revival. The rhetorical high point of the film excerpts a scene from his starring role in the 1937 Rodgers and Hart musical *I'd Rather Be Right*. The emphatic performance of lines added to address current global conflict—"We'll take [France] back from Hitler and put ants in his 'Japants' and that's *for* the record"—underscore the imperative of producers to make this a timely World War II–era film.

Yankee traces Cohan's (James Cagney) rise to fame from his days as a young boy when he traveled as part of the Four Cohans, his family's vaudeville act. This context represents a significant point of departure from many other musical biopics, which typically work in the mode of *The Jazz Singer* (1927), in which the musical prodigy's enthusiasm for popular music is questioned by his religious and traditional family. As George successfully capitalizes on his superior talents at a very early age, it is his own egoism that provides the film's earliest conflict. Cohan outgrows his youthful cockiness and serves his country as a diligent patriot. The film's treatment of the composer as an American icon is, in fact, explicitly discussed when Cohan's producer, Sam (Richard Whorf), tries to recruit a more highbrow Broadway singer, Fay Templeton (Irene Manning), to perform his songs. Fay initially resists, saying she will only perform in a "quiet, dignified musical play," and that Cohan's work represents "loud, vulgar, flag waving." Sam takes Fay to task for her elitism, explaining his understanding of American taste and convincing her to "hitch your wagon to his star right now." Cohan, Sam argues, is "the whole darn country squeezed into a pair of pants . . . [he] invented the success story. And every American loves it because it happens to be his own private dream. He's found the mainspring in the Yankee clock: ambition, pride, and patriotism."

James Cagney performing in *Yankee Doodle Dandy*. Undated movie still. (Bettmann/Corbis)

Fitting this aggrandized portrayal of an American individual, and the reputation of its studio director Michael Curtiz, *Yankee Doodle Dandy* is much more a star vehicle than an auteurist masterpiece. James Cagney, chosen by Cohan himself after Fred Astaire turned down the role, was afforded the opportunity to play against type. Cagney typically played violent, masculine characters, so this film gave the actor a chance to dramatically expand his range. Cagney's upbeat, surprisingly dance-heavy performance was rewarded with his only Academy Award for Best Actor.

Production memos reveal how fully Cohan involved himself in the adaptation process, often to the aggravation of the producers; at one point "Cohan read [the initial] script with great interest—then tossed it aside and immediately countered with one of his own, numbering 170 pages" (Tibbetts, 2005). Along with the new script, Cohan included a revealing note: "To my mind the only sweetheart *your hero* can have in the early stages is the theater itself" (130). Here, far from insisting on any strict fidelity to his life story, Cohan, incredibly, describes himself in the third person, as a stock character under the ownership of the producers. In this respect, the composer and the film's staff were in agreement. Similarly, Cohan cited certain facts of his life—multiple marriages, opposition to labor unions, and disputes with popular critics—that would be best left offscreen (129–30). The producers concurred on these omissions, and the film depicted, according to Cohan's daughter, "the kind of life that Daddy would like to have lived!" (102).

See also: Cagney, James; Music in Film; Musical, The

References

Cameron, Kenneth M. *America on Film: Hollywood and American History*. New York: Continuum, 1997.

Custen, George. *Bio/Pics: How Hollywood Constructed Public History*. New Brunswick, NJ: Rutgers University Press, 1992.

McGilligan, Patrick. *Yankee Doodle Dandy*. Madison: University of Wisconsin Press, 1981.

Tibbetts, John C. *Composers in the Movies: Studies in Musical Biography*. New Haven, CT: Yale University Press, 2005.

—*Jesse Schlotterbeck*

PEOPLE

A

ALLEN, DEDE. Dede Allen was one of Hollywood's most important and innovative screen editors. Indeed, during the 1960s and 1970s, she was one of the most sought-after editors in the industry. Allen was nominated several times for Academy Awards and sat on the Board of Governors of the Academy of Motion Pictures Arts and Sciences.

Born Dorothea Caruthers on December 3, 1923, in Cleveland, Ohio, Allen came from a middle-class family. Her father worked for Union Carbide and, until she was married, her mother was an Edwardian stage actress. Influenced by her mother's love for the movies, Allen viewed as many films as she was able while she was young. Educated in Europe, she left for Hollywood in 1943 in order to become a director. Initially forced to work as a messenger for Columbia Studios, within a year of being hired, she was promoted to the sound editing department, where she began as an assistant sound editor. She spent her nights working at the Actor's Lab, a Hollywood theater company made up mostly of expatriate New Yorkers. Allen credits the Actor's Lab with teaching her how to structure dramatic scenes.

As more and more men who worked in the film industry were sent overseas during WWII, job opportunities opened up for women; it was at this point that Allen became a sound editor at Columbia. In 1945, she married Stephen Fleischman, who would ultimately work as a writer, director, and producer in television. Between 1945 and 1950, Allen took time out to have a family and moved to New York. She had one son, Tom Fleischman, who later became a sound editor. Still in New York, Allen took a job at a commercial movie company, Filmgraphics, working there as an editor, sound editor, and script girl. In 1957, she edited a film short, *Endowing Your Future*, and in 1958, a grade-B feature film, *Terror from the Year 5000*, also known as *Cage of Doom*.

In 1959, director Robert Wise, who edited both *Citizen Kane* and *The Magnificent Ambersons* for Orson Welles, hired Allen to edit *Odds against Tomorrow* (1959), a film noir shot in New York, that featured Harry Belafonte and Robert Ryan. Wise encouraged Allen to experiment with the scenes, and he was very pleased with the final cut. Recognizing her enormous talent, Robert Rossen brought her on to edit his 1961 masterpiece *The Hustler*. The film was nominated for numerous Oscars, including those for Best Picture; Best Director; Best Actor, for Paul Newman; and Best Supporting Actor, for Jackie Gleason (although also nominated for a Best Supporting Actor award, George C. Scott refused the nomination). Allen was nominated by the American Cinema Editors, USA for its award for best Edited Feature Film.

Perhaps Allen's greatest career achievement came with the 1968 film *Bonnie and Clyde*. Allen's editing of this iconic film was revolutionary, innovative, and extraordinarily influential, and after the picture was released, she became one of the most sought-after editors in the industry. Continuing to work on feature films, she also began training novice editors, eventually establishing what came to be known as the New York School of Editing. Her students included Jerry Greenberg, Evan Lottman, Barry Malkin, Richard Marks, Jim Miller, and Steven Rotter.

After her success with *Bonnie and Clyde*, Allen would go on to edit such pictures as *Rachel, Rachel* (1968), *Alice's Restaurant* (1969), *Little Big Man* (1970), *Slaughterhouse Five* (1972), *Serpico* (1973), and *Dog Day Afternoon* (1975), for which she was nominated for an Academy Award. While she did not win the Oscar, she did win the British Academy of Film and Television Arts (BAFTA) award for film editing. She continued her work through the 1970s and '80s, editing such pictures as *The Missouri Breaks* (1976); *Slap Shot* (1977); *The Wiz* (1978); Warren Beatty's *Reds* (1981), which she co-produced and for which she was again nominated for an Academy Award; *The Breakfast Club* (1985); *The Milagro Beanfield War* (1988); *Henry and June* (1990); *The Addams Family* (1991); and 2001's *Wonder Boys*, for which she received yet another Oscar nomination.

In 1992, Warner Bros. executives persuaded Allen to move to California to become the Vice-President in Charge of Creative Development at their studio. She was eventually promoted to Senior Vice-President in Charge of Creative Development. She served on the board of trustees for the Academy of Motion Picture Arts and Sciences, representing the Film Editors branch; and also as the vice president of the Board of Directors of the Motion Picture Editors Guild. Although she never won an Oscar for her work as an editor, Allen won a Crystal Award from Women in Film, a Career Achievement Award from the American Cinema Editors, and a Fellowship and Service Award from the Motion Picture Editors Guild. Allen died on April 17, 2010; she was 86.

Selected Filmography

John Q (2002); *Wonder Boys* (2000); *The Addams Family* (1991); *Henry & June* (1990); *Let It Ride* (1989); *The Milagro Beanfield War* (1988); *The Breakfast Club* (1985); *Reds* (1981); *The Wiz* (1978); *Slap Shot* (1977); *The Missouri Breaks* (1976); *Dog Day Afternoon* (1975); *Night Moves* (1975); *Serpico* (1973); *Slaughterhouse-Five* (1972); *Little Big Man* (1970); *Alice's Restaurant* (1969); *Rachel, Rachel* (1968); *Bonnie and Clyde* (1967); *America, America* (1963); *The Hustler* (1961); *Odds against Tomorrow* (1959); *Because of Eve* (1948)

References

Gentry, Ric, and Dede Allen. "An Interview with Dede Allen." *Film Quarterly* 46(1), Fall 1992: 12–22.

Lumme, Helena. *Great Women of Film.* New York: Billboard Books/Watson-Guptill, 2002.

McGilligan, Patrick. "Dede Allen." In Kay, Karyn, and Gerald Peary, eds. *Women and the Cinema: A Critical Anthology.* New York: Dutton, 1977: 199–207.

McGrath, Declan. *Editing and Post-production.* Boston: Focal Press, 2001.

—*Scott Sheidlower*

ALLEN, WOODY.   A legendary filmmaker and consummate auteur, Woody Allen has been writing and directing films since 1966. Since 1969 he has averaged one movie per year. His unique style generally favors the script and actors over avant-garde cinematic techniques and special effects. While he occasionally experiments with narrative techniques, his films are noted for complex characters, long scenes of dialogue, and location shoots. He is one of a few filmmakers who retains complete creative control over his films.

Allan Stewart Konigsberg was born December 1, 1935 in Brooklyn, New York, to Nettie and Martin Konigsberg. His mother was a bookkeeper and his father a jeweler. While Allen's parents were both born and raised on Manhattan's Lower East Side, Allen and his sister were raised in middle-class Brooklyn, where he attended public schools. After high school Allen attended NYU, but didn't apply himself and was eventually expelled.

Even before he graduated from high school, Allen was ghostwriting jokes for Sammy Kaye, Guy Lombardo, and Arthur Murray. After he dropped out of college, he signed with the William Morris Agency to write comedy skits for Pat Boone, Buddy Hackett, and others. In 1953, he left for Hollywood to work on the *Colgate Comedy Hour* for NBC. While he was in Hollywood he met Danny Simon, the brother of Neil Simon, who became his mentor. In 1956, Allen returned to New York, where he wrote nightclub routines for a number of celebrities. In 1958, he left the William Morris Agency and formed a business relationship with Jack Rollins and Charles Joffe, who launched his film career and continue to work with him, producing most of his films. During the 1960s Allen wrote for television and worked as a stand-up comic, touring the country and appearing frequently on *The Tonight Show.* His film career began in 1965 with the box-office hit, *What's New Pussycat?*, which he scripted. Since then he has written and directed over 40 films.

Allen is a prolific filmmaker. Every year he has a film in release, one in production, and one he is writing. His filmmaking approach, which is based on a restricted number of takes and tight schedules, keeps his budgets low (currently around $12 million per picture) and allows him to keep to his rigorously defined timetable. Allen is philosophical about his filmmaking vision, something reflected in the movies he creates. For instance, in *Manhattan*, which Allen co-wrote, Yale (Michael Murphy) suggests that "the essence of art is to provide a certain working through of the situation for people, so that you can get in touch with feelings that you didn't know that you had." This notion emphasizes the therapeutic value of art for the artist. Indeed, films such as *Stardust Memories, Deconstructing Harry,* and *Vicky Cristina Barcelona,* emphasize the point that art exists for the sake of the artist, often with only a peripheral regard for the

Director Woody Allen attends the premiere of his film *Match Point* at the 58th International Cannes Film Festival on May 12, 2005 in Cannes. From an early career as a gag writer and stand-up comic, Allen became one of America's foremost independent filmmakers. (MJ Kim/Getty Images)

audience. Reflecting this sense of art as a process of creative "working through of the situation," Allen's films frequently repeat subjects he approached in previous work: *Manhattan* is a more refined version of *Annie Hall*, *Hannah and Her Sisters* fleshes out some of the ambiguities in *Interiors*, while *Match Point* deals with the same issues as *Crimes and Misdemeanors*. For Allen, then, it seems that art is also becoming and, perhaps, never arrives.

Allen's films can be divided into three periods: his early slapstick-comedy and Diane Keaton films; his Mia Farrow period; and his post–Mia Farrow period. (Allen had long-term, intimate relationships with both women.) Allen's early films relied heavily on slapstick and visual comedy. During this period he developed the Chaplinesque character, most often played by Allen himself, of the lovable, anxious schlemiel. With *Annie Hall*, Allen moved toward the seriocomedy he would master in the 1980s. A romantic comedy that deals with the complexity of intimate relationships, *Annie Hall* also relies on various forms of comedy to ease the filmic tension Allen masterfully creates in this film. In the 1980s, Allen's films relied more on situational comedy and situational irony than on physical comedy, as his early films had. The result is a period of filmmaking that more closely examines the nature of relationships and growth into middle age, what might be termed "mature comedies."

While many critics consider his Mia Farrow years to be his best, after his relationship with Farrow ended, his films became more diverse in form and content. (An acrimonious split between Allen and Farrow led to court battles over their adopted and biological children and Allen ultimately marrying the much younger Soon-Yi Previn, the adopted daughter of Farrow and Andre Previn, who had lived with Farrow and Allen while the two were together.). *Everyone Says I Love You* (1996) is a musical, while films like *Sweet and Lowdown* (1999) and *Match Point* (2005) bear little resemblance in style to any of Allen's previous films. Also, he began casting other actors in the "Woody Allen" character: John Cusak in *Bullets over Broadway* (1994), Kenneth Branagh in *Celebrity* (1998), and Will Ferrell in *Melinda and Melinda* (2004). In 2004, Allen made the greatest change in his film career: he started shooting films in England. New York City had become an integral part of his films; but artistically the change in location, said Allen, was necessary for him to view the world differently. Many of the themes Allen has dealt with in the past are there, but English and European culture play a role in the narrative. While frustrated with Hollywood's current business model, which favors blockbusters, Allen sees the move in pragmatic terms: European audiences tend to embrace his films more than American audiences.

Interestingly, especially because Allen, both in his personal life and in his films, seems hopelessly unable to determine "what women want," he has directed more women in Oscar-nominated roles than any other living filmmaker. A close examination of Allen's films reveals that most of them reflect his desire to understand women. This may appear directly, as in films such as *Interiors, Alice, Purple Rose of Cairo,* and *Vicky Cristina Barcelona,* or indirectly, through the male characters' relationships with women, in films like *Annie Hall, Crimes and Misdemeanors, Hannah and Her Sisters* (which covers all manner of sins), and *Match Point.* Setting the stage for most of the films that follow, *Annie Hall* explores Alvy Singer's attempt to come to terms with his relationship with women—and Annie in particular. The nature of women is a recurring theme in Allen's films. Films like *Interiors, September, Alice,* and *Vicky Cristina Barcelona* (none of which Allen appears in as an actor) focus on female protagonists and examine personal relationships from the female perspective. These characters are carefully and deeply wrought, and within each film reveal different aspects of the feminine psyche.

Sex is also a prominent and recurring theme in Allen's films. The 1970s emerged as an era in America during which sexuality could be discussed more openly. While never graphically portrayed in his films, the omnipresence of sex through innuendo, jokes, or postcoital conversations, reflected society's changing attitudes toward sexuality. But beneath the jokes and shock value created by the frank discussions of the subject in his early films (*Everything You Always Wanted to Know about Sex* and *Sleeper*), Allen presents viewers epistemological inquiries into human sexuality. For instance, in one scene in *Annie Hall,* also co-written by Allen, in a postcoital moment between Alvy (Allen) and Annie (Keaton), Alvy rolls over, turns on the light, and says, "As Balzac said, 'there goes another novel.'" This statement directly addresses the creative impulse expressed in both the sexual and the artistic moment. Allen, it seems, is suggesting that the creative impulse can be expressed through art or sexuality, but that for the artist, and by extension humanity in general, sexual desire tends to pervert what he understands as the transcendent quality of creativity. Indeed, in many of Allen's films, the artist is compromised by his sexual desires.

Another prominent motif in Allen's films is the city of New York. His recent European films notwithstanding, New York City plays a significant role in almost all of his work. Allen himself has stated that *Manhattan* is his homage to New York, and *Hannah and Her Sisters* offers an architectural tour of the city. The city shapes Allen's characters, and is integral to his plots. Indeed, the *absence* of the city in *A Midsummer Night's Sex Comedy* underscores the *significance* of the city in modern America. As the primary symbol of American modernity, Allen appears to be saying that the city acts to repress humanity's innate carnal desires; only in some Burkeian place of the sublime, then, can humanity's essential self finally emerge. Because Allen's characters, in both his comedies and his dramatic films, are so often repressed, so often representative of charmingly neurotic figures struggling mightily to disclose their own inner selves, it is not surprising that this brilliant director places most of them in the city, in *the* American city, New York City.

Allen continues to make films and gather awards. By 2009, he had received 46 Academy Award nominations and taken home the top prize 10 times. While most of his nominations have been for screenwriting, for which he holds the record at 14, most of his wins have gone to women who have acted in his films.

See also: Annie Hall; Manhattan

Selected Filmography

Midnight in Paris (2011); *Whatever Works* (2009); *Vicky Cristina Barcelona* (2008); *Match Point* (2005); *Deconstructing Harry* (1997); *Mighty Aphrodite* (1995); *Husbands and Wives* (1992); *Shadows and Fog* (1991); *Crimes and Misdemeanors* (1989); *Hannah and Her Sisters* (1986); *A Midsummer Night's Sex Comedy* (1982); *Manhattan* (1979); *Interiors* (1978); *Annie Hall* (1977); *Sleeper* (1973); *Bananas* (1971)

References

Brode, Douglas. *The Films of Woody Allen.* New York: Citadel, 1991.
Girgus, Sam B. *The Films of Woody Allen.* Cambridge, UK: Cambridge University Press, 1993.
Kapsis, Robert E., and Kathie Coblentz, eds. *Woody Allen Interviews.* Jackson: University Press of Mississippi, 2006.
Nichols, Mary P. *Reconstructing Woody: Art, Love, and Life in the Films of Woody Allen.* Lanham, MD: Rowman & Littlefield, 1998.
Pogel, Nancy. *Woody Allen.* Boston: Twayne, 1987.
Silet, Charles L.P., ed. *The Films of Woody Allen.* Lanham, MD: Scarecrow Press, 2006.

—*Dean R. Cooledge*

ALTMAN, ROBERT. Robert Altman's satirical, multi-layered, absurdist, and thematically complex films are reminiscent, in their personal vision and artistic daring, of European art cinema—except that Altman could not touch anything without making it strangely and irreducibly American. Not often a successful box-office director, Altman nevertheless got to do pretty much what he wanted, as he wanted, for most of his career. As he put it late in life, what director could have asked for more?

Born in Kansas City, Missouri, on February 20, 1925, Altman went to private school and joined the Air Force in 1945 to serve as a bombardier in World War II.

After the war he broke into early TV, and cut his teeth in the 1950s and 1960s directing and writing a variety of TV episodes, particularly westerns such as *Bonanza*.

Altman's breakthrough came in 1970 when he was given the chance to direct the Korean War hospital comedy *M*A*S*H** after, as the joke has it, every last director left in Hllywood said no to the project. His two stars, Elliott Gould and Donald Sutherland, thought he was inept, and tried to get him fired. Altman's methods were unconventional to say the least: he threw out most of screenwriter Ring Lardner Jr.'s dialogue, and prompted his ensemble cast to improvise a series of comic moments. If the executives at Twentieth Century-Fox had known that Altman was following no plot, had adopted an impertinent improvisational antiwar tone, and was beginning his experimentation with overlapping dialogue, they probably would have shut the production

Film director Robert Altman poses in New York City on September 20, 1981. (AP/Wide World Photos)

down. But they were preoccupied overseeing their mammoth WWII epic *Tora! Tora! Tora!*, and left Altman alone. By the end of the year *Tora! Tora! Tora!* became one of the biggest box-office and critical disasters of all time, and *M*A*S*H**, setting the tone for a new generation's resistance to staid Hollywood approaches, won the Palme d'Or at the Cannes Film Festival; garnered a host of Academy Award nominations, including Best Picture and Best Director; and was a box-office smash.

The success gave Altman a chance to fulfill his dream of becoming one of the most independent-minded directors in an era of independent-minded directors. After making *M*A*S*H**, Altman began his most fertile creative period—the 1970s. In film after film, he developed a distinct tone and a style, making him one of the most identifiable directors working in Hollywood. He called his method the "Gypsy caravan style" of filmmaking, an unusual collaborative approach enhanced by on-the-set improvisation and his famous roaming, floating camera. The best films of the period included his revisionist western *McCabe and Mrs. Miller* (1971), starring Warren Beatty and Julie Christie in what critic Pauline Kael called a "beautiful pipe-dream"; *The Long Goodbye*

(1973), one of the best and most underrated films of the 1970s, starring Elliott Gould as a mumbling version of Raymond Chandler's Philip Marlowe; *Thieves Like Us* (1974), a lyrical Depression-era crime film that Kael called a masterpiece; and, preeminently, *Nashville* (1975), Altman's political epic centered in America's country music capital, his most ambitious film to date and his most critically acclaimed.

But the critics, with the exception of Pauline Kael, were not always flattering in their reviews, and the box-office results for Altman were usually disappointing. After a series of bizarre critical and financial failures in the late 1970s, including the surreal *3 Women* (1977) and *Quintet* (1979), a futuristic apocalyptic dream set in the Arctic and seen by practically no one, even Kael turned her back on Altman, and he was considered poison by every Hollywood studio. The nadir of his career was when Twentieth Century-Fox refused to release his comedy *Health* (1980), and Altman, faced with debts, was shortly thereafter forced to sell his production company, Lions Gate, and to take jobs shooting wedding videos.

Some American lives not only have second acts, but third and fourth acts, as well. Altman remade himself in the 1980s, directing a series of small-budget film versions of successful contemporary American plays, including David Rabe's *Streamers* (1983) and Sam Shepard's *Fool for Love* (1985). These films were respectful adaptations of stage plays, perhaps not fully conceived as films in their own right, but an antidote to the increasingly blockbuster-conscious Hollywood, and a spur to the growing independent cinema movement. The films kept Altman working and gained him critical respect.

In the 1990s, a few significant films brought him back to new heights of respectability and importance. *The Player* (1992), starring Tim Robbins as a Hollywood studio executive driven to murder, was a stunningly incisive and entertaining critique of Hollywood politics and aesthetics, as well as a devastating moral indictment of yuppie values, and it showed Altman at his most audacious and playful. He followed *The Player* with *Short Cuts* (1993), an adaptation of a series of Raymond Carver short stories that in style and complexity was reminiscent of *Nashville*, had the latter been darker-toned, as it investigated American social decay in and around Los Angeles.

Altman received his fifth Academy Award nomination for *Gosford Park* (2001), a charming 1930s "upstairs downstairs" period piece set in a manor house in England that employed his usual stylistic methods. His last film, the marvelously unpredictable *A Prairie Home Companion* (2006), seemed almost an indirect pastiche of *Nashville*, and reminded audiences of Altman's marvelous capacity to create surprising comic tonalities, and to inform his films with a buoyant atmosphere of happy ensembles.

Having never won a Best Director Oscar, he was awarded the Academy of Motion Picture Arts and Sciences Lifetime Achievement Award in 2006. He died on November 20 of that year. Altman had been working on a number of projects, still seeking to map out his large-spirited and unpredictable vision of America's dreamers and misanthropes.

Selected Filmography

A Prairie Home Companion (2006); *The Company* (2003); *Gosford Park* (2001); *Dr T and the Women* (2000); *Cookie's Fortune* (1999); *The Gingerbread Man* (1998); *Kansas City* (1996);

Prêt-à-Porter (1994); *Short Cuts* (1993); *The Player* (1992); *O. C. and Stiggs* (1985); *Secret Honor* (1984); *Streamers* (1983); *Come Back to the Five and Dime, Jimmy Dean, Jimmy Dean* (1982); *Health* (1980); *A Perfect Couple* (1979); *Quintet* (1979); *A Wedding* (1978); *3 Women* (1977); *Buffalo Bill and the Indians, or Sitting Bull's History Lesson* (1976); *Nashville* (1975); *California Split* (1974); *Thieves Like Us* (1974); *The Long Goodbye* (1973); *Images* (1972); *McCabe and Mrs. Miller* (1971); *Brewster McCloud* (1970); *MASH* (1970); *Countdown* (1968)

References

Cook, David A. *Lost Illusions: American Cinema in the Shadow of Watergate and Vietnam, 1970–1979.* Berkeley: University of California Press, 2000.
Kael, Pauline. *Deeper into Movies.* Boston: Little, Brown, 1973.
Kael, Pauline. *5001 Nights at the Movies.* New York: Henry Holt, 1985.
Sterritt, David, ed. *Robert Altman: Interviews.* Oxford: University Press of Mississippi, 2000.

—*Robert Cowgill*

ARZNER, DOROTHY.   Dorothy Arzner was one of the few female directors ever to achieve prominence in American moviemaking, even earning notice as one of the "Top Ten" directors of the 1920s. When her career ended in 1943, she had directed 17 films, including Paramount's first talkie. Although she never came out publicly as a lesbian, she was among many Hollywood figures during its golden age whose homosexuality was an "open secret" among insiders.

Arzner was born in San Francisco January 3, in either 1897 or 1900 (sources disagree) and grew up in Los Angeles. Her father owned the Hoffman Café in Hollywood, and Arzner met many movie notables while waiting tables there. She did not immediately enter filmmaking, instead enrolling at the University of Southern California as a premed student, dropping out, and driving an ambulance during World War I. Once the war ended, she worked for a newspaper, but by 1919 she had embarked on her movie career. Arzner began as a script typist for William DeMille and was quickly promoted to editing and screenwriting; among her many credits in these capacities are *Blood and Sand* (1922, editor), *The Covered Wagon* (1923, editor and screenwriter), and *Red Kimono* (1925, screenwriter).

Her first film as director was the Paramount silent feature *Fashions for Women* (1927). She stayed with Paramount through 1932, directing three more silent films and, beginning with *The Wild Party* (1929), seven talking pictures. She is the only female director to work in both formats and is credited with inventing the boom microphone. Her last film with Paramount, *Merrily We Go to Hell* (1932), is considered among her most notable, as are most of her post-Paramount films, including *Christopher Strong* (1933), *Nana* (1934), *Craig's Wife* (1936), *The Bride Wore Red* (1937), and *Dance, Girl, Dance* (1940). During World War II she also directed Women's Army Corps training films, returning to the private sector for *First Comes Courage* (1943), her last film. A lengthy illness, followed by postwar social mores that required passive, domestic women, effectively ended her Hollywood career. Arzner then found a niche offering classes at the Pasadena Playhouse and in the film department at UCLA (1959–63), as well as directing dozens of Pepsi-Cola commercials for television.

In her later years Arzner was rediscovered amid second wave feminism and lesbian activism, which generated new scholarship on the intersections between personal and public lives. Her films include stories of female bonding and often feature strong women who question or defy society's sexism. As a result, some of the most memorable actresses of the era play leads in Arzner's productions, a few in their first starring roles: Lucille Ball, Claudette Colbert, Joan Crawford, Katharine Hepburn, Merle Oberon, Maureen O'Hara, Rosalind Russell, and Sylvia Sidney. Interestingly, though she later acknowledged the "shortcomings" of the Hollywood Code of her era, Arzner asserted that "the Code at least forced women on screen to *do*."

Links between Arzner's lesbianism and the content and style of her films have been explored by feminist and queer scholars, most notably Judith Mayne. Like many of her Hollywood cohorts, Arzner was neither in nor out of the closet as understood today; her relationships, including brief affairs with Alla Nazimova and Billie Burke, were known within the industry, as was her lengthy partnership with dancer/choreographer Marion Morgan (who is credited with influencing the use of dance in Arzner's films). In the 1950s, however, the revival of strict gender codes combined with a newer and virulent homophobia to render Arzner and her films both less relevant and potentially dangerous. This context may explain her 1978 remark, "The true reason I retired from Hollywood may forever remain a secret, and I'd rather it does."

Arzner died in California the next year on October 1, 1979, having finally received some of the attention she deserved. In 1975, the Director's Guild of America, of which she was the first female member, honored her with a tribute; reportedly Katharine Hepburn's telegram was read aloud: "Isn't it wonderful that you've had such a great career, when you had no right to have a career at all." Her star was added to the Hollywood Walk of Fame in 1986.

Selected Filmography

Dance, Girl, Dance (1940); *The Bride Wore Red* (1937); *The Last of Mrs. Cheyney* (1937); *Craig's Wife* (1936); *Nana* (1934); *Christopher Strong* (1933); *Merrily We Go to Hell* (1932); *Working Girls* (1931); *Honor among Lovers* (1931); *Galas de la Paramount* (1930); *Anybody's Woman* (1930); *Paramount on Parade* (1930); *Sarah and Son* (1930); *Behind the Make-Up* (1930); *The Wild Party* (1929); *Manhattan Cocktail* (1928); *Get Your Man* (1927); *Ten Modern Commandments* (1927); *Fashions for Women* (1927); *Blood and Sand* (1922)

References

Hadleigh, Boze. *Hollywood Lesbians*, New York: Barricade Books, 1994.

Johnston, Claire, ed. *The Work of Dorothy Arzner: Towards a Feminist Cinema*. London: British Film Institute, 1975.

Mayne, Judith. *Directed by Dorothy Arzner*. Bloomington: Indiana University Press, 1994.

Penley, Constance, ed. *Feminism and Film Theory*. New York: Routledge, 1988.

—Vicki L. Eaklor

ASHBY, HAL. Perhaps because there is no obvious distinctive voice unifying his work, Hal Ashby is often dismissed as a director whose greatest skill was knowing how to pick talented collaborators. A full 10 years older than fellow New Hollywood stalwarts Francis Ford Coppola, Peter Bogdanovich, and Martin Scorsese, he nevertheless grew his hair and beard long and refused to abandon his "hippie" existence, even after his younger contemporaries had embraced far more mainstream lifestyles.

Ashby was born into a Mormon family in Ogden, Utah, on September 2, 1929. His early life was disrupted by his parents divorce and his father's suicide. Leaving Utah as a young adult—having been the one who found his father after he killed himself—Ashby made his way to California, where he took his first job in the movie industry photocopying scripts for a film studio. Learning the business from the ground up, he ultimately became a film editor. Ashby had the good fortune of working on several movies with Norman Jewison, including his 1967 film *In the Heat of the Night*. After Ashby took home the Oscar for editing on that film, Jewison encouraged him to try his hand at directing. When Jewison bowed out of making *The Landlord* (1970), Ashby stepped in and took over the project. Based on the Kristin Hunter novel about a privileged white kid who buys a building in a New York ghetto and is changed by his experiences with his black tenants, the film starred Beau Bridges in the title role. The picture yielded a supporting Oscar nomination for Lee Grant, and was well received for its honest portrayal of the awkwardness of race relations.

Ashby followed *The Landlord* with *Harold and Maude*, the picture with which he is probably most closely associated. A little gem of a film, the movie explores the unique relationship that develops between the title characters, played with quirky grace by Bud Cort and Ruth Gordon. Although it would gain a cult following years later, *Harold and Maude* was neither well received critically nor a commercial success at the time of its release. Respecting Ashby's talent, however, Jack Nicholson suggested he consider directing *The Last Detail*. Robert Towne wrote a screenplay based on Darryl Ponicsan's novel of the same title, with Nicholson in mind for the lead. Beset by production problems—the project was nearly cancelled when Ashby was arrested for marijuana possession in Canada—the film nevertheless proved a success, earning the Palme d'Or and the Best Actor Award for Nicholson at the 1974 Cannes Film Festival. Towne, Nicholson, and Randy Quaid were all nominated for Oscars, although none of them won. Although it never gained the following that *Harold and Maude* did, a case can be made that *The Last Detail* is Ashby's best film, a rare offering that looks at working-class life without irony, condescension, or hand-wringing sentiment.

Ashby followed the success of *The Last Detail* with another collaborative effort with Towne. *Shampoo* (1975), Ashby's biggest commercial success, is a satire set on the eve of Richard Nixon's reelection (it was actually shot as the Watergate scandal unfolded). A drastic departure from the raw, hard-edged *The Last Detail*, *Shampoo* is an engaging film that explores the tangled web of sexual politics navigated by protagonist George Roundy, played with irresistible charm by co-writer Warren Beatty. *Bound for Glory* (1976), a slow-paced Woody Guthrie biopic, came next. Panned by critics and rejected by audiences, perhaps the only memorable thing about the film is that it was the first movie to use the Steadicam. Ashby's only Oscar nomination as Best Director came for *Coming Home* (1978), one of a number of antiwar, Vietnam epics released at the time—Michael Cimino's *The Deer Hunter* (1978) and Francis Ford Coppola's *Apocalypse Now* (1979) were two others. Although Ashby did not win his coveted Oscar for direction, the picture did earn awards for its screenplay and for Best Actress and Best Actor for leads Jane Fonda and Jon Voight.

By 1979, Ashby had given in to eccentricity and become reclusive and paranoid. Indulging in drugs more and more frequently, Ashby spent much of his time by himself, closed off in his Malibu beach house. Nevertheless, he was able to make *Being There*, an adaptation of a Jerzy Kosinski novel starring the extraordinarily gifted Peter Sellers as Chance, a gardener whose innocence is mistaken for wisdom by ever more powerful people.

Plagued by drug abuse and his chaotic lifestyle, Ashby's career went into decline after he made *Being There*. The Neil Simon–scripted *The Slugger's Wife* (1985), meant to be a light romantic comedy, is never light and only occasionally funny or romantic. As America turned increasingly conservative during the Reagan years, Ashby began to realize that his reputation as an eccentric was limiting his cinematic prospects. He cut his hair and trimmed his beard, and reportedly gave up drugs. Even so, there was little work available for him, apart from a pilot for the *Hill Street Blues* spin-off *Beverly Hills Buntz* (1987) and a sword-and-sorcery project with Monty Python's Graham Chapman, which was never completed. Only 59 years old, Ashby died at his Malibu home of pancreatic cancer on December 27, 1988.

Selected Filmography

8 Million Ways to Die (1986); *The Slugger's Wife* (1985); *Let's Spend the Night Together* (1983); *Lookin' to Get Out* (1982); *Second-Hand Hearts* (1981); *Being There* (1979); *Coming Home* (1978); *Bound for Glory* (1976); *Shampoo* (1975); *The Last Detail* (1973); *Harold and Maude* (1971); *The Landlord* (1970)

References

Biskind, Peter. *Easy Riders, Raging Bulls: How the Sex-Drugs-and-Rock-'n'-Roll Generation Saved Hollywood*. New York: Simon and Schuster, 1999.

Dawson, Nick. *Being Hal Ashby: Life of a Hollywood Rebel*. Lexington: University Press of Kentucky, 2009.

Friedman, Lester, ed. *American Cinema of the 1970s*. Newark, NJ: Rutgers University Press, 2007.

Harris, Mark. *Pictures at a Revolution: Five Movies and the Birth of the New Hollywood*. New York: Penguin, 2008.

—Bill Kte'pi

ASTAIRE, FRED. Fred Astaire, the debonair singing and dancing star of dozens of twentieth-century film musicals, is known worldwide as one of Hollywood's most respected and best-liked performers. Always well-mannered, and modest in his view of himself, Astaire managed to avoid celebrity scandal all his life while carving out a unique persona as a genteel yet thoroughly American figure who could casually bring high style to a popular song and, almost at a whim, spring into a dazzling dance solo or duet, captivating in its grace, athletic in its energy.

Born Frederick Austerlitz Jr. on May 10, 1899, in Omaha, Nebraska, Astaire was the second child of an Austrian immigrant, Frederick Austerlitz, and his American wife, Joanna Gelius. His older sister, Adele, demonstrated dance and performance abilities at an early age, and Astaire's mother bundled Fred and Adele off to New York when the boy was four-and-a-half years old in order to find a place for them on the vaudeville stage. In his autobiography, *Steps in Time*, Astaire indicates that this sudden change in his life was not unwelcome—it represented the possibility for adventure, as he and his sister worked the prestigious Orpheum vaudeville circuit for a time, and then began to ascend the show business ladder

One of America's favorite entertainers, Fred Astaire danced with a winning, effortless style that drew life from ingenious combinations of tap, ballroom, and ballet dancing. (Library of Congress)

by making musicals in London and New York. In the late 1920s and early 1930s, they performed in shows written by some of the best composers of the day—George Gershwin, Cole Porter, and the team of Howard Dietz and Arthur Schwartz.

By 1933, Adele Astaire had retired and Fred moved on to Hollywood, where he had been offered a small role playing himself in an MGM musical, *Dancing Lady*. RKO Studios eventually offered him fifth billing in *Flying Down to Rio*, in which he would be teamed for the first time with Ginger Rogers. Cast as a couple, Rogers and Astaire stole the show from the three performers whose names appeared above theirs on the marquee—Dolores Del Rio, Gene Raymond, and Raul Roulien. It was the pair's mesmerizing dance routine of the tango-like "Carioca" that caught the public's eye, something that did not go unnoticed by the studio heads at RKO, which made Rogers and Astaire headliners in their next film. Appearing together in a number of subsequent films, the pair became a top 10 box-office draw for several years in the mid-1930s.

The black-and-white pictures Astaire made with Rogers for RKO ultimately came to define him. Most of these films were directed by Mark Sandrich, with Hermes Pan assisting Astaire in choreographing the dance numbers, Pandro S. Berman producing, and Carroll Clark providing the art direction (within a visual mode originated by Van Nest Polglase). Fairy-tale sets with glossy dance floors and lots of formal wear, especially for the men, characterized these confections.

The Gay Divorcee was the first, and one of the two best, of the six quintessential Astaire-Rogers RKO productions. Rogers was never lovelier than she was when she played Mimi Glossop in this film. Mimi is a reluctant partner to Astaire's Guy Holden, who woos her with his dazzling dance moves. In the film's signature dance sequence, set to Cole Porter's languorous "Night and Day," Holden, in white tie and tails, seduces the shy Mimi, drawing her into an elegant dance floor courtship, the two in perfect romantic harmony.

In the 1940s and '50s, after the Astaire-Rogers team had split, Astaire appeared in several spectacular color film musicals (mostly for MGM), including *Easter Parade*, *Royal Wedding*, *The Band Wagon*, *Daddy Long Legs*, *Funny Face*, and *Silk Stockings*. In these pictures, he was paired with a new generation of dance and film partners, including Judy Garland, Jane Powell, Leslie Caron, and Cyd Charisse.

Noted as a couples dancer, Astaire was often unfavorably compared to Gene Kelly as a solo performer; although in individual sequences such as his Bojangles dance in *Swing Time*, he nevertheless delighted audiences. Although clearly an incredibly gifted dancer, whether performing with a partner or by himself, it may be that Astaire is, indeed, best remembered in top hat and tails, gliding across the dance floor with Rogers in his early RKO musicals.

Astaire was married to Phyllis Livingston Potter for 21 years before her death in 1954; and to Robyn Smith from 1980 until his death on June 22, 1987, in Los Angeles.

See also: Musical, The; Romantic Comedy, The

References

Astaire, Fred. *Steps in Time*. New York: Harper & Brothers, 1959.
Croce, Arlene. *The Fred Astaire & Ginger Rogers Book*. New York: Galahad, 1972.

—*James Delmont*

B

BEATTY, WARREN. In 1967, Warren Beatty starred in and produced Arthur Penn's controversial *Bonnie and Clyde*. The film elicited significant critical debate, pitting traditional critics such as Bosley Crowther against hip, liberal provocateurs such as Pauline Kael. Most importantly, perhaps, the film had far-reaching effects on the Hollywood film industry, supercharging Beatty's career, bringing forward a brace of new talent (Faye Dunaway, Gene Hackman, David Newman, Robert Benton, and others), and inaugurating a profoundly important phase of countercultural American filmmaking at the end of the 1960s.

Interestingly, although Beatty during the late 1960s was emblematic of a new type of Hollywood filmmaking, he also remained wedded to the traditions of the earlier studio system era. Indeed, although he is identified as one of the figures in Hollywood that facilitated the decline of the studio system, it is important to note that Beatty actually provided a bridge between Hollywood's past and its late twentieth-century present. Handsome, hip, and provocative, Beatty embodied the matinee idol ideal of Hollywood's golden era; as a producer, he created affectionate remakes of classic films—*Heaven Can Wait* (1978) and *Love Affair* (1994), for example; and as a director, he provided audiences with pictures that seemed to be homages to cinematic icons—*Bulworth* (1998), for instance, has a Frank Capra-like man-against-corrupt-society feel, while *Reds* (1981) bears the unmistakable mark of David Lean's sweeping period epics. Beatty, then, comes into focus as an intermediate figure straddling old and new Hollywood.

Born Henry Warren Beaty, in Virginia on March 30, 1937, he began to study acting in New York at age 20; his sister, Shirley MacLaine, was already a successful Hollywood actor at this point. Highly regarded roles in television and local theatre led Beatty onto the Broadway stage. He won approving notices for his 1959 debut in William Inge's *A Loss of Roses*, and immediately turned his sights toward movie roles. Elia Kazan's *Splendor in the Grass* (1961) launched Beatty's Hollywood career and brought the young actor almost instant stardom. Playing opposite Natalie Wood, and working from a script penned by Inge, Beatty was called upon to convey to viewers a sense of tormented masculinity; film critics and audiences alike found his performance incredibly

Warren Beatty (right, shown here with his wife, actress Annette Bening) is a popular actor and filmmaker. He began his career as a leading man but has expanded his talents to include producing, writing, and directing. Beatty produced, directed, and starred in the 1981 film *Reds* and won the Academy Award for Best Director. (Getty Images)

moving, and Beatty began to be compared to actors like Marlon Brando and other screen rebels of the 1950s.

Wary of typecasting, Beatty sought to diversify. He was improbably but ingeniously cast as an Italian libertine in *The Roman Spring of Mrs. Stone* (1962), adapted from the only novel by Tennessee Williams. He was even willing to take roles that did not elicit viewer empathy, consciously choosing to play characters that tended to be both apathetic (*All Fall Down*, 1962) and opaque (*Lilith*, 1964). These films, along with Arthur Penn's *Mickey One* (1965), showcased Beatty's steadily expanding screen repertoire. A brief hiatus in Britain yielded two uninspired pictures, *Promise Her Anything* (1965) and *Kaleidoscope* (1966); although he demonstrated a deft comedic touch and deepening screen persona in these films, neither was praised. Against these prosaic comedies, the adventurous *Bonnie and Clyde* stood out in startling relief.

During this period Beatty's screen persona coalesced, and it found an ideal context in the 1970s New Hollywood. Blending character flaws with the Hollywood hero's optimism, the Beatty protagonist proved able to support the sort of pessimistic and revisionist storytelling being imported from European art-house cinema. In Robert Altman's *McCabe and Mrs. Miller* (1971), for instance, Beatty's frontier hero fosters romantic ideals, but his aspirations are dashed thanks to the character's fatal hubris. With its hesitant and ineffectual protagonist, the film constitutes a piercing rebuttal not only of the myths of American ideology and identity, but of the classic Hollywood westerns that promoted and propagated them. *McCabe and Mrs. Miller* also cemented Beatty's taste for entrepreneurial characters blighted by personal failure or external aggressors. Sometimes the Beatty protagonist is motivated by wholly material concerns (*Dollars/$*, a.k.a. *The Heist*, 1971), but often he harbors more exalted aspirations, as in *McCabe and Mrs. Miller* and *Bonnie and Clyde*. Recurrently, the character's psychological flaws accelerate his failure or death. This doomed element of Beatty's persona meshed with the downbeat denouements of New Hollywood pictures, and later films such as *Bugsy* (1991) and *Bulworth* would extend the trope into the age of the blockbuster. For some critics, the bleak climatic sequences of the latter films supplied evidence of Beatty's vanity and narcissism; for others, it revealed the poignancy of curtailed enterprise, delivering affecting stabs of pathos.

By the 1970s, Beatty was becoming increasingly well known not only as an actor/director, but also as a ladies' man and political activist. Significantly, his offscreen pursuits informed his cinematic projects. Agitated by the assassinations of John and Robert Kennedy and Martin Luther King, he embraced subject matter that seemed overtly political. *The Parallax View* (1974), for example, presents a formally spare depiction of political conspiracy and cover-up; shot in the wake of Beatty's Democratic fundraisers for George McGovern, the film's shadowy intrigue offers an apocalyptic view of Nixonian America. Hal Ashby's *Shampoo* (1975) went even further, wedding the erotic to the political by framing Beatty's hypersexualized, anticonformist lead character within the boundaries of the 1968 presidential campaign, which saw the election of Richard Nixon and the first glimpse of the moral-majority America that would emerge in earnest during the Reagan-era 1980s.

Unadorned by political pretensions, *The Fortune* (1975) and *Heaven Can Wait* are apt to look frivolous compared to *Shampoo*, but both films are consistent with Hollywood's growing optimism from 1975 onward. The movies aptly demonstrated Beatty's comedic skills—in *The Fortune* he utilizes darting glances, knitted brows, and clipped speech to create a staid counterpoint to Jack Nicholson's zany swindler, while in the wistful love story *Heaven Can Wait*, he adopted a gentler comedic tone playing opposite his then real-life companion Julie Christie. The latter film in particular generated huge revenues ($80 million worldwide), and at this point Beatty seized greater artistic control of his projects, turning to screenwriting and directing, and assuming the role of producer for the first time since *Bonnie and Clyde*.

Although during the 1980s Beatty's output dwindled, it was during this time that he made one of his most important, ambitious, and highly regarded films, *Reds*, which earned him the Best Director Oscar. A biopic of American John Reed, the film managed to fuse a sweeping historical examination of the masses caught up in the Russian Revolution with intimate portrayals of individuals caught up in the drama of the moment. Unlike Beatty's 1970s films, *Reds* seemed wholly incongruous with its industrial and cultural context. Institutionally, its historical subject matter flouted a current trend for conservative filmmaking based on spectacle. Politically, its sympathetic approach to the Russian Revolution contradicted an ethos of Reaganite capitalism. Clearly an instance of "personal filmmaking," *Reds* is considered by many critics Beatty's major cinematic achievement. Beatty's star dimmed a bit in the late 1980s when he—along with Dustin Hoffman—made the ill-advised decision to participate in Elaine May's disastrous project *Ishtar* (1987), an innocuous comedy with a bloated budget ($40 million) that proved not only a critical disappointment but a complete box-office failure.

As the 1990s opened, Beatty made one of his most provocative pictures, *Dick Tracy* (1990), a triumph of special effects characterized by a splashy comic-strip aesthetic. Steeped in noir iconography, the picture revived classic filmmaking techniques and was heralded as a nostalgic paean to both 1930s Hollywood and Chester Gould's original comic strip. Having become involved with Madonna—who co-starred with him in *Dick Tracy*—Beatty appeared in her filmic memoir, *Madonna: Truth or Dare* (1991), which chronicled the singer's experiences during her notorious "Blond Ambition" tour. Offering up fawning observations about his former lover, Beatty seemed less the self-assured ladies' man and more the awkward adolescent with a school-boy crush on the iconic rock star. Interestingly, the same year that *Madonna: Truth or Dare* was released, Beatty would go on to star in and produce the Barry Levinson gangster biopic *Bugsy* (1991); while making the picture, the long-time bachelor fell in love with his co-star Annette Bening, and they eventually married.

Beatty and Bening would co-star in the less-than-inspired *Love Affair* (1994)—Katharine Hepburn's final screen appearance—before Beatty made the intriguing political satire *Bulworth* in 1998. Increasingly, though, critics began to characterize Beatty as a film industry figure flirting with absence—not only because he made fewer and fewer films, but because to some he seemed almost to be a spectral, remote figure on screen. Significantly, the notorious micro-manager turned over control of the much maligned *Town & Country* (2001) to director Peter Chelsom; and as the early 2000s unfolded, it seemed that Beatty—his cinematic legacy long since assured—favoured familial domesticity over moviemaking, as he limited public appearances to political events and career retrospectives.

Selected Filmography

Town & Country (2001); *Bulworth* (1998); *Love Affair* (1994); *Bugsy* (1991); *Dick Tracy* (1990); *Ishtar* (1987); *Reds* (1981); *Heaven Can Wait* (1978); *The Fortune* (1975); *Shampoo* (1975); *The Parallax View* (1974); *$* (1971); *McCabe and Mrs. Miller* (1971); *The Only Game in Town* (1970); *Bonnie and Clyde* (1967); *Kaleidoscope* (1966); *Promise Her Anything* (1965); *Mickey One* (1965); *Lilith* (1964); *All Fall Down* (1962); *The Roman Spring of Mrs. Stone* (1961); *Splendor in the Grass* (1961)

References

Crowther, Bosley. "*Bonnie and Clyde* Arrives," *New York Times*, August 14, 1967; and Kael, Pauline. "Bonnie and Clyde," *New Yorker*, October 21, 1967. Reviews reprinted in Friedman, Lester D. ed. *Arthur Penn's Bonnie and Clyde*. New York: Cambridge University Press, 2000.

Thomson, David. *Warren Beatty and Desert Eyes: A Life and a Story*. London: Secker & Warburg, 1990.

—*Gary Bettinson*

BERGMAN, INGRID. Ingrid Bergman was born in Stockholm, Sweden, on August 29, 1915, to a Swedish father and German mother. Losing both of her parents at an early age, she went to stay with an aunt and uncle. At the age of 18, Bergman was accepted at the Royal Dramatic Theatre School in Stockholm, where she studied acting and made her stage debut. Her first film role came in Gustaf Molander's *Munkbrogreven* in 1935. A year later she starred in Molander's *Intermezzo*, the film that would propel her to stardom on the big screen. *Intermezzo* caught the attention of Hollywood producer David O. Selznick, who bought the rights to remake the film in English, with Bergman in mind for the lead role. The Hollywood version (1939) of the film was such a success that Selznick signed Bergman to a seven-year contract. Bergman, however, made only two films with Selznick, partly because he took a break from making films, and partly because Bergman was loaned out to other studios by Selznick. She played a variety of roles during this early period in her career, including a Victorian barmaid in MGM's *Dr. Jekyll and Mr. Hyde* (1941), and the iconic Ilsa, opposite Humphrey Bogart's Rick, in Warner Bros.' *Casablanca* (1942).

Selznick persuaded Ernest Hemingway that the beautiful young actress was perfect for the female lead in *For Whom the Bell Tolls* (1943); her performance earned Bergman her first Best Actress Academy Award nomination. She would win the first of her three Best Actress Oscars the following year for *Gaslight* (1944), in which she portrays a naive wife driven toward insanity by her husband. *Gaslight* is one of several films in which Bergman's character suffers at the hands of her husband—others included *Notorious* (1946) and *Under Capricorn* (1949), both directed by Alfred Hitchcock, who also directed Bergman in *Spellbound* (1945). Proving her versatility as an actress, Bergman played Sister Mary Benedict in her next film, *The Bells of St. Mary's* (1945). Featuring fan-favorite Bing Crosby as Father Chuck O'Malley, the friendly rival of Sister Mary at the local parish, the picture proved to be Bergman's biggest box-office success and earned her another Academy Award nomination. In 1946, she returned to the stage, playing the lead role in *Joan of Lorraine* on Broadway. The performance earned her a Tony Award for Best Actress. In 1949, she went on to star in *Joan of Arc*, a screen adaptation of *Joan of Lorraine*. Although the film was a box-office disappointment, Bergman received another Best Actress Academy Award nomination for her performance.

Later in 1949, Bergman made the fateful decision to send Italian director Roberto Rossellini what was basically a fan letter, in which she indicated that she was very much interested in working with him. Rossellini responded by rewriting a part in his script for *Stromboli* and offering the role to Bergman (1949). While filming *Stromboli*, Bergman and Rossellini, both married, began a torrid affair. Both would seek divorces from their current spouses, although Bergman's husband agreed to their split only after she revealed to him that she was carrying Rossellini's child, a son, Roberto, who was born in 1950. Although Bergman and Rossellini ultimately married, news of the couple's affair, and of Bergman's willingness to leave not only her husband but also their daughter to be with Rossellini, cost her many of her American fans and negatively affected her Hollywood career. Bergman and Rossellini lived in Italy and made five films

Film star Ingrid Bergman reclines against the arm of a sofa, 1941. (Getty Images)

together between 1950 and 1955. In 1952, Bergman gave birth to twin girls, one of whom, Isabella, became a noted actress and model.

Bergman worked solely with Rossellini until 1956, when she made *Elena et les hommes* with Jean Renoir, a film that reignited international interest in the actress. During the same year, she was welcomed back to Hollywood, starring in the Twentieth Century-Fox production of *Anastasia*, for which she won another Best Actress Oscar. Although her Hollywood career was back on track, her relationship with Rossellini was deteriorating, and the couple divorced in 1957.

In 1959, Bergman won an Emmy for her lead role in a television production of *The Turn of the Screw*; and in 1965, she made her London theatre debut. She won her third Academy Award in 1974—a Best Supporting Actress Oscar—for her role in *Murder on the Orient Express*. Divorced from her third husband and diagnosed with cancer in 1975, Bergman made her last film in 1978, Ingmar Bergman's *Autumn Sonata*. Her final role came in the television miniseries *A Woman Called Golda*, in which she played the part of Golda Meir. The role won Bergman an Emmy and a Golden Globe. She died in London on August 29, 1989 on her 67th birthday.

References

Benshoff, Harry M., and Sean Griffin. *America on Film: Representing Race, Class, Gender, and Sexuality.* Malden, MA: Blackwell, 2004.
Jewell, Richard B. *The RKO Story.* London: Octopus, 1982.
Macpherson, Don, and Louise Brody. *Leading Ladies.* London: Conran Octopus, 1986.

—*Victoria Williams*

BERKELEY, BUSBY. Busby Berkeley William Enos was a choreographer and a director who helped revitalize the movie musical in the 1930s. Born to a theatrical family in Los Angeles on November 29, 1895, Berkeley served in the U.S. Army during World War I. He eventually made his way to New York, where he became both an actor and a choreographer. His choreography impressed film critics and studio heads alike, and when actor Eddie Cantor went to Hollywood to star in *Whoopee* (1930), Berkeley was sent along to choreograph the film. Prior to Berkeley's work, musical numbers in movies were filmed with a stationary camera. Berkeley freed the camera so that rather than merely showing the chorus girls dance, the camera moved about them as they created various kaleidoscopic patterns that were recorded from the sides, the front, the back, and especially from above.

In 1933, Berkeley moved to Warner Bros. There, for eight years, he choreographed numbers for some of the studio's best musicals, each more sophisticated, larger, and more spectacular than the previous one. Warner Bros. had been on the verge of bankruptcy when Berkeley was asked to choreograph *42nd Street* (1933). In this film he choreographed the dance

A still from Busby Berkeley's *Gold Diggers of 1933*. Berkeley was famous for using his dancers to create stunning geometric patterns on-screen. (Underwood & Underwood/Corbis)

numbers using the same techniques he had employed before: the mobile camera, cutting to expand the dance space, close-ups of beautiful girls, and overhead shots. He also packed the dance numbers together at the end of the movie. The film was a success and established Berkeley as one of Hollywood's most important choreographers. That same year he choreographed *Gold Diggers of 1933*. Like *42nd Street*, this film starred Ruby Keeler and Dick Powell. It is memorable because in one number, "The Shadow Waltz," Berkeley used the new technology of neon lights.

Also in 1933, he choreographed *Footlight Parade*, which included the song "By a Waterfall." This was one of the first cinematic production numbers to be shot as a water ballet. Until he moved to MGM in 1939, Berkeley choreographed and directed 19 more films for Warner Bros. While not all were musicals—he made the crime drama *They Made Me A Criminal* in 1939, for instance—most of the pictures were. They included such visually arresting production numbers as the title song of *Dames* (1934) and "Lullaby of Broadway" in *Gold Diggers of 1935*.

After Berkeley moved to MGM, he directed and choreographed three Mickey Rooney-Judy Garland musicals. He was also in charge of *For Me And My Gal* (1942), and in 1943 he choreographed the "I Got Rhythm" number in *Girl Crazy*. While these numbers were less ambitious than the work he had done at Warner Bros., they were still imaginative. Also in 1943, he directed and choreographed *The Gang's All Here* for Twentieth Century-Fox. This formulaic wartime musical, starring Alice Faye and Carmen Miranda, included some of his most fantastic and creative work. For Carmen Miranda he choreographed "The Lady in the Tutti-Frutti Hat." In the 1960s, this number, which included a 60-foot-high headpiece for Carmen Miranda, was considered the height of camp. He also choreographed the stunning "Polka Dot Polka" for Alice Faye. In the late 1940s and early '50s, he did three films with Esther Williams. The finale of *Easy to Love* (1953), which was filmed in Florida, included Williams diving from a helicopter over 100 water-skiers. Berkeley's last film was as the second-unit director for 1962's *Jumbo*, in which he directed and choreographed most of the musical numbers. In 1971, Berkeley directed and choreographed Ruby Keeler in *No, No Nanette* on Broadway. This was his last professional production. He died on March 14, 1978, at the age of 80, in his home near Palm Springs, California.

Although budget constraints make it almost impossible to include the kind of elaborate song-and-dance productions favored by Berkeley in contemporary musicals, his visual sense, innovative camerawork, and creative staging continue to shape almost every musical from the 1930s forward.

Selected Filmography

Take Me Out to the Ball Game (1949); *Cinderella Jones* (1946); *The Gang's All Here* (1943); *Cabin in the Sky* (1943); *For Me and My Gal* (1942); *Babes on Broadway* (1941); *Ziegfeld Girl* (1941); *Blonde Inspiration* (1941); *Strike Up the Band* (1940); *Forty Little Mothers* (1940); *Fast and Furious* (1939); *Babes in Arms* (1939); *They Made Me a Criminal* (1939); *Comet Over Broadway* (1938); *Garden of the Moon* (1938); *Men Are Such Fools* (1938); *Hollywood Hotel* (1937); *The Go Getter* (1937); *Stage Struck* (1936); *I Live for Love* (1935); *Bright Lights* (1935); *Gold Diggers of 1935* (1935); *Dames* (1934); *She Had to Say Yes* (1933); *42nd Street* (1933)

References

Hanley, Robert. "Busby Berkeley, the Dance Director, Dies." *New York Times (1857-Current file)*, March 15, 1976. Available at http://www.proquest.com.

Pike, Bob, and Dave Martin. *The Genius of Busby Berkeley*. Reseda, CA: CFS Books, 1973.

Rubin, Martin. *Showstoppers: Busby Berkeley and the Tradition of Spectacle*. New York: Columbia University Press, 1993.

Thomas, Tony, and Jim Terry, with Busby Berkeley. *The Busby Berkeley Book*. Greenwich, CT: New York Graphic Society, 1973.

—*Scott Sheidlower*

BERRY, HALLE. Halle Berry, beauty queen, spokesmodel, actress, and producer, was the first woman of color to receive the Academy Award for Best Actress. One of the highest-paid actresses in Hollywood, she is also one of the few African American performers to have received an Emmy Award, Golden Globe, and Screen Actors Guild Award (Ewey Johnson, 2008). She garnered all three of these awards for her work in the HBO biopic *Introducing Dorothy Dandridge* (1998), on which she also served as executive producer. Berry has been instrumental in breaking down barriers that have long restricted women of color from playing roles other than those as maids, servants, or prostitutes.

Actress Halle Berry poses during a press conference for the film *X-Men: The Last Stand*, at the 59th International Film Festival in Cannes in 2006. Berry became the first African American women to win the Academy Award for Best Actress, for her performance in *Monster's Ball*, 2001. (AP/Wide World Photos)

Born Maria Halle Berry on August 14, 1966, in Cleveland, Ohio, to Judith Ann Hawkins, a psychiatric nurse from England, and an African American man Jerome Berry, who worked as a hospital attendant, she changed her name legally to Halle Berry in 1971. Her parents divorced when she was four; she has an older sister, Heide, from whom she is estranged. She graduated from Bedford High School and attended Cuyahoga Community College. Berry began entering beauty contests in the 1980s. She won the "Miss Teen All American" pageant in 1985, and a year later, the "Miss Ohio USA" pageant. She was a "Miss USA" runner-up, and subsequently the first African American entrant in the "Miss World" contest. Deciding to try her hand at acting, she secured a role in the spin-off series *Living Dolls* in 1989, playing the character of Emily Franklin; she followed this with a regular role on the popular television series *Knots Landing*. Appearing in music videos and a significant number of films during the 1990s, she won several important awards for her performances.

In 1991, Berry appeared in what many consider her break-out role in Spike Lee's *Jungle Fever*, which starred Wesley Snipes and Annabella Sciorra. She went on to co-star in the film *Strictly Business* (1991). This was followed by appearances in *The Last Boy Scout*, with Bruce Willis (1991) and *Boomerang* (1992), which starred Eddie Murphy, Martin Lawrence, and Chris Rock. Berry also continued her work in television, starring in the ABC miniseries *Queen: The Story of an American Family* (1992)—adapted from an Alex Haley book—for which she won an NAACP Image Award. In 1994, Berry played the role of the seductive secretary Sharon Stone in the movie *The Flintstones*. A more serious role came in *Losing Isaiah* (1995), in which she played a recovering drug addict attempting to regain custody of her son. Berry became a spokesmodel for Revlon in 1996, and later secured contracts with Versace and Cody Inc. She received critical acclaim for her role in the political satire *Bulworth* (1998), starring opposite Warren Beatty. In 1999, Berry took the role of Dorothy Dandridge in HBO's critically acclaimed biography of the performer. Ironically, the real Dorothy Dandridge was the first African American woman to be nominated for the Academy Award for Best Actress. Berry would go on to win that award in 2001, for her role in *Monster's Ball* opposite Billy Bob Thornton (Mapp, 2008).

Berry starred in several blockbusters after receiving the Academy Award, including the *X-Men* trilogy (2000–2006), *Die Another Day* (2002), and *Catwoman* (2004); she received $12.5 million for the latter picture, an enormous sum for a female actor. In 2005, Berry returned to television, starring in the Oprah Winfrey adaptation of the Zora Neale Hurston novel *Their Eyes Were Watching God*. Berry continues to be one of the hardest-working actors in America.

References

Ewey Johnson, Melissa. *Halle Berry: A Biography*. Westport, CT: Greenwood, 2009.

Farley, Christopher John. *Introducing Halle Berry*. New York: Pocket Books, 2002.

Mapp, Edward. *African Americans and the Oscar: Decades of Struggle and Achievement*. Lanham, MD: Rowman & Littlefield, 2008.

—*Hettie Williams*

BIGELOW, KATHRYN. Of the more than two dozen women who have both written and directed films in the United States over the past three decades, Kathryn Bigelow (born November 27, 1951) has enjoyed a greater measure of critical esteem than many of her contemporaries, though only occasionally an equal measure of box-office success. She has been praised repeatedly—and somewhat ironically—as the most "masculine" of feminine directors working today, chiefly because she continues to display a fascination for action narratives and for characters caught up in violent conflict. Seldom will any reviewer of her films abstain from the use of phrases like "testosterone-charged" and "adrenalin rush" to describe the energy and momentum of the human drama that is indeed central to all of her work, and the implied subtext of such commentary would seem to be that Bigelow has somehow intruded on an otherwise masculine domain once exclusively dominated by a Don Siegel or a Sam Peckinpah.

Curiously, for an action-oriented, high-intensity filmmaker, Bigelow's creative roots lie in the more cerebral forms of painting known as conceptual art, and she continues to think of her work in largely visual terms. Her decision to shift the focus of her art

Academy Award-winning film director Kathryn Bigelow speaks during the 2010 Ernst & Young Strategic Growth Forum in Palm Springs, California, on Saturday, November 13, 2010. Bigelow won an Oscar for Best Director for her film *The Hurt Locker*, which won a total of six Academy Awards, including Best Picture, in 2008. (Bloomberg/Getty Images)

work from painting to cinema—signaled by her move from the Art Institute of San Francisco to the Film Program at Columbia University—was inspired by the belief that filmmaking would allow her to communicate a greater range of expressive possibilities. Her subsequent determination, however, not to enter the industry "ghetto" reserved for novice women directors, making the kind of movies commonly known as "chick flicks," reflects a consistent desire for independence from the studio system and its assumptions about culture and gender, assumptions she has challenged consistently throughout her career.

Bigelow's earliest films are thus both deliberately imitative and just as deliberately transgressive, taking up a familiar genre and then proceeding to twist it out of shape. Her debut film, *The Loveless* (1982), co-directed with Monty Montgomery, is a stylized homage to *The Wild One* (1954) with Willem Dafoe cast in the Marlon Brando role of a moody, impulsively violent leader of a motorcycle gang going "nowhere." Unfortunately, Bigelow's narrative focus constantly shifts away from the impending conflict between unruly outsiders and redneck townsfolk toward the interior conflicts of her biker protagonist, leaving her audience uncertain as to whether she has any story to tell.

Her next venture in genre exploitation/experimentation—a far more successful one, both artistically and commercially—is a fusion of two otherwise unrelated film types: the horror movie and the western. *Near Dark* (1987) follows the gruesome adventures of a family of gypsy vampires, whose violent assaults on an assortment of victims are filmed with an unsettling mixture of humor and film noir dread, and once again

Bigelow seems far more interested in the interpersonal dynamic of this "family" than in accounting for their past or present existence. By taking her nightmare characters out of Transylvania and placing them on the dusty plains of Oklahoma, Bigelow renders the traditional horror tale almost mundane, a tendency that becomes even more marked when the unwitting cowboy protagonist of the film (played by Adrian Pasdar) falls in love with a bloodsucking (but otherwise sweet and affectionate) young blonde (Jenny Wright), shifting the center of this drama away from murder-and-vampire mayhem toward romance and redemption. Curing vampires of their homicidal addiction through blood transfusions risks a descent into comic banality, but Bigelow's determination to bring her cowboy-meets-girl vampire story to a happy ending overrides whatever the conventions of either genre seem to demand.

Bigelow's next experiment in genre-busting is the far more successful *Blue Steel* (1989), which takes the demands of the cop-thriller far more seriously than the aesthetic of the B-horror flick, and as a result she is able to center her film on a complex and conflicted heroine. Jamie Lee Curtis's Megan Turner—a novice cop who must simultaneously defend her own life and rescue New York City from a psychopathic serial-killer (who is also a would-be suitor)—is obliged to play two iconic yet incompatible roles: a castrating urban combatant whose revolver becomes a fetishized object of seduction and destruction, and a daughter-lover whose ambivalence toward the men in her life draws her in several contradictory directions at once. Megan's humiliation of her abusive father, her refusal to be either dehumanized or defeminized by the patriarchal police culture she is a part of, and her steely determination to destroy a virtually demonic predator/lover (played with maniacal charm by Ron Silver), who seemingly cannot be killed by ordinary bullets, all raise her to an almost mythic level of feminist counter-aggression. Yet Curtis's performance intimates both fragility and emotional longing, qualities one would never associate with a stereotyped woman warrior.

Bigelow's next film, *Point Break* (1991), attempts a similar transformation of all-too-familiar action figures into conflicted antiheroes, engaged in an existential test of wills and self-knowledge. Her antagonists this time are a callow FBI agent, Johnny Utah (played with characteristic inexpressiveness by Keanu Reeves), and a surfer-bank-robber-guru named Bodhi—short for *bodhisattva*—played by the late Patrick Swayze in what would become one of his signature roles. That *Point Break* has achieved the status of a cult favorite among Bigelow's admirers should surprise no one: it contains precisely those oppositional themes and subversive ironies that practically all of her films exhibit, only presented here with even greater energy and panache. Her surfer-bank robbers are thus not an ordinary band of thieves but a family of outsiders, dedicated to ridiculing "the system." Disguising themselves as ex-presidents Reagan, Carter, and Nixon, they begin to take on some of the satiric personae these masks connote, culminating in a scene where, in the midst of a bank heist, the "Nixon" robber holds his hands aloft and shouts "I am not a thief." That they are destroyed by an almost adolescent belief in their invincibility rather than by the intelligence and fortitude of the government agents who are hot on their path tells us a great deal about just how ambivalently Bigelow views her criminal protagonists, and a similar inversion of moral perspective occurs when Reeves's boyishly naive hero finally realizes his secret sharer connection to the gang's leader, throwing away his badge and his career in a gesture made famous by Gary Cooper's Marshal Will Kane in *High Noon*.

Bigelow's 1995 sci-fi extravaganza *Strange Days*—written and produced by her ex-husband, James Cameron—failed to attract the audiences that flocked to *Point Break*, in spite of its more ambitious visual style and apocalyptic subject. Set years before the actual fin-de-siècle, the film invokes the specter of the Last Days, with Los Angeles on the eve of the new millennium as the battleground on which the armies of the night will clash, and "civilization as we know it" will move closer to the abyss. Her shambling weakling of a protagonist, Lenny Nero—played with a persistent whine by Ralph Fiennes—moves about in a surreal cyber world of bootleg porno and snuff CDs that tap directly into the cerebral cortex, enabling the user to re-experience the most violent (usually erotic) acts with unbearable intensity. Part *Blade Runner*, part *Day of the Locust*, Bigelow's nightmare future is an obviously derivative dystopia, complete with imminent race wars and pervasive police corruption, and with only a determined African American heroine (played with equal tenderness and ferocity by Angela Bassett) to save the day. Movie critics were largely unimpressed by both the visual razzle-dazzle and the forced romantic denouement of this film, and *Strange Days* was seen by many as an ambitious but expensive flop.

Bigelow's next two films represent a departure from the world of subversive mayhem and existential irony that have marked her work up to this point. *The Weight of Water* (2000), based on a novel of the same title by Anita Shreve, juxtaposes the tortured lives and psyches of two different families, separated by a century but brought together by a dynamic of sexual longing and moral confusion, coupled with betrayal by the men in their lives. Bigelow clearly wants the viewer to see these two family melodramas as reflecting images, one of the other, but the parallel stories never entirely intertwine, and the violent acts that punctuate the lives of both never really move us toward insight or even empathy. *K-19: The Widow-Maker* (2002) is a far more conventional Cold War action-thriller, with practically every movie cliché of submarine warfare dusted off for use in this predictable exercise in testosterone-driven personality conflicts in a very small space. Not even the talents of Liam Neeson and Harrison Ford, as two rival captains of an endangered Russian sub, can rescue this film from ultimate banality.

Bigelow's most recent film, *The Hurt Locker* (2009), has rescued a career that seemed to be moving irresistibly toward the margins of contemporary filmmaking, with a remarkably candid, largely cinéma vérité representation of the face of war in Iraq, and of the inner lives of the men who have fought that war. Her central figure, Sergeant James (superbly underplayed by Jeremy Renner), heads a bomb-disposal squad, and his task is to defuse the omnipresent IEDs without blowing up his comrades or himself in the process. What we (and Renner's character) soon discover is that he enjoys his work—the danger and the resultant adrenalin rush—far more than anything else in his life. Bigelow's observation that "War's dirty little secret is that some men love it" is convincingly borne out when we view her otherwise fearless warrior baffled and distressed while shopping for breakfast cereals in a supermarket, and her protagonist's return to the front follows with a kind of tragic inevitability once we have viewed his extreme discomfort with civilian life. In *The Hurt Locker* Bigelow finally appears to have found an action vehicle that can bear the weight of moral reflection without collapsing under it. This view was obviously shared by members of the Motion Picture Academy, which voted Bigelow Best Director of 2009—the first woman to have received this award in the Academy's history—and also awarded *The Hurt Locker* an Oscar for Best Picture.

Selected Filmography

The Hurt Locker (2008); *K-19: The Widowmaker* (2002); *The Weight of Water* (2000); *Strange Days* (1995); *Point Break* (1991); *Near Dark* (1987); *The Loveless* (1982); *The Set-Up* (1978)

References

Dargis, Manohla. "Action!" *New York Times*, June 18, 2009.

Jermyn, Deborah, and Sean Redmond, eds. *The Cinema of Kathryn Bigelow: Hollywood Transgressor*. London: Wallflower, 2003.

Karnicky, Jeff. "Georges Bataille and the Visceral Cinema of Kathryn Bigelow." *Enculturation* 2 (1), Fall 1998.

Rosefelt, Reid. "Kathryn Bigelow: Don't Look Back." *SpeedCine*, July 13, 2009.

—*Robert Platzner*

BOGDANOVICH, PETER.   Peter Bogdanovich, born on July 30, 1939, in Kingston, New York, is unique in the history of cinema. He is a film critic, film historian, screenwriter, composer, producer, author, actor, and director. As a young boy in New York, he was exposed by his father, a Serbian artist, to the wonder of silent and talking movies. Two films in particular remained in Bogdanovich's psyche, Howard Hawks's *Red River* (1948) and John Ford's *She Wore a Yellow Ribbon* (1949). Bogdanovich's passion for film was firmly in place, and he estimates that between the ages of 12 and 30 he saw over 4,000 movies.

In the late 1950s and early 1960s, Bogdanovich wrote film criticism for various publications, beginning with *Film Culture, Film Quarterly*, and *Movie*, and eventually went on to popular national publications such as *Esquire, Vogue*, and the *Saturday Evening Post*. He produced a series of monographs for the Museum of Modern Art on directors Howard Hawks, Alfred Hitchcock, and Orson Welles, and wrote books on Allan Dwan and Fritz Lang. His first directing experience was in 1959, when he helmed the Off-Broadway theatre production of Clifford Odets's *The Big Knife*.

By the mid-1960s, Bogdanovich had caught the Hollywood bug and started working with producer/director Roger Corman. He worked as assistant director and screenwriter on Corman's *The Wild Angels* (1966), a low-budget biker flick, and credits Corman with teaching him how to plan and make movies on a small budget. He then worked on the less satisfying exploitation picture *Voyage to the Planet of the Prehistoric Woman* (1968); and the same year, he acted in and directed his first feature, the thriller *Targets* (1968), which featured the legendary Boris Karloff in an award-worthy performance. The film, based loosely on the Charles Whitman murders, was shelved by Universal for a brief period because there was some controversy surrounding it. Apparently, the assassin in *Targets* drove the same car and had the same kind of gun as the person who killed Martin Luther King Jr. Some of the crew who worked on *Targets* went on to work on the counter culture classic *Easy Rider* (1969). Bogdanovich also made the documentary *Directed by John Ford* (1971).

Bogdanovich struck pay dirt with his next film, *The Last Picture Show* (1971), which was based on the novel by Larry McMurtry. Shot in black and white and featuring a then 20-year-old Cybill Shepherd, the movie garnered critical praise; some even argued that it was the best film since *Citizen Kane* (1941). The picture was nominated for eight Oscars, including Best Director, and won two: Best Supporting Actor (Ben Johnson) and Best Supporting Actress (Cloris Leachman). Bogdanovich was involved in a highly publicized

Director Peter Bogdanovich attends the TCM Classic Film Festival screening of a *A Star Is Born* at Grauman's Chinese Theater on April 22, 2010, in Hollywood. (Getty Images)

affair with Shepherd and left his wife, Polly Platt, and two children. He continued his winning streak with the Barbra Streisand comedy *What's Up, Doc?* (1972) and the caper film *The Paper Chase* (1973). At this point, it was thought that he could do no wrong in Hollywood, but *Daisy Miller* (1974), the musical *At Long Last Love* (1976), and *Nickelodeon* (1976), while well received critically, were commercial failures.

By 1978, Bogdanovich's affair with Shepherd had cooled, and in 1979 he worked again with Roger Corman on the Ben Gazzara picture *Saint Jack*. He fell in love with the 20-year-old *Playboy* Playmate Dorothy Stratton, who had a small role in 1980's *They All Laughed*. In a jealous rage, Stratton's husband shot her and then shot himself. Bogdanovich, who was crushed, wrote an account of the relationship and murder in *The Killing of the Unicorn* (1984). In the book, there are some strong allegations made against *Playboy* founder Hugh Hefner, which started a well-publicized feud between

Bogdanovich and Hefner. Bogdanovich distributed *They All Laughed* himself and lost several million dollars, despite the fact that the film starred Audrey Hepburn. He then directed the award-winning and critically acclaimed *Mask* (1985), about a young, disfigured boy, which featured singer Cher in the role of the mother. He sued Universal Studios for cutting some footage he deemed important and for replacing songs by Bruce Springsteen, which were originally in the soundtrack. Bogdanovich's next film, *Illegally Yours* (1988), went straight to video. Also, in 1988, he married Dorothy Stratton's younger sister, who was just 20 years old, which led to a minor scandal; they divorced in 2001.

Twenty years after *The Last Picture Show,* Bogdanovich revisited its characters in *Texasville* (1990), which featured a return of the original *Picture Show* cast. In 1991, George Hickenlooper made a documentary, *Picture This: The Times of Peter Bogdanovich in Archer City, Texas,* about the experience of making these two movies.

Throughout the 1990s, Bogdanovich continued to write and publish, and he began to expand into the world of television, directing episodes of the revamped drama *Naked City* and the *Fallen Angels* series. He appeared as a therapist in the highly popular HBO gangster drama *The Sopranos,* and in the Truman Capote biopic *Infamous* (1986). During the early 2000s, he directed *The Cat's Meow* (2001), *Mystery of Natalie Wood* (2004), and *Tom Petty and the Heartbreakers: Running Down the Dream* (2007).

Now in his seventies, Bogdanovich is busier than ever. He is a highly sought after guest for documentaries on DVD releases of the films of directors like Hitchcock and Ford, and he often does commentaries for classic Hollywood films, such as *Bringing Up Baby* (1938). Bogdanovich has often lamented that movies today are all special effects and hype, and show little concern for story. Throughout his career, the one thing that has been foremost in his mind was to make movies that told stories, had substance, but were still entertaining.

Selected Filmography

The Cat's Meow (2001); *The Thing Called Love* (1993); *Noises Off . . .* (1992); *Texasville* (1990); *Illegally Yours* (1988); *Mask* (1985); *They All Laughed* (1981); *Saint Jack* (1979); *Nickelodeon* (1976); *At Long Last Love* (1975); *Daisy Miller* (1974); *Paper Moon* (1973); *What's Up, Doc?* (1972); *Directed by John Ford* (1971); *The Last Picture Show* (1971); *Targets* (1968); *Voyage to the Planet of Prehistoric Women* (1968)

References

Bogdanovich, Peter. *Who the Hell's in It? Portraits and Conversations.* New York: Alfred A. Knopf, 2004.

Bogdanovich, Peter. *Pieces of Time: Peter Bogdanovich on the Movies.* New York: Arbor House, 1973.

Giacci, Vittorio. *Bogdanovich: Peter Bogdanovich.* La nuova: Firenze, 1976.

Yule, Peter. *Picture This: Life and Films of Peter Bogdanovich.* New York: Limelight, 1992.

—*Robert G. Weiner*

BORDEN, LIZZIE.   Lizzie Borden is a feminist filmmaker, artist, and critic who has taken directing to new levels. She has confronted some of the most controversial issues of her time, including sexuality, prostitution, pornography, voyeurism, and women's equality.

Linda Elizabeth Borden was born in Detroit, on February 3, 1954, though some sources list 1950 as her actual date of birth. To the chagrin of her parents, she adopted, and later capitalized on the nickname Lizzie. (The original Lizzie Borden [1860–1927] was tried but acquitted of murdering her parents in Fall River, Massachusetts.) She studied art at Wayne State University, eventually transferring to Wellesley College in Massachusetts, where she completed her BFA in 1973. She then attended Queen's College in New York, where she completed her MFA. A gifted writer, in 1975 she published *Artists' Performance*, a book she coauthored with Susan Brockman. She also began critiquing art in the journal *Artforum* at this time.

Self-taught in film production, Borden made *Regrouping* in 1976, an 80-minute, black-and-white offering in which she explored the idea that women could achieve a sense of solidarity if they were willing to unite toward a common cause, even if they were confronting different issues. She followed *Regrouping* with *Born in Flames* (1983). Set in New York City on the 10th anniversary of a fictitious socialist revolution, the film presents audiences with a dystopic society wherein the government has supposedly taken progressive steps to deal with issues of class, race, gender, and sexual orientation, but where people still suffer from political, economic, and labor abuses. Hard-edged and marked by what was extremely raw language for the time, Borden edited the film's short vignettes together in a fragmented, nonlinear fashion, a process that radically altered the normative viewing experiences of audiences.

In *Working Girls* (1986), the first film in which she used professional actors, Borden examined middle-class prostitution in a documentary fashion. Attempting to deromanticize the process, Borden portrayed prostitution as nothing more than a business, one in which working girls make appointments, keep logs detailing the proclivities of their clients, insure that they are protected by using the proper contraceptives, and sometimes even commute to work on bicycles (Crowdus, 2002). Confronting fantasies about prostitution from the perspectives of both men and women, *Working Girls* also explores capitalism and the employer-employee relationship—especially that between prostitutes and their madams.

An unsettling thriller, *Love Crimes* (1991, 1992—two versions were released) was Borden's first studio film. In the manner of *Sex, Lies, and Videotape*, Steven Soderbergh's 1989 film, Borden explores the disturbing dynamics of voyeurism, desire, control, and degradation. The film follows a hard-driving female district attorney, Dana Greenway (Sean Young), who ignores authority and sets her own rules. She becomes intrigued by the case of a handsome, predatory man, David Hanover (Patrick Bergin, best known for his role as the despotic husband in *Sleeping with the Enemy* opposite Julia Roberts), who poses as a photographer in order to seduce, and abuse, women. When none of Hanover's victims will press charges against him, Greenway goes undercover in an attempt to make a case that she can use to bring the man to justice. After making contact with Hanover, and subjecting herself to his abuse, however, Greenway, like the other women on whom Hanover has preyed, finds herself strangely attracted to her antagonist, and she must reconcile her desire to prosecute this victimizer with her desire to be controlled by him.

In 1994, Borden joined three other women directors—Clara Law, Ana Maria Magalhães, and Monika Treut—to create the anthology *Erotique*. Exploring some of the same themes she addressed in *Love Crimes*, Borden's segment, "Let's Talk About Sex," follows a young Hispanic woman, Rosie (Kamala Lopez-Dawson), who desperately wants to be an actress but continues to run up against stereotypic boundaries that keep all but the blonde-haired, blue-eyed, "pretty" girls on the outside looking in. Working as a phone sex operator in order to support herself, Rosie comes to dread listening to her callers' fantasies. Unfulfilled at every turn, she enters into an increasingly disturbing, sexually charged phone relationship with Dr. Robert Stern (Bryan Cranston), a man who is willing to listen to Rosie's fantasies.

Although Borden has continued to work in the industry, after her work on *Erotique* her production has trailed off. She directed an episode of the *Red Shoe Diaries* for television in 1996 and participated—rather eerily—in a 1995 History Channel production entitled *The Strange Case of Lizzie Borden*. Although most of her work to this point has come early in her career, Borden's talent and her willingness to involve herself in cutting-edge filmmaking have made her an important figure in American cinema.

Selected Filmography

Erotique (1994); *Love Crimes* (1992); *Inside Out* (1991); *"Monsters"* (1988); *Working Girls* (1986); *Born in Flames* (1983); *Regrouping* (1976)

References

Crowdus, Gary, and Dan Georgakas. *The Cineaste Interviews 2: On the Art and Politics of the Cinema*. Chicago: Lake View Press, 2002.

Lane, Christina. *Feminist Hollywood: From Born in Flames to Point Break*. Detroit: Wayne State University Press, 2000.

McDonald, Scott. "Interview with Lizzie Borden." *Feminist Studies* 15(2), Summer 1989: 327–45.

Redding, Judith M., and Victoria A. Brownworth. *Film Fatales: Independent Women Directors*. Seattle: Seal Press, 1997.

—Ralph Hartsock

BRANDO, MARLON. Marlon Brando was arguably the finest screen actor of the twentieth century, winning worldwide acceptance as both a movie star of the first rank and as a performer of uncommon skill. A so-called Method actor, he was a student of the Stanislavski approach to stage acting, which he learned first from his mentor, Stella Adler, and later from Elia Kazan, Lee Strasberg, and others who taught at the famous Actors Studio in Manhattan.

The son of Marlon Brando Sr. and Dorothy Julia Pennebaker, Brando was born in Omaha, Nebraska, on April 3, 1924. His mother had a hand in founding the prestigious Omaha Community Playhouse at a time when Henry Fonda appeared there; and his sister, Jocelyn, also became an actor. After an indifferent school career, Brando set out for New York City in 1943, where he began to study with Adler. It was during this time that he developed the habit of observing people—often with such intensity that he annoyed them—eventually acquiring the ability not only to imitate their mannerisms and vocalisms, but, seemingly, to embody their very essence. Expelled from secondary school for engaging in mildly insurrectionary pranks, Brando retained a streak of mischievousness and rebellion his entire life. In the end, this would serve him well, as in many of his most celebrated film roles he played rebels, criminals, or outlaws.

Early on in his career, he had to settle for small parts in stage productions, such as *I Remember Mama* and *Truckline Café*; but his casual, powerful presence ultimately caught the eye of critics and audiences alike. Despite a tendency to mumble, he brought a fresh, naturalistic style to his roles. Above all, Brando exuded sexuality. An uncommonly handsome young man, he earned a slightly tougher look when the tip of his nose was flattened in a friendly boxing match.

His unique look and style impressed director Elia Kazan and playwright Tennessee Williams, both of whom felt he was right for the part of Stanley Kowalski in the 1947 Broadway production of *A Streetcar Named Desire*. Wearing skin-tight jeans and torn T-shirts, Brando, giving expression to a powerful sense of working-class angst, wowed audiences and stole the show from veteran actress Jessica Tandy, who played the vulnerable, sensitive, but sexually corrupt Blanche, sister to Kowalski's wife, Stella. Brando's fresh, powerful reading of Stanley helped make the play both a sensation and a success. It also earned Brando invitations from Hollywood, which he accepted; he never returned to the stage.

After playing a disgruntled paraplegic in *The Men* in 1950, Brando reprised his role as Stanley Kowalski in Kazan's 1951 screen version of *Streetcar*, garnering an Oscar nomination for his performance. Kazan had a unique skill in handling Brando, and he was able to get the most out of his young star. Indeed, Brando gave one of his finest performances in Kazan's next film, *Viva Zapata* (1952), in which he played the Mexican revolutionary Emiliano Zapata. An atmosphere-soaked period piece, the film sported a superb cast, which included Anthony Quinn (who won a Best Supporting Actor Oscar as Zapata's brother), Jean Peters, and Joseph Wiseman. Brando was again nominated for Best Actor. In what many consider his finest performance, Brando played Terry Malloy in another Kazan film, *On the Waterfront* (1954). The Malloy character was a street tough who betrays his brother and other union-related, local gangsters, and Brando was brilliant in the role. Playing opposite the ingenue Eva Marie Saint and veteran performers Lee. J. Cobb, Karl Malden, and Rod Steiger, Brando gave a naturalistic performance, enhanced by the feature distorting makeup he wore, in a stunning display of Method acting. This bravura performance won Brando a Best Actor Oscar.

Even at this early point in his career, Brando was already world famous. Much of this had to do with his willingness to accept difficult roles. Demonstrating his versatility as a performer, for instance, he took the role of the singing, dancing Sky Masterson in *Guys and Dolls*; he also took up the challenge of playing Mark Antony in a screen adaptation of *Julius Caesar*, a production that featured a star-studded cast, including British acting stalwarts James Mason and John Gielgud. Brando more than held his own in this film, and he was invited by Gielgud to do a run of Shakespeare plays in England, although he declined the invitation.

In the interval between making *Julius Caesar* and *On the Waterfront*, Brando agreed to play a motorcycle hoodlum in the cult film *The Wild One* (1953), forgettable for everything except the brooding, explosive vulnerability Brando brought to his role. Unlike James Dean, another brilliant protégé of Kazan's, who died in a tragic car accident after making only three films, Brando combined vulnerability with menace. Indeed, where Dean touched audiences with his ability to express a certain sense of young, male fragility, Brando's characters, even the young men, seemed wholly grown—and very dangerous. Interestingly, later in his career, Brando would play a series of paternalistic characters, most notably in *The Godfather* (1972), *Last Tango in Paris* (1973), and *Apocalypse Now* (1979), whose rage, carefully controlled and hidden beneath placid exteriors, boils just under the surface, making them threats to everyone around them.

Brando was sometimes accused of being lazy—an extraordinary natural talent, who tended to be self-indulgent and undisciplined, and who never fully realized his true potential. This is often a criticism leveled at those to whom things seem to come too easily. Yet, in Brando's case, starting in his mid-twenties, he made 27 films in 23 years, earning multiple Oscar nominations and working with such heralded directors as Kazan, Bernardo Bertolucci, Arthur Penn, John Huston, Sidney Lumet, Fred Zinnemann, Charlie Chaplin, and Francis Ford Coppola. In his fifties, and having given numerous iconic performances, he was ready for semiretirement, during which he wanted only to play small parts with outsized salaries. Brando made a dozen films at this point, none of them particularly memorable. After providing audiences some of the most viscerally exciting, dynamic, and startling performances in screen history, Brando died in 2004.

References

Brando, Marlon, with Robert Lindsey. *Songs My Mother Taught Me*. New York: Random House, 1994.
Grobel, Laurence. *Conversations with Brando*. New York: Cooper Square Press, 1991.
Manso, Peter. *Brando: The Biography*. New York: Hyperion, 1994.

—*James Delmont*

BROOKS, MEL. A deeply devoted family man who is profoundly committed to his Jewish faith, Mel Brooks has long been one of Hollywood's most influential figures. Known for his outrageous—and some would say offensive—films, Brooks has built a reputation as a master comedic writer.

Mel Brooks poses before the set of his Broadway production *The Producers* in 2001. In that year *The Producers* won a total of 12 Tony Awards, the most ever for a Broadway production.

Born Melvin Kaminsky on June 28, 1926, in New York City to Jewish immigrant parents, Brooks was the youngest child in his family. Following his father's death in 1929, Brooks became preoccupied with his own mortality, paying close attention to his physical well-being. He took great comfort in watching movies—his early favorite was the 1931 production of *Frankenstein*—as well as listening to radio comedies such as *The Yiddish Philosopher* featuring Eddie Cantor. After graduating high school in 1944, Brooks joined the army. Serving in Belgium during World War II, Brooks was frustrated and angered by the anti-Semitism that marked America's armed forces at the time. Following the war, he turned to comedy, accepting a job from Sid Caesar as a writer for *The Admiral Broadway Revue*.

Although the show lasted for only 19 episodes, Brooks impressed Caesar with his abilities as a comedic writer. Caesar eventually hired him to write for *Your Show of Shows*, which he did from 1950 to 1954. In 1961, Brooks was hired to help Jerry Lewis and Bill Richmond write the script for the feature film *The Ladies Man*. In 1963, he wrote and starred in *The Critic*, a short film in which he watches abstract animations and, not understanding their meaning, heckles the cartoons.

Brooks's first stand-alone feature was the 1968 hit *The Producers*. The story follows Max Bialystock (Zero Mostel), a Broadway producer, and his accountant Leo Bloom (Gene Wilder), as they purposely attempt to produce a failed musical. *The Producers*, which won the 1969 Oscar for Best Writing, Story and Screenplay, was a huge hit for Brooks and remains his most successful title. A Broadway adaptation of the film opened in 2001 and went on to win 12 Tony Awards. In 2005, a remake of the original film was released, with Nathan Lane and Matthew Broderick reprising their stage roles as Bialystock and Bloom.

Brooks continued his feature film success with two 1974 spoofs: *Young Frankenstein*, a parody of his favorite childhood movie, and *Blazing Saddles*, which took satirical aim at traditional westerns. His next features, *High Anxiety* (1977) and *History of the World: Part I* (1981), were both met with mixed critical reviews. Brooks's next feature, *Spaceballs* (1987), however, was a critical and commercial success. Apart from writing the sci-fi parody, Brooks also starred as President Skroob, who attempts to steal the air from planet Druidia. The 1990s saw two more parodies: *Robin Hood: Men in Tights* (1993) and *Dracula: Dead and Loving It* (1995). More recently, Brooks wrote a film adaptation of his 1960s television series *Get Smart*; the picture was released in 2008.

Brooks's films are marked by their unpredictability, featuring a surprising mix of crude sight gags and childish jokes. In a 1991 interview, Brooks admitted that this often jarring juxtaposition of forms is a significant part of his comedy. Some film critics have suggested that Brooks seems to have a difficult time maintaining a consistent comedic tone throughout his films. In *History of the World*, for instance, he provides viewers with both a hilarious, even iconic, song-and-dance number concerning the Spanish Inquisition, as well as a tedious, drawn-out musical sequence on the French Revolution. It may be that this qualitative unevenness is largely responsible for the less than positive reviews of some of Brooks's films.

Selected Filmography

Dracula: Dead and Loving It (1995); *Robin Hood: Men in Tights* (1993); *Life Stinks* (1991); *Spaceballs* (1987); *The History of the World: Part I* (1981); *High Anxiety* (1977); *Silent Movie* (1976); *Young Frankenstein* (1974); *Blazing Saddles* (1974); *Twelve Chairs, The* (1970); *Producers, The* (1968)

References

Crick, Robert Alan. *The Big Screen Comedies of Mel Brooks.* Jefferson, NC: McFarland, 2002.
Parish, James Robert. *It's Good to Be the King: The Seriously Funny Life of Mel Brooks.* Hoboken, NJ: John Wiley, 2007.

—*Sean Graham*

BURTON, TIM. Tim Burton was voted the 49th greatest director of all time in 1996 by *Entertainment Weekly*. He was the youngest director on the list. Burton became an influence in Hollywood at a young age due to his unique, darkly humorous, and often quirky cinematic vision. His films are intensely personal and highly stylized.

Born Timothy William Burton on August 25, 1958, in Burbank, California, he spent much of his childhood secluded and entertained himself by watching horror movies and drawing. Burton lived near a cemetery and has commented on the "weirdness" of the situation. His rather macabre childhood has influenced his filmmaking.

After high school, Burton studied animation at the California Institute of the Arts, founded by Disney, from whom he would eventually obtain a fellowship. He worked at Disney on *The Fox and the Hound* (1981) and *The Black Cauldron* (1985), but found that he often had artistic differences with his colleagues. Allowed by Disney to work on personal projects, he created a six-minute tribute to the horror actor Vincent Price titled *Vincent* (1982), and the movie *Frankenweenie* (1984), which was judged by studio administrators as unsuitable for children.

Paul Reubens (a.k.a. Pee-wee Herman) was so impressed by *Frankenweenie* that he asked the then 27-year-old Burton to direct *Pee-wee's Big Adventure* (1985), which, to the delight of studio heads, turned out to be a huge hit. His successful turn with this film led to his being chosen to direct the quirky supernatural comedy *Beetlejuice* (1988), which starred Michael Keaton and which was embraced by critics and audiences alike. Based on the critical and box-office success of these two films, Burton was tapped to direct the enormously expensive *Batman* (1989), on which he again worked with Keaton.

Director Tim Burton, November 2010. (Getty Images)

His next movie, *Edward Scissorhands* (1990), is considered by many his seminal work. The film, which featured the extraordinarily talented Johnny Depp as the eerily seductive Scissorhands, found Burton at the height of his creative powers and showcased his ability to create a highly stylized and painstakingly designed film. The working relationship between Burton and Depp has been a fruitful one, as they have gone on to make five more films together.

Batman Returns (1992) saw Burton once again working with Keaton. The film was darker and stranger than the original, showing how much creative freedom he had won. The film did well, but many people were disappointed by it. While working on *Batman Returns*, he also produced the wildly popular *The Nightmare Before Christmas* (1993), which he had written himself. The stop-motion animation movie emphasized Burton's gothic style and dark humor. Mixing two of his favorite themes, Christmas and Halloween, today it has become a cult classic.

Although *Ed Wood* (1994), his tribute to the legendary "worst director of all time," did poorly at the box office, it received some of the best critical reviews of Burton's career. The vibrant *Mars Attacks!* (1996) was a step away from his typical style and was met with mediocre reviews and little box-office success, despite the appearances by big name stars.

Burton returned to form with *Sleepy Hollow* (1999), where he again worked with Depp. His next two films were more conventional. The remake *Planet of the Apes* (2001) did well at the box office but was panned by critics. He followed with *Big Fish* (2003), which disappointed fans.

Charlie and the Chocolate Factory (2005), a more faithful retelling of Roald Dahl's original story, was a commercial and critical success. His second stop-motion film, *Corpse Bride* (2005), received an Academy Award nomination for Best Animated Feature Film and garnered more critical praise. Many consider it to be the spiritual successor to *The Nightmare Before Christmas*.

His most recent work, *Sweeney Todd: The Demon Barber of Fleet Street* (2007), received a Golden Globe nomination for Best Director and won an Oscar for Best Achievement in Art Direction.

As of 2009, all but three of his feature films have been nominated for an Academy Award in some category. *Sweeney Todd* won the Best Motion Picture (Comedy or Musical) and Best Actor (Comedy or Musical) Awards at the 65th Golden Globe Awards.

Selected Filmography

Alice in Wonderland (2010); *Sweeney Todd: The Demon Barber of Fleet Street* (2007); *Charlie and the Chocolate Factory* (2005); *Big Fish* (2003); *Planet of the Apes* (2001); *Sleepy Hollow* (1999); *Mars Attacks!* (1996); *Ed Wood* (1994); *Batman Returns* (1992); *Edward Scissorhands* (1990); *Batman* (1989); *Beetlejuice* (1989); *Pee-wee's Big Adventure* (1985)

References

Burton, Tim, and Mark Salisbury. *Burton on Burton*. London: Faber. 2000.

Burton, Tim, and Kristian Fraga. *Tim Burton: Interviews*. Jackson: University Press of Mississippi. 2005.

Woods, Paul A. *Tim Burton: A Child's Garden of Nightmares*. London: Plexus. 2002.

—*James Heiney*

C

CAGNEY, JAMES. One of the greatest film actors of all time, and one of the twentieth century's most recognizable faces, James Cagney was the quintessential movie tough guy. Although famous for portraying gangsters, Cagney was also a capable singer, dancer, and light comedian who excelled in a variety of roles. He was nominated three times for an Academy Award, winning once for his performance as lead actor in *Yankee Doodle Dandy* (1942). The unique cadence of his voice also made him one of the most mimicked film personalities of all time.

James Francis Cagney Jr. was born July 17, 1899, in New York City, the son of an Irish American bartender and part-time boxer. One of seven children, Cagney was sickly as a small child but grew up as something of a street brawler. He worked odd jobs to help support his family, including stints as a newspaper copyboy, a waiter, a bellhop and a billiard racker in a pool hall. In 1918, he graduated from Stuyvesant High School and briefly attended Columbia University before dropping out after the death of his father. An excellent athlete, Cagney was an accomplished amateur boxer and baseball player who at one time considered trying to make baseball a career. While working as a package wrapper at Wanamaker's Department Store, Cagney heard from a fellow employee about a vaudeville troupe looking for entertainers and willing to pay $35 a week, good money at the time. Cagney auditioned for the outfit and, ironically, the future tough guy won a place in an all-male chorus that cross-dressed as females. Ignoring his mother's pleas to give up the pursuit of a stage career, Cagney sought out more theater work and eventually joined the vaudeville circuit, touring primarily as a singer, dancer, and comedian. In 1922, he married actress Frances Willard Vernon, with whom he would remain for the rest of his life. The couple had two children.

After years in vaudeville and performing in plays, Cagney got his big break by landing a role starring opposite Joan Blondell in the Broadway production of *Penny Arcade* (1929). He earned rave reviews for his performance, and as a result Warner Bros. signed the actor and cast him in *Sinners' Holiday* (1930), the film version of the play. More films followed, and in 1931 Cagney won widespread praise for his breakthrough performance as a gangster in *The Public Enemy*. In the film, Cagney's character violently smashed a grapefruit into the face of actress Mae Clarke in what many film historians describe as

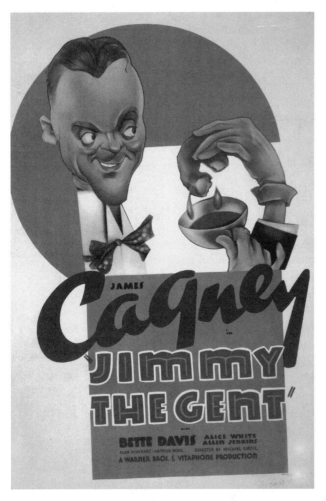

Movie poster for the 1934 film *Jimmy the Gent*, starring Jimmy Cagney and Bette Davis. (Library of Congress)

one of the most significant scenes in movie history. The scene established Cagney's rough-and-tumble reputation in the mind of the public and led to more "darker roles." He starred in a string of successful films with good friend Pat O'Brien, including *Devil Dogs of the Air* (1935), *Ceiling Zero* (1935), *Angels with Dirty Faces* (1938), and *Torrid Zone* (1940). Cagney also gave memorable performances as the gangster who gunned down Humphrey Bogart in *The Roaring Twenties* (1939) and as a blind boxer in *City of Conquest* (1940). As a result, by the beginning of the 1940s the 41-year-old star had established himself as one of Hollywood's biggest box-office draws.

In 1942 Cagney shed his tough-guy image to take on what for him was a dream role, starring as multitalented singer, dancer, composer, and theatrical producer George M. Cohan in *Yankee Doodle Dandy*. Many considered this Cagney's greatest performance, and the patriotic theme of the film played well to an American public only a few months removed from the Japanese attack on Pearl Harbor. The film earned eight Oscar nominations, and Cagney received the Academy Award for Best Actor in a lead role for his performance. That same year, Cagney formed his own production company and was elected president of the Screen Actors Guild. After the release of *Yankee Doodle Dandy*, Cagney raised money for the war effort and tirelessly toured military bases in the United States and Britain, performing for thousands of troops.

Through the 1940s and 1950s Cagney continued making movies, either through Warner Bros. or his own production company. In 1961, at the age of 62, he retired from films after starring in the Billy Wilder comedy *One, Two, Three*. He remained retired for the next 20 years until 1981, when he appeared in Milos Forman's *Ragtime*, his last film performance. During the latter stages of his life Cagney received countless accolades for his body of work, including Lifetime Achievement Awards from the

American Film Institute and the Screen Actors Guild. On March 30, 1986, Cagney died at his farm in Stanfordville, New York, at age 86. President Ronald Reagan delivered the eulogy at the actor's funeral.

References

Cagney, James. *Cagney by Cagney*. New York: Doubleday, 1976.
Dickens, Homer. *The Complete Films of James Cagney*. New York: Citadel, 1989.
McCabe, John. *Cagney*. New York: Carroll & Graf, 1999.
Warren, Doug. *James Cagney: The Authorized Biography*. London: Robson, 1998.

—Ben Wynne

CAMPION, JANE.   Jane Campion is a highly acclaimed director from New Zealand who began her career in the 1980s. Winner of the Palme d'Or for short film in 1986 and feature film in 1993, Campion is also only one of four women nominated for an Academy Award for direction. Her films are known for complex character relationships—often dealing frankly with sexuality and family dysfunction—and rich cinematography and costume design. Campion frequently writes as well as directs her films, and has received awards for original screenplays.

Campion was born April 30, 1954, to Richard Campion, theatrical director and cofounder of the New Zealand Players Company, and Edith Armstrong, a stage actress. She grew up in New Zealand and attended Victoria University, graduating in 1975 with a bachelor's degree in Anthropology. After college, she moved to Australia for art school, graduating from the Sydney College of Arts with a bachelor's in painting in 1979. Scholarly examinations of her work have cited her academic experiences as significant to her filmmaking, pointing to her background in painting as an influence in her use of colored lighting and her background in anthropology as an influence in her explorations of multicultural issues.

It was at the Sydney College of Arts that she made her first film, a short called *Tissues*, about a father who is arrested for child molestation. This film won her entrance to the Australian Film, Television, and Radio School, from which she graduated in 1984. While a student there, she made a number of critically popular short films. Her first effort, *Mishaps of Seduction and Conquest*, wove a parallel story between famed English mountaineer George Mallory's failed attempt to scale Everest and the fictional Geoffrey Mallory's seduction of a female writer. The picture cut between the two stories, utilizing newsreel footage and original film and applying silent movie-style title cards in between the individual scenes. Her first critically successful film, *An Exercise in Discipline-Peel*, was made in 1982. The short film, about the escalating tension between a man, his sister, and his son during a car trip, won Campion her first Palme d'Or at the 1986 Cannes Film Festival. Campion followed *Exercise in Discipline-Peel* with *Passionless Moments*, a series of linked short subjects written and directed by Campion and her boyfriend Gerard Lee. The film, which dealt with inconsequential moments in the lives of various people in a neighborhood, won the most popular short film award at the 1983 Sydney Film Festival. Campion's final film at AFTRS was her thesis project, *A Girl's Own Story*, a tale of adolescent girls in the early 1960s that dealt with themes of family dysfunction and adolescent sexuality.

After graduation, Campion worked on several projects for Australian television, directing the film *Two Friends*, centered on two adolescent female friends and their gradual alienation from one another. The film inverted its plot, telling the story in reverse, from a point of total alienation to the earlier days of friendship. During this period, she also directed an episode of the television show *Dancing Daze* for Australian television and made the miniseries *An Angel at My Table*, based on the autobiographies of New Zealand author Janet Frame, focusing especially on her struggle with mental illness and her emergence as a poet. This miniseries would go on to be adapted into a single film and shown at international film festivals in Venice and Toronto.

Campion's 1989 film *Sweetie* was her feature film debut, based partially on the dissolution of her relationship with Gerard Lee. In *Sweetie*, Campion dealt with one of the themes she would return to again and again, family dysfunction. The film begins by exploring the relationship between Kay and Louis; Kay gets involved with Louis based on a fortune teller's advice. After they move in together, they decide to plant a tree in their small backyard, creating a great deal of tension between them. Their relationship, already dysfunctional, is complicated by the arrival of Kay's mentally unstable sister, Sweetie. The separation of Kay's parents and other complications in her life lead to a confrontation with a naked, painted Sweetie in a wobbly tree house—although a bit heavy-handed, the metaphors of stability/instability are nonetheless touching—that results in Sweetie's death. While this film was shown at Cannes and also nominated for the Palme d'Or for full-length film, it met with a mixed audience response, due in part to its exploration of the controversial theme of mental illness.

It was Campion's second feature, *The Piano*, that would bring her great acclaim. The picture, starring Holly Hunter, Sam Neill, and Harvey Keitel, is set in colonial New Zealand and is based on a love triangle between Alisdair Stewart (Neill), a colonial settler; Ada McGrath (Hunter), his mute mail-order bride who communicates primarily using the titular instrument; and George Baines (Keitel), another settler with close ties to the native Maori. The film was strongly influenced by the European folktale "Bluebeard" and by the novel *Wuthering Heights*, as well as by the history of European-Maori contact in New Zealand. The picture also introduced Anna Paquin as the young Flora McGrath, Ada's daughter. After it was screened at Cannes, Campion became the first female director to win the Palme d'Or; the film went on to win Academy Awards for writing and acting.

In 1996, Campion directed *Portrait of a Lady*, an adaptation of the Henry James novel, starring Nicole Kidman, who Campion had first met back when Kidman was in high school. Although the film featured acclaimed talent—including John Malkovich, Barbara Hershey, and John Gielgud—making it proved challenging for Campion, as much of the tension introduced in the source text is centered within the characters. Kidman in particular had difficulty expressing the emotional struggle waged by Isabel Archer, and the film did not garner the same sort of acclaim that was lavished on *The Piano*.

Campion's follow-up to *Portrait of a Lady* was 1999's *Holy Smoke*. Reuniting with Harvey Keitel, Campion co-wrote the screenplay for the picture—with her sister

Anna—as well as directing it. The film, which explores the complex relationship between a former cult member and the man attempting to deprogram her, stars Kate Winslet as Ruth and Keitel as P. J. Waters. As with her previous films, *Holy Smoke* dealt with complex issues related to sexuality, alienation, and loss. The film does end on a redemptive note, however, with Ruth and P. J. corresponding with each other, even as they involve themselves in their new, happier lives.

Campion had originally intended once again to team with Nicole Kidman for *In the Cut* (2003). Kidman, though, withdrew from the project due to her divorce from Tom Cruise, and Meg Ryan stepped into the starring role. *In the Cut* follows the life of Frannie (Ryan), an English teacher who becomes embroiled in an investigation into a serial killer being carried out by Detective Malloy, played by Mark Ruffalo. Marketed as a thriller, the film received mixed reviews; although some critics found the pacing too slow for a thriller, others pointed out that Campion had done a fine job in exploring the psychological elements that defined the different characters. In the end, the film received more attention for its explicit sexual content than for anything else, especially since Ryan—who was well known for her girl-next-door roles in romantic comedies—had replaced Kidman, who would seem to have been better suited for the role of Frannie.

Campion made two short films after 2000, both as part of larger multidirector projects. She contributed *The Water Diary*, a segment examining the effects of a drought that causes a family to sacrifice their horses in order to secure food and water, to the film *8* (2009), which dealt with various issues of world poverty. Her contribution to *Chacun son cinema* (2007) was a three-minute short titled *The Lady Bug*, which focused on a janitor in a theater poking at a ladybug while a movie in which two women berate a man for his inadequate sexual performance plays in the background.

In 2009, Campion returned to feature films with *Bright Star*, a biographical sketch of the poet John Keats and his romance with Fanny Brawne. *Bright Star* presented a melancholy look at love, focusing on the letters and interactions of the romantic partners rather than on Keats's poetry. The film was praised for the performances of its leads, Abbie Cornish and Ben Winshaw, and was nominated for the Palme d'Or at Cannes.

Campion cites a number of significant directorial influences on her film career, including Akira Kurosawa and Francis Ford Coppola, whose first *Godfather* film she watches religiously once each year. Additionally, she has been influenced by the work of a number of contemporary female directors, including Gillian Armstrong, Alison McLean, Niki Caro, and Sally Potter. Campion continues to speak out about the paucity of woman working in the industry, especially behind the camera. As the only female director to have won the Palme d'Or, and one of only four to have been nominated for an Academy Award for direction, however, she has become an inspiration for other woman trying to break into the field.

See also: Piano, The

Selected Filmography

Bright Star (2009); *In the Cut* (2003); *Piano, The* (1993); *Sweetie* (1989); *A Girl's Own Story* (1984); *Passionless Moments* (1983)

References

Aldred, B. Grantham. "Binary Structures, Clothing and Jane Campion's *The Piano*." *Midwestern Folklore* 31(1–2), 2007.

Hogg, Trevor. "Burning Brightly, a Jane Campion Profile." December 2009. *Flickering Myth* 10, June 2010. http://flickeringmyth.blogspot.com/2009/12/burning-brightly-jane-campion -profile.html.

McHugh, Kathleen Anne. *Jane Campion*. Champaign: Univeristy of Illinois Press, 2007.

Wexman, Virginia Wright, ed. *Jane Campion: Interviews*. Jackson: University Press of Mississippi, 1999.

—B. Grantham Aldred

CAPRA, FRANK.   An Italian immigrant, Frank Capra was a major contributor to the development of the American film industry. A director, writer, and producer of narrative pictures and documentaries, Capra created films characterized by humanistic themes and a unique cinematic style. His enormously popular pictures of the 1930s and 1940s—among them *It Happened One Night* (1934), *Mr. Deeds Goes to Town* (1936), *Mr. Smith Goes to Washington* (1939), and *It's a Wonderful Life* (1946)—are still considered some of the best films ever made.

Frank Russell Capra was born Francesco Rosario Capra in Bisacquino, Sicily, on May 18, 1897, and immigrated to the United States in 1903 with his father, mother, and siblings. The family joined an older brother who had previously settled in California. The youngest child, Capra attended school, sold newspapers, and worked at other jobs to finance his education. He graduated from Manual Arts High School in Los Angeles and then the Throop Institute (now the California Institute of Technology) with a bachelor of science degree in chemical engineering.

During World War I, Capra enlisted in the U.S. Army; allowed to finish his college studies, he entered the military in October 1918. Not yet a naturalized citizen, he was stationed at Fort Winfield Scott, at the Presidio of San Francisco, where he taught ballistics and mathematics to artillerymen. His military career was short-lived, however, as he contracted the Spanish flu and was medically discharged in December 1918. Capra changed his name to Frank Russell Capra when he became a U.S. citizen in 1920.

After leaving the service, Capra tramped through Arizona, Nevada, and California, tutoring, hustling poker, playing guitar, and selling different products door-to-door. In San Francisco, he answered an advertisement from a "movie studio" and learned to make one-reel silent films based on poems. Enthralled by that first, limited experience, he set out to learn every step of the process of making films. He became a prop man, editor, and a gag writer for Bob Eddy. In Hollywood, working for Hal Roach, he wrote gags for the *Our Gang* kids. Writing for Mack Sennett's Keystone Comedies, he learned the dynamics of staging comedy: timing, building a gag, the heaping of "business on business" until the big one, the "topper," was revealed.

Capra made his first feature films, *Tramp, Tramp, Tramp, The Strong Man* (1926), and *Long Pants* (1927), for Harry Langdon, a famous, baby-faced comic with a gift for pantomime and an innocence bordering on the grotesque. Writing for the

Our Gang kids and for Harry Langdon, Capra learned to respect the integrity of characterization: the gag was important, but it had to fit into the plot and be true to the personality of the characters.

Working under Harry Cohn— "His Crudeness"—at CBC, a small "poverty row" studio that later became Columbia, Capra made a series of silent films and began dabbling in the mechanics of sound. It was at this time that he made his first A-picture, *Submarine* (1928), and developed a close working relationship with cameraman Joseph Walker and screenwriters Jo Swerling and Robert Riskin. He also began to develop his own cinematic style.

Convinced that a director should be responsible of every aspect of the filmmaking process, Capra began to make progressively more complex pictures. These included *The Donovan Affair* (1929), *Ladies of Leisure* (1930), *The Miracle Woman* (1931), *Platinum Blonde* (1931), *Forbidden* (1932), and *American Madness* (1932). Working with Riskin, Capra introduced themes of idealism and sentimentality into these early pictures, setting the stage for what was to come in his later films.

Lieutenant Colonel Frank Capra in London on August 19, 1943. Capra, a Hollywood filmmaker who was shocked by Pearl Harbor, enlisted and was assigned to produce war films during World War II. (AP/Wide World Photos)

Although a box-office failure, Capra's *The Bitter Tea of General Yen* (1933) had the distinction of being the first motion picture to make its screen debut in Radio City Music Hall. He followed *Bitter Tea* with *Lady for a Day* (1933), a box-office hit that was nominated for an Academy Award for Best Picture.

His brilliant *It Happened One Night* (1934), generally considered the film world's first romantic comedy, started out with several strikes against it. Its working title, *Night Bus*, was uninspired; and because of the storyline, the actors would have few costume changes and visit a limited number of locales. While the first script was turned down by perhaps a dozen noted actors, Capra was able to convince Claudette Colbert—available for just a few weeks at double her usual salary—and Clark Gable—on loan from his home studio—to come onboard. Capra and Riskin then worked their magic on the script, making it contemporary, witty, and, as it turned out, timeless. A rich and spoiled socialite, literally escaping an arranged marriage—she is forced to dive from her father's yacht and swim ashore—boards a night bus in New York City, where she encounters an unemployed, fast-talking reporter—a man who doesn't even wear an undershirt! The film proved to be a Depression-era fairy tale: the Princess and the Commoner meet, fall in love, and live happily ever after. Opening slowly, the film turned out to be the "must-see" movie of 1935; it also won Academy Awards for Best Picture, Best Director, Best Actor, Best Actress, and Best Screenplay.

The films that followed *It Happened One Night* saw the development of Capra's signature style; his use of themes and visual treatments that came to be described as "Capra-esque." Most of these films were essentially comedies of manners, witty contemporary morality plays that celebrated the values of small-town America and the virtues of democracy. Generally, they pitted a good man—usually a naive, sincere, and unaffected man—against the forces of evil permeating American society: the corruption of the moneyed elite and the ruthlessness of arrogant politicians. Most notable among these films were *Mr. Deeds Goes to Town* (1936), *You Can't Take It with You*—which earned Capra his second and third Oscars for direction—*Lady for a Day* (1933), *Mr. Smith Goes to Washington* (1939), and *It's a Wonderful Life* (1946).

During World II, Capra, commissioned as a major in the U.S. Army Signal Corps, supervised the making of documentary films, in particular his *Why We Fight* series: *Prelude to War* (1942), *The Nazis Strike* (1942), *The Battle of Britain* (1943), *Divide and Conquer* (1943), *Know Your Enemy: Japan* (1945), *Tunisian Victory* (1945), and *Two Down and One to Go* (1945). These documentaries may be understood as thematic montages—not so much directed as edited, or in the case of *Why We Fight*, redacted from existing war-footage, much of it taken from enemy newsreels and Nazi propaganda films. Overlaying this filmic material with anti-Nazi commentary, the pictures in the *Why We Fight* series served as military training films that were supposed to help soldiers, and the American people, understand the ideological background to the war. Significantly, the production of the series earned Capra a Distinguished Service Medal. In addition to be recognized by the armed forces, *Prelude to War* won the 1942 Academy Award for Documentary Feature; by the end of the war in 1945, this film had been seen by nine million people.

Although Capra continued to make films for another four decades after America climbed out of the Depression and helped win World War II in the 1940s, his pictures became less and less popular with audiences. His sentimental idealism and homespun heroes seemed naive and intellectually dishonest to an increasing number of postwar viewers. Yet, even though they fell out of favor in postwar America, Capra's films, with their well-crafted comedic sensibilities, their whimsical characterizations, and their message of the basic goodness of humanity, continue to resonate with contemporary audiences.

In 1982, Capra was honored by the American Film Institute with a "Salute to Frank Capra," and in 1986, he received the National Medal of Arts. Capra died in 1991.

Selected Filmography

Pocketful of Miracles (1961); *A Hole in the Head* (1959); *Here Comes the Groom* (1951); *Riding High* (1950); *State of the Union* (1948); *It's a Wonderful Life* (1946); *Your Job in Germany* (1945); *Arsenic and Old Lace* (1944); *Meet John Doe* (1941); *Mr. Smith Goes to Washington* (1939); *You Can't Take It with You* (1938); *Lost Horizon* (1937); *Mr. Deeds Goes to Town* (1936); *It Happened One Night* (1934); *Lady for a Day* (1933); *The Bitter Tea of General Yen* (1933)

References

Capra, Frank. *Frank Capra: The Name above the Title*. New York: Da Capo, 1997.
Carney, Raymond. *American Vision: The Films of Frank Capra*. Cambridge, UK: Cambridge University Press, 1986.
Doherty, Thomas. Projections of War: Hollywood, American Culture, and World War II. New York: Columbia University Press, 1993.
Gehring, Wes. *Populism and the Capra Legacy*. Westport: Greenwood, 1995.
Glatzer, Richard, and John Raeburn, eds. *Frank Capra: The Man and His Films*. Ann Arbor: University of Michigan Press, 1975.
McBride, Joseph. *Frank Capra: The Catastrophe of Success*. New York: Simon and Schuster, 1992.

—*Arbolina L. Jennings*

CARPENTER, JOHN. John Carpenter is one of the key figures in American horror and science fiction filmmaking. He influenced the direction of the genres through his intelligent and moody films that bear his unmistakable style. His career has spanned four decades and encompassed over 30 movies as producer and director. He has also left his mark as a writer, actor, and composer. His compositions and movies have won numerous special interest awards.

Born John Howard Carpenter on January 16, 1948, in Carthage, New York, he was raised in Bowling Green, Kentucky, where his father, who had a profound musical influence on him, was the head of the music department at Western Kentucky University. Carpenter composes the music for almost all of his films. His most famous theme is that from *Halloween*. His music is generally synthesized with piano accompaniment and atmospherics. He enrolled in the prestigious film program at the University of Southern California. Carpenter's first directorial effort was *Dark Star*, part of his master's thesis. It received limited theatrical release, was praised by critics, and became a cult classic. Notable was his ability to make a good movie on a limited budget, $60,000 for this film. He also began his tradition of formally prepending "John Carpenter's" to the movie title for movies that he directed. This was his only movie not filmed in wide-screen. Carpenter is an advocate of the composition space that wide-screen affords.

Assault on Precinct 13 (1976) was his first professional endeavor and a salute to Howard Hawks. It is an example of the influence that westerns had on Carpenter. *Halloween* (1978) established Carpenter as a master of the horror genre. He avoided the gore of other slasher films and instead built suspense through visual elements, most

Director John Carpenter poses at the 58th International Film Festival, September 2001, in Venice, Italy. (AFP/Getty Images)

notably his hallmark of minimalist lighting and nuance. Part of the movie's success is due to Carpenter's chilling score. *Halloween* grossed more than $65 million in its initial release and went on to become one of the industry's most successful independent films.

Carpenter frequently appears as an actor in his own movies and did so in *The Fog* (1980). He was displeased with the final cut of *The Fog* and, as a sign of his integrity as a director, shot additional scenes until it was acceptable to him. He followed *The Fog* with the critically acclaimed *Escape from New York* (1981), which gained both a cult following and mainstream success. Kurt Russell, with whom Carpenter had previously worked when making the made for TV movie *Elvis*, was featured in *Escape from New York*. Russell became part of the community of actors and crew members with whom Carpenter especially enjoys working.

The Thing (1982), ostensibly a remake of the 1951 picture *The Thing from Another World*, provided Carpenter with his largest budget ($15 million) to date. Although it was his first financial failure, the movie did find an audience on cable and home video and is now regarded as an excellent horror film. Carpenter won over critics with the release of his 1984 picture *Starman*. A departure from his horror films, *Starman* was a science fiction romance featuring Jeff Bridges and Karen Allen. A modest commercial success, many felt that the offering was Carpenter's attempt to make up for the disappointing numbers from *The Thing*.

In 1986, Carpenter released *Big Trouble in Little China*, a big-budget action-adventure comedy that also produced disappointing box-office numbers. After this, he would have trouble finding financing. Returning to his horror film roots, he directed two well-made, low-budget features in the 1980s: *Prince of Darkness* (1987) and *They Live* (1988). The 1990s proved to be a decade in which Carpenter released a series of poorly performing films, the one bright spot being *Vampires* (1998), which starred the always reliable James Woods in the lead role.

Ghosts of Mars, released in 2001, was panned by critics. Carpenter's reputation as a filmmaker who can deliver brilliant horror and science fiction pictures remains intact with his fans, however. His earlier films are considered classics and have continued to perform well on home video. Several have been remade, including *Assault on Precinct 13* and *The Fog* (both 2005). More recently, Rob Zombie has produced and directed *Halloween* (2007), a reimagining of Carpenter's 1978 film.

See also: Halloween

Selected Filmography

L.A. Gothic (2010); *Ghosts of Mars* (2001); *Vampires* (1998); *Escape from L.A.* (1996); *Village of the Damned* (1995); *Memoirs of the Invisible Man* (1992); *They Live* (1988); *Prince of Darkness* (1987); *Big Trouble in Little China* (1986); *Starman* (1984); *Escape from New York* (1981); *Fog, The* (1980); *Halloween* (1978)

References

Boulenger, Gilles. *John Carpenter: The Prince of Darkness*. Los Angeles: Silman-James Press. 2003.

Conrich, Ian, and David Woods. *The Cinema of John Carpenter: The Technique of Terror*. London: Wallflower. 2004.

Muir, John Kenneth. *The Films of John Carpenter*. Jefferson, NC: McFarland. 2000.

—*James Heiney*

CASSAVETES, JOHN. One of the most influential figures in American independent cinema, John Cassavetes was a writer, director, and actor whose uncompromising personal vision made him a perpetual Hollywood outsider during his lifetime and an inspirational legend after his death.

Born on December 9, 1929, in New York City, John Nicholas Cassavetes was the second son of Greek immigrant parents. Shifts in fortunes led to frequent moves throughout the 1930s, including a return to Greece, but the family eventually settled on Long Island in the 1940s. After graduating from Port Washington High School and flunking out of several colleges, Cassavetes decided to become an actor and entered the American Academy of Dramatic Arts in New York City in 1949.

For several years after graduating from the academy, Cassavetes struggled to get parts. Although trained for the stage, he discovered that the new medium of television provided him the best opportunities. Between 1954 and 1959 Cassavetes made close to 100 television appearances, eventually landing the starring role in *Johnny Staccato*, an NBC television series about a piano-playing detective, in 1959. Television led to film roles; and, despite a reputation in Hollywood for being difficult, Cassavetes crafted many memorable characters in the 1960s, such as Johnny North, the willing victim in *The Killers* (1964); Victor Franko, the tough convict turned soldier in *The Dirty Dozen* (1967); and Guy Woodhouse, the deceitful husband in *Rosemary's Baby* (1968).

Actor and director John Cassavetes poses during an episode of the television anthology series *The Alfred Hitchcock Hour* on January 21, 1964. The episode, co-starring Cassavetes's wife Gena Rowlands and directed by John Brahm, was originally broadcast on March 6, 1964. (Getty Images)

Despite his success, Cassavetes was dissatisfied with the parts he was offered and with the bland commercialism of American television and film. He quickly got involved in side projects that allowed him to explore roles and artistic ideas that the mainstream industry considered too radical. His first film project grew from improvisations at the Variety Arts Studio, a workshop he co-founded with Burt Lane in New York in 1957. *Shadows* (1959) was an experimental film that dealt with interracial relationships and racism, featuring a jazz soundtrack by bassist Charles Mingus and saxophonist Shafi Hadi. The improvisational film was championed by *Film Culture* founder Jonas Mekas, and helped launch the New American Cinema movement in the 1960s. Cassavetes's next film, *Too Late Blues* (1961), had a similar focus on jazz and spontaneity. With his third film, *Faces* (1968), Cassavetes came closest to achieving mainstream success. A radical condemnation of middle-class values shot in cinéma vérité style, *Faces* earned three Academy Award nominations, several international prizes, and respectable box-office receipts.

Like many independents, Cassavetes relied on a group of collaborators that consistently helped with his productions. Seymour Cassel remained a close friend throughout Cassavetes's life, and appeared in many of his films. He earned an Oscar nomination as Best Supporting Actor for his role in *Faces*. He also starred in *Minnie and Moskowitz* (1971), playing the zany parking lot attendant, Seymour Moskowitz, who ultimately finds true love. Peter Falk and Ben Gazzara were also close collaborators. Both appeared with Cassavetes in *Husbands* (1970), and both would star in subsequent Cassavetes films. Falk played the oppressive construction worker Nick Longhetti in *A Woman Under the Influence* (1974). Gazzara starred as Cosmo Vitelli in *The Killing of a Chinese Bookie* (1976).

No collaborator worked on more of Cassavetes's films than actress Gena Rowlands, whom Cassavetes married in 1954. Rowlands was twice nominated for Academy Awards as Best Actress in performances that Cassavetes directed. In *A Woman Under the Influence*, Rowlands played Mabel Longhetti, an eccentric housewife and mother who gradually loses her grip on reality. In *Gloria* (1980), she played a gangster's moll who winds up taking care of a child whose parents were murdered. Cassavetes often wrote parts to showcase Rowlands's talent for playing women in crisis. She played an aging actress who has sacrificed everything for her career in *Opening Night* (1977), and a mother whose husband and daughter reject her in *Love Streams* (1984).

Although Cassavetes's films were never widely distributed in his lifetime, he is one of a handful of American artists to be nominated for Academy Awards in three separate categories: acting (*The Dirty Dozen*), writing (*Faces*), and directing (*A Woman under the Influence*).

Cassavetes died on February 3, 1989, of cirrhosis of the liver, leaving behind three children, Nick, Alexandra, and Zoe. A major influence on Martin Scorsese and countless other filmmakers, Cassavetes's films testify to his determination to make profoundly personal statements regardless of cost.

Selected Filmography

Big Trouble (1986); *Love Streams* (1984); *Gloria* (1980); *Opening Night* (1977); *The Killing of a Chinese Bookie* (1976); *A Woman under the Influence* (1974); *Minnie and Moskowitz* (1971); *Husbands* (1970); *Faces* (1968); *A Child Is Waiting* (1963); *Too Late Blues* (1961); *Shadows* (1959)

References

Carney, Ray. *Cassavetes on Cassavetes*. London: Faber & Faber, 2001.
Charity, Tom. *John Cassavetes: Lifeworks*. London: Omnibus, 2001.

—*Joseph Christopher Schaub*

CHAPLIN, CHARLIE.   One of the most famous and recognizable figures in cinema, Charles (Charlie) Spencer Chaplin was born on April 16, 1889, in London. His parents, Charles Sr. and Hannah Chaplin, were both music hall performers on South London's vaudeville circuit. Chaplin's childhood was plagued by poverty and hardship. Following his birth, Charles Sr. abandoned Hannah, a very young Charlie, and his half-brother Spencer Hawks. To help support the family, Chaplin danced and performed in the streets for change.

Chaplin's skills as a performer caused him to be noticed by vaudevillian troupes. In 1898, at the age of nine, he began to tour with a clog-dancing troupe, the Eight Lancashire Lads. Chaplin's talents at improvisation and pantomime opened doors to a number of minor roles in theatrical productions. He returned to vaudeville in 1906, joining Casey's Circus, a troupe that specialized in impersonating prominent personalities of the day. By 1907, Chaplin was brought to the attention of Fred Karno, the founder and leader of England's most famous pantomime troupe. Spencer, already a member of Karno's Troup, lobbied hard to get his brother Charlie a spot in the group.

Mentored by Karno, Chaplin soon emerged as a featured player of the troupe. With the Karno Troup, he toured England, Paris, and, later, the United States, in 1910 and 1913. Praised by critics, he gained the attention of Mack Sennett, founder of the Keystone Film Studio. Chaplin, seeking to expand his career beyond the stage, signed with Keystone in May 1913. After the release of his first film in February 1914, *Making a Living*, he appeared in 33 one- or two-reel comedies and one feature film for Keystone. He immersed himself in the process of filmmaking and soon was writing and directing films for Keystone.

It was with Keystone that he created his most endearing character, the Tramp. Unsure how to utilize Chaplin's talents, Sennett ordered him to develop a costume for his bit part in the film *Mabel's Strange Predicament*. Donning oversized trousers and shoes (size 14, so large they had to be worn on the wrong feet), undersized coat and derby, a cane, and wearing a toothbrush mustache, he created an iconic figure of the early cinema. The Tramp, or a variation of the character, was a Chaplin staple for the next 22 years.

A number of disputes emerged between Chaplin and Keystone, primarily over salary and artistic control. Leaving Keystone, he signed next with Essanay Studios in November 1914. He completed 14 films for Essanay, including *The Tramp* (released April 11, 1915). During his time with Essanay, his popularity continued to soar. Known as "Chaplinitis," his characters inspired fans to imitate their hero. Songs were written about him, merchandise sold, and numerous impersonators emerged. Essanay, seeking to profit from his popularity, pushed him to release more and more films. Chaplin, however, was taking longer to finish each picture. With the end of his Essanay contract, he signed a one-year contract with Mutual Film Corporation worth $670,000 and that gave him complete artistic freedom. He completed 12 two-reel films over the next year.

In June 1917, Chaplin left Mutual and signed with First National Films. First National allowed him to produce his own films and to establish his own studio. His studio, constructed on Sunset Boulevard in Hollywood, was the setting for his films for the next 35 years. His initial First National release, *A Dog's Life*, paired Chaplin's Tramp with the down-and-out dog Scraps. This laid the foundation for his teaming with young Jackie Coogan in 1921's *The Kid*.

It was during his time with First National that Chaplin began to use his influence within the cinematic community to push his political agenda. With the entry of the

United States into World War I, he enlisted, only to fail the physical. Personally anti-militaristic, he aided the war effort by touring with Mary Pickford and Douglas Fairbanks on the third Liberty Bond Drive. Impressed with the support for the war that he witnessed on the tour, he put on a uniform for the 1918 film *Shoulder's Arms*, in which his character actually captures the German Kaiser.

In 1921, Chaplin made a triumphal return to England. Scandal, however, followed. Upon leaving the United States, he was asked his opinion of Bolshevism. His vague comments led many in the United States to the conclusion that he was a communist sympathizer. Upon his return to the United States, he began working for United Artists, a production company founded by Chaplin, Fairbanks, D. W. Griffith, and Pickford. It was while he was with United Artists that Chaplin produced his most famous films, including *The Gold Rush* (1925), *City Lights* (1931), and *Modern Times* (1936). Interestingly, even with the development of talking motion pictures, he remained steadfast in his support of the silent film. *Modern Times*, however, marked the end of his silent career, and also the retirement of his Tramp persona.

His first sound film, *The Great Dictator* (1940), was his most controversial. A satirical look at Hitler and Nazism, the final speech, given by Chaplin's character, led many critics to believe his sentiments lay with communism and the Soviet Union. His next film, *Monsieur Verdoux* (1947), continued to stir up controversy and was banned in parts of the United States.

Controversy and scandal finally caught up with Chaplin. Traveling to England with his family, he was informed in September 1952 that he could not return to the United States until he addressed questions concerning his political affiliations. He decided to remain in exile in Switzerland, returning to the United States only once more, in 1972, to receive a special Academy Award for his contribution to the cinema. Overseas, he produced and starred in two more films, the last being *A Countess from Hong Kong* in 1966. Chaplin died on December 25, 1977.

Selected Filmography

A Countess from Hong Kong (1967); *The Chaplin Revue* (1959); *A King in New York* (1957); *Limelight* (1952); *Monsieur Verdoux* (1947); *The Great Dictator* (1940); *Modern Times* (1936); *City Lights* (1931); *The Circus* (1928); *The Gold Rush* (1925); *A Woman of Paris: A Drama of Fate* (1923); *The Pilgrim* (1923); *Pay Day* (1922); *Nice and Friendly* (1922); *The Idle Class* (1921); *The Kid* (1921); *A Day's Pleasure* (1919); *Sunnyside* (1919); *The Professor* (1919); *Shoulder Arms* (1918)

References

Gehring, Wes D. *Charlie Chaplin A Bio-Bibliography*. Westport: Greenwood, 1983.

Harness, Kyp. *The Art of Charlie Chaplin: A Film-by-Film Analysis*. Jefferson, NC: McFarland, 2008.

Milton, Joyce. *Tramp The Life of Charlie Chaplin*. New York: HarperCollins, 1996.

Smith, Julian. *Chaplin*. Boston: Twayne, 1984.

—Robert W. Malick

CHAYEFSKY, PADDY.   One of the most distinguished dialogue writers in American cinema, Sydney "Paddy" Chayefsky was a multimedia talent, writing for film, radio, television, and the Broadway stage. Born on January 29, 1923, to Jewish parents in the Bronx, New York, Chayefsky played semiprofessional football and studied accounting and languages in college. Serving in World War II until a landmine explosion cut his army career short and earned him a Purple Heart, Chayefsky gained the nickname "Paddy" as a result of his attempts to avoid kitchen duty by attending Catholic mass. While recovering from his injuries in London, Chayefsky began writing the musical *No T.O. for Love* with fellow patient and composer Jimmy Livingston. Actor Curt Conway discovered Chayefsky's script and produced it as a successful Special Services show in London and Paris, with Chayefsky as a cast member. The show ultimately led to Chayefsky spending the rest of his military career working on the war documentary *The True Glory.*

After a brief stint working in his uncle's print shop, Chayefsky made his first attempt at a writing career; he was initially disappointed, however, suffering through a botched move to Hollywood and a brief tenure writing radio gags for Robert Q. Lewis. Chayefsky eventually got his career on track, though, taking on writing assignments adapting plays for radio and television. During his television career, he wrote over a dozen teleplays, some of which—*Printer's Measure* (1953), *Middle of the Night* (1954), and *The Catered Affair* (1955), for example—demonstrated how thoroughly he had been influenced by growing up in a multiethnic, immigrant Bronx neighborhood. Garnering critical acclaim for his work, he became the first television writer to have his collected teleplays published. Of his numerous television successes, his 1953 teleplay for *Marty*—an endearing story about a lonely, lovelorn 34-year-old Bronx butcher—led to a Hollywood contract.

Learning from his earlier Hollywood failures, Chayefsky asked for an unprecedented contract that gave him full creative control over the screenplay for *Marty* (1954), a decision that led to him taking $13,000 and 5 percent of the film's net profit rather than the customary six-figure fee. Enlisting Delbert Mann to direct and Ernest Borgnine to play the lead, Chayefsky embarked on a thorough preproduction rehearsal schedule that sharply contrasted with standard practices in studio film production. Despite his unorthodox methods—or perhaps as a result of them—*Marty* earned him his first Academy Award for screen writing; the film also won Oscars for Best Picture, Best Actor, and Best Director.

In the wake of *Marty*'s success, Chayefsky adapted his teleplays *The Bachelor Party* (1957) and *Middle of the Night* (1959) as feature film screenplays and sold *The Catered Affair* (1956) to MGM. Over Chayefsky's mild objections, the studio hired Gore Vidal to adapt the latter teleplay. He now focused his attention on *The Goddess* (1958), a John Cromwell film loosely based on the life of Marilyn Monroe. Though he received an Academy Award nomination for his work on this picture, it did not prove to be as critically or financially successful as *Marty.*

After *The Goddess* and *Middle of the Night*, Chayefsky's career underwent a change, as his writing shifted away from working-class realism toward an aesthetic rooted in technical jargon and social satire. Adapting William Bradford Huie's novel *The Americanization of Emily* (1964) for Arthur Hiller, he turned his source material into a World War II satire, set in London, that explored notions of bravery and nationalism and led to Production Code clashes over the film's explicit sexuality and nudity. After adapting the Gold Rush musical *Paint Your Wagon* (1969) for his friend Joshua Logan, he reteamed with Hiller to write the script for *The Hospital* (1971). The biting critique of the dehumanization of urban medical centers and the failure of 1960s-style counterculture earned Chayefsky his second Academy Award.

His most enduring work was the screenplay he wrote for Sidney Lumet's 1976 film *Network*. Interestingly, the original screenplay, concerning "the mad prophet of the airwaves" Howard Beale (Peter Finch) and his exploitation by prophet-hungry media executives, took direct aim at the industry that gave Chayefsky his start. Lumet slightly altered his own omniscient narrative format to accommodate Chayefsky's stylized voice-overs, and *Network* won Chayefsky his third Academy Award. His final screenplay was an adaptation of his own novel *Altered States* (1980); the writer clashed violently with director Ken Russell, reaching the point where he demanded that his name be removed from the final credits.

Despite his film success, Chayefsky asserted that the "theater was his homeground," and he worked steadily on Broadway, adapting *Middle of the Night* to the stage and creating original works such as *The Tenth Man* and *Gideon* while collaborating with iconic figures such as Elia Kazan, Joshua Logan, and Arthur Miller. He also became politically active in the 1970s—a move that was reflected in his writing—founding Writers and Artists for Peace in the Middle East and serving as a delegate to the International Conference on Soviet Jewry. Chayefsky died from an unspecified form of cancer on August 1, 1981.

Selected Filmography

Altered States (1980); *Network* (1976); *The Hospital* (1971); *Paint Your Wagon* (1969); *The Americanization of Emily* (1964); *Middle of the Night* (1959); *The Goddess* (1958); *The Bachelor Party* (1957); *Marty* (1955); *As Young as You Feel* (1951); *The True Glory* (1945)

References

Bowles, Stephen E. *Sidney Lumet: A Guide to References and Resources*. Boston: G. K. Hall, 1979.
Cagle, Chris. "Two Modes of Prestige Film." *Screen* 48(3), Autumn 2007: 291–311.
Clum, John M. *Paddy Chayefsky*. Boston: Twayne, 1976.
New Dramatists Alumni Publication Committee. *Broadway's Fabulous Fifties: How the Playmakers Made It Happen*. Portsmouth, NH: Heinemann, 2002.

—*Jerod Ra'Del Hollyfield*

COEN, JOEL AND ETHAN.   Joel and Ethan Coen (born November 29, 1954, and September 21, 1957, respectively, in Minneapolis) have written and directed more than a dozen films that reflect modern American culture on a number of levels. Spanning a range of genres, the brothers are difficult to categorize. Essentially, their films fit into three broad categories: heartland crime thrillers, Great Depression America, and slapstick class commentary.

Screenwriters, producers, and directors, brothers Ethan (left) and Joel Coen. (AP/Wide World Photos)

Apart from their early script for Sam Raimi's *Crimewave* and Ethan's role as co-writer on two small pieces, the Coen brothers have directed all of their scripts. Beginning with their directorial debut, *Blood Simple* (1984), culture and landscape are revealed as major influences on characters. The first of their heartland crime thrillers, this picture sets an eerily calm backdrop for the grim analysis of adultery and murder. The Coen brothers would revisit the vast Texas scenery again in *No Country for Old Men*. Featuring blackmail and a love affair that leads to murder, *The Man Who Wasn't There* (2001) shares plot similarities with *Blood Simple*. Shot in black and white and set in 1959 Santa Rosa, it does differ from the Coen brothers' first feature, as it includes humorous caricatures that offset the dark, somber plot.

Perhaps the brothers' most successful heartland picture to date is *No Country for Old Men* (2007). This picture follows a disturbed bounty hunter and the police officer tracking him across West Texas in 1980. Landscape is a key factor, not only as an arena but also as a representation of the Old West, where cowboys rule. This picture earned Oscars for Best Picture, Best Director, Best Writing, and Best Supporting Actor. Sharing sinister characters with *No Country for Old Men*, *Fargo* (1996) employs the amusing dialect of the Eskimo-hat-wearing citizens of Fargo, North Dakota. Unlike the superficial characters seen in the Coen brothers' slapstick social commentaries, *Fargo* and *No Country for Old Men* explore shadowy criminal personalities juxtaposed with down-home police officers. *Fargo* became famous not only for its shocking conclusion, but also for the unusual timbre and the humorous turns of phrase that characterized the speech of the picture's characters. The film garnered Oscars for Best Writing and Best Actress for Frances McDormand.

In their early work, the Coen brothers wrote and directed two Great Depression period pieces, beginning with *Miller's Crossing* (1990). This Prohibition-era picture follows gang lieutenant Tom Regan as he warily attempts to reconcile a mob war. With careful depictions of bossism and mafia warfare, the film offers a vivid portrayal of crime culture in 1930s America. Interestingly, the Coens wrote *Barton Fink* (1991), a story about a Hollywood golden age screenwriter with writer's block, while they themselves were struggling with the story for *Miller's Crossing*. Set in 1941, it is full of references to classic American film and literature, including loose representations of writers William Faulkner and Clifford Odets.

Later in their careers, the brothers returned to the Great Depression with *O Brother, Where Art Thou?* (2000). Based on Homer's *Odyssey*, this Mississippi travelogue follows three escaped convicts as they weave their way in and out of key moments in American history. The trio encounters crooked politicians, a one-eyed Bible salesman, the KKK, and George "Babyface" Nelson. As with *The Ladykillers* (2004), which is also set in Mississippi, *O Brother Where Art Thou?* incorporates bluegrass, gospel, blues, and country music to help paint a portrait of an era and a culture.

While they have enjoyed more critical success with heartland crime thrillers like *Fargo* and *No Country for Old Men*, the Coen brothers are well known for their love of screwball and slapstick comedies. The first of these projects was *Raising Arizona* (1987). Set in Tempe, Arizona, the film depicts the desert as a mirror of the dull, empty lives of a bumbling petty criminal and his doe-eyed wife. This lower-class couple is envious of the life of a wealthy, obnoxious car salesman. The salesman, they decide, not only has too much money but more than enough children. They decide to kidnap his toddler, resulting in a humorous but cautionary look at class conflict. This commentary is expanded in *The Big Lebowski* (1998), which follows "The Dude" as he stumbles, in a perversely charming way, through the role of a private investigator in early 1990s Los Angeles.

While the Coen brothers touched upon corporate greed in *Raising Arizona, Barton Fink*, and *The Big Lebowski*, this critique took full shape with the metropolitan fantasy *The Hudsucker Proxy* (1994). The film follows a simple-minded mail clerk as he falls backwards into the role of CEO of the corporate giant Hudsucker Industries. A scathing portrayal of fat cats duping stockholders, *The Hudsucker Proxy* sets the tone for future slapstick class commentaries *Intolerable Cruelty* (2003) and *Burn after Reading* (2008). In *Intolerable Cruelty*, the Coen brothers characterize American stereotypes in a higher economic class than *Raising Arizona* and *The Big Lebowski*. The main character is a dim but successful divorce attorney, and his obsession with a vindictive, gold-digging divorcée costs him dearly. *Intolerable Cruelty* places silly people in high places, and assigns each wealthy fool a metaphorical plank from which to jump as the compulsory murder plot comes tragically undone.

Burn after Reading accomplishes a similar critique, but this outlandish vision of modern urban America adds a more diverse selection of pay grades. Adultery and financial tensions abound among personal trainers, CIA officials, a treasury agent, and a pediatrician. And, as usual with the Coen brothers, the punishment is death. This trend is perhaps their most consistent and effective, contributing to their commentary on the social circles they explore. With strange and shocking depictions of past and present American lifestyles, the films of the Coen brothers offer us alternative and penetrating views of our not-so-everyday lives.

See also: Fargo; No Country for Old Men

Selected Filmography

True Grit (2010); *A Serious Man* (2009); *Burn after Reading* (2008); *No Country for Old Men* (2007); *The Ladykillers* (2004); *Intolerable Cruelty* (2003); *The Man Who Wasn't There* (2001); *O Brother, Where Art Thou?* (2000); *The Big Lebowski* (1998); *Fargo* (1996); *The Hudsucker Proxy* (1994); *Barton Fink* (1991); *Raising Arizona* (1987); *Blood Simple* (1984)

References

Cheshire, Ellen, and John Ashbrook. *Joel and Ethan Coen.* Harpenden, UK: Pocket Essentials, 2005.

Coen, Joel and Ethan Coen. *Blood Simple.* New York: St. Martin's, 1988.

The Internet Movie Database. "Ethan Coen." http://www.imdb.com/name/nm0001053/.

The Internet Movie Database. "Joel Coen." http://www.imdb.com/name/nm0001054/.

Luhr, William, ed. *The Coen Brothers' Fargo.* Cambridge, UK: Cambridge University Press, 2004.

—Adam Dean

COLBERT, CLAUDETTE.   Born in Paris on September 13, 1903, Claudette Colbert was one of Hollywood's highest-paid actresses in the 1930s. She began her screen career in 1927, playing Mary in Frank Capra's *For the Love of Mike,* her only silent film. She made 35 movies in the 1930s and 17 in the 1940s, winning an Oscar in 1935 for *It Happened One Night.* Between 1950 and 1990, she made twelve films and appeared in numerous TV series, winning a Golden Globe in 1988 for *The Two Mrs. Grenvilles,* her last film. In 1934, she stared in three films nominated for Best Picture: *Cleopatra, Imitation of Life,* and *It Happened One Night.* In addition to acting in film, Colbert also appeared on the stage between 1919 and 1985; she was nominated for a Tony in 1958 for her role in *The Marriage Go-Round.*

Directed by Capra, *It Happened One Night* (1934) showcased Colbert's comedic talent. Paired with Clark Gable, Colbert plays Ellie Andrews, a rebellious socialite who is engaged to be married to a fortune hunter her father cannot abide. She escapes her father's control by literally jumping ship (the family yacht) in Miami. A madcap romance ensues between Ellie and Peter Warne (Gable), a reporter she meets on the bus to New York, where she plans to reunite with her husband. The risqué hitchhiking scene in which Colbert lifts the hem of her dress to attract a passing motorist after she and Gable are stranded by the side of the road would have been impossible under MPAA scrutiny had that agency enforced 1930 production codes. Indeed, Colbert herself protested the unladylike display of her lower extremity, but when confronted with the chorus girl brought in to double for her, she reportedly said, "Get her out of here. I'll do it. That's not my leg!" At the time of its release, a *New York Times* movie review touted *It Happened One Night* as offering "a welter of improbable incidents" and claimed that "these hectic doings serve to generate plenty of laughter." According to the reviewer, "Colbert [gives] an engaging and lively performance" (Hall, 1934).

Nominated in 1945 for the Best Actress Oscar for *Since You Went Away* (1944), Colbert lost to Ingrid Bergman, who won for her role in *Gaslight*; nevertheless, this is arguably Colbert's most memorable film. In a dramatic role, rather than the comedic ones in which she was usually cast, Colbert plays Anne Hilton, a soldier's wife who keeps things together on the home front (overseeing two children, a maid, a taciturn elderly colonel, a pseudo uncle, and a bulldog) while waiting for her husband's return. Confronting the harsh realities of war (Anne's husband is reported missing and her oldest daughter's fiancé is killed in battle), Colbert offers audiences reassurance through her strength and wisdom, passion and dignity. Originally reluctant to play the role of the mother of teenage daughters, Colbert agreed after Hedda Hopper and David O. Selznick persuaded her it was an important part. As it turned out, she was so convincing in the role that in 2006, critics declared her to be the "perfect choice to embody America's homeland spirit during WWII" (Sarvady, 2006).

Returning to the screen after a 25-year absence, Colbert took on the role of Alice Grenville, widowed mother-in-law of Ann (Ann-Margret), the social-climbing chorus girl who marries (and murders) Alice's son William, in the TV drama *The Two Mrs. Grenvilles* (1987). "While much is lost" in this adaptation of Dominick Dunne's 1985 novel, it is "an intriguing portrait of the rich and powerful closing ranks to protect themselves from outsiders. The well-connected Alice knows precisely which political and journalistic buttons to push when favors are needed" (O'Connor). Like Alice Grenville, Colbert knew how to push buttons, winning the Golden Globe for Best Performance by an Actress in a Supporting Role in a Series, Mini-Series or Motion Picture Made for TV at the age of 85.

After suffering a series of strokes, Colbert died in Speightstown, Barbados, on July 30, 1996.

References

"Biography for Claudette Colbert." *Turner Classic Movies*, 2009. Available at http://www.tcm.com.

Hall, Mordaunt. "*It Happened One Night* (1934): Claudette Colbert and Clark Gable in a Merry Jaunt from Miami to New York." *New York Times*, February 23, 1934: 23. Available at http://movies.nytimes.com.

O'Connor, John. " 'The Two Mrs. Grenvilles' on NBC." February 6, 1987: 30. Available at http://movies.nytimes.com.

Pace, Eric. "Claudette Colbert, Unflappable Heroine of Screwball Comedies, Is Dead at 92." *New York Times*, July 31, 1996: D 26. Available at http://movies.nytimes.com.

Sarvady, Andrea, et al. "Claudette Colbert." In *Leading Ladies: The 50 Most Unforgettable Actresses of the Studio Era*. San Francisco: Chronicle, 2006.

—*Robin L. Cadwallader*

COPPOLA, FRANCIS FORD. Francis Ford Coppola is one of the few Hollywood directors to have earned auteur status. His reputation has largely been built on the foundation of a number of films that he directed and wrote in the 1970s, particularly the first two *Godfather* films and *Apocalypse Now* (1979).

Coppola was born in Detroit on April 7, 1939, although he grew up in Queens, New York. He became interested in theater while recovering from polio when he was 10 and began writing plays six years later. While attending Hofstra University, he directed and wrote scripts for stage productions that were performed by the institution's student theater group. After discovering the work of Russian filmmaker Sergei Eisenstein, Coppola shifted his focus to the cinema. Finishing his BA in 1960, Coppola continued his studies at UCLA and soon began working with the producer and director Roger Corman. Among Coppola's responsibilities while working with Corman was helping to prepare the script for the English version of the Russian film *Nebo zowet* (1959), which appeared in the United States as *Battle beyond the Sun* (1963), and serving as the sound engineer on *The Young Racers* (1963). He was also given the chance to direct his own film, the horror flick *Dementia 13* (1963), while in Ireland working on *The Young Racers*.

Director Francis Ford Coppola arrives for the screening of the film *Marie-Antoinette*, in Cannes, on Wednesday, May 24, 2006. (AP/Wide World Photos)

Coppola then entered the screenplay for *Pilma, Pilma* in the competition for the UCLA Samuel Goldwyn Award and, upon winning, was hired to write for Seven Arts. Leaving UCLA, he wrote a number of scripts over the next few years. None of them made it to the screen, at least as he had conceived them, and he was fired, along with Gore Vidal, for the disaster *Is Paris Burning?* (1966). Coppola's big break came with *You're a Big Boy Now* (1966), a widely praised film that he wrote and directed and that UCLA accepted as his master's thesis in 1968. He would go on to direct *Finian's Rainbow* (1968) and *The Rain People* (1969), which was sound-mixed at American Zoetrope, an independent production house that Coppola set up in San Francisco in order to gain some freedom from the major studios. He also earned accolades at this time for his studio work and won an Oscar for his part in crafting the script for Twentieth Century-Fox's *Patton* (1970).

The first film entirely produced by Zoetrope was George Lucas's *THX 1138* (1971), a futuristic tale that nearly broke the company. The follow-up was Coppola's masterpiece, *The Godfather* (1972). Based on Mario Puzo's best-selling Mafia novel of the same name, *The Godfather* was co-scripted by Puzo and Coppola. The film turned Coppola into a legend, stabilized Zoetrope, and won a slew of Oscars, including those for Best Picture, Best Actor for Marlon Brando, and Best Screenplay Based on Material from Another Medium. Coppola went on to release *The Conversation* in 1974—a mystery that he produced, wrote, and directed, and that won the Grand Prix International prize at the Cannes Film Festival—and *The Godfather, Part II*, once again writing the screenplay with Puzo. Winning Academy Awards for Best Picture and Best Screenplay Based on Material from Another Medium, as its predecessor had, *The Godfather, Part II* also earned Coppola the Oscar for Best Director. Significantly, he would not release another film for five years, largely due to turmoil on the set of *Apocalypse Now*, the Vietnam War epic adapted from Joseph Conrad's *Heart of Darkness* (1899) that Coppola directed, produced, and co-wrote, and for which he won the Palme d'Or at the Cannes Film Festival.

Soon after finishing *Apocalypse*, Coppola produced the children's movie *The Black Stallion* (1979) and teamed up with George Lucas to serve as executive producer on Akira Kurosawa's *Kagemusha* (1980). Over the following years, Coppola directed and/or wrote a number of mostly unmemorable films, including *One from the Heart* (1982), *The Escape Artist* (1982), *Hammett* (1983), *The Outsiders* (1983), *Rumble Fish* (1983), *The Cotton Club* (1984), and *Mishima: A Life in Four Chapters* (1985). He seemed to get back on track with *Peggy Sue Got Married* (1986), a story about a housewife in her forties who travels back to the end of her high school senior year, but this film was followed by another string of less-than-successful projects, including *Gardens of Stone* (1987) and the biopic *Tucker: The Man and His Dream* (1988).

By the end of the 1980s, Coppola, after having refused to do so for years, agreed to make a third *Godfather* film, hoping to inject needed funds into his struggling production company. He again co-wrote the screenplay with Puzo and directed, but *Godfather, Part III* (1990) proved less successful than the previous two films, earning only the disdain of the critics and an adequate audience. Coppola then directed *Dracula* (1992), which received numerous negative reviews but found success at the box office, as the public responded to the visually stunning retelling of the vampire story. Although Coppola's next directorial efforts—the comedy *Jack* (1996) and *John Grisham's The Rainmaker* (1997), for which he wrote the script—extended *Dracula's* success, his *Youth without Youth* (2007), another film that he wrote and directed, proved to be his poorest-performing picture, grossing less than $250,000 domestically. Even though his record as a director has been spotty since the halcyon days of the 1970s, the respect that Coppola has earned in the film industry has allowed him to continue to make films with studio support.

Selected Filmography

Tetro (2009); *Youth without Youth* (2007); *The Rainmaker* (1997); *Jack* (1996); *Dracula* (1992); *The Godfather: Part III* (1990); *Tucker: The Man and His Dream* (1988); *Gardens of Stone*

(1987); *Peggy Sue Got Married* (1986); *The Cotton Club* (1984); *Rumble Fish* (1983); *The Outsiders* (1983); *One from the Heart* (1982); *Apocalypse Now* (1979); *The Godfather: Part II* (1974); *The Conversation* (1974); *The Godfather* (1972); *The Rain People* (1969); *Finian's Rainbow* (1968); *You're a Big Boy Now* (1966); *Dementia 13* (1963); *The Bellboy and the Playgirls* (1962); *Battle beyond the Sun* (1960)

References

Cowie, Peter. *Coppola: A Biography.* New York: Da Capo, 1994.

Phillips, Gene D., and Walter Murch. *Godfather: The Intimate Francis Ford Coppola.* Lexington: University Press of Kentucky, 2004.

Phillips, Gene D., and Rodney Hill, eds. *Francis Ford Coppola: Interviews.* Jackson: University Press of Mississippi, 2004.

—Albert Rolls

CORMAN, ROGER.   Known in the film industry as "King of the B-movie," Roger Corman has been working as a producer and director since the 1950s. His longevity is the result of his ability to balance filmmaking's creative aspects with the financial bottom line. Although he has worked primarily in the straight-to-video/DVD market for some time, his influence is as far-reaching and intensely felt as ever.

Corman was born in Detroit to Ann and William Corman, on April 5, 1926. William, an engineer, was a frugal man who saved enough to retire at 43 and move his family to California. Like his father, Roger also studied engineering (at Stanford), but wanted a career in Hollywood. After graduating, he took several jobs until he was able to parlay a position as a literary agent into film work (McGee, 1996).

His rise to prominence is inseparable from that of American International Pictures. With the release of *The Fast and the Furious* (1954), for which he provided the story and produced, Corman became one of the company's in-house directors churning out low-budget, teen-oriented genre pictures throughout the 1950s and '60s. While most major studios were struggling to bring in audiences after the advent of television, Corman and AIP were able to attract young, drive-in theater audiences by feeding them a steady diet of horror and science fiction fare (Palmer, Del Valle, and Biodrowski, 1998).

The traits of determination and frugality that Corman inherited from his father made him an ideal fit for AIP, which was always interested in getting the most bang for its buck—and no one was better at making "art" out of "schlock" than Roger Corman. Working hyper-efficiently with eager young talent, he was almost always able to bring his films in on time, and sometimes even under budget (Corman 1990). One-week shoots, single takes, and even recycled sets and footage were all commonplace with Corman films. The overt social commentary, *The Intruder* (1962), was an exception to his usual approach; he even put up his own money for lack of other financing. The *Twilight Zone*–style parable about American racism starred a young William Shatner and was shot on location in Missouri under threat of violence from locals. Despite positive critical reception, the film failed at the box office. It remains one of Corman's most personal and palatable films.

Although a progressive sensibility is evident in many of Corman's films, he is still most recognized for lowbrow pictures such as *The Day the World Ended*, *Little Shop of Horrors*, and the Edgar Allan Poe adaptations that featured Vincent Price. He did, however, also direct two serious examinations of '60s counterculture for AIP before leaving the company over editorial conflicts. *The Wild Angels* (1966), a nihilistic depiction of life among a motorcycle gang, displayed graphic violence and sexuality. The film offered clear evidence of the loosening of the Production Code during the '60s, a phenomenon also signaled by the release of studio pictures such as *Who's Afraid of Virginia Woolf?* (1966) and *The Graduate* (1967) (Williams, 2008). Significantly, *The Wild Angels* starred Peter Fonda and Dennis Hopper. Corman's *The Trip* (1967), one of the first American films to address explicitly LSD use, was written by Jack Nicholson and also featured Fonda and Dennis Hopper; all three counterculture icons would appear in the cult classic *Easy Rider* (1967).

Corman directed the gangster film *The St. Valentine's Day Massacre* (1971) for Twentieth Century-Fox, but found his style incompatible with big-studio filmmaking. He formed his own production company, New World Pictures, in 1971. Although he did direct sporadically between the 1970s and the 1990s, most of his attention over the past 40 years has been focused on the nearly 400 films he has produced. Despite this prodigious achievement, Corman's greatest legacy may still turn out to be how influential he was in launching the careers of such important American directors as Martin Scorsese, Ron Howard, Francis Ford Coppola, Jonathan Demme, John Sayles, and Peter Bogdanovich (Silver and Ursini, 2006).

Selected Filmography

Frankenstein Unbound (1990); *Battle Beyond the Stars* (1980); *Deathsport* (1978); *Von Richthofen and Brown* (1971); *Gas! . . .* (1970); *Bloody Mama* (1970); *The Trip* (1967); *The St. Valentine's Day Massacre* (1967); *The Wild Angels* (1966); *The Tomb of Ligeia* (1964); *The Secret Invasion* (1964); *The Masque of the Red Death* (1964); *The Terror* (1963); *The Raven* (1963); *Tower of London* (1962); *Tales of Terror* (1962); *Premature Burial* (1962); *Pit and the Pendulum* (1961); *The Little Shop of Horrors* (1960); *House of Usher* (1960); *A Bucket of Blood* (1959); *Machine-Gun Kelly* (1958); *Gunslinger* (1956); *Day the World Ended* (1955); *Apache Woman* (1955); *Five Guns West* (1955); *Swamp Women* (1955)

References

Corman, Roger. *How I Made a Hundred Movies in Hollywood and Never Lost a Dime*. New York: Random House, 1990.

McGee, Mark Thomas. *Faster and Furiouser: The Revised and Fattened Fable of American International Pictures*. Jefferson, NC: McFarland, 1996.

Palmer, Randy, David Del Valle, and Steve Biodrowski. "Invasion of the Monster Movie Moguls: An Overview of American International Pictures—Part One." *Cinefantastique* 30, 1998: 78–89.

Silver, Alain, and James Ursini. *Roger Corman: Metaphysics on a Shoestring*. Los Angeles: Silman-James Press, 2006.

Will, David, et al., eds. *Roger Corman*. Cambridge: Edinburgh Film Festival in Association with *Cinema* magazine, 1970.

Williams, Linda. *Screening Sex*. Durham, NC: Duke University Press, 2008.

—*Mikal Gaines*

COSTNER, KEVIN.   Kevin Costner has appeared in over 40 movies, and, in the late 1980s and early 1990s, became one of the film industry's biggest box-office draws. Interestingly, although he has been disparaged by film critics for his lack of talent as an actor, he has remained widely popular with film audiences. Critics have been much kinder in regard to his abilities as a director, however, and Costner is considered by many to be an artist behind the camera.

Born in Lynwood, California, on January 18, 1955, Costner was not initially drawn to a career in acting. A sports star in high school, he turned down a basketball scholarship to play baseball at California State University, Fullerton, where he majored in business. It was only on a chance meeting in an airplane with Richard Burton that Costner decided to quit his job and move to Hollywood. He found a few bit parts in the early 1980s, eventually winning the role of Alex in Lawrence Kasdan's *The Big Chill* (1983). Unfortunately for Costner, his scenes were left on the cutting-room floor (he appears as the corpse at the beginning of the film). He made an impression on Kasdan, however, and two years later the director cast him in his western *Silverado* (1985). Costner played Jake, the wild and impulsive younger brother of the Scott Glenn character, Emmett. The film did well at the box office, and audiences liked the Costner character; he also appeared in two other films released in 1985: *American Flyers* and *Fandango*. The films that followed in the 1980s, *The Untouchables* (1987) and *No Way Out* (1987), would solidify the actor's popularity with audiences. In the former, written by David Mamet, Costner was cast as federal agent Elliot Ness, opposite Sean Connery and Robert De Niro; in the latter film, a military thriller, he stars as a young naval officer wrongfully accused of murder.

As the 1980s came to a close, Costner went on to make two sports films that did extremely well at the box office, eventually becoming cult classics. The first was *Bull Durham* (1988), a romantic comedy, with Susan Sarandon, about an aging minor league baseball player and his exploits with a pitching phenom, played by Tim Robbins. (Sarandon and Robbins met and fell in love on the set of *Bull Durham* although they never married, they lived together for years before finally ending their romantic relationship). The second film was an adaptation of W. P. Kinsella's novel *Shoeless Joe* entitled *Field of Dreams* (1989). In this picture, Ray Kinsella, played by Costner, hears voices that prompt him to build a baseball field on his Iowa farm in order to resurrect the ghosts of the game's past, including his own deceased father. Costner played a baseball veteran twice more, in *For Love of the Game* (1999) and *The Upside of Anger* (2005), and a golf-pro in *Tin Cup* (1996).

In 1990, Costner directed his masterpiece, the epic western *Dances with Wolves*, a tale of a Civil War lieutenant who is stationed on the American frontier and encounters a tribe of Sioux Indians. While it has been criticized as overly romantic, idealizing the

Sioux or perhaps even the landscape itself, the film, which depicts the beauty of Native American life and the tragedy of white expansionism, served as an important cinematic step toward deconstructing traditional westerns and their Eurocentric sensibilities. *Dances with Wolves* won seven Academy Awards, including Best Picture and Best Director. Costner would go on to work on two other epics, the futuristic pictures *Waterworld* (1995) and *The Postman* (1997), the latter directed by Costner, both of which were savaged by critics and failed miserably at the box office. Proving that he was still popular with audiences, though, Costner starred in such films as *JFK* (1991), *The Bodyguard* (1992), Clint Eastwood's *A Perfect World* (1993), and *Thirteen Days in October*, all of which did well commercially. Although he seems to struggle with complex roles, such as those he was

A fan favorite, Kevin Costner has starred in such popular films as *Field of Dreams, Bull Durham,* and *JFK.* (AP/Wide World Photos)

required to play in *JFK* and *Thirteen Days in October,* Costner appears much better suited to roles in which he plays laconic characters, such as those in *The Bodyguard* and *A Perfect World.*

Despite some critical and commercial decline in recent years, Costner has continued to show bright spots, such as his portrayal of hired gun Charley Waite in the western *Open Range* (2003), which he directed. He also scored with audiences playing the terse, methodical, antihero serial killer in *Mr. Brooks* (2007).

Selected Filmography

Mr. Brooks (2007); *The Guardian* (2006); *The Upside of Anger* (2005); *Open Range* (2003); *Dragonfly* (2002); *3000 Miles to Graceland* (2001); *Thirteen Days* (2000); *For Love of the Game* (1999); *Message in a Bottle* (1999); *The Postman* (1997); *Tin Cup* (1996); *Waterworld* (1995); *The War* (1994); *Wyatt Earp* (1994); *A Perfect World* (1993); *The Bodyguard* (1992); *JFK* (1991); *Robin Hood: Prince of Thieves* (1991); *Dances with Wolves* (1990); *Field of Dreams* (1989); *The Gunrunner* (1989); *Bull Durham* (1988); *No Way Out* (1987); *The Untouchables* (1987); *Silverado* (1985)

References

Caddies, Kelvin. *Kevin Costner: Prince of Hollywood*. London: Plexus, 1995.

Castillo, Edward D. Review of *Dances with Wolves* by Kevin Costner and Jim Wilson. *Film Quarterly* 44(4), Summer 1991: 14–23.

Klein, Edward. "Costner in Control." *Vanity Fair*, January 1992: 72–77, 131–34.

Wright, Adrian. *Kevin Costner: A Life on Film*. London: Time Warner, 1992.

—*K. A. Wisniewski*

CUKOR, GEORGE.   George Cukor was a Hollywood director from 1930 to 1981. Considered Hollywood's quintessential actor's director, he was also known as Hollywood's quintessential "woman's director," a reference to the fact that he was especially prized by many of Hollywood's leading actresses and also to his open (at least in Hollywood) homosexuality. With a remarkable number of classic pictures to his credit—such as *Dinner at Eight* (1933), *Camille* (1936), *The Women* (1939), *The Philadelphia Story* (1940), and *My Fair Lady* (1964)—Cukor earned his reputation as a filmmaker who confronted American attitudes toward class and gender differences while maintaining an air of sophistication, wit, and urbanity.

Of Hungarian extraction, George Dewey Cukor was born in New York City on July 7, 1899. From 1920 to 1929, he worked extensively in the New York theater community, directing original productions of works such as *The Great Gatsby* (1925) and *Gypsy* (1929) on Broadway. When sound technology took over the movies in the late 1920s, Hollywood looked to Broadway for artists to ease the transition, and in 1929, Cukor was lured west to serve as a dialogue director. He soon began directing, and beginning in 1932, released a series of films starring Constance Bennett: *Rockabye*, *What Price Hollywood?*, and *Our Betters* (1933). In 1933, he adapted the George S. Kaufman and Edna Ferber hit play *Dinner at Eight*, which became a classic for star Jean Harlow. Many of Cukor's future successes were based on theatrical material, such as *Romeo and Juliet* (1936), *Gaslight* (1944), and *A Double Life* (1947).

From the early *What Price Hollywood?* to *A Double Life*, *The Actress* (1953), *A Star is Born* (1954), and *Les Girls* (1957), Cukor focused much of his work on the lives of theatrical and cinematic performers. *A Double Life* is perhaps his darkest examination of the difficulty of earning a living as a professional actor. Ronald Colman stars as an actor unable to separate his offstage and onstage life, which results in tragedy.

Another consistent anxiety for characters in Cukor's films results from the demands placed on them to behave according to socially defined gender categories. In this light, it is no coincidence that Cukor developed a close bond with star Katharine Hepburn. He cast Hepburn in her first film role in *A Bill of Divorcement* (1932), about a woman who relinquishes the possibility of marriage in favor of taking care of her father as he descends into madness. The pair would make 10 films together over almost five decades, including 1933's huge box-office hit *Little Women*. *Sylvia Scarlett* (1936), a film that was embraced by the *Cahiers du cinéma* critics in the late 1960s, tells the story of a girl who poses as a boy. It features several scenes that suggest Sylvia's ambiguous attitude toward her gender identity, as well as the confusion that results for the men who desire her when she appears as "Sylvester." *Adam's Rib* (1949) pits Hepburn against partner Spencer Tracy in a tale of married lawyers on opposing sides of a court case that hinges on issues informing the battle of the sexes. Another Tracy/Hepburn vehicle, *Pat and Mike* (1952), is a romantic comedy about a pants-wearing woman (Hepburn) who expertly plays a multitude of sports. Other Cukor films starring Hepburn include *Holiday* (1938), *The Philadelphia Story*, and *The Corn Is Green* (1979), a made-for-television movie about a Welsh schoolteacher.

Cukor's reputation for evoking quality performances from his actresses was not just a product of his collaborations with Hepburn. He directed Greta Garbo in one of her best films, *Camille*, and worked for two years preparing (and directing a substantial portion of) the women-centered *Gone with the Wind* (1939); and after being replaced on that pic-

Portrait of Oscar-winning film director George Cukor during an interview on January 14, 1982, in Paris. (AP/Wide World Photos)

ture by Victor Fleming (at the request of star Clark Gable), he chose to make a film without a single male actor: *The Women* (1939). In the 1950s, Cukor made a succession of films starring comic talent Judy Holliday. In 1954, he drew out what is perhaps Judy Garland's best performance in *A Star is Born*. Ten years later, Cukor won an Oscar for directing another musical, the classic *My Fair Lady*.

Cukor died on January 23, 1983, at his home in Los Angeles.

Selected Filmography

Rich and Famous (1981); *The Blue Bird* (1976); *Travels with My Aunt* (1972); *Justine* (1969); *My Fair Lady* (1964); *The Chapman Report* (1962); *Something's Got to Give* (1962); *Let's Make Love* (1960); *Heller in Pink Tights* (1960); *Wild Is the Wind* (1957); *Les Girls* (1957); *Bhowani*

Junction (1956); *A Star Is Born* (1954); *It Should Happen to You* (1954); *The Actress* (1953); *Pat and Mike* (1952); *The Marrying Kind* (1952); *The Model and the Marriage Broker* (1951); *Born Yesterday* (1950); *A Life of Her Own* (1950); *Adam's Rib* (1949); *Edward, My Son* (1949); *A Double Life* (1947); *Winged Victory* (1944); *Gaslight* (1944); *Resistance and Ohm's Law* (1943); *Keeper of the Flame* (1942); *Her Cardboard Lover* (1942); *Two-Faced Woman* (1941); *A Woman's Face* (1941); *The Philadelphia Story* (1940); *Susan and God* (1940); *The Women* (1939); *Zaza* (1938); *Holiday* (1938); *Camille* (1936); *Romeo and Juliet* (1936); *Sylvia Scarlett* (1935); *David Copperfield* (1935); *Little Women* (1933); *Dinner at Eight* (1933); *Our Betters* (1933); *A Bill of Divorcement* (1932); *What Price Hollywood?* (1932); *Tarnished Lady* (1931); *The Virtuous Sin* (1930)

References

Long, Robert Emmet, ed. *George Cukor: Interviews*. Jackson: University of Mississippi Press, 2001.

McGilligan, Patrick. *George Cukor: A Double Life*. New York: Harper-Perennial, 1992.

Phillips, Gene. *George Cukor*. Boston: Twayne, 1982.

—Kyle Stevens

CURTIZ, MICHAEL. Michael Curtiz, born in Hungary on December 24, 1886, as Manó Kertész Kaminer, immigrated to the United States in 1926, and would go on to direct over 100 films in Hollywood. Like so many of his émigré colleagues, he brought to Hollywood considerable experience from the European film industry. Curtiz had worked sparingly in Hungary and Denmark in the 1910s, but spent the bulk of his time working in Austria for Sascha Films, directing more than 20 films from 1919 to 1926. *Moon of Israel* (1924) was noticed by Jack Warner, who recruited Curtiz to remake the film for Warner Bros. as *Noah's Ark* (1928).

From 1926 to 1954, Curtiz directed 88 films for Warner Bros., "probably a record for one man's direction of features at a single studio" (Meyer 1978). Highlights of his Warner Bros. work include a series of action-adventure films starring Errol Flynn and Olivia de Havilland in the mid- to late 1930s, most notably *The Adventures of Robin Hood* (1938); the George M. Cohan biopic *Yankee Doodle Dandy* (1941), which netted James Cagney his only Academy Award; Joan Crawford's comeback film *Mildred Pierce* (1945); and *Casablanca* (1942), the Hollywood classic that many have described as an "accidental masterpiece."

Curtiz's most popular pictures, *Yankee Doodle Dandy* and *Casablanca*, exploit a timely connection to World War II. In both films, a struggle between the conflicting demands of individual interest and national service is dramatized. Humphrey Bogart's Rick, a café owner in the colonial city, claims no interest in politics—"I stick my neck out for nobody," he repeatedly declares. The selfishness and bravado of *Yankee*'s Cohan as a young prodigy threatens to undermine his career. By the end, though, the star protagonists come down firmly on the side of sacrifice for the country. Rick forgoes his personal interests for the greater good when he helps his love interest, Ilsa (Ingrid Bergman), to flee safely with Resistance leader Victor Laszlo (Paul Henreid), while Cohan overcomes his self-aggrandizing tendencies to pen patriotic songs that served the national morale in both World Wars.

Curtiz was also the most prolific director of the musical biopic, popular studio fare during the 1940s and '50s. During his time with Warner Bros., in addition to *Yankee Doodle Dandy,* Curtiz directed Cary Grant as a straight Cole Porter in *Night and Day* (1946) and Kirk Douglas as a jazz prodigy resembling Bix Beiderbecke in *Young Man with a Horn* (1950). He also remade *The Jazz Singer* in 1952 and directed *The Helen Morgan Story* in 1957.

The fact that the musical biopic is considered more a producer's than a director's genre fits Curtiz's reputation as a cooperative studio-era director. As opposed to many of his more difficult contemporaries, Curtiz welcomed the collaborative efficiency of studio-era filmmaking, ceding creative control to producers and other technical staff whenever necessary. After his relationship with Warner Bros. disintegrated in the mid-1950s, Curtiz, characteristic of this phase of Hollywood history, worked according to the "package-unit" system, by "short-term film-by-film arrangement" (Bordwell, Staiger, and Thompson, 1985). He would make 15 more films for a variety of studios before he died of cancer on April 10, 1962, but found the new, more star-driven Hollywood less conducive to quality filmmaking than the studio era. In an interview during this period, Curtiz lamented the state of his industry, complaining that the greed of "unions and stars" was "destroying the wonderful machine that was—and still is—Hollywood" (Meyer, 1978, 101).

Selected Filmography

The Comancheros (1961); *Francis of Assisi* (1961); *The Adventures of Huckleberry Finn* (1960); *A Breath of Scandal* (1960); *The Man in the Net* (1959); *The Hangman* (1959); *King Creole* (1958); *The Proud Rebel* (1958); *The Helen Morgan Story* (1957); *We're No Angels* (1955); *White Christmas* (1954); *The Egyptian* (1954); *The Boy from Oklahoma* (1954); *Trouble along the Way* (1953); *The Jazz Singer* (1952); *The Story of Will Rogers* (1952); *I'll See You in My Dreams* (1951); *Jim Thorpe—All-American* (1951); *Force of Arms* (1951); *The Breaking Point* (1950); *Bright Leaf* (1950); *Young Man with a Horn* (1950); *Flamingo Road* (1949); *The Unsuspected* (1947); *Life with Father* (1947); *Night and Day* (1946); *Mildred Pierce* (1945); *Roughly Speaking* (1945); *Janie* (1944); *Passage to Marseille* (1944); *This Is the Army* (1943); *Mission to Moscow* (1943); *Casablanca* (1942); *Yankee Doodle Dandy* (1942); *Captains of the Clouds* (1942); *Dive Bomber* (1941); *The Sea Wolf* (1941); *Santa Fe Trail* (1940); *The Sea Hawk* (1940); *Virginia City* (1940); *Four Wives* (1939); *Essex and Elizabeth* (1939); *Daughters Courageous* (1939); *Dodge City* (1939); *Angels with Dirty Faces* (1938); *Four Daughters* (1938); *The Adventures of Robin Hood* (1938); *Kid Galahad* (1937); *The Charge of the Light Brigade* (1936); *The Walking Dead* (1936); *Captain Blood* (1935); *The Case of the Curious Bride* (1935); *Black Fury* (1935); *Mandalay* (1934); *Female* (1933); *The Kennel Murder Case* (1933); *Mystery of the Wax Museum* (1933); *20,000 Years in Sing Sing* (1932); *Doctor X* (1932); *Noah's Ark* (1928)

References

Bordwell, David, Janet Staiger, and Kristin Thompson. *The Classical Hollywood Cinema.* New York: Columbia University Press, 1985.

Harmetz, Aljean. *Round Up the Usual Suspects: The Making of Casablanca*. New York: Hyperion, 1992.

Kinnard, Roy. *The American Films of Michael Curtiz*. Metuchen, NJ: Scarecrow Press, 1986.

Meyer, William R. *Warner Brothers Directors: The Hard-Boiled, the Comic, and the Weepies*. New Rochelle, NY: Arlington House, 1978.

Robertson, James C. *The Casablanca Man: The Cinema of Michael Curtiz*. London: Routledge, 1993.

—Jesse Schlotterbeck

D

DEMILLE, CECIL B. Cecil B. DeMille's films resonated with audiences wrestling with contemporary changes in 1900s American society. As one of very few producer/directors who used silent-film-era successes to transition into a new era of sound, he made a total of 70 movies between 1913 and 1956. DeMille's evolution from anonymity to fame was in large part propelled by his ability both to express and to question themes within American culture. These changes, occurring within a populace rent by contending visions of society's present and future are embedded in each of DeMille's films.

Born August 12, 1881, in Ashfield, Massachusetts, DeMille enrolled at New York City's Academy of Dramatic Arts, becoming a moderately successful playwright. In 1913, he and his friend Jesse L. Lasky formed the Jesse L. Lasky Feature Play Company, and DeMille began his career as a director and producer. After producing 24 films, the Lasky company merged with Famous Players in 1916, and created a profitable nine-year association that resulted in the production of 28 additional silent pictures. Successful films such as Lasky's *The Squaw Man* (1914, 1931) and *The Virginian* (1914) helped to propel moving pictures into the spotlight of American culture, creating a popular audience and spurring businessmen to invest in the industry.

Perhaps most significantly for DeMille, films like *The Cheat* (1915), *Old Wives for New* (1918), *The King of Kings* (1927), and *The Ten Commandments* (1956) addressed the growing tension between traditional religious values and the values of a new consumer culture. Boldly using high budgets, new lighting techniques, and a blend of the sexual and the religious, DeMille earned a reputation as the "Great Showman," or "Master of Spectacle," even before the advent of sound and color in filmmaking. Astute viewers began to recognize that beneath his showmanship, however, lurked a cinematic critique of early twentieth-century consumer culture. In *The Cheat* (1915), for example, DeMille explored the fall from grace of a society woman who gambles away Red Cross money. In religious epics such as *The Sign of the Cross* (1932) and *Samson and Delilah* (1949), DeMille emphasized Christian religious values in the same moment that he titillated audiences with nude scenes and sexual situations. The inclusion of unpredictable scenes that displayed nudity, wealth, and physical desires in

Cecil B. DeMille sits on his lawn at his home in Hollywood on June 19, 1956. (AP/Wide World Photos)

biblical films and in *Cleopatra* presented to viewers modern moral issues clearly exposed against the backdrop of an ancient setting. They also benefited, however, from DeMille's strict attention to historical detail, as evidenced in *Cleopatra* and *The Ten Commandments*. He believed historical accuracy to be of the greatest importance to a film's integrity, and sought to create innovative films that creatively fit within a historical model rather than existing outside of historical truth.

Often considered a great entertainer and remembered for "bathtub" scenes awash with sexual connotation, DeMille's strengths and skills as an influential, thought-provoking director have at times been overlooked. Having won only one Academy Award throughout his long and very successful career, for *The Greatest Show on Earth*, he was awarded three Oscars in the 1950s, almost as an afterthought for his achievements. In the end, though, his ability to blend the past and the present in popular and thought-provoking films made DeMille one of the most significant figures in the history of American cinema. He died on January 21, 1959, in Hollywood.

Selected Filmography

The Ten Commandments (1956); *The Greatest Show on Earth* (1952); *Samson and Delilah* (1949); *Unconquered* (1947); *The Story of Dr. Wassell* (1944); *Reap the Wild Wind* (1942); *Union Pacific* (1939); *The Buccaneer* (1938); *The Plainsman* (1936); *The Crusades* (1935); *Cleopatra* (1934); *Four Frightened People* (1934); *This Day and Age* (1933); *The Sign of the Cross* (1932); *The Squaw Man* (1931); *Madam Satan* (1930); *Dynamite* (1929); *The Godless Girl* (1929); *Walking Back* (1928); *The King of Kings* (1927); *The Volga Boatman* (1926); *The Golden Bed* (1925); *Feet of Clay* (1924); *The Ten Commandments* (1923); *Adam's Rib* (1923); *Manslaughter* (1922); *Fool's Paradise* (1921); *Why Change Your Wife?* (1920); *Male and Female* (1919); *Don't Change Your Husband* (1919); *The Squaw Man* (1918); *The Devil-Stone* (1917); *The Woman*

God Forgot (1917); *Joan the Woman* (1916); *The Trail of the Lonesome Pine* (1916); *Temptation* (1915); *The Cheat* (1915); *Carmen* (1915); *The Arab* (1915); *The Girl of the Golden West* (1915); *The Ghost Breaker* (1914); *The Virginian* (1914); *The Squaw Man* (1914)

References

Bernardi, Daniel, ed. *The Birth of Whiteness: Race and the Emergence of U.S. Cinema*. New Brunswick, NJ: Rutgers University Press, 1996.

Birchard, Robert S. *Cecil B. DeMille's Hollywood*. Lexington: University Press of Kentucky, 2004.

Essoe, Gabe, and Raymond Lee. *DeMille: The Man and His Pictures*. New York: Castle, 1970.

Higashi, Sumiko. *Cecil B. DeMille and American Culture: The Silent Era*. Berkeley: University of California Press, 1994.

Louvish, Simon. *Cecil B. DeMille: A Life in Art*. New York: St. Martin's, 2007

Ringgold, Gene, and Bodeen, DeWitt. *The Films of Cecil B. DeMille*. New York: Citadel, 1969.

—*Sarah Bischoff*

DE NIRO, ROBERT. One of the most respected actors in the American cinema, much of Robert De Niro's success can be attributed to his collaborations with director Martin Scorsese. Known for his shy and self-effacing manner, De Niro has never made for an easy or particularly riveting interview. His on-screen intensity, however, helps account for his psychologically complex and gripping portrayals of outsiders populating the fringes of society. At his most subtle, De Niro captures the spirit of youth, rebellion, and alienation that figure prominently in New Hollywood cinema. At its most extreme, De Niro's embodiment of marginality has resulted in some of the screen's most violent and frightening outcasts.

Robert De Niro was born in New York City on August 17, 1943. The son of artists, he quit high school, and settled on the idea of becoming an actor at the tender age of 17. In the early 1960s, he pursued his ambition by studying Method acting under Stella Adler at the Conservatory of Acting at the New School. Several of his earliest screen roles came in films by director Brian De Palma: *Greetings* (1968), *The Wedding Party* (1969) and *Hi, Mom!* (1970). Much later, he would star as Al Capone in De Palma's *The Untouchables* (1987), well after they had both become famous.

Significantly, De Niro's partnership with Scorsese has resulted in many of his most iconic and enduring screen performances. Together, De Niro and Scorsese have contributed highly stylized images of the ethnic-American experience while exploring the complex dynamics of urbanity, organized crime, and Catholic and Jewish guilt. In 1973, De Niro starred as Johnny Boy in Scorsese's *Mean Streets*, a film that would prefigure a commitment to an examination of complex cultural themes in a number of the duo's most well-received films, including *Raging Bull* (1980), *Goodfellas* (1990), and *Casino* (1995). Interestingly, although directed by Francis Ford Coppola, his role in *The Godfather II* (1974), for which he won an Academy Award for Best Supporting Actor, was an important marker of his on-screen exploration of Italian American identity.

It may be argued that it was De Niro's realistic and nuanced portrayal of a delusional Vietnam War veteran-turned-cab-driver in Scorsese's *Taxi Driver* (1976) that would make both of them household names. As Travis Bickle, De Niro gave audiences both a highly disturbing glimpse of urban alienation, and one of Hollywood's most well-known and oft-repeated expressions: "Are you talkin' to me?" Another important film that De Niro starred in during this period was Michael Cimino's *The Deer Hunter* (1978). Playing Michael, an angst-ridden war veteran, De Niro captured the anguish of post-Vietnam-era America.

Heavily influenced by Adler's emphasis on physical transformation, De Niro stunned audiences with his portrayal of Jake La Motta in Scorsese's *Raging Bull*. In order to shoot the scenes when La Motta is at his fighting best, De Niro first forced his body into rock-hard physical condition; once those scenes were completed, Scorsese shut down production for four months so De Niro could eat his way across Europe and gain the 60 pounds he needed to add to his frame in order to portray the older, fallen La Motta. De Niro's profoundly unsettling performance in *Raging Bull* ultimately earned him the Academy Award for Best Actor.

De Niro's great versatility as an actor is suggested by his willingness to accept roles in films of divergent genres. He starred in Scorsese's musical *New York, New York* (1977), for example; in Terry Gilliam's science-fiction adventure *Brazil* (1985); in Roland Joffé's period piece *The Mission* (1986); and in the partially animated *The Adventures of Rocky and Bullwinkle* (2000). De Niro also channeled his well-established screen persona as a tough guy for parodic effect in the DreamWorks animation picture *Shark Tale* (2004), for which he provided the voice of Don Lino, a gangster shark boss.

De Niro's various turns at comedy also convey his range as an actor. In Scorsese's darkly humorous *The King of Comedy* (1982), De Niro plays Rupert Pupkin, an aspiring stand-up comic who kidnaps a talk show host played by Jerry Lewis. Playing straight man to other actors, De Niro also appeared in the road-show comedies *Midnight Run* (1988) and *We're No Angels* (1989). More recently, he has appeared in comedic films such as *Analyze This* (1999), in which he plays a gangster undergoing psychoanalysis, and *Meet the Parents* (2000), in which he portrays an intimidating and overprotective future father-in-law intent on tormenting his daughter's fiancé. Both films spawned sequels, *Analyze That* (2002) and *Meet the Fockers* (2004), respectively, although these follow-ups were less successful than the original films.

In 1993, De Niro made his directorial debut with *A Bronx Tale* (1993). Written by and co-starring newcomer Chazz Palminteri, the film revisited a number of the issues concerning Italian American identity that De Niro and Scorsese had explored in some of their earlier films. Like Scorsese's *Mean Streets*, Palminteri's *Bronx Tale* follows the stories of neighborhood gangsters and the hardworking citizens who must share their communal space with these despicable and violent men. The film focuses on Calogero "C" Anello (played brilliantly by De Niro look-alike Lillo Brancato). The teenage son of a hardworking and honest bus driver, Lorenzo Anello (De Niro), C is torn between his loyalty to his father and what he imagines to be his respect for the neighborhood crime boss, Sonny LoSpecchio (Palminteri).

The Good Shepherd (2006), the only other film De Niro has directed, examines the origins of the CIA. Intriguingly, the film takes the viewer back in history in order to examine contemporary, post-9/11 issues regarding national intelligence. Although a much darker film, *The Good Shepherd* is consistent with De Niro's liberal politics, which have playfully materialized on the screen in the satire *Wag the Dog* (1997), in which De Niro plays a spinmeister who creates a fake war in order to divert the public's attention from a presidential sex scandal.

In 1988, De Niro branched out from acting and established Tribeca Films. He would eventually go on to organize the Tribeca Film Festival in 2002. Despite the commercial and critical failures of some of his more recent films, De Niro's legacy as a serious and gifted actor seems assured.

Selected Filmography

Machete (2010); *Everybody's Fine* (2009); *Righteous Kill* (2008); *Stardust* (2007); *Meet the Fockers* (2004); *Analyze That* (2002); *City by the Sea* (2002); *Showtime* (2002); *The Score* (2001) *15 Minutes* (2001); *Meet the Parents* (2000); *Men of Honor* (2000); *The Adventures of Rocky & Bullwinkle* (2000); *Flawless* (1999); *Analyze This* (1999); *Ronin* (1998); *Jackie Brown* (1997); *Cop Land* (1997); *Heat* (1995); *Casino* (1995); *Frankenstein* (1994); *Cape Fear* (1991); *Goodfellas* (1990); *The Untouchables* (1987); *The Mission* (1986); *Brazil* (1985); *Once Upon a Time in America* (1984); *Raging Bull* (1980); *The Deer Hunter* (1978); *New York, New York* (1977); *The Last Tycoon* (1976); *1900* (1976); *Taxi Driver* (1976); *The Godfather: Part II* (1974); *Mean Streets* (1973); *Bang the Drum Slowly* (1973); *The Gang That Couldn't Shoot Straight* (1971)

References

Baxter, John. *De Niro: A Biography.* London: HarperCollins, 2003.

Dougan, Andy. *Untouchable: A Biography of Robert De Niro.* New York: Thunder's Mouth, 2002.

Friedman, Lawrence S. *The Cinema of Martin Scorsese.* New York: Continuum, 1998.

Kolker, Robert P. *A Cinema of Loneliness: Penn, Stone, Kubrick, Scorsese, Spielberg, Altman.* New York: Oxford University Press, 1980.

Smith, Greg M. "Choosing Silence: Robert De Niro and the Celebrity Interview." Henry, Charlotte, and Angela Ndalianis, eds. *Stars in Our Eyes: The Star Phenomenon in the Contemporary Era.* Westport, CT: Praeger, 2002.

—*Linda Mokdad*

DEREN, MAYA. Maya Deren is a figure in the history of cinema referred to with notable frequency as a "legend." Deren's life and work are the stuff of legend, as is well documented by her biographers in their thousand-page (unfinished) work *The Legend of Maya Deren.* At the root of this legend is Deren's first film, *Meshes of the Afternoon* (1943), which set the terms for postwar American avant-garde film and remains a seminal work to this day. Indeed, in 1990, the Library of Congress acknowledged its historical and aesthetic import, preserving it in the National Film Registry. Yet, Deren's significance extends far beyond a single film. In promoting her work, particular *Meshes*, she not only innovatively modified practices of distribution and exhibition for independent film; she also demanded that audiences and cultural institutions take film seriously as an art form. In this way, her limited catalog—a handful of short films, poetry, prose and theory, photographs and an extensive study of Vodoun culture—belie her significance in American film. Deren's aesthetic creativity in filmmaking, her writing and lectures on film art and its place in modernity, and her tireless efforts as an advocate for experimental filmmaking laid the foundation for the independent American cinema. These accomplishments are indeed legendary, especially if one considers that she died when she was only 44.

Born Eleanora Derenkowsky in Kiev, on April 29, 1917, Deren and her parents fled the anti-Semitic pogroms of the Ukraine five years later. They ultimately immigrated to the United States and shortened their name to Deren. Eleanora attended the League of Nations' International School, and then matriculated at Syracuse University. After graduating, she became a key figure in the Trotskyist Young People's Socialist League, and embraced both political activism and the bohemian life of New York's East Village before continuing her education. Upon earning her master's degree from Smith College, she took a job as an assistant to noted choreographer Katherine Dunham and traveled to Los Angeles with the road tour of *Cabin in the Sky* (1941). In Los Angeles, Deren met and married Czech filmmaker Alexander Hammid, who introduced her to visual media by taking her to foreign films and by teaching her still photography and filmmaking. Deren was transformed by this relationship and embraced her new life by changing her name, in 1943, to "Maya," the word for the Hindu concept of illusion as the expression of deeper truth. In that same year, she also bought a 16 mm Bolex camera—purchased with the inheritance money left to her after the death of her father—and made her first film with Hammid, *Meshes of the Afternoon*.

If *Meshes of the Afternoon* were the only film Deren ever made, it alone would mark her place in American film history. The 14-minute silent film (later scored by her third husband, Teijo Ito) won her a Guggenheim fellowship—Deren was the first filmmaker to apply for and to win the prestigious award. *Meshes* would go on to win the Cannes Festival's 16mm "Grand Prix Internationale," the first awarded to an American, or a woman. Although it was made for only $275—"what Hollywood spends on lipstick," as Deren was known to say—*Meshes* heralded the postwar American avant-garde, bringing a more narrative, or personal, style than earlier experimental films, which tended to favor shapes and figures over human subjects. Lauded by East Coast film critics such as Parker Tyler and P. Adams Sitney, the narrative focuses on the experiences of the protagonist (played by Deren) and unfolds within a few circumscribed locations—mostly within the couple's home. *Meshes* appropriates images from both film noir and women's melodrama, reworking them to convey the female protagonist's nightmarish experiences of domestic entrapment and alienation. The film articulates these themes through the use of complex editing patterns and film speeds, techniques that would mark Deren's filmmaking for the rest of her career. *Meshes'* formal experimentation with personal narrative ushered in the "New American Cinema" of Stan

Brakhage, Shirley Clarke, and Kenneth Anger, among others. *Meshes*, in fact, continues to inspire filmmakers to this day: Barbara Hammer pays homage to it in her film *I Was/ I Am* (1973); David Lynch has also honored Deren in his visual and narrative citations of *Meshes*, visible in both *Inland Empire* (2006) and, more strikingly, in *Lost Highway* (1997); and Derek Jarman named it among his 10 favorite films.

What continues to intrigue both artists and audiences alike about Deren are her original, highly aesthetic camerawork and editing, by which she attempts to manipulate filmic images from a specific subjective or "motivated" position. Deren's fascination with the camera's ability seemingly to transport bodies physically can be understood as the filmic translation of her lifelong obsession with dance. Based on her apprenticeship with Dunham, Deren published the article "Religious Possession in Dancing" (1942); she would remain fascinated, both as a scholar and artist, with the idea of ritualistic possession for the rest of her life. Indeed, several years later, Deren received a grant to research Haitian Vodoun practice, which led to the publication of her ethnographic book *Divine Horsemen: The Living Gods of Haiti* (1953); the production of the film *Divine Horsemen* (1985; edited posthumously); and the musical record *Voices of Haiti* (1953). Previous to this project, many of her short films—such as *A Study in Choreography for Camera* (1945), *Ritual in Transfigured Time* (1945–46), *Meditation on Violence* (1948), and *The Very Eye of Night* (1952–55)—included dance and often featured accomplished dancers. Yet, rather than simply photographing dance performances, she used her knowledge of choreography to emancipate the camera from its theatrical moorings. Her camera did not follow a dancer but was itself made to dance, freeing it from spatial and temporal laws of cinematic realism. The ability of film to represent the changing laws of time and space in the twentieth century is a theoretical insight Deren developed in great detail in *An Anagram of Ideas on Art, Form and Film* (1946). Deren's philosophical treatise is a highly sophisticated theoretical engagement with film art that foreshadows much poststructuralist film theory in its examination of cinema's new images of time and space.

Deren's short film *At Land* (1944) exemplifies her ambition to experiment with film's spatiotemporal relations. One of the most famous edited sequences from *Meshes* involves the elliptical cutting of shots of the protagonist walking from sea to sidewalk to carpeted floor. *At Land* builds on these series of images, extending the metaphorical connection of the sea to women's social mobility. Deren, once again the protagonist, is filmed at the beach and then in various enclosed spaces, either with individual men or at a dinner party. The protagonist's connection with nature and the sea is in stark contrast with her disruptive presence in social situations. This discord is expressed through jump cuts and elliptical edits, creating jarring dislocations for the viewer and protagonist alike. Her films experiment with formal qualities to articulate pointed critiques of sexual and gender power relations (and, at times, race and class as well). *Meshes, At Land, Ritual in Transfigured Time* (1946), and the unfinished *Witch's Cradle* (1943) all deal with women's spatial confinement, frequently symbolized as entanglements with little potential for escape. For example, *Meshes* ends with the ambiguous death of the protagonist, draped in seaweed, while *Ritual* concludes with the female African American protagonist (played by dancer Rita Christiani) sinking into the depths of the ocean, a stunning film image that turns from positive to negative print. That Deren was able to convey such complex ideas in powerful images and emotionally compelling narratives begins to explain the lasting influence of her films.

It should be noted that contemporary musicians and filmmakers who pay their respects to Deren are indebted to feminists who spearheaded the women's recovery projects that brought attention to Deren in the 1970s and '80s. After her death in New York City on October 13, 1961, Deren's films fell out of favor and, for the most part, were no longer screened. Fortunately, second-wave feminists introduced them to new audiences at women's film festivals. Although activists and scholars held showings of her films out of the desire to reclaim women artists of the past, it was her tenacious work to organize structures such as the Film Artists Society that especially drew the attention of second-wave feminists, and feminist film collectives, like East London's "Circles." Tireless in her efforts to build collective structures to support artists, she established the Creative Film Foundation to underwrite grants for independent filmmakers as well as to organize film screenings and symposia. She also lectured and published widely, developing a public discourse about cinema in journals and magazines to help build an audience for film art. Organizer, activist, film theorist, ethnographer, auteur—these titles may not sum up Maya Deren, but taken together, they begin to explain why she is one of the most influential and legendary figures of American cinema.

Selected Filmography

Divine Horsemen: The Living Gods of Haiti (1985); *Maeva* (1961); *The Very Eye of Night* (1958); *Meditation on Violence* (1948); *Ritual in Transfigured Time* (1946); *A Study in Choreography for Camera* (1945); *At Land* (1944); *Witch's Cradle* (1944); *Meshes of the Afternoon* (1943)

References

Clark, VèVè A., Millicent Hodson, and Catrina Neiman. *The Legend of Maya Deren: A Documentary Biography and Collected Works.* New York: Anthology Film Archives/ Film Culture, 1988.

Geller, Theresa L. "The Personal Cinema of Maya Deren: *Meshes of the Afternoon* and Its Critical Reception in the History of the Avant-Garde." *Biography: An Interdisciplinary Quarterly* 29(1), Winter 2006: 140–58.

Nichols, Bill, ed. *Maya Deren and the American Avant-Garde.* Berkeley: University of California Press, 2001.

Rabinovitz, Lauren. *Points of Resistance: Women, Power, and Politics in the New York Avant-Garde Cinema, 1943–1971.* Urbana: University of Illinois Press, 1991.

—*Theresa L. Geller*

DISNEY, WALT.   Born into a poor Chicago family on December 5, 1901, Walt Disney achieved the American Dream by becoming a popular filmmaker. He created a number of the world's most famous fictional characters and completely redefined the nature of filmic animation. An admired family man, Disney was an iconic figure whose films came to be understood as symbolic representations of the American way of life.

When still very young, Disney developed a passion for drawing. In 1928, he created what would become perhaps his best-known cartoon character, Mickey Mouse. Originally brought to the big screen during the silent era, Disney's cartoon shorts were soon accompanied by sound, and in 1929 he began to release his *Silly Symphonies*. Although they were not wildly successful, the *Silly Symphonies* series did give rise to Disney's most successful cartoon short *The Three Little Pigs* (1933). By the end of the 1930s, Mickey Mouse would be joined by two steadfast friends: Donald Duck and Goofy.

One of Disney's most important career moments came in 1937 when he released the first full-length animated feature film, *Snow White and the Seven Dwarfs*. The film was a box-office success and laid the groundwork for future extremely popular film animations, including *Pinocchio* (1940), *Fantasia* (1940), *Dumbo* (1941), *Bambi* (1942), and *Cinderella* (1950).

Creator of Mickey Mouse, Walt Disney achieved preeminence in movies and television and revolutionized the leisure industry with his theme park, Disneyland, which opened in 1955. (Library of Congress)

The release of these animated films made the Disney name synonymous with family entertainment. Building on the success of his earlier animated films, Disney would go on to make his first feature film combining live action and animation, *Song of the South* (1946); his first all-live-action feature film, *Treasure Island* (1950); and his second feature combining live action and animation, *Mary Poppins* (1964).

During the 1930s and 1940s, nearly every animated feature film was in some way influenced by Disney. Expressing communal values such as hard work, the triumph of the underdog, national self-definition, and the importance of religious freedom, Disney's cartoons and films reassured Americans confronted with the threats of the Great Depression, World War II, and the looming Cold War. Viewers related to his innocent, defenseless protagonists, who were usually desperate, insecure figures faced with overwhelming challenges, but whose innate goodness and extraordinary will to survive eventually allowed them to overcome evil and set things right in their communities. By the 1950s, Disney had become such a well-known and beloved figure that his face regularly graced the covers of the nation's more popular magazines.

Disney was a self-admitted moralist who saw himself as more than simply a filmmaker; he believed that he had a responsibility to act as an educator, child psychologist—child experts claimed that his films had a healthy impact on young viewers—and even as a pastor. In 1954, the National Education Association actually rewarded him with an American Education Award for his educational work. During the 1950s, millions of ordinary Americans welcomed "Uncle Walt" into their homes by way of their television sets, where he amused children and gave advice to parents, as well as inspiration and reassurance.

Beyond his contributions to film entertainment, Disney also changed the shape of recreation in America. He brought his figures to life and turned amusement into an imaginative experience by building his first Disneyland in Anaheim, California, in 1955, providing park-goers with rides, haunted houses, and jungle adventures. He also planned on opening a Walt Disney World Resort in Florida, but did not live to see the project completed in 1971.

Disney died on December 15, 1966, in Los Angeles, leaving behind a multibillion-dollar business empire. Throughout his life he demonstrated how one could be empowered by fantasy and proved, at least on a certain level, that dreams could come true.

Selected Filmography

Winnie the Pooh and the Blustery Day (1968); *The Happiest Millionaire* (1967); *The Jungle Book* (1967); *Scrooge McDuck and Money* (1967); *Monkeys, Go Home!* (1967); *The Fighting Prince of Donegal* (1966); *Follow Me, Boys!* (1966); *Lt. Robin Crusoe, U.S.N.* (1966); *The Ugly Dachshund* (1966); *Winnie the Pooh and the Honey Tree* (1966); *That Darn Cat!* (1965); *The Monkey's Uncle* (1965); *Emil and the Detectives* (1964); *The Moon-Spinners* (1964); *The Three Lives of Thomasina* (1964); *The Misadventures of Merlin Jones* (1964); *The Sword in the Stone* (1963); *Dr. Syn, Alias the Scarecrow* (1963); *The Incredible Journey* (1963); *Savage Sam* (1963); *Miracle of the White Stallions* (1963); *Son of Flubber* (1963); *Babes in Toyland* (1961); *The Absent-Minded Professor* (1961); *The Saga of Windwagon Smith* (1961); *One Hundred and One Dalmatians* (1961); *Swiss Family Robinson* (1960); *Ten Who Dared* (1960); *Pollyanna* (1960); *Kidnapped* (1960); *Noah's Ark* (1959); *Old Yeller* (1957); *Johnny Tremain* (1957); *The Great Locomotive Chase* (1956); *Davy Crockett, King of the Wild Frontier* (1955); *Contrast in Rhythm* (1955); *20000 Leagues under the Sea* (1954); *Rob Roy, the Highland Rogue* (1953); *The Sword and the Rose* (1953); *The Story of Robin Hood and His Merrie Men* (1952); *Alice in Wonderland* (1951); *Treasure Island* (1950); *Cinderella* (1950); *The Wind in the Willows* (1949); *Johnny Appleseed* (1948); *Song of the South* (1946); *Peter and the Wolf* (1946); *Bambi* (1942); *Der Fuehrer's Face* (1942); *Dumbo* (1941); *Fantasia* (1940); *Pinocchio* (1940); *Snow White and the Seven Dwarfs* (1937); *Three Blind Mouseketeers* (1936); *Three Little Pigs* (1933); *Babes in the Woods* (1932); *Haunted House* (1929); *Hell's Bells* (1929); *Jungle Rhythm* (1929); *Springtime* (1929); *The Plowboy* (1929); *Mickey's Follies* (1929); *Mickey's Choo-Choo* (1929); *The Gallopin' Gaucho* (1928); *Steamboat Willie* (1928)

References

Gabler, Neal. *Walt Disney: The Biography*. London: Aurum Press, 2008.
Watts, Steven. *The Magic Kingdom: Walt Disney and the American Way of Life*. New York: Houghton Mifflin, 1997.

—Daniela Ribitsch

DONNER, RICHARD.   Richard Donner is a director and producer best known for his work on films such as *The Omen* (1976), *Superman* (1978), and the *Lethal Weapon* series of pictures released during the 1980s and 1990s. He has earned a reputation as a director who brings a raw authenticity to his source material and as someone who gives actors a lot of flexibility in their interpretations of roles. Although not as famous as many of his contemporaries, Donner has left an indelible mark on American film, and continues to be active in the industry.

Born in New York City on April 24, 1930, Donner dreamed of becoming an actor, but his cinematic interests eventually shifted to directing. He began his career making travelogues and commercials before moving into television in the late 1950s. Although Donner directed his first feature film, *X-15*, in 1961, his greatest successes came on the small screen. Throughout the 1960s and early 1970s, he directed episodes of series such as *The Rifleman, Combat, Get Smart, Twilight Zone*, and *Kojak*. It was Donner who directed the legendary *Twilight Zone* episode "Nightmare at 20,000 Feet," which featured William Shatner as an airline passenger convinced a monster is trying to crash the plane.

Donner continued working in television throughout the early 1970s, but also began making inroads into feature films. His first feature film of that decade, *Twinky* (1970), also known as *Lola*, was an intriguing yet somewhat derivative picture that failed to generate much interest. It was not until 1976 that Donner made the film that brought him mainstream attention. *The Omen*, the story of the young son of an American ambassador who is actually the Antichrist, became one of the biggest films of that year, earning excellent reviews for its finely crafted suspense. The movie remains one of the best horror films of the decade, an intoxicating brew of social cynicism and apocalyptic dread accentuated by Donner's taut direction. The film mirrored the popular fascination with the supernatural and end-of-the-world scenarios popular in mid-1970s America. The primary credit goes to Donner for taking what could have been a B-movie and turning it into a believable, intelligent thriller.

Donner followed *The Omen*'s success by directing the 1978 hit adaptation of *Superman*. The defining feature of the film is that it took its subject matter seriously, marking a departure from the camp approach so prevalent since the 1960s. *Superman* launched a successful franchise, although Donner never made another film in the series. While making the original film, Donner shot scenes to be included in the sequel, *Superman 2*, but disagreements with producers led to his dismissal from the project in favor of Richard Lester. Donner always hoped to get his version of *Superman 2* released, which became a reality in 2006 when his cut appeared on DVD.

The 1980s saw Donner more active than ever. He directed seven films, spanning the genres of comedy, adventure, and action. Donner's films included *The Goonies*, his 1985 collaboration with Steven Spielberg; his update of Dickens with *Scrooged*; and the first two films of the *Lethal Weapon* series. Both *The Goonies* and *Scrooged* fared well with filmgoers if not with critics, and both remain cult favorites. Yet it was Donner's contributions to the *Lethal Weapon* film series that earned him his greatest hits of the decade. The series took the traditional "buddy film" scenario and applied it to the action genre so prevalent in the 1980s, especially films such as *Rambo* and *Dirty Harry*. What set Donner's films apart was his ability to make the characters likeable and believable. The formula worked so well that Donner directed two more *Lethal Weapon* films in the 1990s, although neither performed as well as the first had at the box office.

Donner remains an active film director in the twenty-first century, although he has yet to recapture his mainstream success of previous decades. Recent years have seen him turn his attention to film production as well as directing. Donner has served as producer or executive producer on numerous projects, including the HBO series *Tales from the Crypt* and the highly popular *X-Men* film series. He is also involved in the writing of graphic novels, serving with Geoff Johns and Adam Kubert as the new team behind *Action Comics*. After four decades of success, Richard Donner shows no signs of slowing down.

Selected Filmography

16 Blocks (2006); *Timeline* (2003); *Lethal Weapon 4* (1998); *Conspiracy Theory* (1997); *Assassins* (1995); *Maverick* (1994); *Lethal Weapon 3* (1992); *Radio Flyer* (1992); *Lethal Weapon 2* (1989); *Scrooged* (1988); *Lethal Weapon* (1987); *The Goonies* (1985); *Ladyhawke* (1985); *The Toy* (1982); *Inside Moves* (1980); *Superman* (1978); *The Omen* (1976); *Lola* (1970); *Salt and Pepper* (1968); *X-15* (1961)

References

Muir, John Kenneth. *Horror Films of the 1970s*. Jefferson, NC: McFarland, 2002.
Rossen, Jake. *Superman vs. Hollywood: How Fiendish Producers, Devious Directors, and Warring Writers Grounded an American Icon*. Chicago: Cappella, 2008.

—Brad L. Duren

DURAS, MARGUERITE. Marguerite Duras is widely known in France as a prolific screenwriter, director, novelist, and playwright. In the United States, however, despite an interested critical reception for her novels among feminist academics, the numerous films that she both wrote and directed are not well known. Instead, her cinematic reputation rests primarily on two films: *Hiroshima, mon amour* (1959), for which she wrote the screenplay, and *The Lover* (1992), directed by Jean-Jacques Annaud, which is based on her "autobiographical" novel *L'Amant*.

Duras's early life experiences in the colonial world of French Indochina serve as the raw material for much of her literary and cinematic work. She was born Marguerite

Donnadieu on April 4, 1914, in Gia-Dinh, a suburb of Saigon. Her parents, Henri and Marie Donnadieu, had immigrated as part of France's "Colonial Army," and were employed there as schoolteachers; following Marguerite's father's death in 1918, her mother raised Duras and her two older brothers alone. Apart from a short trip to France during her childhood, she lived in or near Saigon until she was 18. In her teens, she had an affair with an older, married Chinese man, an experience she would return to in many variations in her work. At 18, she left Indochina to travel with her family to France, where she studied philosophy, law, mathematics, and political science at the École Libre des Sciences Politiques in Paris. In 1937, while working as a secretary at the Ministry of Colonies, she began to read extensively in French and American literature and to attend performances at the Théatre des Mathurins, seeing this as a kind of apprenticeship in the theater. During this time she also joined the Resistance, and formed a friendship with François Mitterand that lasted until his death. Her first novel, *Les impudents*, was published in 1943, and it was at this time that she took the surname Duras, after the district in France were her father had owned a house. She began writing for the screen in1959, when she authored the classic film treatment for *Hiroshima, mon amour*, directed by Alain Resnais.

Hiroshima, mon amour immediately established Duras's international reputation as a screenwriter, and has remained widely popular with both critics and moviegoers. Her script for the film, which has been published in book form, is seen by many as a work of art in its own right. In this film, which tells the story of a brief affair between a French actress and a Japanese man, both married, both nameless, Duras explores many of the themes that have characterized her body of work as a whole. These include the role of memory and forgetting; the links between violence and sexuality, domination and desire; and the process of mourning as a way of working through but never completely healing from the traumas of the past. Duras's commitment to the primacy of the literary over the visual can be seen in this film in the form of a discontinuity between the soundtrack and the images, a technique that serves to disrupt narrative coherence, leaving the viewer out of sync with the moment of the film in much the same way that the protagonists seem caught between past and present. Duras would later use this technique to great effect in her own films, most notably *India Song* (1975). In addition to this auditory discontinuity, *Hiroshima, mon amour* undermines its own narrative development by means of jump cutting to and from multiple flashbacks—some brief, some longer—thereby foregrounding the significance of memories that insist upon erupting into the present.

During the years from 1959 to 1984, Duras wrote numerous novels, including several that were adapted to the screen by directors such as Peter Brooks (*Moderato cantabile*, 1960), Jules Dassin (*10:30 PM Summer*, 1963), and Tony Richardson (*Le marin de Gibraltar*, 1966). She also wrote and directed 19 films of her own. Nevertheless, it was not until the 1984 publication of her novel *L'Amant*—almost immediately published in English translation as *The Lover*—that she found a wide readership in the United States. This novel, which won the 1984 Prix Goncourt, served as the basis for the 1992 film by the same title, directed in English by Jean-Jacques Annaud. It is this film that has secured Duras's reputation among English-speaking audiences, in spite of the fact that she was so outraged by Annaud's treatment of her story that she broke with him during production and subsequently wrote *L'Amant du Chine du nord* (translated into English as *The North China Lover*) as a literary attempt to reclaim her own story from Annaud's filmic version. *The Lover* tells the story of Duras's teenage relationship with her older Chinese lover, and has received a mixed critical response, owing in part to its strange blend of eroticism and emotional distance. Reviewers have commented on the dynamics of colonialism that haunt the film (between a young woman, who nevertheless represents the colonial power of Europe, and an older man, who nevertheless represents the oppressed, colonized Other) and on the undercurrents of masochism that characterize the girl's sexuality—themes that are prominent in many of Duras's films and novels. *The Lover* was nominated in 1993 for an Academy Award for cinematography.

Duras died in her Left Bank apartment in Paris on March 3, 1996.

Selected Filmography

The Children (1984); *Il dialogo di Roma* (1982); *L'homme atlantique* (1981); *Agatha et les lectures illimitées* (1981); *Le navire Night* (1979); *Aurélia Steiner* (Melbourne) (1979); *Cesarée* (1978); *Les mains négatives* (1978); *Baxter, Vera Baxter* (1977); *Le camion* (1977); *Entire Days in the Trees* (1976); *India Song* (1975); *Woman of the Ganges* (1974); *Nathalie Granger* (1972); *Jaune le soleil* (1972); *Détruire dit-elle* (1969); *La musica* (1967); *Mademoiselle* (1966); *Hiroshima mon amour* (1959)

References

Adler, Laure. *Marguerite Duras: A Life*. Trans. by Anne-Marie Glasheen. Chicago: University of Chicago Press, 2000.

Glassman, Deborah. *Marguerite Duras: Fascinating Vision and Narrative Cure*. Rutherford, NJ: Fairleigh Dickinson University Press, 1991.

Harvey, Robert, and Hélène Volat. *Marguerite Duras: A Bio-Bibliography*. Westport, CT: Greenwood, 1997.

Hofmann, Carol. *Forgetting and Marguerite Duras*. Niwot: University Press of Colorado, 1991.

—Judith Poxon

E

EASTWOOD, CLINT.   With a career in motion pictures that has spanned five-and-a-half decades, Clint Eastwood is one of Hollywood's living legends. A talented actor, an Oscar-winning director and producer, and an accomplished composer of scores and soundtracks, Eastwood's versatility has been the key to his enduring success.

Born on May 31, 1930, in San Francisco, Clinton Eastwood Jr. grew up in the Oakland/Piedmont area of Northern California. He served as a swimming instructor in the army from 1950 to 1953, and after a brief stint at Los Angeles City College, signed a bit player contract with Universal Studios in 1954. During his time at Universal, Eastwood landed small roles in B-movies, such as *Tarantula* (1955), then studied acting with Jack Kosslyn, whose maxim—"Don't just do something, *stand* there"— formed the cornerstone of Eastwood's acting philosophy. Seething stillness and brooding intensity became his trademarks, and in time the tall, lean, soft-spoken actor began to attract attention.

Eastwood's first starring role came from the CBS television series, *Rawhide*, where he played the boyish cowhand Rowdy Yates from 1959 to 1965. Occasionally called upon to sing in the show, Eastwood recorded an album, "Cowboy Favorites," in 1962, and made guest appearances on many TV shows, including *Mr. Ed*, in the early part of the decade. In 1964, Eastwood left Hollywood for a long-shot opportunity that would ultimately establish his international stardom. *A Fistful of Dollars* (1964) was the first in Sergio Leone's trio of "spaghetti westerns" featuring "the man with no name." In this Italian remake of Akira Kurosawa's samurai classic *Yojimbo* (1961), Eastwood plays a lone killer who rides into a Mexican border town where two rival gangs hire him for his gunfighting prowess. By the end of the film, the gangs have killed each other off, and Eastwood, the lone survivor, rides out of town.

The European success of *A Fistful of Dollars* led to two sequels, *For a Few Dollars More* (1965) and *The Good, the Bad, and the Ugly* (1966). These three Italian films would redefine the American western by introducing sadistic violence, unorthodox scores by Ennio Morricone, and a new kind of amoral hero driven by self-interest rather than an embedded code of ethics. Draped in a poncho, and clenching a cigarillo between impassive lips, Eastwood gave this enigmatic killer a nonchalant style that had

great appeal throughout Europe. Likewise, the American release of the trilogy in the late 1960s launched Eastwood's career as a Hollywood superstar.

Shortly after forging this iconic image for the Old West, Eastwood created what may be his signature character, the renegade San Francisco police detective "Dirty Harry" Callahan. In *Dirty Harry* (1971), which Eastwood's mentor Don Siegel directed, Eastwood plays a volatile cop with a distrust of authority and a penchant for phrases like, "Do you feel lucky, punk?" A box-office smash, *Dirty Harry* spawned four sequels: *Magnum Force* (1973), *The Enforcer* (1976), *Sudden Impact* (1983), and *The Dead Pool* (1988). Harry's intolerance for bureaucracy, lack of sympathy for criminals, and accuracy with his .44 magnum revolver popularized an image of vigilante justice that

Best-known as a tough, quiet action hero from many westerns and police dramas, Clint Eastwood is one of Hollywood's top film stars. He began a career as a movie director in the 1970s and won wide acclaim for his 1992 film *Unforgiven*. Eastwood also served as mayor of Carmel, California, from 1986 to 1988, declining to run for reelection after his first term. (AP/Wide World Photos)

would peak in the Reagan era. Reagan himself made reference to a line from *Sudden Impact* while threatening to veto a proposed tax increase. Mimicking Harry, Reagan told his congressional opposition, "Go ahead, make my day."

Eastwood has played the avenging stranger role in numerous westerns, such as *Hang 'Em High* (1968) and *Pale Rider* (1985). He has replayed the streetwise cop role in *The Gauntlet* (1977) and *The Rookie* (1990). Laconic action heroes may be Eastwood's specialty, but he has also enjoyed box-office success with comic roles such as Philo Beddoe, the best friend of an orangutan in *Every Which Way but Loose* (1978) and its sequel, *Any Which Way You Can* (1980). He sang show tunes in the musical *Paint Your Wagon* (1969), and played the sensitive romantic lead to Meryl Streep's Oscar-nominated performance in *The Bridges of Madison County* (1995). Streep is just one of many actors to receive Oscar attention in a film that Eastwood directed.

As a director, Clint Eastwood has a reputation for finishing on time and under budget, but he is also increasingly known for his artistry. Eastwood has twice won the Academy Award for directing. Making his debut with the suspense thriller *Play Misty for Me* (1971), Eastwood showed daring in both his subject and his style. As star and director of *High Plains Drifter* (1973), he took an allegorical approach, using a small western town to comment on the cultural malaise surrounding Vietnam. Many of his westerns, such as *The Outlaw Josey Wales* (1976), transcend generic boundaries by expressing ambivalence toward violence. Such was the case with *Unforgiven* (1992), which won Eastwood his first Oscar for directing. He was nominated again for *Mystic River* (2003), a murder mystery that deflates the notion that revenge is satisfying, and won a second Oscar for *Million Dollar Baby* (2004), a boxing film with a complex treatment of euthanasia. Eastwood is also a self-taught jazz pianist and has frequently composed the scores for his films. He received two Golden Globe nominations for music in the same year with *Gran Torino* (2008) and *Changeling* (2008).

Eastwood's recent movies have challenged accepted notions about his right-wing political views. Although he has often supported Republican presidential candidates, and even served as Republican mayor of Carmel, California, from 1986 to 1988, Eastwood characterizes himself as a libertarian. His later films have done as much to deconstruct the image of the right-wing reactionary as his early films did to construct it. He has completed eight films since 2000. He has starred in four of those films, and won many prestigious awards in the process. Now 80, Eastwood shows no signs of slowing down. He continues to make movies that remake his own Hollywood legend.

See also: Flags of Our Fathers; Letters from Iwo Jima

Selected Filmography

Hereafter (2010); *Invictus* (2009); *Gran Torino* (2008); *Changeling* (2008); *Letters from Iwo Jima* (2006); *Flags of Our Fathers* (2006); *Million Dollar Baby* (2004); *Mystic River* (2003); *Blood Work* (2002); *Space Cowboys* (2000); *True Crime* (1999); *Midnight in the Garden of Good and Evil* (1997); *Absolute Power* (1997); *The Bridges of Madison County* (1995); *A Perfect World* (1993); *Unforgiven* (1992); *The Rookie* (1990); *White Hunter Black Heart* (1990); *Bird* (1988); *Heartbreak Ridge* (1986); *Pale Rider* (1985); *Sudden Impact* (1983); *Honkytonk Man* (1982); *Firefox* (1982); *Bronco Billy* (1980); *The Gauntlet* (1977); *The Outlaw Josey Wales* (1976); *The Eiger Sanction* (1975); *Breezy* (1973); *Thunderbolt and Lightfoot* (1974); *Magnum Force* (1973); *High Plains Drifter* (1973); *Joe Kidd* (1972); *Dirty Harry* (1971); *Play Misty for Me* (1971); *The Beguiled* (1971); *Kelly's Heroes* (1970); *Two Mules for Sister Sara* (1970); *Paint Your Wagon* (1969); *Where Eagles Dare* (1968); *Coogan's Bluff* (1968); *Hang 'Em High* (1968); *The Good, the Bad, and the Ugly* (1966); *For a Few Dollars More* (1965); *A Fistful of Dollars* (1964)

References

Engel, Leonard, ed. *Clint Eastwood: Actor and Director*. Salt Lake City: University of Utah Press, 2007.

McGilligan, Patrick. *Clint: The Life and Legend*. New York: St. Martin's, 2002.

—*Joseph Christopher Schaub*

EBERT, ROGER.   Award-winning film critic Roger Ebert is the most prolific voice in American film review today. At an amazing rate of six reviews a week for over four decades, he has critiqued over 10,000 films. Showing a nearly unparalleled love of movies and using his keen eye for exceptional films, Ebert has consistently provided his audience with straightforward and honest critiques.

Ebert was born in Urbana, Illinois on June 18, 1942. An only child, Ebert filled his early years devouring science fiction books and magazines. While in high school, Ebert became a reporter for Champaign-Urbana's *News Gazette* and explored the theatrical world-even making a contemporary version of H.G. Wells's *War of the Worlds* with classmate Dave Stiers (David Ogden Stiers of *M*A*S*H* fame). During his college years at the University of Illinois, Ebert gained notoriety and awards with his column in the campus newspaper.

Following college, Ebert took a post at the *Chicago Sun-Times* as their new film critic. His reviews brought a fresh and youthful spirit to the stodgy and often cantankerous film critics from Chicago's other three newspapers. Early in his career, Ebert showed a knack for sharp wit and a keen eye for talent when he praised an unknown Martin Scorsese's film *Who's That Knocking at My Door* (1967) when it premiered at the Chicago Film Festival (Kelly, 1991).

Roger Ebert had a banner year in 1975, starting with winning a Pulitzer Prize for his film criticisms, the first ever in that category. This was also the year that he joined with Gene Siskel reviewing movies on television. Over the next six years, Siskel and Ebert would hone their craft in the Chicago area and on public broadcasting.

In 1981, Ebert, along with Siskel, signed a syndication deal with Tribune Entertainment that brought their show, "At the Movies," to a national audience. Three years later in 1984, the pair received an Emmy Award nomination in the category of Outstanding Informational Series. This would be their first of six nominations.

In 1986, *Siskel & Ebert* debuted as a weekly syndicated series with Buena Vista Television. Ebert gave the show its future trademark by introducing the thumb's-up/down method of completing each film review. With continued reviews in the *Chicago Sun-Times* and a nationally syndicated show, Ebert was solidifying his status as one of America's premier film critics.

The success and influence of *Siskel & Ebert* came full circle when their glowing review of *One False Move* (1992) transformed this film, planned for video release, to theatrical distribution and box-office success (Hill, 2005). Sparks also flew in 1992 when Ebert chided Siskel for giving out essential plot details while they reviewed *The Crying Game* (1992). The openness and candor of their reviews made *Siskel & Ebert* a program the national audience often used to decide whether or not to see a film.

Gene Siskel died of brain cancer in 1999, ending a remarkable partnership with Ebert that had lasted nearly 25 years. While still mourning the loss, Ebert honored his friend and colleague by continuing the show with guest critics and then permanently teaming with *Chicago Sun-Times* reporter Richard Roeper in 2000. The newly minted *Ebert & Roeper* continued in syndication at the outset of the twenty-first century.

In 2004, Roger Ebert was diagnosed with a form of throat cancer that required debilitating radiation and chemotherapy. During this ordeal, he continued to write over 250 film reviews for the *Chicago Sun-Times*, as well as for other publications (Scott, 2008). This was a staggering number for anyone, especially someone battling cancer. In his absence, Richard Roeper continued the television program with guest stars and occasional contributions from Ebert himself.

During the summer of 2006, Roger Ebert experienced a recurrence of cancer in his salivary gland. An attempt at corrective surgery failed, leaving him without the ability to speak. Undeterred, Ebert continued to be influential through his multifaceted presence as a reviewer. Using his column with the *Chicago Sun-Times* and multiple Internet sites, Ebert employed his sharp wit, ability to put himself in the audience's place, and keen eye for exceptional films to maintain his position as one of America's leading film critics.

See also: Film Criticism

Newspaper columnists and film critics Roger Ebert (left) and Gene Siskel (right). (AP/Wide World Photos)

References

Ebert, Roger. *Your Movie Sucks*. Kansas City, MO: Andrews McMeel Universal, 2007.

Hill, Lee Alan. "30 Years at the Movies with Roger Ebert." *Television Week*, January 24, 2005.

Kelly, Mary Pat. *Martin Scorsese: A Journey*. New York: Thunder's Mouth, 1991.

Scott, A. O. "Roger Ebert: The Critic Behind the Thumb." *New York Times*, April 13, 2008.

—*Lucas Calhoun*

EDISON, THOMAS ALVA.   Thomas Alva Edison was an American inventor and entrepreneur. Filing over 1,000 patents during his lifetime, he influenced several components of the movie industry. He conducted experimental research in lighting, telegraphy, sound recording, and moving photography, and established industry standards, such as 35mm film and sprockets.

American inventor Thomas Edison (1847–1931). (Chaiba Media)

Born February 11, 1847, in Milan, Ohio, Edison attended both public and private schools in Port Huron, Michigan. He held various jobs in the telegraph industry during the 1860s, and in 1868 the journal *Telegrapher* published his design for a duplex telegraph, a system that allowed messages to be sent in opposite directions on one wire simultaneously. He soon gained a reputation as an innovator in the field of telegraphy; he would go on to use his expertise in this area to help him develop landmark technological products.

The filmmaking pioneer Eadweard Muybridge, who had been on the lecture circuit touting his short moving picture *Animal Locomotion*, visited Edison's lab in February 1888. Realizing that Muybridge was on to something with his "zoopraxiscope," a device for projecting filmic images, Edison initially suggested a partnership. Although the partnership never materialized, Edison did adapt Muybridge's zoopraxiscope, turning it into a much more efficient projecting device that came to be called the Kinetoscope. On August 24, 1891, Edison filed patents for the kinetograph (camera) and the kinetoscope (the viewing implement), and Muybridge was largely forgotten.

Edison founded the Edison Manufacturing Company in 1887, building its first studio, which he called the "Black Maria," in 1892. *Scientific American* covered the first public demonstration of the Kinetoscope on May 9, 1893. For the event, Edison created a one reel melodrama, *Dashed to Death* (1909); ever utilitarian in his approach, the inventor recorded a car being driven over a cliff at Palisades, New Jersey, not merely as an aesthetic phenomenon, but to discover a formula for a steel axle that could withstand the fiery crash when the vehicle hit bottom.

Edison used the Black Maria to promote Buffalo Bill's Wild West Show, before that troupe toured Europe, including producing film images of Annie Oakley demonstrating her skills as a sharp-shooter. Edison also shot scenes of boxing at his studio; interestingly, while live boxing was prohibited by law, viewing images of the brutal sport in a kinetoscope was not. In 1894 or 1895, William Kennedy Laurie Dickson (1860–1935) and

William Heise produced the earliest synchronized sound motion picture, the "Dickson Experimental Sound Film," depicting Dickson playing the violin.

A shrewd businessman, Edison wisely secured patents or copyrights where applicable. Significantly, copyright law did not recognize motion pictures as a separate entity until 1912; before this time, Edison sent what were known as positive paper prints—a technique developed by Dickson—to the Copyright Office at the Library of Congress. Derived from short films, these prints were copyrighted as a series of still photographs gathered together in sequence; they provide us with a record of early twentieth-century life, including the attire, popular buildings, and technologies of the time.

Edison and the co-inventors in his employ created films based on popular subject matter that had been captured by still photographers during the post-Civil War period. Of particular note, they produced short scenic and travel films, with images of buildings and natural wonders—Coney Island and Niagara Falls, for example—and new-era modes of transportation. Edison's cameras even recorded significant events of the day, such as President William McKinley's inauguration and assassination, the Galveston hurricane (1900), and the San Francisco earthquake (1906).

Although he was not always the one who invented many of the gadgets on which he worked, Edison had a keen technological eye and improved on several mechanical devices designed by others. This was the case in regard to his work in the burgeoning film industry, as he was able to apply his previously acquired knowledge of telegraphy and sound production in phonographs to the development of other forms of presentation. In essence, then, it may be said that Edison functioned more as what we would understand today as an executive producer of films, rather than as their creator. Remarkably entrepreneurial, Edison realized that he could use the popular new medium of film to advertise his Kinetoscope, which he did in *Moving Picture News* (1913), and elsewhere. After an extraordinarily productive life, Edison died on October 18, 1931.

References

Israel, Paul. *Edison: A Life of Invention*. New York: John Wiley, 1998.
Phillips, Ray. *Edison's Kinetoscope and Its Films: A History to 1896*. Westport, CT: Greenwood, 1997.
Wood, Bret, prod. *Edison: The Invention of the Movies*. DVD. New York: Kino on Video, 2005.

—*Ralph Hartsock*

EISENSTEIN, SERGEI. Sergei Eisenstein was the most famous Soviet filmmaker of the first half of the twentieth century. Today, he is best remembered for his film *Battleship Potemkin* (1925), and for his revolutionary theory of film montage, which is still taught today as one of the few alternatives to traditional Hollywood continuity editing.

Born on January 23, 1898, in Riga, Latvia, Sergei Mikhailovich Eisenstein grew up in a prosperous middle-class Russian family. At an early age he learned French and

German and developed a lifelong passion for the arts. He entered the Institute for Civil Engineers in St. Petersburg in 1915, but was called to military service during World War I. During the Russian Revolution of 1917, he sided with the Red Army and served in the corps of engineers as an explosives technician.

Eisenstein began his artistic career as a cartoonist, publishing his first cartoon in the *St. Petersburg Gazette* in 1917. He soon became fascinated by theater, however, doing set design, costuming, and acting while still a soldier. In 1920, he secured a position as scenic designer of the First Proletkult Workers Theater. During his time at Proletkult, he began his study of stage direction with Vsevelod Meyerhold, whose theory of biomechanics and stagecraft would have lasting impact on him. Eisenstein quickly advanced as a director, and in 1923, he published his first article in *Lef*, the journal of the artistic left front. Entitled "The Montage of Attractions," the piece explained his theory for using all the elements of the dramatic arts to produce specific reactions in the audience.

Through his theatrical work, Eisenstein gradually developed an interest in film. After viewing the films of D. W. Griffith, particularly *Intolerance* (1916), and studying the basics of film editing with Lev Kuleshov and Esther Shub, he created a short film component, entitled *Glumov's Diary* (1923), for one of his stage productions. By the end of 1924, Eisenstein had completed his first feature-length film. *Strike*, which premiered in Moscow early in 1925, told the story of workers who strike to protest labor conditions at a locomotive factory and are brutally crushed by Tsarist forces. In making the film, he had dispensed with the notion of stars playing main characters, which, by the 1920s, had already become an established policy in Hollywood. Instead, he used "typage" (choosing actors with particular looks), and treated the assembled masses as characters. The film had mixed reception, but it was clear that Eisenstein was beginning to revolutionize cinema to further the aims of socialism.

In his next film, *Battleship Potemkin* (1925), he fully realized his desire to express revolutionary ideas through film. *Battleship Potemkin* was originally intended as part of a twentieth-anniversary celebration of the anti-Tsarist uprisings of 1905. Eisenstein, however, reduced the many protests of that year to a single representative episode, the mutiny of a crew of sailors who were being mistreated by the officers on their ship. Told in five acts, *Battleship Potemkin* has a precise dialectical structure specifically designed to foment revolutionary action. Through film editing, Eisenstein was developing a theory of dialectical montage based on Marx's notion of dialectical materialism in which the movement of history is determined by the clashing of economic forces. Using the formula—thesis plus antithesis yields synthesis—Eisenstein proposed that meaning, or synthesis, in film was derived from the collision between two contrasting shots. His technique was profoundly different from the Hollywood style of continuity editing, which strove to combine shots in a seamless, fluid manner so that the audience could be fully absorbed in the story. Unlike his Hollywood counterparts, Eisenstein was not interested in entertaining, but in inspiring revolutionary action.

In each of *Battleship Potemkin*'s sections, an act of injustice is followed by an act of rebellion, with the rebellious acts escalating as the film progresses. In the first act, sailors who are fed rotten meat protest by staging a hunger strike. In the second act, marines who are ordered to shoot the sailors refuse and join the sailors in a mutiny.

In the third act, the battleship pulls into the Odessa harbor displaying a dead sailor before the people of Odessa with a placard indicating he died "for a bowl of soup." Residents of Odessa then support the sailors with gifts of food. In the fourth, and most famous act, "The Odessa Steps," the Tsar's soldiers massacre the supporters on a monumental white staircase, after which the battleship fires on the Tsarist buildings at the top of the stairs. The Odessa Steps sequence features all of Eisenstein's various forms of montage (metric, rhythmic, tonal, overtonal, and intellectual) to create powerful emotional effects in the viewer. In the final act, a squadron of the Tsar's navy is called in to destroy the mutinous battleship, but instead, all the ships join the *Potemkin* in a revolutionary show of solidarity.

Battleship Potemkin made Eisenstein an international celebrity. The film was exhibited around the world, and although it was banned in some countries for its revolutionary content, it was generally seen as heralding the arrival of a new movement in film history, known as Soviet Montage. Following *Potemkin*, Eisenstein made *October* (known in the West as *Ten Days That Shook the World*, 1928), which tells, in compressed form, the story of the Russian Revolution. In *October*, Eisenstein further developed his theories, particularly stressing the intellectual montage that had been the least developed form in *Battleship Potemkin*. Following *October*, Eisenstein completed *Old and New* (*The General Line*, 1929), a film that dealt with the collectivization of a dairy farm. For the first time in this film Eisenstein used a main character, Marfa Lapkina, as the agent driving the process of modernization that brings change to the farming village.

After *Old and New*, Eisenstein traveled, first throughout Europe, then to the United States, where he was contracted by Paramount to direct a number of films, including an adaptation of Theodore Dreiser's *An American Tragedy*, but, predictably, the deal fell through as Eisenstein's complex scenario emphasized the failures of American capitalism rather than the culpability of the main character. Following this disappointment, he went to Mexico in 1930 to make a film that was to be financed by Upton Sinclair. Eisenstein traveled throughout Mexico with Edouard Tisse, his cameraman, and his collaborator, Grigori Alexandrov, but after a year of filming, battling opposition, overstaying his leave from the Soviet Union, and finally losing the support of Sinclair, Eisenstein was forced to leave Mexico without the negatives for *Que Viva Mexico*. Following nearly three years of international travel, Eisenstein returned to Moscow in 1932, shattered by his experiences, and suffered a nervous breakdown.

When he recovered, Eisenstein resumed teaching at GIK (Gerasimov Institute of Cinematography) in Moscow, and chaired the Directing department. He married filmmaker Vera Atasheva, and made his first sound film, *Bezhin Meadow* (1935), based on a Turgenev novel about a father who murders his revolutionary son. Misfortune continued to plague Eisenstein as *Bezhin Meadow* was rejected by the head of Soviet Cinema, Boris Shumyatsky. His attempts to continue making films were often thwarted by Stalinists in the Soviet film industry, who advocated socialist realism over what they saw as his formalist exercises.

Despite constant criticism and threats throughout the Stalinist 1930s and '40s, Eisenstein would make two more film masterpieces. *Alexander Nevsky* (1938) told the story of a Russian prince who repelled a thirteenth-century Teutonic invasion at a time when the threat of Nazi Germany loomed. The film's famous score was composed by Sergei Prokofiev, and its unqualified critical and popular success helped earn Eisenstein the Order of Lenin prize in 1939. *Ivan the Terrible, Part One* (1944) was also a popular and critical success, telling the story of the sixteenth-century grand prince of Moscow who crowned himself Tsar of Russia, and set about reclaiming lost territory. *Part Two*, however, angered Stalin with its critical portrayal of the powerful Tsar's transformation into a cruel dictator, and was not released in the United States until 1959.

In addition to his films, Eisenstein wrote several books and published many articles on various aspects of film theory. Two of his books, *The Film Sense* (1942) and *Film Form: Essays on Film Theory* (1949), still rank as required reading for film students who hope to understand Soviet Montage.

Sergei Eisenstein died of heart failure in Moscow on February 11, 1948, but his impact on successive generations of filmmakers has been vast. His theories of montage proved inspirational for many of the new wave movements that flourished around the world in the 1960s and 1970s. Despite critiques that have painted Eisenstein's theory of montage as propagandistic manipulation, his reputation as a cinematic genius continues to grow with time.

See also: Intellectual Montage.

Selected Filmography

Ivan Groznyy III (1988); *Que Viva Mexico* (1979); *Eisenstein's Mexican Project* (1958); *Ivan the Terrible, Part Two* (1958); *Ivan the Terrible, Part One* (1944); *Seeds of Freedom* (1943); *Conquering Cross* (1941); *Idol of Hope* (1941); *Land and Freedom* (1941); *Mexican Symphony* (1941); *Mexico Marches* (1941); *Spaniard and Indian* (1941); *Zapotecan Village* (1941); *Time in the Sun* (1940); *The Fergana Canal* (1939); *Alexander Nevsky* (1938); *Bezhin lug* (1937); *Death Day* (1934); *Eisenstein in Mexico* (1933); *Thunder over Mexico* (1933); *¡Que viva Mexico!* (1932); *La destrucción de Oaxaca* (1931); *Sentimental Romance* (1930); *Old and New* (1929); *The Storming of La Sarraz* (1929); *Ten Days That Shook the World* (1928); *Battleship Potemkin* (1925); *Strike* (1925)

References

Barna, Yon. *Eisenstein*. Bloomington: Indiana University Press, 1973.
Eisenstein, Sergei. Trans. by Herbert Marshall. *Immoral Memories: An Autobiography by Sergei M. Eisenstein*. Boston: Houghton Mifflin, 1983.

—*Joseph Christopher Schaub*

EPHRON, NORA. Nora Ephron is among the increasing number of women who are working as writers and directors in Hollywood. Ephron was born on May 19, 1941, the first daughter of the playwrights and screenwriters Henry and Phoebe Ephron and grew up in Beverly Hills. After graduating from Wellesley College, Ephron was a reporter at the *New York Post* from 1962 to 1968 and then worked as a freelancer for four years. She served as a contributing editor for *New York* magazine from 1973 to 1974, the year she moved to *Esquire* to write a column and serve as a senior editor. She also published collections of her magazine articles—personal observations on feminist interests and pop culture—in books such as *Wallflower at the Orgy* (1970) and *Scribble Scribble* (1978).

Interestingly, Ephron emerged as a playwright after her parents turned the letters she sent them from Wellesley into a script for the play *Take Her, She's Mine*. Deciding to try her hand at script-writing in the 1970s, she worked on the short-lived series *Adam's Rib* in 1973 and wrote the screenplay for the TV movie *Perfect Gentlemen* in 1978. She turned her attention to the big screen in the early 1980s, writing, with Alice Arlen, the screenplay for the box-office hit *Silkwood* (1983). The film dramatized the harrowing story of Karen Silkwood, a disgruntled employee at a Crescent, Oklahoma, nuclear power plant who died in a mysterious car crash. That same year her novel *Heartburn* appeared. Based on her marriage to the journalist Carl Bernstein, her second husband, the book was eventually turned into a movie, also called *Heartburn* (1986). Although the picture boasted a star-studded cast, including Meryl Streep and Jack Nicholson, it did poorly at the box-office.

Ephron found the filmic success for which she was looking with *When Harry Met Sally* (1989), a delightful romantic comedy starring Billy Crystal and Meg Ryan as longtime friends who find love with each other after years of failed relationships with others. Heralded as the next great writer of romantic comedies, Ephron surprised many people in the industry when she followed *When Harry Met Sally* with *Cookie* (1989)—co-written with Arlen—and *My Blue Heaven* (1990), two crime comedies, and her directorial debut, the drama *This Is My Life* (1992). The latter film, which Ephron co-wrote with her sister Delia, follows a single mother (Julie Kavner) who pursues her dream of becoming a stand-up comic while her children languish at home.

Finally returning to the romantic comedy, Ephron co-wrote the script for *Sleepless in Seattle* (1993) with David S. Ward and Jeff Arch. Drawing on Leo McCarey's *An Affair to Remember* (1957) for inspiration, *Sleepless* stars Tom Hanks and Meg Ryan as star-crossed lovers who finally find each other at the top of the Empire State Building. The film charmed audiences, and although her next project, *Mixed Nuts* (1994), was rejected by viewers, Ephron would go on to pen romantic comedy hits such as *Michael* (1996) and the updated version of *The Shop around the Comer* (1940), *You've Got Mail* (1998), which Ephron directed and co-write with her sister Delia, and which again starred Hanks and Ryan as lovers who must find each other by way of a most circuitous route.

The sisters then adapted Delia's novel *Hanging Up* (2000) into a film of the same name, and Nora directed another crime comedy, the box-office flop *Lucky Numbers* (2000). After that failure, Ephron wrote *Imaginary Friends*, a play that opened at San Diego's Old Globe Theatre in 2002. She returned to Hollywood three years later to co-write—again with Delia—and direct the big-screen adaptation of the 1960s sitcom *Bewitched* (2005). Although it featured Nicole Kidman as the spirited witch Samantha, the film was a critical and box-office failure. Ephron would wait another four years before making her next film, *Julie & Julia* (2009), adapted from the memoirs of Julie Powell and Julia Child.

Turning her writing skills to another medium, Ephron has developed her own blog; in 2006 she gathered her Internet musings into a collection of essays: *I Feel Bad about My Neck: And Other Thoughts on Being a Woman.*

Selected Filmography

Julie & Julia (2009); *Bewitched* (2005); *Hanging Up* (2000); *You've Got Mail* (1998); *Michael* (1996); *Mixed Nuts* (1994); *Sleepless in Seattle* (1993); *This Is My Life* (1992); *My Blue Heaven* (1990); *When Harry Met Sally* (1989); *Cookie* (1989); *Heartburn* (1986); *Silkwood* (1983)

References

Bellafante, Ginia. "Matchmaker, Matchmaker." *Time*, December 21, 1998.

Levy, Barbara. "Nora Ephron: All You Ever Wanted to Know about Control." *Ladies Laughing: Wit as Control in Contemporary American Women Writers.* New York: Routledge, 1997: 35–50.

McCreadie, Marsha. *The Women Who Write the Movies: From Frances Marion to Nora Ephron.* Secaucus: Carol Publishing Group, 1994.

—*Albert Rolls*

F

FAIRBANKS, DOUGLAS, SR.   Referred to by some as "The King of Hollywood," Douglas Fairbanks Sr. was one of the dominant figures of the early film industry. His dashing good looks made him the quintessential leading man of the silent era, and his business acumen and vision helped create United Artists and the Academy of Motion Picture Arts and Sciences. During the 1920s he and his wife, fellow screen star Mary Pickford, reigned as Hollywood's first great "power couple."

Douglas Elton Thomas Ullman Fairbanks Sr. was born May 23, 1883, in Denver, the son of an attorney who abandoned the family when Douglas was five years old. As a child Fairbanks showed an interest in the stage and at the age of 11 began performing in local theater productions in Denver. He won rave reviews for his work and established a reputation in the Denver area as a natural talent. He dropped out of high school during his senior year and in 1900 moved to New York City to pursue acting as a profession. He worked a series of odd jobs before making his Broadway debut in 1902 in a play titled *The Duke's Jester*. In 1907, he married Anna Beth Sully, and the couple had one child, Douglas Elton Fairbanks, who the world would later know as the actor Douglas Fairbanks Jr.

Seeing the potential in the emerging film industry, the ambitious Fairbanks moved to Hollywood in 1915, where he signed a contract with the Triangle Film Corporation and began working with famed director D. W. Griffith. That year he made his first film, *The Lamb*, and within a very short time established himself as one of Hollywood's most popular actors. Fairbanks eventually signed with Paramount, where much of his early work consisted of light-hearted romantic comedies that the public loved. In 1916, he met Mary Pickford, the most popular actress in the country at the time, and the two soon began an affair. In 1917, when the United States entered World War I, Pickford, Fairbanks and their friend Charlie Chaplin toured the country selling war bonds. By 1918, Fairbanks was one of the biggest box-office draws in the movie industry and a keen businessman who continually sought more control over the business end of the motion pictures in which he appeared. Together with Pickford, Chaplin, D. W. Griffith, and attorney William G. McAdoo, he founded United Artists in an

In the post–World War I film industry, Douglas Fairbanks found his niche as an action hero and made the transition to sound through roles in *The Mark of Zorro, Three Musketeers,* and *Robin Hood,* although age began to make swashbuckling more difficult. (Library of Congress)

effort to give the stars complete artistic control over their films and establish a distribution network that would give them a greater share of the profits from their movies.

After beginning his relationship with Pickford, Fairbanks divorced his first wife and married the actress in 1922. Hollywood's first great celebrity union generated a mass of publicity, and huge crowds greeted the couple during a honeymoon tour of Europe. In California their Beverly Hills estate, called "Pickfair," was the social center of Hollywood. During the 1920s, Fairbanks began making the high-energy action pictures for which he would be best remembered. These included pictures such as *The Mark of Zorro* (1920), *The Three Musketeers* (1921), *Robin Hood* (1922), *The Thief of Bagdad* (1924), and *The Black Pirate* (1926). The decade also saw Fairbanks establish a number of Hollywood institutions and traditions that remain an integral part of the film industry. In 1927, he was a founding partner of Grauman's Chinese Theater and, in the first ceremony of its type, Fairbanks and Pickford placed their hand- and footprints in wet cement for the theater's grand opening. The same year Fairbanks won election as the first president of the Motion Picture Academy of Arts and Sciences, and the first Academy Awards were presented in his office.

The end of the silent movie era marked a rapid downturn in Fairbanks's fortunes, and by the early 1930s the aging star had lost interest in the industry that he helped create. No longer up to the physical challenge that some of his earlier roles required, the chain-smoking Fairbanks watched as the American public embraced a new, younger generation of action stars. His personal life also began to deteriorate during the period. After more than a decade as Hollywood's most famous couple, he and Mary Pickford separated in 1933 and divorced three years later. He retired from acting after appearing in *The Private Life of Don Juan* (1934). Fairbanks married his third wife,

Sylvia Ashley, in 1936, and spent much of the remainder of his life travelling. He died of a heart attack at his home in Santa Monica, California, on December 12, 1939.

References

Balio, Tino T. *United Artists: The Company That Changed the Film Industry.* Madison: University of Wisconsin Press, 2008.

Herndon, Booton. *Mary Pickford and Douglas Fairbanks: The Most Popular Couple the World Has Ever Known.* New York: W. W. Norton, 1977.

Tibbetts, John C., and James M. Welsh. *His Majesty the American: The Cinema of Douglas Fairbanks, Sr.* South Brunswick: A. S. Barnes, 1977.

Vance, Jeffrey, and Tony Maietta. *Douglas Fairbanks.* Berkeley: University of California Press, 2008.

—Ben Wynne

FLEMING, VICTOR.   One of the most notable directors of the early film industry, Victor Fleming directed dozens of feature films during a career that spanned more than 30 years. While he worked with most of the notable actors and actresses of Hollywood's golden era, he is probably best known for directing the film classics *The Wizard of Oz* (1939) and *Gone with the Wind* (1939).

Victor Fleming was born on February 23, 1883 (though some sources say 1889), in Pasadena, California. As a young man he worked as a mechanic and racecar driver. In an era when reliable automobile pilots were at a premium, he found work in 1910 as a stunt driver in films, which eventually led to work behind the camera. He served as an assistant cameraman under director Allan Dwan and worked on a number of early films starring Douglas Fairbanks Sr. By 1915, Fleming was director of photography for director D. W. Griffith and well on his way to a successful career in the film industry. During World War I, Fleming served in the army and was the chief cameraman for Woodrow Wilson as Wilson negotiated the Treaty of Versailles in France in 1919. Following the war, Fleming directed his first feature films, *When Clouds Go By* (1919) and *The Mollycoddle* (1920), both of which starred Fairbanks. Working for United Artists and Paramount during the 1920s, he established a reputation as a talented, tough director capable of delivering aggressive dramas that today would be characterized as "action pictures." He also set the standard for directors of the period who were making the transition from silent films to "talkies."

Fleming's career reached a turning point in 1927 when he directed one of the landmark films of early Hollywood, *The Virginian*, an adaptation of the popular Owen Wister western novel. In the film Fleming worked with a young actor named Gary Cooper, and under Fleming's direction Cooper emerged as a star destined to become an American film icon. During the 1930s, Fleming signed with MGM and directed a number of successful films including *Red Dust* (1932), *Treasure Island* (1934), *Reckless* (1935), and *The Farmer Takes a Wife* (1935). As was the case with Cooper, Fleming was credited with helping guide the early career of Spencer Tracy, who starred for the director in *Captains Courageous* (1937) and won an Oscar for Best Actor for his performance.

Director Victor Fleming and actress Jean Harlow stand on a staircase, looking over the railing. Fleming directed Harlow in the films *Red Dust* and *Bombshell*. (Hulton Archive/Getty Images)

The late 1930s represented the high-water mark in Fleming's career, as he directed two of the most beloved motion pictures of all time, *The Wizard of Oz* and *Gone with the Wind* (both 1939), which were both nominated for the Best Picture Academy Award during the same year, with the latter winning the Oscar. Though known as a rough-and-tumble "man's director," he was able to coax stellar performances from a young Judy Garland and from the temperamental Vivien Leigh. Under Fleming's direction Leigh won the Best Actress Oscar for her performance in *Gone with the Wind* and Hattie McDaniel won the Academy Award for Best Supporting Actress. Fleming himself won the 1939 Academy Award as Best Director for his successful efforts in bringing Margaret Mitchell's epic novel about the Old South to the screen. Fleming was also Clark Gable's favorite director, and the two good friends worked together on a number of projects. Fleming continued to direct successful films into the 1940s, but none would match *Gone with the Wind* or *The Wizard of Oz* in long-term appeal. Some of his later works included *Dr. Jekyll and Mr. Hyde* (1941), *Tortilla Flat* (1942), *A Guy Named Joe* (1943), and *Adventure* (1946). In 1948, he directed Ingrid Bergman in *Joan of Arc*, his final film. Fleming died suddenly on January 6, 1949, while vacationing near Cottonwood, Arizona.

Victor Fleming left a rich legacy as a filmmaker, although he has traditionally been underrated. One of the most respected directors in the early period of Hollywood, he deftly navigated the waters from silent pictures to "talkies," and from black-and-white film to color. He also established a cinematic style that many successful directors who followed him sought to emulate.

Selected Filmography

Joan of Arc (1948); *Adventure* (1945); *A Guy Named Joe* (1943); *Tortilla Flat* (1942); *Dr. Jekyll and Mr. Hyde* (1941); *Gone with the Wind* (1939); *The Wizard of Oz* (1939); *Test Pilot*

(1938); *Captains Courageous* (1937); *The Farmer Takes a Wife* (1935); *Reckless* (1935); *Treasure Island* (1934); *The Wet Parade* (1932); *Around the World with Douglas Fairbanks* (1931); *Renegades* (1930); *Common Clay* (1930); *The Virginian* (1929); *The Wolf Song* (1929); *The Awakening* (1928); *Abie's Irish Rose* (1928); *The Rough Riders* (1927)

References

Hakell, Molly. *Frankly My Dear: Gone with the Wind Revisited*. New Haven, CT: Yale University Press, 2009.

Harmetz, Aljean. *The Making of The Wizard of Oz: Movie Magic and Studio Power in the Prime of MGM*. New York: Hyperion, 1998.

Sragow, Michael. *Victor Fleming: The Life and Work of an American Movie Master*. New York: Pantheon, 2009.

Vieira, Mark A. *Hollywood Dreams Made Real: Irving Thalberg and the Rise of MGM*. New York: Harry N. Abrams, 2009.

—*Ben Wynne*

FLYNN, ERROL.   Errol Leslie Thomson Flynn was born in the British Commonwealth seaport of Hobart, Tasmania, on June 20, 1909. He was an Australian film actor descended from an old Antrim Catholic family from Ireland. Famous for his romantic, swashbuckler roles, he became a Hollywood star during the 1930s and 1940s. A compelling screen figure and notorious womanizer, Flynn took roles in costume action-adventures that seemed to match his flamboyant lifestyle perfectly. He was married three times: to Lili Damita, Nora Eddington, and Patrice Wymore. He had four children: a son, Sean, and three daughters, Deirdre, Rory (who wrote *The Baron of Mulholland. A Daughter Remembers Errol Flynn* in 2006), and Arnella Roma. After becoming an American citizen in 1942, Flynn sought to join the American army. To his great disappointment, he was rejected due to having been exposed to several different diseases. Flynn died on October 14, 1959, of a heart attack in Vancouver, Canada, and is interred in Forest Lawn Memorial Park Cemetery, in Glendale, California.

Flynn attended fine schools in Australia and England, but was expelled from most; his rebellious, adventurous nature made him change jobs several times when he was in his late teens and early twenties. In 1933, an Australian film producer saw the tall, athletic, good-looking Flynn and offered him a part in *In the Wake of the Bounty*. After his debut in the role of Fletcher Christian, he passionately embraced acting, which he maintained came quite naturally to him. That same year he went to England, where he gained acting experience with the Northampton Repertory Company. A role in *Murder at Monte Carlo* (1934), a low-budget mystery film made by Warner Bros.-Teddington Studios, UK, led to his first Hollywood contract: Flynn was the last minute replacement for Robert Donat in Warner Brother's pirate epic *Captain Blood* (1935). The role as the dashing swashbuckler Blood brought him instant success and worldwide popularity.

Nicknamed the Tasmanian devil, Flynn despised mediocrity above all things. In *They Died with Their Boots On* (1942), Flynn as General George Armstrong Custer described his artistic credo when asked where he was going: "To hell or glory. It depends upon your point of view." Embodying characters such as Captain Blood, Miles Hendon in *The Prince and The Pauper* (1937), Sir Robin Hood of Locksley in *The Adventures of Robin Hood* (1938), the Earl of Essex in *The Private Lives of Elizabeth and Essex* (1939), Captain Geoffrey Thorpe in *The Sea Hawk*, (1940), James J. Corbett in *Gentleman Jim* (1942), and Don Juan in the *Adventures of Don Juan* (1949), Flynn became a prodigal figure within the motion picture world. He defined the unique male archetype of the noble, dashing hero of the silver screen, creating a constellation of manly virtues that made him, in Jack L. Warner's words, "all the heroes in one magnificent, sexy, animal package." Indeed, Flynn's characterization of the roguish antihero would influence the way other action-movie roles were conceived.

Flynn was notorious for his high-spirited bacchanalias, hedonistic lifestyle, and amorous escapades. His freewheeling life took a serious turn in 1942, when two underage girls accused him of statutory rape. Although he was cleared of the charges a year later, the rape trial had a strong impact on his career. As a result of this experience, Flynn left Hollywood in 1952. After a detour in Europe, he came back in 1956 and played roles of embittered men in *The Sun Also Rises* (1957), *Too Much Too Soon* (1958), and *The Roots of Heaven* (1958).

Flynn was interested in politics, co-authored several screenplays, and wrote three books. He authored *Beam Ends (1937)* and *Showdown (1946)*, as well as a posthumously published autobiography entitled *My Wicked, Wicked Ways* (1959). A leftist, he narrated the documentary film *Cuban Story* (1959) and wrote, narrated, and co-produced *Cuban Rebel Girls* (1959), a semidocumentary tribute to Fidel Castro. These last films made him persona non grata in 1950s Hollywood. Sadly, despite his numerous notable roles, Flynn was never nominated for any awards.

See also: Action-Adventure Film, The

References

Bawden, Liz-Anne, ed. *The Oxford Companion to Film*. New York: Oxford University Press, 1976: 257.

"Biography of Errol Flynn." *The Official Errol Flynn Estate Site* authorized by Patrice Wymore; retrieved January 31, 2009. http://errolflynnestates.com/bio/index.htm.

"In Like Flynn." *Official Web Site of Errol Flynn*, from Rory Flynn; retrieved January 3, 2009. http://www.inlikeflynn.com.

Katz, Ephraim. *The International Film Encyclopedia*, 2nd ed. London: Macmillan, 1982: 428–29.

—*Réka M. Cristian*

FORD, JOHN. One of the most renowned directors in the history of Hollywood, John Ford will always be associated with making movies that captured enduring images of the mythic American landscape. He made over 130 films that spanned from the early silent era to the late 1960s; and while his work encompassed many genres and was set in diverse periods of history, he is best remembered for a cycle of westerns, often filmed in Utah's rugged iconic Monument Valley, in which he explored the myths, archetypes, and jarring contradictions inherent in stories of American exceptionalism. Ford is still Hollywood's most honored director, having won more Oscars (four) than any other director in history. Oddly enough, however, none of his Oscars was awarded for his westerns, an indication of the man's breadth of accomplishment, his complex artistic sensibility, and Hollywood's uncomfortable relationship to the genre.

Born John Martin Aloysius Feeney in Cape Elizabeth, Maine, on February 1, 1894, to Irish immigrant parents, he wandered to Hollywood at the age of 19, following his brother Francis, who was directing and acting in silent films. In later life, Ford maintained he never wanted to

John Ford (seen here in 1934) is the only Hollywood director to win five Academy Awards. Ford is known for films such as his 1940 adaptation of John Steinbeck's novel *The Grapes of Wrath*. (AP/Wide World Photos)

have anything to do with the movies, but was simply broke and did what he could to eat. He rode as a clansman in D. W. Griffith's *Birth of a Nation* (1915), but hurt himself when he ran into a branch on the first day of shooting; he spent several days after the accident observing the master Griffith at his craft. The experience proved significant if not immediately life altering; after years of working for his brother and various other directors as a laborer, actor, stuntman, property man, and general assistant, he got his first chance to direct at the age of 23 when the man assigned to the job he eventually took did not show up. By then John Feeney had changed his name to Jack Ford, altering it again to the more formal-sounding John Ford when he began to be assigned A-pictures.

In 1924, he directed his 50th and most ambitious picture to date, *Iron Horse*, an epic about the building of the transatlantic railroad. Filmed on location in Nevada, often in extreme conditions of cold and snow, the mammoth production traced themes that would emerge throughout Ford's work: the interplay and conflict of ethnic and racial communities during the expansion of the American continent; the effect of landscape on the way Americans imagine their destiny; and the conflict embedded in the

American psyche between community and the individual. The film was also marked by Ford's technique of blending raucous and crude humor into otherwise serious dramatic material, a practice critics never failed to abhor and Ford never stopped practicing.

By the early sound era he had developed into one of Hollywood's most trusted and eclectic directors, making movies ranging from high-toned melodrama (*Arrowsmith* 1931), to adventure (*The Lost Patrol* 1933), to romantic comedy (*The Whole Town's Talking* 1935), to biography (*Mary of Scotland* 1936). But the most representative Ford pictures of this era—ones in which the subject matter began to evolve toward themes he would pursue in the bulk of his career—were those that made up an informal trilogy starring American humorist Will Rogers: *Doctor Bull* (1933) *Judge Priest* (1934), and *Steamboat Round the Bend* (1935). If these films veer toward nostalgia and folksy paternalism—a tendency throughout Ford's work—they nonetheless confront the ugliness of racial prejudice and intolerance in otherwise idealized rural communities.

In 1935, Ford won his first Best Director Oscar for *The Informer*, a dark and shadowy adaptation of the Liam O'Flaherty novel of betrayal and redemption in Ireland during "the troubles." Although stylistically the film owed a great deal to German Expressionist directors like F. W. Murnau and Fritz Lang, it marked the enduring personal interest Ford had in making films set in his often idealized ancestral homeland. Ford remained a self-conscious Irish American, and while it sometimes broadly passed into uncomfortable clichés—the heavy-drinking, brawling, and sentimental Irish braggart is a character that appears even in many of his westerns—the strong Irish ethnic flavor in his work was indicative of the rough-hewn son-of-an-immigrant American identity of which Ford was proud, and that he had no interest in obscuring even after he became a Hollywood legend. Indeed, one of the most personal films of his late career, *The Quiet Man* (1952), filmed on location in County Mayo, Ireland, although invested with a rather sentimental charm and lyricism, did not shy away from exploring the troubling issues of sectarian division, betrayal, sexism, and alcoholism.

In the late 1930s, Ford began to work with two American actors who in their own very powerful ways would develop into iconic presences in the American cultural landscape: Henry Fonda and John Wayne. Indeed, the Ford films that star these two actors form the basis of his most enduring and resonant accomplishment. These films seem to speak to each other, counteract each other, and even debate each other, as Ford critiques and glorifies aspects of the American expansionist past.

In 1939, Ford cast Fonda as a settler caught up in fighting during the Revolutionary War in *Drums along the Mohawk*, an epic in which the director examines the uncertain national affiliation and nascent patriotism of people struggling to survive in the wilderness. In the same year, Ford gave Fonda the career-changing lead role in *Young Mr. Lincoln*. Admired by Sergei Eisenstein for its subtle visual dialectic, the film was in essence a courtroom melodrama in which the young Abraham Lincoln defends a man unjustly accused of murder. Ford coaxed the reluctant Fonda to take the part, helping him understand that the Lincoln he was playing was merely a backwoods hick lawyer with no particular mark of greatness about him; Ford knew the audience would project Lincoln's future greatness onto the actor's every step and word. In these films, and in the documentary-flavored *The Grapes of Wrath* (1940)—a powerful adaptation of the John Steinbeck novel about the migration of sharecroppers from Oklahoma's dust bowl to California's fertile valleys that presented a surprisingly sharp critique of capitalism—Ford helped to shape Henry Fonda's persona as a strong man of quiet integrity in whom the greatest hopes of the common citizen stirred.

If, in Ford's films, Fonda largely came to represent the American individual quietly standing for collective justice and operating within the somewhat porous boundaries of constitutional law (themes Ford exploited beautifully in the poetic 1946 western *My Darling Clementine*, in which Fonda played the awkward lawman Wyatt Earp), John Wayne came to represent the country's conflicted relationship with an ideology of romantic individualism that threatened civil society. Ford made Wayne a star by casting him as the gentle outlaw the Ringo Kid in the classic western *Stagecoach* (1939), a populist saga that suggests that civilization, represented by the microcosmic space of the stagecoach, requires the instinctual abilities and innate morality of an outlaw to save it.

Stagecoach became the first in a series of Ford's westerns in which Wayne was used simultaneously to reflect and to disrupt the audience's attraction to such characters. Notable among these films is the so-called Cavalry Trilogy, beginning with 1948's *Fort Apache* (which co-starred Fonda, cast against his screen image as a Custer-like martinet who leads his regiment to slaughter), *She Wore a Yellow Ribbon* (1949), and *Rio Grande* (1950), three films that together form a complex examination of how military duty and ritual served the purposes of American projects of conquest and expansion even while calling them into question. It may be that Wayne and Ford's most famous collaboration came with *The Searchers* (1955), in which Wayne played the racist former Confederate soldier Ethan Edwards, who leads a search to avenge the murder of his brother's family and the abduction of his niece by Comanche Indians. In that film, the code of individualism seems demonic, and comes close to disrupting the potential for society to heal the wounds inflicted by its racist past.

Ford's work distinguished itself throughout his career by the array of character actors who repeatedly appeared in his movies over the decades. He called them his trademark "John Ford Stock Company," a fluid group that helped deepen his exploration of the nature of community. Part of the pleasure in watching Ford's movies is in seeing these actors continue to play similar roles, to age, and to carry with them the legacies of their past performances.

It may be argued that Ford was an artist of his time, and as such, his films do not always age well. A selective compilation of his western battle scenes would suggest he didn't shy away from the visual cliché of anonymous marauding Indians dying anonymous deaths. Did his films contribute to simplistic and perhaps racist stereotypes of Native Americans? Ford was troubled enough with the question that late in his career he made the epic *Cheyenne Autumn* (1964), which tells the story of conquest from the Native American point of view. The elegiac film was deemed leaden by many critics, and its casting of non–Native American actors in major Native American roles would be more troubling if had not been so typical of Hollywood's casting practices during that period.

Ford served in the Navy during WWII, and he made a series of battle documentaries for the American military that earned him the rank of Admiral. But by the mid-1960s, the director's increasingly nostalgic view of military service, his hardening right-wing politics (he produced for the military in 1971 the prowar documentary *Vietnam! Vietnam!*), and his increasingly positive view of what many perceived of as the problematic American past made him seem reactionary and out of touch with the changing politics of the New Hollywood. Approached by many critics and writers who valued his wisdom and knowledge of the industry, when he did grant interviews he often came off as cynical and disagreeable. Nevertheless, his influence on directors coming of age during the 1960s and '70s was immense. Just as Orson Welles watched *Stagecoach* over 40 times before he filmed *Citizen Kane*, a host of later directors of the New American Cinema studied Ford's work, including Martin Scorsese, whose *Taxi Driver* (1974) reads as a nightmarish urban updating of Ford's *The Searchers* in its relentless exploration of America's violently conflicted attitude toward homicidal heroes.

In 1973 Ford was chosen as the first recipient of the American Film Institute's Lifetime Achievement Award. He died on August 31, 1973, widely acclaimed by his surviving colleagues in the industry as America's greatest film director.

Selected Filmography

7 Women (1966); *Cheyenne Autumn* (1964); *Donovan's Reef* (1963); *How the West Was Won* (1962); *The Man Who Shot Liberty Valance* (1962); *Two Rode Together* (1961); *Sergeant Rutledge* (1960); *The Horse Soldiers* (1959); *Korea* (1959); *The Last Hurrah* (1958); *Gideon of Scotland Yard* (1958); *The Wings of Eagles* (1957); *The Searchers* (1956); *Mister Roberts* (1955); *The Long Gray Line* (1955); *Mogambo* (1953); *The Sun Shines Bright* (1953); *What Price Glory* (1952); *The Quiet Man* (1952); *This Is Korea!* (1951); *Rio Grande* (1950); *Wagon Master* (1950); *She Wore a Yellow Ribbon* (1949); *3 Godfathers* (1948); *Fort Apache* (1948); *The Fugitive* (1947); *My Darling Clementine* (1946); *They Were Expendable* (1945); *How to Operate Behind Enemy Lines* (1943); *German Industrial Manpower* (1943); *December 7th* (1943); *The Battle of Midway* (1942); *Sex Hygiene* (1942); *Torpedo Squadron* (1942); *How Green Was My Valley* (1941); *Tobacco Road* (1941); *The Long Voyage Home* (1940); *The Grapes of Wrath* (1940); *Drums along the Mohawk* (1939); *Young Mr. Lincoln* (1939); *Stagecoach* (1939); *Submarine Patrol* (1938); *Four Men and a Prayer* (1938); *The Hurricane* (1937); *Wee Willie Winkie* (1937); *The Plough and the Stars* (1936); *Mary of Scotland* (1936); *The Prisoner of Shark Island* (1936); *Steamboat Round the Bend* (1935); *The Informer* (1935); *Judge Priest* (1934); *The Lost Patrol* (1934); *Arrowsmith* (1931); *Men without Women* (1930); *The Black Watch* (1929); *Strong Boy* (1929); *Riley the Cop* (1928); *Napoleon's Barber* (1928); *Hangman's House* (1928); *Four Sons* (1928); *Upstream* (1927); *The Blue Eagle* (1926); *3 Bad Men* (1926); *The Iron Horse* (1924)

References

Ford, Dan. *Pappy: The Life of John Ford*. Englewood Cliffs, NJ: Prentice Hall, 1979.
McBride, Joseph. *Searching for John Ford: A Life*. New York: St. Martin's, 2001.
McBride, Joseph, and Michael Wilmington. *John Ford*. New York: Da Capo, 1975.
Place, J. A. *The Non-Western Films of John Ford*. New York: Citadel, 1979.
Sinclair, Andrew. *John Ford: A Biography*. New York: Dial, 1979.

—*Robert Cowgill*

FOSTER, JODIE.   An award-winning American actress, producer, and director, Jodie Foster catapulted to superstardom during the 1990s. Her enormous talents as an actress have earned her worldwide respect. Considered to be one of the most powerful actresses in Hollywood today, it is widely believed in the movie industry that having Foster star in a movie guarantees that it will become a box-office success.

Alicia Christian "Jodie" Foster was born on November 19, 1962, in Los Angeles, California, to parents Evelyn "Brandy" Foster, a film producer, and Lucius Fisher Foster III, a real estate broker. Her first experience with acting came at age three when she was featured in a Coppertone suntan lotion commercial. By age eight, the young actress had performed in more than 45 commercials. Foster made her television acting debut in 1969 on the CBS television show *Mayberry, R.F.D.* In 1972, the young star made her motion picture debut in the Walt Disney film, *Napoleon and Samantha*. Throughout the early 1970s, Foster performed in several additional movies, including *Menace on the Mountain* (1973), *Alice Doesn't Live Here Anymore* (1975), *Bugsy Malone* (1976), and *Freaky Friday* (1976). A pivotal role in her career came in 1976 when Foster co-starred with Robert De Niro in *Taxi Driver*. Her portrayal of Iris, a 12-year-old prostitute, earned her Best Supporting Actress Awards from the New York Film Critics, the National Film Critics, and the Los Angeles Film Critics as well as an Academy Award nomination.

In 1980, Foster graduated valedictorian from the French-speaking prep school the Lycée Francais de Los Angeles. She then took a break from her acting career to attend Yale University. In 1985, she graduated magna cum laude with a BA in literature. While attending the university as a freshman, Foster became a media sensation when John Hinckley Jr. attempted to assassinate President Ronald Reagan on March 30, 1981. Hinckley claimed that his actions were an expression of his love for Foster.

In 1988, Foster's portrayal of Sarah Tobias, a working-class rape survivor, in the critically acclaimed *The Accused* earned her both a Golden Globe Award and an Academy Award for Best Actress. In 1991, Foster won a second Academy Award for Best Actress for her portrayal of FBI agent Clarice Starling in the blockbuster hit *The Silence of the Lambs*. That same year, Foster also starred in and directed her first movie, *Little Man Tate*. In 1992, she founded her own production company, Egg Pictures, which specialized in the production of independent films. In 1994, Foster co-produced and starred in *Nell*, which told the story of a young girl living in total isolation in the back hills of North Carolina. By now an established actress in Hollywood, Foster continued to obtain highly sought-after roles in numerous movies. In 1997, she starred alongside Matthew McConaughey in the science fiction movie *Contact*. *Panic Room* (2002), in which she played the lead, was also a box-office success. In 2004, Foster expanded her acting repertoire when she took on a role in the French-speaking film *Un long dimanche de fiançailles* (*A Very Long Engagement*). The movie gave her the opportunity to showcase her fluency in the French language. In 2005, she starred in the action thriller *Flightplan*, which reached number one at the box office. In 2006, she co-starred with Denzel Washington in the Spike Lee movie *Inside Man*. Finally, in 2007, Foster starred in and produced *The Brave One*, which also reached number one at the box office.

An enormously talented actress and well-educated woman, Foster has achieved superstar status. Her acting, as both a child star and then as an adult actress, has always been consistently strong. On the movie set, she has proven herself to be dependable, professional, and adaptable to a broad range of movie genres, including comedy, drama, science fiction, and the action thriller. Today, Foster continues to be a much sought after actress by movie producers as well as an enormous box-office draw. Her acting has already earned her an important place in American cinema history.

See also: Silence of the Lambs, The; Women in Film

Selected Filmography (Director)

The Beaver (2010); *Home for the Holidays* (1994); *Little Man Tate* (1991)

References

Foster, Buddy, and Leon Wagener. *Foster Child: A Biography of Jodie Foster.* New York: Dutton, 1997.
Hollinger, Karen. *The Actress: Hollywood Acting and the Female Star.* New York: Routledge, 2006.
Lumme, Helena, and Mika Manninen. *Great Women of Film.* New York: Billboard Books, 2002.

—Bernadette Zbicki Heiney

FRANKENHEIMER, JOHN.   An innovative American television and film director known for his distinctive use of dialogue and unconventional camera angles, John Frankenheimer was born on February 19, 1930, in New York City. A 1951 graduate of Williams College, Massachusetts, Frankenheimer had his first experience in filmmaking while a member of the U.S. Air Force Motion Picture Squadron. Following his discharge in 1953, Frankenheimer obtained a position as an assistant director and later as a director of live television with CBS. He worked on a number of shows, including *You Are There, Playhouse 90, Climax!,* and *Danger.* Frankenheimer's work earned him 14 Emmy Award nominations, and he was twice awarded the Television Critics Award for Best Director.

Frankenheimer's first foray into film was *The Young Stranger* (1957). As in many of his later pictures, Frankenheimer sought to address important social issues in this film. Based on an episode of *Climax!, The Young Stranger* explores coming-of-age issues and tensions between a son and his father. Unhappy with the process of making the film, he returned to television. It was not until 1961, when he made *The Young Savages,* that he began exclusively to make films for the big screen. *The Young Savages* also marked Frankenheimer's first collaboration with Burt Lancaster; the director and popular actor would go on to make three more pictures together: *The Birdman of Alcatraz* (1962), *Seven Days in May* (1964), and *The Train* (1964).

Frankenheimer's most controversial and disturbing film may have been *The Manchurian Candidate*, released in 1962. Starring Frank Sinatra, Laurence Harvey, and Angela Lansbury, *The Manchurian Candidate* addressed issues of paranoia and political extremism in Cold War America. The film was well received by critics and audiences alike, receiving 1963 Oscar nominations for Best Supporting Actress for Angela Lansbury and Best Film Editing for Ferris Webster; Frankenheimer was nominated for the Best Director Golden Globe Award.

In 1964, Frankenheimer followed up *The Manchurian Candidate* with *Seven Days in May*, which dealt with the political intrigue swirling around a right-wing plot to overthrow the U.S. government. In 1966, he made *Seconds*, starring Rock Hudson, which, along with *The Manchurian Candidate* and *Seven Days in May*, is considered part of Frank-

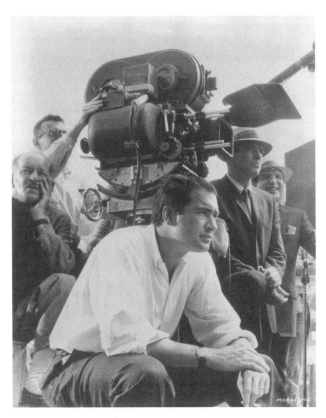

Director John Frankenheimer (center) on the set of his film *Young Savages*. To the right are actors Burt Lancaster and Telly Savalas. (Hulton Archive/Getty Images)

enheimer's "paranoia trilogy." *Seconds* centers on a secretive organization that provides its clients with new identities and lives for the right price. Themes such as the pursuit of youth, perfection, and materialism are addressed. The unusual camera angles, distortions, and the grim narrative, however, did not appeal to audiences, and the film proved to be a disappointment at the box office.

By 1968, Frankenheimer's career faltered. A close friend of Robert Kennedy, Frankenheimer was traumatized by the presidential candidate's assassination. Suffering from depression and alcoholism, he relocated to Europe. Returning to the United States in 1973, Frankenheimer released a number of mediocre thrillers, including *The Iceman Cometh* (1973), *Impossible Object* (1973), *99 and 44/100% Dead* (1974), *French Connection II* (1975), and *Black Sunday* (1977). His alcoholism became an issue while he was filming *The Challenge* in Kyoto, Japan, in 1982.

Struggling with his addiction, Frankenheimer continued to make films of varying quality: while *52 Pick-Up* (1986) was successful, *The Holcroft Covenant* (1985), *Dead Bang* (1989), *The Fourth War* (1990), and *Year of the Gun 1991)* were all box-office failures.

In 1993, Frankenheimer returned to television, directing HBO's *Against the Wall* and *The Burning Season* (both released in 1994). For the two films, Frankenheimer received two Emmy Awards (including Best Director for *The Burning Season*) and three Golden Globe awards. In 1996, Frankenheimer directed the TNT film *Andersonville*, for which he received another Emmy award. He continued his work for TNT with 1997s *George Wallace*, which earned him his fourth Emmy and the Golden Globe Award for Best Motion Picture Made for Television.

While working in television, Frankenheimer also remained active in feature films. Following the removal of director Richard Stanley, Frankenheimer took over *The Island of Dr. Moreau* (1996). Starring Marlon Brando and Val Kilmer, the film was hampered by script and casting problems, and proved to be yet another box-office failure. Frankenheimer's last theatrical releases were *Ronin* (1998) and *Reindeer Games* (2000); his last television movie was HBO's *Paths to War* (2002).

John Frankenheimer died on July 8, 2002, following complications from surgery in Los Angeles.

Selected Filmography

Reindeer Games (2000); *Ronin* (1998); *The Island of Dr. Moreau* (1996); *Year of the Gun* (1991); *The Fourth War* (1990); *Dead Bang* (1989); *52 Pick-Up* (1986); *The Holcroft Covenant* (1985); *The Challenge* (1982); *Prophecy* (1979); *Black Sunday* (1977); *French Connection II* (1975); *99 and 44/100% Dead* (1974); *The Iceman Cometh* (1973); *Story of a Love Story* (1973); *The Horsemen* (1971); *I Walk the Line* (1970); *The Extraordinary Seaman* (1969); *The Gypsy Moths* (1969); *The Fixer* (1968); *Grand Prix* (1966); *Seconds* (1966); *The Train* (1964); *Seven Days in May* (1964); *The Manchurian Candidate* (1962); *Birdman of Alcatraz* (1962); *All Fall Down* (1962); *The Young Savages* (1961); *The Young Stranger* (1957)

References

Armstrong, Stephan B. *Pictures About Extremes: The Films of John Frankenheimer.* Jefferson, NC: McFarland, 2007.

Higham, Charles, and Joel Greenberg. *The Celluloid Muse: Hollywood Directors Speak.* Chicago: Regnery, 1969.

Pratley, Gerald. *The Films of Frankenheimer: Forty Years in Film.* Cranbury, NJ: Lehigh University Press, 1998.

—*Robert W. Malick*

FRIEDKIN, WILLIAM. Unevenness characterizes the career of American director William Friedkin. He is best known for the highly influential films *The French Connection* (1971) and *The Exorcist* (1973), which revolutionized the respective genres of action and horror. Although the success of these films positioned Friedkin as one of Hollywood's elite directors, his career since their release has been plagued by critical and commercial disappointments.

Friedkin was born in Chicago on August 29, 1935, and grew up in a lower-middle-class neighborhood. As an adolescent, he had brushes with the law; growing concerned, his hardworking mother intervened and helped turn him in the right direction. Although his father was multitalented, he lacked ambition, a trait that seems to have motivated young William to make something of himself (Biskind, 1998). Moved by the work of Orson Welles and others, he began working his way up from the mailroom at a local television station. He went on to direct several documentary projects, most notably, *The People Versus Paul Crump* (1962). A taut film about a black man on death row, the documentary won top prize at the 1962 San Francisco Film Festival.

Friedkin continued making documentaries in Chicago, using the experience to hone his trademark visual style (Clagett, 1990). He eventually made his way to Hollywood, but his first feature did not draw on his skills as a documentarian. *Good Times* (1967) was a musical comedy starring Sonny and Cher that sought to capitalize on the success of the Beatles' *A Hard Day's Night*, but which was largely ignored. He followed with more ambitious projects: the period musical *The Night They Raided Minsky's*; a film adaptation of Harold Pinter's play *The Birthday Party*; and an adaptation of Mart Crowley's Off-Broadway play *The Boys in the Band* (Katz, 2001).

The gritty crime drama *The French Connection* (1971) was an aesthetic departure from his earlier films and signaled his turn toward hyperkinetic, sensory experience at the expense of narrative and character development (Saeli, 1997). Remembered for its landmark car chase and morally ambiguous cop protagonists, the film brought Friedkin an Oscar for Best Director. Its $26 million domestic gross (on a $1.8 million budget) afforded Friedkin a certain industry clout, of which he took full advantage in 1973 while making *The Exorcist* (Biskind, 1998). The now notorious horror film, about a pubescent girl possessed by the devil, became a runaway box-office hit; rumors about the long and bloated production, mixed reviews from critics, and a limited initial release, it seems, could not halt the film's word-of-mouth (Klemesrud, 1974).

Friedkin's next film, *Sorcerer* (1977), was a remake of Henri-Georges Clouzot's *Wages of Fear*. Unfortunately for Friedkin, its release coincided with that of another blockbuster, George Lucas's *Star Wars*. *Sorcerer* flopped at the box office, and it marked the beginning of a string of unsuccessful films directed by Friedkin: *The Brink's Job*, *Cruising*, and *Deal of the Century*. *Cruising* (1980), an erotic thriller starring Al Pacino, drew attention from several groups that protested its negative depiction of homosexuality, and Friedkin was forced to cut a good number of scenes in order to secure an R-rating (Williams, 2005). While one might expect that Friedkin's brand of gut-reaction filmmaking would be perfect for the erotic thriller, his attempt to replicate the "sexy violence" formula popularized by Brian De Palma (*Dressed to Kill*) and perfected by Paul Verhoeven (*Basic Instinct*) in his film *Jade* (1995) failed miserably.

There have been some bright spots in Friedkin's career since his halcyon days in the 1970s—*To Live and Die in L.A.* (1985), *Blue Chips* (1994), *12 Angry Men* (1997), and *Bug* (2006), for example—but he has struggled to regain the status he enjoyed after he released *The French Connection* and *The Exorcist*.

Selected Filmography

Bug (2006); *Hunted, The* (2003); *Rules of Engagement* (2000); *Jade* (1995); *Blue Chips* (1994); *The Guardian* (1990); *Rampage* (1987); *To Live and Die in L.A.* (1985); *Deal of the Century* (1983); *Cruising* (1980); *The Exorcist* (1973); *The French Connection* (1971)

References

Biskind, Peter. *Easy Riders, Raging Bulls: How the Sex-Drugs-and-Rock-'n'-Roll Generation Saved Hollywood.* New York: Simon and Schuster, 1998.

Clagett, Thomas D. *William Friedkin: Films of Aberration, Obsession, and Reality.* Jefferson, NC: McFarland, 1990.

Gross, Larry. "What Ever Happened to William Friedkin?" *Sight & Sound*, December 1995.

Katz, Ephraim. *The Film Encyclopedia*, 4th ed. New York: Harper Resource, 2001.

Klemesrud, Judy. "They Wait Hours to Be Shocked." *New York Times*, January 27, 1974: 97.

Saeli, Marie. "William Friedkin." *International Dictionary of Films and Filmmakers, Vol. 2*, 3rd ed. Hillstrom, Laurie Collier, ed. Detroit: St. James Press, 1997.

Weinraub, Bernard. "Friedkin Tries Again for the A-List." *New York Times*, April 2, 2000: AR29.

Williams, Linda Ruth. *The Erotic Thriller in Contemporary Cinema*. Bloomington: Indiana University Press, 2005.

—Mikal Gaines

G

GABLE, CLARK. Between 1930 and 1960, Clark Gable was Hollywood's most popular leading man. Women were drawn to his masculine good looks, while men considered him to be the consummate "man's man." Indeed, in the opinion of many, Gable was the sexiest and most talented leading man of all time.

William Clark Gable was born on February 1, 1901, in Cadiz, Ohio, to parents William H. Gable, an oil driller and farmer, and Adeline Hershelman. After Gable's mother died when he was seven months old, he was placed with his uncle Charles Hershelman, who lived in Vernon, Pennsylvania. In 1903, after his father married his second wife, Jennie Dunlap, Gable returned home and the family settled in Hopedale, Ohio. At the age of 14, he was forced to quit high school in order to help support the family. By the time he was 21, he had worked on the family farm, been employed by the B. F. Goodrich Tire factory and had worked with his father in the oil-drilling business. When he was 17, he decided that he wanted to pursue a career in acting after he saw the play *The Bird of Paradise*. In 1922, Gable joined a traveling troupe, the Jewell Players. In 1924, he joined a Portland, Oregon, theater group that was directed by Josephine Dillon, whom Gable married on December 13, 1924. The couple relocated to Hollywood, where Gable secured work as a movie extra. In 1928, he won the lead in the New York City theater production, *Machinal*. By 1930, his marriage to Dillon had ended, and he had returned to Hollywood to perform in the play *The Last Mile*. Shortly thereafter, he signed a contract with MGM that paid him $350 a week

Gable's first movie with MGM was the western *The Painted Desert* (1931). That same year he also made his Hollywood debut as a leading man in the film, *Dance, Fools, Dance*, co-starring Joan Crawford. His sex appeal and magnetism quickly made him popular with American movie audiences. Throughout the early 1930s he co-starred in several movies with some of Hollywood's most popular leading ladies, including Marion Davies, Carole Lombard, Jean Harlow, and Helen Hayes. In 1934, he won an Academy Award for his leading role in *It Happened One Night*. By the mid-1930s, Gable was considered Hollywood's most popular leading man. His name alone guaranteed that a movie would become a box-office success. True to form, throughout the latter part of the 1930s Gable starred in several commercial hits,

This movie still shows Clark Gable in the Civil War epic *Gone with the Wind*. Gable left his acting career to join the Army Air Corps during World War II. He served as a tail gunner on raids over Nazi Germany. (Library of Congress)

including *Call of the Wild* (1935), *San Francisco* (1936), *Too Hot to Handle* (1938), and *Idiot's Delight* (1939). In 1939, Gable took on the role of a lifetime when he portrayed Rhett Butler in *Gone with the Wind*. The movie catapulted Gable to superstar status. On March 29, 1939, Gable married his third wife, Carole Lombard. Three years later she was killed in a plane crash. Distraught, Gable enlisted in the U.S. Army Air Corps in 1942. After he was discharged in June 1945, he returned to acting and resumed his role as Hollywood's favorite leading man. Throughout the late 1940s and early 1950s, Gable starred in several popular movies, including *Adventure* (1945), *The Hucksters* (1947), *Lone Star* (1952), and *Never Let Me Go* (1953). In 1954, he left MGM and became a freelance actor. In 1955, he was hired by Twentieth Century-Fox for the movies *Soldier of Fortune* and *The Tall Men*. He also starred in *Teacher's Pet* (1958), *But Not for Me* (1959), and *It Started in Naples* (1960) for Paramount Pictures. Gable died of a heart attack in 1960, shortly after finishing *The Misfits*.

For three decades, Gable entertained American movie audiences with his masculine good looks and acting skills. In total, he starred in 67 movies, many of which became box-office successes simply because Gable appeared in them. During his long reign as Hollywood's leading "leading man," Gable embodied what many thought was the ideal of the American male. Women dreamed of being with him, while men dreamed of being him. He died on November 16, 1960, in Los Angeles.

References

Bret, David. *Clark Gable: Tormented Star*. New York: Da Capo, 2007.
Harris, Warren G. *Clark Gable: A Biography*. New York: Harmony, 2002.
Wayne, Jane Ellen. *The Leading Men of MGM*. New York: Carroll & Graf, 2005.

—*Bernadette Zbicki Heiney*

GARBO, GRETA.   Greta Garbo is considered by many to have been the most glamorous actress in Hollywood during the 1920s and 1930s. Her enormous talents as an actress combined with her distinctively husky voice made her one of the few actresses to transition successfully from silent films to talking movies.

Greta Garbo was born Greta Lovisa Gustafsson on September 18, 1905, in Stockholm, Sweden, to parents Anna Lovisa Karlsson, a homemaker, and Karl Alfred Gustafsson, a landscaper. She was the youngest of the family's three children. When she was 14 years old, her father died of tuberculosis. She was forced to quit school and get a job in order to help support her family. Following her first job as a soap latherer in a barbershop, she was hired as a salesperson at the Paul U. Bergstrom Department Store, where she eventually was asked to appear in short promotional films for the store. In 1922, Garbo was one of seven students admitted to Stockholm's Royal Dramatic Theatre School. That same year, she also appeared as a bathing beauty in E. A. Petschler's film *The Vagabond Baron*. While attending the school, Garbo met director Mauritz Stiller, who in 1924 hired Garbo to portray Countess Elizabeth Dohna in her first silent movie, *The Atonement of Gosta Berling*. In 1925, she moved to the United States with Stiller to work at MGM. She arrived in New York City on July 6, 1925, and, shortly thereafter, posed for a series of photographs taken by Arnold Genthe that appeared in the magazine *Vanity Fair*. She arrived in Hollywood on September 10, 1925, and soon became one of MGM's most popular and lucrative silent movie stars. In 1926, her first American film, *The Torrent*, was released, followed by *The Temptress* in 1927. In both films she was cast in extremely "sexy" parts. In 1927, she co-starred with John Gilbert in the popular movie *Flesh and the Devil*. The actors' on-screen chemistry led to a very public offscreen romantic relationship. The publicity surrounding their relationship was in harsh contrast to Garbo's normally very private personal life. Throughout the remaining years of the 1920s, she continued to star in box-office successes, including *Love* (1927), *The Divine Woman* (1928), *The Mysterious Lady* (1928), *A Woman of Affairs* (1928), *Wild Orchids* (1929), *A Man's Man* (1929) and *The Single Standard* (1929). In 1929, she portrayed Madame Irene Guarry in her last silent movie, *The Kiss*. This was also the last silent movie produced by MGM.

In 1930, MGM released Garbo's first sound movie, *Anna Christie*. Its success inspired MGM to release a second, German-language version. Garbo had demonstrated that she could successfully transition from silent films to talking movies. Throughout the 1930s, she maintained her status as one of Hollywood's most glamorous movie stars. In 1931, she starred with Clark Gable in the box-office hit *Susan Lennox: Her Fall and Rise*. In 1932, she starred in three commercially successful movies: *Mata Hari*, *Grand Hotel*, and *As You Desire Me*. During the latter part of the decade, Garbo starred in several additional popular movies including *Queen Christina* (1933), *The Painted Veil* (1934), *Anna Karenina* (1935), *Camille* (1937), *Conquest* (1937), and *Ninotchka* (1939). In 1941, she starred in what would be her last movie role, *Two-Faced Woman*. Unfortunately, this film would be her only box-office failure.

During her career, Garbo appeared in 11 silent movies and 15 talking movies. She also became the highest-paid actress in Hollywood during the 1930s. Today, Garbo

Greta Garbo embodied romance and mystery in the silent era and the 1930s, playing tragic heroines such as Anna Karenina and Camille. (The Illustrated London News Picture Library)

remains a legend in American cinematic history. She died in a New York hospital on April 15, 1990.

References

Paris, Barry. *Garbo*. Minneapolis: University of Minnesota Press, 2002.
Vieira, Mark A. *Greta Garbo: A Cinematic Legacy*. New York: Harry N. Abrams, 2005.
Wayne, Jane Ellen. *The Golden Girls of MGM: Greta Garbo, Joan Crawford, Lana Turner, Judy Garland, Ava Gardner, Grace Kelly, and Others*. New York: Carroll & Graf, 2003.

—*Bernadette Zbicki Heiney*

GIBSON, MEL. With his leading-man good looks, Mel Gibson enjoyed a meteoric rise to fame. Throughout the years, he has proven himself a master of multiple genres ranging from romantic comedy to action to Shakespeare. Gibson has also forged a strong, albeit sometimes controversial, career as a director and writer. Although he starred in *Braveheart* (1995), he proved he was much more than an actor by directing the film, which won both Best Picture and Best Director Academy Awards. He later wrote and directed *The Passion of the Christ* (2004) and *Apocalypto* (2006), both of which were extremely violent and steeped in themes of religion and redemption, and which met with controversy upon their release.

Catholicism has always played a strong role in Gibson's life. In fact, Mel Columcille Gerard Gibson, born in Peekskill, New York, on January 3, 1956, was named after three Catholic saints. His parents moved their large family to Sydney, Australia, when Gibson was 12 years old, apparently to save their older sons from being drafted into the Vietnam War. Gibson attended a Catholic high school prior to studying at the National Institute of Dramatic Art at the University of New South Wales. For many years it appeared that he and his wife, Robyn, were a rarity, bucking the trend of the high Hollywood divorce rate. In a departure from his strong Catholic convictions, the couple—who wed in 1980 and have seven children together—separated in 2006 and divorced in 2009. That same year, Gibson also had a daughter with his girlfriend, Oksana Grigorieva, a singer.

Although he made his film debut in the low-budget surfer flick *Summer City* (1977), Gibson quickly received recognition for *Tim* (1979), a coming-of-age story for which he received the Australian Film Institute Award for Best Actor as the mentally challenged protagonist. Gibson also landed the lead role in *Mad Max* (1979), the first of three films about Max Rockatansky and his fight for survival in a barren, postapocalyptic world. The critically acclaimed sequel, *Mad Max 2: The Road Warrior* (1982), catapulted Gibson to stardom in the United States. A third installment, *Mad Max: Beyond Thunderdome* (1985), was a box-office smash and featured music legend Tina Turner.

A scene still of actor and director Mel Gibson from *Braveheart*. (Icon/Ladd Co/Paramount/The Kobal Collection)

Gibson won his second Australian Film Institute best actor award for Peter Weir's *Gallipoli* (1981), a World War I drama that follows its young protagonists in the Gallipoli campaign in Turkey. He teamed up again with Weir for *The Year of Living Dangerously* (1982). Set in Indonesia during a coup d'etat in 1965, this was the first Australian film to be fully financed by an American studio, MGM. Gibson continued to tackle dramatic roles throughout the 1980s, starring in films such as *The Bounty* (1984), a remake of *Mutiny on the Bounty*; *The River* (1984), which depicted the struggles of a Tennessee farming family; and, *Mrs. Soffel* (1984), a romantic thriller about inmate brothers who escape prison with help from the warden's wife. He became a household name with *Lethal Weapon* (1987), a buddy film featuring Gibson as the impulsive, self-destructive detective Martin Riggs, and Danny Glover as his partner Roger Murtaugh, the voice of reason. The box-office success of the first film—more than $65 million in U.S. ticket sales—led to three more installments: *Lethal Weapon 2* (1989), *Lethal Weapon 3* (1992), and *Lethal Weapon 4* (1998), each of which was wildly successful. Other Gibson action films include *Tequila Sunrise* (1988), in which he played a drug dealer trying to go straight, and *Payback* (1999), a crime thriller that once again found his character on the wrong side of the law. In the Ron Howard thriller *Ransom* (1996), Gibson portrayed a father desperate to find his young son, who was abducted in Central Park; he went on to play a paranoid New York City cabbie in the thriller *Conspiracy Theory* (1997).

Gibson has tackled comedy in a number of films, including *Bird on a Wire* (1990), *Air America* (1990), *Forever Young* (1992), and the western *Maverick* (1994). He also voiced Captain John Smith in the family-friendly Disney animated feature *Pocahontas* (1995). His humorous turn as a chauvinistic, womanizing advertising executive who suddenly can hear the innermost thoughts and desires of women in *What Women Want* (2000) came on the heels of a $25 million paycheck for *The Patriot* (2000). That same year, he voiced the rooster Rocky Rhodes in *Chicken Run*, a claymation feature. Each of his three 2000 releases earned more than $100 million. In 2002, Gibson starred in two films: *We Were Soldiers*, based on the true story of the first major battle of the Vietnam War; and, *Signs*, a sci-fi blockbuster directed by M. Night Shyamalan that featured Gibson as a former minister who has lost his faith and must help his family deal with an alien invasion.

Gibson made his directorial debut with the touching drama *The Man without a Face* (1993), in which he also starred. His directing prowess was acknowledged with *Braveheart* (1995), an epic period piece about William Wallace and the thirteenth-century Scottish fight for freedom from England. *Braveheart* received a total of 10 Academy Award nominations, was named Best Picture, and walked away with Oscars for cinematography, makeup and sound effects editing. Gibson took home the Oscar for Best Director. His devout faith came to the forefront in his next foray into directing, *The Passion of the Christ* (2004). Filmed in Latin and Aramaic, this labor of love depicting the final 12 hours of the life of Jesus Christ proved extremely controversial due to its incredibly graphic, and extra-canonical portrayal of the Passion and what some took to be Gibson's racist representations of Jews—it also did not help that Gibson implied that, like his father, he was sympathetic with the cause of Holocaust deniers. Charges of anti-Semitism were further fueled by remarks that Gibson made following his 2006 arrest for drunk driving—he has intermittently battled alcohol issues for years—for which he subsequently apologized. His next undertaking as a writer/director was the similarly controversial *Apocalypto* (2006), a bloody account of the downfall of Mayan civilization filmed in the dialect of Yucatec, which drove home the theme of redemption. The action movie *Edge of Darkness* (2010) marked Gibson's return to acting following an eight-year hiatus from the big screen.

Selected Filmography

Edge of Darkness (2010); *Paparazzi* (2004); *The Singing Detective* (2003); *Signs* (2002); *We Were Soldiers* (2002); *What Women Want* (2000); *The Patriot* (2000); *Chicken Run* (2000); *Payback* (1999/I); *Lethal Weapon 4* (1998); *Conspiracy Theory* (1997); *Fathers' Day* (1997);

Ransom (1996); *Pocahontas* (1995); *Braveheart* (1995); *Maverick* (1994); *The Man without a Face* (1993); *Lethal Weapon 3* (1992); *Hamlet* (1990); *Air America* (1990); *Bird on a Wire* (1990); *Lethal Weapon 2* (1989); *Tequila Sunrise* (1988); *Lethal Weapon* (1987); *Mad Max Beyond Thunderdome* (1985); *Mrs. Soffel* (1984); *The River* (1984); *The Bounty* (1984); *The Year of Living Dangerously* (1982); *Attack Force Z* (1982); *Mad Max 2: The Road Warrior* (1981); *Gallipoli* (1981); *Tim* (1979); *Mad Max* (1979); *Summer City* (1977); *I Never Promised You a Rose Garden* (1977)

References

Cagle, Jess. "A Softer Side of Mel." *Time*, December 11, 2000.

Corliss, Richard, Jeff Israely, and Jeffrey Ressner. "The Passion of Mel Gibson." *Time*, January 27, 2003.

Current Biography. H. W. Wilson, 2003. http://vnweb.hwwilsonweb.com.rlib.pace.edu/hww/results/getResults.jhtml?_DARGS=/hww/results/results_common.jhtml.33.

Garber, Zev. *Mel Gibson's Passion: The Film, the Controversy, and Its Implications.* West Lafayette, IN: Purdue University Press, 2006.

Levy, Emanuel. "A Fresh Start in the Rainforest." *Financial Times*, December 18, 2006.

Vincent, Mal. "Don't Call It a Comeback, but Mel Gibson Returns to the Big Screen." *McClatchy-Tribune News*, January 30, 2010.

—*Michele Camardella*

GISH, LILLIAN.   The career of Lillian Gish spanned 75 years, during which she made 105 films. As "the first lady of the silent screen," Gish is credited with inventing modern film acting. Her restrained style completely differed from the exaggerated style typical of stage actors at the time. Born in Springfield, Ohio, on October 14, 1893, film and Gish came into the world at approximately the same time. Her father abandoned the family, leaving them destitute. Lillian, her sister Dorothy, and her mother resorted to acting, enduring the social stigma associated with the profession. Lillian's stage career began at age eight in touring companies. Hers was a lonely youth often living separated from her family, in squalid conditions, undernourished, with little opportunity for schooling.

Childhood friend Mary Pickford introduced the Gish sisters to D. W. Griffith. The sisters' film debut came in Griffith's *An Unseen Enemy* (1912). Film acting kept the family together and brought a modicum of economic stability. Together, Griffith and Lillian made over two dozen films, including the infamous *Birth of a Nation* (1915) and *Intolerance* (1916). Devoted to Griffith from the time they began working together, Gish ardently defended him against claims of racism over *Birth of a Nation*. Despite this controversy, she and Griffith dedicated their careers to making film a respected art.

Typecast as the fragile, ethereal beauty at the mercy of men and nature, Gish starred primarily in melodramas. Her virginal, childlike beauty represented the American ideal of femininity at the time. While Gish resented the victim typecast, according to biographer Charles Affron, "Lillian's success had been and would continue to be predicated

In 1915 Gish rose to stardom as Elsie Stoneman in the controversial film *The Birth of a Nation*, directed by D. W. Griffith. (Library of Congress)

on her illusory subservience to strong men, a posture that furthered her own ambitions" (138).

Withstanding WWI air raids, the Gishes and Griffith made films in Europe including the war-mongering *Hearts of the World* (1918). Later, regretting making this film, she committed herself to pacifism.

After the war, notable films of this "Biograph girl" included *Broken Blossoms* (1919); *Way Down East* (1919); and *Orphans of the Storm* (1922). Gish's directorial debut was *Remodeling Her Husband* (1920). After its release, she insisted that directing was men's work, so instead she invested her own money in Inspiration Pictures, making two successful films overseas, *The White Sister* (1923) and *Romola* (1924). In 1925, she left Griffith, accepting a contract from MGM for $800,000. Along with this astounding sum, Gish earned unprecedented power, especially for a woman, to choose projects, directors, and co-stars. Her most notable MGM films were *La Boheme* (1926), *The Scarlet Letter* (1926), and *The Wind* (1928).

Unlike many actors, Gish successfully transitioned from silent cinema to "talkies" in *One Romantic Night* (1930). Yet, with her youth fading, she left Hollywood, resuming a stage career. In 1948, she transitioned to television. She continued to work in theatre, film, radio, and television throughout her life. Her later film career included *Duel in the Sun* (1946), for which she received an Academy Award nomination; *The Night of the Hunter* (1955); *The Unforgiven* (1960); *The Comedians* (1967), for which she received a Golden Globe nomination; and her final film, *The Whales of August* (1987).

Insisting she was not a feminist, Gish nevertheless offered a nontraditional example of femininity as a single career woman. Much was made of her choice not to marry or have children. She rejected several proposals, insisting marriage and career did not mix—and she preferred her career. Gish was a social and political conservative known for her work ethic, social propriety, and devotion to family. In 1941, she preached isolationism at antiwar rallies and on radio as a member of the America First Committee. Some considered her antiwar stance unpatriotic; realizing her career was in jeopardy, she resigned her membership. Although not involved in the House Un-American Activities Committee, Gish feared communism's threat and the role of film in spreading this ideology. She saw films as dangerous instruments of propaganda and spoke of the moral responsibility of the arts to all who would listen. A lifelong Republican, she lobbied government to create a cabinet-level post for the arts and for film preservation funding.

Gish received an honorary Academy Award in 1971, Kennedy Center Honors in 1982, and a Life Achievement Award from the American Film Institute in 1984. She died a film legend, on February 27, 1993, bequeathing millions in continued support of the arts.

See also: Birth of a Nation, The; Griffith, D. W.

References

Affron, Charles. *Lillian Gish: Her Legend, Her Life.* Berkeley: University of California Press, 2002.
American Film Institute, *Lillian Gish.* NY: Worldvision, 1989.
Gish, Lillian. *Lillian Gish: The Movies, Mr. Griffith, and Me.* Englewood Cliffs, NJ: Prentice-Hall, 1969.
Oderman, Stuart. *Lillian Gish: Life on Stage and Screen.* Jefferson, NC: McFarland, 2000.
Sanders, Terry. *Lillian Gish: An Actor's Life for Me.* New York: Thirteen/WNET.

—*Jamie Capuzza*

GRANT, CARY. For more than four decades, Cary Grant was one of Hollywood's most popular leading men. His self-created persona defined the sophisticated leading man for generations. Most popular in the genre of the romantic comedy, Grant obtained a level of superstardom that remains intact today.

Cary Grant was born Alexander Archibald Leach on January 18, 1904, in Bristol, Great Britain. He was raised as an only child by his parents Elias J. Leach, a factory worker, and Elsie Kingdom Leach. His parents had previously lost their first child, John, in 1899; and his mother, who never fully recovered from the loss, was institutionalized when Grant was nine years old. He spent his teenage years being raised by his father. Grant attended the Bishop Road Boys School in Bristol until he won a scholarship to the Fairfield Secondary School in Somerset in 1915. Three years later, when he was 14 years old, he quit school and joined the John Pender Comedy Troupe. In 1920, he traveled to the United States with the troupe to perform in New York City at the Globe Theater. When the troupe returned to Great Britain, Grant remained in New York City and took a job with the Steeplechase Amusement Park on Coney Island as a stilt walker. In 1927, he was hired for a role in the play *Golden Dawn*, on Broadway. Although the play was only a marginal success, it afforded him the opportunity to acquire other acting jobs on Broadway.

In 1931, Grant signed a contract with Paramount Pictures. That same year, he made his acting debut in the movie *Singapore Sue* and also began to use exclusively Cary Grant as his professional name. An instant Hollywood success, Grant quickly rose to superstar status. His on-screen persona epitomized America's image of what a handsome and sophisticated Hollywood movie star should be. Throughout the 1930s, he co-starred in several pictures alongside some of Hollywood's most famous leading ladies. In 1933, he starred in two movies with Mae West, *She Done Him Wrong* and *I'm No Angel*. In 1936, he co-starred with Katharine Hepburn in the film *Sylvia Scarlett*, and in 1937 with Irene Dunne in the box-office hit *The Awful Truth*. Grant co-starred with Hepburn in several other popular movies during the latter part of the 1930s, including *Bringing Up Baby* (1938), *Holiday* (1938), and *The Philadelphia Story* (1940). He also starred in numerous romantic comedies, including the hits *Thirty-Day Princess* (1934), *Kiss and Make-Up* (1935), and *Wedding Present* (1936). By the end of the decade, Grant had found his niche in romantic comedy feature films.

In 1942, he became a U.S. citizen and legally changed his name to Cary Grant. During the 1940s, some of his most successful comedies included *His Girl Friday* (1940), *The Talk of the Town* (1942), *Arsenic and Old Lace* (1944), and *Mr. Blandings Builds a Dream House* (1948). Surprisingly, it was his performance in the drama *Penny Serenade* (1941) that earned him his first Academy Award nomination. He earned a second nomination in 1944 for his role in the drama *None but the Lonely Heart*. Throughout the 1950s and 1960s, he continued to excel in the romantic comedy genre. Some of the more notable pictures in which he starred during this period included *Monkey Business* (1952), *An Affair to Remember* (1957), *That Touch of Mink* (1962), and *Father Goose* (1964).

Although the romantic comedy had become his specialty, Grant had the opportunity to explore more dramatic roles in four Alfred Hitchcock films. In 1941, he was cast as Johnnie, a husband who appeared to be trying to murder his wife, in *Suspicion*. His success in *Suspicion* led to roles in three additional Hitchcock films: *Notorious* (1946), *To Catch a Thief* (1955) and *North by Northwest* (1959). In 1966, Grant took on his last movie role before retiring, starring in the romantic comedy *Walk, Don't Run*.

For more than 40 years, the name Cary Grant was synonymous with the Hollywood romantic comedy. He entertained American movie audiences with both his acting skills and his sophisticated charm. This sophistication ultimately became America's definition of an elegant gentleman. He died on November 29, 1986, but is still considered one of Hollywood's most popular leading men.

References

Duncan, Paul. *Cary Grant*. New York: Barnes & Noble, 2008.
Eliot, Marc. *Cary Grant: The Biography*. New York: Harmony, 2004.
McCann, Graham. *Cary Grant: A Class Apart*. New York: Columbia University Press, 1998.

—*Bernadette Zbicki Heiney*

GRIER, PAM. Pam Grier, the "Queen of Blaxploitation," not only revolutionized the way women in general are portrayed on-screen but, more specifically, how African American women are portrayed. In the 1970s she became one of the first African American female superheroes, garnering fame, fans, and of course, critics.

Born Pamela Suzette Grier on May 26, 1949, in North Carolina, Grier spent most of her early years living on multiple Air Force bases with her family. Her father and mother, an Air Force mechanic and a nurse respectively, were the parents to four children. When Grier was nine years old, her family finally settled in Denver. Having become accustomed to the middle-class lifestyle she experienced on military bases, Grier later stated that she felt ostracized in the primarily black and working-class neighborhood in which she found herself in Colorado.

Grier's film career began when Roger Corman cast her in *The Big Doll House* in 1971. The small role led to several other supporting appearances in *The Arena* (1971), *Black Mama/White Mama* (1972), and *The Big Bird Cage* (1972), and ultimately led to her signing a five-year contract with the production company American International Pictures.

In the 1970s, a new genre of film, dubbed "blaxploitation" because it featured African American actors in exploitative roles, became popular among urban African American audiences. These films featured mostly African American male protagonists living out urban action-adventure narratives supported by the hippest clothes and music of the times. These male-centered narratives were expanded when Pam Grier was cast in *Coffy*.

Directed by Jack Hill, *Coffy* was released in 1973. The stunning, sexy Grier starred as a seemingly demure nurse who, after her sister is put into a comma from a drug overdose, dons skin-tight clothing and holstered guns and proceeds to wreck uber-violent revenge on the neighborhood drug dealers. The film earned $8 million for the studio and fame for Grier.

As a result of her performance in *Coffy*, Grier was cast in several more blaxploitation films. In 1974, she starred in *Foxy Brown* as a woman who poses as a prostitute in order to avenge her boyfriend's death; in 1975, she starred in *Friday Foster* as a fashion photographer trying to stop an assassination attempt on African American politicians; and in what turned out to be her final film for AIP, 1975's *Sheba Baby*, Grier portrayed a private eye who protects her father, whose business is being threatened by the mob. In all of these films, Grier's beauty—and body—was highlighted as much as her acting and action skills. While this intentionally exploitative formula attracted millions of moviegoers, it also made her the target of a great deal of criticism.

Her fans and a good number of film critics applauded Grier for bringing a new kind of African American woman to the screen. They contended that, first and foremost, Grier broke down barriers for actresses, and more specifically for African American actresses. Not only did she earn starring roles and huge salaries (she was one of the highest-paid actresses in the 1970s), but ultimately the power to shape what kind of characters she would play. Supporters of Grier argued that her performances—with their expression of overt sexuality, beauty, and physical and emotional strength—acted to break down negative stereotypes of African American women (especially that of the "mammy," the desexualized mother figure). This appealed not only to white feminists in the 1970s, who featured her on the cover of *Ms.* magazine, but also to the growing Black Power movement, which stressed race pride. Grier, they proclaimed, had redefined the public image of black female beauty, bringing Afros and black skin to posters all over America.

Blaxploitation films, however, were unpopular with many leaders in the black community because they portrayed African Americans as violent, oversexed criminals. These leaders also criticized the films for what they believed was their lack of positive social messages. Grier's roles, especially, were attacked by many black feminists as merely filmic depictions of African American women as sexual objects.

Ultimately Grier's career stalled with the demise of blaxploitation films. In the 1970s and 1980s, she made a number of unmemorable films—*Greased Lightning* (1977), *Fort Apache: the Bronx* (1981), *Above the Law* (1988), and *The Package* (1989), for example. Her career was revived in 1995, however, when Quentin Tarantino cast the still stunning, 45-year-old Grier in his homage to blaxploitation films, *Jackie Brown*. In *Jackie Brown*, Grier was cast as a beautiful, strong, self-possessed woman— who happens to be African American—who faces down drug dealers and manipulators. After making this film, and attracting a whole new generation of film fans, Grier went on to play numerous television roles and to star in the hit Showtime cable series *The L Word* (2004).

References

Bogle, Donald. *Toms, Coons, Mulattoes, Mammies, and Bucks: An Interpretive History of Blacks in American Films.* New York: Viking, 1994.

Dunn, Stephane. *"Baad Bitches" & Sassy Supermamas: Black Power Action Films.* Urbana: University of Illinois Press, 2008.

Howard, Josiah. *Blaxploitation Cinema: The Essential Reference Guide.* Guildford, UK: FAB Press, 2008.

Sims, Yvonne D. *Women of Blaxploitation: How the Black Action Film Heroine Changed American Popular Culture.* Jefferson, NC: McFarland, 2006.

—*Katharine Bausch*

GRIFFITH, D. W.   Born on January 22, 1875, David Wark Griffith has long been considered the founder of American cinema as a serious art form. His extraordinarily controversial 1915 Civil War epic, *The Birth of a Nation*, was shown in theatres for the amazing price of two dollars a ticket, with musical accompaniment by a full orchestra; it was also the first moving picture screened in the White House. On a commercial level, he was a pioneer of the feature film—as opposed to the mass-market two-reelers that were standard fare at the time—and helped to create some of the first movie stars, including Lillian and Dorothy Gish, and Mae Marsh.

Born in Kentucky a decade after the end of the Civil War, Griffith was the son of Jacob Wark Griffith, a Confederate Army veteran. Although Jacob died when Griffith was only 10 years old, it seems that he had already passed along to his son a taste for Victorian Age romanticism and fierce pride in his Southern identity. Jacob's death left his widow, the former Mary Perkins Oglesby, to care for their two children by herself. Unable to keep their farm afloat and overwhelmed by debt, Mary moved the family to Louisville, where she opened a boardinghouse, which also failed. The family's misfortunes eventually forced Griffith to drop out of school and take a job in a dry goods store; later, he took a job in a bookstore, where he embarked on a course of interdisciplinary self-study.

Griffith was nearly 25 years old when the cinema began to emerge and 30 when it was still in its primitive, nickelodeon stage. Thus, it was the theatre

Film director D. W. Griffith. (Library of Congress)

and stage plays that formed him, in particular the Victorian melodrama, which supplied him with the narrative archetypes for his films. Griffith eventually began selling scripts to the Biograph Company, a major studio of the silent era, and began to act in early films. He soon started directing—making numerous one- and two-reelers—and gathering together a company of actors and technicians, most notably the pioneering cameraman Billy Bitzer. Making his many film shorts allowed Griffith to experiment with diverse source material, locations, techniques, and methods of storytelling. The prolific director ultimately made more than 450 short films with Biograph, which constituted an important part of the work of his early career. He concentrated on making domestic melodramas (*The Painted Lady*, 1912); urban dramas (*The Lily of the Tenement*, 1911); and adaptations of the literary works of authors such as Jack London and Frank Norris (*A Corner in Wheat*, 1909). One of his best known two-reelers, *The Musketeers of Pig Alley* (1912)—now celebrated for its brilliant technique—is considered the first crime movie.

The success of an Italian adaptation of the Roman epic *Quo Vadis?* demonstrated both the artistic and commercial potential of longer motion pictures. Griffith's first attempt at the new form was a Biblical epic, *Judith of Bethulia* (1913), an adaptation of a play written by the popular writer Thomas Bailey Aldrich. The film starred Blanche Sweet, and featured the actresses who would later become stars while working with Griffith, Mae Marsh and the Gish sisters. The film combined two elements that Griffith would use again in his other great epics, spectacular battle scenes and the depiction of more intimate expressions of pathos, especially from vulnerable, virtuous women. Resistant to long features, Biograph delayed the release of the film, perhaps for budgetary reasons—the picture reputedly cost an unprecedented $50,000—or because of doubts about the public's patience for multireel films. Nevertheless, the film was well received when it was released. Angry at the studio's lack of support, Griffith decided to leave Biograph, taking with him his stock company; he soon began working on what would become his most important and most controversial film, *The Birth of a Nation*.

Technically brilliant, *The Birth of a Nation* was an adaptation of Thomas Dixon's novel *The Clansman*. A paean to the eighteenth-century Ku Klux Klan, Griffith's film at least seemed to suggest that the latter-day formation of such a group was the last best hope for saving white America. Despite its controversial subject matter, the picture was initially well received when it premiered in New York City; Dixon even talked then-president Woodrow Wilson into screening *Birth of a Nation* in the White House. Many Americans, though, felt that the film was racist, a charge with which Griffith would have to contend for the remainder of his career.

Perhaps in response to these accusations of racism following the release of *Birth of a Nation*, Griffith produced the monumental *Intolerance* in 1916. Made up of four narrative threads—stories concerning the Passion of the Christ, ancient Babylon, the St. Bartholomew's Day Massacre, and then-contemporary issues of injustice and redemption—*Intolerance* sought to explore "love's struggle through the ages." As the title implies, the separate narratives are linked by the theme of intolerance, and they progressively converge to form a masterful mosaic. While *Intolerance* was the most expensive movie made to that point in time, it did not match the success of *Birth of a Nation*. Griffith's insistence, it seems, on building up a complex filmic structure supported by four narrative strands, coupled with his decision to crosscut among these narratives with little if any explanation, made the film too intricately demanding for almost all audiences.

At this point, Griffith's career entered another major phase, as he made a series of films focusing on characters played by Lillian Gish: *True Heart Susie* (1919), *Broken Blossoms* (1919), *Way Down East* (1920), and *Orphans of the Storm* (1921)—which also starred Gish's sister, Dorothy. Although these films were not as materially ambitious as pictures like *Birth of a Nation* and *Intolerance*, they had a dramatic sensibility that the earlier, epic films lacked. The latter three films are all domestic melodramas played out against evocative backdrops (slum, nature, historical turbulence), with visually arresting images that are romantic and genuinely poetic. Although there is typically a male romantic lead who may or may not be successful in rescuing an endangered woman, the female protagonists in these films are clearly the dominant figures. Much of this is no doubt a result of Gish's strong characterization; but some of it must also be attributed to Griffith's skills as a "woman's director," one who was able consistently to draw powerful performances from the actresses with whom he worked.

More than just an extraordinarily talented director, Griffith also contributed to organizing American cinema as an industry. Along with Mary Pickford, Douglas

Fairbanks, and Charlie Chaplin, Griffith was one of the founding partners of United Artists, which ultimately became a major studio. As was his habit, though, Griffith quickly grew restless, and he chose to leave UA; his professional relationship with Lillian Gish also began to deteriorate at this time, and the two finally stopped working with each other altogether. After his break with Gish, Griffith's work went into artistic and commercial decline. Trying to rekindle the magic he had developed with Gish, he turned to another leading lady, Carol Dempster, but she proved to be a far from satisfactory replacement for the ethereal Gish. Experimenting with story formulas in films like *America* and *Isn't Life Wonderful?* (both 1924) did not help matters, either, and Griffith closed his career with an uninspired biographical picture about Abraham Lincoln. Never having accumulated the wealth that others in the industry had been able to gather, Griffith lived out his life in Hollywood, a man of modest means. He died on July 23, 1948, at the age of 73, and was buried near his birthplace in Kentucky.

Selected Filmography

The Struggle (1931); *Lady of the Pavements* (1929); *The Battle of the Sexes* (1928); *Drums of Love* (1928); *The Sorrows of Satan* (1926); *That Royle Girl* (1925); *Sally of the Sawdust* (1925); *Isn't Life Wonderful* (1924); *America* (1924); *The White Rose* (1923); *Mammy's Boy* (1923); *One Exciting Night* (1922); *Orphans of the Storm* (1921); *The Mother and the Law* (1919); *The Fall of Babylon* (1919); *True Heart Susie* (1919); *Broken Blossoms or The Yellow Man and the Girl* (1919); *The Girl Who Stayed at Home* (1919); *A Romance of Happy Valley* (1919); *The World of Columbus* (1919); *The Greatest Thing in Life* (1918); *The Great Love* (1918); *Hearts of the World* (1918); *Intolerance: Love's Struggle Throughout the Ages* (1916); *The Birth of a Nation* (1915); *The Avenging Conscience: or "Thou Shalt Not Kill"* (1914); *The Escape* (1914); *Home, Sweet Home* (1914); *The Primitive Man* (1914); *The Battle of the Sexes* (1914); *Judith of Bethulia* (1914); *The Massacre* (1914); *The Battle at Elderbush Gulch* (1913)

References

Drew, William M. *D. W. Griffith's Intolerance: Its Genesis and Its Vision*. Jefferson, NC: McFarland, 2002.

Everson, William K. *American Silent Film*. New York: Da Capo, 1998.

Gordon, Andrew, and Vera Hernan. *Screen Saviours: Hollywood Fictions of Whiteness*. Lanham, MD: Rowman & Littlefield, Inc, 2003.

Hansen, Miriam. *Babel and Babylon*. Cambridge, MA: Harvard University Press, 1991.

Lang, Robert, ed. *The Birth of a Nation: D. W. Griffith, Director*. Piscataway, NJ: Rutgers University Press, 1993.

Schickel, Richard. *D. W. Griffith: An American Life*. New York: Limelight, 2004.

Simmon, Scott. *The Films of D. W. Griffith*. New York: Cambridge University Press, 1993.

Stokes, Melvyn. *D. W. Griffith's The Birth of a Nation: A History of the Most Controversial Motion Picture of All Time*. New York: Oxford University Press, 2008.

—*Dimitri Keramitas*

H

HAWKS, HOWARD.   Since the 1960s, Howard Hawks has been recognized as a great artist, a true auteur of international cinema. By his own admission, however, he was a diverse and unabashedly commercial director, with a gift for discerning what film audiences liked. He worked in all major American film genres, most notably gangster, screwball comedy, film noir, and westerns. Of the 47 films he is officially credited with having directed, his reputation rests on 10, a number that could readily be expanded by scholars and critics who continue to reevaluate his work, believing that additional films deserve further scrutiny. The films for which he is best known and which continue to garner critical attention are *Scarface* (1932), *Bringing Up Baby* (1938), *Only Angels Have Wings* (1939), *His Girl Friday* (1940), *Sergeant York* (1941), *To Have And Have Not* (1944), *The Big Sleep* (1946), *Red River* (1948), *Gentlemen Prefer Blondes* (1953), and *Rio Bravo* (1959).

A distinctive characteristic of a Howard Hawks film is overlapping dialogue, in which one or more persons speak before another has completely finished. It was a device that became a sort of trademark, giving pace, energy, and forward movement to dialogue sequences. It often enhanced comedy, as in the three person "trialogue" in *His Girl Friday*, in which Cary Grant, Rosalind Russell, and Ralph Bellamy conduct a decidedly hectic but completely comprehensible conversation. The overlapping dialogue could also further the sense of tension in an action film, evident in the conversations that take place among scientists and military men in *The Thing from Another World* (1951). (It should be noted that the credited director of this science-fiction thriller is Christian Nyby, but Nyby had never directed before, and the directorial hand of the producer, Hawks, is readily apparent throughout.) Another characteristic was his avoidance of complex camera work, such as sweeping panoramas, dolly or crane shots, and other forms of cinematography that he felt distracted from or at least did not add to his story. He favored eye-level camera placement, and his films, more often than not, took place indoors.

Born in Goshen, Indiana, on May 30, 1896, Hawks was a child of wealth and privilege who readily availed himself of all the advantages of such good fortune. He was schooled at exclusive Phillips Exeter Academy in New Hampshire and later at Cornell, where he studied engineering. In the early 1920s, he became intrigued with Hollywood. Following the whim of the dilettante rather than any calculated career plan, he worked college summers at Famous Players-Lasky (later Paramount Studios), starting out as an assistant prop man, and quickly rising to associate producer and writer, turning out silent screen scenarios, and editing those of others.

The story of his rise in the industry, particularly the early part of his career, is open to interpretation. Hawks was known as an unremitting teller of tall tales, and seemed to take a certain perverse delight in "rewriting" his life story. His version of his experiences over the years, related in numerous interviews, often varies in detail. His account of his life and his film industry successes is consistent, however, in that it presents Hawks as a man who won all the arguments with studio executives and triumphed in all significant conflicts. Undoubtedly there is some exaggeration, but to his credit, little contradictory evidence to the facts as he presented them. He was admired by those who worked with him, and his many talents were recognized and appreciated from the beginning. He was a true independent, a director who early in his career served as his own producer, and never hesitated to rewrite a script or change a set if he deemed it necessary. Allowing directors such latitude was highly unusual in the days of the studio system; Hawks, though, resisted attempts by producers to control the filmmaking process. Indeed, he usually signed contracts to direct only one or two pictures for any single studio at a time.

Hawks was particularly adept at recognizing and seizing opportunities. When an art director at Famous Players was unavailable to create a modern set requested by Douglas Fairbanks, the studio's biggest star of the silent era, Hawks volunteered to design and build it. He had had some training in architecture at Cornell, and his success with this venture led to the development of a strong friendship with Fairbanks. By his own account, Hawks was an excellent golfer and a skilled tennis player, attributes that impressed Fairbanks, Hollywood's reigning hero of swashbuckling adventure films and a man who took great pride in doing his own film stunts. The friendship with Fairbanks led the latter to recommend Hawks to Mary Pickford, one of the most prominent stars of the silent screen, and, at the time, Fairbanks's fiancée. Hawks seized another opportunity when one day the director of one of Pickford's films did not appear on the set as scheduled. The supremely confident Hawks volunteered to step in and direct the scenes scheduled to be shot that day, allowing the studio to avoid costly delays. Building on this first foray into directing, he moved into producing and writing stories and scenarios for films that he would go on to direct.

During World War I, Hawks served in the Signal Corps, gaining extensive experience with airplanes. He developed a lifelong interest in aviation, an enthusiasm that informed his direction of action-adventure films with aviation themes, including *The Air Circus* (1928), *The Dawn Patrol* (1930), *Ceiling Zero* (1936), *Only Angels Have Wings* (1939), and *Air Force* (1943). Inherently fond of risk, he had a similar passion for auto racing; in fact, for a time he designed racing cars and drove professionally. These experiences found their way into films such as *The Crowd Roars* (1932) and *Red Line 7000* (1965). In the years between 1926 and 1929, Hawks directed eight full-length motion pictures: *The Road to Glory* (1926), *Fig Leaves* (1926), *The Cradle*

Snatcher (1927), *Paid to Love* (1927), *A Girl in Every Port* (1928), *Fazil* (1928) *The Air Circus* (1928), and *Trent's Last Case* (1929). Of these eight films directed prior to the advent of sound, only *A Girl in Every Port* has merited any critical attention, largely because of the engaging performances by Victor McLaglen and Robert Armstrong, who played career sailors living in a Hawksian man's world, unencumbered by domesticity and doing what a man's got to do—in this case, getting drunk and pursuing women.

In *A Girl in Every Port*, McLaglen's character, Spike, momentarily succumbs to the allure of domesticity but quickly recovers his senses, forsaking an impending marriage with Marie (Louise Brooks). Interestingly, in *His Girl Friday*, the formidable Hildy Johnson (Rosalind Russell) sidesteps her impending marriage so that she might continue unfettered in her career in journalism as the ace reporter working for her less-than-scrupulous editor, former husband Walter Burns (Cary Grant). In the original play, written by Ben Hecht and Charles MacArthur, Hildy ("Hildebrand") Johnson was a male role, which was also the case in the 1931 film version of the play directed by Lewis Milestone. In his remake, however, Hawks changed the title, and, in an inspired moment, changed the role of Hildy to a woman. In the end, she becomes a Hawksian woman, talented, strong-willed, but one who discovers that what she really wants in life is to follow her man—the right man—please him, and ask few, if any, questions.

Hawks had a very distinct idea of how he wanted to portray women in his films. The female protagonists in Hawks's action films were largely devoid of the attributes of conventional femininity—they were also completely comfortable in a man's world. Sophisticated, confident, and self-possessed, they were complementary figures able to engage and hold their own in exchanges with their male counterparts. Once they recognized that certain men were worthy of them, however, they quietly and unconditionally surrendered themselves to these men. Hawks, it seems, began to develop this idea of the strong/compliant filmic woman during the 1930s, giving inchoate expression to it in *Only Angels Have Wings* (1939), where Bonnie Lee (Jean Arthur) discovers, after tears, confusion, and a great deal of frustration, precisely what she has to do to snare Geoff Carter (Cary Grant): "I'm hard to get, Geoff," she says, "all you have to do is ask me." Seemingly quite pleased with this terse expression of surrender, Hawks has Vivian Rutledge (Lauren Bacall) utter the same words to Philip Marlowe (Humphrey Bogart) in *The Big Sleep*, and Feathers (Angie Dickinson) speaks a variant of the declaration to Sheriff John T. Chance (John Wayne) in *Rio Bravo*. It may be argued, though, that the Hawksian woman achieves her fullest expression in Hawks's adaptation of Ernest Hemingway's *To Have and Have Not*. Casting 19-year-old model Lauren Bacall in her first screen role as Marie Browning, Hawks fashioned her character after his current wife, socialite Nancy Gross, whom the tall, slightly gaunt, beautiful, and seductively clever Bacall resembled somewhat. Hawks even gave the Bacall character the nickname "Slim," his term of endearment for his wife. Playing opposite her future husband Humphrey Bogart—the pair absolutely sizzled on the screen—Bacall embodied the Hawks woman: dangerously attractive, mouthy, and, in the end, totally devoted to her man.

Not surprisingly, the men in Hawks's action films are bulwarks of conventional masculinity, idealized and mythic. Hawks stressed the theme of "professionalism" in these action pictures: men—real men—recognized that they had jobs to do, and they set out in single-minded fashion to do them. Fear, doubt, or any other emotion that might undermine a man's confidence and determination had no place in the makeup of the Hawksian hero. If you were a professional, if you were good enough, you did the job or died honorably in the attempt. Nowhere is this ideal more powerfully expressed than in *Rio Bravo*, a picture that Hawks admitted was a response to Fred Zinnemann's 1952 film *High Noon*. Hawks—and star John Wayne—could not abide the Zinnemann characterization of Sheriff Will Kane (Gary Cooper) as a figure who is not good enough to deal with crazed killers by himself or wise enough to hire professionals to help him with the job. When Wayne's Sheriff John T. Chance is asked if wants to deputize some ranch hands, he brusquely rejects the idea: "Well-meaning amateurs," he says, "most of them worried about their wives and kids."

Significantly, Hawks is the only notable director in American cinema to have given audiences an acknowledged classic motion picture in four of the primary film genres that define American cinema. *Scarface* would certainly be in the top five of any film scholar's list of significant American films in the gangster genre. *Bringing Up Baby* and *His Girl Friday* are Hawks's definitive contributions to screwball comedy, pairing Katharine Hepburn in the first and Rosalind Russell in the second with the redoubtable Cary Grant. *The Big Sleep* is quintessential noir, while *Red River* rivals the films of the man many consider to be the undisputed master of the American western, John Ford.

In his last two films, *El Dorado* (1966) and *Rio Lobo* (1970), Hawks once again gave expression to his ideas concerning heroic men, "professionals" acting out their predestined roles as communal saviors. These pictures, though, proved to be little more than thinly veiled remakes of *Rio Bravo*, none of which, most would agree, compared to *Red River*, perhaps his best film in the western genre and one of his best films generally. An iconic figure in the cinematic world, Howard Hawks died on December 26, 1977, at the age of 81 in Palm Springs, California.

Selected Filmography

Rio Lobo (1970); *El Dorado* (1966); *Red Line 7000* (1965); *Man's Favorite Sport?* (1964); *Hatari!* (1962); *Rio Bravo* (1959); *Land of the Pharaohs* (1955); *Gentlemen Prefer Blondes* (1953); *Monkey Business* (1952); *The Big Sky* (1952); *The Thing from Another World* (1951); *I Was a Male War Bride* (1949); *A Song Is Born* (1948); *Red River* (1948); *The Big Sleep* (1946); *To Have and Have Not* (1944); *Air Force* (1943); *Ball of Fire* (1941); *Sergeant York* (1941); *His Girl Friday* (1940); *Only Angels Have Wings* (1939); *Bringing Up Baby* (1938); *Come and Get It* (1936); *The Road to Glory* (1936); *Ceiling Zero* (1936); *Barbary Coast* (1935); *Twentieth Century* (1934); *The Prizefighter and the Lady* (1933); *Today We Live* (1933); *Tiger Shark* (1932); *The Crowd Roars* (1932); *Scarface* (1932); *The Criminal Code* (1931); *The Dawn Patrol* (1930)

References

Bogdanovich, Peter. *The Cinema of Howard Hawks*. New York: Museum of Modern Art, 1962.

Hawks, Howard, with Joseph McBride, ed. *Hawks on Hawks*. London: Faber & Faber, 1996.

Hillier, Jim, and Peter Wollen, eds. *Howard Hawks: American Artist*. London: British Film Institute, 1997.

Pippin, Robert B. *Hollywood Westerns and American Myths: The Importance of Howard Hawks and John Ford for Political Philosophy*. New Haven, CT: Yale University Press, 2010.

—*Richard C. Keenan*

HECKERLING, AMY.   Amy Heckerling, one of the few female movie directors to achieve both commercial and critical success, is perhaps best known for films that provide audiences with sharp insights into teen life.

Heckerling was born May 7, 1954, in the New York City borough of the Bronx. She attended the High School of Art and Design, a public school in Manhattan. She graduated from New York University in 1975 and immediately enrolled in the prestigious American Film Institute (AFI) in California. A film she completed at AFI caught the attention of producers who were creating a movie about teenagers at a California high school. They tapped Heckerling to direct the film, *Fast Times at Ridgemont High*. Released in the fall of 1982, the picture became the sleeper hit of the year. It also launched Heckerling's career, along with those of its young stars, Sean Penn, Jennifer Jason Leigh, and Nicolas Cage.

Fast Times vaulted Heckerling into an exclusive club: female directors who were sought after by Hollywood studios. Significantly, she became known as a filmmaker who paid special attention to female characters. In *Fast Times*, for example, young women contemplate sex, relationships, and even difficult issues such as abortion. In 1984, Heckerling made *Johnny Dangerously*. Featuring Michael Keaton and Marilu Henner, the picture was a spoof of traditional gangster movies. Unfortunately for Heckerling, it was a critical and box-office flop. She bounced back in 1985 with *National Lampoon's European Vacation*, which featured Chevy Chase and Beverly D'Angelo. Heckerling's next big hit was 1989's *Look Who's Talking*, starring Kirstie Alley and John Travolta as friends, and potential romantic mates, Mollie and James. The story is told from the perspective of Mollie's baby (brilliantly voiced by Bruce Willis), who desperately wants his mother and James to get together. Heckerling has said that the birth of her own daughter, Mollie, in 1985 prompted her to write a screenplay that focused on the thoughts of an infant (Sjursen, 1999).

In the early 1990s, Heckerling hit a rough patch. Seeking to capitalize on the success of the first film, she quickly wrote and directed *Look Who's Talking Too* (1990), but the sequel failed miserably at the box office. Then in 1991, Heckerling and her husband were divorced. That same year, she settled a lawsuit with two women who claimed that Heckerling had really based *Look Who's Talking* on a student film they had shown her in 1986 (Horowitz, 1991).

Undaunted, Heckerling went back to work, crafting a movie script inspired by Jane Austen's novel *Emma*. Her efforts paid off, and *Clueless* hit the big screen in 1995. An endearing exposé of teen angst, the coming-of-age comedy centers around a rich Beverly Hills High School student named Cher Horowitz. Cher, delightfully played by Alicia Silverstone, although eager to correct the faults and weaknesses of others, doesn't seem to realize that she has many of her own. Adored by both fans and critics, *Clueless* earned Heckerling a National Society of Film Critics Award for best screenplay. While studio executives initially balked at making a film that featured female characters, Heckerling stood her ground, resisting the suggestion that more male characters be added to the film and insisting that the story be told from Cher's point of view (Heckerling and Firstenberg, 1995).

Heckerling has produced two television series: *Fast Times*, a short-lived 1986 series based on *Fast Times at Ridgemont High*; and *Clueless*, a sitcom inspired by the 1995 film that had a three-year run. Her next two films, 1998's *A Night at the Roxbury*, based on a *Saturday Night Live* skit, and *Loser* (2000), which tells the story of two young college students, were coolly received, both by audiences and critics. In 2005, seeking to address a movie studio culture that consistently denies film leads to older women, Heckerling made *I Could Never Be Your Woman*, which featured Michelle Pfeiffer, who, interestingly, is one of the few actresses who can still carry a Hollywood picture despite being in her fifties. Plagued by postproduction problems, the film made little impact, going straight to DVD.

Independence and passion may very well be Heckerling's most enduring qualities. She has said that she's been offered formulaic movies to direct, but would rather write and direct her own projects (Schwartz, 2008). She continues to be a director who resolutely refuses to step behind the camera until the right project comes along.

Selected Filmography

I Could Never Be Your Woman (2007); *Loser* (2000); *Clueless* (1995); *Look Who's Talking Too* (1990); *Look Who's Talking* (1989); *European Vacation* (1985); *Johnny Dangerously* (1984); *Fast Times at Ridgemont High* (1982); *Getting It Over With* (1977)

References

Heckerling, Amy, with Jean Picker Firstenberg. Edited transcript of Harold Lloyd Master Seminar at American Film Institute, September 14, 1995. Available at www.fathom.com.

Horowitz, Joy. " 'Look Who's Talking' Suit on Plagiarism Is Settled." *New York Times*, June 14, 1991.

Schwartz, Missy, et al. "Would You Dump This Woman?" *Entertainment Weekly*, February 8, 2008: 30–33.

Sjursen, Katrin. "Amy Heckerling." *Current Biography* 60, July 1999: 27–29.

—*Rachael Hanel*

HEPBURN, KATHARINE.   Katharine Hepburn was one of America's most successful and influential performers. She presented audiences with strong female characters in over 50 films and across a seven-decade career. Her offscreen persona heightened her legacy as an outspoken and determined woman who challenged—and changed—the nation's attitudes toward sexual difference.

Katharine Houghton Hepburn was born on May 12, 1907, to upper-middle class and politically progressive parents in Hartford, Connecticut. When she was 14, Hepburn's beloved older brother, Tom, hanged himself. Hepburn discovered the body, a traumatic experience that caused her to withdraw from her peers. She attended Bryn Mawr College, graduating in 1928 with a degree in philosophy and history. Hepburn pursued a career in acting after graduating college, and performed in a variety of small roles until her athletic performance in *The Warrior's Husband* on Broadway in 1932 drew attention. A screen test for RKO Studios in Hollywood (which was regularly recruiting Broadway stars as talking movies began to be made) landed her a leading role opposite John Barrymore in *A Bill of Divorcement* (1932), the first of 10 films she would make with director George Cukor. Indeed, much of

Studio portrait of actress Katharine Hepburn in 1957. (Getty Images)

Cukor's reputation as a "woman's director" may be due to his collaborations with Hepburn, most of which demonstrated atypical sensitivity to gender issues.

Hepburn made her second film, *Christopher Strong* (1933), with director Dorothy Arzner, Hollywood's sole female director during its classical period. That same year, Hepburn earned her first Academy Award for playing Eva Lovelace, an ambitious stage actress, in *Morning Glory*. She also starred as Jo in Cukor's 1933 adaptation of *Little Women*, which was a huge hit. Hepburn did not fare as well in pictures such as *Spitfire* (1934) and *A Woman Rebels* (1936). Audiences even steered clear of her respectable efforts in director John Ford's admittedly rather maudlin *Mary of Scotland* (1936), and the underappreciated *Quality Street* (1937). However, during the latter 1930s, Hepburn had some of her best roles, in films that are now considered classics: *Alice Adams* (1935), *Sylvia Scarlett* (1935), *Stage Door* (1937), *Holiday* (1938), and *Bringing Up Baby* (Howard Hawks, 1938). Giving expression to her own feminist views, Hepburn chose to play strong female characters who made—and owned—their choices. She bestowed her characters with an intelligence and articulateness all too rare for the time. This, coupled with Hepburn's reluctance to give interviews and her penchant for being photographed wearing slacks (a remarkable behavior for a female public figure at the time), created a persona that mass audiences rejected as haughty and unsympathetic.

Hepburn's attitude, both on the screen and off, may have had much to do with her lack of commercial success in the second half of the 1930s. Audiences turned away from her films in such numbers that she was pronounced "box-office poison" in 1938. This decree drove her back to Broadway, where she appeared in *The Philadelphia Story* (1939), a play written specifically for her by playwright Philip Barry. Hepburn received stellar reviews for her performance as Tracy Lord, an arrogant socialite who must learn to temper her expectations of others with a "regard for human frailty." Having bought the rights to the play, Hepburn was able to cast herself in the film version, which she made with Cukor. The story, in which a series of men chastise Tracy for her proud manner, addressed viewer's objections to what they perceived as Hepburn's arrogance, and the film once again made her an audience darling.

Following *The Philadelphia Story* in 1940, she appeared as renowned journalist Tess Harding in George Stevens's *Woman of the Year* (1942). This film also starred Spencer Tracy, with whom she would make nine films (and share a romantic relationship until his death in 1967). Hepburn and Tracy became one of Hollywood's most celebrated couples; their films confronted the changing dynamics between men and women in America during and following World War II. The best-known among them are *Without Love* (1945), *Adam's Rib* (1949) and *Pat and Mike* (1952), the latter two both Cukor films, and *Desk Set* (1957). Their last film together was *Guess Who's Coming to Dinner* (1967), for which they both received Academy Awards.

Prior to *Guess Who's Coming to Dinner*, Hepburn made a number of memorable films, such as *The African Queen* (John Huston, 1951). She published her experiences about making the film in *The Making of the African Queen or How I Went to Africa with Bogart, Bacall and Huston and Almost Lost My Mind*. In 1955, David Lean cast her in *Summertime*, the story of a lonely middle-aged woman traveling in Venice. Hepburn played the villainous Mrs. Venable in Joseph L. Mankiewicz's adaptation of Tennessee Williams's *Suddenly Last Summer* (1959) before giving a highly affecting performance as a morphine-addicted mother in *Long Day's Journey into Night* (1962).

Hepburn received another Academy Award the year after Tracy's death for her tragicomic turn as Eleanor of Aquitaine in *The Lion in Winter* (Anthony Harvey, 1968). She returned to the theater in the 1970s, though she also appeared in a handful of quality television movies, notably *Love among the Ruins* (1975), with Laurence Olivier, and *The Corn is Green* (1979), both directed by Cukor. In 1981, Hepburn starred with Henry Fonda in *On Golden Pond* (1981); the two played aging parents coming to grips with their relationship with their adult daughter, played by Fonda's real daughter, Jane Fonda. For her moving performance, Hepburn won her record fourth Best Actress Oscar.

In 1999, the American Film Institute declared Hepburn the Greatest Female Star in the history of American cinema. She died on June 29, 2003, in her home in Old Saybrook, Connecticut.

References

Berg, Scott A. *Kate Remembered.* New York: Berkley Books, 2003.
Hepburn, Katharine. *Me: Stories of My Life.* New York: Random House, 1996.
Phillips, Gene. *George Cukor.* Boston: Twayne, 1982.

—*Kyle Stevens*

HESTON, CHARLTON.   As both actor and political activist, Charlton Heston captivated audiences with his portrayal of strong, masculine leaders in films while publicly promoting conservative religious and social values to the American public. Born into a hardworking Michigan family on October 4, 1923, Heston attended Northwestern University before serving in the army briefly before the end of World War II. He and his wife Lydia worked as actors, earning roles on Broadway and directing at small theaters until Heston's first major role as Cinna in the 1949 television broadcast of *Julius Caesar.* After this initial achievement, his career rose with the advent of television, and Heston won his first star role in the 1950 film *Dark City.* Though he did not earn the Academy Award for Best Actor until 1959, amidst the stunning success of William Wyler's *Ben-Hur,* Heston's iconic representation of Moses in Cecil B. DeMille's *The Ten Commandments* (1956) established his image as a bold, strong-willed leader on the screen. Throughout the 1960s his roles in films such as *El Cid, Khartoum, The Greatest Story Ever Told, The Agony and the Ecstasy,* and *Planet of the Apes* met with critical and box-office success and solidified his reputation as an actor, while numerous forays into the American political scene made him increasingly visible to the American public.

An active member of the Democratic Party, Heston threw his support behind Presidents Kennedy and Johnson, marched on Washington in favor of the Civil Rights bill, and supported Great Society programs. He also began serving on the board of the Screen Actors Guild (SAG), and promoted "enlightened trade unionism" throughout his six years as president of the organization. As such, Heston fought for actors' rights to withdraw personal dues from the guild and thus to maintain an independent working status if they disagreed with the union's political philosophy and policies. As liberalism came to dominate the policies of both the U.S. government and SAG, Heston's formerly Democratic position turned increasingly toward the right, and he aligned with neoconservatives in support of Ronald Reagan's election, officially registering with the Republican Party in 1987.

Though Heston's career as actor and political spokesperson may seem like two distinct phases, with the success of his 1950s–60s acting career as the first and his 1970s–2000s political activism as the second, his actions in regard to both endeavors remained intertwined. Switching from the Democratic to Republican parties, Heston's shift in allegiance occurred as Americans formerly united over Cold War–era concerns became increasingly divided over national issues. As Heston faced radical liberalism from the SAG, U.S. politicians, and independent social groups in the 1970s, '80s, and '90s, he turned to leaders whom he had vivified onstage as true exemplars of American heroism and Christian morality. Speaking to voters in favor of the conservative

Pictured here in 1981, Charlton Heston was known both as an Academy Award–winning actor and a spokesperson for conservative causes, most notably as president of the National Rifle Association (1998–2003). (National Archives)

right-to-work campaign of 1986, the well-known public figure informed his audience that the very men he had portrayed on stage and screen, such as Thomas Jefferson and Abraham Lincoln, had held upright American freedoms.

In the 1990s, Heston won the offices of vice president and president of the National Rifle Association (NRA). Arguing that the Second Amendment is essential to upholding American liberty, Heston made reference to one of his most iconic roles in a speech he gave to the National Press Club in 1997. Utilizing his popular public image as the character Moses, the experienced actor linked the Ten Commandments to the Bill of Rights in an effort to emphasize the importance of basic American freedoms, such as the right to own and use a firearm. Both an inspirational and a polarizing figure at this point in his life, Heston's personal, political, and artistic choices during the last half-century have revealed just how complex America's evolutionary process has been.

References

Berkvist, Robert. "Charlton Heston, Epic Film Star and Voice of N.R.A., Dies at 84." *New York Times*, April 6, 2008. http://www.nytimes.com/2008/04/06/movies/06heston.html.

Heston, Charlton. "The Second Amendment: America's First Freedom." In Dizard, Jan E., et al., eds. *Guns in America: A Historical Reader*. New York: New York University Press, 1999.

Heston, Charlton. "Winning the Cultural War." Harvard Law School Forum Speech. February 16, 1999. http://www.grossmont.edu/bertdill/docs/Winningculturewar.pdf.

Raymond, Emilie. *From My Cold, Dead Hands*. Lexington: University Press of Kentucky, 2006.

Raymond, Emilie. "The Agony and the Ecstasy: Charlton Heston and the Screen Actors Guild." *Journal of Policy History* 17(2), 2005: 217–39.

—*Sarah Bishoff*

HILL, GEORGE ROY.   Although George Roy Hill made only 14 feature films, he showed a remarkable talent for deftly telling stories that explore the complexity of marginalized characters that exist on the outskirts of mainstream society and the close relationships they form. An intensely private man, Hill's life as a member of the cinematic community seemed to reflect the lives of many of his characters, as the Oscar-winning director remained on the edge of Hollywood culture throughout his career.

George Roy Hill was born in Minneapolis, Minnesota, on December 21, 1921, to George Roy and Helen Frances Owens Hill. His affluent Roman Catholic family was involved in newspaper publishing and owned the Minneapolis Tribune. He attended The Blake School, one of Minnesota's most prestigious private schools. Hill developed a love of flying when he was young and served as a cargo pilot in the U.S. Marine Corps during World War II. After the war, he studied at Trinity College in Ireland.

Hill was 40 when he directed his first film, coming to Hollywood by way of military service, flying with the Marine Corps in both World War II and the Korean War; from academia, earning a BA in music from Yale and a B. Litt from Trinity University in Dublin; from television, winning Emmy nominations for writing and directing; and from directing on Broadway. Adapted for the screen, one of the plays that Hill directed onstage, *Period of Adjustment* by Tennessee Williams, was the first feature film that he directed. His second film, *Toys in the Attic* (1963), was also based on a stage play.

Hill's third film, *The World of Henry Orient* (1964), concentrates on the lives of two 14- year-old girls who seek adventures in New York City. Even in this early film, Hill's attention is focused on dispossessed individuals—the girls, who are on the verge of entering the messy relational world of adulthood after growing up in dysfunctional families. Together, they dedicate themselves to the "world of Henry Orient," a modern concert pianist with whom one has fallen in love. Although Orient turns out to be a fraud as an artist, his world still provides the girls with the love, community, and acceptance for which they hunger. Hill would revisit these themes in *A Little Romance* (1979), in which two 13-year-olds, an American girl and a Parisian boy (a devotee of American films, chiefly Hill's), who meet and ultimately pledge their eternal love for each other with a sunset kiss under the Bridge of Sighs in Venice. As with the girls in *Henry Orient*, the characters in *A Little Romance* enlist the help of an aging con artist who can provide the support that their families, apparently, cannot.

Clearly the most successful of Hill's films, both critically and commercially, were *Butch Cassidy and the Sundance Kid* (1969) and *The Sting* (1973). (Hill was nominated as Best Director for both pictures, taking home the Oscar for *The Sting*.) Companion pieces starring Paul Newman and Robert Redford, both films focus on the friendship between men who exist outside the borders of polite, legal society. While seemingly perfect examples of traditional genre films, *Butch Cassidy* and *The Sting* actually act to subvert the normative structures of genre itself. The Newman and Redford characters in each film portray "old-world" men committed to a dying way of life that favors partnership over the individual accumulation of wealth. Although Hill allows audiences to identify strongly with the roguish male protagonists in each of these pictures, he also leaves viewers uneasy by weaving a dark existentialist thread through the narrative fabrics of the films. Ostensibly celebrations of American culture, in the end, the films prove to be unsettling critiques of that culture. Redford and Newman would each work with Hill again, although not together. Redford starred in *The Great Waldo Pepper* (1975), a film about a barnstorming flying ace that, given Hill's experience as a Marine pilot and his joy of flying his open-cockpit Waco, was particularly close to the director's heart. Two years later, Newman would take the lead in *Slap Shot* (1977), which explored the trials and tribulations of a losing hockey team. Although in these films Hill sought to explore the same themes he had addressed in *Butch Cassidy* and *The Sting*, *The Great Waldo Pepper* and *Slap Shot* did not enjoy the same success as Hill's earlier, iconic pictures.

Though a number of his films did extremely well at the box office, Hill's concern as a director was never simply to make money. One of a wave of 1960s and 1970s proto-independent American filmmakers—along with others such as Robert Altman, Martin Scorsese, Arthur Penn, and Mike Nichols—Hill strove to make pictures that would appeal to cinematically intelligent audiences. Toward this end, he adapted for the screen two modernist novels that focused on the existential struggles of the individual in history: *Slaughterhouse-Five* (1972), based on Kurt Vonnegut Jr.'s work of the same name, and *The World According to Garp* (1982), based on John Irving's work of the same name. Although these quirky little pictures did not prove popular with audiences, they remained true to Hill's commitment to create films that sought to explore the deepest levels of the human experience.

George Roy Hill died in 2002 from complications related to Parkinson's disease.

Selected Filmography

Funny Farm (1988); *The Little Drummer Girl* (1984); *The World According to Garp* (1982); *A Little Romance* (1979); *Slap Shot* (1977); *The Great Waldo Pepper* (1975); *The Sting* (1973); *Slaughterhouse-Five* (1972); *Butch Cassidy and the Sundance Kid* (1969); *Thoroughly Modern Millie* (1967); *Hawaii* (1966); *The World of Henry Orient* (1964); *Toys in the Attic* (1963); *Period of Adjustment* (1962)

References

Horton, Andrew. *The Films of George Roy Hill*. Jefferson, NC: McFarland, 2005.
Shores, Edward. *George Roy Hill*. Boston: Twayne, 1983.

—*Sarah N. Petrovic*

HITCHCOCK, ALFRED. Sir Alfred Hitchcock (1899–1980), the acknowledged master of the spy-thriller genre during his lifetime, is still regarded as one of the supreme auteurs of the twentieth century. Few directors are as often cited or imitated by filmmakers eager to claim a measure of creative cachet for their suspense-based plots; but as yet, no one can reasonably claim to have surpassed Hitchcock in his ability to evoke a world of fear, intrigue, and hidden guilt.

Hitchcock's middle-class upbringing and Catholic education afford few clues to an understanding of his future career, which began formally at the age of 21 when he was hired by the British branch of Paramount's Famous Player-Lasky studio to draw dialogue title cards. Hitchcock's literary as well as artistic talents were soon recognized, and he quickly made the transition from art director and scriptwriter to director, thanks to the support of Michael Balcon, for whose Gainsborough Pictures Hitchcock directed several silent features. The most important of these early films was unquestionably *The Lodger* (1926), a romantic thriller based loosely on the real-life crimes of Jack the Ripper. Hitchcock's mysterious "lodger" is suspected of being a serial murderer of women, but by film's end his innocence is established and

Alfred Hitchcock, who began directing motion pictures in his native Great Britain, immigrated to the United States, where he directed and produced his most well-known films. (AP/ Wide World Photos)

the movie's heroine is his. This is the first instance of Hitchcock's use of the "wrong man" motif, a theme that will appear and reappear in nearly all of his major works. Hitchcock's preference for evocative imagery, oblique angles, and dramatic lighting—reminiscent of the German expressionist movement, which influenced him profoundly during his year directing films in Germany—is equally evident in this film.

Hitchcock made the transition to synchronized sound in 1929 with the film *Blackmail*, where a plot that turns on sexual violence, unsolved murder, and secret guilt becomes the dramatic focus of this work. Hitchcock released two versions of this film—one silent, the other with sound—but it is only in the latter that he is able to fuse an obsessive visual motif with auditory clues that rivet the audience's attention on an instrument of death. Hitchcock's work in his native England came to an end in 1939 when he accepted an invitation from legendary producer David O. Selznick to join him in Hollywood, but during the decade from 1929 to 1939, he directed some of the more memorable films of his career. Three films that stand out from this period are *The Man Who Knew Too Much* (1934), *The 39 Steps* (1935), and *The Lady Vanishes* (1938), and all three fall squarely within the spy-thriller category. In swift pacing and deft characterization, each of these films demonstrates Hitchcock's ability to construct a suspenseful (if not always plausible) narrative, complete with touches of humor and romance. However, to draw his audience into the controlled mayhem of a spy story, Hitchcock also employs an additional plot device that he described as the "MacGuffin," meaning any dramatic conflict that sets the story in motion or provides a pretext for action. And in each of these films, Hitchcock's favorite MacGuffin is a conspiracy, inimical to England (or to all freedom-loving people, as the case may be), hatched by agents of a "foreign" power, against which the seemingly inadequate resources of his unpolitical protagonists are pitted. The exposure and defeat of this conspiratorial group then becomes the mainspring of the film's plot. Hitchcock's fondness for this peculiar storyline is evident throughout his career, and it remains the one structural motif that viewers of his major films can easily trace.

Hitchcock's debut film in the United States was *Rebecca* (1940), based on Daphne du Maurier's wildly popular novel of that title. Selznick offered Hitchcock his choice of A-list actors (in this case, Laurence Olivier and Judith Anderson) and outstanding production facilities, but he also insisted on an intrusive regime of constant supervision of scripts, and shooting schedules, and even camera set-ups, and before long Hitchcock realized it would be impossible for the two of them to work together. Thus, *Rebecca's* success notwithstanding—it won an Academy Award for Best Picture—Selznick chose to rent out Hitchcock to other studios like Universal, United Artists, RKO, and Twentieth Century-Fox, where he made the next six of the next eight films, most of which either reflect a wartime atmosphere or carry an explicit anti-Nazi message: *Foreign Correspondent* (1940), *Saboteur* (1942), *Lifeboat* (1944), and *Notorious* (1946). Of these, *Notorious* has proven to be the most enduringly popular, in part because of its stellar performances, but also because of Hitchcock's masterful use of the camera both to capture emotional nuance and build suspense. In addition to these American productions, Hitchcock took time out to make two short films for the British Ministry of Information, *Bon Voyage* (1944) and *Aventure malgache* (1944), the latter in support of the French Resistance.

Not all of Hitchcock's work during this period, of course, was political in nature. *Suspicion* (1941) marked the beginning of a more than decade-long professional relationship with Cary Grant (they made four films together), but it is also remembered for its tentative multiple endings, and RKO's insistence that Grant could not, under any circumstances, be cast as a wife-murderer (thereby necessitating a last-minute plot change). Nor was this the last time that studio heads would intervene to alter a Hitchcock script, and his desire to achieve complete directorial autonomy began to grow from this period on. However, Hitchcock's experience directing *Shadow of a Doubt* (1943) for Universal proved a happier experience, and once again he was able to take the story of a serial murderer of women (shades of *The Lodger*) and humanize his killer by surrounding him with a loving and ultimately uncomprehending family. Returning to Selznick in 1945, Hitchcock also directed *Spellbound*, one of the earliest films to make explicit use of Freudian psychotherapy. Hitchcock had planned to incorporate a series of elaborately designed dream sequences—drawn by Salvador Dali—only to have this segment of the film sharply reduced by Selznick, who had convinced himself that Hitchcock's work was too cerebral for popular audiences. Hitchcock's last attempt to work with Selznick was in 1947, when he directed *The Paradine Case*, a poorly scripted courtroom drama that proved to be one of Hitchcock's greatest box-office flops.

Now free from any further contractual obligations to Selznick International, Hitchcock attempted to form his own production company, Transatlantic Pictures, which proved to be a short-lived venture. However, he did manage to make one daringly experimental film during this period entitled *Rope* (1948), an adaptation of a stage play based on the infamous Leopold and Loeb murders. *Rope* is best remembered for its innovative use of extended takes (creating the illusion of one continuous shot throughout) and its emotionally heightened use of color, though film historians have also noted an interest in implied homoerotic relationships between the two principal male characters that will resurface in some of Hitchcock's later films as well. It also marks the first of four films that Hitchcock would make with Jimmy Stewart in a lead role. As for Hitchcock's interest in the psychopathic mind—a critical dimension of *Rope*—that would increase over the years until it became the obsessive focus of his later films.

The films made during 1951 to 1964 are often referred to by Hitchcock's biographers as the work of his "golden years," and in swift succession he completed films that won him both critical acclaim and immense box-office success. The first of these, *Strangers on a Train* (1951) continues a theme that runs like a thread through many of Hitchcock's films, namely, the idea of a shared guilt (or in Joseph Conrad's phrase a secret sharer) that binds together the innocent and the truly guilty. In this case, the seemingly fortuitous, yet fateful, connection that is established between a tennis pro, Guy Haines (Farley Granger), and a talkative stranger he meets on a train, Bruno Anthony (Robert Walker), leads to Bruno's murder of guy's estranged wife, and the expectation that Guy will reciprocate by killing Bruno's hated father. Guy's refusal to "exchange murders" leads to a typical Hitchcockian cat-and-mouse chase in which Guy must prove his innocence while exposing Bruno as the real killer, and once again we are confronted with the moral dilemma of the "wrong man." Hitchcock's obvious fondness for this narrative construct suggests a deep authorial suspicion that clear moral distinctions are often a camouflage for partly buried but undeniably powerful unconscious desires.

Dial M for Murder (1954) explores similar terrain, albeit in a much more conventional setting, by making an unhappy wife (famously played by Grace Kelly, in the first of three Hitchcock films she would star in) as the target of a murder-for-hire plot from which she must extricate herself, only to find that she has become the prime suspect in the killing of her would-be assassin. Husbands in Hitchcock's films tend, on the whole, to be treacherous, and even homicidal, and Ray Milland's Tony Wendice is no exception, and his exposure and apprehension at the conclusion of the film provides the kind of moral-emotional closure that popular audiences craved throughout the 1950s.

Hitchcock's next major work, *Rear Window* (1954), provides many of the melodramatic effects and emotional satisfactions of his earlier films, and certainly benefits from a stellar cast; nevertheless, it presents us with an unsettling portrait of the artist as a largely neurotic voyeur, and intimates a general view of marriage that is more subversive than one would expect. Its protagonist, L. B. Jeffries, played with consummate irony by Jimmy Stewart, is an action photographer who has been immobilized by an injury and whose sole form of entertainment is the opportunity to spy on his neighbors. The murder mystery that subsequently plays out before his prying eyes is complicated by the tentative love affair that Jeffries maintains with his glamorous and increasingly demanding girlfriend, Lisa Fremont (once again, Grace Kelly). Together, they track down a wife killer (yet another!) whose attempt to kill Jeffries (by throwing him out of his "rear window") ends unsuccessfully. But in the process of unfolding his convoluted plot, and allowing the viewer to glimpse the troubled lives of Jeffries's stereotypically maladjusted neighbors, Hitchcock exploits our willingness to invade another's privacy. And out of this guilty pleasure arises yet another ironic insight: the realization that practically all forms of intimate knowledge, even in the most innocent-seeming of circumstances, are fraught with the possibility of danger and death.

By this time Hitchcock was safely ensconced at Paramount Studios, and there he produced a series of entertaining films of somewhat lesser artistry, including *To Catch a Thief* (1955), *The Trouble with Harry* (1955), and a remake of an earlier spy thriller, *The Man Who Knew Too Much* (1956). Of this group, *To Catch a Thief* remains a perennial favorite, chiefly owing to the comic/romantic pairing of Cary Grant and Grace Kelly, whose clever verbal foreplay turns out to be far more interesting than the unlikely tale of deception and detection that surrounds them. The closing years of this decade, however, saw the production of two of Hitchcock's undisputed masterpieces—*Vertigo* (1958) and *North by Northwest* (1959)—and in both, Hitchcock is in full command of his powers of visualization and his talent for intricate plot construction. Based on a French mystery novel (*D'entre les morts* by Pierre Boileau and Thomas Narcejac), *Vertigo* invites the viewer to enter a world of terrifying dreams and erotic obsessions, bound up in a story of deception and murder. Once again, a scheming husband executes an elaborate plan to do away with his wife, enlisting the unknowing support of a former detective and college acquaintance (John "Scottie" Ferguson, played by Jimmy Stewart) whose paralyzing acrophobia has led to his premature retirement from the police force. Scottie's discovery of the murder plot, however, is virtually displaced by a romantic subplot that raises disturbing questions about the nature of identity and the reality of love.

North by Northwest, by contrast, marks Hitchcock's return to a far more conventional narrative tradition of espionage and romantic entanglements. Centering on the misadventures of Roger O. Thornhill, ad agency executive and ladies' man (played by Cary Grant in his last Hitchcock film), *North by Northwest* carries us along at breakneck speed, as its protagonist is compelled not only to prove his innocence of a murder he did not commit (echoes of the "wrong man" theme), but also rescue a beautiful counterspy with whom he has fallen in love. Hitchcock's wildly implausible plotline is more than redeemed, however, by witty dialogue and extraordinary camera work that transforms a clichéd cliffhanger into a seriocomic melodrama of self-discovery. Hitchcock's filming of a chase scene across an empty field, in which his hero is pursued by a deadly crop-duster (whose bullets, curiously, never find their mark) has become one of the truly iconic images of American filmmaking, as well as a textbook illustration of Hitchcock's talent for narrative/visual construction.

The creative surge of this extraordinary decade reaches its point of climax with the filming of two memorable thrillers, *Psycho* (1960) and *The Birds* (1963), and in both of these films Hitchcock attempts to shock his audience in a more direct and violent manner than in any of his earlier movies. Of the two, *Psycho* is the more brutal and explicitly terrifying work, much closer in subject matter and tone to contemporary "slasher" films, in which innocent victims of a deranged killer are literally cut to shreds. Both films, however, abound in images of entrapment and paranoia, and both reflect a sudden darkening of Hitchcock's vision of life. *The Birds* especially conjures up an apocalyptic view of nature, as flocks of otherwise harmless birds suddenly descend on Bodega Bay, attacking every human who comes across their path. In each of these works, death comes suddenly and with a ferocity that defies rational explanation; never have Hitchcock's characters appeared quite so fragile or defenseless as in these experiments in terror, and critics of his work have observed a growing nihilism in these late films.

Hitchcock's next three films—*Marnie* (1964), *Torn Curtain* (1966), and *Topaz* (1969)—all reveal a perceptible decline of creative energy and directorial control, and not surprisingly all three did poorly at the box office. Changes in popular taste made Hitchcock's attempts to revisit the world of Cold War spies seem dated, and problems of casting compounded Hitchcock's inability to find scriptwriters and cinematographers whose gifts matched his storytelling abilities. His last two films, *Frenzy* (1972) and *Family Plot* (1976), however, constitute an interesting coda to his remarkable career, as Hitchcock recovers through both a measure of audience appeal and critical esteem that he had lost in his later years. For many viewers, *Frenzy* seemed a companion piece to *Psycho*, projecting us into the mind of a psychopathic murderer of women whose seeming innocuousness belied his terrifying erotomania. Unlike the protagonist of *Psycho*, however, *Frenzy*'s homicidal greengrocer has no revealing backstory that helps us to understand his violent obsessions, and inevitably Hitchcock's drama devolves into a case of untimely (but ultimately successful) police work, as the "wrong man, unjustly sentenced for another man's crimes, leads authorities to the actual murderer.

Family Plot, by contrast, exhibits no grisly crimes, but rather adopts an almost humorous tone, reminiscent of some of Hitchcock's earlier films (for example, *Rear Window*) in which a macabre sense of social satire and comedy merges with a suspense plot and an atmosphere of imminent danger. That Hitchcock returned to the study of moral perversity—in this case, a "family" of kidnappers whose greed and sense of empowerment through crime drives the plot—in his last work is in many ways a fitting finale for an artist whose work turns constantly on the struggle between innocence and evil. No other Anglo-American director has yet managed to turn the resources of the suspense genre to the purposes of psychological and moral analysis more compellingly than Alfred Hitchcock, and his six decades of innovative filmmaking, in retrospect, appear to be an amazing record of sustained creativity.

Selected Filmography

Family Plot (1976); *Frenzy* (1972); *Topaz* (1969); *Torn Curtain* (1966); *Marnie* (1964); *The Birds* (1963); *Psycho* (1960); *North by Northwest* (1959); *Vertigo* (1958); *The Wrong Man*

(1956); *The Man Who Knew Too Much* (1956); *The Trouble with Harry* (1955); *To Catch a Thief* (1955); *Rear Window* (1954); *Dial M for Murder* (1954); *I Confess* (1953); *Strangers on a Train* (1951); *Rope* (1948); *The Paradine Case* (1947); *Notorious* (1946); *Spellbound* (1945); *Lifeboat* (1944); *Shadow of a Doubt* (1943); *Saboteur* (1942); *Suspicion* (1941); *Mr. & Mrs. Smith* (1941); *Foreign Correspondent* (1940); *Rebecca* (1940); *Jamaica Inn* (1939); *The Lady Vanishes* (1938); *Sabotage* (1936); *Secret Agent* (1936); *The 39 Steps* (1935); *The Man Who Knew Too Much* (1934); *Number 17* (1932); *The Skin Game* (1931); *Murder!* (1930); *Blackmail* (1928); *The Manxman* (1928); *Champagne* (1928); *Easy Virtue* (1928); *The Farmer's Wife* (1928); *When Boys Leave Home* (1927)

References

McGilligan, Patrick. *Alfred Hitchcock: A Life in Darkness and Light.* New York: HarperCollins, 2004.
Mogg, Ken. *The Alfred Hitchcock Story.* London: Titan, 2008.
Spoto, Donald. *The Art of Alfred Hitchcock.* New York: Anchor, 1992.
Wood, Robin. *Hitchcock's Films.* New York: Paperback Library, 1970.

—*Robert Platzner*

HOPPER, DENNIS. Dennis Hopper, in his more than 50 years as an actor and director, has known extraordinary success and astonishing failure. Indeed, his career appeared dead a number of times, but defying convention—as many of his on-screen characters do—and showing uncanny survival abilities, he has always orchestrated comebacks, becoming an iconic countercultural figure and one of the few Hollywood legends in the process.

Hopper was born on May 17, 1936, in Dodge City, Kansas. In his early teens, he moved with his parents to San Diego, California, and showed promise as an actor, winning a scholarship to study at San Diego's Old Globe Theatre, where he performed Shakespearean roles. After high school, Hopper went to Los Angeles and got parts on episodes of various television series, most notably as an epileptic on *Medic*. His performance in that role impressed Hollywood studio heads. Harry Cohn of Columbia Pictures agreed to meet him but made the mistake of belittling Hopper's Shakespearean background. Hopper told him off, in no uncertain terms, and was banned from Columbia Pictures' studios.

Hopper signed on with Warner Bros. and landed small roles in *Rebel Without a Cause* (1955) and *Giant*, two pictures featuring James Dean. Dean, who introduced Hopper to Stanislavsky's style of "Method acting," would die tragically in a car accident in September 1955, just as shooting on *Giant* was coming to a close. Dean's death devastated Hopper, and he decided to leave Los Angles and go to New York to study Method acting at the Lee Strasberg Institute, as Dean had done. When Hopper returned to Hollywood, his devotion to the Method put him at odds with the Hollywood establishment. Having developed a reputation for being difficult, Hopper had trouble landing big roles; he continued to work, however, garnering supporting roles in major films such as *Cool Hand Luke* (1967), as well as small parts in episodic television.

In 1968, Hopper, who had also been working as a photographer, directed and co-starred, with Peter Fonda, in *Easy Rider*, a landmark and extremely controversial film about two pot-smoking bikers who are attempting to escape straight America. Tapping into the 1960s counterculture, the picture, which cost less than $400,000 to make, earned $40 million after it was released in 1969, and was a driving force in the burgeoning movement of independent filmmaking. Hopper, who earned his first Oscar nomination as one of the film's co-writers (Peter Fonda and Terry Southern were the others), was declared a genius; within two years, however, it seemed that he had sabotaged his own career. Attempting to undermine further the established process of Hollywood filmmaking, Hopper made *The Last Movie*, a film that sought to expose the illusionary character of the American movie industry. After taking home top honors at the Venice Film Festival, the picture was a box-office disaster and Hopper once again found himself struggling to get work.

Director and actor Dennis Hopper in 1971. (AP/Wide World Photos)

Throughout the 1970s and early 1980s, Hopper did find parts—most notably in Francis Ford Coppola's *Apocalypse Now* (1979)—but these were usually small roles in marginal films. His problems were exacerbated by his extensive drug use, which led to hallucinations and his eventual commitment to a psychiatric ward in 1984. After being released, Hopper bounced back. In 1986, he played Shooter, an alcoholic ex-basketball star, in *Hoosiers*—which earned him an Oscar nomination for best supporting actor—and Frank Booth, a drug-crazed dealer in *Blue Velvet*. Building on these performances, Hopper proved his versatility, performing in pictures such as *The Indian Runner* (1991) and *Super Mario Brothers* (1993). He has since shown that he can tackle almost any role, playing villainous parts in *Speed* (1994) and *Waterworld* (1995), romantic parts in *Carried Away* (1996) and *All the Way* (2003), and comedic parts in *EdTV* (1999) and *Knockaround Guys* (2002). Hopper also returned to the director's chair for *Colors* (1988), *The Hot Spot* (1990), *Chasers* (1994), and *Homeless* (2000); and to television for the miniseries *Paris Trout* in 1991, for which he won an Emmy, and for episodes of *Flatland* and *24* in 2002, *E-Ring* in 2006, and *Crash* in 2008 and 2009. Dennis Hopper died on May 29, 2010, at the age of 74, after a 10-year battle with prostate cancer.

Selected Filmography

Homeless (2000); *Bad City Blues* (1999); *The Venice Project* (1999); *Jesus's Son* (1999); *Waterworld* (1995); *Straight Shooter* (1999); *EdTV* (1999); *Chasers* (1994); *True Romance* (1993); *Red Rock West* (1993); *Super Mario Bros.* (1993); *The Indian Runner* (1991); *Paris Trout* (1991); *The Hot Spot* (1990); *Catchfire* (1990); *Colors* (1988); *The Pick-up Artist* (1987); *Straight to Hell* (1987); *Hoosiers* (1986); *Blue Velvet* (1986); *River's Edge* (1986); *The Osterman Weekend* (1983); *Rumble Fish* (1983); *Out of the Blue* (1980); *Apocalypse Now* (1979); *The Last Movie* (1971); *True Grit* (1969); *Easy Rider* (1969); *Head* (1968); *Panic in the City* (1968); *Hang 'Em High* (1968); *The Glory Stompers* (1968); *Cool Hand Luke* (1967); *The Trip* (1967); *From Hell to Texas* (1958); *Gunfight at the O.K. Corral* (1957); *Giant* (1956); *I Died a Thousand Times* (1955); *Rebel Without a Cause* (1955)

References

Gates, David and Devin Gordon. "Newsmakers." *Newsweek* (2003). http://www.newsweek.com/id/58705/page/2.

Martin, Adrian. "The Misleading Man: Dennis Hopper." In Ndalianis, Angela, and Charlotte Henry, eds. *Stars in Our Eyes: The Star Phenomenon in the Contemporary Era*. Westport, CT: Greenwood, 2002: 3–20.

Rodriguez, Elena. *Dennis Hopper: A Madness to His Method*. New York: St. Martin's, 1988.

—*Albert Rolls*

HUSTON, JOHN. One of the twentieth century's most successful filmmakers, John Huston directed a number of American classics and also excelled as a screenwriter and actor. During a career that spanned a half-century, he was a larger-than-life presence in Hollywood who worked with the greatest film stars of his generation. He was nominated for 10 Academy Awards.

John Marcellus Huston was born in Nevada, Missouri, on August 5, 1906, the son of stage and screen actor Walter Huston and newspaperwoman Rhea Gore. Huston's childhood was unconventional, to say the least. After his parents divorced, he traveled the country with his father on the vaudeville circuit and spent considerable time at major news and sporting events that his mother covered. Though sickly as a child, he eventually conquered his physical frailties and became a capable amateur boxer. Dropping out of school at 14, he worked a variety of jobs, including breaking horses and performing street theater, before winning his first Broadway role in the 1925 production *Ruint*. Never one to stay in one place for long, Huston traveled to Mexico, London, and Paris as he tried to chart a course for his life; he eventually ended up back in the United States penniless. After lackluster attempts at newspaper and magazine reporting, he finally found his calling as a screenwriter and part-time actor. Catching the eye of Warner Bros. executives, Huston got his big break in 1941 when the studio signed him to direct the screen adaptation of Dashiell Hammett's popular mystery *The Maltese Falcon*. One of the most popular films of all time, *The Maltese Falcon* established Huston as a director and Humphrey Bogart as a Hollywood star. The film also was the first of a string of films directed by Huston and featuring Bogart, including *Across the Pacific* (1942), *Key Largo* (1948), and *Treasure of the Sierra Madre* (1948). *Treasure of the Sierra Madre* was an especially important film for the Huston family, as John won the Academy Award for Best Director while his father Walter won the Oscar for Best Supporting Actor. During World War II, Huston served as an officer in the signal corps, where he produced documentaries for the U.S. government. These included the controversial film *Let There Be Light*, which dealt with the mental and physical problems experienced by returning World War II veterans.

For Huston, more success followed during the 1950s with a wide range of films including his landmark effort *The African Queen* (1951), starring Bogart and Katharine Hepburn; *The Red Badge of Courage* (1951), starring Audie Murphy; the Toulouse-Latrec biographical film *Moulin Rouge* (1952); and the epic *Moby Dick* (1956), starring Gregory Peck. In 1961, Huston directed Clark Gable's last film, *The Misfits*, which also featured Marilyn Monroe. During the same period, the director began acting in films for the first time in years, usually playing small character roles. He received an Oscar nomination for his performance as a supporting actor in the 1963 feature *The Cardinal*. Although Huston peaked as a director during the 1950s, he continued working on well-received films into the 1980s. His last major success as a director came in 1985 with *Prizzi's Honor*, which was nominated for the Best Picture Oscar and in which Huston directed his daughter Angelica, who won the Academy Award for Best Supporting Actress.

Perhaps a product of his unconventional childhood, Huston was known as one of Hollywood's great eccentrics and a man who did his best, for better or worse, to live life to the fullest. In addition to his film pursuits, he was an accomplished painter and sculptor and an avid outdoorsman who counted Orson Welles and Ernest Hemingway as two of his closest friends. He was also known as a hard and sometimes ill-tempered drinker and an aggressive gambler. Huston was married five times and had five children. During the latter stages of his life, he was plagued by a number of illnesses but he continued to pursue various projects. He literally worked up until his last breath, dying of emphysema on August 28, 1987, in Middleton, Rhode Island, on location for a film in which he had a small role.

Selected Filmography

The Dead (1987); *Prizzi's Honor* (1985); *Under the Volcano* (1984); *Annie* (1982); *Victory* (1981); *Phobia* (1980); *Wise Blood* (1979); *Independence* (1976); *The Man Who Would Be King* (1975); *The MacKintosh Man* (1973); *The Life and Times of Judge Roy Bean* (1972); *Fat City* (1972); *The Kremlin Letter* (1970); *A Walk with Love and Death* (1969); *Sinful Davey* (1969); *Reflections in a Golden Eye* (1967); *Casino Royale* (1966); *The Bible: In the Beginning . . .*

(1966); *The Night of the Iguana* (1964); *The List of Adrian Messenger* (1963); *Freud* (1962); *The Misfits* (1961); *The Unforgiven* (1960); *The Roots of Heaven* (1958); *The Barbarian and the Geisha* (1958); *Heaven Knows, Mr. Allison* (1957); *Moby Dick* (1956); *Beat the Devil* (1953); *Moulin Rouge* (1952); *The African Queen* (1951); *The Red Badge of Courage* (1951); *The Asphalt Jungle* (1950); *We Were Strangers* (1949); *Key Largo* (1948); *The Treasure of the Sierra Madre* (1948); *Let There Be Light* (1946); *San Pietro* (1945); *Report from the Aleutians* (1943); *Across the Pacific* (1942); *Winning Your Wings* (1942); *In This Our Life* (1942); *The Maltese Falcon* (1941)

References

Brill, Lesley. *John Huston's Filmmaking*. Cambridge, UK: Cambridge University Press, 1997.
Grobel, Lawrence. *The Hustons*. Lanham, MD: Cooper Square Press, 2000.
Huston, John. *An Open Book*. London: Macmillan, 1981.
Long, Robert Emmet. *John Huston: Interviews*. Jackson: University of Mississippi Press, 2001.

—*Ben Wynne*

K

KASDAN, LAWRENCE. Born in Miami Beach, Florida, on January 14, 1949, Lawrence Kasdan began his adult life receiving his MA in education from the University of Michigan. Beginning as an award-winning advertising copywriter, Kasdan eventually made his way to Hollywood to pursue a career as a screenwriter. Early on, he sold two screenplays that would go on to become successful films: *Continental Divide* (1981) and *The Bodyguard* (1992). Having caught the attention of Steven Spielberg with *Continental Divide*, he soon met with the famed director and was introduced to George Lucas. Kasdan, then, would be a key figure in the creation of three of the biggest Hollywood blockbusters of the 1980s: *Star Wars: The Empire Strikes Back* (1980); *Raiders of the Lost Ark* (1981); and *Star Wars: Return of the Jedi* (1983). During this period of collaboration, he would also direct the 1980s hit *Body Heat* (1981), the steamy romance starring William Hurt and Kathleen Turner, before co-writing and directing his biggest hit, the baby-boomer nostalgia flick *The Big Chill* in 1983.

Kasdan's place in Hollywood history, it seems, would have been assured by way of his work with George Lucas alone. As co-writer of the last two films of the original *Star Wars* trilogy—*The Empire Strikes Back* is perhaps the most beloved of the *Star Wars* films—Kasdan will forever be a pop culture icon. His contribution to another pop culture phenomenon, the *Indiana Jones* franchise, only adds to his luster. More than simply a screenwriter on the first *Indiana Jones* film—Kasdan began the process by sitting in a room with Lucas and Spielberg, tape-recorder preserving their conversations—Kasdan was instrumental in sculpting the character and personality of one of Hollywood's most enduring heroes. In fact, characterization has always been one of his greatest skills.

Kasdan broke new ground with *Body Heat* (1981), a controversial noir thriller that titilated audiences. The picture became one of the most popular films of the 1980s, launching its stars, Turner and Hurt, into superstardom. Hurt would once again connect with Kasdan as part of the director's ensemble cast for *The Big Chill*. In addition to Hurt, *The Big Chill* featured Kevin Kline, Tom Berenger, Jeff Goldblum, Glenn Close, Meg Tilly, JoBeth Williams, and Mary Kay Place as former college classmates who gather for the funeral of one of their dear friends. A critical and commercial success, the film became a cultural icon of the 1980s, linking the decade with the 1960s.

Though the two periods could not be more different politically, the soundtrack of the film introduced teenagers of the Reagan era to the music of the 1960s, having a lasting impact on the latter decade. The film itself also showed that the baby-boomer generation, teenagers in the '60s, could still be considered "cool" and "hip" despite having become part of the thirty-something establishment.

For the next decade, Kasdan's record in the industry would be decidedly uneven—just as many of the films on which he worked missed the mark as became hits. Still, he was attached as either a writer or director—or both—to a number of popular films during this period: *Silverado* (1985); *The Accidental Tourist* (1988); *Grand Canyon* (1991); *The Body Guard* (1992); and *Wyatt Earp* (1994). In 1997, Kasdan would finally appear in front of the camera, playing Dr. Green in the Oscar-award-winning picture *As Good As It Gets*.

Though some have suggested that Kasdan's star has dimmed since his halcyon days of the 1980s, he is still considered a writer/director of distinction. Aside from playing a key role in creating and deepening some of the most beloved characters in film history, he contributed to defining popular culture in the late twentieth century.

Selected Filmography

Dreamcatcher (2003); *Mumford* (1999); *Wyatt Earp* (1994); *The Bodyguard* (1992); *Grand Canyon* (1991); *The Accidental Tourist* (1988); *Silverado* (1985); *The Big Chill* (1983); *Star Wars: Episode VI—Return of the Jedi* (1983); *Continental Divide* (1981); *Body Heat* (1981); *Raiders of the Lost Ark* (1981); *Star Wars: Episode V—The Empire Strikes Back* (1980)

References

Indiana Jones: Making the Trilogy. Documentary. Paramount DVD, 2003.
Kasdan, Lawrence, and Jake Kasdan. *Wyatt Earp: The Film and the Filmmakers.* New York: New Market Press, 1994.
Lawrence Kasdan. DVD: The Directors Series. American Film Institute, 2000.
Star Wars: Empire of Dreams. Documentary Twentieth Century-Fox DVD, 2004.

—*Richard A. Hall*

KAZAN, ELIA. Elia Kazan gained a reputation for being an actor's director over the course of a stunningly successful career, both on Broadway and in Hollywood. His work won him three Tony awards and two Oscars—and his skill benefited actors (indeed, those who worked with him in films alone garnered 21 Best Actor nominations and 9 Oscars for Best Actor). But in spite of his justifiable renown for being the guiding hand behind some of the most powerful dramas of stage and screen of the 1940s and 1950s, he never escaped the stigma that followed him after he agreed to testify in 1952 to the House Committee on Un-American Affairs (HUAC) and "named names" of friends and colleagues whom he claimed were communist sympathizers.

Born in Constantinople, Turkey in 1909 to Greek parents, Kazan moved with his family to the United States when he was four, and grew up in the suburbs outside New York City. His personal story is an example of American immigrant drive, determination, and success: son of a rug merchant, he went to public school, then to college, receiving his BA at Williams College, where he became interested in drama, and then moved on to Yale Drama School. He never fully lost his sense of being an outsider at Yale. And while what he learned there deepened his understanding of how a director, as Kazan put it in his memoir, performs an "overall task", he found the model of theater the school taught to be polite and sterile, and he balked at it.

He landed his first professional position not as a director but as an actor in the company of the far from sterile or polite Group Theater in 1933. Recently founded by Harold Clurman, Cheryl Crawford, and Lee Strasberg, the Group was a leftist modern theater collective that emphasized ensemble acting and a cooperative approach to developing theater works. They integrated in their practices acting techniques derived from the theories of Russian theater master Constantine Stanislavsky, techniques Strasberg dubbed "the Method," a way in which actors created authentic performances by remembering personal moments of intense feeling. Even though it was as an actor that Kazan earned a major critical success, his experience performing for the Group is significant mostly for two reasons: it later served his ability to direct a rising generation of Method actors, including Marlon Brando, Julie Harris, Lee J. Cobb, and James Dean, on stage and screen; and it provided him left-wing (some have said even Stalinist) political affiliations that later he "named" to HUAC. Although the Group Theater disbanded in 1942, Kazan along with Strasberg and other Group alumni established in 1948 the Actors Studio, a school of Method acting in New York City that serves to this day as a training ground for American actors in Group techniques.

Kazan received the New York Drama Critics Award for directing Thornton Wilder's *The Skin of Our Teeth* (1942), and from that point he began the legendary period during which he directed a series of extraordinary plays that defined American drama of the mid-twentieth century. His collaboration with Tennessee Williams resulted in four seminal Broadway productions, including Williams's Pulitzer Prize–winning plays *A Streetcar Named Desire* (1947) and *Cat on a Hot Tin Roof* (1955). His direction of Arthur Miller's *All My Sons* (1947) and the Pulitzer Prize–winning *Death of a Salesman* (1949) cemented his reputation as a director of deeply American-themed works that called for outsized raw emotionality in performance.

A man of exceeding ambition, Kazan launched a successful film career even while he was America's foremost theater director. His first major film, *A Tree Grows in Brooklyn* (1945), a melodrama about an Irish family and their alcoholic father, began what seemed to be a penchant to direct "social problem" pictures. *Gentleman's Agreement* (1947), for which he won his first Oscar, dealt with anti-Semitism; *Pinky* (1949) with miscegenation; *Panic in the Streets* (1950), a noirish thriller, with disease control. But it was the 1951 film version of *A Streetcar Named Desire*, the only one of his stage works Kazan directed for the screen, that established Marlon Brando as the most compelling film actor of his generation, and Kazan as the master director of the Method in cinema. Kazan's films from then on were marked by powerful star performances, most notably

On the Waterfront (1954) (another Best Director Oscar) in which Brando was a conscience-stricken former prizefighter turned mob informer; and *East of Eden* (1955), an adaptation of John Steinbeck's novel, in which James Dean captured the angst of misunderstood adolescence caught in archetypal Oedipal conflict.

Kazan struggled with his decision to provide names to HUAC, but once he testified—naming, among others, former Group colleagues Clifford Odets, John Garfield, and Lee Strasberg—he maintained he was glad he had done it, a position he modified later in life. The decision seems even today to affect readings of his work: *On the Waterfront* has been seen as a treatise defending the morality of informing; *America, America* (1963), a semiautobiographical film about Kazan's family emigrating from Greece, proclaims his deep roots in a particularly American story of identity and self-denial. After his testimony, he had no trouble getting work, but many of the writers and actors and directors who had refused to testify were blacklisted, and had trouble getting jobs for the rest of their lives. So deep was the rift in the Hollywood creative community that almost 50 years after his Congressional testimony, when Kazan was awarded a special Lifetime Achievement Oscar in 1999, his appearance at the Academy Awards ceremony prompted a flurry of protestations and denunciations.

In the 1960s Kazan turned the majority of his creative attention to becoming a best-selling novelist; he succeeded, though with limited critical success. He died, in 2003, at the age of 94.

See also: East of Eden; On the Waterfront; Splendor in the Grass; Streetcar Named Desire, A

Selected Filmography

The Last Tycoon, The (1976); *Splendor in the Grass* (1961); *A Face in the Crowd* (1957); *East of Eden* (1955); *On the Waterfront* (1954); *A Streetcar Named Desire* (1954); *Gentleman's Agreement* (1947); *A Tree Grows in Brooklyn* (1945)

References

Kazan, Elia. *A Life*. New York: Alfred A. Knopf, 1988.
Murphy, Brenda. *Collaborative Drama: Tennessee Williams and Elia Kazan*. Cambridge, UK: Cambridge University Press, 1992.
Schickel, Richard. *Elia Kazan: A Biography*. New York: HarperCollins, 2005.

—*Robert Cowgill*

KEATON, BUSTER.   Once considered a lesser talent than Charlie Chaplin and Harold Lloyd, Buster Keaton is now regarded by many as the most modern and influential of the silent comedians, and as one of the greatest directors and actors in the history of cinema. Though known as the "Great Stone-Face," Keaton's unsmiling visage was subtly mobile, and his minimalist acting was ahead of its time. A daredevil athlete and acrobat who performed his own stunts and directed his own films, his comedies operate on a grand scale, as Keaton's characters contended against the overwhelming forces of nature and machinery, all the while keeping their mysterious inner equilibrium.

Born Joseph Frank Keaton on October 4, 1895, he was allegedly nicknamed by Harry Houdini after taking a "buster" of a fall down a staircase. By the age of five he was starring in vaudeville with his parents as one of "The Three Keatons." Playing in an almost violent roughhouse act with his father, he received an informal education in timing, pratfalls, and perhaps most importantly, in how not to smile. As an adult, Keaton had a chance encounter with Roscoe "Fatty" Arbuckle, then the second most popular film comedian in America, who invited him to appear in a short, *The Butcher Boy* (1917). Keaton became Arbuckle's sidekick and eventually his co-star and co-director. He embarked on a more

Actor/director Buster Keaton in costume in 1939. (Library of Congress)

sophisticated and intricate form of comedy when he went solo, making 19 shorts between 1920 and 1923 and 10 features between 1923 and 1928.

One Week (1920), his first important film, followed the construction of a mail-order house and inaugurated Keaton's technique of grappling with immense mechanical props. He used this technique, with great comic effect, in *The Boat* (1922), in which he struggles with a hopelessly sinking watercraft. *The Scarecrow* (1920) and *The Electric House* (1922) showcased Keaton's love of gadgetry: unlike Chaplin, who stressed machinery's alienating potential, Keaton strove to master technology. In *The Navigator* (1925), for instance, Keaton is pitted against his largest prop, an eerily empty, drifting ocean liner. Significantly, *The Navigator* featured Keaton in one of his favorite roles: as a sheltered, hapless young man forced to rise to some overwhelming occasion. This character would be reprised in a rather unsettling way in the *Battling Butler* (1926), in which the Keaton character must prove his manhood by entering into a savage, and disturbingly realistic, boxing match. In *Steamboat Bill, Jr.* (1928), an effete Buster braves cyclones and floods to prove himself to his overbearing father and undergoes his most famous (and dangerous) stunt: a house-front falls on top of him and he passes through an open window, inches away from cinematic—and literal—death.

Like Lloyd, Keaton's characters succeeded through the classic American formula of hard work and self-reliance. Unlike Lloyd's, however, Keaton's characters tended to be ethereal loners, whose goals of making good occasionally descend almost to the point of bleak pessimism. This can be seen in the Sisyphean image of Keaton caught in a giant paddlewheel in *Daydreams* (1922), or in the nightmarish *Cops* (1922), where he is hunted down by hordes of policemen who multiply with geometric regularity, much like the mobs that pursue Keaton in *Seven Chances* (1926). The coda of *College* (1927) telescopes a happy-ever-after ending into quick dissolves of parenthood, decrepitude, and death. Keaton also turned a dispassionate eye toward Hollywood, lampooning western masculinity in *The Frozen North* (1922) and *Go West* (1925)— in the latter the leading lady is a cow—turning the conflict between Indians and whites into a grotesque burlesque in *The Paleface* (1921), and derisively mimicking D. W. Griffith's triptych *Intolerance* (1916) in *The Three Ages* (1923).

As a director (frequently an uncredited one), Keaton was concerned with the authenticity of action and space. His preference for long takes and long shots preserves the fluidity of motion in continuous space, creating comedy from within the frame's depth of field and presenting his miraculous stunts as they were actually performed, instead of cheating his audiences by relying on camera tricks and editing. Keaton's concern for authenticity included the incredible historical accuracy of his excursions into period Americana. *Our Hospitality* (1923) recreates antebellum America by way of its story of a Hatfield-McCoy type feud, for example, while *The General* (1926)—which most critics claim is his masterwork—captures the Civil War in a way that many consider more convincing than any other Hollywood production, even inviting comparisons to Mathew Brady's stunning photographs. Named after the locomotive whose theft triggers two chases across battle lines, it is Keaton's most perfect stylistic integration of comedic and dramatic storylines.

Although his pictures were generally characterized by a certain cinematic realism, he was not altogether adverse to using sight gags. In his short film *Hard Luck* (1921), for instance, Keaton flubs a pool dive, leaving a hole in the earth from which he emerges years later with a Chinese wife and kids; he also made an exception to the demand for realism with the oneiric passages of *Sherlock Jr.* (1924)—one of the most self-reflexive features ever made in Hollywood—which showcased the stunning special effect of Keaton falling asleep and walking into the screen of the film he's projecting, interacting with a movie within a movie.

Early in his career, Keaton's films had been independently produced by financier Joseph Schenck, who distributed them through different Hollywood studios. In 1928, Schenck persuaded Keaton to sign with Metro-Goldwyn-Mayer. Keaton would come to regard his decision to follow Schenck's advice as the worst mistake of his life, although he had few options in a period of studio monopolization that drove out the first generation of independent filmmakers. Although it may be argued that *The Cameraman* (1928) and *Spite Marriage* (1929) approached the quality of his independent work, after he made these films for MGM, the studio stripped Keaton of his creative independence, forbidding him from using the improvisational style that had made his films unique. The advent of sound made things even worse, as the newly developed cameras used to lift filmmaking out of the silent era functioned at a painstakingly slow speed, limiting Keaton's ability to shoot his pictures at the frenetic pace he preferred. Sound also revealed Keaton's own deep, husky Midwestern voice, leading the studio to cast him as a graceless rube in progressively worse films. Frustrated, Keaton turned to alcohol, with not unexpected results—he was fired in 1933.

Though no longer a star, Keaton continued to work hard for the rest of his life, eventually returning to MGM as a gagman, making shorts for Columbia and Educational Pictures, appearing on TV and in Samuel Beckett's *Film* (1964) and Chaplin's *Limelight* (1953), and regaining a measure of creative independence by making commercials and industry-sponsored films, such as *The Railroader* (1965). Keaton's reputation was revived after the 1949 publication of James Agee's landmark essay "Comedy's Greatest Era," leading to the rerelease of many of his silent films. He died a happy man on February 1, 1966, acclaimed as a genius around the world.

Selected Filmography

A Funny Thing Happened on the Way to the Forum (1966); *How to Stuff a Wild Bikini* (1965); *Beach Blanket Bingo* (1965); *Pajama Party* (1964); *It's a Mad Mad Mad Mad World* (1963); *The Adventures of Huckleberry Finn* (1960); *Around the World in Eighty Days* (1956); *Limelight* (1952); *In the Good Old Summertime* (1949); *God's Country* (1946); *She Went to the Races* (1945); *San Diego I Love You* (1944); *Li'l Abner* (1940); *The Villain Still Pursued Her* (1940); *The Taming of the Snood* (1940); *Pardon My Berth Marks* (1940); *Nothing But Pleasure* (1940); *One Run Elmer* (1935); *Palooka from Paducah* (1935); *The Invader* (1935); *Allez Oop* (1934); *The Gold Ghost* (1934); *What! No Beer?* (1933); *Speak Easily* (1932); *The Passionate Plumber* (1932); *Parlor, Bedroom and Bath* (1931); *Doughboys* (1930); *Free and Easy* (1930); *The Cameraman* (1928); *Steamboat Bill, Jr.* (1928); *College* (1927); *The General* (1926); *Battling Butler* (1926); *Go West* (1925); *Seven Chances* (1925); *The Navigator* (1924); *Sherlock Jr.* (1924); *Our Hospitality* (1923); *Three Ages* (1923); *The Balloonatic* (1923)

References

Agee, James. *Agee on Film: Criticism and Comment on the Movies.* New York: Modern Library, 2000.

Keaton, Buster. *Interviews.* Sweeney, Kevin, ed. Jackson: University of Mississippi Press, 2007.

Kerr, Walter. *The Silent Clowns.* New York: Da Capo, 1975.

Smith, Imogen Sara. *Buster Keaton: The Persistence of Comedy.* Chicago: Gambit, 2008.

—Ihsan Amanatullah

KEATON, DIANE. Diane Keaton's Oscar-winning turn as Annie Hall, the spirited, slightly scattered romantic interest at the center of Woody Allen's eponymous 1977 romantic comedy, remains one of her best-remembered roles. More than her contemporaries Meryl Streep and Glenn Close, Keaton has perfected a type of character during her years in the movies: charmingly vulnerable, independent, a bit flighty. Yet Keaton's four-decade career in film belies the notion she is primarily a comedic actress. She showed dramatic range in Oscar-nominated roles as Louise Bryant, radical writer and wife of the communist journalist Jack Reed, in *Reds* (1981); and as Bessie, the selfless, caregiving aunt struck with leukemia in *Marvin's Room* (1996). Collaborators and critics have remarked on Keaton's incisive intelligence and work ethic, qualities that also account for the actress's staying power in Hollywood.

Born Diane Hall in Los Angeles on January 5, 1946, Keaton enjoyed a comfortable upbringing in Southern California. In 1965, she moved to New York City to study under Sanford Meisner, mentor of acting luminaries including Gregory Peck, Grace Kelly, and Robert Duvall. In New York, Keaton landed a part in the Broadway ensemble cast of *Hair*, the musical celebration of 1960s free love, and performed in numerous cabaret acts. Breakout film roles came in *Lovers and Other Strangers* (1970), *The Godfather* (1972), and *The Godfather: Part II* (1974). From the beginning, Keaton displayed an independent streak that put her somewhere on the peripheries of both youth culture and mainstream American femininity. She gained press attention as the only one of *Hair*'s cast members who refused to disrobe; and of her *Godfather* role as Kay Adams-Corleone—the willfully innocent, WASPy wife of Al Pacino's Michael Corleone—Keaton has remarked that she had "no interest in that woman" (Mitchell, 2001).

Keaton's collaborations with Woody Allen better capture the tenor of her rise to stardom during a tumultuous period in America's collective sex life. Many of the Hollywood productions she had grown up with during the 1950s had celebrated the self-sacrificing, stay-at-home housewife as the keeper of domestic calm in a chaotic "man's world." A wave of films during the 1960s and 1970s broke apart the stratified gender roles of postwar Hollywood. After she played comic roles in early Allen films like *Play It Again, Sam* (1972), *Sleeper* (1973), and *Love and Death* (1975), the nervous energy and humor Keaton brought to Annie Hall—the name combines Keaton's nickname and her birth surname—epitomized the excitements and anxieties of women searching for personal and professional independence at a time of reinvigorated feminism. On the heels of *Annie Hall*, Keaton starred in two more Allen films: the somber *Interiors* (1978) and *Manhattan* (1979). In *Interiors*, Keaton played Renata, the eldest daughter of a well-off family who struggles to accommodate her success as a published poet with spousal jealousy and family turmoil. *Manhattan* was a return to comedy for Allen; but unlike Annie Hall, Keaton's Mary Wilke wastes no opportunity to show off her intellect. The modern American woman could be assertive, aggressive even, Keaton seemed to be saying through her character in *Manhattan*.

Keaton's extremely successful career on the big screen has included its misfires. Her turn as an American actress recruited to work for the Israeli intelligence services in *The Little Drummer Girl* (1984), a cinematic adaptation of a John le Carré novel, received mixed reviews; as did her performance—with its failed attempt at a Southern accent—in *Crimes of the Heart* (1986), in which she starred with Sissy Spacek and Jessica Lange as one of a trio of eccentric Mississippi sisters.

Keaton continues to thrive, however, as more recently she has defied the common wisdom that there are no parts for older actresses in Hollywood. In the 1990s and

2000s, she anchored several lighthearted box-office successes, including *Father of the Bride* (1991), *Father of the Bride: Part II* (1995), *The First Wives Club* (1996), and *Something's Gotta Give* (2003). She received a Best Supporting Actress Oscar nomination for her work on the last film. Keaton has also spent time on the other side of the camera. Directing ventures have included an episode of David Lynch's television series *Twin Peaks* and her debut behind the camera on a feature film, the family drama *Unstrung Heroes* (1995). An interest in photography has involved Keaton in several book projects. She dedicated *Local News* (1999), a collection of mid-century photographs culled from the archives of an out-of-print Los Angeles tabloid, to "those who slip away unnoticed." The line captures something of Keaton's offbeat celebrity: she has parlayed movie success into examining facets of American life deemed less than glamorous by Hollywood standards.

References

Ferriss, Suzanne, and Mallory Young. *Chick Flicks: Contemporary Women at the Movies*. New York: Routledge, 2008.

McMurtry, Larry. "Diane Keaton on Photography." *New York Review of Books* 54(17), November 8, 2007.

Mitchell, Deborah C. *Diane Keaton: Artist and Icon*. Jefferson, NC: McFarland, 2001.

—*Diana Lemberg*

KUBRICK, STANLEY. Stanley Kubrick was a prominent director from the mid-1950s until the end of the twentieth century. His films covered a wide range of subject matter and were known for their bizarre, creative, and sometimes controversial subject matter. A director who eventually rejected the Hollywood establishment, he left behind a catalog that includes some of the greatest films of the second half of the twentieth-century.

Kubrick was born on July 26, 1928, in the Bronx, New York. His father, Jacques Kubrick, was a prominent physician, while his mother, Gertrude, was a housewife. Kubrick was not a stellar student, but early on demonstrated a talent for photography. While at Taft High School, his father gave him a 35mm camera, and he immediately took an active interest in the art form. Kubrick's big break occurred when one of his pictures was purchased by *Look* magazine. Upon graduation he was hired by *Look* as a staff photographer. During his time with the magazine, Kubrick also enrolled in classes at Columbia University but never sought a degree. His real education came from his work as a photographer and also by attending film screenings at the Metropolitan Museum of Art (Turner, 1988).

His first foray into movies was a film short based on a picture story he had done for *Look*. *Day of the Fight* (1950) focused on the life of boxer Walter Cartier. Kubrick bankrolled the film from his own savings and sold the piece to RKO—netting a $100 profit. His next work, *Flying Padre* (1951), was partially subsidized by RKO, and its minor success led to his decision to become a feature filmmaker. Borrowing

Film director Stanley Kubrick during production of *The Shining*. (AP/Wide World Photos)

money from his father and uncle, Kubrick embarked on his first full-length film project (Phillips, 2002).

Fear and Desire (1953) was shot on location in the San Gabriel Mountains and tells the story of a chance meeting between two American soldiers and two enemy soldiers. The movie played the art-house circuit and received some favorable reviews. Though Kubrick himself would later dismiss the film, at the time it did serve to encourage him to borrow more money from another family member and to begin work on a second full-length project. *Killer's Kiss* (1955) was set in New York and revolved around the life of a boxer and the girl he desired. It is in this picture that one sees what would be a recurring theme in Kubrick's pictures—dark visions of society engulfed in surreal imagery.

Kubrick's next picture was a foray into film noir. *The Killing* (1956) told the story of a racetrack heist, filmed partially as a series of flashbacks. For the movie Kubrick partnered with producer James Harris, with whom he would work on three additional films. *The Killing* was a critical success and set the stage for the film that would place him in the forefront of Hollywood directors. *Paths of Glory* (1957), starring Kirk Douglas in the title role, still ranks today as one of the greatest antiwar films ever made. Set during the World War I, the film is a condemnation of a system that led to the horrors of trench warfare while simultaneously reflecting the callous attitudes of officers toward their men—man's inhumanity toward man. Douglas was so impressed by Kubrick's work that he hired him to take over the direction of his next film, *Spartacus* (1960), a Roman-era epic based on the life of a gladiator who led a rebellion against the empire. Unlike his previous films, Kubrick did not have complete control over the picture and often found himself at odds with Douglas, who was not only the film's star but also its executive producer. Despite their differences, however, the two men were able to create a final product that was both a critical and financial success.

Stung by his experiences during the filming of *Spartacus*, and disillusioned by the limitations of Hollywood's studio system, Kubrick made the momentous decision to leave the United States in 1962 and relocate to England, where he bought a small estate in Hertfordshire. He would remain there for the rest of his life. The first picture he shot in England was *Lolita* (1962), an adaptation of Vladimir Nabokov's novel about a professor who marries a widow simply because he is obsessed with her adolescent daughter. In order to heighten the sexually charged character of the film, Kubrick provided viewers with a disturbing twist by emphasizing the black-comedy nature of the illicit relationship.

His next three films formed a trilogy dealing with controversial themes through the lens of science fiction and biting satire. Building on the black-comedy theme from *Lolita*, Kubrick now turned his attention to the futility of war in the nuclear age. *Dr. Strangelove or: How I Learned to Stop Worrying and Love the Bomb* (1964) was an offbeat portrayal of nuclear holocaust, a condemnation of militarism run wild, and a savage parody of the Cold War and its fears. Kubrick's next film, *2001: A Space Odyssey* (1968), turned out to be a visual, sensorial, and technological masterpiece, and still ranks today as one of the top science fiction films of all time. The third film of the trilogy, *A Clockwork Orange* (1972), is set in England during a dystopic future in which a youth gang, led by a Beethoven-obsessed sociopath, engages in extraordinarily unsettling, ecstatic acts of rape, torture, and physical assault.

In a departure from what had come before, Kubrick next made a long, sprawling period piece, *Barry Lyndon* (1975), which turned out to be his only real commercial failure. A five-year gap between films ended with his adaptation of a Stephen King novel and a return to the themes that had made his previous films so successful. In *The Shining* (1980), viewers enter the nightmarish world of a man (disturbingly portrayed by Jack Nicholson) slowly going insane while he and his family act as caretakers of an isolated mountain lodge. While receiving mixed reviews from critics, it proved to be a box-office success.

In 1987, Kubrick made his third antiwar film, *Full Metal Jacket*. Shot in England, and following filmic offerings such as Francis Ford Coppola's *Apocalypse Now*, Michael Cimino's *The Deer Hunter*, and Oliver Stone's *Platoon*, *Full Metal Jacket* was Kubrick's statement on the senselessness of the Vietnam conflict. Not surprisingly, his last film, *Eyes Wide Shut* (1999), proved controversial. Starring Tom Cruise and Nicole Kidman, who were then married, the picture follows a wealthy, New York City couple into a debasing world of eroticism and sexual perversion; a world in which, the director seemed to be saying, there is little hope for redemption. Ironically, Kubrick would not live to see his final cinematic work released, as he died in his sleep on March 7, 1999, just four days after he had delivered the final print of his film.

Selected Filmography

Eyes Wide Shut (1999); *Full Metal Jacket* (1987); *The Shining* (1980); *Barry Lyndon* (1975); *A Clockwork Orange* (1971); *2001: A Space Odyssey* (1968); *Dr. Strangelove or: How I Learned to Stop Worrying and Love the Bomb* (1964); *Lolita* (1962); *Spartacus* (1960); *Paths of Glory* (1957); *The Killing* (1956); *Killer's Kiss* (1955); *The Seafarers* (1953); *Fear and Desire* (1953); *Day of the Fight* (1951)

References

Abrams, Jerold, ed. *The Philosophy of Stanley Kubrick*. Lexington: University Press of Kentucky, 2007.

Lane, Anthony. "The Last Emperor: How Stanley Kubrick Called the World to Order." *New Yorker*, March 22, 1999: 120–23.

Phillips, Gene, and Rodney Hill. *The Encyclopedia of Stanley Kubrick*. New York: Facts on File, 2002.

Turner, Adrian. "Stanley Kubrick." In Wakeman, John, ed. *World Film Directors, Vol. II, 1945–1985*. New York: H. W. Wilson, 1987.

—*Charles Johnson*

L

LANG, FRITZ.   Fritz Lang was one of the most notable of the Austrian and German directors who fled to the United States after Adolf Hitler came to power in the 1930s. Already acclaimed as a major filmmaker after making masterpieces such as *Metropolis* (1927) and *M* (1931), Lang did not quite match the success he had enjoyed in Europe after he arrived in America. He did, however, work steadily for more than two decades and was one of the major forces in creating what came to be known as film noir. Lang's bitterness and cynicism found an unusually suitable outlet in this genre, with his protagonists constantly struggling against their fates.

Born in Vienna in 1890, the son of an architect, Lang studied art in Munich and Paris before serving in the Austrian army during World War I. Convalescing from wounds he had received in battle, Lang tried writing screenplays. His film career began in Berlin as a script reader, and by 1919 he was directing films, many written in collaboration with his second wife, Thea von Harbou. In films such as *Dr. Mabuse: The Gambler* (1922), Lang displayed a deliberate pace and the expressionistic visual style that dominated German filmmaking during the 1920s; *Dr. Mabuse: The Gambler* also introduced Lang's obsession with the shady world of criminals, police, and spies. A visit to America in 1925—especially his experiences in Hollywood and the sight of the New York City skyline—inspired him to make the futuristic *Metropolis*, which would become one of the most iconic films of cinema's early history. In 1931, Lang made the first German sound film, *M*, a haunting portrait of a child killer that served as a template for the director's later film noirs. *M* was characterized by a claustrophobic urban setting, streets that feel like steel traps, and a perverse protagonist (Peter Lorre, in a masterful performance) overwhelmed by forces he cannot evade.

Although the director expressed his concerns about what he felt was the increasing threat of National Socialism in *The Testament of Dr. Mabuse* (1933), he was asked to work for the Nazis by propaganda minister Joseph Goebbels. Instead, Lang fled to Paris, leaving behind his fortune—including a large art collection—as well as his wife, who was a member of the Nazi Party. Although Lang's mother was Jewish, she had converted to her husband's Catholicism when their son was ten. Lang was raised as a Catholic and always identified himself as such.

Austrian-born film director Fritz Lang during his days at Germany's UFA studios in 1927. (Time Life Pictures/Getty Images)

After making the romantic drama *Liliom* (1934), which was later adapted as the Broadway musical *Carnival*, Lang was signed by MGM. This studio was not known for the dark, socially conscious films Lang wanted to direct, and he left after making *Fury* (1936)—an attack on lynch-mob hysteria that starred Spencer Tracy and Sylvia Sidney—and began to make freelance films. He reunited with Sidney for *You Only Live Once* (1937), about a young couple on the run from the law. Co-starring Henry Fonda, the film was inspired by the real-life outlaws Bonnie and Clyde. With their violence and dark, atmospheric lighting, these first two American films were tentative steps in Lang's evolution toward his fully developed noir style.

Fascinated by the American West, Lang spent periods on a Navaho reservation and used what he observed there to help him make two westerns: *The Return of Frank James* (1940), with Fonda and Gene Tierney, and *Western Union* (1941), with Randolph Scott and Robert Young. Interestingly, while most of Lang's films are set in urban locations and filmed in black and white, his westerns demonstrate a talent for composing striking Technicolor landscapes.

With World War II raging in Europe, Lang next turned to more topical films. *Man Hunt* (1941) involves a big-game hunter (Walter Pidgeon) on the run from Nazis. The picture co-starred Joan Bennett, who went on to make three more films with Lang and reportedly had an affair with the director. Another example of his early noirs, *Man Hunt* gave Lang a chance to make a personal statement dramatizing the gathering Nazi threat. Released in June 1941, before the United States entered the war and was thus officially neutral, the film attracted the attention of members of Congress, who began an investigation to determine whether the picture could be considered subversive; the investigation was dropped after the events at Pearl Harbor occurred in December of that year.

After *Moontide* (1942), a melodrama with Jean Gabin and Ida Lupino, Lang explored the Nazi occupation of Czechoslovakia in *Hangmen Also Die!* (1943); the film was based on a story by Bertolt Brecht. *Moontide* and *Hangmen Also Die!* were poorly received, but Lang quickly redeemed himself with films such as *Ministry of Fear* (1944). Based on a Graham Greene novel, *Ministry of Fear* concerns a man (Ray Milland) who has just been released from a mental institution and finds himself forced to flee from both the Nazis, who are pursuing him because he has accidentally been given a secret document, and the police, who suspect him of murder.

Along with films such as Otto Preminger's *Laura* (1944) and Billy Wilder's *Double Indemnity* (1944), Lang's next two offerings were characterized by the mixture of sex, greed, murder, and mystery that are the fundamental elements of film noir. In *Woman in the Window* (1944), for instance, a mild-mannered professor (Edward G. Robinson) finds himself the victim of capricious fate as he falls for a mysterious beauty (Joan Bennett), kills someone in self-defense, and is blackmailed. Lang carried the theme of the random character of fate even further in *Scarlet Street* (1945), often cited as one of his best American films. A meek married man (Robinson again) becomes entangled with an avaricious woman (Bennett), who persuades him to embezzle from his employer. This story of innocence corrupted is one of Lang's most pessimistic.

Lang's next four films are less highly regarded. The talky espionage thriller *Cloak and Dagger* (1946), with a miscast Gary Cooper, is notable as the first film about atomic scientists, though Warner Bros. angered Lang by removing the final scene warning of the dangers of atomic power. In *Secret beyond the Door* (1948), Lang's final film with Joan Bennett, a newly married woman discovers her husband (Michael Redgrave) is unbalanced. Despite similarities to the director's earlier psychological thrillers, *Secret beyond the Door* seems muddled. Widely considered one of Lang's weakest films, *An American Guerilla in the Philippines* (1950) is the story of an American sailor (Tyrone Power) stranded in Japanese-occupied territory during World War II. In *The House by the River* (1950), a minor but efficient noir, a wealthy man (Louis Hayward) kills the family maid (Dorothy Patrick) and tries to frame his brother (Lee Bowman) for the murder.

Lang began his return to form with *Clash by Night* (1952), a love-triangle melodrama with noir touches, featuring standout performances by Barbara Stanwyck, Robert Ryan, Paul Douglas, and, in one of the best of her early efforts, Marilyn Monroe. Lang followed *Clash by Night* with his final western, the truly strange *Rancho Notorious* (1952), with Marlene Dietrich as a singer who runs a hideout for outlaws. Despite interference from producer Howard Hughes, Lang created a stylish blend of western and noir with this film, as a man (Arthur Kennedy), seeking revenge for the murder of his fiancée, poses as an escaped prisoner to infiltrate the hideout.

In *The Big Heat* (1953), Glenn Ford plays a Los Angeles police detective whose wife (Jocelyn Brando) dies in a car bombing intended for him. This portrayal of a dehumanizing quest for revenge is sometimes cited as Lang's best American film. In *The Blue Gardenia* (1953), Norah Larkin (Anne Baxter) believes that while she was drunk, she killed a man (Raymond Burr) who had been making unwanted advances. A remake of Jean Renoir's *La Bête Humaine* (1938) and adapted from an Emile Zola novel,

Human Desire (1954) is one of Lang's darkest noirs. It stars Glenn Ford as a railroad engineer having an affair with the wife (Gloria Grahame) of a drunken, violent co-worker (Broderick Crawford).

The swashbuckler *Moonfleet* (1955) was Lang's first foray into CinemaScope, although it appears that Lang was not particularly comfortable with the wide-screen process. Lang was more successful with his final two American films, both noirs. In *While the City Sleeps* (1956), journalists Edward Mobley (Dana Andrews), Mildred Donner (Ida Lupino), and Mark Loving (George Sanders) stalk a serial killer, Robert Manners (John Barrymore Jr.), with unforeseen consequences. Several plot elements come together during a thrilling chase that winds through New York City streets and down into the underground spaces of the subway system. In the similar *Beyond a Reasonable Doubt* (1956), a publisher, Austin Spencer (Sydney Blackmer), convinces a writer, Tom Garrett (Andrews again), to implicate himself in a murder so that an incompetent district attorney, Roy Thompson (Philip Bourneuf), can be exposed; not surprisingly, the plan backfires. It is noteworthy that his final American film focuses on a consistent Langian theme: the individual struggling against his or her tragic fate.

During the mid-1950s, Lang returned to Germany to realize a film project adapted from a novel written by Lang and his then wife von Harbou. An exotic, mystical story set in India and divided into two films, *The Tiger of Eschnapur* (1958) and *The Indian Tomb* (1959), the project gave the director a chance to try something new. In the end, the pictures did not represent Lang's best efforts, and the U.S. distributor American International reedited the films into a single 90-minute offering, *Journey to the Lost City* (1959).

Lang retreated to firmer ground for his final film, *The 1000 Eyes of Dr. Mabuse* (1960), a continuation of his earlier Mabuse films. Unable to secure financing for further films, the director made his first acting appearance since 1919 in Jean-Luc Godard's *Contempt* (1963). Lang plays himself, a once-great filmmaker relegated to doing work-for-hire, on an ill-conceived adaptation of *The Odyssey*, for a bullying Hollywood producer, Jeremy Prokosch (Jack Palance). Godard's screenplay gave Lang opportunities to reflect upon his career. It may be that his best moment in *Contempt* comes when Brigitte Bardot tells him she likes *Rancho Notorious*, and his expression moves quickly from pleasure to wishing she had picked a better film.

Lang made 25 American films during the studio system era in Hollywood, working on some projects for which he had little affinity and making certain pictures less dark, brutal, sexy, or political than he would have liked. Nevertheless, most of his Hollywood efforts convey his unsentimental personality and eerie, atmospheric style. Although he fit the cliché of the monocled Teutonic perfectionist who demonstrated an antagonistic attitude toward those with whom he worked, he was still able to elicit dozens of outstanding performances from his actors. Initially considered inferior to the films he made in Germany, Lang's American films have now been accepted by critics and fans alike as extremely important cinematic works. Lang died in 1976, in Beverly Hills, California; he was 86.

See also: Big Heat, The; Film Noir; Metropolis; Studio System, The

Selected Filmography

Beyond a Reasonable Doubt (1956); *While the City Sleeps* (1956); *Moonfleet* (1954); *Human Desire* (1954); *The Big Heat* (1953); *Blue Gardenia* (1953); *Clash by Night* (1952); *Rancho Notorious* (1952); *American Guerrilla in the Philippines* (1950); *House by the River* (1950); *Secret beyond the Door* (1948); *Cloak and Dagger* (1946); *Scarlet Street* (1945); *The Woman in the Window* (1944); *Ministry of Fear* (1944); *Hangmen Also Die!* (1943); *Moontide* (1942); *Man Hunt* (1941); *Western Union* (1941); *Return of Frank James, The* (1940); *You Only Live Once* (1937); *Fury* (1936); *M* (1931); *Metropolis* (1927)

References

Eisner, Lotte. *Fritz Lang*. New York: Oxford University Press, 1977.

Gunning, Tom. *The Films of Fritz Lang: Allegories of Vision and Modernism*. London: British Film Institute, 2000.

Humphries, Reynold. *Fritz Lang: Genre and Representation in His American Films*. Baltimore and London: Johns Hopkins University Press, 1989.

McGilligan, Patrick. *Fritz Lang: The Nature of the Beast*. New York: St. Martin's, 1997.

—*Michael Adams*

LAUREL AND HARDY. Stan Laurel and Oliver Hardy were members of one of the most influential comic duos in American movies. Among those who brought the world of vaudeville to the big screen during the transition period from silents to sound movies, they excelled in slapstick comedy, parodies, and situations that would be taken up and used by later generations of admiring artists.

Born Arthur Stanley Jefferson, in Ulverston, Lancashire, England, on June 16, 1890, Stan Laurel was the son of actor-manager Arthur J. Jefferson and actress Madge Metcalfe. He performed with the Levy and Cardwell Juvenile Pantomimes Company from 1907 to 1909. Prior to his meeting with Hardy, he appeared in vaudeville shows and pantomimes in Great Britain. He was an understudy to Charlie Chaplin before appearing in American vaudeville in the 1910s.

Hardy was born Norvell Hardy, on January 18, 1892, in Harlem, Georgia, near Augusta. His father, Oliver Hardy, who served in the Georgia Volunteer Infantry during the Civil War, died when the young Norvell was only 10 months old. In honor of his father, Norvell adopted his name, calling himself Oliver Norvell Hardy. As Hardy grew, he began to fabricate stories about his family and himself. He claimed, for instance, that his father had been an attorney and that at age eight he had sung with Coburn's Minstrels (Gehring, 1990). In reality, after her husband's untimely death, Hardy's mother, Emily (Emmie) Norvell Tant, operated hotels in Madison, and later in Milledgeville, Georgia.

Hardy eventually enrolled at the Atlanta Conservatory of Music, and later at the Georgia Military College in Milledgeville. He worked as a film projectionist from 1910 to 1913, after which he migrated to Jacksonville, Florida, at that time a minor center of film production. An endearingly portly presence on screen, Hardy worked

Portrait of comedy duo Laurel and Hardy. (Michael Ochs Archives/Getty Images)

for various studios and appeared with a slimmer comedic partner, Bobby Ray, in *The Paperhanger's Helper* (1925). Significantly, this union with the slender Ray would foreshadow his iconic pairing with Stan Laurel.

In his first short film, *Nuts in May* (1917), Laurel portrayed a mentally challenged man who escapes an institution dressed as Napoleon. In *A Lucky Dog* (1917), he played a poor dog owner, while Hardy was cast as a crook attempting to rob him. In 1921, film producer Hal Roach created a series of short comedy films with Laurel; four years later Roach persuaded Laurel to join the new Comedy All-Stars, a troupe that included Hardy. The first Laurel and Hardy films were *The Second Hundred Years* and *Putting Pants on Philip*, both released in 1927. Between 1927 and 1932, Laurel and Hardy would make 65 films with Roach,

The duo's first sound film was *Unaccustomed as We Are* (1929). Their innovative sound effects and sight gags would eventually be picked up by other early sound filmmakers. During World War II, they made more feature films together, among them *Air Raid Wardens* (MGM, 1943), and *The Bullfighters* (Twentieth Century-Fox, 1945). The government even issued a short film, *The Tree in a Test Tube* (1943), in which the pair demonstrated conservation tips recommended by the U.S. Department of Agriculture.

In their work ethic, they differed greatly: Laurel was a workaholic and designed many of the duo's acts. Extremely creative, he kept notepads throughout his house, using them to record his thoughts as they came to him. Hardy, on the other hand, was less interested in working when he was not on the set, enjoying diversions such as gourmet cooking, golf, and gambling. Although master comedians, their films often raised important social questions, as they poked fun at authority figures and members of the upper classes. Vastly significant figures in the early American cinema, Laurel and Hardy would profoundly influence other comedians such as Jack Benny, Lucille Ball, Jackie Gleason, Jerry Lewis, Danny Kaye, and Dick Van Dyke. Oliver Hardy died on August 7, 1957, the result of three debilitating strokes; Stan Laurel died on February 23, 1965, after suffering a heart attack.

References

Gehring, Wes D. *Laurel & Hardy: A Bio-Bibliography.* Westport, CT: Greenwood, 1990.

McCabe, John. *Babe: The Life of Oliver Hardy.* New York: Carol Publishing Group, 1989.

McCabe, John. *The Comedy World of Stan Laurel.* Garden City, NY: Doubleday, 1974.

Nollen, Scott Allen. *The Boys: The Cinematic World of Laurel and Hardy.* Jefferson, NC: McFarland, 1989.

—Ralph Hartsock

LEE, ANG. Ang Lee is a Taiwanese American director, producer, and writer of international renown. Critics widely consider Lee to be one of the most significant filmmakers working today. Over the past 15 years, his reputation has grown considerably, and he has acquired worldwide audiences with films as varied as *The Wedding Banquet* (1993), *Sense and Sensibility* (1995), *The Ice Storm* (1997), *Crouching Tiger, Hidden Dragon* (2000), *The Hulk* (2003), and *Brokeback Mountain* (2005). *Crouching Tiger, Hidden Dragon* garnered Lee a 2001 Oscar for Best Foreign Language Film, and the controversial but extremely popular *Brokeback Mountain* earned him a 2005 Academy Award for Best Director.

Ang Lee was born in Pingtung, Taiwan, on October 23, 1954. Early on, Lee showed a preference for the arts and for drama in particular; however, his father, a school administrator and stern patriarch, strongly dissuaded him from pursuing the arts and demanded that he follow what was considered a more intellectual, honorable profession (Berry, 2005). Having fared poorly in his university entrance exams, Lee opted to enroll in Taiwan's National Art School, where he received his first formal exposure to theater and graduated in 1975. He then moved to the United States to further his studies, eventually receiving his bachelor's of arts in theater at the University of Illinois Urbana-Champaign, in 1980, and acquiring his MFA in theater from New York University in 1984. During his time as a student filmmaker, Lee developed his skills and defined his vision as an artist, showing preferences for technically sophisticated works that explore the notion of identity and tradition. Lee's talent was not lost on the artistic and academic community, as he won student awards for Best Director and Best Film while at NYU.

Given the filmmaker's connections to Taiwan, China, the United States, and Europe, it is not surprising that Lee's work is both expansive and decidedly cross-cultural. It is also marked by a willingness on Lee's part to openness and risk, from both a formal and a thematic standpoint. Indeed, Lee has a history of utilizing young, unknown actors; taking on difficult topics; and utilizing a range of experimental technical approaches in an attempt to enhance the narrative and visual elements of his films. As is often the case with innovative artists, the quality of Lee's work has proven to be uneven: for instance, while film critics praised him for his stunning use of color and magical realism in *Crouching Tiger, Hidden Dragon*, most found what he did in *Hulk* to be awkwardly executed.

While Lee's films are diverse in terms of subject matter, certain themes and motifs continually emerge within them. The pressures of family and society are given

In 2001, Taiwanese director Ang Lee's *Crouching Tiger, Hidden Dragon* became the first foreign-language film to earn more than $100 million in the United States. (AP/Wide World Photos)

expression in his work by way of examining the conflicted relationships that exist among wives, partners, children, and different examples of filmic "father figures," many of whom have an overbearing and unhealthy influence on those around them. Lee has reflected on this focus, noting that in addition to giving his films more emotional and psychological complexity, it also offers him an artistic means by which to work through his relationship with his own father (Berry, 2005, 336). He has also examined the repression—both conscious and unconscious—of heterosexual and homosexual desire in characters forced to function within the restrictive boundaries of what are often stifling social constraints. For Lee, repression is a fundamental element that is woven through all of his work, one that he believes humanizes his characters and helps to drive the storylines of his films (Crothers Dilley, 2007).

Selected Filmography

Taking Woodstock (2009); *Lust, Caution* (2007); *Brokeback Mountain* (2005); *Hulk* (2003); *Chosen* (2001); *Crouching Tiger, Hidden Dragon* (2000); *Ride with the Devil* (1999); *The Ice Storm* (1997); *Sense and Sensibility* (1995); *Eat Drink Man Woman* (1994); *The Wedding Banquet* (1993); *Pushing Hands* (1992)

References

Berry, Michael. "Ang Lee: Freedom in Film." In *Speaking In Images: Interviews with Contemporary Chinese Filmmakers*. New York: Columbia University Press, 2005.
Cheshire, Ellen. *Ang Lee*. North Pomfret, UK: Trafalgar Square, 2001.
Dilley, Whitney Crothers. *The Cinema of Ang Lee*. London: Wallflower, 2007.

—*Caleb Puckett*

LEE, SPIKE. Spike Lee has been one of the most prolific and controversial film-makers working in American cinema over the past three decades. He occupies a special position in film history as one of the only African American directors to work steadily on films of his own choosing, maintain his creative autonomy, and showcase his work through mainstream studio outlets.

Shelton Jackson Lee was born to musician/composer Bill Lee and schoolteacher Jacquelyn Shelton on March 27, 1957, in Atlanta, Georgia. The family moved to Brooklyn, New York, while Lee was still young. Growing up in New York seems to have influenced his filmmaking, as the city serves as the backdrop for most of his films. Lee enrolled at his father's alma mater, Morehouse College, in 1975. Many of his experiences there were dramatized in his film *School Daze* (1988). After graduating, Lee entered the Tisch School of the Arts at New York University. A friendship between Lee and another black film-maker, Ernest Dickerson, formed while he was there. The friendship has endured, and Dickerson has worked as the director of photography on seven of Lee's pictures, including his film school thesis at NYU, *Joe's Bed-Stuy Barbershop: We Cut Heads* (1981), which won the Academy Award for Best Student Film.

Success beyond film school was hard earned. Lee's first post-film school project, about a bike messenger who is forced to become the family breadwinner in the wake of his mother's death, had to be abandoned after financing disappeared (Lee et. al., 1991). The setback seemed to fuel Lee's passion for filmmaking, however; it also taught him valuable lessons about the practical end of the industry, lessons that he put to good use in making his first feature, *She's Gotta Have It* (1986). The story of a black woman, Nola Darling (Tracy Camilla Johns), and her relationships with three very different men, the picture was shot independently over 12 days on a budget of $175,000 and went on to make $7 million. Interestingly, one of Nola's relationships is carried out with "Mars Blackmon," played by Lee, who would become a recurring figure in a string of Nike commercials featuring Michael Jordon.

Lee continued working at a breakneck pace, putting out a film every year between 1988 and 1992. While *School Daze* (1988), *Do the Right Thing* (1989), *Mo' Better Blues* (1990), *Jungle Fever* (1991), and *Malcolm X* (1992) proved to be somewhat controversial offerings, their critical and box-office success made it clear that audiences would turn out to view "A Spike Lee Joint." The films also demonstrated Lee's commitment to empowering black talent. Indeed, several of the actors who worked in these early Lee films—including Laurence Fishburne, Samuel L. Jackson, Wesley Snipes, Martin Lawrence, and Oscar winners Denzel Washington and Halle Berry—would go on to become Hollywood stars.

Lee stayed productive through the mid-1990s, working on a wide range of films. The semiautobiographical *Crooklyn* (1994), written by his sister Joie and brother Cinque, explored the challenges of a black Brooklyn family facing the death of its matriarch. (Lee has taken advantage of his talented family on a number of occasions: Beyond co-writing the script for *Crooklyn*, Joie has also starred in several of Lee's other films; his brother David has worked for Lee as a composer and his father as a cinematographer.) In 1995, Lee directed the crime thriller *Clockers*, based on a Richard Price novel; Martin Scorsese, one of Lee's cinematic influences, produced the film. He released two films in 1996: *Girl 6*, about a black actress who becomes a phone sex

Filmmaker Spike Lee arrives at the Bellas Artes museum in Caracas, July 24, 2009. Lee was in Venezuela to give a seminar to young film students. (AP/Wide World Photos)

operator because she cannot find work, and *Get on the Bus*, an intimate look at a group of men headed to the Million Man March.

In 1997, Lee partnered with HBO to make the documentary *4 Little Girls*. An examination of the 1963 bombing of the 16th Street Baptist Church in Birmingham, Alabama, the film was nominated for an Academy Award. He has made two other, Emmy Award-winning documentaries for the cable network: *Jim Brown: All American* (2002), and *When the Levees Broke: A Requiem in Four Acts* (2006). Lee teamed up with Denzel Washington for a third time in *He Got Game* (1998) and rounded out the decade by directing his first film with a predominantly white cast, *Summer of Sam* (1999).

The start of the new millennium found Lee exploring the issue of racial stereotyping in the biting satire *Bamboozled* (2000). A powerful examination of the historical legacy of denigrating black images in popular media, the film was a box-office failure. Still, Lee understood how important the issue of stereotyping was in America, and the concert film *The Original Kings of Comedy* (2000), as well as his film adaptation of Roger Guenveur Smith's Obie Award–winning *A Huey P. Newton Story* (2001), can be read as critical companion pieces to *Bamboozled*.

Neither of Lee's next two narrative features was financially successful, although both addressed significant cultural issues. *25th Hour* (2002) was one of the first major studio films to address the aftermath of the 9/11 terrorist attacks; while *She Hate Me* (2004), explored shifting familial mores, reproductive rights, and economic corruption.

Lee's feature output has slowed, although he has directed several short films and done television work including the short-lived drama series *Sucker Free City* (2004).

Teaming once again with Denzel Washington, Lee scored with *Inside Man* in 2006, although his *Miracle at St. Anna* of 2008 failed. Lee has claimed that critics and audiences cannot separate his public persona from his work, but he has expressed no desire to make a clean break between the two.

Selected Filmography

Miracle at St. Anna (2008); *Lovers & Haters* (2007); *Inside Man* (2006); *She Hate Me* (2004); *25th Hour* (2002); *Bamboozled* (2000); *The Original Kings of Comedy* (2000); *Summer of Sam* (1999); *He Got Game* (1998); *4 Little Girls* (1997); *Get on the Bus* (1996); *Girl 6* (1996); *Lumi-ère and Company* (1995); *Clockers* (1995); *Crooklyn* (1994); *Malcolm X* (1992); *Jungle Fever* (1991); *Mo' Better Blues* (1990); *Do the Right Thing* (1989); *School Daze* (1988); *She's Gotta Have It* (1986)

References

Crowdus, Gary, and Dan Georgakas. "Thinking about the Power of Images: An Interview with Spike Lee." *Cineaste* 26(2), January 2001: 4–9.

Guerrero, Ed. *Framing Blackness: The African American Image in Film.* Philadelphia: Temple University Press, 1993.

Lee, Spike, and Terry McMillan, et al. *Five for Five: The Films of Spike Lee.* New York: Stewart, Tabori, and Chang, 1991.

Massood, Paula J. *The Spike Lee Reader.* Philadelphia: Temple University Press, 2007.

Reid, Mark. "Spike Lee." In Gates, Henry Louis Jr., and Evelyn Brooks Higginbotham, eds. *African American National Biography. Vol. 5.* New York: Oxford University Press, 2008.

—*Mikal Gaines*

LEWIS, JERRY. A popular comedian and actor during the 1950s and 1960s, Jerry Lewis achieved worldwide fame both on stage and in film for his slapstick comedy routines. He also proved himself to be an equally talented screenwriter and director. Lewis's numerous accomplishments as a comedic actor and filmmaker have earned him an important place in American cinematic history.

Jerry Lewis was born Jerome Levitch on March 16, 1926, in Newark, New Jersey. His parents, Daniel Levitch and Rae Brodsky, were both actors who performed onstage professionally as Danny and Rae Lewis. In 1932, when Lewis was six years old, he made his acting debut when he performed a rendition of the song "Brother, Can You Spare a Dime?" in the Catskills, New York. In 1942, when Lewis was 16 years old, he quit high school to perform professionally as a comedian. On July 25, 1946, he performed onstage with singer Dean Martin at the 500 Club in Atlantic City, New Jersey. This performance, in hindsight, was a pivotal moment in Lewis's acting career. Their onstage chemistry and comedy routine quickly became popular. They performed regularly in nightclubs and theaters across the country. From April 1949 through June 1953, the duo also performed on their own radio show, the *Dean Martin & Jerry Lewis Show.*

Actor and comedian Jerry Lewis shares a banana split with Pierre, a five-year-old chimpanzee who's trying to make a name for himself in the movies, 1950. (AP/Wide World Photos)

In 1949, the comedy team made their motion picture debut with *My Friend Irma*. The popularity of this first movie led to the duo's collaboration on 16 other movies between 1949 and 1956. In all of their films, Martin played the straight man to Lewis's slapstick comedy acts. Some of their most popular movies included *At War with the Army* (1950), *The Stooge* (1953), and *Money from Home* (1953). The team's last two movies, *Artists and Models* (1955) and *Hollywood or Bust* (1956), are considered by many critics to be their best two movies. In 1956, Martin and Lewis ended their working relationship.

Following his split with Martin, Lewis embarked on a very successful solo acting career. In 1960, he also made his screenwriting and directorial debut with the movie *The Bellboy*. In 1960, he produced and starred in the smash hit *Cinderfella*. Lewis also wrote, directed, and performed in *The Ladies Man* (1961), *The Errand Boy* (1961), and *The Nutty Professor* (1963). Many critics consider *The Nutty Professor* to be Lewis's movie masterpiece because it highlighted his skillful use of the camera to execute a comedy routine. Other popular movies made by Lewis included *The Patsy* (1964), *The Disorderly Orderly* (1964), *The Family Jewels* (1965), in which Lewis took on seven different roles, and *Three on the Couch* (1966), in which he played four different roles.

In 1967, Lewis taught a graduate course in film direction at the University of Southern California. Some of his students included George Lucas, Francis Ford Coppola, and Steven Spielberg. In 1971, he published the book *The Total Film-Maker*.

During the early the 1970s, Lewis directed and starred in two additional movies. In 1970, *Which Way to the Front* was released; and *The Day the Clown Died*, shot in 1972, was never released due to conflicts among the backers, producers, and Lewis. Throughout the rest of the decade, Lewis devoted most of his attention to being the National Chair and spokesman for the Muscular Dystrophy Association. Actively involved in the fight for a cure since the 1940s, Lewis has been a tireless host and fund-raiser on the annual Labor Day Muscular Dystrophy Telethon, which began in 1966. In 1983, he returned to acting in his critically acclaimed role in the Martin Scorsese film *The King of Comedy.*

In total, Lewis starred in 63 motion pictures, 17 of which he directed, 14 of which he produced, and 11 of which he wrote. His brilliant comedy routines established him as one of the world's most famous funnymen. Equally important, the Martin and Lewis comedy team is also considered to be one of the most successful teams in American cinematic history. Lewis's talents as a comedic actor, screenwriter, producer, and director have earned him an important place in America cinematic history.

References

Levy, Shawn. *King of Comedy: The Life and Art of Jerry Lewis.* New York: St. Martin's, 1997.
Lewis, Jerry, and James Kaplan. *Dean & Me: (A Love Story).* New York: Doubleday, 2005.
Neibaur, James L., and Ted Okuda. *The Jerry Lewis Films: An Analytical Filmography of the Innovative Comic.* Jefferson, NC: McFarland, 1994.

—*Bernadette Zbicki Heiney*

LLOYD, HAROLD.　Harold Clayton Lloyd was one of the most successful actor/comedians of the silent film era. Between 1913 and 1947, he made almost 200 films, both silents and "talkies," rivaling Charlie Chaplin as one of the industry's top money-makers. Lloyd's on-screen persona the "Glass Character," with his signature tortoise-shell horn-rimmed glasses, was an earnest mild-mannered character who faced adversity and triumphed, a man to whom people in the 1920s could relate. Known for his very physical comedy, Lloyd has been characterized as "The King of Daredevil Comedy." In addition to his acting career, Lloyd produced several movies and film compilations and was involved in radio and television. In 1953, at the 25th annual Academy Awards, he received an honorary Oscar for Lifetime Achievement, recognizing nearly a half-century of filmmaking.

Lloyd was born April 20, 1893, in Burchard, Nebraska, to James Darsie "Foxy" Lloyd and Elizabeth Fraser. His father had several unsuccessful business ventures and moved his family from town to town after each failed attempt to strike it rich. Elizabeth Fraser had dreamed of becoming an actress, but while visiting relatives in Nebraska she met and married Lloyd. The stress of Foxy's financial failures and constant relocation, however, took its toll, and Lloyd's parents divorced in 1910. After receiving a $6,000 cash settlement in a lawsuit and splitting the enormous sum with his attorney, Foxy moved to San Diego, where Harold was enrolled in high school and began starring in high school plays. By 1912, Harold had joined the Burwood Stock Company, which was headed by John Lane Connor, an early mentor to Lloyd. Continuing to act in school plays, Lloyd also began teaching at the San Diego School of Expression, another one of Connor's enterprises.

Lloyd arrived in Hollywood in 1913 and found work with Universal as an extra. It was there that he met Hal Roach, who would be an important force in Lloyd's career. Roach soon began making one-reel comedies starring Lloyd as "Willie Work," and Pathé Films eventually offered Roach a distribution contract after the release of *Just Nuts* (1915), one of the few surviving films of that period. Lloyd next developed the character of "Lonesome Luke," a variation on Charlie Chaplin's Little Tramp; but it was his "Glasses Character" that allowed him to transform his acting career.

The first of the glasses films was *Over the Fence* (1917). Lloyd convinced Pathé that such "one-reelers" were ideal for distribution while he was developing the character. Released every week or so, these short films allowed audiences to familiarize themselves with the new character. In 1919, he began to make more complex films, such as *Ask Father* (1919), considered one of the best one-reel comedies of the time. Unfortunately, while posing for publicity photos that same year, Lloyd had the thumb and index finger of his right hand ripped off when a prop bomb accidentally exploded, leaving him hovering near death for days. Recovering fully, he wore a prosthetic thumb and finger thereafter.

His most memorable film may be the feature *Safety Last* (1923), where his character is seen hanging from the hands of a clock high above a busy street. Audiences loved these stunts, and Lloyd, it seems, enjoyed his reputation as a daredevil actor willing to take chances with his life. *Safety Last* turned out to be a wildly popular film, one of the last he would make with Hal Roach. In 1924, he became an independent producer, releasing *Girl Shy* (1924), *The Freshman* (1925), *Kid Brother* (1927), and his last silent film, *Speedy* (1928). In 1929, he made the transition to sound with *Welcome Danger* (1929). Sadly, he released only six more films between 1929 and 1947.

Harold Lloyd married his leading lady, Mildred Davis on February 10, 1923. They had two children: Gloria and Harold Clayton Lloyd Jr. (b. 1931). They also had an adopted daughter, Gloria Freeman, renamed Marjorie Elizabeth Lloyd. In 1926, Lloyd started construction on his Beverly Hills estate, "Greenacres," a 44-room mansion on 16 sprawling acres. Lloyd died of prostate cancer at the age of 77 on March 8, 1971. After his death, Lloyd's beloved Greenacres was opened for public tours from May 1973 to February 1974.

Selected Filmography (Director)

Just Neighbors (1919); *The Lamb* (1918); *Over the Fence* (1917); *Pinched* (1917)

References

Baer, William. *Classic American Films, Conversations with Screenwriters.* Westport: Praeger, 2008.

Dardis, Tom. *Harold Lloyd: The Man on the Clock.* New York: Viking, 1983.

Vance, Jeffrey, and Suzanne Lloyd. *Harold Lloyd: Master Comedian*. New York: Henry N. Abrams, 2002.

—*Katie Simonton*

LUCAS, GEORGE. As a screenwriter, director, and producer, George Lucas has been one of the most influential figures in the American cinema. Not only did he craft some of the most successful films of all time, he pioneered—through his production company Lucasfilm and its many subsidiaries—a number of innovative technologies that continue to reshape modern cinema.

Even before his graduation from the film school at the University of Southern California, Lucas had become associated with a number of young filmmakers who wanted to escape the constraints of Hollywood's studio system. With Francis Ford Coppola, he was instrumental in creating American Zoetrope, a production company headquartered in San Francisco that was designed to utilize younger talent and engage in a type of cinéma vérité. Coppola became an early mentor who helped Lucas create and sell his first professional films, *THX 1138* (1971) and *American Graffiti* (1973). The latter was a coming-of-age film loosely based on Lucas's own adolescent years of "cruisin' " in Modesto, California, just prior to the cultural convulsions of the 1960s. Although the film sparked a nostalgia for this American "age of innocence" (leading to television series such as *Happy Days* and its own multitude of spin-offs), it also employed several innovative techniques—such as intertwining several unrelated narrative threads and integrating original period songs into the narrative schema—that became conventions in subsequent films and even television dramas. Produced on a shoestring budget, the film was a huge commercial success and provided Lucas with the finances and clout he needed to create his own production company (Lucasfilm), which in turn allowed him to pursue other, original projects.

Lucas's next film would become a cultural phenomenon. Originally envisioned as a swashbuckler set in outer space, *Star Wars* (1977) became an industry unto itself in more ways than one, ultimately giving rise to five sequels and prequels and revolutionizing filmmaking in the process. Unable to use existing technology to achieve the effects he envisioned, Lucas established his own special effects studio, Industrial Light and Magic (ILM), and hired John Dykstra to create the technology required. Famously, Dykstra spent over $1 million before a single frame of film was shot, but the computer-controlled camera he developed forever transformed special effects. Eventually, ILM would become an independent subsidiary of Lucasfilm, winning multiple Academy Awards for its sophisticated visual effects.

As with special effects for his film, Lucas desired sound effects for *Star Wars* that exceeded the capabilities of existing systems, so he experimented with the new sound recording and mixing techniques that would become the basis for Skywalker Sound, another subsidiary of Lucasfilm. By the third installment of the original trilogy, *The Return of the Jedi* (1983), the engineers at Skywalker Sound had developed a state-of-the-art digital system, THX Sound (after *THX 1138*) that has become an industry standard. Like ILM, Skywalker Sound, now completely digital, has won numerous Academy Awards as well as multiple Clio Awards for its successes in television.

Film director George Lucas, shown here in 1974, has directed such films as *American Graffiti* and *THX 1138* and is the creator behind the entire *Star Wars* series. (AP/Wide World Photos)

Beyond its inspiring special effects, *Star Wars* has endured because of the archetypal power of its rather simple narrative. As an undergraduate, Lucas had been introduced to Joseph Campbell's interpretations of world mythology, and it was Campbell's influential study of the hero myth that informed the storyline of the *Star Wars* series. Other films, such as *Labyrinth* (1986, produced by Lucas and directed by Muppets creator Jim Henson), *Willow* (1988, co-written and produced by Lucas), and the *Indiana Jones* series (all co-written and produced by Lucas and directed by Steven Spielberg) reflect similar themes of the heroic quest.

Convinced that the future of filmmaking lay in digital image and sound, Lucas rereleased the original *Star Wars* trilogy in the late 1990s with new digital enhancements. This served as a prelude to the digital technology used in the prequel trilogy that began with *The Phantom Menace* (1999) and continued with *The Attack of the Clones* (2002), which was the first "virtual" commercial film shot entirely in a high-definition digital format.

In addition to ILM and Skywalker Sound, Lucasfilm has been an incubator for other digital projects. The graphics division was sold in 1986 to Steve Jobs of the Apple Corporation and became Pear, but Lucas has retained the game division (Lucas Arts) and the eponymous educational foundation and its clearinghouse for interactive technology for home and school known as Editorial.

Selected Filmography

Star Wars: Episode III, Revenge of the Sith (2005); *Star Wars: Episode II, Attack of the Clones* (2002); *Star Wars: Episode I, The Phantom Menace* (1999); *Star Wars: Episode IV, A New Hope* (1977); *American Graffiti* (1973); *THX 1138* (1971)

References

Baxter, John. *Mythmaker: The Life and Work of George Lucas.* New York: Avon, 1999.

Hearn, Marcus. *The Cinema of George Lucas.* New York: Harry N. Abrams, 2005.

—*Rodger M. Payne*

LUMET, SIDNEY.   A venerated American filmmaker, Sidney Lumet directed more than 40 films over a career that lasted longer than half a century. His most notable films include *12 Angry Men, Serpico, Dog Day Afternoon, Network,* and *The Verdict.* He received an honorary Academy Award in 2005, after having received five previous Oscar nominations. Throughout his career, Lumet's films often sympathized with the political left and made arguments for social justice.

Born in Philadelphia on June 25, 1924, Lumet moved with his family to New York City two years later. As a child, he acted in New York's Yiddish Theatre, and he continued to act onstage as a young adult before transitioning to directing television for CBS in the early 1950s. Lumet is strongly identified as a New York filmmaker, with many of his films having been shot on location in the city.

Lumet directed his first feature film, *12 Angry Men,* in 1957. The film is woven through with elements that would become trademark features of the director's subsequent work, including an urban, realist aesthetic and a focus on matters of social justice. In the film, Henry Fonda plays a juror, the only one of 12, who initially believes that a teenage boy on trial for murder may be innocent of the charges against him. Throughout the film, Fonda attempts to convince the other jurors that the boy, who is understood to be poor and of color, is a victim of social prejudice. Although his arguments are at first rejected by his fellow jurors—who are hot, hungry, and, because in their minds the boy is clearly a delinquent, unconcerned that they are making a life and death decision—Fonda slowly brings them around to his socially enlightened way of thinking. Lumet would return to the courtroom as a setting for several other films, including *The Verdict* (1982) and *Find Me Guilty* (2006).

Lumet's characters frequently challenge authority figures. In the Arthur Miller adaptation *A View from the Bridge* (1961), an Italian immigrant community in Red Hook bands together against immigration officials. The story, which Miller penned as a response to Elia Kazan's anticommunist allegory *On the Waterfront,* acts as a critique of the House Un-American Activities Committee and of red-baiting informants. And in one of his best-known films, *Dog Day Afternoon* (1975), Al Pacino plays a likeable bank robber who connects with a New York City crowd that represents a post-Watergate America disillusioned by corrupt authority figures.

In addition to *A View from the Bridge,* several of Lumet's films are sympathetic to the people and ideals of the political left. *Fail-Safe* (1964), for instance, presents viewers with a story in which the United States and the Soviet Union come to the verge of nuclear war, serving as an argument for nonproliferation; and in *Daniel* (1983), an adaptation of E. L. Doctorow's novel *The Book of Daniel,* the children of a fictionalized Julius and Ethel Rosenberg wrestle with the legacy of their parents in the midst of the Vietnam

Director Sidney Lumet arrives at the 2007 LA Film Critics' Choice Awards held at the InterContinental on January 12, 2008, in Los Angeles. (Frederick Brown/Getty Images)

War era. More recently, Lumet's cable television movie *Strip Search* (2004) critiqued the deterioration of civil liberties under President George W. Bush with a story concerning the detainment of an Arab American man.

Arguably Lumet's greatest film, *Network* (1976) takes a satirical behind-the-scenes look at television network news. The Academy Award-winning screenplay, written by Paddy Chayefsky, tells the story of Howard Beale (Peter Finch), an anchorman who suffers an emotional breakdown while on the air. After ratings soar, Diana Christensen (Faye Dunaway), a cutthroat, ratings-driven junior executive, seizes the opportunity to revamp the network's programming schedule, filling it with sensationalistic shows. She develops the "Mao Tse Tung Hour," hosted by a communist and featuring a radical guerrilla group, along with a new show for Beale in which psychics forecast the news. A cautionary tale, the film predicts the rise of reality television and "entertainment" cable news programs. It is number 66 on the American Film Institute's list of their top 100 movies.

Lumet's diverse filmography ultimately defies rigid definitions, as evidenced by his adaptations of Agatha Christie's *Murder on the Orient Express* (1974) and the Broadway musical *The Wiz* (1978). The latter film, having been poorly received by critics and audiences alike, also exemplifies the somewhat uneven nature of his work. Despite this unevenness, Lumet remained a deeply influential and highly lauded director. Sidney Lumet died of lymphoma on April 9, 2011, at his home in Manhattan.

See also: Serpico

Selected Filmography

Before the Devil Knows You're Dead (2007); *A Stranger Among Us* (1992); *Q and A* (1990); *Verdict, The* (1982); *Network* (1976); *Dog Day Afternoon* (1975); *Serpico* (1973); *The Appointment* (1969); *The Deadly Affair* (1966); *Fail-Safe* (1964); *Long Day's Journey into Night* (1962)

References

Cunningham, Frank R. *Sidney Lumet: Film and Literary Vision*. Lexington: University Press of Kentucky, 2001.

Lumet, Sidney. *Making Movies*. New York: Alfred A. Knopf, 1995.

Rapf, Joanna E., ed. *Sidney Lumet Interviews*. Jackson: University Press of Mississippi, 2006.

—Andrew Paul

LUMIÈRE, AUGUSTE AND LOUIS.   Auguste Marie Louis Nicolas Lumière was born on October 19, 1862 in Besançon, France, while Louis Jean Lumière was born in the same town on October 5, 1864. Known as the Lumière brothers, they patented the groundbreaking optical device called Cinématographe Lumière, or the cinematograph, on February 13, 1895.

The Lumière family lived in Besançon, where they owned a photographic studio that developed into a prosperous company of photo products. Their family name, meaning "light," epitomized their business. Auguste and Louis helped their father, Charles Antoine Lumière, run and expand the family enterprise until the beginning of the 1890s. Inspired by Thomas Alva Edison's Kinetoscope peep-show or viewing machines consisting of individual looking boxes, the Lumière brothers decided to take the images out of the box and make them available for larger audiences. For this they needed a new apparatus. The Lumières were determined to construct a complex device with a threefold function: a camera, a projector, and a film developer or printer (that used perforated paper strips to advance the film roll), all assembled in one tool.

After the Kinetoscope show, the technically talented Louis designed the Lumière film camera. Louis was responsible for the step-by-step development of the cinematograph, a lightweight, handheld motion picture camera, with a mechanism similar to that of a sewing machine. Despite the initial success of his project, Louis was skeptical about the prospects of motion pictures; he believed that cinema was an invention without a future. Instead of pursuing a career in film, he became interested in creating color photography called Autochrome Lumière (1903) and with the autochrome transparency system (1907), followed by Photo-Stereo-Synthesis plates. The latter were three-dimensional images that are the antecedents of today's holograms. In the 1930s, Louis was still involved with the study of relief cinematography: he explored stereoscopy and stereoscopic films. Meanwhile, Auguste directed many Lumière movies and even appeared in several of their early films. Although he had the idea of constructing the cinematograph, his interest focused rather on medical research on tuberculosis, cancer, and related medical fields, and less on further developments in film.

The first public screening of 10 short Lumière films took place on December 28, 1895, at Salon Indien, the basement of the Grand Café in Paris. Viewers were charged an admission fee to watch filmed reality projected on a large canvas, a screening that afterwards led to many other small group projections and then to mass viewing of moving images, first across Europe and then throughout the whole world. This event inaugurated the birth of cinema as a mass medium and also prefigured the commercial potential of the movies.

The Lumières were fascinated by the idea of capturing reality on film; they recreated the world in a total of over 1,420 films and experimented with a fixed camera on various mundane subjects and episodes of public and private events recorded in black-and-white short, silent films that had a running time ranging from 40 to 50 seconds. Some of their most famous movies include the *Workers Leaving the Lumière Factory* (1895) *Arrival of a Train at La Ciotat Station* (1895), *Baby's Breakfast* (1895), and *Teasing the Gardener* (1895). The last two films can be considered the forerunners of today's home videos; additionally, the latter is the precursor of chase movies and comedy films. However, all Lumière films are prototypes of documentaries and newsreels.

The Lumières did not recognize the narrative and entertainment potential of moving pictures; and soon the novelty of their invention ebbed and their popularity faded, along with their financial success. Toward the end of their careers, they worked primarily as inventors and manufacturers of cameras; eventually, however, they were unable to fill the numerous orders they received for film equipment, and ultimately sold their cinematograph patent to the talented entrepreneur Charles Pathé.

Auguste died on April 10, 1954 in Lyon, while Louis died on June 6, 1948 in Bandol. Today, the Institut Lumière in Lyon, established in 1982, commemorates the pioneering work of the Lumière brothers in the film world.

See also: Silent Era, The

References

Cook, David A. *A History of Narrative Film*, 2nd ed. New York and London: W. W. Norton, 1990.

Herbert, Stephen. "Louis Jean Lumière. Inventor of the Cinématographe and the Autochrome Colour Photography Process." *Who's Who of Victorian Cinema*. http://www.victorian-cinema.net/louislumiere.htm.

Herbert, Stephen. "Auguste Marie Nicolas Lumière. Medical Researcher and Co-Patentee of the Cinématographe." *Who's Who of Victorian Cinema*. http://www.victorian-cinema.net/augustelumiere.htm.

Kracauer, Siegfried. 1999. "Basic Concepts." In Braudy, Leo, and Marshall Cohen, eds. *Film Theory and Criticism. Introductory Readings*, 5th ed. New York: Oxford University Press, 1999: 171–82.

—*Réka M. Cristian*

LUPINO, IDA. Ida Lupino had a successful acting career in the 1930s and 1940s. However, she is best known as one of the few successful women directors in post-World War II cinema. Lupino's films addressed the traumatic aspects of life during the Cold War with a particular focus on women's limited public roles.

Lupino was born on February 4, 1918, in London to Stanley Lupino, a comedian and playwright, and Connie Emerald, a musical-comedy performer. A child actress, Lupino attended the Royal Academy of Dramatic Art. She came to Hollywood in 1933, signing with Paramount as "the English Jean Harlow." Lupino generally played older women in B-films such as *Peter Ibbetson* (1935) with Gary Cooper and *The Adventures of Sherlock Holmes* (1939) with Basil Rathbone. A bout with polio in the late 1930s almost terminated her career, and Lupino would later use the experience in her film *Never Fear*. Lupino's greatest success came in the early 1940s when she worked alongside Humphrey Bogart in *High Sierra* (1941) and Edward G. Robinson in *The Sea Wolf* (1941). She won a New York Film Critics award for her work in *The Hard Way* (1942).

Lupino never seemed satisfied with just acting. In the 1930s, she had some success as a classical musical composer. She appeared on several movie soundtracks, including *The Man I Love* (1947), as a singer and piano player. By the mid-1940s, she expressed aspirations to direct or produce. In 1946, she became an uncredited co-producer on *War Widow*. Two years later, she coproduced a low-budget thriller, *The Judge*. In 1949, Lupino and television producer Anson Bond formed Emerald Productions, later renamed The Filmmakers. When the director of Emerald's 1949 feature film, *Not Wanted*, suffered a heart attack, Lupino stepped in to complete the film. She also co-wrote and co-produced it. Like many of The Filmmakers' productions, the film is a melodrama that focuses on a social problem and possesses elements of film noir. *Not Wanted* addressed unwed motherhood. *Outrage* (1950) focused on rape, *Never Fear* (1949) centered on polio, and *Hard, Fast, and Beautiful* (1951) told the story of a young tennis player with a dominating mother. Lupino directed these films along with *The Hitchhiker* (1953) and *The Bigamist* (1953). She also wrote the screenplays for *Never Fear, Outrage,* and *The Bigamist,* as well as the script for *Private Hell 36* (1954). None of the films were successes at the box office, and The Filmmakers collapsed in 1954. However, Lupino's peers recognized her talents by giving her the honor of presenting the Oscar for Best Film Direction at the 1950 Academy Awards. She was one of a very few women directors at the time. She directed her last Hollywood feature film, *The Trouble with Angels,* in 1966.

Lupino, who once stated that she preferred to focus on the talents of others, seemed most comfortable behind the camera. As an actress, she worked slowly. As a director, she gained a reputation for working quickly and staying on budget. She also used location shooting long before it became common to do so. Much as she enjoyed directing, however, acting paid the bills. Lupino continued to act through the 1950s, in films such as *On Dangerous Ground* (1951) and in the 1957–1958 television comedy series *Mr. Adams and Eve.* Lupino earned two Emmy nominations for her acting. In the 1960s and 1970s, she only acted occasionally, undoubtedly because she did not need to do so. She derived more satisfaction from directing. Lupino appeared in Sam Peckinpah's *Junior Bonner* (1972) before making her final big-screen appearance in *My Boys Are Good Boys* (1978). A 1977 *Charlie's Angels* episode served as her last television appearance.

Lupino, who wrote scripts for several television shows in the 1950s, became one of the busiest directors in the medium in the 1960s. She directed episodes of *Dr. Kildare, The Ghost and Mrs. Muir, The Virginian, Gilligan's Island, The Twilight Zone, 77 Sunset Strip,* and *Alfred Hitchcock Presents.* Although honored by film societies and museums today, ironically, Lupino was slow to recognize her own contributions to cinema and television. She seemed to think that any attention she received was due only to the fact that she was a woman who had worked in an almost exclusively male field. After fielding numerous queries about her directorial accomplishments, Lupino realized at the end of her life that she was an exceptional director. She died on August 3, 1995.

See also: Women in Film

Selected Filmography (Director)

The Trouble with Angels (1966); *The Bigamist* (1953); *The Hitchhiker* (1953); *Hard, Fast, and Beautiful* (1951); *Outrage* (1950); *Never Fear* (1949); *Not Wanted* (1949)

References

Donati, William. *Ida Lupino: A Biography.* Lexington: University Press of Kentucky, 1996.
Kuhn, Annette, ed. *Queen of the 'B's: Ida Lupino behind the Camera.* Westport, CT: Greenwood, 1995.

—*Caryn E. Neumann*

LYNCH, DAVID. Emerging from a background in painting, David Lynch, born on January 20, 1946, in Missoula, Montana, is Hollywood's most unlikely filmmaker—a creator of dreams and alternative realities, abstractions and textures, deformity and viscera, and mystery and darkness. Despite a relatively meager output of films—only six in 17 years (and one of those an offshoot of his television work)—Lynch's twisted vision has been carved into the minds of moviegoers on the strength of his visual imagery.

After making a couple of short films and attending the American Film Institute's Center for Advanced Film Studies, Lynch completed *Eraserhead*, the bizarre tale of a man living with his deformed baby in an industrial wasteland. Featuring the work of two frequent Lynch collaborators—the crisp black-and-white photography of Frederick Elmes and the aural constructions of soundman Alan Splet—the film eventually became a *succès de scandale*. In an odd embrace by Hollywood, the perceptive Mel Brooks offered Lynch the job of directing *The Elephant Man*, the Victorian-era story of the hideously deformed, but internally pure, John Merrick. Eight Oscar nominations followed, and so did an offer from the less perceptive Dino De Laurentiis to direct the $60 million sci-fi adaptation of Frank Herbert's opus *Dune*, a monumental failure on every level. Lynch, however, returned with *Blue Velvet*, a strange film noir that continues the explorations begun in *Eraserhead*.

Since then, Lynch's film work has been both sparse and subpar—his *Wild at Heart* took the top prize at the Cannes Film Festival, but its excessive violence turned off most viewers, while his *Twin Peaks: Fire Walk with Me* seemed a lazy way of squeezing a theatrical release out of his television series. *Twin Peaks*, ABC television's gutsy foray into experimental drama, has proven to be Lynch's chief contribution to popular culture. Producing the series and directing numerous episodes, Lynch managed to bring his vision of a dark and troubled America directly into America's living rooms. While several film projects such as *Ronnie Rocket* and *One Saliva Bubble* have been rumored but have never materialized, Lynch has been branching out into music (producing an album by singer Julee Cruise and creating the *Industrial Symphony #1* at the Brooklyn Academy of Music in 1991), photography, installations, and a return to painting. "All my films are about trying to find love in hell" (quoted by Greg Olson in *Film Comment*, May-June 1993).

Selected Filmography

Mulholland Dr. (2001); *Wild at Heart* (1990); *Blue Velvet* (1986); *Dune* (1984); *The Elephant Man* (1980); *Eraserhead* (1978)

References

Lewis, Jon. *American Film: A History.* New York: W. W. Norton, 2008.
Olson, Greg. "Heaven Knows, Mr. Lynch: Beatitudes from the Deacon of Distress." *Film Comment* 29, no. 3 (May-June 1993): 43–6.
Sklar, Robert. *A World History of Film.* New York: Harry N. Abrams, Inc., 2002.

—Daniel Curran

M

MANN, MICHAEL. Michael Kenneth Mann was born in Chicago, Illinois, on February 5, 1943. His father was a Ukrainian immigrant, his mother a local girl. He earned an English degree from the University of Wisconsin (Madison), followed by graduate studies at the London International Film School. Although from the same generation as New Hollywood directors like Coppola, Scorsese, Spielberg, and Lucas, Mann's Midwestern roots and international education set him apart. His most significant formative cinematic influence was *Dr. Strangelove* (1964). Mann claims to have learned from Stanley Kubrick's Cold War satire that filmmaking could be simultaneously accessible and socially conscious. His early work reflects *Strangelove*'s radical impulses. The nonfiction *Insurrection* (1968) documented the Paris student revolts, which also inspired the rarely seen experimental short *Juanpuri* (1971). His interest in 1960s politics also surfaced in *Ali* (2001).

Mann's cinematic skills are readily discernible in his work; and, in the manner of many latter-day filmmakers, Mann often directs, writes, and produces his pictures. He uses a coterie of cast and crew (which has included two of the biggest names in American film acting, Robert De Niro and Al Pacino), and has perfected a powerfully expressive mise-en-scène. Many of his films contain distinctive color schemes, and he has used high-definition video in films and television shows such as *Ali*, *Robbery Homicide Division* (CBS, 2002–03), *Collateral* (2004), and *Miami Vice* (2006). As Mann makes clear, he uses the latter process not to reduce costs, as it does not, but because it enhances the specific qualities of the film image. Interestingly, his narratives are almost exclusively concerned with men who exist in morally decaying societies. He valorizes protagonists who obey a code of morality and duty, and demeans their antagonists who do not. Clashes between pairs of strong but divergent male characters drive the plots of *Manhunter* (1986), *Heat* (1995), *The Insider* (1999), and *Collateral*.

Mann's fondness for buddy narratives appears in his early television work. He wrote for *Starsky and Hutch* (ABC, 1975–79), and in 1979, he directed the made-for-television movie *The Jericho Mile*, about a Folsom State Prison inmate who was persuaded to try out for the Olympic track team. Committed to narrative realism, Mann employed several Folsom inmates as actors in this picture. The film proved popular with both viewers and critics, winning multiple Emmy Awards, including one for Mann's co-written script. Following the success of *Jericho Mile*, Mann became the executive producer for *Miami Vice* (NBC, 1984–89), a character-driven cop show that focused, rather atypically for the period, on moral questions. (In 2006, Mann directed the film version of *Miami Vice*.) Putting his stamp on the show, Mann helped to shape 1980s pop culture. Adopting an "MTV" aesthetic, consisting of glossy advertising images and a prominent soundtrack, *Miami Vice* provided audiences with glamorous characters and showcased pop songs, cutting-edge fashion, luxury brands, and Miami itself. The show's soundtrack topped the charts for months, and young men adopted the fashion sense of the leading male characters, marking the birth of the "metrosexual." Sonny Crockett's (Don Johnson) ensembles, including pastel T-shirts under expensive Italian suits and sockless loafers, remain emblematic of the decade.

In order to become intimately familiar with the literal, psychological, and emotional spaces that his characters inhabit, Mann does extensive research on his films. His obsessive attention to detail and procedural verisimilitude tends to be expressed in powerful and provocative ways in the cold, clinical, compulsive professionalism of his films' male characters. Even though he has not yet compiled an extensive filmography, the pictures that he has made reflect the painstaking work process that he employs.

Again, Mann's films tend to be character-driven examinations of angst-ridden men. This has remained the case even when he has ventured into the realm of the genre film. In his 1992 adaptation of James Fenimore Cooper's *The Last of the Mohicans*, for example, Mann produced what, on one level, was a traditional genre film, although he sought to trope the Eurocentrism that marked both the novel and other film adaptations of this literary work. Similarly, in *Heat*, Mann generally stayed with the framework of the conventional detective/gangster film, yet he also sought to expose the psychological and emotional wounds suffered by both the good cop (Al Pacino) and the bad criminal (Robert De Niro). This sense of depicting male characters marked by a certain tortured masculinity has become a trademark of Mann's films.

See also: Ali; Insider, The

Selected Filmography

Public Enemies (2009); *Miami Vice* (2006); *Ali* (2001); *The Insider* (1999); *Heat* (1995); *Last of the Mohicans* (1991); *Thief* (1981); *Insurrection* (1968)

References

Marc, David, and Robert J. Thompson. *Prime Time, Prime Movers*. Boston: Little, Brown, 1992.
Zoglin, Richard. "Cool Cops, Hot Show." *Time*, September 16, 1985: 61.

—*Gerald Sim*

MARX BROTHERS, THE. If you have never seen one of the Marx Brothers' movies, then stop reading and find a way to watch one—now. Not one of the tired later pictures like *Go West* (1940) when the brothers worked under the formulaic thumb of MGM, but an early MGM delight like *A Night at the Opera* (1935) before the formula had calcified. Or better yet one of their anarchic Paramount productions like *Horsefeathers* (1932), which will prove to you that the movies have lost their capacity to be this strange, this mad, and this funny.

If you *have* laughed at the Marx Brothers, then the only question that matters is what is your favorite Marx Brothers movie? For many it is *Duck Soup* (1933): Groucho as Rufus T. Firefly, leader of Freedonia, leading the whole cast as he sings "to war, to war/ to war we gotta go/ hi-dee hi-dee/ hi-dee hi-dee/ hi-dee hi-dee ho": it's one of the transcendent moments in the movies. If you are ever lucky enough to see it in a theater, stand in the back of the house and wait until the laughter rolls toward the screen in an explosive wave of joy that at times drowns the punch lines.

There were four of them (yes, brothers in real life), and then there were three when deceptively funny straight man Zeppo was shed after the brothers moved from Paramount to MGM in 1934. Their act could only have grown from vaudeville. Chico (Leonard by birth), the oldest, affected an Italian accent and played piano in a swaggering, finger-pointing style; Harpo (Adolph), mute (in the act, not in life), donned a curly wig, played the harp, and chased scantily clad women (not in life), behavior lewd enough in the pre-Code Paramount Pictures to lead some of the audience in repertory screenings in the 1930s to hiss the screen. Groucho (Julius Henry) used greasepaint to smear a huge mustache and eyebrows on his face and delivered a steady mixture of deadpan sarcasm, caustic insults, and brilliant wordplay; but if any of his jokes was worth a groan, he always let the audience know he knew it. By 1925, they had a Broadway hit, *The Cocoanuts*, written by George S. Kaufman with help from Morrie Ryskind and songs by Irving Berlin, and it ran 375 performances; it was turned into a dreadfully stagy early sound film in 1929. It was followed by another Broadway show, *Animal Crackers*, also by Kaufman and Ryskind, and it became their second dreadfully primitive and stagy early sound film in 1930. Small matter: the Marx Brothers could survive bad sound, and they *thrived* on clunky supporting acting; it was the slick studio work in their later MGM films that they couldn't overcome.

Irving Thalberg, chief of production at MGM, tried to shape their act by making them appear lovable to everyone except themselves and the tiffany studio's safely snooty villains. His meddling had mixed artistic and financial results: receipts for the Marx Brothers MGM films, even their most successful ones, indicate they never attained the box-office success of, say, Charlie Chaplin, or even the later Abbott and Costello. And the most loving fans will admit that of the 13 movies they made together, the 4 that were produced after 1940 are depressing. The old fizz flattened, exhaustion haunts the proceedings.

But as Clifton Fadiman put it in his rave review for *A Night at the Opera*, "the Marxes are quite funny enough to be taken seriously"; and while he flatly vowed not to construe "their impertinent treatment of the social properties . . . as a revolt against the constrictions of American life, or as proletarian propaganda" (1935, 322)—a

vow all true Marxists are willing to take—it's clear the Marx Brothers have shown to nearly every comic who has been influenced by them (and that includes Woody Allen and Jerry Seinfeld and Chris Rock and Jon Stewart) that the only way to combat the restrictions, class absurdities, and ethnic barriers of American life is to find a way to reiterate Groucho's declaration in *Duck Soup*: "This is war!"

The Marx Brothers, a team of sibling comedians, appeared in vaudeville, stage plays, film, and television in a successful career spanning five decades. Pictured from top to bottom are Zeppo, Harpo, Groucho, and Chico Marx. (Library of Congress)

References

Eyman, Scott. *Lion of Hollywood: The Life and Legend of Louis B. Mayer.* New York: Simon and Schuster, 2005.

Fadiman, Clifton. "A New High in Low Comedy." In Kauffmann, Stanley, ed. *American Film Criticism: Reviews of Significant Films at the Time They First Appeared.* New York: Liveright, 1972: 322–28.

Kanfer, Stefan. *Groucho: The Life and Times of Julius Henry Marx.* New York: Vintage, 2001.

—*Robert Cowgill*

MAY, ELAINE.   Elaine May began her rise to fame by performing in America's first improvisational theater, The Compass Theater (which evolved into The Second City). She became a household name in 1957 as half of Nichols and May, the comedy partnership she formed with Mike Nichols (who would later become known as a director of Broadway and Hollywood). In the 1970s and 1980s, she emerged as one of Hollywood's first and most successful female directors and screenwriters.

May was born Elaine Berlin on April 21, 1932, in Philadelphia. As a child, she performed on stage and on radio with her father, Jack Berlin, who led his own traveling Yiddish theatrical company. She studied acting under Maria Ouspenskaya before moving to Chicago to sit in on classes at the University of Chicago. There she involved herself in improvisational theater, where she met Nichols. Nichols and May utilized improvisational techniques in television and radio appearances before appearing on Broadway in a hit revue show, *An Evening with Mike Nichols and Elaine May* (1959). The pair produced three successful albums: *Improvisations to Music* (1958), *An Evening with Mike Nichols and Elaine May* (1960), and *Nichols and May Examine Doctors* (1963). Nichols and May exposed clichéd 1950s American middle-class attitudes toward sex, gender, class, race, celebrity, psychoanalysis, the arts, and more.

May's career as a film director began in 1971 with *A New Leaf*, which she also wrote and starred in (and for which she was nominated for a Golden Globe Award for Best Actress). She plays Henrietta, a dizzy heiress and botanist who becomes the target of a bankrupt playboy, played by Walter Matthau. She followed in 1972 with *The Heartbreak Kid*, based on a screenplay by Neil Simon. The story follows a nice Jewish boy (Charles Grodin) who marries a shrill, stereotypical Jewish American Princess (played by May's daughter, Jeannie Berlin). On their honeymoon, he falls for his blonde fantasy shiksa (Cybill Shepherd), inspiring a series of humorous deceptions.

Her next feature, *Mikey and Nicky* (1976), starred John Cassavetes as a nervous small-time crook who contacts his old friend, played by Peter Falk, to help him evade a hitman (Ned Beatty). The narrative extends over the course of one night, as the men descend into the dark recesses of Philadelphia's back alleys. The film made extensive use of improvisation, and legendary acting teachers Sanford Meisner and William Hickey appear in cameos as mob bosses. The raw sensibility of May's direction and the improvised performances make the film more about male friendship and the psychology of American masculinity than a traditional gangster picture. May clashed with studio executives over the final edit. It was not until a decade after its initial release that audiences were able to view May's preferred version.

Ishtar (1987) was the final film May directed. Although the film has gained a cult following for its Orwellian vision, critics and audiences at the time rejected it. Dustin Hoffman and Warren Beatty (who also served as producer) play untalented musical lounge performers who book an engagement in the fictional nation of Ishtar. There they become entangled in a political revolution when the CIA enlists them to interfere with a plot to overthrow Ishtar's government.

As an actress, May also appeared in *Enter Laughing* (Carl Reiner, 1967); *Luv* (Clive Donner, 1967); *In the Spirit* (Sandra Seacat, 1990), co-written by Berlin; and *Small Time Crooks* (Woody Allen, 2000).

Beginning with the 1969 Drama Desk Award for Most Promising Playwright (for *Adaptation*), May has also enjoyed success as a writer. For the screen, she co-wrote *Heaven Can Wait* with Warren Beatty (Beatty and Buck Henry, 1978). She also contributed to the scripts of *Such Good Friends* (Otto Preminger, 1971), *Reds* (Warren Beatty, 1981), *Tootsie* (Sydney Pollack, 1982), and *Labyrinth* (Jim Henson, 1986). She reunited with Nichols by writing screenplays for *The Birdcage* (1996) and *Primary Colors* (1998), both of which he directed. May was nominated for an Academy Award for her work on *Heaven Can Wait* and *Primary Colors*, for which she won a British Academy of Film and Television Award. She has been nominated for three Writer's Guild of America awards, and has won one, for *Heaven Can Wait*.

Selected Filmography

Down to Earth (2001); *Primary Colors* (1998); *The Birdcage* (1996); *Ishtar* (1987); *Labyrinth* (1986); *Tootsie* (1982); *Reds* (1981); *Heaven Can Wait* (1978); *Mikey and Nicky* (1976); *Such Good Friends* (1971); *A New Leaf* (1971); *Bach to Bach* (1967)

References

Kercher, Stephen. *Revel with a Cause: Liberal Satire in Postwar America*. Chicago: University of Chicago Press, 2006.
Probst, Leonard. *Off Camera: Leveling about Themselves*. New York: Stein and Day, 1975.
Sweet, Jeffrey. *Something Wonderful Right Away: An Oral History of The Second City and The Compass Players*. New York: Limelight, 2003.

—*Kyle Stevens*

MCDANIEL, HATTIE. Hattie McDaniel—singer; songwriter; radio, stage, and film actress—is best known for her role as "Mammy" in the David O. Selznick movie *Gone with the Wind* (1939). This role earned her the honor of being the first African American to be nominated for an Academy Award; when she won the Oscar for Best Supporting Actress, she became the first African American to win an Academy Award. She was also the first African American woman to sing on radio and the first African American Academy Award winner to appear on a U.S. stamp. McDaniel had a prolific career in film. She appeared in well over 100 productions, usually as a domestic, and was befriended by some of the leading stars of her day, including Clark Gable, who routinely attended parties at McDaniel's home and who worked with her on several films (Watts, 2007). Believing she deserved to be buried in Hollywood Cemetery, she requested this honor in her will; when she died in 1952, the owner of the cemetery refused McDaniel's request, pointing out that African Americans were not allowed to be buried there.

Hattie McDaniel was born on June 10, 1895, in Wichita, Kansas, to Civil War veteran Henry McDaniel and Susan Holbert, a former slave (Jackson, 1993). She was the youngest of 13 children. The McDaniel family moved to Colorado in 1900, and Hattie was raised in Denver. She and her brothers Sam and Chris eventually began touring with their father's Henry McDaniel Minstrel Show. In 1910, she won an award for reciting a poem at a Women's Christian Temperance Union event, and this contributed to her desire to perform. In 1920, she joined a popular all-black band called George Morrison's Jazz Orchestra and toured with them through 1925. Her radio career began on KOA radio station in Denver. She appeared in a touring company of "Showboat" as the character "Queenie" from 1929 to 1930. McDaniel joined her brother Sam, who had become a film actor, and sisters Etta and Orlena in Los Angeles in 1931. She teamed with Sam on KNX radio, playing the bossy maid "Hi-Hat Hattie" on *The Optimistic Do-Nut Hour*.

McDaniel secured her first film role in *The Golden West* (1932); she followed this picture with appearances in *Love Bound*, *Impatient Maid*, and *Are You Listening?*, all of which were released in 1932. She joined the Screen Actors Guild (SAG) in 1934, and in 1935 the Fox Film Corporation offered her a contract to appear in *The Little Colonel* with Shirley Temple and Bill "Bojangles" Robinson. Amazingly, she appeared in 70 films in the 1930s alone. She was routinely cast as a maid, nanny, cook, or servant in these films (Bogle, 1994). Although she would win an Oscar for her role in *Gone with the Wind*, McDaniel, along with the other African American actors who appeared in the picture, was barred from the film's 1939 Atlanta, Georgia, premiere. Protests by David O. Selznick and Clarke Gable fell on deaf ears. Even after she took home the Academy Award in 1940, she continued to be cast as a domestic throughout her career.

McDaniel was active in film and then in television throughout the 1940s. During this period in her career, she co-starred in pictures such as *In This Our Life*

Hattie McDaniel plays a tune as she portrays the title role of *Beulah* in the CBS Radio Network's comedy series in New York City, 1951. (AP/Wide World Photos)

(1942), with Bette Davis, and *Since You Went Away* (1944). Her last film appearances were in *Mickey* and *Family Honeymoon*, both of which were released in 1949. She starred in *The Beulah Show* on radio in 1947; the show was later adapted for TV and shown on ABC during 1950s. McDaniel was diagnosed with breast cancer in 1951, having appeared in only a few episodes of the television version of *The Beulah Show*. She died from the disease on October 26, 1952, in Woodland Hills, California.

One of the most important contributors to the development of American radio and film, McDaniel was a trailblazer, opening the way for future African American actresses (Jackson, 1993). She has two stars on the Hollywood Walk of Fame, one for her contributions to film and another for her accomplishments in radio.

References

Bogle, Donald. *Toms, Coons, Mulattoes, Mammies, and Bucks: An Interpretive History of Blacks in American Film.* New York: Continuum, 1994.

Jackson, Carlton. *Hattie: The Life of Hattie McDaniel.* Lanham: Rowman & Littlefield, 1993.
Watts, Jill. *Hattie McDaniel: Black Ambition, White Hollywood.* New York: HarperCollins, 2007.

—*Hettie Williams*

MÉLIÈS, GEORGES. Marie-Georges-Jean Méliès (December 8, 1861–January 21, 1938) was a crucial figure in the development of motion pictures. Méliès, the youngest son of a wealthy French family, was a man of startling artistic virtuosity who introduced seminal changes to early filmmaking. Charlie Chaplin appropriately called him "the alchemist of light."

A talented man with a classical education, Méliès began his career drawing caricatures under the anagrammatic pseudonym "Geo Smile" for the satirical journal *La Griffe.* Attracted by the subversive dream-world of the stage, he bought the Théâtre Robert-Houdin in 1888, where he worked as director, inventor, performer, producer, conjurer, and designer until 1895, establishing himself as a successful and respected personality in the Parisian entertainment world. Enchanted by the Lumière brothers' show at the Grand Café in 1895, Méliès wanted to purchase a cinematograph but Antoine Lumière refused to sell him one. A year later, Méliès constructed his own camera modeled after R. W. Paul's cinematic device, built the first European glass-structure film studio, and began the production of his own films.

Méliès understood that a movie is more than a simple process of reality recording. Unlike the Lumière brothers, who saw film as no more than a scientific curiosity employed in the mimesis of the world, Méliès recognized the artistic, entertaining, and narrative potential of movies. He combined theatrical skills and filmmaking, turning from being a conjuror of the stage into a magician of the screen. Méliès realized that film as new technology was to make magic shows available for large audiences in a place that combined the technical potential of the film medium with the artistic values of the theater: the film theater.

He created the basic grammar of special effects and trick pictures in movies. Méliès used the reversal of time, the split screen, the overlapping process, the double and multiple exposure, time-lapse, and the dissolve process; he was the first to shoot the stop trick, afterwards used in *Disappearance of a Lady* (1896). The stop trick and the time-lapse were techniques that later would create the need for professional film cutters. Long before Technicolor's three-color pellicle format, Méliès had his own color films, which were manufactured by 21 women employed at a special studio to hand-tint his films individually, frame by frame.

Méliès was, at the turn of the twentieth century, the most inventive filmmaker in the world. Today he can be considered the first cinematic auteur. His early films were groundbreaking artifacts that have influenced mainstream and avant-garde filmmakers alike. The 14-minute epic *A Trip to the Moon* (1902) was the first movie in film history to employ animation; together with *Impossible Voyage* (1904) it was the precursor of science fiction and fantasy films. *The Devil's Manor* (1896) is the prototype of thriller and horror films, while the reconstructed reality of the *Dreyfus Affair* (1899) posits Méliès as the pioneer of the docudrama.

The films of Méliès enjoyed enormous worldwide popularity and began to be plagiarized. In 1903, he decided to fight his film imitators in America—where copies of *A Voyage to the Moon* were widely pirated—by opening his STAR-FILM company in New York to rent his films. This investment failed because his small company was incapable of fighting the intensifying commercialism of the rapidly growing film industry. Despite his active involvement in early cinema, Méliès finally went bankrupt.

Fewer than 140 of his 520 films survive. A considerable number of valuable movies were melted down during World War I in order to produce a chemical for the manufacturing of boot heels needed by the French army; in addition, in a moment of financial and emotional crisis, Méliès destroyed a batch of his film negatives and sold his remaining stock of prints by the kilogram to a second-hand film dealer in 1923.

In 1931, Méliès was awarded the Legion of Honor by the French Government. Twenty-two years later, Georges Franju produced, with the assistance of the Méliès family, a stylish bio-documentary entitled *Le Grande Méliès* in which he pays tribute to the first wizard of cinema, who created a coherent artistic world of blissful escapism in films.

See also: Silent Era, The

References

Bawden, Liz-Anne, ed. *The Oxford Companion to Film*. New York: Oxford University Press, 1976: 459–60.

Cook, David A. *A History of Narrative Film*, 2nd ed. New York and London: W. W. Norton, 1990: 16–20.

Gronemeyer, Andrea. *Film: A Concise History*. London: Laurence King Publishing, 1999: 30–31.

Kracauer, Siegfried. "Basic Concepts." In Braudy, Leo, and Marshall Cohen, eds. *Film Theory and Criticism. Introductory Readings*, 5th ed. New York: Oxford University Press, 1999: 171–82.

—*Réka M. Cristian*

MICHEAUX, OSCAR. Novelist, producer, director, and actor, Oscar Micheaux was the first African American to produce a feature-length film (1919) and a sound feature-length film (1920). He was also one of the first African Americans to write a best-selling novel—*The Case of Mrs. Wingate* (1943), which sold 55,000 copies. Micheaux, active primarily from 1919 to 1948, participated in more than 40 film productions as a writer, director, producer, or actor. Upon his death on March 25, 1951, in Charlotte, North Carolina, it was noted that of the 82 all-black films made to date, Micheaux was responsible for creating more than half of them. Having served as a Pullman porter and a homesteader in the American West, he was also a pioneering black filmmaker during the Harlem Renaissance era (1919–1934). His films were often classified as "race films" because he challenged the stereotypical depictions of

African Americans presented in the popular pictures of the day while maintaining a black visual iconography and giving expression to a more positive representation of "blackness" (Bowser, Gaines, and Musser, 2001).

Micheaux was born January 2, 1884, in Metropolis, Illinois, one of 13 children. His parents were former slaves. He was raised in Great Bend, Kansas. Leaving home at age 17, he made his way to Chicago, where he became a Pullman rail car porter. Influenced by the self-help philosophy of Booker T. Washington, he moved West with thousands of other African Americans at the end of the nineteenth century. He became a homesteader, eventually acquiring a 160-acre plot of land in Gregory County, South Dakota, in 1905 (McGilligan, 2008).

Micheaux published his first novel in 1913. Titled *The Conquest: The Story of a Negro Pioneer*, it was based on his experience as a homesteader. This book became the basis of a later cinematic work. Micheaux often wrote his life story into the narrative structure of his films, thereby documenting the historical experience of African Americans through personal biography (Bowser, Spencer, 2000). In 1915, he lost his farm due to financial hardship; he relocated to Sioux City, Iowa, where he established the Western Book Supply Company. He continued to write, self-publishing and selling his novels door-to-door. Micheaux wrote the novels *The Forged Note* in 1915 and *The Homesteader* in 1917. He made Western Book Supply viable by selling stock in the company to businessmen and farmers in Sioux City. After rejecting an offer from African American filmmakers George and Noble Johnson—owners of the Los Angeles-based Lincoln Motion Picture Company—to make *The Homesteader* into a film, Micheaux transformed his Western Book Supply Company into the Micheaux Film and Book Company. Through his fund-raising efforts, he secured enough capital to develop *The Homesteader* himself. The film premiered February 20, 1919; it was the first feature-length picture developed by an African American (Cripps, 1977).

Micheaux is recognized as an important personality in American filmmaking for several reasons. His films were both controversial and progressive for the times during which they were produced. The African American newspaper *The Chicago Defender* heralded the coming of a "new epoch" in black culture with the premiere of *The Homesteader* in 1919. Micheaux directly challenged prevailing racial attitudes with his productions. His picture *Within Our Gates*, released in 1920, was a direct challenge to the romanticized depiction of the Ku Klux Klan presented in D. W. Griffith's 1915 film *The Birth of a Nation*. Griffith's film is often lauded as a cinematic masterpiece, but it aroused a great deal of criticism from the African American community due to its blatant stereotypes of blacks. Micheaux's response was an attempt to showcase a more realistic depiction of white supremacy and the brutality leveled at African Americans in the South. Micheaux also sought to highlight controversial racial issues in *Body and Soul*, released in 1924. The story of *Body and Soul* concerned a corrupt minister, played by Paul Robeson (1898–1976), an African American performer who was introduced to movie audiences in this film, who beats and rapes a black woman. Micheaux's 1931 picture *The Exile* was the first sound feature-length film created by an African American.

Oscar Micheaux produced and directed 44 movies and wrote a total of seven novels including *The Winds from Nowhere* (1941), *The Case of Mrs. Wingate* (1943), *The Story of Dorothy Stanfield* (1946), and *Masquerade, a Historical Novel* (1947). He has been recognized by both the Producers Guild of America, which honored his work by creating the Oscar Micheaux Award, and the Directors Guild of America, which acknowledged his work by creating the Golden Jubilee Special Award in 1986. Micheaux is recognized by many as one of the most influential African Americans in American history. As a writer, director, and producer of American films, he embodied the self-help ethic central to the development of the black experience in America.

Selected Filmography

The Betrayal (1948); *The Notorious Elinor Lee* (1940); *God's Step Children* (1938); *Swing!* (1938); *Underworld* (1937/I); *Murder in Harlem* (1935); *Harlem after Midnight* (1934); *The Exile* (1931); *Darktown Revue* (1931); *Wages of Sin* (1929); *The Millionaire* (1927); *The Spider's Web* (1927); *The Broken Violin* (1927); *The House behind the Cedars* (1927); *Body and Soul* (1925); *The Gunsaulus Mystery* (1921); *The Symbol of the Unconquered* (1920); *The Brute* (1920); *Within Our Gates* (1920); *The Homesteader* (1919)

References

Bowser, Pearl, and Louise Spence. *Writing Himself into History: Oscar Micheaux, His Silent Films, and His Audiences.* New Brunswick, NJ: Rutgers University Press, 2000.

Bowser, Pearl, Jane Marie Gaines, and Charles Musser, eds. *Oscar Micheaux and His Circle: African American Filmmaking and Race Cinema of the Silent Era.* Bloomington: Indiana University Press, 2001.

Cripps, Thomas. *Slow Fade to Black: The Negro in American Film, 1900–1942.* Oxford, UK: Oxford University Press, 1977.

Green, J. Ronald. *With a Crooked Stick: The Films of Oscar Micheaux.* Bloomington: Indiana University Press, 2004.

McGilligan, Patrick. *Oscar Micheaux, the Great and Only: The Life of America's First Black Filmmaker.* New York: HarperCollins, 2008.

—*Hettie Williams*

MILLER, ARTHUR. Arthur Miller is primarily remembered for writing plays that deal with tortured individuals facing what might be understood as existential injustice, but early in his career he was connected with the film industry. That connection grew as his career progressed, partially because his plays were turned into films and partially because he married movie star Marilyn Monroe. Although he eventually saw his screenplays produced for television and the big screen, he never committed himself fully to the cinematic community.

Arthur Miller was born on October 17, 1915, in New York City. He began making a name for himself as a playwright while attending college in Michigan in the 1930s, winning the Avery Hopwood Award twice and the Theatre Guild National Award. After college, he returned to New York and took a job at the Brooklyn Navy Yard. In

Arthur Miller, along with William Inge and Tennessee Williams, was an influential voice in the American theater in the 1950s. His best works are characterized by concerns for societal problems and a passion for social liberation. (Library of Congress)

his spare time, he wrote radio scripts for *The Dupont Cavalcade of America*, a weekly serial broadcast on NBC, among other programs. In 1944, he began to expand his horizons, signing a contract to do research for the script of *The Story of G.I. Joe* (1945), based on the war correspondence of Ernie Pyle. Although he was not credited for his work on the film script, he did turn his research into a book, *Situation Normal* (1944). The following year he published the novel *Focus*, which was ultimately adapted for the screen in 2001; he also found success on the stage with the plays *All My Sons* (1947) and *Death of a Salesman* (1949), both of which were adapted as films, the first in 1948 and the second in 1951.

Late in the 1940s, Miller completed a screenplay that bore the title *The Hook*. The script was rejected by studio executives, even though Miller's friend, the influential Elia Kazan, who had directed *All My Sons* and *Salesman* on stage, pushed to have it made. The script was thought too "leftist" for the Cold War times—too "communist"—as it suggested that America's workers were being exploited by their capitalist employers. Interestingly, even though Kazan had pushed to have Miller's screenplay made into a movie, he went on to testified before the House Un-American Activities Committee (HUAC), informing on "communist colleagues" and damaging his friendship with Miller. Miller's plays continued to be adapted for television throughout the 1950s. Significantly, one of them, *The Crucible* (1953), turned the Salem witch trials of the 1690s into an allegory of the HUAC hearings.

Cognizant that he could be caught up in the political controversies of the day, and seeking to avoid charges that his work was merely a veiled attempt to indict figures such as Joseph McCarthy in the court of public opinion, Miller had sought to make *The Crucible* as historically accurate as possible. Nevertheless, he developed a reputation as a political dissident, and HUAC influence prevented him from making a movie about juvenile delinquency in 1955. The following year, shortly after he married Monroe, he was called to testify before HUAC and was convicted of contempt of Congress for refusing to cooperate; the conviction was ultimately overturned on appeal. Monroe stood by Miller during his trouble with HUAC, even though she had been warned by Hollywood insiders that she should distance herself from her husband. Miller also stood by Monroe, even as her insecurities led her to suffer mood swings, to abuse drugs and alcohol, and to become increasingly unhappy. Attempting to lift her spirits, Miller adapted his story "The Misfits" into a screenplay and a star vehicle for Monroe; by the time *The Misfits* arrived in theaters, however, Miller and Monroe had divorced. He married the Hollywood photographer Inge Morath in 1962, six months before Monroe died of a drug overdose.

After his marriage to Monroe ended, Miller largely devoted himself to writing for the theater. He did remain tangentially connected to the film industry, however. For example, his play *After the Fall* (1964)—a statement about both HUAC and his first two wives—was adapted for the screen in 1964. He also wrote screenplays for television projects in the 1970s and 1980s—*Fame* (1978), about a playwright's overnight success, and *Playing for Time* (1980), an adaptation of Fania Fenelon's Holocaust memoirs—and the screenplay for the movie *Everybody Wins* (1984), a hard-boiled detective film about corruption in a Connecticut town. He also adapted *The Crucible* for the 1995 film version of the play. Yet Miller remained first and foremost a playwright—certainly one of America's greatest. He died on February 10, 2005, a respected man of letters.

References

Abbotson, Susan C. W. *Student Companion to Arthur Miller.* Westport, CT: Greenwood, 2000.
Gottfried, Martin. *Arthur Miller: His Life and Work.* Cambridge, MA: Da Capo, 2004.
Miller, Arthur. *Timebends: A Life.* New York: Grove Press, 1987.

—Albert Rolls

MONROE, MARILYN. Marilyn Monroe became a global sex symbol as a result of playing coquettish blondes in mid-1950s Hollywood movies. Born Norma Jean Mortenson on June 1, 1926, she was baptized Norma Jean Baker, the surname of her mother's ex-husband. After her mother was committed to a mental institution, Monroe lived in a series of foster homes. The last of these was run by family friends Grace and Erwin Goddard, with whom Monroe lived until she was 15. Facing reassignment to another foster home when the Goddards decided to relocate to a different area, the teenage Monroe married James Dougherty, a 21-year-old neighbor, to avoid her fate. The marriage disintegrated after Dougherty joined the Merchant Marines in 1944, and Monroe took a job at airplane factory. While working at the factory, she was discovered by photographer David Conover; she eventually became a model and came to the attention of Hollywood studio executives.

Movie legend Marilyn Monroe, appearing with the USO Camp Show "Anything Goes," poses for photos after a performance at the Third U.S. Infantry Division area in Korea on February 17, 1954. (National Archives and Records Administration)

Near the end of the summer of 1946, Monroe signed a contract with Twentieth Century-Fox. Shortly afterwards, Norma Jean Baker bleached her hair blonde and changed her name to Marilyn Monroe. For the next few years, she played a series of small parts in movies such as *The Shocking Miss Pilgrim* (1947), *Love Happy* (1949), and *A Ticket to Tomahawk* (1950). Larger parts in *The Asphalt Jungle* (1950) and *All about Eve* (1950) earned her fans and the attention of critics; a number of more visible roles followed, including the lead in *Don't Bother to Knock* (1952). Her performance in *Niagara* (1953), as a wife plotting to kill her husband, propelled her to stardom and began to establish her as a major sex symbol of the silver screen. Monroe became Hollywood's preeminent "Blond Bombshell" after *Gentlemen Prefer Blondes* and *How to Marry a Millionaire* were released in 1953.

Monroe married New York Yankee superstar Joe DiMaggio at the beginning of 1954; the marriage did not last, however, largely because of Monroe's sex-symbol status and DiMaggio's insecurity. Monroe's career had taken off, and even a stilted performance in *River of No Return* (1954) and the negative box-office figures of *There's No Business Like Show Business* (1954) could not derail it. Repeatedly cast as the sexy, dimwitted blond, however—a type she once again portrayed in 1955's *The Seven Year Itch*—Monroe became disheartened. In an effort to escape that image and become a serious screen performer, she travelled to New York City and studied at Lee Strasberg's Actors Studio. While in New York, she met playwright Arthur Miller, whom she married in 1956. That same year she returned to Hollywood and starred in *Bus Stop* (1956), a film partially financed by her own production company, Marilyn Monroe Productions. Her character in that film, Cherrie, was the first well-rounded filmic figure that she had portrayed; critics and moviegoers alike appreciated the change in her screen persona.

Bus Stop was followed by *The Prince and the Showgirl* (1957), the only movie entirely produced by Marilyn Monroe Productions; it co-starred Laurence Olivier, who also directed. Monroe again played a showgirl, Elsie Marina, but an intelligent one who controls much of the film's action. Although the picture failed at the box office, Monroe's performance earned her a David Di Donatello Award, the Italian Academy Award. In 1959, Monroe appeared as Sugar Kane Kowalczyk in *Some Like It Hot*. Playing opposite Tony Curtis and Jack Lemmon, Monroe starred as a singer in an all-girl band infiltrated by two men in drag, who are hiding from the mob after witnessing the St Valentine's Day Massacre. It was the most successful film of her career and won her a Golden Globe.

Her next film, *Let's Make Love* (1960), based on a terrible script that Monroe was forced to accept by Fox, was a flop. Worse, her life seemed to be unraveling; she had been using prescription drugs to escape her insecurities for years but was now suicidal. Miller had attempted to help by adapting his story "The Misfits" into a screenplay for her, but when *The Misfits* (1961) appeared, their marriage was over. She did not live to finish her next film, *Something's Got to Give* (1962). Monroe was found dead on August 5, 1962, having overdosed on barbiturates.

References

Churchwell, Sarah Bartlett. *The Many Lives of Marilyn Monroe*. New York: Macmillan, 2005.
Leaming, Barbara. *Marilyn Monroe*. New York: Crown, 1998.
Rollyson, Carl Edmund. *Marilyn Monroe: A Life of the Actress*. Cambridge, MA: Da Capo, 1993.

—*Albert Rolls*

MOORE, MICHAEL. A talented yet controversial figure, Michael Moore uses his films to promote his worldview and challenge the status quo. A self-described populist, Moore has long been interested in social activism and fights fervently for his causes.

Born April 23, 1954, in Flint, Michigan, where his father worked for General Motors, Moore was raised in nearby Davison. Growing up, Moore was a highly motivated student, winning a library award for reading more books than any other seven-year-old. Raised in a blue-collar Catholic family, his first foray into politics came in 1972, when he won a seat on the local school board. Following high school, Moore started an area hotline for people struggling with issues related to unwanted pregnancies, drug addiction, and suicidal thoughts; he also began publishing *Free to Be*, a community newspaper. After dropping out of the University of Michigan, Moore

started *The Flint Voice*—which became *The Michigan Voice* in 1982—as a liberal alternative to the conservative *Flint Journal*. A National Public Radio commentator by the time he was 31, Moore became editor of the progressive magazine *Mother Jones* in 1986; he was fired a short time after taking the position. While details of his dismissal are unclear, Moore received a $58,000 wrongful dismissal settlement, although *Mother Jones* never publicly admitted any wrongdoing. Moore used the settlement monies to fund his first full-length documentary, *Roger & Me* (1989).

Roger & Me details Moore's failed attempts to interview Roger Smith, then CEO of General Motors, about the company's closure of its plant in Flint. Moore depicted company officials as hardhearted bureaucrats who cared nothing about their employees or about the community; he even went so far as to blame General Motors for the economic woes plaguing his hometown. Holding the film's premiere at

Michael Moore, American filmmaker and liberal political activist (1954–). (Shutterstock)

Flint's Rainbow Cinemas, he donated a large portion of the proceeds to the community. In 1994, Moore created *TV Nation*, a television program devoted to political satire. The program fed his next film, *Canadian Bacon* (1995), a narrative comedy in which the President (Alan Alda) attempts to cast Canada as an American enemy. The film did not do well in the United States, but was well received in Canada.

Moore's next documentary, *Bowling for Columbine* (2002), tackled gun control. Moore argued for stricter regulations while criticizing the National Rifle Association, President George W. Bush, and the media for creating a culture of violence through fomenting fear. The film became the top-grossing documentary of all time, and won the 2003 Best Documentary Oscar. During his acceptance speech, Moore openly criticized President Bush; his comments elicited mixed reactions from audience members.

His vehement disapproval of Bush administration policies led him to make *Fahrenheit 9/11* (2004). While critical of Bush's policies in general, the film focused on the administration's decision to invade Iraq in 2003. Despite winning the top prize at the Cannes Film Festival, Disney-owned Miramax, Moore's distributor, dropped the project before the film was released in the United States. Miramax executives cited what they said was Moore's politically motivated decision to release the film in the midst of the 2004 presidential campaign, claiming that he was attempting to influence the election. Interestingly, Moore accused Miramax of playing politics, claiming that studio heads had actually been pressured by Florida Governor Jeb Bush, the president's brother. Ironically, the controversy only increased interest in the film, which ended up grossing $222 million worldwide, surpassing *Bowling for Columbine* as the all-time highest-grossing documentary.

Moore continued to push for social reform in the projects that followed *Bowling for Columbine*. In *Sicko* (2007), for instance, he examined what he believes is the critical state of the American health care industry, suggesting that the United States desperately needs some form of universal health care; and in *Capitalism: A Love Story* (2009), he explored the faltering economy that accompanied the 2008 election.

Moore's commercial success can be attributed to his unique cinematic style. Relentlessly making his case—his critics, and even his supporters, point out that his films are hardly representative of objective documentary filmmaking—Moore manages to inject his films with a great deal of humour. His goal, it seems, is not to present a balanced discussion of an issue, but rather to provoke an emotional response from viewers in order to convince them of his side of the argument.

Although Moore has proven to be a polarizing figure, he has nevertheless become the most successful documentary filmmaker in cinematic history. Undaunted by his critics, Moore continues to champion his causes and, in the process, to produce entertaining and controversial films.

Selected Filmography

Capitalism: A Love Story (2009); *Slacker Uprising* (2007); *Fahrenheit 9/11* (2004); *Bowling for Columbine* (2002); *The Big One* (1997); *Canadian Bacon* (1995); *Roger & Me* (1989)

References

Larner, Jesse. *Moore and Us: One Man's Quest for a New World Order*. London: Sanctuary, 2005.

Rapoport, Roger. *Citizen Moore: The Life and Times of an American Iconoclast*. Muskegon, MI: RDR Books, 2007.

Schultz, Emily. *Michael Moore: A Biography*. Toronto: ECW Press, 2005.

—*Sean Graham*

MULVEY, LAURA.   Laura Mulvey is a filmmaker, film historian, and theorist best known for her contributions to feminist film theory.

Mulvey was born August 15, 1941 in Oxford, UK. From 1960 to 1963, she attended St. Hilda's College, University of Oxford, receiving an honors bachelor's degree in history. After writing a number of essays on psychoanalysis and film theory, as well as venturing into filmmaking, in 1975 she published "Visual Pleasure and Narrative Cinema" in *Screen* magazine.

Influenced by theorists such as Christian Metz, who used psychoanalytic theory to establish a relationship between the viewer and the camera (usually referred to as "Apparatus Theory"), the essay attempted to explain how women are seen through the lens, and, by extension, how men and women are conditioned to view women. According to Mulvey, the subjectivity of cinema is almost invariably male. Therefore, cinema is a place where women are denied independence of thought and motion. Women become a spectacle whose purpose is almost exclusively defined in sexual terms. Female sexuality is given only a passive space in cinema, where women are characterized as preferring to be looked at than to look themselves. It is from this essay that the concept of the domineering "male gaze" became widely introduced into film and media studies.

Mulvey applies her theory of male-dominated cinematic scopophilia to textual analysis. Discussing Joseph von Sternberg's relationship with Marlene Dietrich, Mulvey states that his films are "one-dimensional" in their fetishizing of Dietrich's form. This erotic worship allows the male viewer a pure appreciation of sexual difference without the castration anxiety that Freud explored. Alternatively, Alfred Hitchcock provided a "more complex" scopophilia, both fetishizing the female form in a manner similar to Sternberg's and reducing it through either voyeurism or sadism. In the case of both directors, female stars were invariably weakened through the cinematic process.

Subsequent pieces clarified her position on the very polemical essay. She expanded her theoretical viewer to include multiple perspectives and even, functioning as more of a film historian than theorist, uncover areas of more complex female spectatorship. Avant-garde works, such as *Meshes of the Afternoon* by Maya Deren, and certain more mainstream works, such as Douglas Sirk's melodramas and the films of Rudolph Valentino, provided at least some space for women viewers.

Mulvey also directed, from 1974 to 1983, six films with her partner Peter Wollen, also a film theorist. The films were intended to apply their theoretical explorations to film production. They were known for confronting the concept of male spectatorship and denying traditional cinematic pleasures and viewer passivity.

Riddles of the Sphinx (1977) consists of a 13 360-degree shots of different environments, using cinema's ability to create a "psychic" space to find new spaces for women. *Amy!* (1980) examines British aviatrix Amy Johnson using a jarring, cinematic collage approach. It has been called an "antidocumentary." *Crystal Gazing* (1982) is known as Wollen and Mulvey's most conventional film, about Thatcherite Britain's social conservatism and economic decline.

Mulvey has since expanded into a number of new theoretical and disciplinary arenas. In 1991, she returned to filmmaking with *Disgraced Monuments*, about the fate of communist imagery after the fall of the Berlin Wall. Her contribution to the British Film Institute's Film Classics series of short monographs was on *Citizen Kane*. Her writing was heavily historical, not theoretical, in its intent to use the film as a barometer of American political thinking on the verge of WWII. The Criterion DVD release of Michael Powell's *Peeping Tom* (1960) included Mulvey reading a short essay of appreciation for the film.

In 2006, Mulvey published a book of essays, *Death Twenty-Four Times a Second: Stillness and the Moving Image*. She is currently Professor of Film and Media Studies at Birkbeck College, University of London.

See also: Feminist Film Criticism; Male Gaze, The

References

Burke, Eleanor. "Laura Mulvey." *Screen Online*, 2003. http://www.screenonline.org.uk/people/id/566978/index.html.

Hill, John, and Gibson, Pamela Church, eds. *The Oxford Guide to Film Studies*. New York: Oxford University Press, 1998

Mulvey, Laura. "Visual Pleasure and Narrative Cinema." *Screen* 16(3), Autumn 1975.

Murphy, Robert. *Directors in British and Irish Cinema: A Reference Companion*. London: British Film Institute, 2006.

Reynolds, Lucy. "Riddles of the Sphinx." *Screen Online*, 2003. http://www.screenonline.org.uk/film/id/567526/index.html.

—*Alan C. Abbott*

MURNAU, F. W. Friedrich Wilhelm Murnau was a prominent German film director of the 1920s. During a brief career spanning only 12 years, Murnau was credited with pioneering many of the techniques still used in film today.

Murnau was born Friedrich Wilhelm Plumpe on December 28, 1888, in Bielefeld, Westphalia, to a family of Swedish ancestry. His education included time spent at universities in Heidelberg and Berlin, where he studied art history, literature, and philosophy. It is during this period of his life that he came under the influence of director Max Reinhardt (*Deutsches Theatre*) and decided to pursue a career in acting. A subsequent rift between father and son caused by this decision resulted in Friedrich changing his name to Murnau (after a Bavarian town) and the father cutting the son off financially. It was only through the help of his grandfather that Plumpe (now Murnau) was able to complete his education (Wakeman, 1987). With the outbreak of World War I, Murnau served first in the infantry on the Russian front and later in the air corps as a pilot. Forced to land in Switzerland during a heavy fog, he was interned there for the remainder of the conflict.

Murnau's initial foray into film occurred during his Swiss internment, where he worked on propaganda films for the German embassy. At the end of the conflict he returned to Berlin and formed a film company with actor Conrad Veidt (Murnau Veidt Filmgesellschaft). Murnau's directorial debut came in the 1919 production of

Onboard the *Demeter*, the vampire Count Orlok, played by German actor Max Schreck (1879–1936), emerges from one of his coffins before they can be destroyed by the ship's first mate, played by Wolfgang Heinz, in a scene from F. W. Murnau's expressionist horror film *Nosferatu, Eine Symphonie Des Grauens*, 1921. The film is based on Bram Stoker's novel *Dracula* and was released in 1922. (Hulton Archive/Getty Images)

Der Knabe in Blau (*The Blue Boy*). This interpretation of a Gothic melodrama introduced techniques such as the inventive use of light and space and the use of the camera to interpret character emotions that would reappear over the course of his career (Mauro, 1997).

Of the 21 films directed by Murnau, the most influential was *Nosferatu* (1922). During an age when most films were still done on soundstages, Murnau deliberately chose to shoot on location in order to achieve a greater sense of realism. To further enhance the film's supernatural mood, he drew upon expressionist film techniques such as the use of shadows and light as well as stop-action and accelerated motion. *Nosferatu* is considered one of the classic works of the German Expressionist film genre and the benchmark by which all subsequent vampire films are measured.

From 1924 to 1926, Murnau directed three films for UFA Studios: *Der letzte Mann* (*The Last Laugh*), *Tartuffe* (1926), and *Faust* (1926). The release of these films continued not only to solidify his reputation as a director in Germany, but also to earn him international recognition. A combination of factors, including problems in his personal life and the financial failure of *Faust*, led him to accept an offer from William Fox of Fox Studios to move to Hollywood, in 1926 (Wakeman; and Tibbetts, 2002).

Murnau was given full control as a director; he was also allowed to bring over his film crew. In his first picture for Fox, *Sunrise* (1927), Murnau employed many of the techniques he had perfected in his German films, with the result being a very "German" English-language film (it also helped that the film was based on German author Herman Sudermann's *Die Reise nach Tilsit*). Critically successful, *Sunrise* garnered three Academy Awards, including Best Actress for Janet Gaynor. Unfortunately for Murnau, the picture was a box-office flop, which resulted in his losing control over his subsequent films with Fox (*Four Devils* and *City Girl*). Disheartened and disenchanted with Hollywood and the studio system, Murnau broke his contract with Fox in 1929 and became an independent director.

By this time Murnau was financially well off (he now owned a farm in Oregon and a luxury yacht) and could afford to embark on a documentary project with fellow filmmaker Robert Flaherty. *Tabu* (1931) was filmed on location in Tahiti, focusing on the lives of Polynesian pearl divers. In this, his last film, Murnau reflects and draws upon all his previous techniques to create what Gary Lewis called the "metaphysical and tragic themes which always interested him" (Lewis, 1966)—in essence, German Expressionism fused with an idyllic South Pacific to create the ultimate escape from reality.

The film opened on March 18, 1931, although Murnau did not live to celebrate the moment. One week earlier, on March 11, he was killed in a tragic car accident near Santa Barbara, California. Influential beyond the grave, Murnau's legacy lived on in future generations of filmmakers—most notably Orson Welles and Alfred Hitchcock—as well as in the horror and film noir genres.

Selected Filmography

Tabu: A Story of the South Seas (1931); *City Girl* (1930); *4 Devils* (1928); *Sunrise: A Song of Two Humans* (1927); *Faust* (1926); *Tartuffe* (1925); *The Last Laugh* (1924); *The Phantom* (1922); *Nosferatu, eine Symphonie des Grauens* (1922); *The Haunted Castle* (1921); *Desire* (1921); *The Dark Road* (1921); *Abend—Nacht—Morgen* (1920); *The Two-Faced Man* (1920); *Der Bucklige und die Tänzerin* (1920); *Satanas* (1920); *Emerald of Death* (1919)

References

Kemp, Philip. "F. W. Murnau." In Wakeman, John, ed. *World Film Directors, Vol. I, 1890–1945*. New York: H. W. Wilson, 1987.

Mauro, Laurie, ed. "F. W. Murnau." In *Twentieth-Century Literary Criticism, Vol. 53*. Detroit: Gale Research, 1997: 237–38.

Tibbetts, John C. "F. W. Murnau." In *The Encyclopedia of Great Filmmakers, Vol. 2, L-Z*. New York: Facts on File, 2002: 456–58.

—*Charles Johnson*

MUYBRIDGE, EADWEARD.   Edward James Muggeridge, later known to the world as Eadweard Muybridge, was born in Kingston-upon-Thames, England, on April 9, 1830. He had a flamboyantly odd personality and was known as an eccentric photographer, whose interest in biomechanics set the stage for the invention of the motion pictures.

Muybridge moved in his youth to the United States and became, after a New York commercial career in book binding and selling, a professional photographer. Known also by the artistic name of "Helios," he specialized in landscape views of the American West after he moved to California in 1855. His outstanding stereoscopic pictures and stunning wet collodion shots of Yosemite Valley (1867, 1872) established his reputation as the top photographer of the West Coast. As official photographer for the government departments, he recorded pictures of Alaska (1868), of the Pacific Railroad, of armed conflicts between the United States Army and the Modoc Indians, and created uniquely detailed pictorial information in the panoramic pictures of San Francisco before the 1906 earthquake. After the tragic events in his personal life, when Muybridge was tried for murdering his wife's lover and then acquitted on the paradoxical grounds of justifiable deeds, he went into a self-imposed working exile and joined an expedition to Central America, which he richly documented in photos. After he returned, he dedicated his work almost entirely to high-speed photography and to the studies of motion.

In 1872, Muybridge was commissioned by the railroad baron Leland Stanford to settle an incisive dispute among racing men about the position of hooves during a horse's gallop. The scheme, constructed at Palo Alto, California, was designed to investigate the phases of rapid equine locomotion. Muybridge first used 12 cameras in a row along a track. He attached a high-speed shutter mechanism to each camera and used a long trip wire that he stretched across the track so Leland's trotting racehorse could trigger each shutter as it went past the cameras. These caught each phase of the movement in a series of 12 photographs. This experiment proved that the horse in swift movement lifted all four feet off the ground simultaneously at a given point during the gallop. For a more precise recording of movement, Muybridge used 24 cameras, as well as lateral cameras with oblique views and more sophisticated shutter-release methods that led to substantial motion studies on animals and even people. The automated shutters Muybridge used in high-speed photography were later adopted for the first movie cameras.

Muybridge invented the zoopraxiscope, also known as zoopraxinoscope or zoogyroscope, which was the projection version of the earlier spinning picture disk, the phenakitoskope. The zoopraxiscope was the forerunner of the movie projector and the first machine to project sequential images of animals, birds, and humans from a dinner-plate-sized rotating glass disk, which produced the illusion of animation by concatenating images into a primitive version of moving images. The zoopraxiscope was the most sophisticated projector of successive photographs at the time and preceded Étienne Jules Marey's chronophotographic gun or the shotgun camera and Thomas Edison's and William Kennedy Laurie Dickson's Kinetoscope.

By 1887, Muybridge's studies incited broad scientific interest, and in the same year he published an 11-volume summary of his experiments at the University of Pennsylvania entitled *Animal Locomotion: An Electro-Photographic Investigation of Consecutive Phases of Animal Movements.* This was the most comprehensive and richly illustrated study on movement and is used even today as a primary work of reference. Muybridge lectured widely in America and Europe and used the zoopraxiscope for projections during his presentations. Additionally, he published other notable "dictionaries" of animal and human motion: *Descriptive Zoopraxography or the Science of Animal Locomotion Made Popular* (1893), *Animals in Motion, an Electro-Photographic Investigation of Consecutive Phases of Animal Progressive Movements* (1899), and *The Human Figure in Motion: An Electrophotographic Investigation of Consecutive Phases of Muscular Actions* (1901).

The self-proclaimed artist-photographer retired to his birthplace and died on May 8, 1904. The complete collection of his photographic plates and lantern slides, his zoopraxiscope and other miscellaneous materials, preserved in London's South Kensington Museum, document the innovative spirit of the man who believed in the technological potential of the medium and also in the power of photography as an art form.

See also: Silent Era, The

References

Coe, Brian. "Eadweard James Muybridge. British Photographer." *Who's Who of Victorian Cinema*, March 2004. http://www.victorian-cinema.net/muybridge.htm.

Katz, Ephraim. 1982. *The International Film Encyclopedia*, 2nd ed. London: Macmillan, 1982: 844–85.

Mitchell, Leslie. "The Man Who Stopped Time." *Stanford* magazine, May/June, 2001. http://www.stanfordalumni.org/news/magazine/2001/mayjun/features/muybridge.html.

Pioneers of Early Cinema: 12, Eadweard Muybridge (1830–1904). http://www.nationalmediamuseum.org.uk/~/media/Files/NMeM/PDF/Collections/Cinematography/PioneersOfEarlyCinemaMuybridge.ashx.

—*Réka M. Cristian*

INDEX

Note: Page numbers in **bold font** refer to main entries in this encyclopedia.

ABOUT THE EDITOR

PHILIP C. DIMARE is a lecturer in the departments of Humanities and History at California State University, Sacramento. He has published numerous articles and book chapters on Religious Studies, Multicultural Studies, and American History. He is the General Editor for the forthcoming ABC-CLIO offerings *Encyclopedia of Religion and Politics in America* and *Ethnic America on Film: The Complete Resource*, and is completing work on a two-volume U.S. history text, *American Visions: A History of the American People*. He is also working on a new book, *Cinemas of Turmoil: American Myth-Making and Hollywood Genre Films*.